(ALL ▪ IN ▪ ONE)

HTI+™

Home Technology Integrator and CEDIA® Installer I

EXAM GUIDE

Ron Gilster
with Helen Heneveld

McGraw-Hill/Osborne

New York • Chicago • San Francisco • Lisbon
London • Madrid • Mexico City • Milan • New Delhi
San Juan • Seoul • Singapore • Sydney • Toronto

*The **McGraw·Hill** Companies*

McGraw-Hill/Osborne
2100 Powell Street, 10th Floor
Emeryville, CA 94608
U.S.A.

To arrange bulk purchase discounts for sales promotions, premiums, or fund-raisers, please contact **McGraw-Hill**/Osborne at the above address. For information on translations or book distributors outside the U.S.A., please see the International Contact Information page immediately following the index of this book.

HTI+™ Home Technology Integrator and CEDIA® Installer I All-in-One Exam Guide

1234567890 DOC DOC 01987654

Book p/n 0-07-223133-5 and CD p/n 0-07-223134-3
parts of
ISBN 0-07-223132-7

Publisher
Brandon A. Nordin

Vice President & Associate Publisher
Scott Rogers

Director of New Program Development
Gareth Hancock

Project Editor
Julie M. Smith

Acquisitions Coordinator
Jessica Wilson

Contributing Editor
Helen Heneveld

Copy Editors
Nancy Rapoport
Lauren Kennedy

Proofreader
Susie Elkind

Indexer
Valerie Perry

Composition
Apollo Publishing Services

Illustrator
Melinda Lytle

Series Design
Peter F. Hancik

This book was composed with Corel VENTURA™ Publisher.

To my loving wife, Connie, and family,
Jeana, Rob, Carly, Markus, Kirstin, and Jessica

ABOUT THE AUTHOR

Ron Gilster is the author of several best-selling books on networking, PC hardware, and IT career certifications, Ron holds a variety of IT certifications and has worked in networking and computing for over 25 years. Ron has served in a variety of small business and corporate technical, management, and executive positions and is currently a university instructor at several university and colleges in the Spokane, Washington area.

About the Contributing Editor

Helen Heneveld, MBA, CEDIA Installer I, HTI+ is a recognized industry expert who speaks, trains, and consults worldwide in the converging home systems industry. Helen is a former CEDIA board member and former Chair of CEDIA's Systems Integration Council.

CONTENTS AT A GLANCE

CONTENTS

FOREWORD

The pace of new technology continues to accelerate. Consumers are constantly bombarded with news and advertising that sings the praises of a connected home and a digital lifestyle. Yet the average consumer is far from comfortable with how new home technologies work and far from confident about whom to trust to make it all work in their homes. Consumers want these new technologies for entertainment, comfort, convenience and peace-of-mind. They want and need technically competent professionals who can design, install, maintain, and upgrade their electronic systems. This is the landscape that has given rise to a new industry, new businesses, and a new profession—Electronics Systems Contractor.

The opportunities for home systems integrators continue to grow and show no sign of slowing down. It is the natural desire of product and technology developers to make their products 'plug 'n play' or even self-installing. And as a given technology matures, those aims are often realized. But the newest, coolest, most powerful technologies always are born in need of help from technical experts who use their skills to smooth out the wrinkles and make them work reliably in consumers homes.

Consumers don't see lines dividing the technologies we work with. They don't expect to have one person or company supply their entertainment system, another install their network, and another design and install their home automation system. To normal people, all the things we do are magic. So we must become skilled and competent in all the disciplines of the connected home. We must become experts in home systems *integration*. That's why I'm pleased to lend my personal support, as well as CEDIA's, to this book and its aims.

The training that is has been available through electrical apprenticeship programs is not adequate for the demands of new digital technologies. Not only is the new Electronics Systems Contractor faced with previously unanticipated applications of low voltage, the phrase 'low voltage' fails to describe what we do. It simply is *not* about copper wire and voltage. It's about protocols and connectivity and interfaces, about bandwidth, frequencies, and packets.

CEDIA Professional Certification and HTI+ Certification fill a critical need in our industry. By establishing best practices and standards for home electronics system design and installation we raise the bar for ourselves. In doing so, we gain credibility with our building industry partners —architects, designers, and homebuilders. And within the context of consumers' understandable reluctance to adopt new technologies, the public will benefit through the establishment and application of objective standards for new technologies the people who deliver them.

As CEDIA president my role is to lead our association into the future and help prepare our members to be successful in it. The mission of CEDIA is to "advance our members' position in the market place and be a core component of their prosperity." It is

CEDIA's goal to make our members the best in the business. The foundation of achieving that goal is technical competence. This book will be invaluable to individuals who want to gain the understanding and learn the skills necessary to be successful in our industry.

As you embark upon a career in Electronic Systems Integration (and I hope you will) remember this: The technology is cool and very engaging. But human beings are still very analog creatures and the people who pay us for our skills and expertise are more interested in the results than how smart or technically competent we are. They hire us because they want someone to make technology easy, reliable, and painless. If we are to become respected professionals in the home building industry we *must* develop our business practices and processes so that the *way* we deliver an integrated home system is as easy, reliable, and painless as the system itself.

One final thought. Within the technology sector of the U.S. economy there is an increasing trend to move high-tech jobs off shore. Across the country there is intense political debate about the effects this trend will have. But as long as people value service, and ours is most definitely a service industry, there will be an opportunity for companies and individuals who can 'do it for you.' Happily, the fact is you can't export these jobs.

Ray Lepper
President, CEDIA
4/22/2004

Updates and Errata

Though every effort has been made to provide complete and accurate information, home technology integration is a complex subject and it is possible that corrections will be identified after publication. Please visit www.osborne.com and click on 'Errata' to access any confirmed fixes.

If you would like to comment on this book, please email the author at feedback@rongilster.com. We are interested in hearing from you, though be aware that we may not be able to respond to your note due to the volume of mail received.

ACKNOWLEDGMENTS

I'd like to thank several individuals whose support and contributions have help to create this book:

- Helen Heneveld, the major contributor and truly our guru of home automation
- Markus H. Burns for his photography and insights
- Joel Silver and Bob Fucci of Imaging Science Foundation, Inc. for their input on imaging technology and products
- Scott Lohraff of The Symphony House for his input on audio
- Neilfred Picciotto for his photographs
- Connie J Price for her photographs
- Mark Stiving of Destiny Networks for his contributions on home control systems and programming
- Gordon van Zuiden of cyberManor for his contributions on integrated home network systems
- Frank White of Custom Metrics, for his help outlining video knowledge areas
- Tom Lyga and Pass & Seymour/Legrand (www.passandseymour.com) for general support and for providing an image for the cover of the book.
- Julie Smith, Jessica Wilson, and the Osborne editorial and production teams for managing the production of this book.

I also wish to acknowledge the contributions of information and art from the following companies:

Access Lighting, Inc. www.accesslighting.com
Ademco (Honeywell) www.ademco.com
Almex Ltd www.almexltd.com
American Fluorescent Corporation www.americanfluorescent.com
American Power Conversion Corporation www.apcc.com
Amerillum www.amerillum.com
Amtel Security Systems, Inc www.amtel-security.com
AMX Corporation www.amx.com
Asante Technologies, Inc. www.asante.com
ATI Technologies, Inc www.ati.com
AudioControl www.audiocontrol.com
Audio, Security & Automation Providers, Inc. www.automation-providers.com
AverMedia Technologies, Inc www.aver.com
BEAMEX www.beamex.com

Belden, Inc. www.belden.com
Boca Automation, Inc/S D Synder & Associates http://home.earthlink.net/~bocasite
Broan-NuTone, LLC www.broan.com
Brookstone Company, Inc www.brookstone.com
Cabinet Tronix www.cabinet-tronix.com
Cadet Manufacturin www.cadetco.com
Canadian Standards Authority www.csa.ca
Canare Corporation www.canare.com
Channel Vision www.channelvision.com
Cisco Systems, Inc (LinkSys) www.linksys.com
Cogency Semiconductor, Inc www.cogency.com
Crestron Electronics, Inc. www.crestron.com
Crutchfield New Media, LLC. www.crutchfield.com
cyberManor www.cybermanor.com
Delphi Technologies, Inc. www.delphi.com

Destiny Networks, Inc
www.destinynetworks.com

Digital Rapids Corporation
www.digital-rapids.com

DITEK Corporation   www.ditekcorp.com

Dynaquip Controls - www.dynaquip.com

FBII (Honeywell)   www.fbii.com

Fluke Networks   www.flukenetworks.com

FutureSmart Systems, Inc. (Honeywell)
www.futuresmart.com

GE Interlogix   www.ge-interlogix.com

General Electric Company   www.ge.com

Gepco International   www.gepco.com

Harris Corporation   www.harris.com

HDCI, Heneveld Dynamic Consulting, Inc.
www.hheneveld.com

Hewlett Packard Company   www.hp.com

HID Corporation   www.hidcorp.com

Home Automation, Inc.   www.homeauto.com

Honeywell International, Inc.
www.honeywell.com

Innovative Telecom Industries -

Intellikey Corporation   www.intellikey.com

Intrigue Technologies, Inc
www.harmonyremote.com

Invensys Building Systems, PLC
www.invensysibs.com

JVC Professional Products Company
www.jvc.com

Klipsch Audio Technologies
www.klipsch.com

Koninklijke Philips Electronics NV
(Philips USA)   www.philipsusa.com

Lamson & Sessions (Carlon)
www.carlon.com

Lantronix Corporation   www.lantronix.com

Leviton Manufacturing Company (Voice and Data Division)   www.levitonvoicedata.com

Leviton Manufacturing Company (Lighting Division)   www.leviton.com

LG Electronics   www.lge.com

Lindows.com, Inc.   www.linspire.com

LiteTouch, Inc.   www.litetouch.com

Lutron Lighting Controls   www.lutron.com

Mediatrix Telecom, Inc.   www.mediatrix.com

Megger Limited   www.megger.com

Mier Products, Inc   www.mierproducts.com

Molex, Inc.   www.molex.com

Monster Cable Products, Inc.
www.monstercable.com

Mordaunt-Short   www.mordaunt-short.co.uk

NetGear, Inc.   www.netgear.com

Niles Audio Corporation
www.nilesaudio.com

Onkyo USA Corporation
www.onkyousa.com

OnQ Technologies   www.onqtech.com

Pacific Digital Corporation
www.pacificdigitalcorp.com

Paladin Tools, Inc   www.paladin-tools.com

Pegasus Communications Corporation
www.pegasuscom.com

Pelco   www.pelcom.com

Philex Electronic, Ltd   www.philex.co.uk

Precise Biometrics
www.precisebiometrics.com

ProjectorPeople.com
www.projectorpeople.com

Rain Bird Corporation   www.rainbird.com

RCI Automation, LLC   http://ourworld
.compuserve.com/homepages/rciautomation/

Residential Control Systems, Inc.
www.resconsys.com

Ronfell Lighting Group   www.ronfell.com

Russound   www.russound.com

Rutherford Controls International Corporation
www.rutherfordcontrols.com

Scan Technology, Inc   www.scantec.com

Seatek Company - www.seatek.com

Siemens Information and Communication
Mobile, LLC   www.siemens.com

Signamax, Connectivity   www.signamax.com

Silent Witness Enterprises, Ltd (Honeywell Video Systems)   www.silentwitness.com

Skylink Group   www.skylinknet.com

Smarthome, Inc   www.smarthome.com

Sonance   www.sonance.com

Sony Corporation   www.sony.com

Sound Advance Systems, Inc.
www.soundadvance.com

SpeakerCraft   www.speakercraft.com

Streamzap, Inc - www.streamzap.com

Telect, Inc.   www.telect.com

3Com Corporation   www.3com.com

Toro Company   www.toro.com

TriangleCables.com   www.trianglecables.com

2Wire, Inc.   www.2wire.com

Underwriters Laboratories, Inc.   www.ul.com

Universal Electronics, Inc.   www.uei.com

Universal Remote Controls, Inc
www.universal-remote.com

Velux Group   www.velux.com

ViewSonic Corporation   www.viewsonic.com

Voyetra Turtle Beach, Inc.
www.voyetra-turtle-beach.com

Vutec Corporation   www.vutec.com

Weiser Lock   www.weiserlock.com

X-10 Wireless Technology, Inc.   www.x10.com

INTRODUCTION

The Benefits of Certification

The emergence of Computing Technology Industry Association (CompTIA) Home Technology Integrator+ (HTI+) certification and the Custom Electronic Design and Installation Association (CEDIA) Installer I certification are clear indications that the home automation market is expanding. In addition, both homeowners and home technology companies and contractors wish to have a common frame-of-reference that verifies the training and knowledge of technicians.

The HTI+ and CEDIA Installer I certifications provide benefits to both the technician and the employer, as well as the homeowner.

The benefits to the technician include:

- A proof of his or her professional achievement and knowledge

- A clear career path

- Improved job opportunities

- A foundation for additional higher-level certifications

The benefits to the employer and homeowner include:

- Verified skills of job candidates simplifies recruitment and hiring

- Reduced entry-level training costs

- Measurable job performance and competency standards

- Increased customer satisfaction and repeat and follow-up business

- Reduced warranty repair work and costs

- Increased competitive advantage over companies without certified technicians

CEDIA and CompTIA

CEDIA and CompTIA are computing and electronics industry associations that promote the development of workplace and product standards.

CEDIA

CEDIA, the Custom Electronics Design and Installation Association, is a worldwide trade association of companies that design and install residential electronic systems. CEDIA was founded in 1989 and currently has about 3,100 member companies.

The objectives of the CEDIA Installer certifications is to establish consistent, clear, and objective standards that employers and customers can use to define the skill sets of technicians.

 NOTE For more information on CEDIA and its Installer Level I and Level II certifications, visit its website at HYPERLINK "http://www.cedia.org" www.cedia.org.

CompTIA

CompTIA, the Computing Technology Industry Association, was founded in 1982 with a focus on advancing the growth of the information technology (IT) industry and to improve the skills and knowledge of IT professionals. Because CompTIA has over 19,000 individual and institutional members in nearly 90 countries, it has become one of the more influential IT trade associations in the world.

CompTIA's commitment is to help facilitate the growth and quality of the IT industry through the development of IT industry standards, the skills and expertise of IT professionals, and the development of ongoing skills education. The areas of focus for CompTIA are currently convergence technology, e-commerce, IT training, software services, IT career certification, and workforce development.

 NOTE For more information on CompTIA and its programs, visit its website at www.comptia.org.

The HTI+ and CEDIA Installer I Certifications

Both the HTI+ and CEDIA Installer Level 1 certification tracks, provide a comprehensive and complete launching pad for a professional desiring to enter the automated or connected home industry. While both certification programs have some similarities and some overlap, most of the content is different allowing the combination of programs to truly strengthen a professional's knowledge and skills that are required to perform well on the job!

Some of the differences between both programs include knowledge domains and the depth of knowledge that is covered. CEDIA Installer Level 1 certification focuses in depth on audio/video along with the fundamentals of wire and cable, connectors, installation and safety practices. HTI+ covers structured wiring and computer networking technologies and protocols, including wireless, in detail and gives the fundamentals of wire and cable and all the subsystems in the home. The basics of audio/video, lighting, telecommunications, heating, air conditioning and control (HVAC), water systems, security, surveillance, and home access systems are covered in HTI+ exams.

NOTE The HTI+ certification consists of two exams: the Residential Systems exam and the Structural Infrastructure and Integration exam. The CEDIA Installer I exam is a single exam.

About thirty percent of overlap exists between the HTI+ and the CEDIA Installer I exams in the technical areas covered, especially in some specific knowledge areas: audio/video, telecommunications, lighting controls, and low-voltage and high-voltage wiring. However, much of the overlap occurs at different skill levels, with some tested at the entry-level and others at the intermediate level. The HTI+ exams assume the certification candidate has at least one year of experience on the job, while the CEDIA exam is less specific about the experience or knowledge you should have when attempting the exam, but the assumption is that it is more intermediate than entry-level.

Matching Your Experience to the Exams

Which certification program is best for you depends on you, your skills, experience, and knowledge. The CEDIA exam is focused heavier in the area of audio and video systems and the HTI+ exams are heavier on multiple function networks, cabling characteristics, connectors, and the integration of subsystems. Ultimately, the combination of both certifications should give you a competitive advantage in the home automation job market.

The following sections provide an overview on the background, content, and the testing and certification procedures for both the HTI+ and CEDIA Installer Level 1 certification programs.

HTI+ Certification Overview

The Home Technology Integrator (HTI+) certification initiative is a partnership between CompTIA and the Internet Home Alliance. The HTI+ certificate is a cross-industry credential providing recognition that a Home Technology Integrator (HTI+) professional has attained a standard of excellence in the integrated home network industry.

The HTI+ certification program covers a broad range of basic entry-level knowledge required of a home technology installer/integrator. It represents a good balance of skills and knowledge required to perform well on the job. The development of the objectives involved nationally recognized subject matter experts (SMEs) from each the different subsystem areas.

There aren't any prerequisites to take the HTI+ certification exams, however on-the-job experience and training is highly recommended. The technician that earns HTI+ certification demonstrates he or she has the equivalent knowledge and skill levels of a working professional with at least 6 months of hands-on experience in each set of standards designed to measure your mastery of the core competencies involved in the installation, integration, and troubleshooting of residential technology subsystems.

Tables 1 and 2 list the subject matter areas of each of the HTI+ exams along with the percentage of the exam dedicated to each area.

Domain	Subject Area	Percentage of Exam
1.0	Computer Networking Fundamentals	25%
2.0	Audio/Video Fundamentals	20%
3.0	Home Security and Surveillance Systems	10%
4.0	Telecommunications Standards	10%
5.0	Home Lighting Control	10%
6.0	HVAC Management	10%
7.0	Water System Controls	10%
8.0	Home Access Controls	3%
9.0	Miscellaneous Automated Home Features	2%
	TOTAL	100%

Table 1-1   HTI+ Residential Systems Exam Subject Area Domains

There are no formal prerequisites you must meet before taking the HTI+ exam, but it is recommended that you have at least 6 months experience in each of the domain subject areas. If you pass both exams, the HTI+ certification is awarded for life, with no recertification requirements.

 NOTE   These certification objectives are subject to change. For the most current information, visit www.comptia.org.

Domain	Subject Area	Percentage of Exam
1.0	Structured Wiring	50%
1A	Low-voltage wiring	25%
1B	High-voltage wiring	25%
2.0	Systems Integration— User Interface and Control Processors	50%

Table 1-2   HTI+ Systems Infrastructure and Integration Exam Subject Area Domains

About the CD-ROM

The CD-ROM located in the back of this book includes the following software and files:

- A practice exam for both of the HTI+ certification exams to help you get a feel for the type of questions you may face on the actual certification exams. Though these practice exams provide no guarantees for your performance on the actual exam, they are valuable tools for making sure you understand the knowledge in this book and that you have some familiarity with electronic exams before taking the real exam.

- A practice exam for the CEDIA Installer Level I certification exam. As with the HTI+ practice exams, the CEDIA Installer Level I practice exam doesn't precisely replicate the actual exam but will give you a feel for the type of questions you may face on the actual exam and will provide feedback as to how well you've mastered the information in this book.

- A PDF document that shows CEDIA's planning icons, important tools for effectively mapping out home technology systems. These icons are available directly from CEDIA in various print and electronic forms to help design systems for your customers (www.cedia.org).

For detailed information on the CD-ROM software, please see the About the CD-ROM appendix at the back of this book.

The logo of the CompTIA Authorized Curriculum Program and the status of this or other training material as "Authorized" under the CompTIA Authorized Curriculum Program signifies that, in CompTIA's opinion, such training material covers the content of the CompTIA's related certification exam. CompTIA has not reviewed or approved the accuracy of the contents of this training material and specifically disclaims any warranties of merchantability or fitness for a particular purpose. CompTIA makes no guarantee concerning the success of persons using any such "Authorized" or other training material in order to prepare for any CompTIA certification exam.

The contents of this training material were created for the CompTIA HTI + exam covering CompTIA certification exam objectives that were current as of July, 2004.

How to Become CompTIA Certified

This training material can help you prepare for and pass a related CompTIA certification exam or exams. In order to achieve CompTIA certification, you must register for and pass a CompTIA certification exam or exams.

In order to become CompTIA certified, you must:

1. Select a certification exam provider. For more information please visit http:// www.comptia.org/certification/general_information/test_locations.asp

2. Register for and schedule a time to take the CompTIA certification exam(s) at a convenient location.

3. Read and sign the Candidate Agreement, which will be presented at the time of the exam(s). The text of the Candidate Agreement can be found at http:// www.comptia.org/certification/general_information/candidate_agreement.asp

4. Take and pass the CompTIA certification exam(s).

For more information about CompTIA's certifications, such as their industry acceptance, benefits, or program news, please visit http://www.comptia.org/certification/ default.asp

CompTIA is a non-profit information technology (IT) trade association. CompTIA's certifications are designed by subject matter experts from across the IT industry. Each CompTIA certification is vendor-neutral, covers multiple technologies, and requires demonstration of skills and knowledge widely sought after by the IT industry.

To contact CompTIA with any questions or comments , please call + 1 630 268 1818; questions@comptia.org.

PART I

Home Technology Installation Basics

Wire and Cable Basics

In this chapter, you will learn about:
- Wire types, insulation and jacket materials
- Cable types, construction, and characteristics
- Cable performance, attenuation, cancellation, and interference

Just like a house is built on its foundation, a home automation network is built on its wiring. Home networks of all types, and yes, even wireless networks, are built on a network of electrical, communications, and audio/visual wiring.

The myriad standards, guidelines, and cable and wire types can be a bit confusing, but when you organize them by the various systems in a house, it's really not all that complicated. This chapter focuses on the different cable types and their construction, performance, specifications, and how each is typically used in a home automation project. A variety of different wire and cable is used in home electrical, audio, video, and control systems. This chapter provides you with the basics on the wire or cable used in each of these different applications in a home.

Electrical Wiring and Cable

Residential electrical wiring actually includes all of the wiring in a home, but for now we want to focus on the low voltage wiring. If you plan on using any of this wiring as a component of a home network, of any kind, it is important for this wiring to conform to certain standards and codes.

Low Voltage versus High Voltage

When installing wire and cable in a home, you must be aware of the voltage specification of the cable in use. There are certain cable types that are specified as low voltage and those specified as high voltage. Low voltage cable is designed to carry lower levels of alternating current (AC) and direct current (DC) voltages than is high voltage. I know that may sound like a no-brainer, but there is enough of a difference between these two cabling types that electricians are certified separately for installing one or the other. Table 1-1 lists the basic cable categories and the voltage range each is specified to carry.

Cable Type	DC Voltage	AC Voltage	Usage
Extra Low Voltage (ELV)	< 120 volts (V)	< 50V	Audio, video, telephone, data cables
Low Voltage	120V – 750V	50V – 500V	Standard household electrical wiring
High Voltage	> 1.5 kV	> 1 kV	Power lines to a home

Table 1-1   ELV, LV, and HV wiring and their voltage specifications

Low Voltage Wiring

No specific definition exists for what is generally called low voltage wiring. In some references, low voltage is circuit wiring of less than 30 volts (V) of alternating current (AC) or 60V of direct current (DC). Another reference defines it as being less than 50V AC and yet another defines it as being between 0 and 150V AC and DC. In effect, the term low voltage wiring, which typically is used to describe communications, speaker, security and control signal wiring, is more of a slang term than a specific reference. However, in common usage, electricians use low voltage to refer to less than 50 volts and wire gauges less than 16 AWG.

Low voltage wiring is defined as being one of five types of circuits:

- **Communication circuits**   These circuits carry data signals between devices, typically connected to a network of devices. Communication circuits, such as data networking, telephone, and in some cases, electrical cabling, are explained in detail in Chapters 3 and 10.

- **Signal circuits**   A signal circuit is an electrical circuit that supplies power to an appliance or electrical device that produces a visual light signal or audible sound signal. Examples of signals circuits are doorbells, buzzers, signal lights, fire or smoke detectors, alarm systems, and other types of security systems.

- **Remote control circuits**   A remote control circuit is an electrical circuit that controls one or more other circuits, motor controllers, magnet contacts, or electrical relays. A remote control circuit controls the supply of power to electrical equipment like appliances, lighting, and heating devices or provides command signals to control their operation.

- **Motor control circuits**   A circuit that carries electric signals that control the function of a device or motor controller, but not the main electrical power service.

- **Power-limited circuits**   Circuits that aren't used for signaling or remote control where the power on the line is limited are power-limited circuits. A low voltage lighting circuit that includes 120V to 12V transformers to drive 12V lamps is an example of a power-limited circuit. Power-limited circuits are limited to 30V.

Voltages

There are many voltage numbers around. You may read or hear about 110V, 117V, 120V, 208V, 220V, or even 480V. Different countries or regions of the world have different electrical systems and each electrical system may support a different voltage.

In North America, the electric companies supply a split-phase 240V feed, which is two 120V (plus or minus 5V) feeds, to its residential and commercial customers. The wiring in each building has built-in resistance that can drop the voltage in the raw feed to 110V or 220V at the outlet. So, for all purposes, 110V is the same as 120V, regardless of how electrical devices or installation specification are labeled. If a product is labeled as 110V, it merely means that the product is capable of operating at electrical levels as low as that.

However, 208V is not a reduction of 240V. This is the voltage of a 3-phase Y-circuit that has 120V from any neutral to hot. The voltage of a 3-phase Y-circuit that runs 277V from hot to neutral is 480V. However, most motors intended to run on 480V are typically labeled as 440V. Confused? Don't be. Home networking is mostly a 12 and 24 volt environment.

Low Voltage Classes

Low voltage circuits are divided into three circuit classes, as detailed in Table 1-2.

A few examples of Class 2 circuits are low voltage lighting control, thermostats, security systems, intercoms, audio systems, and computer networks. Some security systems, intercoms, and audio systems can also be Class 3 circuits. Each circuit class also defines the cable class that must be used. On Class 2 and 3 circuits, the cable used must be rated for Class 2 and 3 circuits, respectively. The manufacturer's specifications should indicate the rating class of each cable it sells and the class rating should be marked on the cable as CL2 (Class 2) or CL3 (Class 3).

Electrical Wiring

Generally, home automation projects rarely have to deal with electrical wiring, except to plug a controller or network adapter into an outlet. However, if you are installing home

Class	Type	Volts	Volt-Amps (Power)
1	Power-limited,	30	1000
1	Remote control and signaling	600	No limits
2	DC	30	100
3	DC	>30V	>0.5, but not more than 100 VA

Table 1-2   Low voltage circuit classes

network wiring into open walls or retrofitting wiring into an existing wall, you should be able to at least recognize common electrical service wiring and its characteristics.

 NOTE Most of these electrical wire characteristics also are found in low voltage wiring as well.

The most common electrical wiring used in home construction today are

- **Modern non-metallic (NM)** This wire is made up of two solid copper or aluminum core wires insulated with plastic vinyl and a bare copper ground wire sheathed with a paper layer and an outer vinyl jacket. Modern NM wiring is flexible, durable, and moisture-resistant, which is why it is the most popular choice for residential electric wiring. See Figure 1-1.

- **Underground feeder (UF)** This wire, which is also referred to as NMC cable, is very much like NM cable, except that the three copper wires (two insulated and one bare) are embedded in solid plastic vinyl sheathing. UF wire is the best choice for damp or buried installations.

- **Zip wire** This wire type is lighter duty than most residential wiring and has very limited use. Most lamp cords are zip wire, which gets its name from the fact that the two conductors are molded together, but can be easily separated by pulling them apart manually. Figure 1-2 illustrates the composition of a zip wire.

Voltages Around the World

Voltage can have different values, especially when it comes to wiring ratings and specifications. For example, common voltages used in wiring specifications are 110V, 117V, 120V, 208V, 220V, and 480V. Different countries and world regions have different electrical systems and each electrical system could specify and carry a different voltage than its neighboring countries.

In North America, the electric companies supply a split-phase 240V, 60 Hertz (Hz) feed, which is made up of two 120V (plus or minus 5V) feeds, to residential and commercial customers. The wiring in each building has built-in resistance that drops the voltage of the raw feed down to 110V or 220V at the outlet. As a result, electrical service in North America is referred to as 110V (the net of the nominal 120V feed) or 220V (net of nominal 240V).

In European countries, electricity is supplied at the nominal voltage of 220V to 230V. Like electricity in North America, the actual voltage can vary by 10 percent. Some countries offer 110V at the outlet, but all European electricity is 50 Hz (aka 50 cycles), and this difference is enough to require North American travelers to use a converter, just like European travelers must do in North America.

Figure 1-1
The construction
of modern non-
metallic electrical

Some older wire types you may encounter in a house ar

- **Flexible armored cable** This two-wire type of electric cable, which is also called Greenfield or BX wire (see Figure 1-3), was very popular from the 1920s to the 1940s. The metallic armoring around the outside of the cable provides the grounding.

- **Metal conduit** From the 1940s to the 1970s, two insulated wires were installed in rigid metal conduit tubing. The metal of the conduit provided the grounding. Metal conduit installation is still required in some areas for bare wire installations in basements, foundation crawl space, attics, and garages. It is also required in some cities. Check your local codes.

- **Early NM** This two-wire cable was popular from the 1930s to the mid-1960s. It is made up of a flexible rubberized fabric jacket that surrounds two solid copper wires with rubber insulation and paper sheathing inside the outer jacket. Early NM wire had no grounding wire.

- **Knob and tube** Wires covered with a rubberized fabric material, called "loom," was strung over ceramic insulators (knobs) and ceramic tubes through studs and joists (see Figure 1-4). This is a very old and obsolete wiring system found in homes constructed before 1940.

Figure 1-2
The makeup
of zip wire

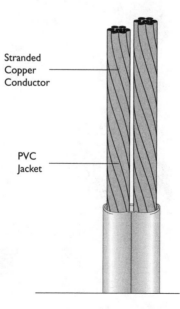

Stranded
Copper
Conductor

PVC
Jacket

Figure 1-3
BX cable is a type
of armored cable.

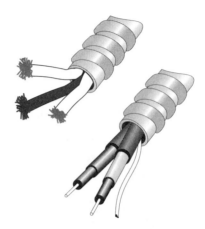

Residential Wire Gauge and Characteristics

The wire gauge used in a home depends on the number of amperes on a particular circuit. For example, if a circuit has 20 amps, a 12-gauge wire should be used. See Table 1-3 for a listing of a few of the common circuit amps and the appropriate wire gauge to use. Remember that a smaller gauge means a bigger and less flexible wire. For wire runs longer than 100 feet, or placed inside a conduit, or installed in a bundle with other wires, the next heavier gauge wire should be used to avoid voltage drops and to overcome heat problems.

Figure 1-4
Knob and tube
insulators were
used in homes
built before 1940.

Photo courtesy of
Markus Burns.

AWG/B&S*	CSA	Circuit Amps	Ohms per 1K feet	Common Usage
24 /Cat 5e	0.205	2.1	28.6	Communications
18 – 22	0.0480 – 0.0280	10 – 8	6.386 – 16.200	Thermostats, doorbells, security systems
16	0.051	12	4.016	Audio
14	0.0800	15	2.524	Light fixtures, receptacles
12	0.1040	20	1.619	Light fixtures, receptacles
10	0.1280	30	1.018	Air conditioner (AC), clothes dryer
8	0.1600	40	0.641	Electric range, central AC
6	0.1920	60	0.403	Central AC, electric furnace

Table 1-3   Wire Gauge to Circuit Amperes Chart
* AWG stands for American Wire Gauge; B&S refers to Brown and Sharpe, which
is equivalent to AWG; and CSA refers to the Canadian Standards Association.

Twisted-Pair Cable

Twisted-pair wiring is by far the most popular installed media for networking in just about any type of network for many reasons, including that it is inexpensive, easy to handle, and readily available. Twisted-pair (TP) wire is the de facto standard for both Ethernet and Token Ring networks.

Twisted-pair wire gets its name from its construction. Pairs of 24-gauge (or heavier) wire are twisted around each other to reduce the impact of cancellation between the two wires. Two types of twisted-pair wire are available: unshielded and shielded. Unshielded twisted-pair (UTP) wire, shown in Figure 1-5, doesn't include any EMI shielding

Figure 1-5
The construction
of unshielded
twisted-pair
(UTP) wiring

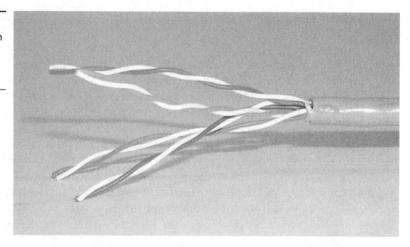

AWG and Metric Wire Sizes

Wire, including the wires bundled into a cable, is measured in a variety of sizes throughout the world. In the U.S., wire is measured using the AWG or American Wire Gauge standard. AWG measures the diameter of the wire using a fairly complicated formula that boils down to for every 6 gauge decrease (say, from 24 AWG to 18 AWG), the diameter of the wire doubles in measurement.

Many countries around the world use metric wire gauges that states a wire gauge as ten times the wire's diameter in millimeters (mm). For example, a 40 gauge metric wire is 4 mm in diameter. So, using the metric wire gauge system, as the wire diameter increases so does the wire gauge. This can cause some confusion between the AWG system and the metric wire size system, so generally metric wire sizes are stated in millimeters and not as metric gauges. Table 1-4 shows a comparison of AWG wire gauge and metric wire size of wires commonly used in structured wiring systems.

Table 1-4	AWG (in millimeters)	Metric Wire Size
Comparison of	10	2.588
AWG gauge and	12	2.304
Metric wire sizes	14	1.628
	16	1.290
	18	1.024
	20	0.081
	22	0.065
	24	0.511
	26	0.404
	28	0.320

to speak of, while shielded twisted-pair (STP) wire, shown in Figure 1-6, has an extra wrapping of foil to help protect the inner wires from EMI and cancellation effects.

UTP cable is designated for various usages through a wire category specification that divides the various grades of UTP into a series of categories. Each category, of the seven defined to date, defines a specific number of wire pairs, a number of radial twists per foot (or twists per inch), the number of wire pairs, the bandwidth rating, the maximum segment (run) length for performance, and its recommended networking usage. Table 1-5 details the various UTP wire categories, which are referred to as "Cats." The most common cable categories used in structured wiring systems are Cat5, Cat5e, and Cat 6.

Twisted pair cable gets its name from its construction style. Most TP cables have multiple pairs of wire, typically two or four pairs. Each wire pair is wrapped or twisted around

Figure 1-6
Shielded twisted-
pair (STP) wiring
has a foil wrapper
to protect
it from EMI.

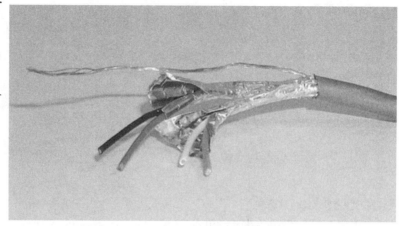

one another to help protect the wires from interference and crosstalk . The more twists
in the wires, the better the protection.

In North America, UTP is the most commonly used cable for low voltage (LV) installations. However, outside of North America, shielded twisted-pair (STP), and its two
variations, screened twisted-pair (ScTP) and foil twisted pair (FTP) wiring (see Figure 1-7)
are commonly used. ScTP and FTP include an overall shielding layer, but don't provide
as much protection from interference as STP.

UTP cable carries a variety of rating codes, which are assigned by the product performance and safety authorities and testing laboratories. The primary rating codes for UTP
cable are defined by the NEC (National Electric Code), published by the National Fire
Protection Association. Table 1-6 lists the primary UTP cable ratings.

Category	Bandwidth	Wire Pairs	Maximum Segment Length	Applications
Cat 1	128 Kbps	2	100 meters	POTS, ISDN, door bell wiring, speaker wire
Cat 2	4 Mbps	4	100 meters	Token Ring networks
Cat 3	10 Mbps	4	100 meters	10BaseT
Cat 4	10 – 16 Mbps	4	100 meters	10 Mbps Ethernet 16 Mbps, Token Ring
Cat 5	100 Mbps	4	100 meters	100BaseT, ATM, CDDI
Cat 5E	200 Mbps	4	100 meters	1000BaseT
Cat 6	600 Mbps	4	100 meters	CDDI, 1000BaseT
Cat 7	1 Gbps		Undefined	Multiple wire pairs with each twist insulated

Table 1-5   ANSI/TIA/EIA UTP Cabling Standards

Figure 1-7
Foil-wrapped twisted pair cabling (FTP) is commonly used outside of the U.S.

Photo courtesy of Berk-Tek.

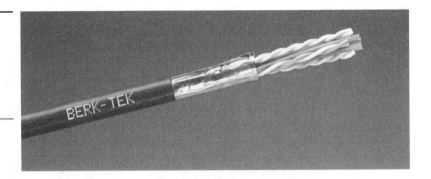

Coaxial Cable

Coaxial cable is constructed of a single inner core wire conductor that is encased in a layer of dielectric insulation, which is then wrapped by a wire mesh outer conductor and shield. A plastic sheathing covers the cable. Some manufacturers also add additional layers of mesh or foil shielding between the mesh and the outer jacket. Figure 1-8 illustrates the construction of a coaxial cable.

Coaxial cable is called single-ended cable because it has a single signal path and a single return path. The core wire carries the positive signals to the next device and the braided mesh layer of the cable carries any return signals.

The different classes of coaxial cabling that are commonly used in residential systems are

- **RG6** This type of coaxial cable is a 75-ohm cable commonly used with digital satellite systems, analog television, VCRs, CCTV, CATV. RG6 coaxial cable is the minimum requirement for many digital television systems and for television antenna system in multidwelling buildings. RG6 cables are typically terminated with F-type connectors.

- **RG11** This type of coaxial cable is fairly stiff and difficult to work with. It was once fairly popular with Ethernet data networks and is included in the IEEE 802.3 Ethernet specifications as 10Base2. RG11 coaxial cabling is most commonly terminated with BNC connectors. This cable is occasionally used for long cable runs for digital television feeds.

Rating	Description
CM	General building cables suitable for non-plenum and riser application.
CMP	Horizontal cabling that is suitable for installation in ducts and plenums without conduit.
CMR	Riser (vertical) cabling that is suitable for use in vertical shaft installations.

Table 1-6   NEC cable ratings

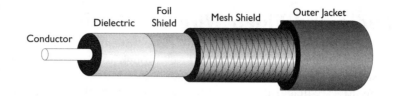

Figure 1-8
The layers of an RG6 coaxial cable

Conductor   Dielectric   Foil Shield   Mesh Shield   Outer Jacket

- **RG58**   This type of low-loss coaxial cable is a 50-ohm cable with a diameter of 0.195-inches that is a good general purpose cable commonly used for security systems and video display applications. RG 58 cables are commonly terminated with BNC connectors.

- **RG59**   This coaxial cable type is a low-loss 100-ohm cable with a diameter of just under 1/4-inch that is a general purpose cable that can carry about 20 percent higher frequencies and a bit longer attenuation limit than RG58 cable. RG59 cable is suitable for basic analog television antennas in homes and for CCTV on short cable runs. RG59 cable is commonly terminated with F-type connectors.

Fiber Optic Cable

Fiber optic cabling (see Figure 1-9) is certainly an option for installing a home network, but it's not usually a particularly practical one. While fiber optic is extremely fast, it can be difficult to work with, its interface devices are relatively expensive, and copper wire technologies have advanced to the point that they are capable of transmitting multiple CD- or DVD-quality streams simultaneously. Wiring with fiber optic cabling in home is getting it ready for the future and probably won't be connected and used at the time of installation.

The fiber optic cabling used in home installations is typically multimode cable. Fiber optic cable is either single-mode or multimode. Single-mode cable carries a single system, but over very long distances. Multimode fiber optic cable is capable of carrying multiple signals, but over a shorter distance, which are still far beyond the requirements of just about any home.

Figure 1-9
A multi-strand fiber optic cable

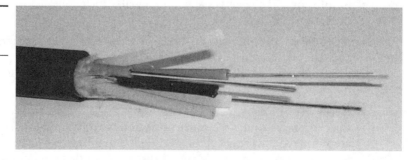

Audio and Video Wire and Cable

If you understand how water flows through a hose, then you essentially understand the physics of how electrical waveforms travel through an audio/video cable. Just like a water hose stores and releases water, when an audio signal is transmitted, the audio/video cable stores (voltage) and releases (current) an electrical wave at certain frequencies and amplitudes and are generally combined under the term frequency. An audio/video signal consists of a collection of high and low frequency waves.

Another function of an audio/video cable is its ability to release or pass the audio signal to the next component (amplifier, speaker, or the like) at the right time, without slowing down the signal. A cable with the ability to release the signal at the right time is called in-phase. Not all cables are able to efficiently carry (store and release) audio signals at all frequencies. Virtually every audio cable can carry high frequencies (above 1 KHz) fairly efficiently. However, the ability for a cable to remain in-phase diminishes as the frequencies drop below 450 Hz. When this happens, the lower frequencies are produced out-of-phase, or reproduced later than the higher frequencies.

Balanced Audio Cables

A balanced audio cable uses both positive and negative carriers, like a coaxial cable, but they also add a grounding carrier as well. In what I'll call an unbalanced cable, the grounding signals are combined onto the negative carrier.

A balanced audio cable is used in high-end or professional microphone, line-level balanced analog audio, extended distance runs, and wiring interconnected to a patch panel, is made up of two twisted-pair insulated wires, commonly copper, and a separate grounding wire or mesh shield (see Figure 1-10).

Frequency, Amplitude, and Hertz

No, this isn't the name of an audio industry law firm; these are the properties that characterize the parts of an audio signal.

- **Amplitude**   The height of an audio signal, which translates into the volume of each part of the signal.

- **Frequency**   The number of cycles (waves) for a sound in a second. Frequency translates to the pitch of a sound. Every sound has pitch, a tiny bell has high pitch and a high frequency, and a bass drum has low pitch and a low frequency. Frequency is measured in Hertz.

- **Hertz**   The measurement of the number of cycles occurring in an audio wave in one second. One wave, measured from the center of the raise in amplitude to the center of the decline in amplitude is one Hertz, which is named after Heinrich Hertz, the discoverer of this phenomenon.

Figure 1-10
Samples
of balanced
audio cables

*Photo courtesy of Gepco
International, Inc.*

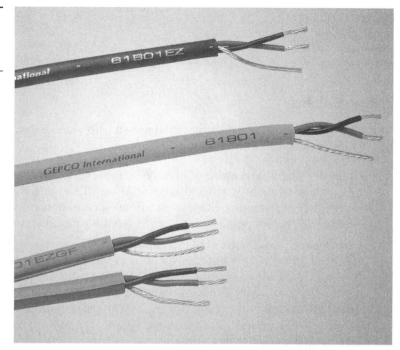

Parallel Pair Wiring

This type of wiring, which resembles lamp cord, is made up of two separate conductors (a positive and a negative) that are encased in a single plastic or rubber insulating jacket (see Figure 1-11). This type of wiring is inexpensive, but doesn't provide much protection from external interference. Parallel pair wiring is commonly referred to as speaker wire.

Parallel wire is available in a variety of wire gauges, ranging from 8-gauge on the high-end to 24-gauge on the low end. However, the gauge that should be used is dependent on a number of factors. A cable with conductors too thin for the signals generated by the amplifier will produce a degraded sound quality with loss in the lower frequencies. In contrast, a cable that is too heavy may be too awkward to work with easily and will definitely cost more.

CROSS-REFERENCE   Chapters 15 and 16 discuss speaker and audio cabling in detail.

NOTE   Speaker wire and parallel cable are often advertised as "oxygen-free." What this means is that the cable has no corrosion. As a cable is exposed to the air, it can begin to darken in color, which means it is oxidizing. In fact, if a copper wire is green, it is likely fully oxidized.

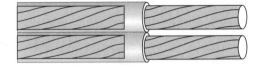

Figure 1-11
Parallel pair wire is commonly used for speaker wire.

Video Cables

There are a variety of cables that can be used with video systems. The primary types of video cable are

- **Coaxial**   This cable is the standard used for cable television connections. Coaxial cable can be terminated with either a BNC or an RCA connector (see Chapter 2). Although it is developing other applications, such as transmission of IR signals, coaxial cable is used primarily for antenna and cable inputs and video distribution.

- **Component (also called digital component)**   The newest of the cable and connector types that provides the best picture quality. The video signal is separated into individual red, green, and blue (RGB) color components, which results in better color and clarity. The connection for a 3-channel component cable has three plugs, one for each color component. Component cable is available in 3, 4, or 5 channel (wire run) configurations. Figure 1-12 shows a component video cable with 4 coaxial cable channels.

- **Composite**   A standard video signal format that contains the color, brightness, and synchronization information. Virtually all VCRs and other legacy video equipment have a composite video input or output. Composite video cables are a single cable carrying only the video signal component. Composite A/V cables that also carry the right and left channels of the audio are terminated with three connectors that are typically color coded with a yellow jack for the video, a white jack for left-side audio, and a red jack for right-side audio. The jack and plug used for composite video are RCA connectors or F-type or BNC coaxial connectors. Figure 1-13 shows a terminated composite video cable.

Speaker Wire

There are several types of speaker wire on the market. Typically, 16-gauge stranded twisted-pair wire or 14- to 18-gauge audio cable is used for an average length speaker run, with

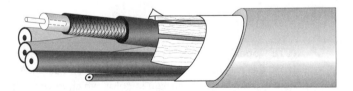

Figure 1-12
A video component cable with four channels

Figure 1-13
A composite video cable terminated with RCA connectors

Photo courtesy of Canare Corporation of America.

heavier wiring used for very long runs. The twist in the wire helps reduce the amount of EMI the wiring picks up.

The following terms are commonly used to describe speaker wire and its characteristics:

- **Cable Ratings**   The cable designed for a specific use is rated for that use. For example, a cable designed for installation inside a wall carries a premise wiring rating. Most speaker cable is not premise wiring rated. Premise wiring rated cable complies with the National Electric Code (NEC) and provides assurance to you and your customer that the design of the cable meets fire safety standards as well.

- **Gauge**   The wire gauge selected for a home A/V system should be chosen based on its properties and the distance of the wiring runs. Speakers have low impedance (4 to 8 ohms), which means the resistance in the wiring is key to determining how much of the audio signal will reach the speaker. For example, a 100-foot run of 16- gauge twisted pair wiring has a round-trip resistance of 0.8 ohms. When this wire is used with a 4-ohm speaker, 17 percent of the signal is lost to the resistance on the wire, which means only 83 percent of the sound signal actually reaches the speaker. The solution to this is the use of heavier wire. The wire sizes typically used for home A/V systems are 16 or 14 AWG (American Wire Gauge), which provide good compromises against signal loss, cost, and ease of installation. On top of that, the connectors on most audio devices are designed for these wiring sizes.

- **Signal (power) loss**   Table 1-7 lists the maximum cable run distances for 16- and 14-gauge speaker wiring given the percentage of power lost to the cable due to line resistance. If you know the speaker's impedance and acceptable loss numbers, you should be able to look up the right size wire to use and its maximum run length.

Speaker Ohms	Decibel Loss	Signal Loss	16 AWG Max. Run (feet)	14 AWG Max. Run (feet)
4	0.5	11%	60	100
4	1	21%	130	210
4	2	37%	290	460
4	3	50%	500	790
8	0.5	11%	120	190
8	1	21%	260	410
8	2	37%	580	930
8	3	50%	990	1580

Table 1-7   Speaker Wire Signal (Power) Loss Table

Wire and Cable Characteristics

All wire has a number of performance properties and characteristics that limits the use of just any wire in any situation. The primary performance properties of metallic wire are

- **Attenuation**   As an electrical signal moves through a wire, it eventually reaches a point where it begins to lose its strength—the attenuation point. Beyond this point, the signal may become distorted or lost altogether. Every cable type is rated with an attenuation distance, which indicates its maximum run length.

- **Cancellation**   When two wires are not properly insulated or placed too closely together, the signal in one wire can be significantly impacted by the signal in the other wire. This is also referred to as phase cancellation.

- **Crosstalk**   This condition is caused when the signal in one conductor, which is also referred to as a channel, leaks into another channel and distorts its signal.

- **Interference**   Electrical signals, in the form of electromagnetic (EM) or radio frequency (RF) waves, can penetrate a cable and distort or disrupt the signals being transmitted over the cable. The two most common types of interference are electromagnetic interference (EMI) and radio frequency interference (RFI). EMI is caused by strong electromagnetic fields emanating from nearby electrical devices, such as electrical motors, magnetic ballasts, and the like. RFI is caused by radio frequency electromagnetic waves, like radio and TV signals, that travel through the air and are picked up by the conductors or shielding of a cable.

- **Inductance**   Signals carried on a wire typically have a varying current that produces a varying magnetic field and can create additional current in the same cable or a nearby cable. In a TP cable, the wires in each wire pair are twisted around each other to reduce electromagnetic induction between the wires.

Control Wiring

There are many different types of control systems in an automated home: lighting control, climate control, security, and perhaps even water control (as in controlling the lawn sprinklers).

The wiring that supports and interlinks the control system's elements is readily available, inexpensive, and easily installed, especially in a new construction situation. Installing new control system wiring in an existing house can be more difficult, but there are alternatives to new wiring in these situations, such as powerline carrier (PLC) and phoneline systems, discussed in Chapter 10.

NOTE   Most control systems don't require heavy duty wiring, generally only 22-gauge wiring or Cat 3 UTP cable, at a minimum.

Bundled Cable

Structured wiring involves the installation of wire homeruns to each room, zone, or area of a home. There are two ways this can be accomplished: pulling each individual cable required separately or pulling in a cable bundle that includes all of the cabling runs required to support the needs of the room, zone, or area.

Using a structured cable bundle eliminates the guesswork of pulling individual cable runs to areas of the home in attempts to provide future capability to the home. A cable bundle pulled throughout a home provides additional capability and expandability to all areas of a home and can save on installation time.

Some cable bundles are enclosed inside a plastic outer sheathing to facilitate pulling the cable through the walls. Others connect the wires together in a zip wire form and others wrap the bundle with strands of plastic ribbons that can be easily removed to terminate the cables in the bundle at the distribution panel or the room outlets. Figure 1-14 illustrates some of the different cable bundle enclosures.

2+2 Bundled Cabling

A standard cable bundle is the 2+2 cable that includes two runs of UTP Cat 5e cable and two runs of RG-6 coaxial cable. Since these four cable runs typically satisfy the distributed system needs of most homes, it is a very popular cable bundle for structured wiring.

Figure 1-14
Examples of
structured wiring
cable bundle
enclosers

*Photo courtesy of
Smarthome, Inc.*

2+2+2 Bundled Cabling

Another popular cable bundle adds two runs of fiber optic cable to 2+2 bundle to provide for even more current capability and future proofing to a home. The two fiber optic cables are multimode strands that can be used for a wide range of current and certainly future applications.

Control Wire Bundles

There are several other types of structured wiring cable bundles, each with its own purpose. Some are variations of the 2+2 bundle with an additional run or UTP or coaxial cable included. However, one special purpose cable bundle is the control wire bundle.

Control wire bundles typically include a single run each of RG-59 or RG-6 coaxial cable and Cat 5e cable and two runs of 18-gauge stranded wire, which are used to cable keypads, room controls, intercoms with video, and for supplying power.

Common Home Automation Wire Types

For reference purposes, I've included Table 1-8, which lists some industry designations for common audio and video cable and wire types. Although there are no industry standards for the colors of the individual wires or the outer sheathing of structured wiring

Subsystem	Usage	AWG	Conductors	Conductor Type	Shielded?	Cable Color
Audio	LV audio	22	4	Stranded	Shielded	Yellow
	Speakers, security siren	14	2	Stranded	None	Green
	Speakers	16	4	Stranded	None	Blue
Baseband video	Composite video (cameras)	RG6/RG59	1	Solid	Shielded	Black/White
Communications	Telephone and data	25 (Cat 5e)	8	Solid	None	Blue
Fire detection	Smoke and heat detectors	18	4	Solid	None	Red
IR control	IR, LV wiring	22	4	Stranded	None	Pink
Security	Door & window contacts	22	2	Stranded	None	Gray
	Motion sensor, glass break	22	4	Stranded	None	Gray
	Keypads	22	4	Stranded	None	Gray
	Advanced keypad with voice pickup and playback	18	2	Stranded	Shielded	Pink
	Driveway probe	18	3	Stranded	Direct burial	Black
Video	Video signal	RG6	1	Shielded Solid	Shielded	Black/White

Table 1-8   Recommended structured wiring cable application

cables. For the most part, category UTP wiring has the same eight wire colors in four matched pairs, but the outer covering of other types of wire is available in a rainbow of colors. For best results, use the same color wire or cable for the same purpose throughout a home. This will make installation and troubleshooting a lot easier.

Table 1-8 provides includes some guidelines on which wiring type is recommended for particular subsystems, including a suggestion outer jacket color for the cables.

Test the Wiring

After what typically seems like miles of cable, speaker, coaxial, composite, and Cat 5 have been pulled into the walls, under the floor, or above the ceiling, and all of the connectors are attached and the wall plates are mounted, a second round of testing should be performed. Yes, a second round. The first round of continuity and attenuation testing should have been done immediately after each cable segment was pulled into place. At this point the wiring should be subjected to a full range of tests.

Even if you are absolutely sure of your work in soldering on the connectors and the connections made at the punch down block, always test the cable at this point in the process.

Especially in new construction, a cable can be "nailed" or "screwed" when the drywall was attached to the wall.

The testing process includes two steps: a visual inspection and a "buzz out" of the wire. Of course, a visual inspection must be done before new walls are completed or from down in the basement or crawl space or up in the attic. You are looking for the obvious, nails or screws piercing the cable, or cuts, gashes, kinks, and breaks in the cable.

A buzz out test of the cabling involves the use of a cable tester, which is also referred to as a "fox and hound." What a cable tester does is send an electrical signal through the cable. Some testers require connectors to work; others use a vibrating electrical noise that is placed on the wire by one device (the fox) and, hopefully, detected by the other device (the hound). This is a two-person job, period. Of course, all of the cables are labeled and documented on a wire chart. Completely test all wiring before beginning the fix-it process, if necessary.

For RG6 coaxial cabling, the testing should include a test for shorts, cable length, continuity, and cable termination. For Cat-5 or Cat-6 cables, testers are available that will verify compliance of your wiring runs and terminations to these standards.

 CROSS-REFERENCE   Chapter 3 covers cable installation and testing in more detail.

Chapter Review

When installing wire and cable in a home, you must be aware of the voltage specification of the cable in use. There are certain cable types that are specified as low voltage and those specified as high voltage. Low voltage cable is designed to carry lower levels of alternating current (AC) and direct current (DC) voltages.

Low voltage wiring is defined as being one of five types of circuits: communication circuits, signal circuits, remote control circuits, motor control circuits, and power-limited circuits. Low voltage circuits are divided into three circuit classes: power-limited, remote control and signaling, and direct current.

The most common types of electrical wiring used for home construction today are: modern non-metallic (NM), underground feeder (UF), and zip wire. Some older wire types you may encounter in a home are: flexible armored cable, metal conduit, early NM, and knob and tube.

The wire gauge used in a home depends on the number of amperes on a particular circuit. Remember that a smaller gauge means a bigger and less flexible wire. Heavier gauge wire should be used to avoid voltage drops and to overcome heat problems.

Twisted-pair (TP) wiring is by far the most popularly installed media for networking in just about any type of network for many reasons, including that it is inexpensive, easy to handle, and readily available. TP wire, Cat5, is the de facto standard for both Ethernet and Token Ring networks.

UTP cable carries a variety of rating codes, which are assigned by the product performance and safety authorities and testing laboratories. The primary rating codes for UTP cable are defined by the NEC (National Electric Code), published by the National Fire Protection Association, as CM, CMP, CMR. Twisted pair cable is available as shielded twisted pair (STP) and unshielded twisted pair (UTP).

Coaxial cable is constructed of a single inner core wire conductor that is encased in a layer of dielectric insulation, which is then wrapped by a wire mesh outer conductor and shield. A plastic sheathing covers the cable. Coaxial cable is single-ended cable with a single signal path and a single return path. RG6 is the most common coaxial cable installed in homes.

When an audio signal is transmitted, A/V cable stores (voltage) and releases (current) an electrical wave at certain frequencies and amplitudes and is generally combined under the term frequency. An audio/video signal consists of a collection of high and low frequency waves. An audio/video releases or passes an audio signal to the next component without slowing down the signal. A cable with the ability to release the signal at the right time is called in-phase.

A balanced audio cable uses both positive and negative carriers with a grounding carrier added. In an unbalanced cable, the grounding signals are combined onto the negative carrier.

Parallel or speaker wire is available in a variety of wire gauges, ranging from 8-gauge on the high end to 24-gauge on the low end.

There are a variety of cables that can be used with video systems. The primary types of video cable are: coaxial, component, and composite. Typically, 16-gauge stranded twisted-pair wire or 14- to 18-gauge audio cable is used for an average length speaker run.

The primary performance properties of metallic wire are: attenuation, cancellation, crosstalk, interference, and inductance.

Structured wiring involves the installation of wire homeruns to each room, zone, or area of a home. Structured wiring can be installed in two ways: pulling each individual cable separately or pulling a cable bundle. A 2+2 cable includes two runs of UTP Cat 5e cable and two runs of RG-6 coaxial cable. The 2+2+2 cable adds two runs of fiber optic cable to 2+2 bundle.

Control wire bundles typically include a single run each of RG-59 coaxial cable and Cat 5e cable and two runs of 18-gauge stranded wire, which are used to cable keypads, room controls, intercoms with video, and for supplying power.

Questions

1. Which of the following is not a home circuit type?

   A. Communication circuits

   B. Signal circuits

   C. Wireless communication circuits

   D. Power-limited circuits

2. What is the term that describes the metallic core of a wire?

   A. Armor

   B. Conductor

   C. Insulator

   D. Jacket

3. What is the general name used for common household electric cable?

   A. Modern NM/Romex

   B. NMC

   C. UF

   D. Zip wire

4. According to Table 1-2, what wire gauge should be used for a circuit with 30 amperes?

   A. 20 AWG

   B. 18 AWG

   C. 14 AWG

   D. 10 AWG

5. When an audio cable is able to release all audio frequencies without adding delay, the cable is said to be

   A. Out-of-phase

   B. In-sync

   C. In-phase

   D. Synchronous

6. Which cable type has a single inner core wire conductor and a wire mesh outer conductor?

   A. UTP

   B. STP

   C. Coaxial

   D. 16g-4

7. Which type of audio/video cable includes carriers for both positive and negative signals, but also includes a grounding carrier as well?

   A. Coaxial

   B. Balanced

C. UTP

D. Parallel pair

8. Which cable type resembles a lamp cord?

A. Coaxial

B. Balanced

C. UTP

D. Parallel pair

9. What is the cable property that states the distance at which the signal traveling on a cable begins to weaken?

A. Attenuation

B. Cancellation

C. Crosstalk

D. Interference

10. What is the common used term that describes a bundled cable with two runs of UTP and two runs of coaxial cable?

A. UC cable

B. Structured bundle

C. 2+2

D. 2+2+2

Answers

1. **C.** Wireless communication circuits. By being wireless, these systems are not part of a house's wiring structure.

2. **B.** Conductor. A conductor has the ability to store and release an electrical current.

3. **A.** Modern NM/Romex. Non-metallic cable is the currently accepted standard for general household electrical wiring.

4. **D.** 10 AWG. This wire is rated for a 30-amp, 240-volt system.

5. **C.** In-phase. The opposite is true when a cable releases lower frequencies later than its higher frequencies.

6. **C.** Coaxial. Both the inner core (positive) and the outer conductor (negative) carry signals.

7. **B.** Balanced. The balance comes from having conductors for both positive and negative signals and a separate conductor for grounding but on other cables may be combined onto the negative carrier.

8. **D.** Parallel pair. This cable looks very much like a lamp cord and is also referred to as rip cable for the ease with which the two conductors can be separated.

9. **A.** Attenuation. Attenuation can be overcome with shorter cable runs or a signal extender, such as a repeater.

10. **C.** 2+2. This type of cable combines two runs of UTP and two runs of coaxial cable into a single cable bundle that is easier to install and provides for future expansion of the home system.

Connector Types and Uses

In this chapter, you will learn about:
- Structured wiring connectors
- Specialized connectors
- Cable preparation and connector installation

Connectors are a major part of home technology integration and home automation. Properly installing the right connector on the right cable is very important to the success of a home's system. Connectors (and their receptacles) create the interfaces that allow electrical signals to flow over the cables between devices. Without them there would be no data, sound, images, or control on the network.

In the structured wiring environment, not that many different types of cable and wiring are used. Typically, the majority of the cabling is twisted-pair (TP) and coaxial, with some quad wire and speaker wire used as required. As a result, the number and types of connectors used is also fairly limited. However, in different applications, you have connector choices based on the type of connection or interface a particular system may require.

This chapter focuses on the connectors commonly used with the cable and wire used in a structured wiring system and the processes used for their installation.

Connector Terminology

There is a definite set of terms used to specify, describe, and name connectors. Some of these terms represent the name of the standards authority that defined a certain connector; others are shorthand or abbreviations for technical terms; and still others are names that describe the shape, use, or application of a connector or are names that have just caught on.

Here is a list of terms common to just about all connectors that describe parts and components of connectors in general:

- **Backboard**   A plywood panel mounted on the wall of a telecom or distribution where a cross-connect device is mounted.

- **Connector**   A device that allows electrical signals to flow from one wire or cable to another.

- **DB-n connector**   Also called D-shell connector, this type of connector facilitates parallel signal transfers. The housing is D-shaped and contains either a male or female plug. The "n" in DB-n represents the number of pins or contacts (male or female) in the connector. For example, a DB-9 connector has 9 pins or contacts and a DB-25 has 25 pins or contacts. Figure 2-1 shows an example of a data bus (DB) connector.

- **Female**   A type of connector plug that has pin receptacles in its housing. See Figure 2-2.

- **Male**   A type of connector plug that has one or more pins extending from its housing. See Figure 2-2.

- **Mass termination**   Although gruesome sounding, this means that all of the wire in a cable are terminated into a connector in a single operation.

- **Molded cable**   A cable assembly that has molded connectors terminating one or both of its ends. Figures 2-2 and 2-3 show molded cables.

- **Plug**   A male connector housing with male or female contacts (see Figure 2-2).

- **Receptacle**   A female connector housing with either male or female contacts.

- **Strain relief**   A molded sleeve or a clamping device that is either incorporated into the connector body or can be attached during termination that provides mechanical support to ensure the cable and wires are not pulled out of the connector and the contacts broken during installation, handling, or from the weight of the cable itself. See Figure 2-4.

Figure 2-1
Examples of male (right) and female (left) DB-9 connectors

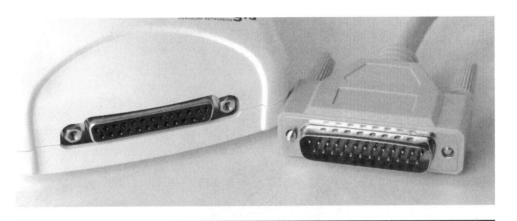

Figure 2-2   Examples of connector plugs with male contacts (right) and female (left) contacts

 CROSS-REFERENCE   The glossary contained in Appendix B of this book contains additional connector, cable, and wiring terms and their meanings.

Power Connectors

When installing some systems in a home technology project, it may be necessary to connect to the AC power system. As a part of this activity, you may need to use one or more power connectors.

Figure 2-3
An example of
a molded cable

*Photo courtesy of
Canare Corporation
of America.*

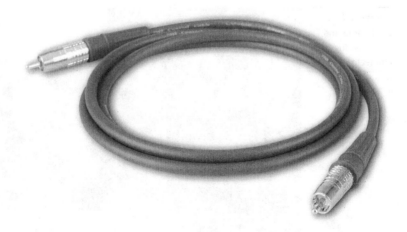

Figure 2-4
The strain relief
on a molded
audio cable

*Original image courtesy
of Canare Corporation
of America.*

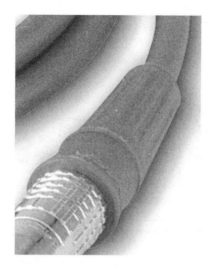

The basic types of power connectors are

- **Lug**   Also called a compression lug, this connector is attached to the end of a power cable. When used with stranded wire, a lug is crimped onto the wire; when used with solid core wire, the lug should be soldered to the wire. Lugs come in a variety of types: single-hole or dual-hole flat connectors, ring connectors, forked connectors, and spade connectors. Figure 2-5 shows a selection of a variety of lug connectors. Lugs have different ratings for use with different wire sizes and some require specialized crimping tools.

- **Plug**   As shown in Figure 2-6, the standard three-contact electrical plug is commonly attached to the power cord of virtually all electrical appliances,

Figure 2-5
Single-hole and
dual-hole lug
connectors

*Photo courtesy
of Telect, Inc.*

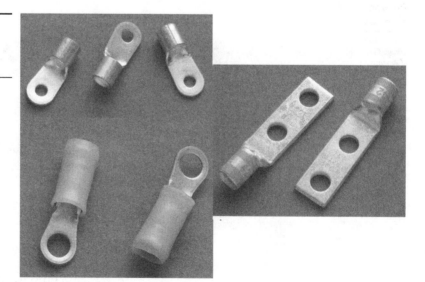

Figure 2-6
A standard three-contact U.S. electrical plug

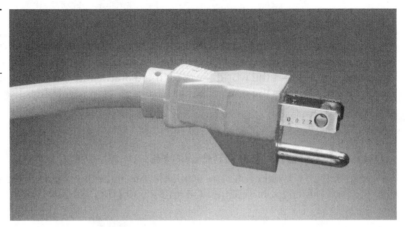

control systems, and power supplies in North America. Lamps and other low-voltage devices use only a two-contact plug. There are several types of electrical plugs used in the United States, with different plugs used for different applications. Around the world, electrical plug patterns, shapes, and sizes vary by country and region (see the following section).

- **Receptacle**   A device with female contacts that makes an electrical contact with an inserted plug.

- **Terminal strip**   Not to be confused with a plug strip, a terminal strip is used to make multiple connections by either soldering a wire to a contact, connecting with a lug style connector, or connecting with a screw terminal. Figure 2-7 shows an example of a solder terminal strip. Terminal strips are used in a variety of systems, including AC and DC power and telecom cabling.

Figure 2-7
A terminal strip on which connecting wires are soldered

Photo courtesy of Molex, Inc.

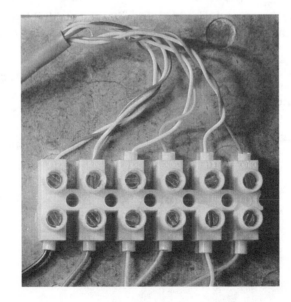

Electrical Plugs

As I discuss in the preceding section, electrical plugs vary from country to country, depending on the electrical system in use. Figure 2-8 illustrates some of the various types of plugs used throughout the world. In the United States and Canada, Type A and B plugs are used. Table 2-1 lists the power characteristics and electrical plugs used in a sample of other countries.

Coaxial Cable Connectors

A wide variety of coaxial cables are available, but in a structured wiring system, the primary coaxial cable types used are RG6 and RG59 ("RG" stands for Radio Guide).

F-Type Connectors

The F-type connector is the most commonly used connector for home systems that apply coaxial cabling. F-type connectors are available as either a screw-on or a crimp-on type connector.

F-Type Twist-On Connectors

To terminate a coaxial cable with a crimp-on F-type connector (see Figure 2-9), use the following steps:

1. Use a knife to cut around the plastic outer layer about 1-inch (25 millimeters) from the end of the cable. Take care not to cut the mesh or braided copper shielding under the outer jacket of the cable. Remove the cut away outer covering and separate wires of the braided shielding so that they can be twisted together to create a "pigtail."

2. After removing the braided shielding, a metal foil layer should be exposed. Cut off the exposed portion of the foil shielding.

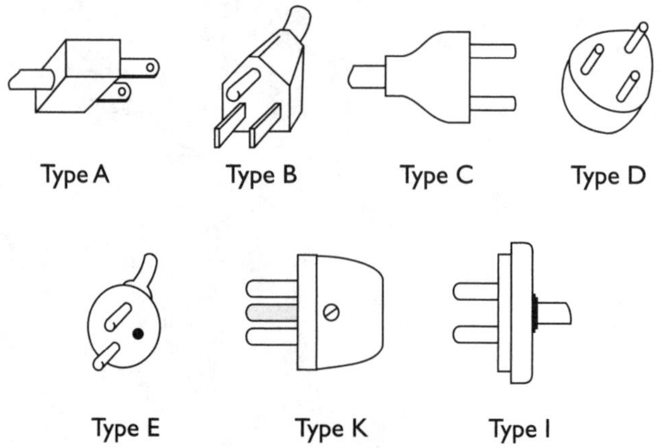

Figure 2-8
A sampling of the different electrical plugs used around the world

Type A   Type B   Type C   Type D

Type E   Type K   Type I

Country	Voltage	Frequency	Plug Type
Australia	230V	50 Hz	I
China	220V	50 Hz	A and I
Colombia	110V	60 Hz	A and B
Czech Republic	230V	50 Hz	E
Denmark	220V	50 Hz	C and K
Egypt	220V	50 Hz	C
France	230V	50 Hz	E
Germany	230V	50 Hz	C
India	240V	50 Hz	C and D
Ireland	230V	50 Hz	E
Japan	100V	50/60 Hz	A and B
Mexico	127V	60 Hz	A
Russian Federation	220V	50 Hz	C
Sweden	220V	50 Hz	C

Table 2-1
Electrical Characteristics and Electrical Plugs in Use Around the World

3. Use a knife to cut off the white dielectric material, leaving about 1/8-inch (3 mm) of the dielectric material extending out onto the center core to serve as an insulator that prevents the metallic braid "pigtail" from making contact with the center conductor. Be careful not to cut into or through the center conductor wire.

4. Pull the shielding "pigtail" back over the uncut portion of the cable's outer jacket and twist or screw the F-type connector plug over the cable end as far as it can go. The sleeve of the connector should also cover a portion of the "pigtail," trapping it against the outside of the cable. Cut off any exposed portion of the "pigtail."

5. Use wire cutters to cut the end of the exposed center conductor wire at a 45-degree angle, leaving about 1/8-inch (3 mm) extending beyond the end of the F-type jack body. Be careful when handling the terminated cable and jack, the end of the center wire should be a very sharp point.

NOTE If the F-type connector is to be used outside the home, such as to an antenna or satellite dish, it must be sealed to prevent water from getting inside the cable or connector body. The recommended way to seal the cable against water seepage is to wrap the connector sleeve and a portion of the cable with waterproofing or self-amalgamating tape.

Figure 2-9
An F-type twist-on connector for coaxial cabling

F-Type Crimp-On Connectors

Some technicians believe that a crimp-on style F-type connector (see Figure 2-10) provides a tighter and more secure connection. To terminate a coaxial cable with a crimp-on F-type connector, use the following steps:

1. Use a knife to cut away about 3/8-inch (9.5 mm) of the cable's outer covering, exposing the braided metal shielding. Be careful not to cut the braided shielding.

2. Fold the braided shielding back over the outer jacket of the cable.

3. Cut away the metal foil shielding and cut the white dielectric material so that only 1/4-inch (6.3 mm) of the dielectric material is exposed (and 1/8-inch of the center conductor wire is exposed). Take care not to nick, cut, or ding the center conductor wire when cutting the dielectric material. Clean away any dielectric material dust or fuzz that may be on the center wire.

4. Slide the crimp ring over the folded back braided metal shielding and over the cable's outer jacket.

5. Check the exposed edge of the foil shielding that was cut away earlier and ensure that it is lying flat against the dielectric material under the edge of the outer jacket. If any burrs or flags are sticking up, they need to be smoothed down by twisting them flat against the dielectric material.

6. Push the connector sleeve (mandrel) back under the uncut portion of the cable so that the mandrel is placed between the braided shielding and the foil shielding inside the uncut cable.

7. Slide the crimp ring towards the stripped end of the cable so that it fits over the mandrel inside the cable.

8. Use a coaxial crimping tool to secure the connector to the cable.

Coaxial Cable Strippers and Crimpers

When working with coaxial cable, or any cable or wire for that matter, it's best to use tools specifically designed for use with that particular cable type. Several specialized tools are available for stripping and terminating coaxial cable. However, not every tool is designed to work with every type of coaxial cable, so you need to be sure that your tools are specifically designed for RG58, RG59, or RG6, depending on which coaxial cable you are installing.

Figure 2-10

An F-type crimp-on connector for coaxial cabling

Strippers   Coaxial cable strippers are designed to cut through the outer jacket and dielectric layers of a cable, leaving the proper amount of conductor wire for installing any of the various coaxial cable connectors. Figures 2-11 and 2-12 show the two most common types of coaxial cable strippers. Remember that cable strippers are specified to a certain cable type, so be sure you match the tool to the cable and the task.

Coaxial Cable Crimpers   Crimpers are used to clamp a metal connector to a cable. Coaxial cable crimp-on connectors require the use of a crimper tool, but not just any crimper. Crimpers are typically designed to work with a specific type of cable and, in many cases, a special type of connector. Typically, when you are working with coaxial cabling in a home system, the crimper you use is a specialized coaxial cable F-type connector crimper like the one shown in Figure 2-13.

Coaxial Cable Termination Kits   Several cable and connector vendors have prepared connector kits for use with coaxial cable. A typical kit includes all of the pieces and tools commonly needed to terminate coaxial cable in a home system, including a number of professional grade F-type plugs, a coaxial cable stripping tool, an F-type connector crimping tool, and a small tone testing device. In most cases, the tools are specialized for either RG59 or RG6 cable.

BNC Connector

Another type of coaxial connector that could be used in a residential system on RG58 and RG6 cable in data networking and some audio/visual applications is the Bayonet Neill Concellman (BNC) connector. The male portion (plug) of a BNC connector has a bayonet-like shell with two small pins that fit into spiral slots located on the female portion (receptacle) of the connector. The plug is inserted into the receptacle and twisted into a locked position.

There are two styles of BNC connectors used: a BNC-T connector and a BNC barrel connector. The BNC-T connector is commonly used for Ethernet data networks to interconnect

Figure 2-11
A handheld
coaxial cable
stripper

Photo courtesy of
Paladin Tools, Inc.

Figure 2-12
A plier-type
coaxial cable
stripper

*Photo courtesy
of Harris Corp.*

a computer's network adapter to the coaxial cable. However, a BNC barrel connector can also be used with some network adapters as well. When used with video and Community Antenna Television (CATV, which is better known as cable TV) systems, the barrel style connector is the most common. Figure 2-14 shows a BNC-T connector and Figure 2-15 shows a barrel style BNC connector.

Figure 2-13
A coaxial cable
F-type crimper
tool

*Photo courtesy of Graber
Bender.*

PART I

Figure 2-14
A BNC-T style connector

TP Cable Connectors

Depending on the application, Category (Cat) 3, 5, 5e, and higher TP cable use one of the following modular connectors (which are also referenced as keystone connectors because of the shape of their plugs and jacks):

- **Registered jack (RJ)-11** This is the standard two- or four-conductor telephone connector used to connect telephone handsets to telephone outlets. Figure 2-16 shows an RJ-11 plug.

Figure 2-15
A BNC barrel-style connector

Figure 2-16
An RJ-11 plug

- **RJ-31x** This is the connection type used to interface a security system into a home's telephone system. Figure 2-17 shows an RJ-31x modular jack.
- **RJ-45** This is the standard TP connector used for data networking. Figure 2-18 shows an RJ-45 connector.

Registered Jacks

The "RJ" in each of the jacks listed above stands for registered jack, which means that the jack and plug conform to the standards specified in the Universal Service Order Code (USOC), published by the U.S. Federal Communications Commission (FCC), which defines the standard telephone and data communications jacks and plugs. Table 2-2 lists the most common USOC jacks. Although the standard refers mostly to jacks, it also includes the plugs that fit the jacks.

 NOTE You will commonly see the registered jack designations in Table 2-2 listed with a suffix of C, W, or X, which refers to the type of connection and equipment in which they are most commonly used. The C refers to desk sets; the W refers to wall sets; and the X refers to special-purpose jacks.

Figure 2-17
An RJ-31x
modular jack

Figure 2-18
An RJ-45 plug

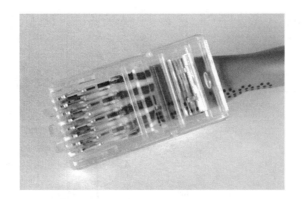

Wiring RJ-11 Jacks and Plugs

To attach an RJ-11 jack or plug to a run of TP wiring, the first thing you must know is how many lines the jack will be supporting. If the jack and plug are being used to connect a single telephone line, then only two conductors are needed to make the connection; however, it is always best to connect four or more conductors to provide for expansion of the telephone system in the future. As listed in Table 2-2, two-line connections use four conductors (which is technically an RJ-14 configuration) and three-line connections use six conductors (RJ-25).

Registered Jack	Contacts	Conductors Used	Usage
RJ-11	6	2	Single-line telephone
RJ-12	6	4	Single-line telephone on key system
RJ-13	6	6	Single-line telephone on key system
RJ-14	6	4	Two-line telephones
RJ-15	3	3	Single-line weatherproof telephone connections
RJ-17	6	2	Medical equipment
RJ-21X	50	50	Amphenol connector for 25-pair 66-style punchdown blocks
RJ-22	4	4	Telephone handset connector
RJ-25	6	6	Three-line telephones
RJ-31X	8	4 or 6	Security system to telephone interface
RJ-45	8	4 or 8	Data networking connector
RJ-48	8	4 or 8	T-1 networking connections
RJ-61X	8	8	Eight-conductor version of RJ-45

Table 2-2   Common USOC Registered Jacks

Figure 2-19
A diagram of
the wiring used
with an RJ-11
connector

Jack

Plug

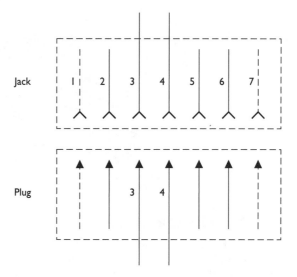

The reason each line requires two conductors is that two contacts are required for telephone communications. These two lines, which are referred to as "Tip" and "Ring" are the modern-day equivalents of the plugs used by switchboard operators years ago. When the operator inserted the plug into the jack to complete a circuit between an incoming call and a telephone in her office or building, the tip of the plug completed one loop and the metal ring around the shaft of the plug completed the other, linking the incoming circuit to a particular line and handset.

To terminate TP wire in an RJ-11 configuration, one wire pair (typically the blue and white-blue) is connected to contacts (pins) 3 and 4 (the center two contacts) of the jack and plug, as illustrated in Figure 2-19.

Most RJ-11 jacks and plugs use a 66-type punchdown or insulation displacement connector (IDC) into which each wire is inserted using a punchdown tool fitted with a 66-type blade. The photo in Figure 2-20 of an RJ-45 jack shows IDC contacts on the back of the connector. The punchdown tool, see Figure 2-21, pushes an individual wire into an IDC slot and cuts away any excess insulation and wire. The contact is made by the IDC piercing the insulation on the wire.

Figure 2-20
An RJ-45 jack
with IDC
contacts

*Photo courtesy of
SignaMax Connectivity
Systems.*

Figure 2-21
A punchdown
tool is used to
insert wires into
the IDC on
punchdown
connectors.

*Photo courtesy
of Harris Corp.*

 NOTE   The 66-style punchdown is used for telephone and other voice
connections. If data networking connections use an IDC-type connector,
they use the newer 110-type punchdown.

RJ-11 jacks and plugs can also be attached to TP wiring using a crimper with the
proper attachments. After the appropriate wires are placed into the slots corresponding
to the proper pins on the jack or plug, the crimper is used to cinch clasping material on
the connector to hold the wire in place. Figure 2-22 shows a TP wiring crimper.

Figure 2-22
A crimper can
be used to attach
RJ jacks and plugs
to a cable.

*Photo courtesy of
Tecra Tools, Inc.*

Wiring RJ-31X Jacks and Plugs

An RJ-31X jack can be connected to one of the outside phone lines of a home and optionally to the home's inside phone lines. It seizes an outgoing phone line, alerting the monitoring station when there is a security event. If you wish to allow the security system to seize more than one line to prevent interruptions, then separate RJ-31X jacks can be connected to each of the inside phone lines.

If the RJ-31X is only being connected to the outside lines, then only two of its conductors need be connected. However, if one inside line is to be made available for line seizure by the security system, two additional conductors are connected for that line. If more than one inside line is to be connected to the security system, multiple RJ-31X jacks are required.

RJ-31X jacks have a small 66-type punchdown block inside the housing of the jack. Punchdown blocks make it easy to connect inside lines to outside lines. Assuming an RJ-31X jack has eight inside IDCs and eight outside IDCs in the punchdown block, Table 2-3 lists the configuration of the punchdown to connect the jack to the telephone lines and Figure 2-23 illustrates this connection.

Wiring RJ-45 Jacks and Plugs

The RJ-45 jacks and plugs are the standards for terminating TP cable used for data networks. However, these connectors are more commonly known by the networking standards (568a and 568b) that are used to configure the jack and plug connections. While RJ-45 describes the USOC jack and plug used to make the connections in a data network, other standards are used to describe the actual wiring of the jack and plug.

TP Wire Color

In a standard four-pair unshielded twisted-pair (UTP) cable (Cat 5, Cat 5e, Cat 6, and Cat 7), each pair of wires shares a base color. As shown in Figures 2-24 and 2-25, the base colors are orange, blue, green, and brown. One of the wires in each pair has a solid color jacket and one has a jacket with a color strip alternating with a white strip.

Wire	Source	Inside Phone Line #1	Inside Phone Line #1	Outside Phone Line #2	Outside Phone Line #2
White (TP)	Jack	Tip			
Blue (TP)	Jack	Ring			
White-Blue (TP)	Internal wiring		Tip		
Blue (TP)	Internal wiring		Ring		
Red (Quad)	Telco central office (CO)			Tip	
Green (Quad)	CO			Ring	
Red (Quad)	Jack				Tip
Green (Quad)	Jack				Ring

Table 2-3   RJ-31X Wire Connections

From Internal
Phone Wiring
Blue
White/Blue
From Outside
Telephone Lines
Blue
Green
White
Red

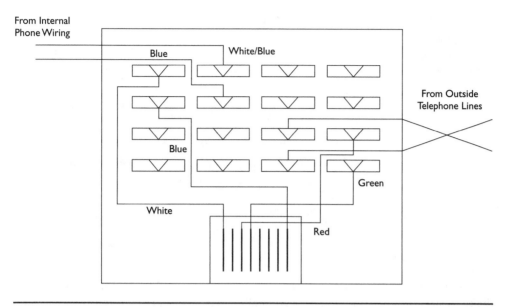

Figure 2-23 A diagram of wiring for a single telephone line in an RJ-31X jack

The color-coding on the wires provides you with end-to-end consistency when you are terminating a cable with connectors. If the wires were all one color, it would be easy to get your wires crossed.

Installing an RJ-45 plug on a UTP cable is a matter of orientation and color. Orienting the plug to receive the cable wires consists of turning the plug so that the locking tab, or what the Telco people call the "hook," is on the bottom and the open end of the connector is towards you.

Figure 2-24 The Electronics Industry Association/Telecommunications Industry Association (EIA/TIA) 568A RJ-45 wiring configuration

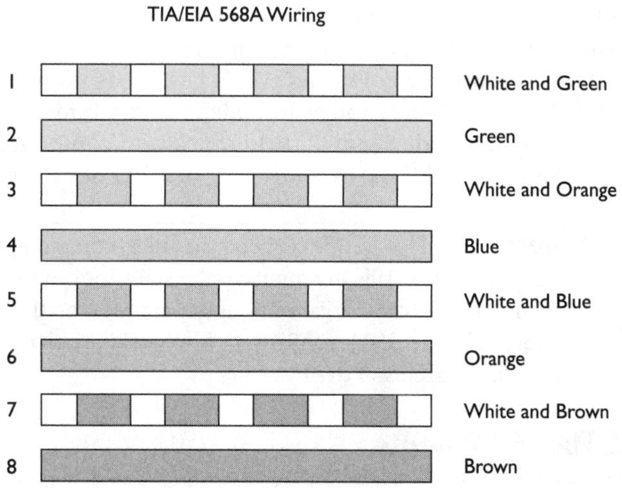

TIA/EIA 568A Wiring
1
White and Green
2
Green
3
White and Orange
4
Blue
5
White and Blue
6
Orange
7
White and Brown
8
Brown

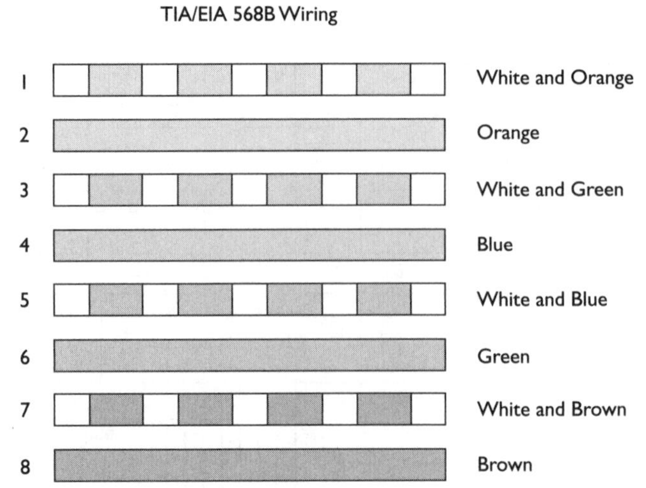

Figure 2-25

The EIA/TIA 568B RJ-45 wiring configuration

TIA/EIA 568B Wiring

1	White and Orange
2	Orange
3	White and Green
4	Blue
5	White and Blue
6	Green
7	White and Brown
8	Brown

With the plug in this position, Pin 1 is located on the left side and Pin 8 is located on the right side. It's important to know where Pin 1 is located so that the correct wires are inserted into the correct pins.

Most quality jacks are color-coded on their IDC contacts or if the jack is a crimp-on type, on a bar located above the pin contacts. On a punchdown block, Pin 1 is indicated with the number 1 and on a crimp-style jack, Pin 1 is on the far-left side and Pin 8 is on the far-right side (looking at the jack from the front).

TP Wiring Standards

The two wiring standards used to define how TP cable is attached to an RJ-45 jack or plug are Electronics Industry Association/Telecommunications Industry Association (EIA/TIA) 568A and 568B.

The primary difference between these two cable standards is the sequence and placement of the green and orange wire pairs on the plug or receptacle. Actually, for a computer network installation, there is actually no difference in performance between the two standards because the color of a wire's jacket has no bearing on the signal being transmitted. However, if the cable is intended to carry both data and voice (telephone) traffic, the 568A standard (Figure 2-26) is backward compatible with the older USOC telephone standards and EIA/TIA 568B (Figure 2-27) doesn't support voice signals.

 NOTE Although 568B has been the most commonly used of the two 568 standards, especially in commercial installations in the United States, most technical and trade organizations generally agree that all future installations should use the 568A configuration to avoid problems with integrated voice and data systems in the future.

TP EIA/TIA 568 Pinouts

When you install an RJ-45 jack or plug on the end of a UTP cable, it is very important that you match the correct pin to the correct wire color. However, beyond the differences

Figure 2-26

The EIA/TIA 568A cable termination standard for TP cable also supports voice signals.

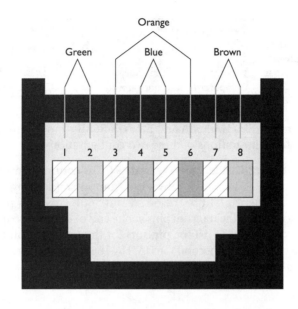

between 568A and 568B, there are differences between the pinout (which pin is connected to which wire) patterns required to support different types of connections made between different types of hardware. The pattern you use depends on the requirements of the equipment to which the cable will be attached. Table 2-4 lists the types of wiring patterns used in common network situations.

Straight-Through Pinout A straight-through pinout on an RJ-45 connector matches the same color wires on both the plug and the receptacle. In other words, the orange, blue, green, and brown wires on the plug match up and connect to the orange, blue, green, and brown wires on the receptacle. Tables 2-5 and 2-6 list the pinouts for

Figure 2-27

The EIA/TIA 568B cable termination standard for TP cable

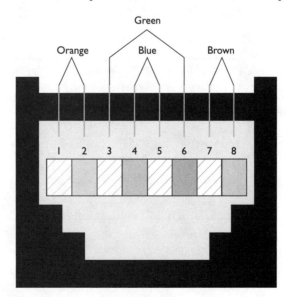

Table 2-4	Connection Type	Pattern
Pinout Patterns for Certain Network Connection Types	Computer-to-hub/hub-to-computer	Straight-through
	Computer-to-computer	Cross-connect (crossover)
	Computer-to-Internet gateway	Cross-connect (crossover)

straight-through EIA/TIA 568A and EIA/TIA 568B connections, respectively. Figures 2-26 and 2-27 show illustrations of these two configurations.

Cross-Connect/Crossover Pinout   Cross-connect connector configuration is used when the cable is installed between a computer (actually, the computer's network adapter) and a network hub. The 568A and 568B crossover patterns reverse two of the wire pairs to connect the transmit pins at one end of the cable to the receive pins at the other end. Tables 2-7 and 2-8 list the pinouts for the jacks and plugs at each end of a cross-connect or crossover connection for EIA/TIA 568A and 568B, respectively, and Figures 2-28 and 2-29 illustrate these wiring patterns.

Table 2-5	Pin	Wire Color
Pinout for Straight-Through EIA/TIA 568A Connection	1	White-green
	2	Green
	3	White-orange
	4	Blue
	5	White-blue
	6	Orange
	7	White-brown
	8	Brown

Table 2-6	Pin	Wire Color
Pinout for Straight-Through EIA/TIA 568B Connection	1	White-orange
	2	Orange
	3	White-green
	4	Blue
	5	White-blue
	6	Green
	7	White-brown
	8	Brown

Table 2-7
EIA/TIA 568A
Crossover
Pinouts

	Connector		
A			B
Pin	Wire Color		Pin
I	White-green		3
2	Green		6
3	White-orange		I
4	Blue		7
5	White-blue		8
6	Orange		2
7	White-brown		4
8	Brown		5

Table 2-8
EIA/TIA 568B
Crossover
Pinouts

	Connector		
A			B
Pin	Wire Color		Pin
I	White-orange		3
2	Orange		6
3	White-green		I
4	Blue		7
5	White-blue		8
6	Green		2
7	White-brown		4
8	Brown		5

Figure 2-28
Pinout for
crossover
EIA/TIA 568A
connection

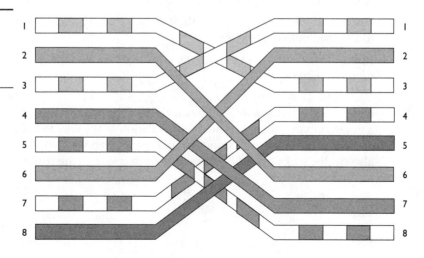

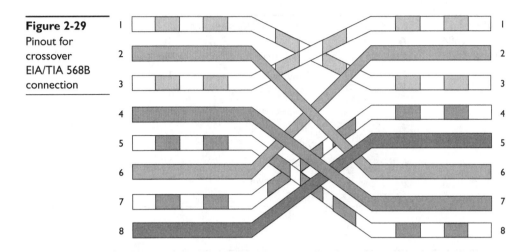

Figure 2-29
Pinout for
crossover
EIA/TIA 568B
connection

Attaching an RJ-45 Connector

To attach an RJ-45 plug to a UTP cable, follow these steps:

1. Strip away about 1.25-inches of the outer jacket of the UTP cable. Use a CatX (the X represents category cables 3 and above) cable stripper, if one's available. The cable sheathing should not be stripped more than 1.25-inches from the connection end of the cable and 1-inch is best.

2. Untwist the exposed wire pairs, but avoid untwisting the wires at the end of the jacket. UTP wire should not be untwisted more than 0.5-inch and 0.375-inch is best.

3. Arrange the wires in a flat row in the order that matches the pinout pattern for the cable purpose (see the preceding sections). For example, for a straight-through connector, arrange the wires left to right as white-green, green, white-orange, blue, white-blue, orange, white-brown, and brown.

4. Use wire-cutters to trim the length of the wires to 0.5-inch. There is no need to strip the individual wires.

5. Insert the wires into the RJ-45 plug, ensuring that the wires remain in the required pattern.

6. Use an RJ-45 crimping tool (see Figure 2-30) to push the gold insulation displacement contacts into contact with the wires. The crimper also pushes down a hinged tab that presses against the insulation of the wire to hold it into the plug and create a strain relief. Some crimper tools when used with special connectors also cut the wires extending beyond the other side of the connector.

Figure 2-30

A crimping tool used to install RJ-45 plugs on UTP cable

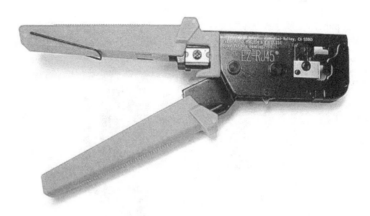

NOTE Actually, you can buy UTP cables with RJ-45 connectors attached. This can be very expensive for longer run cables. However, it is a good option for patch cords and cables.

Punchdowns and IDC Connectors

In many networking situations, centralizing the network resources provides for better control, maintenance, and security. Not all home networks are large enough to require centralization, but in a larger home with several networked subsystems, having the servers, controllers, and source devices in a central location is generally a good idea.

Using a central wiring closet or panel simplifies network maintenance, troubleshooting, and expansion. The central wiring panel terminates all of the network cabling and provides an interface for all of the controlling devices to all of the home automation network as is needed.

For the TP cable part of a home network, a patch panel can be used as the clustering device. A patch panel looks, and in many ways functions, like the old operator-controlled telephone switchboards (see Figure 2-31). Cable home runs terminate to the back of the patch panel using IDC contacts. A patch cord is then used to connect each run to the next upstream device as appropriate. For example, the patch panel can interconnect a networked computer to a network switch that supports both voice and data services.

The two most common types of IDC contacts are the 66 block and the 110 block. The 66 block is used primarily in telephone and voice system connections. The 110 is used for data networks. The wires of the TP cable are pressed into the IDC contacts using a punchdown tool, shown earlier in Figure 2-21.

Figure 2-31
A patch panel
with RJ-45 jacks

Photo courtesy of
SignaMax Connectivity
Systems.

Fiber Optic Connectors

Fiber optic cable is included in several types of structured wiring cable bundles and often installed in homes for two reasons: for its speed and bandwidth, and for future-proofing the home. Few home system devices currently exist that connect to fiber optic cable.

Fiber optic cable is terminated using one of three general types of connectors:

- **Interface connectors**   Connectors that connect a fiber optic cable to a networking device

- **Inline connectors**   Connectors that mates two glass or plastic fibers from separate cable runs to form a temporary joint

- **Splices**   Connectors that create a permanent joint between two fiber optic cable runs

In each of these connections, the termination must use an approved connector that is properly installed to minimize light loss and protect the cable from dirt or being damaged. More than 75 different interface and inline connectors are available on the market that can be installed in several different ways, but luckily only a few are commonly used in most residential applications. And fortunately, there are only two ways to splice a cable.

As I discussed in Chapter 1, fiber optic cable is single-mode, multimode, or plastic optical fiber (POF). Different connectors and splicing methods are used for each type of fiber optic cable. When connecting or splicing fiber optic cable, you must first know which type of cable you are working with.

Fiber Optic Connector Basics

The two basic types of fiber optic connectors are butt-jointed and expanded-beam connectors.

Butt-jointed connectors align two prepared fiber ends into very close proximity or in contact with one another. There are two types of butt-jointed connectors: ferrule and biconical.

- **Ferrule connectors**   This type of butt-jointed fiber optic connector uses two cylindrical ceramic plugs (called ferrules) and an alignment sleeve. The exposed and prepared fiber strand is inserted into precision holes through the center of each ferrule, which aligns it properly. The quality of this type of connection is dependent on how accurately the center holes of each ferrule are in alignment. Epoxy resin adhesive is used to permanently hold the fiber strand in the ferrule. The ends of the fiber strands must be polished so that they are flush with the end of the ferrule to prevent light loss in the connection. The ferrules are inserted into the alignment sleeve, which by aligning the ferrules, aligns the fiber strands. This is the method used for straight tip (ST) connectors.

- **Biconical connectors**   This type of butt-jointed connector uses two cone-shaped plugs that are inserted into a double cone-shaped alignment sleeve. Springs in each plug provide the tension that joins the two fiber strands. Epoxy resin is used to secure the plugs into the alignment sleeve. A threaded outer shell is then used to lock in the alignment of the fibers.

Expanded-beam connectors use lenses to expand and refocus light from one fiber to another. Like butt-jointed connectors, expanded-beam connectors are made up of two plugs and a coupling alignment device.

Fiber Optic Connectors

When choosing a fiber optic connector for residential structured wiring, there are four criteria to consider:

- **Availability**   Is the connector a standard connector and will it be readily available for future expansion or repair work?

- **Compatibility**   Is the connector compatible with the bridging and source equipment?

- **Tools**   Are special tools required to install or test the connector?

- **Reliability**   Is the connector reliable and subject to certain environmental conditions?

NOTE Of the connectors listed in this section, the ST connector is considered to be the most reliable, available, and compatible of the fiber optic connectors.

The most common fiber optic connectors that should be used in a residential situation are

- **SC** This connector, shown in Figure 2-32, is a push-pull snap on and off connector that is very similar to audio and video connectors in that it is small enough in size to allow multiple connectors to connect into a patch panel or other networking devices. SC (568SC) is the connector currently specified by TIA 568 for both single-mode and multimode fiber cable.

- **Straight tip (ST)** The ST connector (see Figure 2-33) was the original standard for fiber optic connections, but is no longer recommended by TIA for new installations. It has been replaced by the SC (568SC) connector in the current standards.

- **Lucent connector (LC)** The LC connector (see Figure 2-34) looks just like an SC connector, but is one-half its size. The size of the LC is based on the size of the RJ-45 connector and is designated as a small form factor (SFF) connector for fiber optic cable.

Figure 2-32
An SC fiber
optic plug

Figure 2-33
An ST fiber
optic plug

*Photo courtesy of
Fiber Connections, Inc.*

- **Face contact (FC)**   The FC connector (see Figure 2-35) uses a threaded plug and sockets to create a secure connection.

- **SMA**   The SMA connector uses a threaded plug and socket that is the first connector standardized in the industry. (See Figure 2-36.)

- **Physical contact (PC)**   Actually, PC is used to describe the end-face polishing used in a connector. The most common of the PC connectors is the FC/PC. A variation of PC is angled polished connector (APC).

- **MT-RJ**   A small form factor two-fiber connector, the MT-RJ connector (see Figure 2-37) is based on the form and size of the RJ-45 connector, which accounts for the RJ in its name.

Figure 2-34
LC fiber optic
connectors

*Photo courtesy of
FiberSource Inc.*

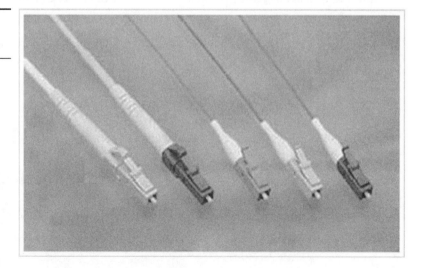

Figure 2-35
FC fiber optic connectors

Photo courtesy of FiberSource Inc.

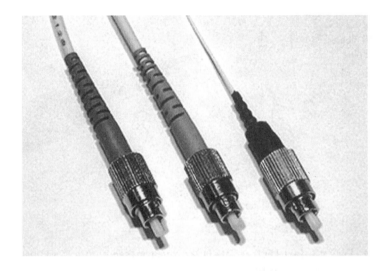

 NOTE I've tried to provide a meaning for the acronyms or abbreviations used for the different fiber optic connectors. However, some meanings are lost to history, assuming that they existed at some point.

Fiber Optic Cable Preparation

In order for fiber optic connections to be secure, the fiber strands must be cleaned before they are mated. Even at the size of a fiber optic strand, dust particles can cause up to 1 dB of signal loss if the cable ends aren't properly cleaned. Dust can be easily removed from the cable and its glass or plastic strands with a blast from a can of compressed air.

Figure 2-36
An SMA fiber optic connector

Photo courtesy of FiberSource Inc.

Figure 2-37
An MT-RJ fiber
optic connector

*Photo courtesy of
Fiber Connections, Inc.*

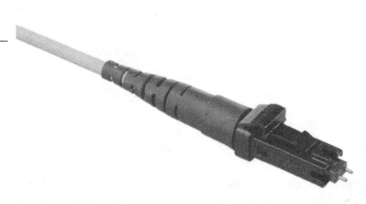

Anytime a cable connection is unmated (disconnected), a rubber or plastic boot should be immediately placed over the ends of the cable or its ferrule to prevent dust from contaminating the cable end.

In addition to removing any dust from the end of the cable, the cable end should also be cleaned using a lint-free cloth or tissue, denatured alcohol, and canned dry air. Saturate the cloth or tissue in alcohol and use it to clean the sides of the connector ferrule. Immediately after cleaning, make the connection. Use the compressed air to clean the outside of the connector housing and receiver ports, if any.

NOTE   Here's a very important safety tip: Never, I repeat never, look directly into the end of a fiber optic strand. It only takes milliseconds for the intense light in the cable to damage your eye permanently. You should also never touch the end of a fiber strand, but this has more to do with cleanliness.

Stripping a Fiber Optic Cable

To strip a fiber optic cable (see Figure 2-38), you should perform these steps:

1. Remove the outer jacket of the cable using an electrical stripping tool.

2. Use a knife or scissors to remove the Kevlar (the same stuff used in bullet-proof vests) strength member. Avoid cutting too deeply into the buffer, coating, and sealing layers around the glass or plastic fiber strand.

3. Carefully remove the buffer, coating, and sealing layers around the fiber strand using a special fiber stripper tool to avoid creating surface flaws or scratches, which could cause the cable to fail.

Figure 2-38
The construction
of a fiber optic
cable

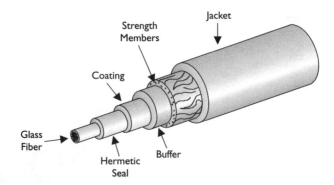

Each fiber optic connector has a unique and required process when it comes to installing the components of the connector. Follow the manufacturer's instructions to the letter to ensure a proper connection that minimizes light loss.

Fiber Optic Connector Standards

Like TP cabling, the standard for cabling and connectors for fiber optic cabling is defined in American National Standards Institute/ Electronics Industry Association/Telecommunications Industry Association (ANSI/EIA/TIA) 568A and soon in a new section for the ANSI/EIA/TIA 568B standard that's currently under development. At present, the 568A standard specifies the SC connector as the 568SC connector, but TIA has published a standard called the Fiber-Optic Cable Intermatability Standard (FOCIS) that recognizes, among others, the fiber optic connectors, listed in Table 2-9 with their standard commercial names.

Computer Data and Cable Connectors

In addition to the RJ connectors I described earlier in the chapter, personal computers (PCs) use a variety of other connectors. These connectors are used to connect to peripheral and other devices, such as printers, scanners, and the like.

Three basic types of physical connectors are most commonly used with PCs:

- Data bus (DB) series connectors
- Universal Serial Bus (USB) connectors
- Institute of Electrical and Electronic Engineers (IEEE)-1394 connectors

Table 2-9	Connector Type	FOCIS Designation
FOCIS Fiber Optic Connectors	FC	FOCIS-4
	SC	FOCIS-3
	SMA	FOCIS-1
	ST	FOCIS-2

Serial Versus Parallel

External connections made to a PC use either serial or parallel data transmission modes. Serial transmissions transfer data one bit at a time in series using a form of single-file transmission over a single transmission line. Parallel transmissions transfer data in waves that are made up of several parallel bits moving on separate transmission lines. Figure 2-39 illustrates the basic difference between these two transmission modes.

DB Series Connectors

As I defined earlier in the chapter, a DB connector is a computer and device connector that is used to transfer data between two serial or parallel interface devices. Typically, the number of pins available in its plug and the matching number of receptacles in its jack are used to specify a DB connector. For example, a DB-25 connector (see Figure 2-2 earlier in the chapter) has 25 pins and 25 receptacles in its plug and jack, respectively. Likewise, a DB-9 connector has nine pins and receptacles.

USB Connectors

The USB provides a high-speed data bus that provides an easy way to connect peripheral devices to a PC. A USB port supports data transfer at speeds of 12 million bits per second (Mbps), which is much faster than the interface available on a standard serial port. USB ports are standard to most newer PCs. Figure 2-40 illustrates a USB connection being made on a PC.

There are two types of USB connectors, see Figure 2-41. Type A connectors are found on PCs and some device interfaces. Type B connectors are found on devices that connect to a PC over a USB connection.

Figure 2-39
Serial data is transmitted one bit at a time over a single line (bottom) and parallel data is transmitted as a wave of bits on several parallel lines (top).

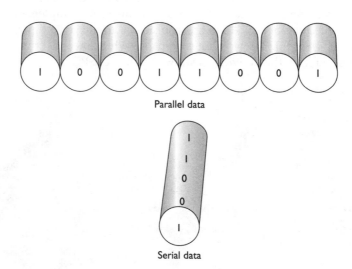

Parallel data

Serial data

Figure 2-40
A USB plug being
inserted into a
USB jack on a PC

IEEE-1394 Connectors

IEEE-1394 connectors are more commonly known by the brand or model names given to them by manufacturers. Perhaps the best-known commercial names for IEEE-1394 connections are FireWire, which is the name used by Apple Computer, and iLink, the name used by the Sony Corp.

IEEE-1394 transfers data in speeds up to 800 Mbps and a single 1394 port can support up to 63 additional external devices. IEEE-1394 uses a transfer technology that is similar to USB, but these two data bus technologies are more complementary than competitive. The connectors for IEEE-1394 are also similar to the USB connectors (see Figure 2-42) and, like USB, IEEE-1394 is hot swappable, which means it can be connected and disconnected from the PC without shutting down the PC.

Figure 2-41
USB cables have
different plugs for
the computer or
hub (right) and
the peripheral
device (left) jacks.

Photo courtesy of
Belkin Components.

Figure 2-42
An illustration
of top and front
views of an
IEEE-1394 plug

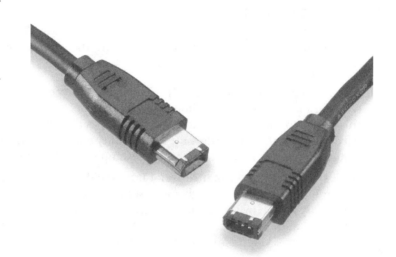

Audio/Video Cable Connectors

The connectors used to terminate the various wire and cable types used on audio systems are fairly standardized. Some systems have multiple connector choices, like the system shown in Figure 2-43.

Figure 2-43
The back panel
of an audio/video
device showing
the jacks for a
variety of signal
and connector
formats

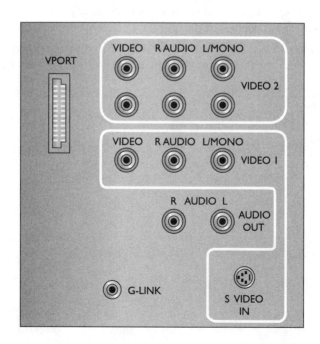

Audio Connectors

Audio connections use many of the same connectors as data networks and video systems. However, while the connection is very much the same, the application is different. The primary connectors used for audio systems are

- **Bayonet Neill Concellman (BNC)** This connector type provides a mechanically solid twist-lock connection. Although it's most commonly used with coaxial cable, this connector can be used with other cable types as well. BNC connectors are used in high-end installations for high-quality audio and video systems. See Figure 2-15 earlier in the chapter for an example of a BNC connector.

- **IEEE 1394 (High Performance Serial Bus [HPSB])** Like USB, IEEE 1394, shown in Figure 2-42, is a high-speed serial interface for computers. More commonly known by vendor names, such as FireWire (Apple) and iLink (Sony), IEEE 1394 allows for high-speed connection between a computer and digital devices, such as video cameras, digital still cameras, and digital sound devices.

- **Radio Corporation of America (RCA) connector** RCA connectors are a plug and jack combination designed for use with coaxial cable. This connector style is designed to carry a wide range of audio frequency (AF) signals, from very low to several megahertz. RCA connectors are also called phono plugs and jacks. Figure 2-44 shows a crimp-on RCA plug.

- **TOSLink (a.k.a. Optical Digital Audio Output)** If TOS has a meaning, it is lost forever. However, TOSLink is a fiber optic digital audio interface commonly used to connect a digital source (typically a DVD or CD player) to a digital receiver or pre-amplifier. Data is passed as laser (light) pulses that minimize interference and signal degradation. Figure 2-45 shows an example of a TOSLink cable.

- **Triple RCA** An enhanced version of component video and standard RCA connectors, this connector type is used for component video signals (red, green,

Figure 2-44

A crimp-on
RCA plug

*Photo courtesy of
Canare Corporation
of America.*

and blue). High-definition television (HDTV) uses this special type of component video cable (see Figure 2-46).

- **USB**   USB is a high-speed serial interface for computers that allows peripheral devices to be added to the system on a plug-and-play basis without the need to shut down the computer before or after the device is added. USB is a digital data interface and will allow USB CD, DVD, speakers, and other audio devices to be connected to a computer using what is called hot-swap. See Figures 2-40 and 2-41 earlier in the chapter for views of USB connectors.

- **XLR**   XLR connectors are primarily used for professional-level analog audio connections. XLR cables use positive and negative ground carriers, as do RCA cables, but the XLR cable adds a ground circuit. Figure 2-47 shows an XLR connector jack.

Figure 2-46
A triple RCA
cable

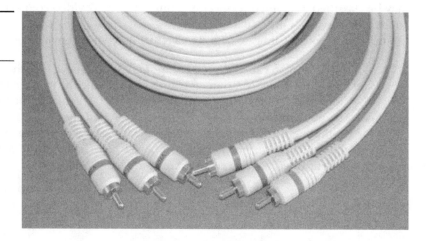

Figure 2-47
The jack of an
XLR connector

Preparing Audio Cable

In a structured wiring environment, audio signals can be distributed over either speaker wire, coaxial cable, or fiber optic cable. TP cable may also be used, but that is generally not a good first choice for this purpose unless it is digital audio.

CROSS-REFERENCE See Chapter 16 for information on installing RCA and other audio connectors.

NOTE The process used to prepare coaxial, fiber optic, or TP cabling for termination with an audio connector is the same as described earlier in the chapter for each of these cable types.

Video Connectors

Video systems and audio systems have many connector types in common. In fact, what may be classified as a video connector is often an audio/video connector in that the connection services both media.

The primary video connectors used in a structured wiring environment are

- **Component (also called digital component)** The newest of the cable and connector types, component connectors provide the best picture quality. The video signal is separated into individual red, green, and blue (RGB) color components, which results in better color and clarity. The connection for a component cable has three plugs, one for each color component. Make sure the colors are matched to the device jack colors. The connectors for a component video connection are shown in Figure 2-48.

Figure 2-48
A component
video cable
showing the
component video
connectors

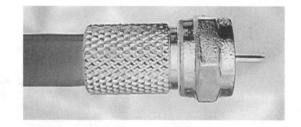

- **Composite**   A standard video signal format that contains color, brightness, and synchronization information. Virtually all VCRs and other legacy video equipment have a composite video input or output. The most commonly used jacks and plugs for composite video are RCA connectors. This signaling and connection format is distinctive in that it uses a yellow jack for video, a white jack for left-side audio, and a red jack for right-side audio.

- **Digital Video Interface (DVI)**   This interface connector, shown in Figure 2-49, provides connections for both analog and digital monitors on a single cable. Each of the three DVI configurations is designed to accommodate either analog (DVI-A), digital (DVI-D), or integrated (DVI-I) signals. When a DVI connector and port are used, the digital signal sent to an analog monitor is converted to an analog signal. If the monitor is a digital monitor, such as a flat panel display, no conversion is performed.

  Because Hollywood and the movie industry fears the image quality possible with DVI may make it possible to illegally copy and distributed high-quality bootlegs of their films, the High-Bandwidth Digital Content Protection (HDCP) standard has been developed to work with DVI circuits. HDCP circuitry is added to the DVI connection on both the transmitter (DVD player, cable box, and the like) and to the receiver (projector, LCD TV, etc.). The HDCP circuits encrypt the video content, which prevents a copy of the original content from being played.

Figure 2-49
A DVI-I cable
with connectors

*Image courtesy of
Texas Instruments, Inc.*

Figure 2-50
An HDMI plug

Image courtesy of Texas Instruments, Inc.

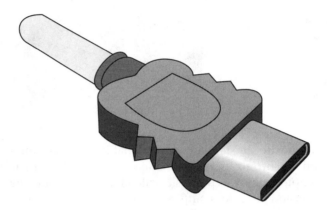

- **F-type connector**   This is the common connector used for video signals such as connecting a cable television service or an Internet connection service to a TV set, receiver, or Internet gateway using coaxial cable. This connector is secured by screwing its locking cap onto a threaded jack.

- **High-Definition Multimedia Interface (HDMI)**   An improvement over the DVI interface, HDMI (see Figure 2-50) supports either RGB or YcbCr digital video at rates well above the 2.2 Gbps required by HDTV. HDMI also supports up to eight channels of digital audio.

- **Super Video (S-Video)**   The signal is split into two color groups: Chrominance and Luminance. Chrominance carries color information and Luminance carries brightness and lighting information. S-Video is used primarily to transmit video signals to a television from a VCR or game device. The pin configuration on the jack and plug (see Figure 2-51) on a S-Video connection prevent the connection from being made incorrectly.

- **Video Port (VPort)**   This connector type is primarily used to connect video game devices that have a VPort connector that carries a composite video signal. VPort was originally designed to host the Microsoft Xbox video gaming device on RCA televisions.

Figure 2-51
An S-Video plug.

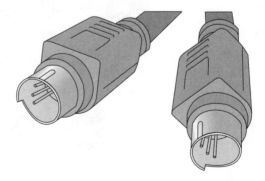

Speaker Connectors

Speaker wire is typically connected to a speaker using one of six common attachment methods:

- **Banana plug** The single prong on this connector is slightly bulged in the center, which gives it a banana look. A banana plug, see Figure 2-52, is attached to the stripped end of a speaker wire inserted through a hole in the body of the connector using a set screw. Banana plugs can be used on either end of a speaker patch cord and a banana jack used to terminate the distributed speaker wire in a wall outlet.

- **Binding post** A binding post, see Figure 2-53, is a five-way connector to which a speaker wire can be attached in a variety of ways. Its primary connection method is a threaded shaft on which a screw knob can be tightened to anchor a spade lug or a loop of bare wire. However, the post shaft is hollow and will accept a banana plug or, like a banana plug, there is a horizontal hole in the shaft through which a speaker wire can be inserted and anchored with the knob. The shaft is also sized to accept a pin connector.

- **Pin connector** Although they're most commonly used for test equipment, pin connectors, like the one in Figure 2-54, can be attached to a speaker wire and used to connect to a binding post by inserting the pin of the connector into the top of the binding post's shaft.

- **Screw terminal** Some older speakers may have screw terminals, which are used to anchor a speaker wire terminated with a spade lug or a loop of bare wire. The

Figure 2-52
A banana plug attached to a speaker wire

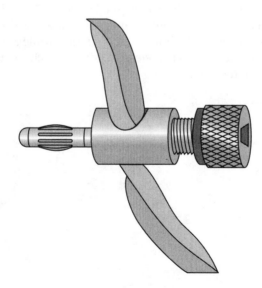

Figure 2-53
A pair of binding post connectors on the back of a speaker

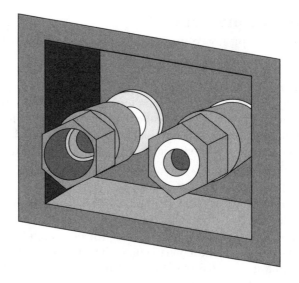

setscrew is either a screw that is tightened with a screwdriver (see Figure 2-55) or a metal or plastic knob that can be tightened by hand.

- **Spade (lug)**   Spades, see Figure 2-56, and other types of lug connectors are connections commonly used for terminating a speaker wire at the speaker. Spades are crimped or soldered on individual speaker wire conductors. Spades, also called Y-posts, and other lugs are placed at the end of the patch cord that connects a wall outlet to a speaker (the other end of the patch cord is usually a banana plug).

- **Spring clip**   This connector (see Figure 2-57), which is also called a push terminal, is a very common connector on lower-end speakers. A stripped speaker wire is inserted in the hole of the connector while a spring-loaded lever is pressed down. When the lever is released, gripping teeth on the inside of the connector clamp on the wire.

Figure 2-54
A screw-on pin connector can be used to connect speaker wire to a binding post.

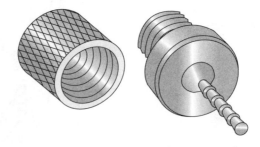

Figure 2-55
A two-post screw terminal

Figure 2-56
A spade is a type of lug connector that is commonly used with speaker connections.

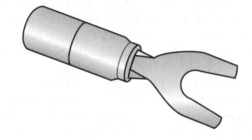

Figure 2-57
Spring clip connectors are commonly found on less expensive speakers.

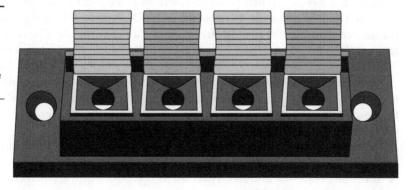

Chapter Review

The basic types of power connectors are: lugs, plugs, receptacles, and terminal strips. Electrical plugs and electrical power characteristics vary from country to country.

In a structured wiring system, the primary coaxial cable types used are RG6 and RG59 and the common coaxial connector is the "F" connector. The two methods used to attach an F-type connector are crimp-on and twist-on.

Cat 3, 5, 5e, and higher TP cable typically use one of the following modular connectors: RJ-11, RJ-31x, or RJ-45. The connector used depends on the number of lines the jack is supporting and its application. These modular connectors are standardized in the USOC, which defines the standard telephone and data communications jacks and plugs.

RJ-11 jacks and plugs use a 66-type punchdown with IDC contacts into which wire is inserted with a punchdown tool. RJ-31X jacks are connected to outside phone lines and optionally to a home's inside phone lines to allow a security system to seize the line and prevent interruptions when it is alerting a monitoring service. RJ-45 jacks and plugs are standard for terminating TP cable for data networks.

In a standard four-pair UTP cable, each pair of wires shares a base color: orange, blue, green, and brown, and one of the wires in each pair has a solid color and the other wire is marked with its color alternated with a white strip. The two wiring standards used to define TP cable connections in a network are EIA/TIA 568A and 568B. The 568A standard is backward compatible with the older USOC telephone standards and 568B doesn't support voice signals.

To install an RJ-45 jack or plug, it is very important that you match the correct pin to the correct wire color. Which wiring pattern you use depends on the requirements of the networking equipment. A straight-through pattern is used to connect computers to hubs and a crossover pattern is used to link computers to other computers.

The use of a central wiring closet or panel simplifies maintenance, troubleshooting, and expansion for a network. The central wiring panel terminates all of the network cabling and provides an interface for all of the controlling devices to all of the home automation network as it needs. A patch panel can be used as a clustering device. Cable home runs terminate to the back of the patch panel using IDC contacts. A patch cord is then used to connect each run to the next upstream device as appropriate. The two most common types of IDC contacts are the 66 block and the 110 block. The 66 block is used primarily in telephone and voice system connections; the 110 block is used for data networks.

Fiber optic cable is included in several types of structured wiring cable bundles and is being installed in homes for two reasons: its speed and bandwidth and it future-proofs the home. Fiber optic cable is terminated using one of three general types of connectors: interface connectors, inline connectors, and splices.

The two basic types of fiber optic connectors are butt-jointed and expanded-beam connectors. Butt-jointed connectors align two prepared fiber ends into very close proximity or in contact with one another. There are two types of butt-jointed connectors: ferrule and biconical. Expanded-beam connectors use lenses to expand and refocus light from one fiber to another. The most common fiber optic connectors and those that should be used in a residential situation are: SC, ST, LC, FC, SMA, and MT-RJ. Fiber strands must be clean before being mated. The standard for fiber optic cabling and connectors is ANSI/EIA/TIA 568A and 568B.

The three basic types of physical connectors most commonly used with PCs are: DB series, USB, and IEEE-1394 connectors. External connections made to a PC use either serial or parallel data transmission modes. USB provides a high-speed data bus that provides an easy way to connect peripheral devices to a PC. IEEE-1394 connectors are known as FireWire and iLink. USB and IEEE-1394 connections are hot swappable.

Audio connections use many of the same connectors as data networks and video systems. The primary connectors used for audio systems are: BNC, IEEE 1394, RCA, TOSLink, USB, and XLR. Audio signals can be distributed over either coaxial cable or fiber optic cable. The primary video connectors are: component, composite, DVI, F-type, HDMI, S-video, and VPort.

Speaker wire is typically connected to a speaker using one of six common attachment methods: banana plug, binding post, pin connector, screw terminal, spade lug, and spring clip.

Questions

1. A connector plug that has one or more pins extending from its housing is commonly called a

   A. Female plug

   B. Male plug

   C. Negative connector

   D. Positive connector

2. Which of the following is the most commonly used connector for terminating coaxial cable as a part of a structured wiring system in a home?

   A. RJ-11

   B. F-type

   C. RJ-45

   D. Spade

3. What connector type is used to interconnect telephone lines with a security system?

   A. RJ-11C

   B. RJ-21X

   C. RJ-31X

   D. RJ-45

4. Which type of punchdown block is used to terminate data networking cable?

   A. 66 block

   B. 88 block

   C. 110 block

   D. 240 block

5. What tool is used to connect a Cat 5e cable wire to an IDC contact?

   A. Punchdown

   B. Screwdriver

   C. Spring clip

   D. Twist-on

6. What are the four wire colors used in a Cat 5e cable?

   A. Blue, green, red, black

   B. Orange, blue, green, brown

   C. Orange, blue, green, yellow

   D. White, black, red, green

7. What is the wiring and connector standard that governs data networking?

   A. EIA/TIA 568

   B. NEC 411

   C. USOC

   D. NFSB

8. Which of the following is not a commonly used fiber optic connector?

   A. RJ

   B. SC

   C. SMA

   D. ST

9. What type of video signal interface separates the video images into RGB color components using three plugs, one for each color component?

   A. Composite

   B. Component

   C. DVI

   D. S-Video

10. What type of speaker wire connection is a five-way connector that can be used to anchor a lug, bare wire loops, stripped wire, a banana plug, and a pin connector?

    A. Binding post

    B. Screw terminal

    C. Spade

    D. Spring clip

Answers

1. **B.** A plug that has one or more receptacles in its housing is referred to as a female.

2. **B.** F-type connectors are commonly used in home systems for coaxial cable terminations. RJ-45 and RJ-11 connectors require multiple wires and a spade connector may not provide the contact required for high-speed signal transmissions.

3. **C.** RJ-11 and RJ-21 are other telephone line connections and an RJ-45 is used with data networking.

4. **C.** A 66 block is used in telephone applications. An 88 block terminates up to 256 wire pairs in large telephone applications, such as a telephone company CO. As far as I know, I made up the 240 block.

5. **A.** This tool is especially made to strip, cut, and insert a wire into an IDC contact.

6. **B.** The only other choice listed that you may actually encounter is yellow, black, red, and green, which are the colors in telephone quad wire.

7. **A.** Actually, the standards are 568A and 568B. The newer EIA/TIA 570 also specifies residential wiring standards. National Electric Code (NEC) Article 411 governs electrical connections. The other choices are not relevant at all.

8. **A.** RJs (registered jacks) are communication connectors for TP wiring.

9. **B.** Composite breaks the signal into two audio and one video channels, DVI is a Digital Video Interface, and S-Video breaks the signal into two components for chrominance and luminance.

10. **A.** Screw terminals can anchor lugs or bare wire, a spade is a type of lug, and a spring clip connector only terminates bare wire.

Wiring Installation Practices

3

In this chapter, you will learn about:
- Pre-wire planning and documentation
- Pre-wire installation tools
- Cable installation techniques
- Cable termination
- Trim-out installation and testing

The structured wiring performance is determined more by the quality of the installation practices used than the quality of the wire or cable. Not that the quality of the cabling isn't important, but good cable can't overcome a poor installation.

This chapter provides an overview of the wire and cable installation practices that should be used for installing cabling in a new construction environment. However, these practices and processes should also be applied to remodeling and retrofit projects, as appropriate, to ensure that the end result provides a high-quality wiring infrastructure to the homeowner. This chapter provides a general overview of the pre-wire phase of a structured wiring project. The general structured wiring planning, installation, and finish topics discussed in this chapter are covered in more detail in Part II's Chapters 6 through 8.

Pre-Wire Planning

As entertainment, networking, and communication technologies continue to emerge, homeowners are beginning to see the value of pre-wiring new homes not only for existing services, but also for those yet to come. In fact, the pre-wiring of a home with a structured wiring environment has virtually become a must feature for new home construction.

Assuming that the decision to pre-wire a home has been made, you and the homeowners should sit down as there are some planning issues that must be considered, such as:

1. What types of Internet connections are available to the home and what type of service(s) do the homeowners wish to connect initially?

2. What type(s) of video and television service is available to the home and to which type do the homeowners wish to connect initially?

3. How many telephone lines do the homeowners plan to install?

4. Is a distributed audio or video system planned for the home, now or in the future?

5. What type of security system is planned?

6. What type of HVAC system is planned? Is automated control desired?

7. How do the homeowners see the house being zoned for each system (audio, security, HVAC, etc.)?

8. Do the homeowners want systems integrated and controlled by a central control system?

The above list is certainly not complete for every situation, but it does cover the basics. Be sure to cover every subsystem that you offer for the home. The list considered should include some or all of the following:

- Structured Wiring
- Whole-house Music System
- Telephone/Intercom System
- Security System
- Lighting Control System
- HVAC Interface Control System
- Motorized Devices
- Integrated Control System
- Surge Protection

The idea of this step is for you, the pre-wiring planner, to gain a shared vision of the home's structured wiring environment with the homeowners, and vice versa.

As a result of this dialogue, you should develop a rough sketch of the home that includes the locations of the devices and the home's wiring requirements. Figure 3-1 shows one example of what this sketch might look like. In new construction situations, a walking tour of the home may be impossible, but in remodeling situations, walking through the home with the floor plan in hand will save time and money later.

NOTE   The pre-wiring plan should also include any wiring that can be installed at this time to provide support for a feature that may be added in the future.

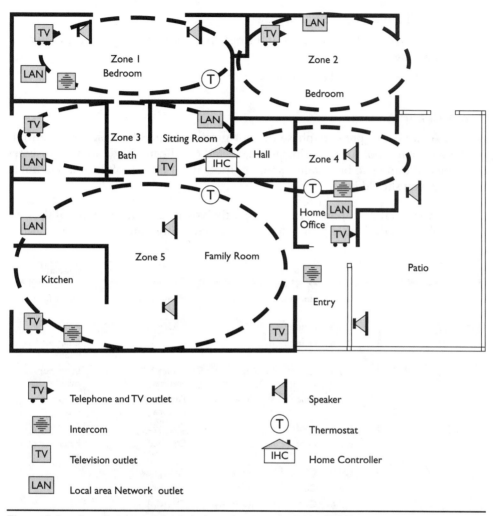

Figure 3-1   A preliminary workup of a home's wiring plan using CEDIA icons

The Pre-Wire Process

The process of pre-wiring a house consists of the following major activities:

1. Determine the locations of the distribution panel, outlets and devices.

2. Create wire chart (see Table 3-1).

3. Place outlet boxes or mud rings at each location.

4. Pull the appropriate type and number of cable runs to each outlet and device location.

5. Label all cables at distribution panel.

6. Terminate or protect the cables at the outlets with the appropriate connecters or bagging.

7. Test all cable runs and connections.

Pre-Wiring Tools

Before beginning the pre-wire phase of your project, ensure that you have the tools you'll need to drill holes, pull, strip, terminate, and test the installed cabling. The types of wiring and cabling to be installed should dictate the specific tools in your kit, but at minimum, you should have:

- **Cordless hand drill and drill bits slightly larger than the diameter of the cables**   To drill cable path holes through studs, floors, and ceilings, as required

Pulled	Tested	Run #	Type	Source	Destination	Device	Length	Special Instructions
		1	Cat 5	House feed	Control center (CC)	Phone feed		Phone feed
		2	Cat 5	House feed	CC	Future		Future
		3	RG-6	House feed	CC	Future		Cable feed—Future
		4	RG-6	Attic	CC	Future TV antenna		Loop extra cable
		5	RG-6	Attic	CC	Future FM antenna		Loop extra cable
		6	RG-6	Roof	CC	DSS feed		Satellite TV
		7	RG-6	Roof	CC	DSS feed		Future satellite service
		8	Cat 5	CC	Studio A	Phone jack		
		9	Cat 5	CC	Studio A	Data jack		
		10	RG-6	CC	Studio A	TV jack		
		11	Cat 5	CC	Studio B	Phone jack		
		12	Cat 5	CC	Studio B	Data Jack		
		13	RG-6	CC	Studio B	TV jack		
		14	Cat 5	CC	Living room Ent.	Phone jack		
		15	Cat 5	CC	Living room Ent.	Data jack		
		16	RG-6	CC	Living room Ent.	TV jack		
		17	Cat 5	CC	Up bedroom	Phone jack		
		18	Cat 5	CC	Up bedroom	Data jack		
		19	RG-6	CC	Up bedroom	TV jack		

Table 3-1   A Home System Wire Chart. Used with permission from Heneveld Dynamic Consulting, Inc.

Pulled	Tested	Run #	Type	Source	Destination	Device	Length	Special Instructions
		20	Cat 5	CC	Living room	Phone jack		
		21	Cat 5	CC	Living room	Data jack		
		22	Cat 5	CC	Up hallway	Phone jack		
		23	Cat 5	CC	Up hallway	Data jack		
		24	Cat 5	CC	Master bedroom	Phone jack		
		25	Cat 5	CC	Master bedroom	Data jack		
		26	Cat 5	CC	Up bedroom	Phone jack		
		27	Cat 5	CC	Up bedroom	Data jack		
		28	Cat 5	CC	Kitchen	Wall phone jack		Mount jack high on wall
		29	Cat 5	CC	Front door	Future doorbell/ intercom		Pre-wire for doorbell
		30	16-4	Living room Entertainment	Living room Stairway wall	Speakers		Pre-wire for speakers— located on stairway wall, either side of opening

Table 3-1   A Home System Wire Chart. *(continued)*

- **Wire cutter/stripper**   For cutting the cable to length and stripping its outer jacket during termination

- **Needle-nose pliers**   For use when terminating all cable types

- **Screwdrivers**   For the most part, you need both slotted head and crosshead recessed (Phillips) screw drivers

- **Volt meter/continuity tester**   For testing each cable run before termination and trim out

Wire Chart

Table 3-1 shows an example of a wire chart that should be created during the planning phase of a structured wiring project and used as a guide for the pre-wiring, rough in, and trim out of the structured wiring of a home. The format shown in Table 3-1 is only an example and you may want to include additional columns for other information, but the columns shown represent the minimum information needed during the complete wiring project.

A wire chart, like the one in Table 3-1, should be created during the planning phase of a structured wiring project and used to track the installation of the wiring throughout the remaining phases of the project. The information in the wire chart is taken directly from the project design and planning documents. If abbreviations are used on the wire chart, a legend should be created to ensure that everyone associated with the project understands their meaning.

The columns included in this wire chart example are

- **Pulled**   After each cable run is installed (pulled) from the source indicated in the "Source" column to the location listed in the "Destination" column, this column can be checked off and initialed by both the installer and whomever inspects his or her work. A double-check of the work is highly recommended to prevent oversight, errors, and omissions.

- **Tested**   During trim out and after each cable run is terminated and tested, the corresponding box in this column for the cable run can be checked off and initialed by the tester and the person verifying the test. A double-check of the work is highly recommended to prevent oversight, errors, and omissions.

- **Run #**   This column is used to create a unique identity and reference number for each cable run. The number or code assigned in this column can later be used in cable documentation and when labeling each cable. Cable number labeling systems provide self-adhesive numbered labels that can be affixed to each cable run at the distribution panel or control center (CC) end.

- **Type**   The type of cable to be used is entered into this column for each cable run.

- **Source**   The location from where the cable run is to begin is entered into this column. The Source and Destination columns provide the starting point and the ending point of the cable run.

- **Destination**   The location to where the cable run is to be pulled is entered into this column. The Source and Destination columns provide the starting point and the ending point of the cable run.

- **Device**   The source, distribution, control, or outlet device to which the cable run is to be connected or will support is identified in this column. When a cable run is being installed for future-proofing (see Chapter 5) purposes, this information should be recorded as well.

- **Length**   This is an optional column but can be helpful when comparing wire usage estimates to the actual installation. After guess-timating or length testing is completed on each cable run record the length in this column. Wire types used can be totaled up and compared to total usage wire estimates for the project. The information in the Length column may come in handy later when you are troubleshooting a cable for possible attenuation problems.

- **Special Instructions**   Because it is common for one technician to design and plan a structured wiring job and another technician to install its cable, this column can prove valuable in noting any issues or instructions the installer should know before beginning his or her work such as device height. Any problems encountered by the installer should also be recorded should yet another technician perform the cable testing. This column can also be used to record any other information relating to a particular cable run that may be valuable for future reference.

PART I

Wall Outlets

The system plan that was developed earlier in the project (and discussed earlier in this chapter) reflects where you and the homeowners have decided the connections, speakers, and controls for home's integrated system should be placed. However, it's one thing to mark it on a floor plan and quite another to religiously follow the plan exactly. Sometimes the wall studs, pipes, vents, or another room feature may not support the original place-ment of a system device. In these cases, you should coordinate with the homeowner to decide on a new location for the device.

Locate Outlets

The first step in the pre-wiring process is to install the outlet boxes and mud rings or plas-ter rings. In each location, an outlet box or mud ring should be nailed to a wall stud at the same height from the floor as the electrical outlets placed by the rough-in electricians and should be 12-inches or 300 millimeters above the floor. The boxes should also be from 12- to 16-inches from any nearby electrical outlets. A standard recommendation is locate low voltage outlets at least one wall-stud cavity away from an electrical outlet.

The outlet box (see Figure 3-2), backless outlet box, or mud ring should be of ap-propriate size to accommodate the size and amount of cabling that is to terminate or pass through that location, as well as the number of connectors and jacks to be installed. Outlet boxes should be placed so that when the drywall is installed they are flush with the front edge of the drywall. A mud ring will be stuck to the back of the drywall by joint compound.

Sidecar Brackets

Several manufacturers make specialized low-voltage boxes and brackets that are able to service both AC electrical power lines and low-voltage structured wiring lines. The double-gang box shown in Figure 3-3 includes a separator panel in the center that meets the re-quirements of the NEC and EIA/TIA standards 568 and 570 for the separation of these lines.

Figure 3-2
A standard electrical outlet box can be used to mount connectors and faceplates for structured wiring.

Photo courtesy of Lamson & Sessions.

Figure 3-3
A double-gang box that uses a separator panel to segregate AC power lines and structured wiring lines

Photo courtesy of Lamson & Sessions.

Another box type attaches to the side of an electrical service outlet box to create a tandem box that will appear, after the drywall is installed, to be a two-gang box. Add-on or side-car brackets (see Figure 3-4) allows the outlet box to be paired with an electrical outlet, creating the finished look of a two-gang box rather than two separate outlets a short distance from each other on the same wall.

When using sidecar brackets be sure to wire the low-voltage wire as far away as possible from the electrical wires. For example, the electrical wiring comes down the stud that the electrical box is mounted on, so wire the low-voltage wire down the opposite stud of that stud opening, wiring into the two-gang box at a right angle to the electrical wiring.

Figure 3-4
An add-on bracket can be attached to the side of an electrical box for structure wiring that creates the appearance of a two-gang box.

Photo courtesy of Lamson & Sessions.

Figure 3-5
An example
of a composite
cable with 2 RG-6
and 2 Cat 5 runs

*Photo courtesy
of Smarthome, Inc.*

Cable

A variety of composite cable systems, like the one shown in Figure 3-5, are available that combine coaxial cable and Cat 5e cables into a single bundle, called a "2 + 2" bundled cable. Some manufacturers also offer what amounts to a "2 + 2 + 2" that includes two runs of fiber optic cable as well.

Cable Schemes

Table 3-2 lists the recommended cables that should be installed for a variety of structured wiring applications. Remember that this is only a recommendation, but it does adhere closely to most of the recognized standards.

Cable Installation

After the outlet boxes and mud rings have been installed, the next step in the pre-wire process is to install the cabling. In a new construction pre-wire situation, the structured cable runs through holes drilled in the wall studs and runs parallel to the electrical wiring that should already be in place.

As a general rule, the path through the wall studs used for the structured cable should not be placed too close to the electrical power lines to avoid the possibility of electrical

Table 3-2 Structured cabling recommendations for various room types as recommended in the TIA/EIA standards	Space	Wire Types	Number of Runs	Applications
	Typical room	Cat 5e/RG-6	2/2	Phone/TV/Data/Satellite
	Media center	Cat 5e/RG-6	3/3	Phone/TV/AV/Data
	Home office	Cat 5e/RG-6	3/3	Phone/TV/Data/AV

interference on the structured cabling. The general guidelines for how far a structured cable should be placed from an electrical line vary from 6- to 24-inches (with 6-inches the absolute minimum distance). However, the generally accepted standard and convention is that 12-inches is the minimum that should be used, unless for some reason the structure doesn't permit it. If the electrical cable in question is a high-voltage line, such as a 240V line, the minimum distance moves out to 24-inches. If an electrical cable must be crossed, the structured cabling should do so at a 90-degree angle.

Nearly all structured wiring cable products are designed for installation in residential settings, so by and large, the bend radii required to pull a cable down between two wall studs is well within its specifications. However, sharp bends or kinks should be completely avoided.

The primary concern for pulling cable into an existing structure is to spread the runs of the various cable types over as wide a space as possible. If it is absolutely necessary to cross cabling, there are standards and guidelines for the installation of low-voltage cabling that covers overlap, separation, and crossing angles.

In general, structured wiring cable should be installed using the following guidelines:

- Use no more than 25 pounds of pull on the cable.

- Use at least 12-inches of separation between 120 volt power and structured wiring cables, and at least 24-inches of separation for 240 volt lines.

- If a low-voltage cable crosses a power cable, it must do so at a 90-degree angle.

- The low-voltage cable should avoid fluorescent light fixtures, and if you must run a cable by a fluorescent fixture, treat it like a 240 volt electrical line.

- Cable sheathing should not be stripped more than 1.25-inches from the connection end of the cable and 1-inch is better.

- UTP wire pairs should not be untwisted more than 0.5-inch and 0.375-inch is even better.

- The bend radius of a cable should be at least 1-inch, but some cable types are more sensitive than others.

- Between a transmitting source and a terminating (receiving device), a UTP cable segment should not be longer than 100 meters or a bit more than 300 feet.

 NOTE In North America, UTP is the most commonly used cable for low voltage (LV) data networking installations. However, outside of North America, shielded twisted-pair (STP) and screened twisted-pair (ScTP) wiring are commonly used.

Cable Path

In a structured cabling environment, one or more separate cable runs are strung between the outlet location and the central distribution panel so that each outlet has its own home-run of cable back to the panel.

When routing the structured cable through a wall stud, you should use a 5/8-inch auger drill bit to drill a hole in the horizontal center of the stud. This provides both a hole big enough for most cable bundles and composite cabling, but also enough wood is left in the stud on each side (at least 1-inch) of the hole to retain the strength of the stud. If you are concerned that the dry wall installers may penetrate your cable when they screw on the dry wall, place a nail plate on the front edge of the stud even with the cable hole. Minimize the number of holes drilled through a wall stud to maintain the integrity of the stud.

Another cable path that can be used is to pass the cable through a hole drilled in the header of the wall (the boards to which the studs are fastened) and run the cable through the attic or crawl space above or below the house. Using this path, the cable can be placed on J-hooks (see Figure 3-6) or tie wraps that hold the cable in place without the threat of damage from nails, staples, or other fasteners used to secure the cable to wall studs.

Service Loops

At the outlet end of the structured cable pulled through the walls, leave at least 2 feet of cable length to work with during the trim-out phase of the cabling project. At the distribution panel have at least 2 feet of cable after the panel location, or better yet, have all cables reach the floor. Having ample cable in a service loop provides some flexibility when you are terminating the cable at an outlet or the distribution panel.

Tuck the service loop into the outlet opening of the wall in such a way that it can later be pulled out through the outlet or mud ring after the wallboard is installed.

It is beneficial to protect the distribution panel cable by putting a large piece of cardboard to fit in the panel opening to cover all the cables.

Cable Handling

Cat 5 and RG-6 are high-frequency cables and must not be damaged during installation. This means that staples or any other type of cable fastener that dents, pierces, or crimps the cable in any way shouldn't be used. Also avoid bending these cable types too sharply when entering or exiting a wall stud cavity. The minimum bend radius for Cat5 is 1-inch, or 25.4 millimeters (mm), and for RG-6 is 2.5-inches, or 63.5-mm, (see Figure 3-7).

Another important part of cable handling is to label or tag each run of cable per the wire chart. Each cable should be numbered per the wire chart and the number recorded on its labeling. This identification links the cable back to the cable plan created during the design and planning phases.

Figure 3-6
A J-hook can be used to suspend cable in open spaces.

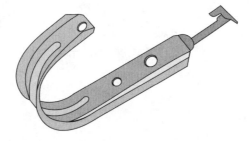

Figure 3-7
The bend radii
of Cat 5 and
RG-6 cables

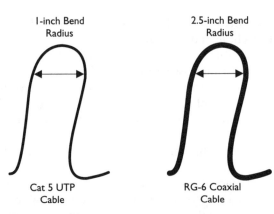

1-inch Bend
Radius

2.5-inch Bend
Radius

Cat 5 UTP
Cable

RG-6 Coaxial
Cable

Cable Trays, Conduits, and Chases and Other Cable Supports

Most often, residential cables are routed through stud walls. However, if the cable has to be routed through an attic, basement, or another open space, the cables must be supported and organized, so typically they are routed through cable (J) hooks (see Figure 3-8) or tie-wraps nailed to the rafters (Figure 3-8).

Cable Trays   In residential settings, it is rare that you would need to install cable trays that look something like a ladder installed horizontally. A cable tray is used to bridge cable runs that must run over areas that have no natural support features. For example, if you were to run cable through an attic, a cable tray hung from the roof rafters provides a secure and safe pathway for the cabling.

Conduits   Conduits can be rigid aluminum tubing or plastic piping or flexible plastic tubing. In most areas, conduit is not required for home structured wiring but can be a wise choice when the pathway available for the structured cable is too close to electrical wiring or other interference sources.

Figure 3-8
Cable ties nailed
to the overhead
beams can be
used suspend and
support a cable
run through an
open space.

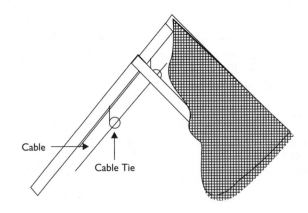

Cable

Cable Tie

EIA/TIA 570, the standard for residential cabling, recommends that data cabling is segregated into its own pathway, which has been interpreted in some municipalities as requiring conduit for all wiring, and especially data network cabling. So, be sure and check your local building and electrical codes.

Some technicians, especially those working with fiber optic cable, recommend the use of conduits for a variety of reasons, including ease of cable installation, ease of cable upgrades, ease of new outlet installation, and protection of the cable from damage.

Chases   A chase is a tube or a three-sided frame placed horizontally on a wall or in a slot cut into a floor. A chase permits cabling to be suspended and protected along a wall or beneath a floor. Chases are commonly used in multistory buildings in the space between the floors. Typically, a lid or cap is placed over the chase to protect the wire. There are vertical chases as well, which are on walls or in shafts to provide a protective path for riser cables, something that is rare in most home-wiring installations.

As a part of future-proofing a home, it's wise to install 2-inch plastic pipe (conduit or chase) between the distribution panel and some key areas of a home, such as the attic, home office, and media center.

Trim Out

The final step in the wiring process is called trim out, during which the cable runs are terminated and installed in the distribution panel and the appropriate connectors and outlets at the in-room end are installed. The trim-out phase is done after the wallboard installers have put up the drywall to cover the wall studs and the painters are finished.

The Distribution Panel

Whether the structured wiring scheme comes together in a small distribution panel, like the one shown in Figure 3-9, or a large fully-integrated panel, like that in Figure 3-10, what makes the system structured is that the home-run cable runs all terminate in this one location.

The structured wiring distribution panel is the central hub for the communications lines and connections in a home. It serves as the interconnection point between service lines that enter the home and the cabling that distributes the various services to the rooms, areas, and zones of the house. The panel also provides an interconnection point for the data networking cabling throughout the home.

A distribution panel doesn't have to be as commercial as those shown in Figures 3-11 and 3-12; the various interconnecting devices could actually be mounted on a sheet of plywood and hung on a wall. However, commercially available distribution panels typically have basic service connections included and a variety of optional modules for different connection types and quantities.

Figure 3-9
A residential
structured wiring
distribution panel

*Photo courtesy
of Channel Vision*

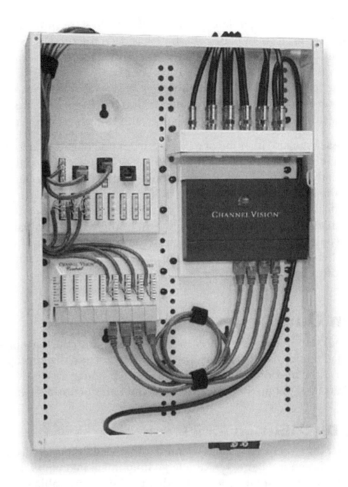

A common distribution panel supports a coaxial signal splitter, a telephone distribution block, and a data networking distribution block. Other devices, such as a telecom distribution block, audio distribution, and a video distribution block can be added to the panel, if required.

Outlet Installation

At the outlet end of the cable pulled during pre-wire, the cable must be terminated with the appropriate jack or plug to provide connection to the distribution panel and the service it delivers.

Terminator Types

The type of termination placed on a cable run depends on the intended use for the cable. Typically, Cat 5e cabling is terminated with an RJ-45 jack (see Figure 3-11), and RG-6 is

Figure 3-10

An integrated structured wiring distribution panel

Photo courtesy of Leviton Manufacturing Company.

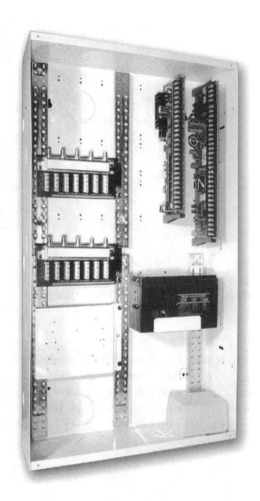

terminated with a Type F connector (see Figure 3-12). However, as I discuss in later chapters, other connectors can be placed on these cables—again, depending on the intended use of the connection.

Figure 3-11

An RJ-45 jack is used to terminate Cat 5/Cat 5e cabling intended for use with a data network.

Figure 3-12
An F Type connector is used to terminate RG-6 coaxial cable runs.

Cat 5 connectors typically require the use of a 110-type punch down tool, but toolless models are also available. Attaching either an F-type male end on the end of a coaxial cable or attaching the cable directly to an F-type jack requires the use of a coaxial cable crimper.

Faceplates

After the cable is terminated (and the wall is completely finished—texturing, painting, wall paper, etc.), the connector or jack on the end of the cable can be installed into a faceplate. In some cases, the jack is integrated into the faceplate, but most connector manufacturers now provide faceplates that can hold a variety of snap-in connectors (see Figure 3-13). If the jacks on a faceplate don't follow a standard pattern that is used

Figure 3-13
A faceplate with two RJ-45 and two RG-6 snap-in modular jacks, with the jacks identified

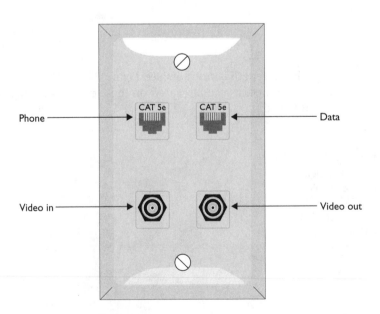

throughout a home, each jack on the faceplate should be labeled. If a standard pattern is used, labeling should be optional. If used, faceplate labels should be simple and to the point.

Cable and Outlet Testing

After each cable run is in place, and even before the cable is terminated, is a very good time to test the continuity of the cable. Testing the cable continuity enables you to check for any crimps, breaks, or other installation problems that may have happened while the cable was being pulled into the walls. A cable with poor or no continuity should be replaced; it is just not good practice to leave a spliced cable in the wall of a structured wiring installation.

A voltage meter or special cable continuity testers, like the one shown in Figure 3-14, that have settings or adapters for various types of wire and cable, is the best tool for this task. It is also a good idea to check continuity after each cable is terminated to ensure that problems weren't introduced with the attachment of a connector or jack.

NOTE The specific tests that should be run on each specific type of cable, in addition to continuity checking, are detailed in the chapters relating to specific cable applications.

Figure 3-14
A cable tester is useful for testing a cable for continuity problems.

Photo courtesy of Fluke Networks.

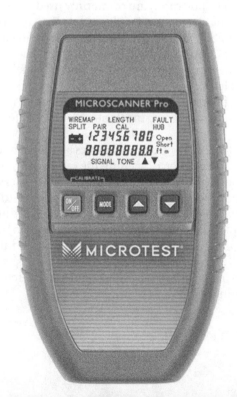

Chapter Review

Before beginning the pre-wire process, you should meet with the homeowners and discuss room use issues that impact the installation of the wiring and its connectors. This action ensures a shared vision of the home's structured wiring environment and should result in a rough sketch of the home, the devices, and the home's wiring requirements.

The process of pre-wiring a house consists of several major activities: determine the locations of the distribution plan and the outlets; create a wire chart, place outlet boxes or mud rings at each location, pull the appropriate type and number of cable runs to each outlet location, label all cables at distribution panel, terminate or protect the cables at the outlets with the appropriate connecters; connect the cable runs into the home's distribution panel and test all cable runs and connections.

Before beginning the pre-wire phase of your project, ensure that you have the tools you'll need to drill, pull, strip, terminate, and test the cabling installed.

The first step in the pre-wiring process is to install the outlet boxes and mud rings or plaster rings. Outlet boxes or mud rings are nailed or screwed to wall studs at 12-inches or 300 millimeters above the floor and 12- to 16-inches from any nearby electrical outlets. The outlet box or mud ring should be of appropriate size to accommodate the size and amount of cabling that is to terminate or pass through it. Sidecar brackets allow for two-gang boxes with both electrical and low-voltage wiring. Be sure to follow installation practices to avoid interference.

Four standard types of wiring are typically used to pre-wire a home in a structured wiring scheme: Cat 5e, coaxial, fiber optic, and quad-wire. Bundled cables that combine coaxial cable and Cat 5e cables into a single bundle, and those that also include one or more runs of fiber optic cable, are commonly used.

Structured cable should not be placed less than 12-inches to electrical power lines to avoid the possibility of electrical interference. If an electrical cable must be crossed, the structured cabling should do so at a 90-degree angle. One or more separate cable runs are used to connect an outlet to the distribution panel using a home run or dedicated cable scheme. At least 2 feet of extra cable length should be left at the outlet end of the cable during rough-in to provide working cable for trim out. At least 2 feet beyond the distribution panel location, or down to the floor, of cable should be left at the distribution panel location.

Cat 5 and RG-6 are high-frequency cables and must not be damaged by staples or any fastener that may dent, pierce, or crimp the cable in any way. Avoid bending these cable types too sharply when entering or exiting a wall stud cavity.

Each cable run should be labeled per the wire chart to identify its cable type and intended use. Each cable should also be numbered and the number recorded on its labeling and the wiring plan diagram. Cable hooks can be used to bridge cable runs over areas with no support features, such as across an attic. Aluminum tubing or plastic piping conduits are not required for most home structured wiring, but should be used when the pathway available is too close to electrical wiring or other interference sources. Include a chase of 2-inch plastic piping for future use from key areas.

In the trim-out phase, cable runs are terminated and installed in the distribution panel and terminated with the appropriate connector at the outlet end. The trim-out phase is done after the wallboard installers have put up the drywall to cover the wall studs and the painters have finished.

The structured wiring distribution panel is the central hub for the communications lines and connections in a home. It serves as the interconnection point between service lines that enter the home and the cabling that distributes the various services to the rooms of the house.

Cables must be terminated with the appropriate jack or plug at the outlet or in-room end of the cable to provide connection to the distribution panel and the service it delivers. The type of termination used depends on the intended use of the cable. Cat 5e cabling is terminated with an RJ-45 jack and RG-6 is terminated with a Type F connector. After the cable is terminated, the connector or jack is installed into a faceplate. Each outlet jack inserted into a faceplate can be identified or a standard layout in the faceplate followed.

Performing continuity testing checks each cable for any crimps, breaks, or other installation problems that may have been introduced when the cable was pulled into the walls or when the drywall was hung. A cable with poor or no continuity should be replaced; it is just not good practice to leave a spliced cable in the wall of a structured wiring installation. A voltage meter or cable tester is used for this testing.

Questions

1. Before beginning the process of pre-wiring a home, what document, form, or chart should be completed?

   A. Materials list

   B. System documentation

   C. User training guide

   D. Wire chart

2. With whom should the home technology integration contractor meet before beginning the actual work of the pre-wiring process?

   A. Cable manufacturer representative

   B. Audio/video technicians

   C. Homeowners

   D. Building contractor

3. Which of the following is not performed as part of a pre-wire project?

   A. Locating outlets and connectors

   B. Installing the distribution panel

   C. Fine-tuning receivers, amplifiers, and speakers

   D. Pulling wire into the walls

4. What is the recommended minimum separation distance between a structured wiring cable and an AC electrical cable?

A. 6-inches

B. 18-inches

C. 24-inches

D. 12-inches

5. Which of the following cable types is not commonly used for structured wiring?

A. Cat 5e

B. Cat 3

C. RG-6

D. Fiber optic

6. If a structured wiring cable must cross an AC power cable, at what angle should the cables be crossed?

A. 30 degrees

B. 45 degrees

C. 75 degrees

D. 90 degrees

7. Which of the following would not be an option for running cable through an open attic or empty building space?

A. Cable trays

B. J-hooks

C. Cable ties

D. Nails

8. What is the reason to install extra wiring and conduit in a home along with its required structured wiring?

A. In case of errors

B. In case of faulty cable runs

C. To increase profitability

D. To provide future-proofing

9. What is the central device in a structured wiring scheme that provides an interconnection between external services and internal cabling?

A. Hub

B. Switch

C. Distribution panel

D. Outlet box

10. What cable test should be performed immediately after installing a structured cable, typically before the cable is terminated?

   A. Fox and hound

   B. Attenuation

   C. Crosstalk feedback

   D. Continuity

Answers

1. **C.** The wire chart summarizes the cabling to be installed and identifies the placement and purpose of each cable run, something that should be understood clearly before beginning the pre-wiring of a home.

2. **C.** Not that meeting with any of the other choices would be a bad idea, but only the homeowners know exactly what they wish their home systems to provide and where.

3. **C.** This part of the project comes much later in the process. All of the other choices are performed during the pre-wire process.

4. **A.** Although the recommended distance is 6- to 24-inches between structured wiring and electrical lines, the minimum distance should be 24-inches to avoid interference from 240V lines.

5. **B.** This cable type doesn't provide enough bandwidth to handle today and tomorrow's system requirements. The other cable types listed as choices are structured wiring cable types.

6. **D.** Crossing structured wiring cables and electrical cables at right angles minimizes the potential for interference.

7. **D.** Regardless of the type of space a cable is running through, nails or any other fastener that may dent, pierce, or damage a cable should not be used. The other choices, either individually or together, work nicely to string cable through an open space. There are curved cable staples that work.

8. **D.** Extra cable runs and conduit help to reduce the cost of future additions to the structured wiring system and to provide flexibility for the support for subsystems expanded or added at a later date. If you answered "C," shame on you!

9. **C.** Hubs and switches are connectivity devices used primarily for data networking. Outlet boxes are used to mount terminators and connectors to cable runs.

10. **D.** This check verifies that the cable is free of breaks and shorts end-to-end. The other choices are cable tests that are used for locating, identifying, and verifying cable performance capabilities.

Codes, Standards, and Safety Practices

In this chapter, you will learn about the following:
- The organizations that develop and publish residential wiring and safety standards.
- Residential wiring and safety standards and guidelines.

To protect a home from fire or other dangers related to its electrical and structured wiring, a variety of product, installation, and safety standards, guidelines, and practices are published by a number of trade, industry, and specialty organizations and associations. Many of these standards have been incorporated into local building codes, so they aren't something that can be ignored.

In this chapter, I discuss the standards that impact the design and installation of structured wiring systems, including audio, speaker, video, and control wiring, as well as the safety practices that should be followed on a job site.

Residential Standards Organizations

The materials and practices used when installing structured wiring in a residential setting are developed by a group of industry, governmental, and trade organizations. The standards produced by these organizations are adopted to ensure the success and performance of electrical and communication systems and the safety of the technicians and the residents and occupants of buildings.

In this chapter, we first look at the organizations publishing residential system standards and then at the standards that govern the materials and practices that should be used when installing structured wiring and devices in a house. The organizations that develop and publish standards that cover the specification and installation of residential system wiring are

- American National Standards Institute (ANSI)
- Electronic Industries Alliance (EIA)
- Institute of Electrical and Electronic Engineers (IEEE)
- International Organization for Standardization (ISO)

- National Fire Protection Association (NFPA)
- Telecommunications Industry Association (TIA)
- Underwriters Laboratories, Inc. (UL)
- Occupational Safety and Health Association (OSHA)

American National Standards Institute (ANSI)

ANSI, pronounced "ann-see," is an agency of the United States federal government that is charged with the responsibility of developing and approving standards that cover a variety of technology, including computers and data communications, and weights and measurements. ANSI is the U.S. representative to the International Organization for Standardization (ISO) that is the worldwide standards authority.

ANSI works with several other agencies to develop and publish (for a fee) its standards, including the Electronic Industries Alliance (EIA) and the Telecommunication Industry Association (TIA), and often publishes standards in conjunction with these independent trade organizations. Examples of jointly issued standards are the ANSI/TIA/EIA 568, 569, and 570 wire and cabling standards.

Electronic Industries Alliance (EIA)

EIA ("ee-eye-aa") is an alliance of trade and industry associations that work together to sponsor and promote data communication standards. The member associations of the EIA are

- Consumer Electronics Association (CEA)
- Electronic Components, Assemblies, and Materials Association (ECA)
- Government Electronics and Information Technology Association (GEIA)
- National Science and Technology Education Partnership (NSTEP)
- Solid State and Semiconductor Technology Council of the Joint Electron Devices Engineering Council (JEDEC)
- Telecommunications Industry Association (TIA).

Most of the EIA standards that apply to residential wiring are issued jointly with ANSI and TIA, including the ANSI/EIA/TIA 568 and 570 standards.

Institute of Electrical and Electronic Engineers (IEEE)

The IEEE ("eye-triple-ee") is a worldwide, technical, professional association of engineers that is a leading standards authority in a variety of technical areas that includes aerospace, biomedical, computer, electrical power, telecommunications, and consumer electronics engineering, and more. The IEEE has over 900 published standards with several hundred more in development.

The IEEE standards that most impact residential systems are its 802 computer networking standards. The number 802 refers to February 1980, which is when the committees working on networking standards were first organized. The IEEE 802 committees are numbered to differentiate their responsibilities and the standards each committee develops. Table 4-1 lists the committees of the IEEE 802 project and the networking specification associated with home networking each is charged with defining.

International Organization for Standardization (ISO)

The ISO ("eye-ess-oh") is an international, non-treaty organization of voluntary members that develops and maintains a variety of technology standards, including standards governing computers, networking, and communications. In fact, the ISO's Open System Interconnect Reference Model (the OSI model for short) is the globally accepted international networking standard model. The ISO is organized as a working network of the national standards authorities of 147 countries, including ANSI from the U.S.

An emerging standard of ISO is the residential gateway, which defines a network interface device that provides service access to a home for such services as telephone, cable television, and Internet access. The ISO standard defines a residential gateway (RG) as the physical devise that terminates all external access networks to a home and also serves to terminate all internal networks as well. The ISO's RG Group sees a residential gateway as a single device that consolidates, coordinates, and integrates communication signals from both internal and external networks. The development of the RG standard by ISO and the International Electrotechnical Commission (IEC) is in conjunction with the proposed Home Electronic System (HES), also called HomeGate, now under development. The IEC is an international organization that publishes electrical and electronic compatibility, design, and safety standards.

IEEE 802 Committee	Responsibility
802.1	Overall specification for a local area network (LAN) and LAN connectivity.
802.2	Logical Link Control (LLC) standards that define the transmission of data from one device to another.
802.3	Media Access Control (MAC) standards that define the control of access to a network – commonly referred to as the Ethernet standards.
802.7	Defines broadband LANs, common to home networks.
802.9	Defines the integration of voice and digital data on a network.
802.10	Defines the standards for security between networked devices.
802.11	Defines the standards for wireless infrared (IR) or radio frequency (RF) networks.
802.15	Defines personal area networks (PANs)

Table 4-1   The IEEE 802 Project Committees

National Fire Protection Association (NFPA)

The NFPA is an international association with well over 75,000 members representing more than 80 national trade and professional organizations that are focused on the development and publishing of fire safety codes, standards, and research to minimize the possibilities and impact of fire and other safety risks. In terms of home automation projects and structured wiring, the NFPA's most important standard is the National Electrical Code® (NEC®), which was last published in 2002 and is scheduled for revision in 2005.

The NEC® (also known as NFPA 70) is the most widely adopted building code component in the world, including the United States, for electrical installations. The NEC® covers the installation of electrical conductors, including the wiring used in structured residential wiring systems.

Telecommunications Industry Association (TIA)

TIA is a trade organization of telecommunication product and service providers that among other industry activities, develops and publishes a variety of wire and media specifications and testing standards, including those for commercial and residential applications.

TIA is organized into five product-specific divisions: User Premises Equipment, Network Equipment, Wireless Communications, Fiber Optics, and Satellite Communications. The primary TIA standards that apply in home networking situations are those that govern Cat 5 wiring connections and testing, which are TIA/EIA 568 and 570.

Federal Communications Commission

The U.S. Federal Communications Commission (FCC) oversees the telecommunications industry through the issuance of regulations and operating rules. Two FCC rules apply to the installation of a home communication system:

- **FCC Part 68**   This FCC rule (actually 47 C.F.R Part 68) governs the connection of terminal equipment, such as the network interface device (NID), to the Public Switched Telephone Network (PSTN) or other Telco facilities or equipment involved in providing private wire line services, as well as the technical rules for inside telephone system wiring. Although the technical and administrative activities of Part 68 have been delegated to the telephone service providers, the FCC still has the authority and responsibility to enforce these rules.

- **FCC Docket 88-57**   These rules allow non-Telco companies or contractors to connect wiring and other devices to the Telco's network. Before 1980, only Telco employees were permitted to service any lines connected to a Telco's equipment or network, including inside wiring and jack. However, since the FCC issued Docket 88-57, customers and non-Telco contractors are permitted to connect to Telco lines and equipment. In fact, this rule transferred the responsibility for customer premise inside wiring (CPIW) from the Telco to the customer. As it stands now, unless otherwise contracted, the Telco's responsibility ends at the NID or demarc.

Figure 4-1
The UL "Listed"
product mark

Underwriters Laboratories (UL)

Perhaps the best known for product testing, UL is an independent, nonprofit product safety testing organization. Most cable and wire manufacturers voluntarily submit their products to UL for fire and electrical safety testing against the NEC and other NFPA standards.

Primarily, the testing performed by UL on cable and wiring is for compliance with Articles 725, 760, 800, and 820 of the NEC, which define the standards for communications, fire protection, and cable television wiring, respectively. A cable or other electric or electronic device bearing the UL logo is certified to meet the requirements of the applicable standards.

UL issues a variety of certification labels to certify conformance of wiring and electrical products to a variety of national and proprietary standards, including:

- **"Listed" wire and cable products**   Wire and cable that are intended for use in residential, commercial, and industrial buildings and aren't a part of another manufactured product and conform to the National Electrical Code (NEC) standards are classified as "listed" products by the UL. The marking used with this certification is shown in Figure 4-1, above.

- **Appliance Wiring Material (AWM) recognized wiring components**   This certification indicates wire or cable that can be used for either internal or external wiring as a component of a product. The marking used with this certification is shown in Figure 4-2.

The UL also issues Canadian versions of these certifications that are based on the Canadian Standards Authority (CSA) using the C-UL recognized component mark. The CSA is a nonprofit, independent testing laboratory that performs essentially the same services in Canada as the UL provides in the U.S. An important wire and cable certification issued by the CSA is the vertical flame testing (FT1/FT4) certification that specifies the flame resistance of wire and cable. Conforming products are marked with the symbol shown in Figure 4-3.

Another standards testing certification is the Conformity to European Directive (CE) that covers virtually all of the same standards used by UL and CSA for products sold in the European Economic Community (EEC). Figure 4-4 shows the mark carried by CE certified products.

Residential Systems Standards

There are several construction, safety practices, materials, and wiring standards that govern how a house is built, including wiring the house for electrical and communications systems. The primary standards a home technology technician should be familiar with are

- ANSI/EIA/TIA wiring standards

Figure 4-2
This UL mark on a cable certifies that it is in compliance with the AWM standards.

- IEEE Ethernet wire standards
- National Electrical Code® (NEC®)
- OSHA job safety practices
- International Building Code (IBC)

ANSI/TIA/EIA Standards

The standards that are jointly sponsored by ANSI, the TIA, and the EIA cover a variety of cabling and cable installation requirements. However, the specific standards that come into play in home systems are those dealing with data, audio, video, and other cabling and termination, particularly ANSI/TIA/EIA 568a and 568b and ANSI/TIA/EIA 570.

ANSI/TIA/EIA 568

The 568 standard is the Commercial Building Telecommunications Cabling Standard. Although this standard was initially developed for commercial building telephone and data cabling systems, it is also the accepted standard for data cabling in a home setting as well.

The purpose of these standards is to provide the specification for generic telecommunication cabling and to assist technicians with the planning and installation of telecommunication cable. These standards also prescribe the performance testing criteria for standard system configurations and their components. Specifically, the 568 standards specify the component elements used in designing and installing the following home cabling types:

- **Horizontal cable** The 568 standards call for cabling running horizontally through a building to be installed using a star topology (see Chapter 10) with each room cable connected back to a central distribution facility or distribution panel. Horizontal cabling runs should not exceed 90 meters (approximately 295 feet), which should be adequate for virtually any home network requirements. An additional 10 meters (just under 30 feet) can also be used for patch cabling and connector cords.

Figure 4-3
The CSA certified product mark

Figure 4-4
The CE certified
product mark

There are other horizontal cabling requirements as well. At least two connector outlets should be installed in each work area (room). In addition, Cat 5 wire should not be untwisted (for termination purposes) more than one-half inch and the bend radius of the cable should never be less than four times the cable's diameter.

- **Central distribution facility or telecommunications closet**   A distribution or integration device, if used, must conform to ANSI/EIA/TIA 569, which virtually all distribution devices do. The distribution panel's function is to terminate and interconnect the horizontal cabling.

UTP Cabling Systems

The 568 standards also specify the UTP cabling categories that are acceptable for use as horizontal cabling and patch cords. Table 4-2 lists the characteristics for the UTP cabling that is acceptable for use as horizontal cabling.

Cat 5 wire is the most commonly used cabling on Ethernet and Token Ring networks. However, while Cat 5 wiring is required for 100 Mbps networks, how the cable is installed can have a huge impact on whether or not the cable will actually support that much bandwidth.

Three specific and very important guidelines are as follows:

- Only 0.5 inch of untwisted wiring at each end of the cable (to avoid near and far near crosstalk)

- No bends in the cable in excess of a 1.25-inch bend radius (in other words, no kinks)

- Cable was not stressed beyond 25 pounds of pull during installation (stretching the cable removes twists)

Category	Bandwidth	Wire Pairs	Maximum Segment Length	LAN Applications
Cat3	16 MHz	2	100 meters	10BaseT, 4 Mbps
Cat4	20 MHz	2	100 meters	16 Mbps, Token Ring
Cat5	100 MHz	4	100 meters	100BaseT, ATM, CDDI
Cat5e	100 MHz	4	100 meters	1000BaseT

Table 4-2   ANSI/TIA/EIA UTP Cabling Standards

Table 4-3	End 1 Pin	Wire	End 2 Pin
The EIA/TIA	1	White green	1
568a Cable	2	Green	2
Termination	3	White orange	3
	4	Blue	4
	5	White blue	5
	6	Orange	6
	7	White brown	7
	8	Brown	8

568a and 568b Standards

Within the 568 standard are two separate cable termination standards for UPT cabling: 568a and 568b. Each of the termination standards prescribes the wires in a UTP cable that are to be connected to specific pins on an RJ-45 connector. Which of the two termination standards are used depends on the intended use of the cable. The basic difference between these standards is that the 568a specification can be used for both voice and data transmission and 568b is more suitable for data transmission only.

Tables 4-3 and 4-4 show the RJ-45 plug pin and wire match-ups for 568a and 568b, respectively.

The 568 standards also specify IDC (Insulation Displacement Connector) connectors at the distribution or telecommunications center and an 8-position modular jack in the work area (rooms of the house), which means an RJ-45 connector. These standards also specify two distinct wire/connector pinouts, which are identified as 568a and 568b. The primary difference between the two is that 568a supports telecommunications (meaning voice telephone signals) and 568b doesn't. Figures 4-5 and 4-6 show the pin/ wire pattern (pinout) for these two standards.

ANSI/TIA/EIA 569

The 569 standard deals with telecommunications design and installation of devices used inside and between buildings and for rooms or work areas where cable media and

Table 4-4	End 1 Pin	Wire	End 2 Pin
The 568b pinouts	1	White orange	1
for the RJ-45	2	Orange	2
connectors on a	3	White green	3
Cat 5 UTP cable	4	Blue	4
	5	White blue	5
	6	Green	6
	7	White brown	7
	8	Brown	8

PART I

Figure 4-5
The pinout (wire and connector pin pattern) defined by ANSI/ EIA/TIA 568a for UTP cabling

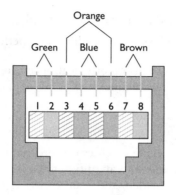

equipment are installed. This standard applies to home networking situations where a central distribution facility is installed and defines the construction and termination method used for horizontal cabling connected into distribution panels.

TIA/EIA 570A

The 570 standard defines the basic requirements for residential structured wiring. This standard was developed by a panel of cabling experts that included cable professionals, telephone companies, cable system manufacturers, and the like. It is the nationally accepted standard covering the design and installation of low voltage wiring in residential dwellings.

However, the primary achievement of the 570 standard is that it consolidates the specifications, installation practices, and performance criteria for the media used in audio, control, data, and video systems into a single conformance standard.

The 570 standard defines the following specifications:

- Grades of houses and residential buildings
- Wiring topologies
- Twisted pair, coaxial, and fiber optic cabling

Figure 4-6
The pinout defined by ANSI/ EIA/TIA 568b for UTP cabling

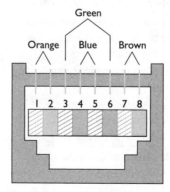

- Termination and connector jacks and plugs
- Installation and testing procedures and performance criteria

One of the specific areas of specification in the 570 standard is in communication outlets. The 570 standard defines two standard grades for communication outlets:

- **Grade 1**   This grade specifies a cable that combines UTP Cat 3 with an RG6 coaxial cable for providing basic telephone and video services to each outlet.
- **Grade 2**   This grade specifies cabling that combines two Cat 5e UTP with two RG6 coaxial cables and an optional two-strand fiber optic cable for providing enhanced voice, video, and data services to each outlet.

IEEE Ethernet Cable Standards

The IEEE 802 standards designate cabling standards for use on an Ethernet network with a special coding scheme that generally describes a cable's characteristics. The most common of the Ethernet cable specifications are listed in Table 4-5.

The coding scheme shown in Table 4-5 has three parts to it: a number (10/100/1000), the word "Base," and a number or letter indicating the media type (2, T, F, and X). For example, 10BaseT, 100BaseT, and 1000BaseT all specify cables that carry 10 Mbps, 100 Mbps, and 1 Gbps (1,000 Mbps) of bandwidth, respectively.

The word "Base" indicates that baseband signaling is used to transmit the data, as opposed to narrowband or broadband. Baseband is a network technology that sends its data over a single carrier frequency. Baseband networks require all nodes to participate in every message sent over the network.

The final part to the cable specification designator is one or two characters that indicate a variety of information, depending on the cable and its speed. In the case of 10Base2, the "2" indicates a maximum segment length of approximately 200 meters (actually it's 185 meters). Cables may also have a T or an F, which refer to twisted-pair wire and fiber optic cable, respectively.

Ethernet Cable Standard	Cable Defined by Standard	Minimum Cable Type
10Base2	10 Mbps thin coaxial network cable	50-ohm RG-58 coaxial cable
10BaseT	10 Mbps unshielded twisted-pair network cable	Cat 3 unshielded twisted pair (UTP)
100BaseT	100 Mbps unshielded twisted-pair network cable	Cat 5 UTP
100BaseF	100 Mbps fiber optic network cable	Single-mode optical fiber
1000BaseT	1 Gbps copper cable	Cat 5e UTP
1000BaseF	1 Gbps fiber optic cable	Multimode optical fiber

Table 4-5   The IEEE 802 Ethernet Cable Standards

The IEEE 802 specification includes standards for wireless networking media as well. The primary two standards in the IEEE 802 are 802.11, which deals with wireless Ethernet, and 802.15, which deals with wireless personal area networking (PAN). I discuss the wireless media standards later in the chapter.

National Electric Code® (NEC®)

The National Electric Code®, or NEC®, is a trademarked standard. It is also known as NFPA 70 and is published by the National Fire Protection Association (NFPA) as a guideline to avoid and prevent electrical shock and fire hazards from residential wiring systems. The NEC® is published periodically and the current (at the time of this writing) version of the standard is 2002, with the next updated version due in 2005.

There is essentially an NEC® standard for every electrical circuit in a home. Most of the NEC® standards cover electrical power circuits, but there are also sections that govern communications media and the transmission of electrical signals over that media. To give you an idea of the extensiveness of the NEC® standards, we have listed a sampling of the NEC® standards that could impact a structured wiring system in Table 4-6.

Job Safety Regulations

Virtually every industrialized country in the world has a governmental agency that creates, publishes, and administers job safety and health codes and regulations. In the United States, the agency is the Occupational Safety and Health Administration (OSHA) of the U.S. Department of Labor. In Canada, the Human Resources Development Canada (HRDC) has this responsibility; in England, the government's Health and Safety Executive (HSE) oversees job safety; and in Japan, the Japan Occupational Safety and Health Office (JOSHO) administers worker safety issues.

Working in an alliance with the National Home Builders Association (NHBA), OSHA has developed and published a Code for Federal Regulations (CFR) specifically addressing job safety issues for construction trades, entitled "Selected Construction Regulations (SCOR) for the Home Building Industry (29 CFR 1926)." Table 4-7 lists a few of the section titles included in this section of the OSHA codes.

Table 4-6	NEC® Section	Applies To
A Sampling of NEC Standards Sections and the Electrical Area Defined	250-104	Using water pipes as grounding conductors
	300-4	Size of bored holes in joists, rafters, or wall studs
	300-15	Wire splices
	300-22	Type NM cable used in HVAC cold air returns
	336-18	Non-metallic cable (Type NM)
	370-16	Outlet box volume and size
	370-23	Electrical boxes
	370-25	Outlet box covers
	410-8	Lighting fixtures in clothes closets

Table 4-7	Section	Topic
A sampling of the coverage included in the SCOR published by OSHA for the home building trades	1926.20	General safety and health provisions
	1926.23	First aid and medical attention
	1926.24	Fire protection and prevention
	1926.28	Personal protective equipment
	1926.55	Gases, vapors, fumes, dusts, and mists
	1926.102	Eye and face protection
	1926.302	Power-operated hand tools
	1926.400	Electrical – General
	1926.404	Wiring design and protection
	1926.405	Wiring methods, components, and equipment for general use
	1926.417	Lockout and tagging of circuits

OSHA and NHBA Job Safety Standards

The National Homebuilders Association (NHBA) in conjunction with OSHA publishes the *Jobsite Safety Handbook*, something that all home automation professionals should be very familiar with. In fact, if you are considering CEDIA certification, it is a must-read before taking the exams.

The portion of the handbook that relates directly to the work of a home technology integration or home automation professional is the "Electrical" section, which includes safety guidelines that cover how to work with electrical and electronic systems safely. The safety guidelines cover the following:

- Working on new or existing electrical circuits only after all power is shut off

- Maintaining electrical tools in a safe working condition that is free of defects

- Using a Ground Fault Circuit Interrupter (GFCI) with all temporary power sources and connecting cords

- Being aware of all overhead and underground electrical power lines and handling tools and equipment around them

Building Codes

In the not-so-distant past, many countries had their own version of a national or uniform building code aimed at protecting the health, safety, and welfare of the public, which means homeowners or occupants. Prior to 1999, the International Conference of Building Officials (ICBO) published the Uniform Building Code (UBC). However, in 2000, the ICBO joined with the International Codes Council to publish a single guideline called the International Building Code (IBC).

The intent of the IBC is to ensure that a building's occupants are protected from fire and structural collapse by developing construction material and practice guidelines that provide for proper design, construction, and code compliance. Another important part of the IBC is to provide uniformity in the construction industry worldwide, including consistent minimum quality, durability, and safety in constructed buildings.

Local Building Codes and Standards

Each state, province, county, parish, shire, city, town, and township can, and most do, develop local building codes that incorporate or extend the national and international building, product, and safety codes and regulations.

For example, in its "Computing and Telecommunications Architecture Standards for Building Wiring," the State of Washington includes the standards listed in Table 4-8, among others, as the basis for its regulations.

Powerline Standards

The term "powerline" is used frequently to describe the electric lines inside the walls of a home. Technically, "powerline" refers to the system used by most electric utility companies to transmit information across their electrical power grid using narrowband communications. The powerline technology is now available for use with home networks to transmit data across the existing electrical wiring.

When you think about it, powerline technology makes a lot of sense. If you are introducing a network into a home, there are already more electrical outlets installed than the number of Ethernet jacks you'd need to install. Powerline technology is a very low-cost alternative to wiring a home with Cat 5 wiring.

There are three primary standards for powerline technology:

- **CEBus (Consumer Electronic Bus)** This media standard is defined in the EIA 600 standard and provides for communication and control networks using powerline and also for a variety of media, including UTP, coaxial, fiber optic,

Wiring Standard	Description
TIA/EIA-568A	Commercial Building Telecommunications Wiring Standard
TIA/EIA-569A	Commercial Building Standard for Telecommunications Pathways and Services
TIA/EIA-570A	Residential and Light Commercial Telecommunications Wiring Standard
TIA/EIA 594	Private Digital Network Synchronization
TIA/EIA 596	Network Channel Terminating Equipment for Switched Digital Devices
TIA/EIA-606	Administration Standard for Telecommunications Infrastructure of Commercial Buildings
TIA/EIA TSB 67	Transmission Performance Specifications for Testing UTP Cabling Systems
TIA/EIA TSB 75	Additional Horizontal Cabling Practices Open Offices
TIA/EIA TSB 95	Additional Transmission Performance Guidelines for 4-pair 100 Ohm Category 5 Cabling

Table 4-8   Example of the Individual Standards included in the State of Washington's Computing and Telecommunications Wiring Standard

infrared, and radio frequency. The CEBus standard is implemented through devices that have adopted the CEBus Home Plug and Play standard that allows CEBus devices to communicate directly with each other without the need for a separate controller.

- **HomePlug**   This powerline technology is the result of an association of networking manufacturers (The HomePlug Alliance) wishing to perform Ethernet functions over the electrical lines in a home. HomePlug is not technically a certified standard, but almost 100 manufacturers now support it, including some heavies such as Linksys and NetGear. HomePlug operates at a maximum of 14 Mbps currently, but development is underway to increase the data speed of this system.

- **X-10**   This powerline technology has been around for some time and is available from a variety of home automation vendors. X-10 uses a controller device to signal a remote device, such as a PC sending a signal over the electrical wiring of a home to a particular electrical outlet to turn on the power to a lamp. X-10 supports baud rates (yes, just like older modems) of 1200 to 38400. X-10 is a full-duplex system, which is actually bad news. Any X-10 device can send a signal at any time, which means that collisions do occur and on occasion, control signals or responses can be lost, without a recovery methodology. X-10 technology is typically used only for residential control networks and is not commonly used for data networking.

Phoneline Standards

In a similar manner to the way that powerline technologies use the existing electrical lines in a home to transmit data, phone line communications technologies use the existing telephone wiring in the walls of a home to communicate.

The leading technology of phone line communications is the standard developed by the Home PhoneLine Networking Association (HPNA). Many vendors, including several also supporting powerline communications, are supporting this standard as well. HPNA currently operates at 10 Mbps and can coexist with DSL systems that may also be on the phone lines.

Wireless Media Standards

Another network media choice available is wireless networking and it eliminates the concern for wiring altogether. However, there are pros and cons for each media so each should be carefully considered before choosing it as a networking solution. The primary wireless media standards are as follows:

- **IEEE 802.11a**   This wireless networking standard defines a radio frequency technology in the 5-gigahertz (GHz) band that offers very high bandwidth (as much as 54 Mbps) over short distances, which makes it a good choice for home audio/video networks.

- **IEEE 802.11b** This is the most common of the wireless networking standards in use today. Virtually every wireless network gateway, access point, or PC Card produced is based on one variation of 802.11b or another. This standard defines a 10 Mbps Ethernet network operating over a radio frequency technology in the 2.4 GHz band.

- **IEEE 802.11g** This standard complements the 802.11a standards by adding an additional three channels in the 2.4 GHz band to increase bandwidth.

- **Bluetooth** Bluetooth is a radio frequency personal area networking (PAN) standard emerging from the cellular telephone industry. The benefit of Bluetooth, named after an ancient warrior king of Sweden, is that it is self-discovering and self-configuring among Bluetooth-capable devices, which means that you can roam freely within a Bluetooth area, and when you leave one server's range, another automatically picks you up. At the present, this is not a totally viable option for whole-house networking due to the lack of compatible products. However, as products are developed, its 10-meter range limit seems to be well-suited for many home networks.

- **HomeRF** This is a radio frequency technology developed specifically for use in wireless home networking. The recently announced HomeRF 2.0 standard has received some strong support and products may soon be available, something that has hindered its adoption in the past.

Other Standards

In the preceding sections, I discussed the primary standards that cover the design, installation, termination, and testing for the media included in a home's structured wiring. However, there are several other standards that apply to the applications and technologies implemented across the wiring. Table 4-9 lists a sampling of other standards and standards organizations that could apply to a whole-house networking implementation, depending on the applications it supports.

Organization	Standard	Description
EIA	EIA-600	CEBus powerline networking
CIC	HomePnP	Home Plug-and-Play
Cable Labs	DOCSIS	Data Over Cable Service Interface Specification
TIA	TR41.5	Residential Gateway
IEEE	IEEE 1394	Standard version of high-speed interface, implemented by Apple Computer as FireWire
VESA	VESA Home Network	High-speed whole-house baseband networking using IEEE 1394
HAVi Consortium	Home Audio Video interface	Digital AV networking interface standard
HomeAPI Working Group	HomeAPI	Programming routines for residential control systems

Table 4-9   Other Residential Network Technology Standards

Chapter Review

The organizations that develop and publish the primary standards covering the specification and installation of residential system wiring are: ANSI, EIA, IEEE, ISO, NFPA, TIA, UL, and OSHA.

ANSI is an agency of the United States federal government that is charged with the responsibility of developing and approving standards that cover a variety of technology, including computers and data communications, and weights and measurements. ANSI works with other agencies to develop and publish standards. Examples of jointly issued standards are the ANSI/TIA/EIA 568, 569, and 570 wire and cabling standards.

EIA is an alliance of trade and industry associations that work together to sponsor and promote data communication standards. Most of the EIA standards that apply to residential wiring are issued jointly with ANSI and TIA, including the ANSI/EIA/TIA 568 and 570 standards.

The IEEE is a worldwide, technical, professional association of engineers that is a leading standards authority in a variety of technical areas. The IEEE standards include the 802 computer networking standards.

The ISO is an international, non-treaty organization of voluntary members that develops and maintains a variety of technology standards, including standards governing computers, networking, and communications. An emerging standard of ISO is the residential gateway, which defines a network interface device that provides service access to a home for such services as telephone, cable television, and Internet access.

The NFPA is an international association focused on the development and publishing of fire safety codes, standards, and research to minimize the possibilities and impact of fire and other safety risks. The NFPA publishes the National Electrical Code (NEC), which includes coverage for the installation of electrical conductors, including the wiring used in structured residential wiring systems.

TIA is a trade organization of telecommunication product and service providers that develops and publishes a variety of wire and media specifications and testing standards for residential applications. The TIA/EIA 568 and 570 standards govern Cat 5 wiring connections and testing for home networking installations.

UL is an independent, nonprofit product safety testing organization that tests cable and wire products for fire and electrical safety testing against the NEC and other NFPA standards.

The primary home technology standards are ANSI/EIA/TIA wiring standards, IEEE Ethernet wire standards, the NEC®, the OSHA job safety practices, and the International Building Code (IBC).

The ANSI/EIA/TIA 568 standard provides specification for generic telecommunication cabling that prescribe the performance testing criteria for standard system configurations and their components. The 568 standards specify horizontal cable, work area or room cabling, and central distribution termination. The 568 standards also specify the UTP cabling categories for use as horizontal cabling and patch cords.

The 568 standard defines two separate cable termination standards for UPT cabling: 568a and 568b. The 568 standards also specify IDC (Insulation Displacement Connector) connectors at the distribution or telecommunications center and the use of the RJ-45 connector.

The EIA/TIA 570 standard defines the basic requirements for residential structured wiring and is the nationally accepted standard covering the design and installation of low voltage wiring in residential dwellings.

The IEEE 802 standards designate network media standards for use on an Ethernet network with a special coding scheme that generally describes a media's characteristics. The National Fire Protection Association (NFPA) publishes the National Electric Code® (NEC®) as a guideline to avoid and prevent electrical shock and fire hazards from residential wiring systems.

Each country has a governmental agency that publishes job safety and health codes and regulations. In the United States, it's the Occupational Safety and Health Administration (OSHA); in Canada, it's the Human Resources Development Canada (HRDC); in England, it's the Health and Safety Executive (HSE); and in Japan, it's the Japan Occupational Safety and Health Office (JOSHO). OSHA publishes the "Selected Construction Regulations (SCOR) for the Home Building Industry (29 CFR 1926)."

The term "powerline" describes the use of the electrical lines inside a home's walls to transmit information. The three primary standards for powerline technology are CEBus, HomePlug, and X-10. Phoneline communications technologies use the existing telephone wiring or coaxial cable in the walls of a home to communicate. The leading phoneline standard is the Home PhoneLine Networking Association (HPNA) standard. The primary wireless media standards are IEEE 802.11a, IEEE 802.11b, Bluetooth, and HomeRF.

Questions

1. Which of the following is not a standards organization listed in this chapter?

   A. ANSI

   B. EIA

   C. NEA

   D. NFPA

2. Which of the IEEE 802 standards is considered to be the Ethernet standard?

   A. IEEE 802.1

   B. IEEE 802.3

   C. IEEE 802.5

   D. IEEE 802.15

3. What organization publishes the NEC®?

   A. ANSI

   B. ICC

   C. EIA

   D. NFPA

4. What is the EIA/TIA standard that governs Cat 5 wiring connections?

   A. 232

   B. 402

   C. 568

   D. 570

5. Which of the UTP cable categories is recommended as 100BaseT media?

   A. Cat 2

   B. Cat 3

   C. Cat 4

   D. Cat 5

6. Which of the following lists the 568b pinout sequence of the wire colors from Pin 1 to 8?

   A. White green, green, white orange, blue, white blue, orange, white brown, brown

   B. White green, blue, white blue, green, white orange, orange, white brown, brown

   C. White orange, orange, white green, blue, white blue, green, white brown, brown

   D. White green, blue, white blue, green, white brown, brown, white orange, orange

7. What is the TIA/EIA standard that specifies residential structured wiring?

   A. 568a

   B. 568b

   C. 570

   D. 802

8. In the term 10BaseT, what does the "Base" refer to?

   A. Broadband

   B. Baseband

   C. Narrowband

   D. Base rate interface

9. Which of the IEEE 802 network standards defines wireless Ethernet standards?

   A. 802.3

   B. 802.10

   C. 802.11

   D. 802.15

10. What government agency publishes the "Selected Construction Regulations (SCOR) for the Home Building Industry (29 CFR 1926)"?

    A. Occupational Safety and Health Administration (OSHA)

    B. Department of Agriculture

    C. Housing and Urban Development (HUD)

    D. American National Standards Institute (ANSI)

Answers

1. **D.** The National Education Association doesn't publish home wiring system standards.

2. **B.** The other standards listed are for LAN connectivity, Token Ring networks, and personal area networks, respectively.

3. **D.** The National Fire Protection Association publishes the NEC approximately every 3-4 years.

4. **C.** Actually there are two standards, the 568a and the 568b.

5. **D.** Cat 2 isn't used for networking. Cat 3 and Cat 4 are recommended for 10BaseT and Token Ring networks.

6. **C.** The difference between the 568a and 568b is the placement of only one pair.

7. **C.** The 568 standards deal with UTP cable and its termination, and the 802 standards are published by IEEE.

8. **B.** Baseband refers to the fact that the cable media is able to carry only a single signal.

9. **C.** The other 802 standards deal with Ethernet media access, metropolitan area networking (MAN), and personal area networking (PAN), respectively.

10. **A.** This agency is charged with issuing worker and workplace safety standards and practices.

PART II

Structured Wiring

Infrastructure Wiring Basics

In this chapter, you will learn about

- Structured wiring
- Future proofing a home's communication systems
- Structured wiring installation requirements and techniques

If you haven't already figured it out, structured wiring is a primary element of a home technology integration or home automation project. Even without installing automated systems and controls, structured wiring makes sense if all that it is used for is distributing telephone, audio, video, or data networking systems.

This chapter covers some of the basics of structured wiring and its components and why and when they are included in a system. The chapters in Parts 3 through 8 of this book cover each of the separate subsystems in much more detail, but this chapter provides you with an overview of why structured wiring is installed in a home and how it benefits the homeowner.

Structured Wiring

There is a big difference between structured wiring and wiring that is not structured. A home's structured wiring system facilitates the delivery of services and the interconnection of the various subsystems to create an integrated technology environment. Structured wiring is the foundation on which a home automation network is built because it provides a planned and organized method of residential low voltage wiring allowing for efficient hook-up and future changes and additions.

The term structured when applied to the wiring of a home's voice, data, audio, video, and control networks means that the wiring for all of these systems was designed as a single entity to be installed in a single operation and not as separate and discrete systems to be installed individually. When properly designed and installed, a structured wiring system should minimize the amount of cable to be installed and maximize the capabilities and flexibilities of the systems attached to the structured cabling. Structured wiring provides several advantages over unplanned and unstructured wiring when designing and installing a wiring infrastructure in a home. As indicated in Table 5-1, structured wiring's characteristics are more conducive to supporting a home network than an unstructured approach to system wiring.

Characteristic	Structured Wiring	Unstructured/Free-Form
Appearance	In or behind a wall	In the walls, over the wall, or across the floor
Installation	Pre-wire, during remodel, or retrofit	As required
Availability	Wall outlets	Where required
Form	Planned distances and topology	Free form
Planned/Unplanned	Planned	Unplanned
Flexibility	Cross-connecting Changes and upgrades in the future	No cross-connecting
Documentation	Labeled and documented	May be labeled, but usually not documented

Table 5-1   Structured and Unstructured Wiring Characteristics

Structured Wiring Components

The three primary components of a structured wiring system are as follows:

- Cable or wiring
- Distribution panel
- Outlets or access points

Cabling and Wiring

In any hard-wired system, the quality of the wiring installation is far more important than the quality of the wire. Don't misunderstand, the quality of the wire is important, but how well the wiring is installed can have a major impact on how well the network implemented on the wiring supports the needs of the customer.

New Construction

The type of wiring you install depends on what the customer defines as the requirements of the network. As specified in the various cable standards (see Chapter 4), there are cable types to support virtually any requirement the customer may define.

The current data and voice standards are Cat 5 cabling (actually Cat 5e, the "e" means extended) and RG6 coaxial cabling. In a new construction situation, installing these cable types in the walls throughout the house provides an infrastructure that should support the networking needs of the home for years to come. As a rule of thumb, each room in a home (those rooms to which the home network will be extended) should have at least two runs of Cat 5 cable—one each for voice and data—and two runs of RG6 coaxial cable for video—one for upstream and one for downstream. In addition, you may want to also add speaker wiring, control wiring, and possibly runs of twisted-pair wire to all rooms for use with a security system.

Cat 5 Versus Cat 5e

Cat 5 and Cat 5e UTP cabling are essentially the same. However, Cat 5e's specification includes some additional limits that extend the bandwidth capability of Cat 5e. In reality, nearly all currently manufactured Cat 5 cable is equivalent to Cat 5e cable, but just hasn't been certified to the higher standards. Table 5-2 compares the basis characteristics of Cat 5 and Cat 5e cable.

Category	Cable Type	Bandwidth	Maximum Segment Length
Cat 5	UTP	100 Mpbs	100 meters
Cat 5e	UTP	1000 Mbps	100 meters

Table 5-2   Cat 5 versus Cat 5e

In summary, the recommendations for the minimum wiring for each room of a new house are (per the TIA standards)

- 2 runs of Cat 5e (UTP)
- 2 runs of RG6 coaxial cable

Optional in each room:

- Additional runs of coaxial cable for use with in-room audio devices and speakers
- 1 or 2 runs of UTP cable to connect door and window contacts to a security system

NOTE   Whether or not fiber optic cabling should be installed in new home construction for both data and video systems is something the customer should decide. The primary reason not to install fiber optic cable is cost; fiber can run up to $2 more per foot than UTP cabling. In addition, standards have not been settled on for the type to use and connectors for fiber optic cable. On the other hand, fiber can carry an extremely large amount of data and may be just the thing to carry the data and video speeds and bandwidth of the future.

Existing Structures

Retrofitting a home for Cat 5 wiring can be troublesome in many situations. It is always better to have a dedicated wire. When that is not possible, however, the use of Powerline, HPNA (see Chapter 10 for more information), or wireless systems should be seriously considered. Of course, you must determine which of these systems will best support the requirements of the network. In any case, these systems may not support the planned video or audio systems and cable must be installed in the walls anyway. If this is the case, we advise that the same amount of cabling be installed as recommended for new construction.

Integrated Cable Bundles

The growing popularity of structured wiring in homes has spawned new cable bundle types that incorporate all of the wiring recommended for a structured wiring installation. These bundles, like the one shown in Figure 5-1, include 2 Cat 5e cables for voice and data, 2-shielded RG6 coaxial cables for video, and in some bundled cables, 2 multimode fiber optic cables for present or future applications.

Distribution Panels

One of the primary components in a structured wiring system is a centralized distribution panel. The distribution panel (see Figure 5-2) provides the system and the homeowners with a single central location where all incoming source signals are integrated and then distributed throughout the home. It also allows for the sharing of signals within them.

Depending on the needs of the system, the distribution panel can be used to connect incoming video, audio, telephone, and data signals to the appropriate wiring that will carry the signals to an outlet for connection and use.

The distribution panel also can serve as the hub of the star topology recommended for home automation and multimedia distribution systems. Each structured wiring run is installed as a home run from the room to the distribution panel. Panel boxes range in size to accommodate a variety of modules.

Modularity is a primary characteristic and key benefit of a structured wiring distribution panel. Service unit modules, such as an audio distribution module, data hub, or the like, can be added to the distribution panel at any time, not just at installation, and allow for services to be added to the system in the future.

Figure 5-1
A structured
wiring cable
bundle

*Photo courtesy
of FutureSmart
Systems, Inc.*

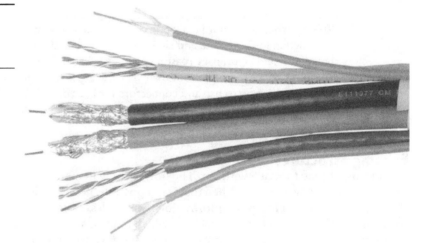

Figure 5-2
A structured
wiring distribution
panel

*Photo courtesy of
Smarthome Inc.*

Distribution Panel Subsystems

There are high-end, fully populated distribution panels, mid-range panels with the basic connecting systems, low-end simple panels with only voice, data and video, and modular distribution panels that can be assembled to fit a particular situation exactly.

Higher-end distribution panels, like the one shown in Figure 5-3, which most manufacturers refer to as their "pro," "gold," or "platinum" series, typically include pre-installed modules to support what could be considered to be the standard subsystems of a structured wiring scheme: data, telephone, audio, and video. In cases where there is a need to support a modem, DSL, ISDN, cable or satellite TV, and other audio/video source devices, optional modules can be added to the distribution panel's housing for integration of these devices.

Figure 5-3
A distribution
panel with
some modules
pre-installed

*Photo courtesy of
General Electric
Company.*

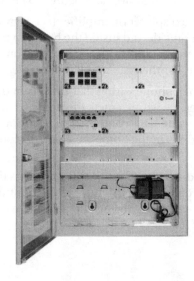

For a more customized system, the distribution control panel can be purchased as an empty enclosure or panel (see Figure 5-2) and separate system modules and assembled to support the signal distribution requirements of the home's structured wiring system. Figures 5-4, 5-5, and 5-6 are examples of modules that can be installed in the distribution panel.

Using a distribution panel provides several benefits to the homeowners:

- The ability to alter the mix of incoming source signals without rewiring

- The ability to easily change the interconnections and distribution of services to outlets

- The ability to upgrade services in the future without wiring

Distribution Panel Components

Structured wiring distribution panels organize the wiring supporting multiroom television, video, telephone, audio, and data networks and distribute it to each room. Of course, it depends on the systems included in the home, but some distribution modules are considered to be fairly standard:

- **Audio** A sound distribution amplifier (see Figure 5-4) that is able to patch incoming audio sources to usually two to eight different speaker sets.

- **Data** A data patch panel with IDC (Insulation Displacement Connector) connectors is used to connect the Cat 5 cabling distributed in the structure wiring system to distribute the signal on the Internet Gateway device.

- **Surge suppression** Few, if any, of the amplifiers, interconnects, or control modules installed in the distribution panel include surge suppression circuits themselves. So, it's a very good idea to protect the modules and devices in the distribution panel from power spikes on the electrical power source by installing a surge suppression device (see Figure 5-5) in the distribution panel.

- **Video** A video splitter or amplifier (see Figure 5-6) distributes the video signals from outside and inside the home to the outlets over the structured wiring. However, multiple video in and out connectors provide better distribution and flexibility for the system to handle cable, satellite, or HDTV signaling.

- **Voice** The telephone wiring that runs from the demarcation point, where the telephone service wiring enters the home, is interconnected into a distribution patch panel using IDC contacts. The telephone wiring (Cat 5) that runs to the various handsets in the home are also interconnected into the distribution panel.

- **Wireless audio/video/data** Even if wireless distribution is to be used for one or all of the distributed systems, the distribution panel can provide the link between the incoming wiring and source devices and the wireless network access point (NAP).

Figure 5-4

An audio/video amplifier module of the type that can be installed in a distribution panel

Photo courtesy of Smarthome, Inc.

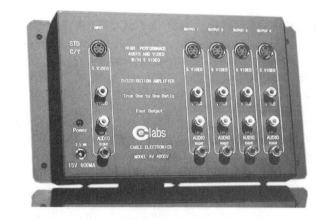

Figure 5-5

A low-voltage surge suppression module should be installed in the distribution panel

Photo courtesy of CyberResearch, Inc.

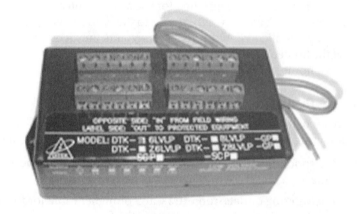

Figure 5-6

A video amplifier and splitter that can be installed in a distribution panel

Photo courtesy of Channel Vision.

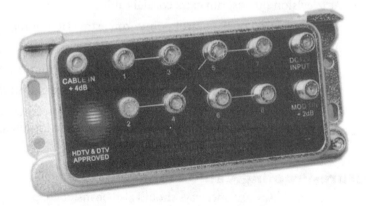

Future-proofing the System

One of the best benefits of modifying distribution or installing a structured wiring system in a home is that it helps to future-proof the home, at least in terms of adding future audio/video and data systems. By future-proof we are referring to structured wiring adding flexibility to any home because of the inclusion of its centralizing and interconnecting distribution panel.

Beyond the distribution panel, using state-of-the-art cabling, such as the bundled cabling, can also help to future-proof a home's networked systems. When the time comes to implement any unused or underused cabling in the structured media, it is a simple matter of adding or connecting the appropriate device in or to the distribution panel.

A key element in future-proofing a structured wiring system, and the home it supports, is the installation of extra (unused) wiring and conduits (raceways) in the structured wiring system. The extra wiring is unterminated and the raceways are unused at the time of installation, but are installed for use at some future date. When the time comes to expand existing or add new subsystems to the home, having the extra wiring and raceways already installed provides for an easy and inexpensive installation should the needs of the homeowner change or new technology emerges to provide expanded capabilities to a home.

Future-Proofing Structured Wiring

To future-proof the structured wiring, extra wiring should be installed and left unterminated at the following locations (the other end is, of course, at the central distribution center):

- At telephone outlets, run extra Cat 5e or higher for additional services in the future
- At networking outlets, run extra Cat 5 or higher cable for future data networks, communications, audio, or whatever the future may bring
- At television outlets, run extra coaxial cable
- At future keypad or IR control points, run extra Cat 5 or higher
- At audio volume control, run extra Cat 5 or higher
- At thermostats, run extra Cat5 or higher and STP for future control wiring
- At HVAC units, run Cat 5 or higher and STP for future control wiring
- At any location where a future sprinkler, spa, pool, weather station, door phone, door strike, garage door opener may later be installed, run Cat 5 or higher for control, sensor, and interface uses

Future-Proofing Cable Management

Extra conduits, chases, and raceways should also be installed, partly to hold the extra cabling and partly to provide inside-the-wall paths for future cabling installations. Conduit is available in a variety of forms and sizes, but as a hedge against the future, flexible conduit is likely the best bet. Flexible conduit for structured wiring is typically orange in color, like that in Figure 5-7, in keeping with wiring conventions, but blue tubing, which is called "smurf tube," is also available.

Figure 5-7
Flexible
structured
wiring conduit

*Photo courtesy of
Lamson & Sessions.*

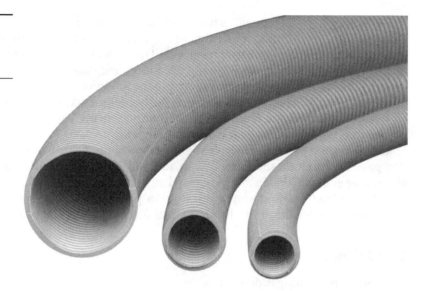

A chase is a channel placed in a floor to provide an enclosed and out-of-the-way path for cabling that must cross a room or travel between two floors. Typically, chases are either inserted between floors of a multiple story home or, in the case of a concrete floor, cut into the floor and fitted with a cover. Raceways are trays and molded covers that provide both support and a path for cable crossing an open area.

To provide for future proofing and to support any future cable installations, install conduit or raceway or install chases between floors between key device locations and future access points.

Chapter Review

Structured wiring facilitates interconnection of the data, video, and audio systems in a home to create an integrated environment. Structured wiring means the wiring for the home's voice, data, audio, video, and control networks are all home run to a central location.

The three primary components of a structured wiring system are: cable or wiring, distribution panel, and outlets or access points.

The recommendation for the minimum wiring to each room of a new house includes: 2 runs of Cat 5e (UTP) and 2 runs of RG6 coaxial cable at minimum. Additional runs of RG6 coaxial cable and UTP cable should be pulled to support audio, video, speakers, controls, and any other devices located in a room, along with any cable being installed for future-proofing. The primary concern for pulling cable into an existing structure is to spread the runs of the various cable types over as wide a space as possible.

New cable bundle types are now available that incorporate all of the wiring recommended for a structured wiring installation. These bundles include 2 Cat 5e cables for voice and data, 2-shielded RG6 coaxial cables for video, and sometimes 2 multimode fiber optic cables for present or future applications.

The distribution panel provides the system and the homeowners with a single central location where all incoming source signals are integrated with the structured distributed wiring in the home. Depending on the needs of the system, the distribution panel can be used to connect incoming video, audio, telephone, and data signals to the appropriate wiring that will carry the signals to an outlet for connection and use.

The distribution panel can also serve as the hub of the star topology recommended for home automation and multimedia distribution systems. Each structured wiring run is home run from the room to the distribution panel.

Modularity is a primary characteristic and key benefit of a structured wiring distribution panel. Service unit modules, like an audio distribution module, data hub, or the like, can be added to the distribution panel anytime, not just at installation, as services are added to the system. Using a distribution panel provides several benefits to the homeowners: added flexibility, future adaptability, and future upgrade.

Questions

1. Structured wiring is defined as

    A. The electrical wiring running from the electrical distribution box to each room.

    B. The wiring for audio, video, data, and control systems designed and installed as a single wiring system.

    C. The wiring running from a source device to an outlet device.

    D. The use of a single cable that incorporates all of the wiring in a home.

2. Which one of the following is not a primary component of a structured wiring system?

    A. Cabling

    B. Speakers

    C. Distribution panel

    D. Outlets and access points

3. Which of the following is the minimum recommended cabling that should be pulled into each room of a home being constructed?

    A. 1 run of UTP and 2 runs of coaxial cable

    B. 1 run of coaxial cable and 2 runs of UTP

    C. 2 runs of UTP and 2 runs of coaxial cable

    D. 3 runs of UTP and 1 run of coaxial cable

4. What are the two structured wiring components recommended for installation to help future-proof a home?

    A. Extra cabling and conduit

    B. Extra outlets and connectors

C. Extra remote controls and IR receivers

D. Extra source equipment and distribution devices

5. What device or module should be installed in a distribution panel to protect other modules and distribution devices from spikes on its power supply line?

A. DC transformer

B. Line filter

C. Surge suppressor

D. UPS

6. What is the current UTP cable standard for structured wiring?

A. RG6

B. Fiber optic

C. Cat 3

D. Cat 5

7. Which structured wiring device is used to interconnect cabling in a centralized location?

A. Ethernet hub

B. Internet Gateway

C. Distribution panel

D. Outlet box

8. When is the best and usually easiest time to install structured wiring?

A. Retrofit

B. Before wall studs and joists are installed

C. Before the wall surface or drywall is installed

D. After the wall surface or drywall is installed

9. Which of the following is not typically integrated into a distribution panel in a structured wiring system?

A. Electrical cabling

B. Telephone cabling

C. Audio cabling

D. Video cabling

10. The term "future-proofing" refers to

A. Preventing expansion of a system beyond its intended design.

B. Ensuring that changes to a home's systems are compatible with existing systems.

C. Ensuring that a system has the capability to support new or expanded systems.

D. Providing a means to remove a cable-based system in favor of a wireless system.

Answers

1. **B.** Structured wiring is installed as a structured system with centralized control and distribution.

2. **B.** Only the cabling, distribution panel, and access outlets are considered as a part of a structured wiring system. External source and playback devices are not.

3. **C.** Two runs of UTP and 2 runs of coaxial cable is the minimum cable service recommended for each room of a home with a structured wiring system.

4. **A.** Pre-installing extra cabling and conduits not only helps to prepare a home for future system changes and additions, but it is much less expensive to install the extra components while the structured wiring components are being installed at the same time.

5. **D.** A DC transformer is not a protective device and the other two are usually too large for inclusion in a distribution panel. However, a UPS is not a bad idea for installation between the main power connection of the distribution panel and the electrical power outlet.

6. **D.** In fact, the standards now specify Cat 5e, where the "e" represents enhanced cable.

7. **E.** This device provides interconnection for each cable system included in the structured wiring of a home.

8. **C.** The wall studs and ceiling and floor joists are important to the path of the structured cable and after the walls are finished, all work is retrofit.

9. **A.** A home's AC power lines are typically interconnected in the electrical panel or fuse box.

10. **C.** Installing extra infrastructure to provide support for future systems extends the value of the installation system.

Planning a Structured Wiring Installation

In this chapter, you will learn about:
- Structured wiring cable installation methods
- Planning for remodeling or new construction settings
- Planning for equipment and component placement

Structured wiring and its concepts, methods, and objectives, are the cornerstone of the home technology integration movement, as well as the certifications offered by CompTIA (HTI+), CEDIA (CEDIA Professional), and even a few manufacturers. In addition to all of this, structured wiring just makes sense for new homes. It provides the homeowner with value, convenience, and perhaps best of all, a home that has a flexible infrastructure that will be able to accommodate changes and future systems.

This chapter looks at the issues that should be considered when planning a structured wiring project and the methods that should be used to improve the design and installation phases of the project.

What Is Structured Wiring?

A good place to start a discussion on how to plan for a structured wiring installation is with an explanation of just what structured wiring is and isn't.

Structured wiring combines all of the communications data, signal, and control cabling in a home into a single consolidated wiring system. This means that all of the cabling, including the network, telephone, video, audio, security, heating and cooling control, lighting control, and other control wiring in a home, is planned, designed, installed, and managed as a single system.

In a nonstructured wiring situation, the wiring supporting each of a home's systems is often installed independently, using what is referred to as a daisy chain. This means that the wiring for one device is typically an extension of the wiring to another device (looped) without a central distribution and management point.

Figure 6-1 shows a slightly exaggerated illustration of a home that has been wired with a nonstructured daisy chain wiring style. As new services are added to the home,

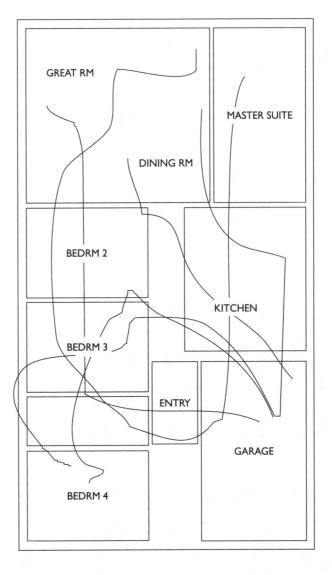

Figure 6-1
An example
of a home with
daisy chain wiring
installed

new wires are attached to the end of existing wiring and new wiring is routed using the easiest path available. Daisy chained wiring typically has been spliced to attach new runs or extend existing runs and often involves splitters and connectors embedded in walls, under floors or in attics.

On the other hand, Figure 6-2 illustrates a simplified view of how structured wiring improves the wiring infrastructure in the same home. Each of the cable runs shown in

Figure 6-2

An example of a home with structured wiring installed

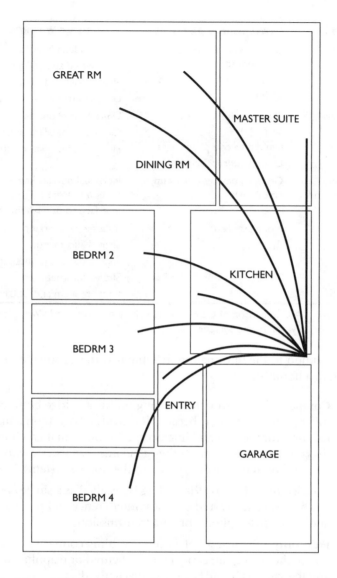

Figure 6-2 includes all of the cabling a room requires, typically with extra wires to accommodate future needs. Two fundamental rules of a structured wiring system are that there should be no splices and each cable bundle should be installed as a home run from the room back to a central distribution center.

Table 6-1 compares just a few types of conventional wiring to a structured wiring system. However, the capabilities provided to the homeowners of a home with structured wiring are obvious.

System	Conventional Wiring	Structured Wiring
Audio/Video	Usually no pre-wire so wires are exposed Separate source devices for each room	Wires hidden in walls Distributed audio/video Shared source devices Local control for source selection and volume
Telephone	Separate phone lines for each phone Limited to two phone lines Dial-up Internet access	Up to four phone lines to each space Capable of handling phone system High-speed or dial-up Internet access
Security (put at end)	Grouped devices (for example, first floor)	Individual devices known (for example, kitchen motion sensor) Interface to other home systems
Data	None installed	In-home networking Shared information Shared devices (printer, scanner) Shared Internet access Cable modem and DSL ready

Table 6-1 A Comparison of Conventional Wiring to Structured Wiring for Typical Home Systems

In addition to the information in Table 6-1, the advantages of installing structured wiring in a home are

- **Compatibility**   Structured wiring builds a bridge between devices from different manufacturers because it provides a common and consistent platform for communications and interaction. Products that aren't in compliance with the communications and wiring standards that also support or require structured wiring should not be designed into the home's systems.

- **Consistency**   Because the cabling is installed as a single system, all of the wiring can be installed to avoid electrical interference and provide a more consistent audio, video, telephone, or data transmission.

- **Flexibility**   Because all of a home's cabling connects to a central distribution center, the wiring can easily be reconfigured or reapplied to other applications and the systems in the home can be changed.

- **Integrity**   Because there are no wire or cable splices in the system, there are no failure points such as a location deep in a wall where a cable might pick up interference.

- **Maintenance and management**   Each cable in the home is individually accessible for testing and troubleshooting.

Planning for Structured Wiring

To begin planning a structured wiring installation you must first identify systems it is intended to support now and in the future. The choices for integrated and distributed systems that can be incorporated into a home's infrastructure seem to grow daily.

System Choices

- The following are the major home automation and technology integration systems that structured wiring is installed for
  - Distributed audio
  - Distributed video
  - Voice communications (telephone/intercom)
  - Heating, ventilation, and air conditioning (HVAC) interface
  - Security and surveillance

Data Networking

Ten years ago, a home may have had only one personal computer (PC) that was used for mostly personal information processing. With the exploding popularity of the Internet and the rapid developments in virtually all areas of software, it's common for a home to now have multiple PCs used for telecommuting, personal entertainment, correspondence, and so much more.

Homes with multiple PCs commonly find themselves constrained by their dial-up or high-speed Internet connection when two or more of the users in the home wish to access the Internet at the same time. Networking a home's PCs so that they can share a single Internet connection, as well as files and peripheral devices, is the best solution. The installation of structured wiring can link each PC in a home directly to the residential gateway of a high-speed Internet connection or a shared modem.

Distributed Audio

In the past, "whole-house audio" meant that you had really large speakers with lots of watts and turned up the volume so everyone in the house could hear it (not to mention the neighbors who were trying to sleep). Often, these speakers were freestanding and hooked only to a local system in the same room.

Structured wiring makes it possible to install speakers in every room of a house while maintaining audio equipment in one central location. The room's occupants can choose the sound they wish to hear and control volume with controls that are set locally.

Distributed Video

What if one person wants to watch a baseball game, but someone else, in another room, wants to watch a DVD? Not a problem with a distributed video system installed on a structured wiring platform. Any video source device around the home can be selected and viewed on any TV. Local control is also possible with a structured wiring system.

Voice Communications

If properly planned, installing a home's telephone system using a structured wiring plat-form can in the long run save money and nuisance for the homeowners by providing telephone outlets in every room of the house. For a home without structured wiring, the homeowner must hire a contractor or the phone company to come in and install a tele-phone outlet should one be needed where none exists and this could lead to yet another daisy chain wire run or cables tacked to the outside of the home or on the inside walls.

In situations where a home is serviced by multiple phone lines, the mix-and-match process of which lines are available on what phones becomes much more manageable. With a structured wiring system, a phone system that can handle multiple phones can easily be added.

Structured wiring can also easily support the installation of in-house intercom systems that can be a headache to install as a retrofit.

HVAC Control

Structured wiring and specialized HVAC systems can together provide the capability to create heating and cooling zones in a home. The benefit here is that unused areas of the home aren't heated or cooled, thereby saving energy and money. In addition, the temper-ature settings for one or more rooms can be managed from a remote location or auto-matically based on time or occupancy.

Security and Surveillance

Structured wiring provides the means to interconnect all of a home's sensors, detectors, locks, surveillance cameras, and lighting to a central location for control management and monitoring. Another benefit of a security system installed on structured wiring is the capability to easily link a telephone line into the security system for use with an out-side monitoring service or to automatically contact the owner in the event of an alarm.

Wireless Systems

It is conceivable that a homeowner may not wish to install a structured wiring system, preferring instead to use wireless devices. This is, of course, the homeowner's choice, but because of a lack of industry-wide standardization in the wireless industry, the task of mixing devices from several manufacturers may be formidable. In addition, wireless performance is not as consistent or dependable as hardwiring a home.

Even radio frequency (RF) and infrared (IR) technology can be integrated into a structured wiring environment. These wireless devices often need to connect to outside services, such as telephone or data networking and have their control or base units inte-grated into the distribution panel.

The Planning Process

Perhaps the most important part of any planning process, including the planning of structured wiring, is an understanding of exactly what it is the homeowner (customer) wishes to accomplish in the end. A homeowner views a structured wiring project in terms of the finished product and experience: the audio system (listening to music throughout the home), video system (watching TV and movies), security system (protecting the home and family), voice system (intercom to the front door), data networking system (sharing computer printer), and so on. To properly plan a structured wiring installation, you must understand the homeowner's vision for the outcomes of the entire project. Without understanding how the systems of a home are to perform and interact, the structured wiring installation may fall short.

Locating the Central Distribution Panel

The location of the central distribution panel, also referred to as the central wiring panel, is extremely important to the success of the installation, and it can also have a direct impact on the overall cost of the project.

If the panel is located in an extreme corner of a home, forcing long cable runs to every room, the cost of cabling will definitely be higher than if the panel is centrally located. Understand that "central" is a generic term when used with wiring systems. Practically, the distribution panel should be as central as possible.

There are several candidates for the location of the distribution panel in every home, such as utility or mechanical rooms, large closets, workshop, basement, accessible attic space, or even an attached garage. The distribution panel isn't the type of thing you want on display in a living area; not that they are ugly, but wiring is wiring and it should be located where curious minds and idle hands don't have direct access to it. Remember that the distribution panel is the central nervous system of an automated home's structured wiring scheme. As such, it should be somewhat secured.

The primary consideration for locating the distribution panel is that it must be kept at a distance from electrical generators and motors, fluorescent lamps, transformers, electrical wiring, and any other potential interference producing device. The space should not be either too hot or too cold and you want to be able to maintain a lower to normal humidity level. The panel is normally wall-mounted, so its location should provide ample wall space that is devoid of the aforementioned hazards. This alone should narrow down the choices for its location. Of course, if the homeowner is really into the home technology integration thing, then it is likely the home design includes a wire closet just for this purpose.

Structured wiring distribution panels can be either surface-mounted or flush-mounted. Surface-mounted panels can be installed during trim out, but a flush-mounted panel must be installed during rough-in so that it is inside the walls prior to drywall.

Developing the Planning Detail

The steps that should be used to develop the plan for a structured wiring project are

1. **Identify the systems to be supported and work backward.**

   The ultimate goal of the planning process is to identify all of the cabling that must be installed as a structured wiring system. The first step is to identify all of the systems to be installed on the structured wiring. You can then work backward from each system to determine the cabling, outlets, and locations required by each system.

2. **Consolidate the cabling requirements.**

Each system to be integrated into the home has its own cabling requirements, most of which can be satisfied by the cabling most commonly included in structured cabling bundles: Cat 5e, coaxial cable, quad wire, and, on occasion, fiber optic cable. You should check the building and local wiring codes to ensure that each of the cable types included in a commercial structured wiring bundle is acceptable for use in your area.

Assuming a location has been chosen for the structured wiring central distribution panel, you can then map out the cable runs required for each system, determine their length, and create a consolidated list of the cabling, outlets, and faceplate components required for the job. Always provide a bit extra of everything, especially cabling, to allow for rough-in, trim-out, mistakes, and, well, you understand.

3. **Create a wire chart.**

In the preceding step, the cable types and outlet boxes were identified, which means that you have the information required to create a wire chart that includes the information needed by the wire installers during rough-in. Table 6-2 is a sample of a wire chart that lists the first ten cable runs planned for a home. In addition to the information listed in this sample form, the length of each cable run, and perhaps status boxes that show when and who pulled, terminated, and tested each run should be added to create a complete record of the cable installation.

4. **Identify and sequence the installation tasks.**

The wire chart lists the cables to be pulled and outlet locations so you have the information required to begin identifying and sequencing the specific tasks to be

#	Type	Source	Destination	Device	Use/Comments
1	Cat 5	House feed	Distribution Panel (DP)	Phone feed	Phone feed
2	Cat 5	House feed	DP	Future	Future
3	RG-6	House feed	DP	Future	Cable feed-future
4	RG-6	Attic	DP	Future TV antenna	Loop extra cable
5	RG-6	Attic	DP	Future FM antenna	Loop extra cable
6	RG-6	Roof	DP	DSS feed	Satellite TV
7	RG-6	Roof	DP	DSS feed	Future satellite service
8	Cat 5	CC	Living room.	Phone jack	
9	Cat 5	CC	Living room	Data jack	
10	RG-6	CC	Living room	TV jack	

Table 6-2   A Sample of a Structured Wiring Planning Chart

performed. The generic steps used to install structured wiring are rough-in, trim-out, and finish. However, the approach used to accomplish these steps can vary.

- **Room-by-room**   With this approach, you complete one room or zone and then move on to the next room or zone. When you use this approach, all of the cabling and rough-in devices required for a room or zone are installed to complete the rough-in for each room or zone. After the wallboards are installed, this same approach can then be used for trim-out and finish work.

- **System-by-system**   With this approach, you install the components required for each system, one at a time. The downside is that pulling cable for each system separately adds more labor and cost to the job. In addition, separately pulling cabling for each system prevents the use of some prepared structured wiring bundles that are commercially available.

- **Rough-in devices, then cabling**   Perhaps the best approach is a combination of the two preceding approaches. You first install the rough-in devices for all systems in each room and then install cabling on a room-by-room basis.

- **Draw cable route map**   In addition to a sequenced list of the tasks to be performed during the installation, you should also finalize a cable route map, typically using a floor plan of the home.

5. **Perform a practice pre-wire walk-through.**

   After the wall studs are in place and the plumbers and electricians have completed their work, perform a dry run of the tasks that have been identified in the project planning.

   The primary purpose of this step is to verify not only the planned cable runs, but to identify any possible problems that impact the project as planned. Use the wire chart and the marked up floor plan that shows your planned cable runs as a map and follow the cable runs in the sequence you set in the preceding step of the planning phase.

   Mark the location of the cable termination on every stud, header, or floor that must be drilled. It is far better to address any problems and possible work-arounds at this time than when you are pulling cable. In fact, it's a good idea to pre-drill all of the holes needed in the cable path *before* you begin actually pulling cable.

Don't cheat on this process. Physically move through the steps and locations included in the planning. This is your ounce of prevention towards ensuring an efficient installation. If necessary, make any adjustments needed to the project plan before beginning the actual work.

Cable Planning

As mentioned earlier in this chapter, as well as the preceding chapters, the specific cabling types that are installed are determined by the systems to be installed on the structured wiring and the physical and electrical conditions through which the cable will run.

The amount of cable to be installed should be measured from the central distribution panel through the walls to the location of a room outlet box. In a home with 2,500 square feet or less, allow 75 feet for each cable run; in a home with between 3,000 and 4,000 square feet, use 100 feet per run; and in a 4,000-square foot home, use an estimate of 125 feet per run when planning the cable lengths. Table 6-3 summarizes the estimating number used in for the various home sizes. Never use exact measurements to estimate the amount of cabling required. Be generous and add at least 20 percent on the estimates and then allow extra cabling for cable loops at each outlet during rough-in.

Planning Cable Runs

For nearly all situations, the following cabling is recommended:

- To each room:
  - **Two runs of Category 5e cable**   For use with data networking and up to four standard telephone lines or a phone system per room.
  - **Two runs of RG-6 coaxial cable**   RG-6 has the properties and characteristics required for cable or satellite television. One cable is installed for downstream (video signal coming into the room) and the second cable is for upstream (video signal out from the room).
- Where required:
  - **One run of 4-conductor speaker wire**   For use with an audio system. Four-conductor wire allows for two stereo speakers, each using one pair of the 4-conductors.
  - **Various runs of twisted pair wire (quad wire or two-pair wire such as 22-2 and 22-4)**   For use with security system components.
  - **Additional runs of coaxial cable, Cat 5e cable, or other cable**   As required by specific system requirements, such as for a driveway loop controller, a door telephone intercom, a connection to a sprinkler system controller, or the like.

Table 6-3	Square Footage of Home	Planning Length for Cable Runs
Estimating Cable Run Lengths	2,500 or less	75 linear feet per run
	3,000 to 3,999	100 linear feet per run
	4,000 to 4,999	125 linear feet per run
	5,000 or more	150 linear feet per run

Cabling Planning Issues

There are some basic electrical issues that need to be addressed during the planning phase for a structured wiring project as well. Even the best cable installation can have problems if the following issues aren't addressed prior to installation:

- **Current** Verify for each system the type of current (AC versus DC) the cable is to carry.

- **ESD (Electrostatic Discharge)** Ensure that all cable or computer technicians wear antistatic devices when working with circuit boards and computer components. Even very small static electricity discharges can damage the delicate circuitry of electronic components.

- **Grounding** Ensure that the distribution panel has a connection to an earth ground. If available, a separate earth ground from that of the home's electrical system should be used.

- **Placement** Verify that each cable run is the proper distance from AC power lines and that if the structured cabling must cross an AC line, that it does so at a 90-degree angle.

- **Electrical event protection** The distribution panel should be protected from unwanted events on the source AC power line, such as brownouts and power sags and spikes. A brownout occurs when the voltage of the AC line drops below the standard range of operation and stays there for an extended time. Power sags are actually short-term brownouts and power spikes are sharp, but short, increases in the line voltage. A variety of devices can be used to protect the distribution panel and the systems it supports: surge suppressors, uninterruptible power supplies (UPS), line filters, and power regulators. Many structured wiring distribution panels come with built-in surge protection. Another less common event is a blackout, which is a complete power failure. Of the protection devices I've just listed, only a UPS, which acts as a battery backup, can provide power for some time after a blackout occurs.

 CROSS-REFERENCE Chapters 1 and 2 cover the basics of wire choice and installation guidelines.

Another issue that you must consider when planning a structured wiring system is whether or not any cabling will run through air supply ductwork. If so, you will need to check the local, state, and national building and electrical codes to determine the required fire safety rating for the cabling that can be installed in a duct. Also, there are different standards and codes for wiring used as riser cables (between floors) and cabling that is to be installed underground. Be sure to check your local codes.

Planning for Electrical Protection

The fact that any incoming AC power required by the devices in a structured wiring project should be something you can take for granted and allow the electricians to worry about is the good news. However, the bad news is that you need to protect the structured wiring system and any devices or subsystems connected to it from that very same AC power. For reasons too numerous to list here, the normal electrical power supply system experiences random spikes, surges, and lulls almost every day. Exactly why these happen isn't really the issue anyway. What is the issue is that protection must be designed into the system to prevent these events from damaging the devices on the structured wiring system.

Electrical Events

External AC power sources can pass on a variety of power-related problems, including the following:

- **Line noise** Consists of small variations in the voltage of the power line. A small amount of line noise is normal in just about every system and all but the very low-end devices can handle it. An electrical device connected to its own circuit (an unshared power line) should have little trouble with line noise. However, for a device that shares a circuit with a refrigerator or a megaton air conditioner, line noise is not only a certainty, but it's likely that the line noise will cause problems. For example, if a transformer is connected to an AC power source with high levels of line noise, it may eventually have its power-regulating circuits burn out, after which time the line noise would pass through to the devices connected to the transformer.

- **Power surge** A power surge or spike, which is also called an over voltage event, occurs when electrical disturbances, such as distant lightning strikes or other anomalies in the electrical supply grid, create a sharp rise in the voltage level that is passed onto the power supply lines. In most situations, a spike or surge lasts only a few thousandths of a second, but, depending on the amount of the rise in the line voltage, that is plenty of time for the voltage to increase to double, triple, or spike even higher. High voltage spikes and surges, if frequent enough, can degrade the electrical circuits of a home's electrical devices. In fact, multiple surges occurring frequently enough can eventually destroy some electrical devices, such as a computer's power supply.

- **Brownouts** Called an under voltage event, a brownout is the opposite of a power surge (over voltage event) and occurs when there is a sudden dip in the power line voltage. In most cases, the power level drops below normal levels for a time and then returns to normal. Brownouts are extremely common during periods of heavy load on the electrical system, such as hot afternoons or cold mornings. The reduced voltage level causes many devices to run slower than normal or malfunction in other ways. Low voltage for an extended time can do just as much damage as spikes. A brownout doesn't typically last too long, but it can.

- **Blackouts** A blackout occurs when the power fails completely. The problems caused by a blackout are usually more frustrating than damaging, but the fluctuation of power surrounding a blackout can cause harm. Typically, any damage associated with a blackout occurs when the power returns suddenly, usually in the form of a huge spike.

- **Lightning strikes** This is the big spike, and it can deliver a million volts or more. I don't need to tell you what would happen if one were to hit a home directly. However, a strike even in the vicinity can result in a very high voltage spike.

 NOTE Electrical events can cause two types of damage to an electrical device: catastrophic, which means a device is destroyed all at once by a single event, and degradation, which means a device is damaged slowly over a period of instances and begins to have intermittent problems before failing altogether.

Surge Suppression

The most common electrical system event is a power surge or spike, which is a temporary increase in the voltage supplied on the electrical lines. For the most part, any power surge to a home is passed on through the electrical distribution panel to the circuits in the home. The installation of surge suppression devices is the best and most economical way to prevent damage to any of the devices on the structured wiring system.

The least expensive and perhaps the least protective way to protect against electrical surges are power strip surge suppressors, like the one shown in Figure 6-3. Surge suppressors are generally available and the most commonly used protection device. The device shown in Figure 6-3 provides protection not only for electrical devices, but provides surge suppression to telephone and data network links as well.

Figure 6-3

A high-end surge suppression plug strip

Photo courtesy of American Power Conversion Corporation.

The primary component of a surge suppressor is a Metal Oxide Varistor (MOV), which, in effect, takes the hit from voltage spikes. However, an MOV can be defeated by one big spike or an accumulation of small surges over time, which is why some surge suppressors have an LED to indicate that the MOV is still intact. A surge suppressor absorbs spikes and surges and smoothes out line noise, which is called line conditioning. The rule-of-thumb for selecting a surge suppressor is that you get what you pay for.

The two main features for choosing a surge suppressor are

- **Clamping voltage**   The voltage at which the suppressor begins to protect the circuit.

- **Clamping speed**   The amount of time that elapses between detection and protection.

Here are some other characteristics to consider when selecting a surge suppressor for a home system:

- **Energy absorption**   Surge suppressors are rated in joules, which is a measure of their capability to absorb energy. The higher the joules rating, the better the protection. Basic protection is 200 joules; 400 joules represents good protection; and 600 joules is better protection.

- **Line conditioning**   The line conditioning capability of a surge suppressor is measured in decibels. The more decibels of noise reduction, the better the line conditioning.

- **Protection level**   Surge suppressors have three levels of protection indicated as the maximum number of watts a suppressor allows to pass through. The standard ratings are (better to good) 330, 400, and 500.

 NOTE   Underwriters Laboratories (UL) standard 1449 covers the construction and performance of surge suppressors. A suppressor with a UL approval has met this standard and will provide protection to its rated capacities.

Protecting Telephone Lines

In the event of an electrical storm or lightning strike, power can surge up the telephone lines just as fast as on power lines. Surge protectors should also be installed to protect any distributed phone lines between the NID and the distribution panel. In addition, surge protect any door intercoms before they connect to the house phone system as they are located outside and susceptible to lightning hits.

Protecting Coaxial Cable Lines

Surge suppression should also be added to coaxial cable lines that connect exterior sources to interior systems, such as the lines that provide cable television, an exterior antenna, or the lines connecting a digital satellite receiver to its dish outside the home.

Three Ways An Electrical Surge Can Enter a Home

Any electrical or signal line that penetrates the shell of a home, or in other words, any line that enters a home from its exterior, is capable of carrying an electrical over voltage surge inside the home. The most common sources for surges are

- Thunder or electrical storms
- Lightning strikes on or near a home
- Extreme weather conditions, such as snow, ice, or gusty winds

A surge can be carried into a home on any or all of the following lines:

- Electrical power lines
- Telephone lines
- Video (cable, satellite, or antenna) or data service lines

To really protect a home from over voltage surges, a transient voltage suppression system (TVSS) should be installed inside the home as near to the point where an exterior line enters the home.

As a general rule, it is always a best practice to install surge protection for any of the most costly or required electronic devices, such as entertainment equipment, computers, printers, and copy machines or faxes, in a home.

The best devices for this purpose include a silicon avalanche diode (SAD) as their primary level of protection from over voltage surges that may enter and be carried on a coaxial cable into a home. SAD devices provide fast and nondegrading surge protection for coaxial data and video source lines.

Battery Backup

An uninterruptible power supply (UPS) provides a constant (uninterrupted) power stream to the electrical devices connected to it. Under normal operating conditions, most surge suppressors can handle short brownout conditions. However, when the AC voltage drops below a certain level or is disrupted completely, a UPS is designed to provide power for a certain amount of time.

All UPS units have two sets of circuits. One side is an AC circuit that provides surge suppression. The other side is a battery and a DC to AC converter. The batteries inside a UPS store a DC charge that must be converted to AC when needed to replace lost voltage.

There are two types of UPS units available, which differ in the following ways:

- **Standby**   This type of UPS operates normally from its AC side. When the power drops, it switches over to its battery backup side.

- **In-line UPS**   Operates normally from its DC or battery backup side. The AC side is used only to maintain the power stored in the batteries or in the event of a problem with the battery-powered circuits.

 NOTE   UPS units are often confused with a standby power supply (SPS), or battery backup, which supplies power only when none is available and has no power-conditioning capabilities.

The use of a UPS unit with home automation systems is optional, but in the case of electrically power telephones and security systems, having power for even a short period of time after a power failure may be a necessity in some home situations.

Chapter Review

Structured wiring combines all of the communications data, signal, and control cabling in a home into a single consolidated wiring system. This means that all of the cabling, including the network, telephone, video, audio, security, heating and cooling control, lighting control, and other control wiring in a home, is planned, designed, installed, and managed as a single system.

The advantages of installing structured wiring are compatibility, consistency, flexibility, integrity, and ease of maintenance and management.

To begin planning a structured wiring installation you must first identify systems it is intended to support now and in the future. The major home automation and technology integration systems that structured wiring is installed for include: data networking, distributed audio, distributed video, voice communications, HVAC control, and security and surveillance.

Perhaps the most important part of any planning process, including the planning of structured wiring, is an understanding of exactly what it is the homeowner (customer) wishes to accomplish in the end.

The location of the central distribution panel is extremely important to the success of the installation, as well as the overall cost of the project. The distribution panel should be as central as possible. The distribution panel must be kept at a distance from electrical generators and motors, fluorescent lamps, transformers, and electrical wiring. The space should not be either too hot or too cold and you must be able to maintain a lower to normal humidity level. Structured wiring distribution panels can be either surface-mounted or flush-mounted.

The steps that should be used to develop the plan for a structured wiring project are: identify the systems to be supported and work backwards; consolidate the cabling requirements; create wire chart; identify and sequence the installation tasks; and perform a practice pre-wire walk-through.

The amount of cable to be installed should be measured from the central distribution panel through the walls to the location of a room outlet box. For nearly all situations, each room should have two runs of Category 5e cable and two runs of RG-6 coaxial cable. Speaker wire, additional Cat 5, and coaxial cable should be installed where required.

There are some basic electrical issues that need to be addressed during the planning phase for a structured wiring project: current, ESD, grounding, placement, and electrical event protection.

External AC power sources can pass on a variety of power-related problems, including: line noise, power surge, brownouts, blackouts, and lightning strikes. Surge suppressors are generally available and the most commonly used protection device. Surge protectors should also be installed to protect any distributed phone lines between the NID and the distribution panel and any coaxial cable lines such as cable service, antenna or satellite. An uninterruptible power supply (UPS) provides a constant (uninterrupted) power stream to the electrical devices connected to it.

Questions

1. Which of the following best describes structured wiring?

    A. All home cabling uses the same path through the walls.

    B. A consolidation of the communications and control cabling in a home.

    C. The integration of the communications and control cabling with the electrical lines in a home.

    D. The design and installation of communications and control cabling in a home as a single system.

2. Which of the following "no-new-wire" solutions can be integrated into a structured wiring environment?

    A. Powerline

    B. HomePNA

    C. RF and IR

    D. All of the above

3. Which of the following is not an advantage of a structured wiring system?

    A. Compatibility

    B. Rigidity

    C. Consistency

    D. Integrity

4. Before beginning the planning for a structured wiring project, what should you first have?

   A. Blueprints

   B. Certification

   C. An understanding of the homeowner's objectives

   D. Experience

5. Which one of the following would not be an ideal location for the central distribution panel of a structured wiring system?

   A. A damp basement corner

   B. A utility closet with no electrical appliances

   C. A small room designed for use as a wiring closet

   D. A garage wall near an electrical panel

6. After you've identified the systems to be supported by the structured wiring system, how should you proceed?

   A. Plan the installation of each end-user system to be installed.

   B. Determine the exact amount of cabling required for the job.

   C. Identify the systems to be installed and work backward to determine the cabling standards that must be satisfied.

   D. Begin pulling the general cable requirements and add any specific requirements as a later step.

7. What method should be used to estimate the amount of cabling required for a structured wiring system?

   A. Identify the cable type and standards required by each system.

   B. Purchase two rolls of each type of cable to cover all possibilities.

   C. Measure the length of the AC lines installed.

   D. Determine the shortest path to each device to be installed.

8. A home that has a conventional wiring scheme likely uses which type of cable installation method?

   A. Structured

   B. Daisy chain

   C. Ring

   D. Home run

9. What is the minimum number of Cat 5e runs that should be installed to each room?

   A. 1

   B. 2

  C. 4

  D. Varies with types of systems in use

10. Which of the following is not an electrical issue that should be considered during the planning for a structured wiring system?

  A. ESD

  B. Grounding

  C. Electrical events

  D. Number of electrical outlets in home

Answers

1. **D.** Choice B also comes close, but structured wiring is designed and installed as a single system.

2. **D.** All of the other choices listed (A, B, and C) are "wireless" technologies that can be integrated into a structured wiring system.

3. **B.** To the contrary, structured wiring is a very flexible system that helps to future-proof a home.

4. **C.** I know, this is a no-brainer, but we can all use a reminder on occasion. The other choices represent nice-to-haves, but you absolutely must know what the project is and what you plan to accomplish before you can begin.

5. **A.** Choice D could have been another choice had I not limited you to one choice. How close the panel would be to the electrical panel would determine if the garage were a good or bad choice. Choices B and C are great locations for a distribution panel.

6. **C.** At least in my opinion, this is the best way to proceed. This approach ensures that every system requirement is addressed in the planning.

7. **A.** Okay, so this is another no-brainer. The cable type and standards requirements are vital to planning the installation of the cabling.

8. **B.** Conventional wiring schemes (meaning nonstructured wiring) are typically the result of several installation phases where new wire was added to the end of an existing wire run.

9. **B.** At least two runs of Cat 5e should be installed in each room that will be occupied in a home.

10. **D.** Actually, the number of outlets in a home has no bearing on the design and planning of a structured wiring system, beyond their use as a guideline to the placement of structured wiring outlet boxes.

Rough-In Installation

In this chapter you will learn about:
- Structured wiring rough-in installation procedures
- Cabling and building standards

After the electricians and plumbers complete their work installing the electrical lines and plumbing in the open walls of a new home, a structured wiring project can proceed with the installation of the cabling, and placement of the distribution panel and outlet boxes. This phase of the project is commonly referred to as the rough-in phase because after this work is completed, the dry wall installers come in and put the wallboard up. Following this step, the next phase of the structured wiring project – trim-out (see Chapter 8) – can be performed.

This chapter focuses on the steps performed during the rough-in phase of a structured wiring project, which is primarily include locating the distribution panel, locating the outlet boxes or mud rings, and pulling cable through the wall studs, headers, joists, and floors.

Rough-in Preparation

Using the information developed in the planning phase of the project (see Chapter 6), you should have a very good estimate of the amount of cabling and outlets required for the project. You should also be able to determine the best type and size of distribution panel for the home.

Outlets

The National Electric Code (NEC) requires all residential wiring be inside an electrical box (see Figure 7-1) whenever it connects to a receptacle, switch, fixture, or another wire. This practice is also good for low-voltage connections, such as Cat 5, coaxial, and twisted pair cabling.

Structured Wiring Outlet Boxes

The best place to begin the rough-in process is by mounting either outlet boxes or mud rings around the house in their designated locations. Deep or backless low-voltage

Figure 7-1
An electrical
outlet box.

*Photo courtesy of
Lamson & Sessions.*

brackets, such as those shown in Figure 7-2, are sometimes referred to as mud rings and are a good choice for use with communications and structured wiring.

As shown in Figure 7-3, double-gang boxes are also available that can be used to combine electrical (110 volt) and structured wiring (low voltage) at the same location. The box features a center divider, which is required by the NEC for dual-purpose boxes, and prevents crosstalk and electrical interference from reaching the low-voltage (structured wiring) side of the box.

There are also "sidecar" brackets (see Figure 7-4) that allow a low voltage outlet to be attached to an electrical outlet. Sidecar brackets go around and over a standard electrical box. After the faceplate is installed, the two boxes give the appearance that the electrical and low voltage outlets are in a common two-gang box.

Figure 7-2
An assortment
of low voltage
brackets.

*Photo courtesy of
Lampson & Sessions.*

PART II

Figure 7-3
A double-gang box used to mount both electrical and structured wiring in a single location.

Photo courtesy of Lampson & Sessions.

 NOTE   It is common practice to use blue outlet boxes for AC or high-voltage connections and orange boxes for structured wiring and low-voltage connections.

Installing Outlet Boxes and Brackets

Outlet boxes are secured to a wall stud by either nailing them to the inside edge of a stud (as shown in Figure 7-5) or by screwing them to the face of a stud. If the building is using steel studs, the wall box will have to be fastened with screws.

The front edge of the outlet box or bracket should extend beyond the stud so that it will be flush with the front surface of the drywall when it's installed. Most outlet boxes have a raised line or mark for where the front of the stud should be. Once the drywall is in place, you can cut out only a portion of the wall to access the outlet box or bracket, so be sure of your measurements before you nail or screw the box in place.

Outlet boxes that are to support data or video connectors should be placed so that the bottom of the box or bracket is at the same height from the floor as the electrical boxes on the same wall and should be in the range of 12 to 16-inches from the floor.

Outlet boxes or brackets that will support volume controls, wall telephones, or other types of local units should be placed at the same height as any light switch boxes on the same wall and should be between 46 to 48-inches above the floor.

Figure 7-4
A sidecar bracket allows a low voltage box to be attached to the side of an electrical outlet box.

Photo courtesy of Lampson & Sessions.

Figure 7-5
An outlet box
nailed to a
wall stud.

*Photo courtesy of
Lampson & Sessions.*

 NOTE   If the job requires the use of floor-mounted boxes, be sure you use
outlet boxes specifically manufactured for that purpose to overcome any bend
radius issues inside the floor joists.

Don't take the term rough-in too literally. Take the time to line up the outlet boxes or
brackets so that they are straight. A box or bracket that is not aligned will result in a faceplate that isn't straight on the wall.

Ceiling Installation

Some ceiling mounted devices (and wall mounted speakers) either come with a rough-
in kit or have one available. This kit contains either a mud ring or a mounting ring, like
the one shown in Figure 7-6 provides a template for the drywall to be cut for the speaker.
The speaker is then attached during trim out. Be sure to leave enough wire to allow for
easy installation of the device at trim-out.

Pre-Wiring

During the pre-wire or when locating speakers during trim-out that didn't have speaker
brackets, the cabling or wire should be installed using a zigzag pattern between the wall
studs, as illustrated in Figure 7-7. The cable should be stapled loosely to the studs so that
the staples can be easily removed during trim-out by lightly tugging on the cable.

Figure 7-6
A rough-in
mounting bracket
for a speaker.

*Photo courtesy of
Crutchfield New
Media, LLC.*

Figure 7-7
Zigzag wiring
between wall
studs during
pre-wire.

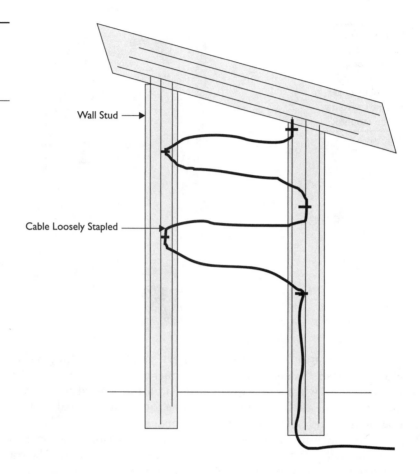

Wall Stud →

Cable Loosely Stapled —

It's a good idea to photograph the placement of the cabling during pre-wire to show a reference point, such as a door or window corner, to aid in locating the cable behind the drywall during trim-out.

Distribution Panel

The distribution panel in a structured wiring system, like the empty one shown in Figure 7-8, interconnects all of the external communications lines, such as television, telephone, and Internet, with the interior structured wiring running throughout a home. Inside the distribution panel, each incoming signal is divided and, in most cases, amplified before being sent out on the structured wiring throughout the home.

If the distribution panel for the structured wiring system is housed in an in-wall or flush-mounted box, the mounting box (without components) should be installed during

Figure 7-8
An open design
distribution panel
into which the
control units for
a home's systems
can be mounted.

*Photo courtesy of
Smarthome, Inc.*

rough-in. They are made to fit easily between standard stud dimensions on 16-inch centers. Otherwise, the installation of the panel can be delayed until the trim-out phase when the panel will be surface mounted. Locate the panel at about eye-height, similar to the height of the electrical panel. If multiple panels are installed, they should be side-by-side on the same level with conduit between them inside the wall for interconnectivity.

During rough-in, the location of the distribution panel must be decided and set permanently so that the structured cable runs have a starting point. There are two methods that can be used to install the cable during rough in:

- A cable run can be started at an outlet location and pulled back to the distribution panel.

- Cable can be pulled from the distribution panel toward the outlet boxes.

Be sure and label each wire as you begin pulling so that when you reach the distribution panel or destination room you know where each wire goes. Leave at least a 2-foot length of extra cable at the outlet and at least 3 feet at the distribution panel (or better yet, let it hang and touch the floor) to enable termination of the cable during trim out.

CROSS-REFERENCE The details of connecting structured wiring into the distribution panel are covered in Chapters 7 and 8.

Cable Rough-In

The process used to install cable is very different in a new construction situation than it is in a remodel or retrofit situation:

- In new construction, the walls are open and you have complete access to the wall studs, headers, and joists to create a pathway for the cable; and you can plainly see any obstacles in the walls that may later cause system performance issues.

- In a remodeling situation, with the walls closed, your best bet is often to minimize the unknown problems in the walls and install the cabling in the attic, basement, or crawl space under the floor wherever possible.

In either case, the guidelines for installing, handling, and routing the structured wiring cable remains the same. These guidelines are specific to each type of structured wiring cable and are discussed in the following sections.

CROSS-REFERENCE See Chapters 1 and 2 for more information on individual cables and their installation requirements.

Structured Wiring Bundles

Several manufacturers offer pre-bundled structured wiring cable that can be installed as a single set. Like the bundle shown in Figure 7-9, these cable bundles come in a variety of individual cables to satisfy the cable requirements of virtually every structured wiring requirements. At minimum, commercial structured cabling bundles include two runs each of Cat 5e (or better) and RG-6 coaxial cable. However, higher-end bundles may also include fiber optic cabling (included for future-proofing a home).

Figure 7-9
A commercially
available
structured
wiring bundle.

*Photo courtesy
of Belden Inc.*

PART II

Structured wiring bundles are typically wrapped with a twist wrap, with an attachment method called "banana peel," such as the one shown in Figure 7-9, or a with a flexible outer jacket to improve their pull-ability. At the point where the outer wrapping needs to be removed to route individual wires to outlets or controls, the binding is easily removed by cutting or a pull-string.

"Bonded" bundled cable is also available and makes individual cable preparation easy. In a bonded cable, the outer sheathing is attached to the shielding layer, which is attached to the insulation around the inner conductors. The benefit of bonded cable is that it is highly waterproof and is a more rugged cable.

Audio Cable

Audio cable is typically made up of two or four stranded wires of 16-gauge or larger wire. There are no standard color-coding schemes for audio wiring, but in most cases, one wire can be distinguished from the other by its jacket color, markings, ridges or other jacket features. In some cables, one conductor wire may be copper-colored and the other silver-colored. The ability to tell one conductor from another in the audio cable is important because this allows you to ensure the polarity of its connections.

During rough-in, audio cabling home runs can be pulled starting at the control amplifier or equipment and toward the speakers and controls in each room or zone. Multiple cables can be pulled together to an area of the house and then branch off separately to their designated room locations. Cables can also be pulled from the room locations, and merged together as they leave an area of the house and head back to the equipment. Remember to label all wiring per the wire chart.

Cable should also be pulled to all volume control, keypad, and speaker locations with a service loop of extra cable length (about 2 feet) provided at the volume control/keypad location. One way to reduce the task of pulling speaker wiring during rough-in is to install a multiple conductor cable to service more than one speaker. Each speaker requires two conductors and if a 4-conductor cable is pulled into a room, two conductors can be routed to each speaker location. This allows a single pull of cable to service the two speakers instead of pulling two 2-conductor cables by just pulling the cable to the first speaker and then looping it on to the second speaker.

Coaxial Cable

Some controversy exists as to which type of coaxial cabling is best for video distribution. Some prefer the more rigid and less flexible RG-6 while others prefer the flexible and more easily installed RG-59. RG-6 has become the preferred coaxial cable of residential system installers because of its ability to handle a wider range of RF channels. In either case, coaxial cabling should be chosen to match the application in use, per the system manufacturer's specifications. Remember that different sized coaxial cable, single-braid coaxial cable and quad-shield types of coaxial cable require different types of terminators and connectors.

CROSS-REFERENCE   See Chapter I for guidelines on installing coaxial cable.

Coaxial cabling, of either specification, is easily pulled through walls, open or closed. However, you should avoid tight bends or kinks in the cabling because they can change the impedance of the cable and this can lead to signal loss.

Category 5e Cable

The current standards for data networking cabling in business (EIA/TIA 568) and homes (EIA/TIA 570) call for Category (Cat) 5 or Cat 5e cabling, respectively. This four-pair twisted-pair cable is available as shielded (STP), screened (ScTP), or unshielded (UTP) cable. The most commonly used cabling for residential installations is UTP cable.

UTP cabling is also the cable type most often included in structured wiring bundles. For areas where this cabling must be installed nearer to potential interference sources, such as fluorescent lighting fixtures or electrical motors, ScTP or STP would be a better choice than UTP.

The handling guidelines for installing category cabling are:

- Install the cable so that there are no kinks or sharp bends that can cause performance problems.
- Limit the pulling tension to 25 pounds or less (per EIA/TIA 568).
- Pull cables slowly and use constant pressure.
- Don't pinch or crush the cable by stepping, sitting, or setting any object on it. Also don't use grasping tools, such as pliers or vise grips at the end, to pull the cable.
- Avoid pulling cable over protruding nails or sharp edges that may damage the outer jacket/insulation of the cable.
- If cable lubricant is used, be sure that it is not harmful to the cable's outer jacket material.
- Ensure that no cable home run is longer than 90 meters (295 feet) from the distribution panel.
- In metal studs, use plastic grommets in the holes to protect the cable jacket and don't pull category cable through a metal stud with an electrical line passing through it.
- If a cable breaks, don't splice the cable; instead, pull a new clean run.
- Don't pull category cable through the same hole in a stud or wall as the electrical wiring.

Cable Management

The orderly arrangement of all cabling in a residential installation is not only for aesthetic reasons, but it can simplify maintenance, troubleshooting, and later additions to the system.

Cable management begins in the placement of the cabling. The standards permit running cable over ceiling joists, but in longer open spaces, it may be better for the safety of the cable and its performance to use some form of cable management.

Here are a few guidelines for the use of cable management devices.

- **Cable staples   Although most types of staples should not be used, if staples are** the only choice available for securing a cable in place, avoid crushing or compressing the cable. There are curved staples available that are made for securing bundled cables and are designed to avoid these problems. The use of plastic standoff cable staples should be used instead of metal staples; and staple guns should never be used.

- **Cable ties**   Cable ties should be applied loosely and spaced randomly. Over-tightening cable ties may crush the cable and damage its interior wires. Crush-proof cable ties are available and Velcro cable ties are an even better choice over nylon or plastic cable ties. To use a cable tie as a cable hanger, the cable tie can be stapled or nailed to a stud or joist to hold a cable bundle in place. Figure 7-10 illustrates how cables can be bundled using cable ties.

- **Cable trays**   When longer open spaces must be crossed by long runs of cable, the use of a cable tray prevents sag in the cable and helps keep the cable out of harm's way. Refer to the EIA/TIA 569A standard for the guidelines for installing cable trays. Figure 7-11 illustrates the use of a cable tray.

- **Conduit**   Flexible structured wiring conduit is available that provides ample room to pull even structured wiring cable bundles through (see Figure 7-12).

- **J-hooks**   This cable management device (see Figure 7-13) can be used in lieu of cable trays across long open runs. Avoid using "wedding band" or "bridle ring" cable supports because they can be over-tightened and crush the cable.

Pull-Cords

In some situations, especially when not enough time is available to pull the cabling in the walls of a new construction project or should the cable not be available when this step

Figure 7-10
Cable ties are
used to bundle
cables together.

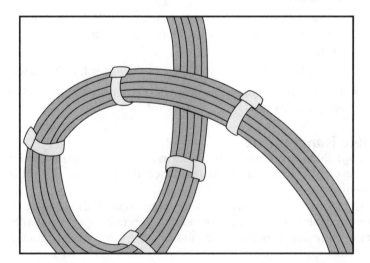

Figure 7-11
A ladder style cable tray can be used to bridge large amounts of cable across open spaces.

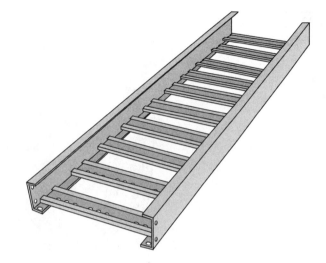

must be performed, installing a pull-cord instead of the actual cable is a faster way to go. A pull-cord is a stiff cord that can be placed through the cable path and later used to pull the structured wiring cable into place. Although a pull-cord can be used to install structured wiring, whenever possible, it's always best to pull the actual cable.

However, there are a few downsides to using pull-cords:

- **Additional step** Using a pull-cord adds an additional step and additional time to the project; time you may not always have.

- **Cable path** Pull-cords are typically limited to pulling a structured wiring bundle into a cable path that runs in a straight-line. Structured wiring bundles are relatively stiff and if there are any bends or sharp turns in the cable path the

Figure 7-12
Flexible residential structured wiring conduit.

Photo courtesy of Lampson & Sessions.

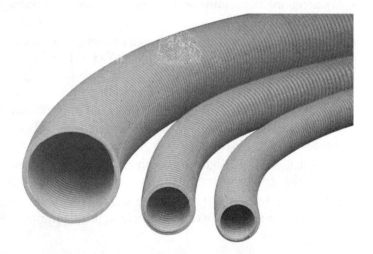

Figure 7-13
A J-hook cable management device with a built-in Velcro cable tie.

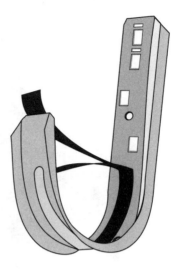

cable can get stuck. Another problem may exist if the cable path wasn't sized properly for the size of the cable bundle as it is always thicker than the pull-cord.

- **Pull-cord breakage**   There are commercially available pull-cords that are stronger than just using heavy twine, but all pull-cords can, and do, break on occasion. If the pull-cord breaks, the only way to correct the problem is to cut open a wall and repair the cord.

Cabling for New Construction

The cable guidelines that apply to new construction situations (in addition to those listed previously) are:

- Route cabling along joists to minimize the number of holes drilled through wall studs.
- Any holes drilled through a stud, header, footing, or joist should be large enough to accommodate all cables to be pulled to a location.
- Cable runs through a stud must be 1.25 inches or more from the nearest edge of the board. This allows for a maximum of a 1.25-inch hole in a standard 2 x 4 stud. If that distance cannot be met, the board must be reinforced with a metal plate or bushing that is at least 0.0625 inches thick. This requirement doesn't apply to cabling placed in conduit.
- Cable that is run through a metal stud (without conduit) must be protected by a bushing or grommet in hole.
- Label each cable run as it is pulled; label both the cable and the outlet box to coincide with the wire chart prepared in the planning phase of the project.

Cabling for Retrofit

Several obstacles exist for installing structured cabling in an existing home, including outside walls filled with insulation, horizontal cross-members in walls, and the lack of pre-existing pathways through wall studs.

One solution is to install the cabling in the attic, placing the cabling in J-hooks or attached to the rafters with cable ties. Another is to pull the cabling underneath the house in a basement with an open ceiling or in the crawlspace under the house. On some homes, the only choice may be to run the cabling on the exterior of the home. Other solutions include using commercially available cable raceways – some styles can be used in front of or to replace wall baseboards.

Chapter Review

The NEC requires that all residential electrical wiring be inside an electrical box wherever it connects to a receptacle, switch, fixture, or another wire and this is considered to be a good practice for low voltage structured wiring as well.

To begin the rough-in process, mount the low-voltage outlet boxes or brackets throughout the home. Outlet boxes or brackets are secured to a wall stud by either nailing them to the inside edge of a stud or by screwing them to the face of a stud. If the building is using steel studs, the wall box will have to be fastened with screws. The front edge of the outlet box or bracket should extend beyond the stud so that it will be flush with the front surface of the drywall when it's installed. Most ceiling and wall-mounted devices have rough-in kits available that contain a rough-in mounting bracket.

The distribution panel interconnects external communications lines to interior structured wiring. Inside the distribution panel, incoming signals are divided and distributed to the structured wiring. If the distribution panel for the structured wiring system is housed in an in-wall or flush-mounted box, the mounting box should be installed during rough-in. Otherwise, the installation of the panel will be surface mounted and can be delayed until the trim-out phase. During rough-in, the location of the distribution panel must be decided and set permanently.

Several manufacturers offer pre-bundled structured wiring cable that can be installed as a single cable pull. These cable bundles usually include two runs each of Cat 5e and RG-6 coaxial cable. Higher-end bundles may include an additional two runs of fiber optic cabling.

During rough-in, audio cabling home runs should be pulled starting at the control amplifier and toward the speakers and controls in each room or zone. A service loop of cable should be placed at each end of the cable. Coaxial cabling is easily pulled through walls, but tight bends or kinks in the cabling should be avoided. All cabling should be labeled during rough-in per the wire chart. The EIA/TIA and NEC standards require certain handling rules for installing Cat 5e cabling.

Cable management is important for more than aesthetic reasons. It can simplify maintenance, troubleshooting and later additions to the system. Options available for mounting cable include special cable staples, cable ties, cable trays, conduit, and J-hooks.

Questions

1. Which national standard requires that all residential wiring be inside an electrical box wherever it connects to a receptacle, switch, fixture, or another wire?

   A. EIA/TIA

   B. NEC

   C. IEEE

   D. UL

2. What is the recommended length of the service loop that should be provided at the distribution panel for each cable run during rough in?

   A. 6-inches

   B. 1 foot

   C. 2 feet

   D. 3 feet or to the floor

3. What is the generally accepted color for low-voltage or structured wiring outlet boxes?

   A. Blue

   B. Green

   C. Orange

   D. Yellow

4. Which two of the following best describe how far data or video connector outlets should be placed above a floor?

   A. At the same height of any electrical switches on the same wall

   B. At the same height of any electrical outlets on the same wall

   C. 12 to 16-inches above the floor

   D. 46 to 48-inches above the floor

5. Which two of the following best describe how far volume controls and wall telephone outlets should be placed above a floor?

   A. At the same height as any electrical switches on the same wall

   B. At the same height as any electrical outlets on the same wall

   C. 12 to 16 inches above the floor

   D. 46 to 48 inches above the floor

6. Which structured wiring device interconnects external communications lines to interior structured wiring?

   A. Distribution panel

   B. Multiplexer

   C. Outlet box

   D. Patch panel

7. What cable sets are typically included in a structured wiring cable bundle?

   A. Two runs of RG-59 or RG-6 and one run of Cat 5e

   B. One run of RG-59 or RG-6 and two runs of Cat 5e

   C. Two runs of RG-59 or RG-6, one run of fiber optic, and two runs of Cat 5e

   D. Two runs of RG-59 or RG-6 and two runs of Cat 5e

8. Which one of the following is not a guideline for installing category cable?

   A. Limit pulling tension to 25 pounds or less.

   B. Lubricants should be safe for the cable's outer covering.

   C. No cable runs can exceed 90 meters.

   D. If a cable breaks, splice the cable using standard connectors.

9. Which one of the following should not be used when installing structured wiring cable?

   A. Velcro cable ties

   B. Nail gun

   C. Cable trays

   D. Conduit

10. What is the type of coaxial cabling preferred by most home system designers and technicians?

    A. RG-6

    B. RG-59

    C. RJ-45

    D. 10Base5

Answers

1. **B.** Each of the standards organizations listed in the other choices have similar standards or recommendations, but the NEC rules.

2. **D.** Service loops of 3 feet should be provided at the distribution panel end of a cable and 2 feet should be provided at the outlet end of a cable during rough-in to facilitate installation activities during trim out.

3. **C.** Blue is typically used for electrical wiring and green and yellow are rarely used, if ever.

4. **B and C.** Connector outlets should match up with electrical outlets on the same way.

5. **A and D.** Outlets that will support controls or wall-mounted telephones should line up with the wall switches on the same wall.

6. **A.** Okay, so this was an easy one—as well it should be.

7. **D.** I'm sure cable bundles are available that may contain the other combinations listed, but two runs each of coaxial and category cable are standard for structured wiring cabling.

8. **D.** If a cable breaks, splice the cable using standard connectors. No splices; no splices; and no splices. Got it?

9. **B.** Because they can pierce a cable, nail and most staples should be avoided. If you absolutely must use staples, use the type designed for bundled cabling or the plastic standoff type.

10. **A.** Because of its ability to carry multiple signals and frequencies, RG-6 has largely replaced RG-59 in home systems.

Trim-Out Installation

In this chapter, you will learn about:
- Cable termination
- Wall plate installation
- Distribution panel installation
- Cable testing

Following the rough-in phase of a home technology integration project, after the wallboard has been put up, finished or repaired, the next phase to be performed is the trim-out. In this phase of the project, the structured wiring, at least from its outward appearance, begins to take shape with the cables terminated at the outlets, the distribution panel components installed and connected, and the cabling tested and verified.

Cable Termination

A structured wiring cable is terminated at each end, one end at the outlet and the other at the distribution panel or an intermediate device, such as a patch panel or hub. The type of termination applied depends on the cable and its intended use at the outlet. For example, coaxial cabling being terminated at an outlet to provide a connection for distributed video or a Cat 5e cable being terminated for a data network connection will each be connected to the outlet connections with a device and method specific to the cable and its application.

Telephone Cable

The trim-out work for a home telephone system involves the termination of Cat 5 UTP at both the telephone block, either inside or outside of the central distribution panel, and at the telephone outlets.

Terminating at the Telephone Block

The cabling installed to provide telephone links throughout a home are connected into the telephone system using a telephone panel or block located inside or very near the structured wiring distribution panel.

The telephone block, shown in Figure 8-1, is commonly referred to as a 110 punch-down block and commonly consists of two columns of 50 IDC contacts. Each row of contacts, which is or can be connected to one another as one circuit of the panel consists of

Figure 8-1
A telephone block
with 110-type
IDC contacts

*Photo courtesy of the
Dynacom Corporation.*

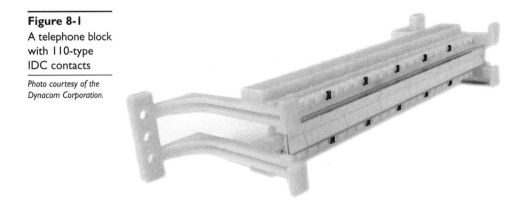

one contract from each column. On some blocks, the pairs are internally linked and on others a bridging clip must be inserted over the inner two contacts to bridge the outer contacts.

When terminating Cat 5 cabling for a telephone system, a 110-type block should be used. Typically, a 66-type block is used in telephone systems where quad wire is in use, but the 110-type IDC contacts, which have shorter contacts, are better suited to Cat 5 cable.

A punch-down tool is used to press the unstripped wire into the IDC contact, which cuts through the conductor's insulation and makes connection with the inner conductor. Another approach that works a lot better in situations where the terminations may need to move at some point in the future are patch cables that are terminated with a 110-pattern plug on one end and an RJ-45 plug on the other.

The standard wire pattern, meaning the color sequence of the wire as it is placed into the 110 block, is shown in Figure 8-2 and listed in Table 8-1.

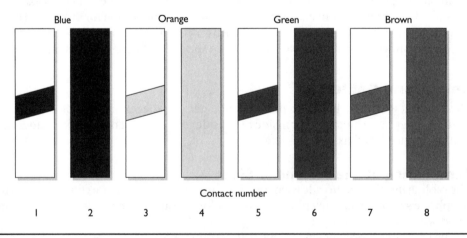

Figure 8-2   The color scheme used for Cat 5 cabling in a 110 punchdown block

	Wire Color	Pair	Contact
Table 8-1 Cat 5/5e 110-block Wire Color Scheme	White/Blue	1	1
	Blue or Blue/White	1	2
	White/Orange	2	3
	Orange or Orange/White	2	4
	White/Green	3	5
	Green/Green/White	3	6
	White/Brown	4	7
	Brown or Brown/White	4	8

NOTE If you consistently reverse one or more of the wire colors, not to worry. As long as the wire pattern is exactly the same on each end of a terminated cable, everything should still work. However, following the standard removes all guesswork about how consistent you've been.

Telephone Outlets

Telephone cabling should be terminated at the wall outlet with an RJ-11 jack, using either a one, two, or three-pair configuration, depending on the number of lines to be connected through the wall outlet. Figure 8-3 illustrates the wire configuration of the RJ-11 terminations at a wall outlet and Table 8-2 lists the wire configurations for RJ-11 wall jacks.

Audio Cable

Most audio cabling is actually speaker wire and can be terminated in two ways: directly at an in-wall or in-ceiling speaker or at a wall outlet for hookup with external speakers. The wall outlet can be a stand-alone outlet or part of a multiple-connection outlet that includes other types of connections.

In situations where the audio cable or speaker wire terminates directly on a speaker, the wire must be prepared or terminated to connect to the connection type or types available on the speaker. Chapter 16 covers the specifics of terminating speaker cable and the various connector types that may be used.

Figure 8-3
A one-pair (single line) and a two-pair (two line) RJ-11 connection

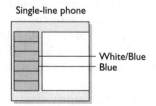

Single-line phone

White/Blue
Blue

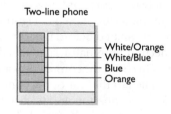

Two-line phone

White/Orange
White/Blue
Blue
Orange

PART II

Wire Pair	Function	Position	UTP Wire Color	Quad Wire Color
1	Tip	Pin/Slot 4	White/Blue	Green
	Ring	Pin/Slot 3	Blue (Blue/White)	Red
2	Tip	Pin/Slot 2	White/Orange	Black
	Ring	Pin/Slot 5	Orange (Orange/White)	Yellow
3	Tip	Pin/Slot 1	White/Green	n/a
	Ring	Pin/Slot 6	Green (Green/White)	n/a

Table 8-2   RJ-11 jack wiring scheme for UTP cable

Speaker Outlets

Figure 8-4 shows an example of a speaker outlet with four 5-way binding post connectors where local freestanding or bookshelf speakers can be connected. Binding posts are the most commonly used connector for audio system outlets.

Speaker wire is secured to a binding post connector with a setscrew. Care should be taken to ensure that the right and left speaker wires are connected properly and the plugs on the face of the outlet are labeled properly. Audio cabling can also be terminated on simple screw connectors as well.

Audio Cable Termination

To properly terminate audio cabling, follow these guidelines:

- Split the insulation between the conductors of the audio cable about 1-inch.

- Remove ½-inch of insulation from each conductor.

- If using screw-type or binding post connectors, wrap the stripped wire 180 degrees around the screw post in a clockwise direction and then tighten the setscrew. Don't wrap the bare wire completely around the post, because when the setscrew is tightened, the wires could be damaged or broken, keep some of the insulation under the screw post.

Coaxial Cable

Coaxial cabling, meaning RG-59 or RG-6 cable, is terminated at an outlet box using a variety of connector types (see Figure 8-5). The most common connector used is the F-type connector, shown in Figure 8-5 . Many coaxial outlet connectors require the cable to be terminated before it is connected to the back of the outlet. In others, the coaxial connection terminator is attached to the cable and then inserted into the outlet faceplate. On some, the connector is a permanent part of the faceplate and the cable must be terminated to the rear of the connection.

Coaxial connectors are attached to the cable using a variety of methods, including crimp-on, compression lock, threaded or twist-on, and several proprietary types of connectors. Some require standard crimper tools and other require a crimper made specifically for a particular brand or style of connector.

Figure 8-4
A four-connector
speaker outlet

*Photo courtesy of Niles
Audio Corporation.*

 CROSS-REFERENCE   See Chapter 2 for more information on coaxial cable terminations and connectors.

Data Outlets

Twisted-pair (TP) wiring, such as Cat 5 and Cat 5e, is terminated with an 8-pin RJ-45 connector using a method called punch down. There are RJ-45 connectors that can be attached to the cable with a crimper and others than merely clamp down on the individual wires with a clamping action or a snap close (see Figure 8-6).

 CROSS-REFERENCE   See Chapter 2 for more information on twisted pair cable terminations and connectors.

Figure 8-5
An F-type jack is
used to terminate
coaxial cable at
a wall outlet

*Original photo courtesy
of Channel Vision.*

Figure 8-6
A snap-in
modular RJ-45
connector

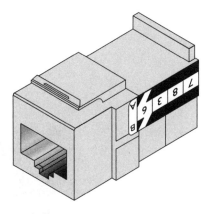

The best practice is to terminate TP and coaxial cabling with connectors (see Figures 8-5 and 8-6) that can be snapped into an open slot faceplate.

Video Outlets

Coaxial cabling is used for distributed video service lines. The best connectors to use when terminating video cabling are either compression lock or threaded male F-type coaxial connectors. As indicated above, the best practice is to use snap-in connectors that can be inserted into an open-slot faceplate at the outlet.

To terminate a video line, follow these guidelines: Use a coaxial cable stripping tool to remove ¾-inch of the cable's outer jacket.

- Remove ½-inch of the center conductor wire.
- Remove about ¼-inch of the metal mesh and foil wrapping.
- Create a slight gap between the mesh and the white dielectric insulator so that the dielectric insulation will fit into the F-type connector.
- The back of an F-type connector has a channel (see Figure 8-7) where the cable is inserted. This channel has an outer chamber and an inner chamber. Gently push the cable into the back of the F-connector so that the dielectric insulation fits inside the inner channel of the connector and the metal mesh fits around the outer chamber. The dielectric insulation should make contact with the end of the channel.

Figure 8-7
An F-type
connector body
and sleeve to
form the inner
and outer
channels

- If the cable is properly inserted, the center conductor wire should stick out at least ¼-inch from the front of the connector.

- Using a coaxial (F-type) crimper, crimp the connector on the cable.

- Trim the center conductor wire using a 45-degree angle so that it is not more than ¼-inch beyond the front of the connector.

CROSS-REFERENCE   Chapter 2 includes more information about coaxial and twisted pair cable termination.

Faceplates

If modular or keystone faceplates, like the one shown in Figure 8-8, are used to hold multiple cable termination jacks, a consistent pattern of placement should be used in every

Figure 8-8

An open slot faceplate can accommodate any arrangement of cable connectors.

location. A fairly commonly used convention (for a four slot faceplate) is to place the RJ-11 telephone jack in the upper-left position, the data network RJ-45 jack in the upper-right position, the video coaxial F-type jack in the lower-left position, and, if used, a video out coaxial F-type connector in the lower-right position. Figure 8-9 illustrates this arrangement.

Modular jacks are inserted into keystone and modular faceplates and wall plates by inserting them from the rear of the faceplate, as shown in Figure 8-10. Although this figure shows only a single jack being inserted, the process is essentially the same for multiple jacks.

Testing Network Wiring

The good news about planning a network before installing it is that you and the customer both know what to expect when you are done, right? Unfortunately, the bad news is that both you and the customer know what to expect.

Figure 8-9
An illustration of a commonly used convention for arranging modular jacks in a keystone faceplate.

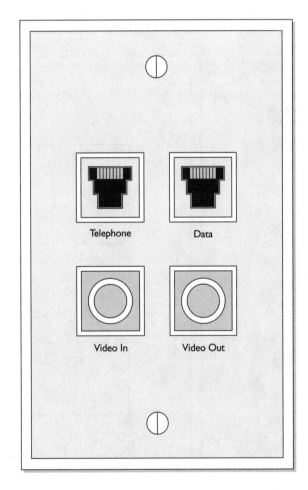

Figure 8-10

Modular RJ-45 jacks inserted in a keystone faceplate

Original image courtesy of Smarthome, Inc.

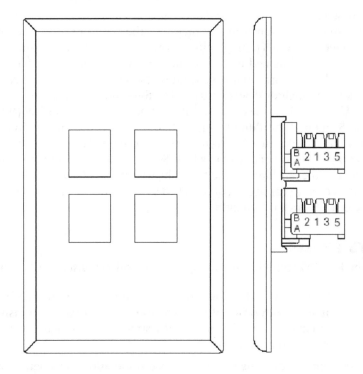

The first test, a visual test, should actually be performed during the rough-in phase as the cabling is installed. However, the cable ends where termination is applied should also be carefully examined. Also, be sure the cables have been properly labeled so that your hookup is correct for testing.

Standards Testing

The only way you can assure yourself and demonstrate to the customer that the network's wiring and infrastructure supports the network to be installed on it is with a planned and formal test procedure that incorporates the TIA/EIA TSB-67, the Transmission Performance Specifications for Field-Testing of Unshielded Twisted-Pair Cabling Systems (TSB-67 for short), and the TSB-95, which provides additional test parameters for Cat 5 wiring.

A number of handheld devices are available to perform the tests prescribed in these two TSB standards. In fact, Cat 5 testers perform what is called a certified test that should assure your customer that his or her network wiring is installed per specification and is ready to support any network-capable devices attached to the network. Certifying the cable provides a benchmark for any future network or cable problems. However, you should know that Cat 5 testing devices can be quite expensive. Cable testing units include a master unit and a slave unit that are attached to the end of the cable segment being tested, and an auto-test function that measures the results of the test as either a pass or a fail.

Essentially, Cat 5 testing units perform two tests: a link test and a channel test. The link test measures the end-to-end connectivity of a cable segment and is typically done on the cable running from the distribution panel to a wall outlet. A channel test extends the link test to include devices attached to the cable segment.

A Cat 5 link (cable only) should not be more than 295 feet (90 meters) in length. A Cat 5 channel shouldn't be more than 328 feet (100 meters) in length. The difference of 33 feet or 10 meters between a link and a channel represents the cables used to connect a computer or other device to a link. So what this boils down to is that the cable running between the patch panel and the wall jack can only be 90 meters in length and all of the cables used to connect a computer to a central device (like a gateway or router) cannot exceed 100 meters in length.

TSB Tests

The EIA/TIA TSB-95 standards specify the following standard testing procedures:

- **Attenuation test**   This test measures the attenuation affect on a signal transmitted on a cable. A series of frequencies up to 100 MHz is transmitted on each wire pair at one end of a link and the strength of the signal received at the other end of the cable is measured.

- **Length test**   As it sounds, this test measures the length of a cable segment. In addition to displaying the distance of the cable in feet or meters (at least to the point where the signal is reflected in the cable), this test checks the links and channels of a cable using Time Domain Reflectometry (TDR) technology. TDR emits a signal pulse and then calculates the length of the cable based on what is called nominal velocity of propagation (NVP). If the test fails, the cable is too long.

- **Near-end crosstalk test (NEXT)**   This test places a test signal on one pair of wires and then measures all of the other wire pairs for signal presence to see how much crosstalk the cable is allowing. Crosstalk is electromagnetic signals on one wire being picked up by another wire.

- **Wire-map test**   Tests each individual wire in the cable and whether or not it maps to the same pin at each end of the cable. This test is used to identify connector and pinning errors on a cable segment.

Any link that fails one of these tests should be replaced, rewired, reconnected, or, in the case of the length test, shortened or replaced. If a channel fails, you may need to test the patch cords used to connect the networked device to the link.

Distribution Panel Trim-Out

The distribution panel provides the interconnectivity of the structured wiring system, along with versatility and flexibility. It also provides for a single access point for all of the various home technology systems and communication services integrated into a home.

Typically, the only distribution panel found in an average home is the electrical panel. The electrical panel is the central point for incoming and service wiring in the home's electrical system. In the same way, a structured wiring distribution panel simplifies and centralizes the design, installation, and perhaps more importantly, maintenance for the home's structured wiring system.

The distribution panel should ideally be centrally located in a home. However, it's far more important that it be central to the structured wiring to minimize the length of cable runs as much as possible. On the other hand, if a home has a natural location for its distribution panel, cable is relatively inexpensive.

Figure 8-11 illustrates how a room in the center of a home serves as a central distribution panel for the structured wiring installed throughout the home.

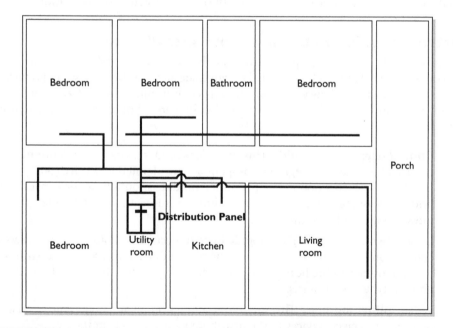

Figure 8-11   A central point in the home should be chosen for the location of a home's distribution panel.

Distribution Panel Installation

The distribution panel should be mounted on a wall at a safe distance from possible interference sources and at about eye-level. If the panel is mounted too low or too high, access to the panel could be cumbersome later. Distribution panels are either flush-mount, which means they are mounted into the wall (this type should be installed during rough-in), or surface-mount. In either case, if multiple panels are installed, they should be set side-by-side on the same level. If the distribution panel is a flush mount, run conduit between the multiple panels to allow for easy hookup.

Following the manufacturer's documentation, remove the appropriate knockouts or plugs from the top or sides of the distribution panel's cabinet. If the cabinet has metal knockouts, you should install protective grommets in each hole to protect the cabling that will pass through them.

All cabling in the distribution panel should be labeled about 6 to 10 inches below where the cable enters the cabinet. Actually, this step is included in the TIA/EIA standards, and each cable should be individually identified both at the termination point and on the cable.

The cables terminating in the distribution panel should be organized by room, zone, or system using Velcro ties, cable ties, or another form of cable management. A bit of organization now will save time during troubleshooting or system reconfiguration later.

Distribution Panel Components Installation

Structured wiring distribution panels are available from panel shells (see Figure 8-12) that contain none of the modules needed to terminate and distribute the systems attached to the structured wiring all the way to fully populated distribution panels (see Figure 8-13). In most residential installations, a typical distribution panel should contain the following modules:

- **Bridged telephone module** This module is used to bridge the telephone line connections from the telephone company's network interface device (NID) to the telephone lines in a home. The telephone module should have the capacity to bridge at least the number of incoming lines to at least the number of telephone lines being installed in the home.

- **Data network module** This module interconnects the incoming Internet service connection (DSL, ISDN, or cable) to the residential gateway and the distributed network outlets in the home. The connections supported should include RJ-45 and 110-type IDC contacts.

- **Video splitter module** This module combines off-air antenna, cable television, or satellite receiver services to the distributed video outlets in the home.

NOTE Extra capacity in these modules, in the form of connections for additional incoming and distributed lines beyond a home's current requirements, helps to future-proof a home.

Figure 8-12

An unpopulated
distribution panel

*Photo courtesy of
Channel Vision.*

Additional modules can also be installed, such as telephone or data security modules, video surveillance splitters, audio distribution modules, security system, and electrical surge suppressors or power line filters.

Figure 8-13

A fully populated
distribution panel

*Photo courtesy of
Channel Vision.*

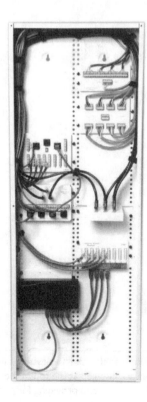

If the distribution panel modules must be installed into the distribution panel separately, a logical layout must be used to support cable management, ease of connection and troubleshooting, and perhaps most important, fit.

Placing Modules in the Distribution Panel

If the distribution panel is not pre-configured with the basic modules or if additional modules are being added to a pre-configured panel, the modules should be placed into the panel in the location where it can be easily attached and that provides the shortest path to the cabling to which it will connect.

There is no standard way to configure a distribution panel, but typically the modules are added starting at the top of the panel to simplify the cable management inside the panel. The panel shown in Figure 8-14 shows a completed distribution panel with its telephone and television distribution modules installed.

Mounting Distribution Panel Modules

Distribution panel modules typically include a mounting bracket kit that can be adjusted to fit the openings available in the panel back and allow some flexibility in their placement

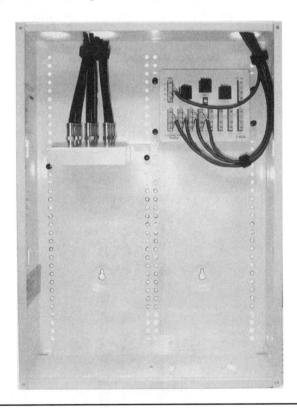

Figure 8-14   A distribution panel with its television and telephone modules installed. Notice how the modules are installed at the top of the panel maximizing the remaining space in the panel for future use and providing for good cable management.

inside the panel. However, some add-in modules have screw-type connectors that are fixed in place (see Figure 8-15).

Snap-in standoffs, like the one shown in Figure 8-16, are commonly used to mount add-in modules into a distribution panel.

Distribution Panel Connections

The cable terminations made at the distribution panel mirror those made at the outlet end of each cable. Twisted-pair cabling is most commonly terminated using 110-style punch-down connections and coaxial connections are made using F-type connectors. For audio connections that terminate into a distribution panel, screw-down terminals are usually used in the distribution panel. Depending on the complexity of the systems being installed in a home, the distribution panel may connect to other distribution devices. For example, the data network lines may first connect to a hub or bridge before connecting into the distribution panel. In this case, patch cords, shorter runs of TP cable, are used to connect the hub into the distribution panel. The same goes for coaxial cabling for the video and CAT5 cabling for a telephone system, where the distribution panel may connect into the video cable head-in or the telephone system demarcation point using patch cords.

When installing the AC power for the distribution panel, the appropriate national, state, and local electrical codes must be followed. For best results, the distribution panel should be wired into a dedicated 15-amp circuit using standard high-voltage electrical wiring. Many brands and models of structured wiring distribution panels void their warranties if their electrical guidelines aren't followed exactly.

Photo courtesy of Channel Vision.

Figure 8-15   An audio distribution module with fixed-position mounting screws

Photo courtesy of Channel Vision.

Figure 8-16   A snap-in standoff like this one is commonly used to attach add-in modules into a distribution panel

Distribution Panel Grounding

It is important that the distribution panel be grounded to an earth ground. The panel itself, a power module, or a surge suppression module, should have a grounding connection (typically a screw) that can be connected to the earth ground of the main power line to the panel (see Figure 8-17).

Grounding the panel's AC power input provides grounded power distribution to any of the modules connecting to it, including DC power converters.

Patch Panels

In the network shown in Figure 8-18, five separate cable runs are coming into the distribution panel, which presents a design problem. It is always better to install extra distribution capability than just enough. For instance, if a 5-port hub or patch panel is used in the situation illustrated in Figure 8-18, in order to troubleshoot any of the connections, one of the other cables must be disconnected. So, in this particular case, an 8-port distribution device would be better.

Figure 8-17
The location of the grounding screw in a typical distribution panel

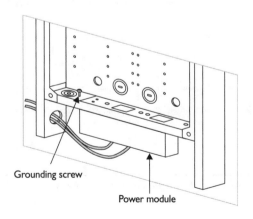

Grounding screw

Power module

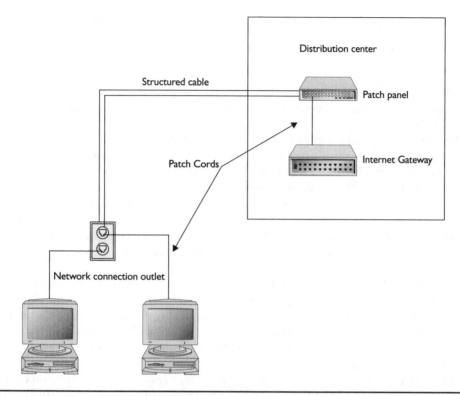

Distribution center

Structured cable

Patch panel

Internet Gateway

Patch Cords

Network connection outlet

Figure 8-18 Basic elements of a home data network

A better way to go would be to install a small patch panel that could be used as a distribution facility for telephone and data wiring as well. Figure 8-19 shows a patch panel of the type that can be installed inside a distribution panel. Patch panel models are available

Figure 8-19
A distribution
panel mountable
patch panel

*Photo courtesy of
Channel Vision.*

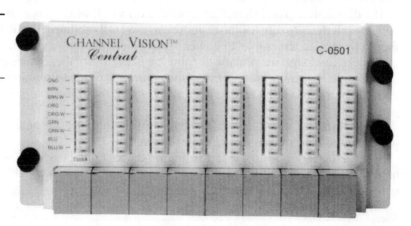

with 4 to 24 connections for home use. Data and voice cables are attached to the back of a patch panel jack using a 110-style punch-down connection.

Chapter Review

A structured wiring cable is terminated at each end, one end at the outlet and the other at the distribution panel or an intermediate device, such as a patch panel or hub. The type of termination applied depends on the cable and its intended use at the outlet.

Speaker wire can be terminated in one of two ways: at an in-wall or in-ceiling speaker or at a wall outlet, either as a stand-alone outlet or as a part of a multiple-connection outlet that includes other types of connections.

Coaxial cabling, meaning RG-59 or RG-6 cable, is terminated at an outlet box/wall plate using an F-type connector. Coaxial connectors are attached to the cable using crimp-on, compression lock, threaded or twist-on, as well as several proprietary connectors. Some require standard crimper tools and others require a crimper made specifically for a particular brand or style of connector.

Twisted-pair (TP) wiring, such as Cat 5 and Cat 5e, is terminated with an 8-pin RJ-45 connector using a method called punch down or using a crimper tool. The punch-down process of terminating twisted-pair cabling involves the use of a tool designed for the 110-style block, which is the type most commonly associated with data networking and TP cable. Punch-down connections use an insulation displacement connector (IDC) that penetrates the insulation of each wire to create a contact.

A formal test procedure that incorporates the TIA/EIA TSB-67, the Transmission Performance Specifications for Field-Testing of Unshielded Twisted-Pair Cabling Systems (TSB-67 for short), and TSB-95, which provides additional test parameters for Cat 5 wiring, should be used to test all structured wiring cable installed for use with a data network. The TSB-95 standards specify the following standard testing procedures: attenuation test, length test, near-end crosstalk test (NEXT), and wire-map test.

The distribution panel provides the interconnectivity of the structured wiring system, along with versatility and flexibility. It also provides for a single access point for all of the various home technology systems and communication services integrated into a home.

The distribution panel should be mounted on a wall where it is a safe distance from possible interference sources and at about eye-level. All cabling in the distribution panel should be labeled about 6 to 10 inches below where the cable enters the cabinet.

Cable terminations made at the distribution panel mirror those made at the outlet end of each cable. A distribution panel may also connect to other distribution devices, such as hubs, demarcs, and other service devices. Typically, these connections are made using patch cords.

When installing the AC power for the distribution panel, the appropriate national, state, and local electrical codes must be followed.

A patch panel can be used as a distribution device for data, telephone, and audio cabling. Data and voice cables are attached to the back of a patch panel jack using a 110-style punch-down connection.

Questions

1. What type of connector is commonly used to terminate speaker wire?

   A. RCA

   B. Type-F

   C. Binding post

   D. Spade

2. When speaker wire is attached to a setscrew connection, how should the wire be wrapped around the post?

   A. Counter-clockwise, 360 degrees

   B. Counter-clockwise, 180 degrees

   C. Clockwise, 360 degrees

   D. Clockwise, 180 degrees

3. What is the most commonly used connector for terminating coaxial cabling?

   A. F-type

   B. RJ-45

   C. RG-6

   D. RG-59

4. Twisted-pair cabling for a data network is terminated with what type of connector?

   A. RJ-11

   B. RJ-45

   C. IEEE 1394

   D. EIA/TIA 568

5. What termination method is used to terminate twisted-pair cabling at the distribution panel?

   A. 66-style

   B. 110-style

   C. EIA/TIA 570

   D. Telco standard

6. How far should each wire pair be untwisted when terminating twisted-pair cabling?

   A. ¼-inch

   B. ½-inch

   C. ¾-inch

   D. 1-inch

7. Which standard should be used when terminating twisted-pair cabling for residential data networking use?

   A. IEEE 802.3

   B. EIA/TIA 568a

   C. EIA/TIA 568b

   D. EIA/TIA 570

8. Which of the following EIA/TIA standards specifies transmission performance standards testing UTP cable?

   A. 568a

   B. 568b

   C. TSB 67

   D. 570

9. Which of the following tests measures how much of a transmitted signal is present on other wire pairs in the same cable?

   A. Attenuation

   B. Length

   C. NEXT

   D. Wire-map

10. At what level should a distribution panel be installed?

   A. Floor level

   B. Side-by-side with an electrical panel

   C. Eye-level

   D. Shoulder-height

Answers

1. **C.** Binding post. RCA connectors are commonly used to interconnect audio source devices; Type-F connectors are used with coaxial cabling; and a spade connector is used to connect directly to a speaker.

2. **D.** Clockwise, 180 degrees. Wrapping the wire completely around the post may cause damage to the wire when the setscrew is tightened.

3. **A.** F-type. The other choices are a TP connector and two types of coaxial cabling, respectively.

4. **B.** RJ-45. An RJ-11 connector is used with standard telephone (2 wire) connections; IEEE 1394 is commonly known as FireWire; and EIA/TIA 568 is a business environment cabling standard.

5. **B.** 110-style. This punch-down type block is used to connect TP cable to RJ-45 connectors as well as distribution panels and patch panels.

6. **B.** ½-inch. This amount of stripping provides adequate insertion into an IDC or snap-on connection.

7. **B.** EIA/TIA 568a. This is the cabling standard recommended by the residential data network cabling standard, EIA/TIA 570.

8. **C.** TSB 67. Along with TSB 95, these are the testing standards required by EIA/TIA 568 and 570.

9. **C.** NEXT. This stands for near-end crosstalk, a test to see if pairs or wires in the same cable are interfering with a signal transmitted on a wire in the same cable.

10. **C.** Eye-level. This level provides for easy access and work inside the panel.

Troubleshooting Structured Wiring

In this chapter, you will learn about:
- Problem identification and diagnostics
- Cable testing procedures
- Cable testing devices

The structured wiring system installed in their home should be something homeowners can take for granted. Homeowners can't be faulted for believing that if the system is properly installed, it should never break or have problems. In fact, that was the basic idea behind all of the precautions and extra steps you took during the installation.

However, it is possible for a structured wiring system to develop problems. Assuming the cabling was properly installed and all of the appropriate standards were observed and implemented, rarely will a problem be with the cable itself. That is, unless something has happened to the wire, such as a nail or screw being driven through it or a wire tugged on a bit too much, or if the system has plainly been abused. There is also the possibility that a connector or termination wasn't installed exactly right or the cable was installed improperly.

Nonetheless, should one or more of a home's systems stop performing or perform oddly, a problem source possibility that must be eliminated is the structured wiring cabling. This chapter focuses on the process and tools used to identify and isolate a cabling problem, should one exist.

Diagnosing a Cable Problem

Cables and connectors can and do fail. However, one of the best benefits of a structured wiring environment is that when a cable problem does occur, rarely is the entire system affected. Because each outlet has a home run directly back to the distribution panel, a problem on one cable impacts only the devices connected to that cable run. Structured wiring cable makes it far easier to isolate and fix problems.

Isolating a Problem

A suspected cabling problem must be identified and isolated before an appropriate solution can be applied. Each type of system, which means each type of cable, has its own unique potential problems and each potential cable problem should be eliminated through a methodical diagnostics process.

Here is a recommended approach for identifying a cabling problem:

1. **Listen** Unless you have witnessed the symptoms of a problem first-hand, you must rely on information provided by the homeowner. Listen carefully and actively to their description of the problem and interact with the customer enough to fully understand what he or she believes to be the issues.

2. **Look** Ask the homeowner to re-create the problem for you. If the customer is able to re-create the problem for you, make a note of exactly what you observe, hear, or smell. Your senses are your best fact-gathering tools. From what you have learned, you should be able to determine what your next diagnostic steps should be. If the problem cannot be re-created, a test procedure should still be performed, but its nature will be more generic.

3. **Inspect** Starting at the malfunctioning device, begin checking the integrity of all visible components and connections of the system. Check connections for fit and snugness, watching for loose wires, broken or pierced insulation, smashed or kinked cable, and any other obvious conditions that could be causing the problem. In many cases, the problem can be found on an exterior (patch cord) cable rather than in the wall.

   If no problems can be found with the existing patch or connector cabling, you can replace or remove them to minimize the variables that could be the source of the problem. Next, your diagnostics should move to the distribution or patch panel. If possible, connect the incoming suspected cable to a different port on the distribution panel or source device to see if the problem may be with the jack on that device. If the problem still exists, check the termination of the cable very closely and verify the connector pinout (the placement of the cable wires in the connector). See Chapter 2 for details of connectors and termination. If the termination of the cable is good, the problem is likely within the cable run.

4. **Test** If the source of the problem hasn't been identified to this point, the cable run should be tested for shorts, crosstalk, and attenuation. These tests are discussed later in this chapter.

Documenting the Problem

Before you go much further, we need to discuss documentation. A written record should be maintained of any and all problems reported or even suspected about the structured wiring system of a home. Actually, this maintenance record should have been created at the end of the trim-out phase of the installation project when cable verification testing was performed to create a benchmark against which later testing can be compared.

Anytime a technician responds to a home to diagnose, troubleshoot, or resolve a cabling problem, the suspected problem, the actions taken to diagnose the problem, the steps used to isolate the problem, and the solution applied should be recorded in a main-tenance log. Often, any problems that develop after one problem has been solved are the cause of changes made to the system or a problem introduced during the testing or resolution of the earlier problem. This documentation makes it much easier to trouble-shoot the next problem.

Cable Testing

In a residential structured wiring installation, typically the runs are not long enough to develop attenuation problems and because of the shorter runs, the signal tends to be stronger so crosstalk and signal return loss aren't typically problems either. However, this doesn't mean that these issues can't happen; it just means that in a typical structured wiring installation they are usually uncommon.

Cable Diagnostics

Cable problems in structured wiring systems are more likely to be caused by damage to the cable, improper termination, or mis-wiring caused during rough-in and trim-out. The construction crew can also damage a cable during their finish work, when a cable can be nailed, stapled, cut, crimped, or crushed.

Testing TP Cable

Common TP cable problems include the following:

- **Cable impedance**   If the wrong type or quality of cabling is installed, the cable may not support the proper impedance levels required to correctly transmit signals over the cable.

- **Cross-pinning**   If the pinout (wiring pattern) of a TP cable is incorrect at one or both ends of the cable (for example, the receive pin on one end of the cable is connected to the receive pin on the other end of the cable), the transmitted signal will not be transmitted or received correctly. Figure 9-1 shows the correct configuration of a TP connection and Figure 9-2 illustrates a crossed or switched pinning condition. A similar condition where wire pairs are crossed is called a reversed pair fault (see Figure 9-3).

- **Open**   An open circuit lacks continuity between the pins on each end of the cable, indicating that a wire has been broken or one of the pins is not properly attached (see Figure 9-4).

- **Short**   A short occurs when two or more conductor wires in a cable are in contact or if a metal object, such as a nail or staple penetrates the cable and creates a contact between two or more conductors (see Figure 9-5).

- **Split pair**   If one conductor of a wire pair is connected to the wrong pin at each end of the wire, which in effect splits the pair, the cable will not function properly. Figure 9-6 illustrates this condition.

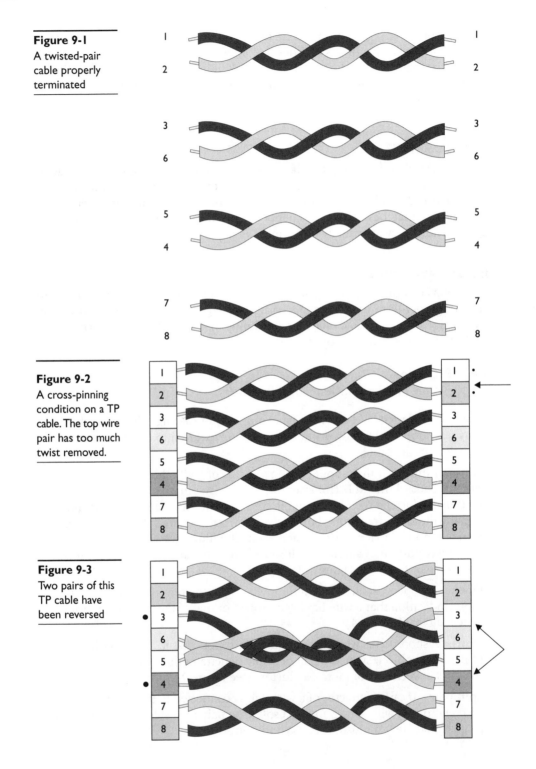

Figure 9-1
A twisted-pair cable properly terminated

Figure 9-2
A cross-pinning condition on a TP cable. The top wire pair has too much twist removed.

Figure 9-3
Two pairs of this TP cable have been reversed

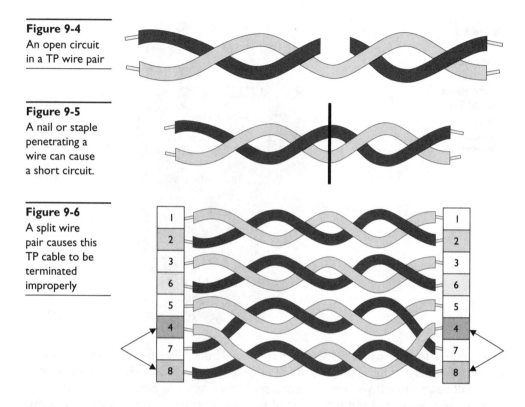

Figure 9-4
An open circuit in a TP wire pair

Figure 9-5
A nail or staple penetrating a wire can cause a short circuit.

Figure 9-6
A split wire pair causes this TP cable to be terminated improperly

- **Termination**   If a cable termination changes the impedance of the cable, which should be 100 ohms on a TP cable and 75 ohms on a coaxial cable, the transmitted signal may be reflected by the terminator and cause data loss.

Diagnosing TP Cable

When a cable is suspected to have a fault, you must be able to locate it in order to fix it. You need to be able to identify whether or not the fault is on a certain pin or at some distance along the cable, or even as far away as the far-end connector.

The two test procedures that can be helpful in determining where a fault may exist on a cable—if one exists at all—are Wiremap and Time Domain Reflectometry (TDR).

Wire Map Testing   When a cable fault is first suspected as the source of a problem, perhaps the most useful and informative test that can be performed on residential structured wiring, especially TP cable, is a wire map test.

Wiremap testers are often incorporated into a TDR tester. The tester shown in Figure 9-7 verifies the pin-to-pin connectivity between the ends of a cable and in doing so eliminates or finds any of the problems described in the preceding section.

TDR Testing   A Time Domain Reflectometer (TDR) transmits a signal on a conductor and measures the time required for the signal, or some part of the signal, to return. If a fault exists on a conductor, the signal is reflected at the point of the fault. The amount of

Figure 9-7
A data
communication
tester that
performs wire
map and TDR
testing

*Photo courtesy of Everett
Communications.*

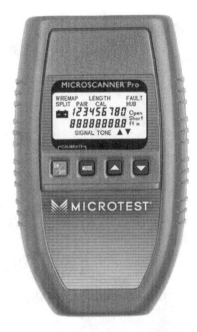

time required for this to take place is then converted into a distance using a formula that involves the speed of light, the velocity of propagation, and some simple arithmetic.

A TDR tester can tell you only where a problem may be, meaning at what distance from the test point, and not what type of problem may exist. Any cable that has two metal conductors can be tested using TDR, which makes it perfect for testing twisted-pair cabling (refer to Figure 9-7).

Figure 9-8
A handheld digital
multimeter

Multimeter   A commonly used tool for testing cable is a multimeter, shown in Figure 9-8, which can be used for testing voltage, current, resistance, and continuity on a copper wire. The most common problem with copper wire cabling is an open-circuit. Using the resistance test (or ohm test) of a multimeter is the easiest way to test for this problem.

Toner/Probe Testing   Another common testing procedure uses a tone generator and probe to identify one cable from a bundle or find a cable inside a wall or under a floor. This test is also referred to as "fox and hound." The tone generator generates a specific signal on the cable and the probe converts it to an audible tone. The closer the probe is placed to the cable carrying the generated signal, the louder the audible tone is sounded. Figure 9-9 shows both a tone generator and probe.

Testing Coaxial Cable

Testing coaxial cabling is less complex than testing TP cable. First of all, there is only one conductor, so the tests performed by a tone generator and probe, a multimeter, and a TDR are typically sufficient for tracking down any problem.

Figure 9-9

A tone generator and probe are used to locate cables and wires

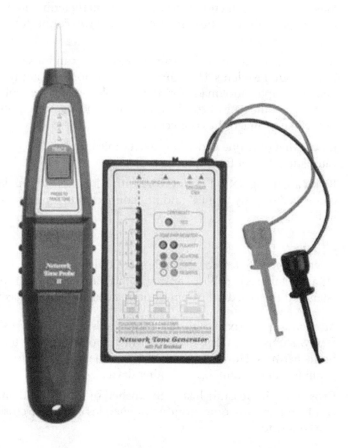

Coaxial cable is generally more durable than TP cable, but it can develop many of the same types of cable faults. However, problems on a coaxial cable are typically caused by improper termination or damage to the cable.

Coaxial cable can exhibit many of the same cable faults as a TP cable, except, of course, those involving wire pairs specifically. However, although a coaxial cable has only one center conductor, remember that the metallic shielding on the cable also carries current and between these two conductors some faults can occur.

When troubleshooting a coaxial cable, here are some physical conditions to check for:

- The coaxial cable must match the impedance requirements of the equipment to which it is attached. Coaxial cable with a cable TV system must be 75 ohm. The coaxial cable for a data network must be 50 ohm. If 75-ohm cable is used for a data network intermittent data errors, which are very hard to track down, are likely to occur.

- Be sure the connectors and terminators attached to the cable are the correct size and match the impedance of the cable. Using the wrong connectors or terminators can cause signal faults on the cable.

- Make sure that each end of the cable is properly terminated and, although this is somewhat obvious, be sure that there are two connectors or terminators on each cable segment.

- Avoid using twist-on connectors because they can loosen easily and cause intermittent problems. Use crimp-on connectors and apply them with a good quality crimping tool made for coaxial cable. Be sure the tool and the connectors are fitted for the type of coaxial cable you are using, such as RG6. Don't use pliers or the like to attach the connectors.

- Ensure that only one end of a coaxial cable is grounded. Grounding both can cause intermittent transmission problems.

- If you are using BNC-T connectors with a PC network, make sure the "T" is connected directly to a PC and not connected to a patch cord that connects to the PC.

Cable Tests

Cable testers designed to test coaxial cable specifically are available, but a better investment is usually a tester that is capable of testing both TP and coaxial cabling (see Figure 9-10).

The standard tests used for troubleshooting coaxial cable are as follows:

- **Attenuation** Coaxial cable has a segment length limit of 185 meters (about 607 feet) when used in a data network, which should be more than adequate for any home network. However, attenuation can be a problem for coaxial cabling that is run to exterior cameras and other devices.

- **Crosstalk** If the cable has been crushed or otherwise damaged, the inner conductor and the outer conductor energies can cause crosstalk between the two conductors.

Figure 9-10
Many testers
include testing
capabilities for
both coaxial
and TP cabling.

*Photo courtesy of
Fluke Networks.*

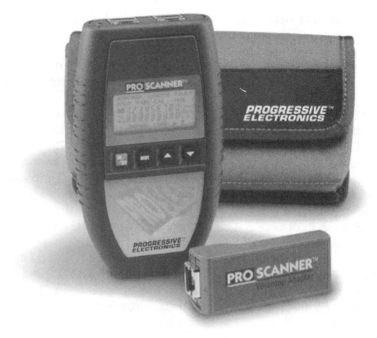

- **Impedance**   The impedance of the cable should match the requirements of the equipment to which it's connected, and the impedance of the connectors must match that of the cable.

- **TDR**   The TDR testing of a coaxial cable measures the length of the cable to a reflection point, which (one hopes) is the terminator or connector on the end of the cable. If the TDR test detects a short or open circuit that causes the test signal to reflect before the termination, the point in the cable where the problem exists is returned.

Chapter Review

A suspected cabling problem must be identified and isolated before an appropriate solution can be applied. Each type of cable has its own unique potential problems and each of these problems should be eliminated through a methodical diagnostics process. A recommended approach for identifying a cabling problem involves the following steps: listen, look, inspect, and test.

A written record should be maintained for all problems reported or even suspected. Whenever a technician responds to diagnose, troubleshoot, or resolve a cabling problem, the problem, diagnostics, and the solution should be recorded in a maintenance log.

Cable problems are most likely caused by damage to the cable, improper termination or mis-wiring that may have been introduced during rough-in, trim-out, or during construction. The cable may have been nailed, stapled, cut, crimped, or crushed. Common TP cable problems include: cable impedance, crossed pinning, open circuit, short circuit, split pair, and improper termination.

Two test procedures can be helpful in determining where a fault exists on a cable: Time Domain Reflectometry (TDR) and wire map. The most commonly used tool for testing cable is a multimeter, which is used for testing voltage, current, resistance, and continuity on a copper wire.

A Time Domain Reflectometer (TDR) transmits a signal on a conductor and measures the time required for the signal, or some part of the signal, to return. If a fault exists on a conductor, the signal is reflected at the point of the fault. The amount of time required for this to take place is then converted into a distance.

When a cable fault is first suspected as the source of a problem, perhaps the most useful and informative test that can be performed on residential structured wiring, especially TP cable, is a wire map test. Wiremap testers verify the pin-to-pin connectivity between the ends of a cable. A tone generator and probe are used to identify one cable in a bundle or to find a cable inside a wall.

Testing coaxial cabling is less complex than testing TP cable. First of all, there is only one conductor, so the tests performed by a multimeter, TDR, and a tone generator and probe are typically sufficient for tracking down any problem. The standard tests used for troubleshooting coaxial cable are: attenuation, crosstalk, impedance, and TDR testing.

Questions

1. Which of the following are advantages of structured wiring over conventional "daisy chained" wiring schemes?

   A. No splices

   B. Home runs

   C. Central maintenance and configuration point

   D. All of the above.

2. Which of the following is not listed in this chapter as an approach for identifying a cable problem?

   A. Listen

   B. Look

   C. Replace suspected cable runs

   D. Test

3. When should a record be created that documents the testing and performance of a structured wiring system?

   A. On the first visit to investigate a problem

   B. During trim-out

   C. After solving a problem

   D. Only after fixing "real" problems

4. Which of the following problems is not a common issue with a structured wiring system?

    A. Attenuation

    B. Reversed pairs

    C. Open circuits

    D. Improper termination

5. After completing the trim-out and finish work of a structured wiring system, the homeowner calls to complain that one of the PCs attached to the data networking system cannot be reached from other PCs in the home for file sharing. After diagnostic testing, you discover that the fault is a short about 20 feet up the TP cable connecting the PC to the patch panel. What diagnostic test was likely used to determine this information?

    A. Ohm (resistance) test

    B. Tone generator/probe test

    C. Wire map test

    D. TDR test

6. The pinout of the connector on a TP cable is incorrect at one end of the cable and the transmitted signal is not being received correctly. What type of problem does this describe?

    A. Impedance

    B. Cross pinning

    C. Open circuit

    D. Short circuit

7. What impedance level should a TP cable have?

    A. 50 ohms

    B. 75 ohms

    C. 100 ohms

    D. 150 ohms

8. Which type of test device is able to verify the pin-to-pin connectivity between two ends of a cable?

    A. TDR

    B. Multimeter

    C. Tone generator/probe

    D. Wiremap

9. Which type of cable testing device can be used to locate a single cable in a wall that is a part of a cable bundle?

A. TDR

B. Multimeter

C. Tone generator/probe

D. Wiremap

10. Which of the following is not a common cable fault of a coaxial cable?

A. Improper termination

B. Cable damage

C. Impedance of 35 ohms

D. Split pairs

Answers

1. **D.** All of these choices represent advantages of structured wiring over conventional wiring schemes.

2. **C.** During diagnostics, this action may be wasteful and unnecessary. First gather some facts and then act.

3. **B.** The first testing cycles performed on the cable should begin the record into which all maintenance activities are recorded.

4. **A.** Because the cable runs tend to be less than the maximum segment length for TP cabling, attenuation is rarely an issue in residential systems.

5. **D.** A TDR test is able to locate the position of a fault on a cable and report the distance from the test point to the fault.

6. **B.** Because of the size of the wires and the connectors, this is a common problem for TP cabling.

7. **C.** A TP cable that tests for less than 100 ohms may be of insufficient quality or a termination error may be causing the problem.

8. **D.** A multimeter is also able to test for continuity, but not to identify the pins in question.

9. **C.** The probe uses induction amplification to sense the tone generator's signal and sound an audible tone when the cable carrying the signal is located.

10. **D.** A coaxial cable has only a single conductor wire.

PART III

Home Computer Networks

199

Computer Network Basics

In this chapter, you will learn about:
- Home networks and what they are
- Data versus control networks
- Network topologies
- Networking technologies and standards

The foundation of home technology integration (HTI) is a computer network in some form. It's the emergence of the computer network and the number of options available to create a network in a home that has given rise to the idea that just about any electrical, audio, visual, lighting, or control system can be connected to a network.

Networking a home and a good number of its sight, sound, comfort, and security features provides the homeowner with centralized control and security, not to mention a lot fewer stubbed toes. There are as many reasons to integrate the technology in a home using a network as there are homes and homeowners. However, in the end, all of these reasons are based around a single concept—the home network.

Computer Networks in the Home

A home computer network can be as simple as two PCs connected by a communications medium that share files, perhaps a printer, or maybe even an Internet connection. However, a home computer network can also be something very complex and sophisticated such as an integrated music, video, lighting, and security system that at the touch of a button arms the security system in home mode, turns the audio video (AV) equipment on, closes the drapes, drops the video screen, and starts the movie playing. There are no actual configuration limits to what a home computer network can be designed to do. Computer networks, including home computer ones, exist for the sole purpose of sharing resources, such as peripheral devices (like a printer, scanner, or audio source), data files, and other computer-connected resources.

Computer Networks

A computer network is created whenever two or more computers are directly connected using a communication medium, such as a parallel port, serial port, network cable, or a wireless connection, and some level of resource sharing is initiated by or for the computer's users.

Figure 10-1 illustrates a very basic computer network, representative of what might be found in a home computer network. The two computers shown have the capability to share data files, provided each user has granted permission to the other user, and they share a printer.

The computers that make up a home network can be connected to each other in a variety of ways, including dedicated network cabling or wiring, a wireless radio frequency (RF) signal, or perhaps the alternating current (AC) electrical wiring, cable TV wiring, or telephone wiring in the home.

More often than not, a home network is installed for the purpose of sharing a single Internet connection. Regardless of the type of Internet service in use, having separate lines for every computer in a home is not only very expensive, but also with today's technology, completely unnecessary. The PCs on a home network can share not only a connection to the Internet, but also virtually every peripheral and data file on any computer on the network. In some instances, users on the network can even share software, such as multiplayer games.

Most high-speed broadband services (cable, digital subscriber line (DSL), Integrated Services Digital Network (ISDN), and fixed terrestrial wireless) provide an in-home device (modem, bridge, or router) that can be used to share the communications line (and the access to the Internet) directly. The latest versions of Windows and the Apple MAC Operating System (OS) include software support for sharing a single dialup connection as well as connections across a local network.

A home computer network can be used to share or distribute digital audio or video files between devices in a home. For example, digital music can be transmitted over the network to other PCs or stereo receivers in the home and played through their speakers. Separate rooms can receive a different digital music stream, depending on who's in the room and his or her taste. The same is true for digital video streams.

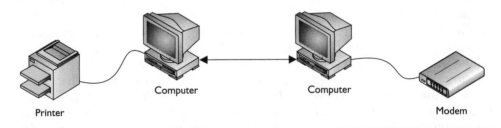

Figure 10-1 A computer network in its most basic form allows two computers to share information and devices.

Control Networks

The type of network described in the preceding section is also called a data network, because the signals transmitted between the computers (also referred to as nodes) on the network represent various forms of data, including text, graphics, and sound signals encoded in digital/data form.

Another type of network is a control network, which is used to manage and control lighting, Heating, Ventilating, Air Conditioning (HVAC), appliances, and home security systems. Control networks use computer-based controllers and receivers. Control networks are also called home automation networks and home technology integration networks. A common control network found in most modern homes is that made up by the heating and cooling system and a thermostat.

The essential components in a control network are the controller and receivers. The controller and receivers can either be hardware devices or software running on a computer. The controller transmits commands and control data across the network to the receiver, which either acts on the incoming data or retransmits to another device, such as an appliance, stereo, light fixture, or whatever has been attached to the network for automation purposes. For example, if you wish to have your home's outside lighting and a random set of inside lights turned on and off while you are away on vacation, you program the controller with the pattern you wish to use and as the scheduled events are triggered, the controller transmits the appropriate on or off signal to the receivers managing the applicable lighting fixtures.

As illustrated in Figure 10-2, a control network in a home can manage the heating and cooling, security cameras inside or outside of the home, the lighting inside and outside the home, and even the lawn sprinklers or the coffee pot using localized or built-in receivers.

Figure 10-2

A control network is used to control, monitor, and manage one or more of a home's systems.

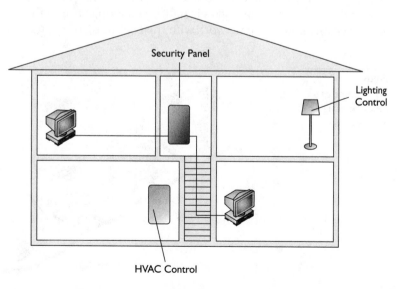

Security Panel

Lighting Control

HVAC Control

Network Topologies

The physical layout of a network is its topology. A network can be set in a single serpentine line that winds through the rooms of a home; it can be set in a loop that runs throughout the home starting and stopping in the same place; or each of the networked devices can have its own direct line to a central point. These three options are the basic topologies used to define the layout of a network. Respectively, they are called bus, ring, and star, also called "home run."

Bus Topology

A bus topology gets its name from the term electrical bus, which is a circuit wire that carries an electrical signal. The central element of a bus topology network is a single cable that runs the length of the network—the network trunk line or "backbone" cable. Devices attaching to the network are connected directly to the cable or through clustering devices, such as a hub. Figure 10-3 illustrates a bus topology network connected in what is called a "daisy-chain." The arrangement shown in Figure 10-1 is common when coaxial cable is used as the network backbone.

Another example of a bus topology network is shown in Figure 10-4. In this illustration, the networked devices connect to the backbone using short cables, called patch cables or cords. Understand that this illustration is highly simplified. Later in this chapter, we look at exactly how the connection is made, but for now, understand that the networked devices connect to the network backbone.

Ring Topology

The second of the top three network topologies is the ring topology, which gets its name from the fact that this topology is installed in a loop (or ring) that circles back around to connect the end of the network with the beginning of the network. To understand

Figure 10-3
An example of a network using a bus topology

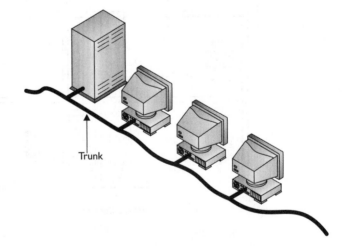

Trunk

Figure 10-4
Another view of
a bus topology
network

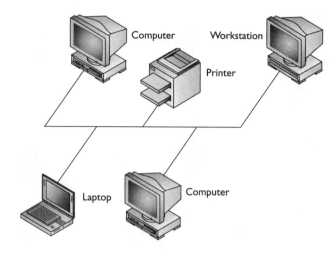

the concept behind a ring topology, take a pencil and begin drawing a circle on a piece of paper. If the line you drew were the network cable, the fact that the end of the cable connects back to the beginning of the cable is what makes it a ring topology.

Figure 10-5 illustrates how a ring topology might actually look when installed in a home or an office building. Only starting and ending the network backbone cable at the same place creates the "ring." Placed into a home networking situation, a ring network might look something like the network shown in Figure 10-6.

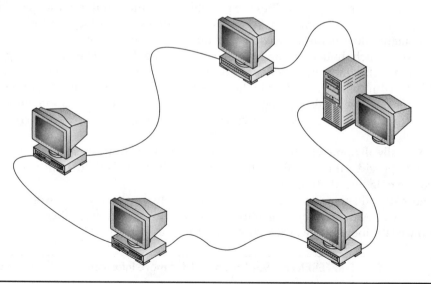

Figure 10-5   An example of a ring topology network

PART III

Figure 10-6
A ring topology used with a home network might not actually look much like a "ring."

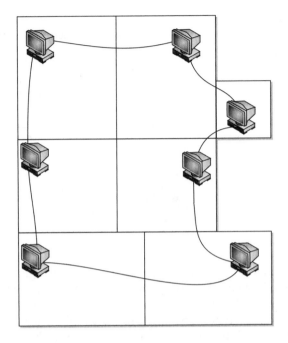

Star Topology

The third of the three most common network topologies is the star topology. In much the way that the name "ring" describes the general layout and topological shape of a ring topology network, the name "star" does the same for a star topology network.

The star topology defines a network structure that emanates from a central unit, such as a server, switch, hub, or another type of networking device. The star topology may resemble a starfish more than it does a heavenly body, but the fact that its network devices each have a direct line connection to the central unit like the points of a star, or the arms of a starfish, is where this topology gets its name. The star topology is sometimes also called hub-and-spoke because of its central device and the home run to each connected device.

In virtually all home situations a star topology is usually the least expensive, the easiest to install, provides the most flexibility, and offers the most fault tolerance, or built-in resistance to failure, than the other topologies.

Figure 10-7 illustrates a very basic star topology network that uses a network hub as its central device. Actually, the configuration shown is very common to Ethernet networks, which we talk about in the next section, "Hybrid Star Topologies."

 CROSS-REFERENCE   See Chapter 11 for more information on hubs and other networking hardware.

Figure 10-7
A network
segment using
a star topology

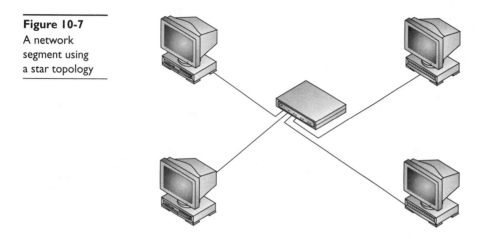

Hybrid Star Topologies

A hub is a networking device that clusters several devices together and connects them either directly or indirectly to the network backbone or trunk line. Chapter 11 explains the function of a hub in more detail, but for now just see it as a way to connect multiple devices that are located in close proximity to the network trunk.

If the starred cluster shown in Figure 10-7 were connected to the backbone cable along with a few other stars created in the same way, the resulting topology would look something like the one shown in Figure 10-8. Figure 10-8 is a hybrid topology that combines the bus and the star topologies.

Figure 10-9 illustrates another hybrid star topology. Only this time, the star topology is combined with the ring topology to create a ringed-star or a star-ring hybrid.

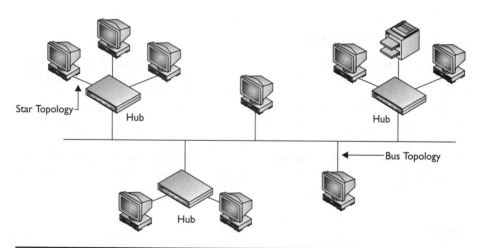

Figure 10-8 An example of the hybrid star-bus network topology

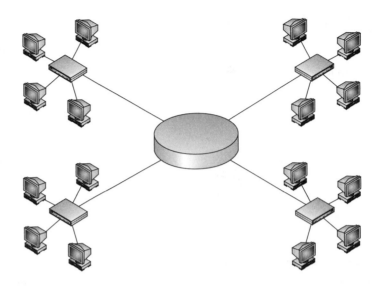

Figure 10-9
An example of the hybrid star-ring network topology

In their purest form, bus, ring, and star topologies can be implemented fairly easily. However, in practice, it is much more common for a topology to be installed in one form of hybrid topology or another.

Another hybrid network topology is the mesh topology. This topology, which provides the ultimate in fault tolerance, requires that every network device be connected directly to every other network device, creating a mesh of wiring. With this topology in place, the network isn't dependent on any one path through the network.

When we discuss Ethernet and Token Ring networking in the next section, "Networking Technologies," you should get a better understanding of why a hybrid is commonly used.

Networking Technologies

While network topologies provide a general guideline for the layout of a network, the primary two networking technologies, Ethernet and Token Ring, provide the specifications and rules that define the functionality of the network itself.

Of these two, Ethernet is by far the most commonly implemented and most likely the one you'd choose to install in a home networking environment. Token Ring networking technology is harder to find, more expensive, and more complicated to configure. On the other hand, it is very dependable. Ethernet networking components are readily available, inexpensive, and relatively simple to install and configure, which are most of the reasons it is also the more popular choice.

Ethernet

Ethernet is not actually a thing; it is a standard specification for a networking technology that defines the types of wiring that should be used, the type and speed of the signals transmitted over the wiring, and how to control and restrict access to the network to prevent an electrical signal logjam on the wire.

The Ethernet standard was developed by the Institute of Electrical and Electronics Engineers (IEEE, pronounced as "eye-triple-eee"), a trade organization that took it upon itself to standardize the specification and characteristics of low-voltage networks, including data networks. In February of 1980, the IEEE gathered groups of interested parties, divided them into narrowly focused subcommittees charged with defining network standards compatible with the networking model standard published by the International Organization for Standardization (ISO), the Open Systems Interconnect Reference Model, or the OSI reference model, as it is more commonly called.

The IEEE 802 (802 is for 1980, February) committees were numbered to differentiate their responsibilities, and the standard each committee produced took on the number of the committee writing it. Table 10-1 lists the committees of the IEEE 802 project and the networking specification each is charged with defining.

Token Ring

Originally Token Ring, the common implementation of ring topology networks, was an IBM thing. However, in today's world there are a number of vendors providing Token Ring equipment. Apple Computer supports a version of ring networking it calls TokenTalk, in contrast to its Ethernet product, AppleTalk.

IEEE 802.3 Subcommittee	Responsibility
802.1	Internetworking
802.1d	Spanning Tree Protocol
802.1s	Multiple Spanning Trees
802.1q	VLAN Frame Tagging
802.2	Logical Link Control
802.3	Ethernet (CSMA/CD)
802.3u	Fast Ethernet
802.3z	Gigabit Ethernet
802.3ae	10 Gigabit Ethernet
802.4	Token Bus
802.5	Token Ring
802.6	Distributed Queue Dual Bus (MAN)
802.7	Broadband Technology
802.8	Fiber Optic Technology
802.9	Voice/Data Integration
802.10	LAN Security
802.11	Wireless Networking
802.11a	54 Meg Wireless Network
802.11b	11 Meg wireless Network
802.12	Demand Priority Access LAN (100BaseVG-AnyLan)

Table 10-1 The IEEE 802 Project Committees and Their Areas of Responsibility

PART III

802.15	Wireless Personal Area Network
802.16	Wireless Metropolitan Area Networks
802.17	Resilient Packet Ring
802.18	LAN/MAN Standards Committee
802.19	Technical Coexistence
802.20	Mobile Broadband Wireless Access (MBWA).

Table 10-1   The IEEE 802 Project Committees and Their Areas of Responsibility *(continued)*

In a home networking setting, installing a ring network is not typical, but doing so is completely possible provided you have the budget for the hardware, which tends to be more expensive than Ethernet equipment.

The OSI Model

The OSI model is something you need to know because it is used as the common frame of reference in networking. Typically, networking devices and software are discussed in regard to the OSI layer on which they are defined.

Reasons for a Layered Model

A networking model defines the formats, functions, and services performed to transmit data from a sending device across a network to a destination device. However, a layered networking model defines these activities in discrete, yet interoperable, layers. The benefits of working with a layered model are that developments or changes to one layer's specification should have very little or no impact on the other layers and it provides a structured approach to troubleshooting. In a networking model, a router manufacturer can modify the functionality of its equipment operating at Layer 3 (see "The Layers of the OSI Model") and the manufacturers of equipment operating at Layers 2 or 4 would remain compatible and able to communicate with the Layer 3 devices.

The Layers of the OSI Model

The OSI reference model is separated into seven layers. Each one specifies a distinct group of functions that must be performed to transmit data from one network node to another. Figure 10-10 shows the layers of the OSI reference model from Layer 1 (Physical layer) to Layer 7 (Application layer).

TIP   Bear in mind that the OSI reference model isn't software or even firmware, (programming statements embedded in an electronic circuits). The OSI reference model is a written specification that defines what must happen on each of its seven layers to get data from point A to point B.

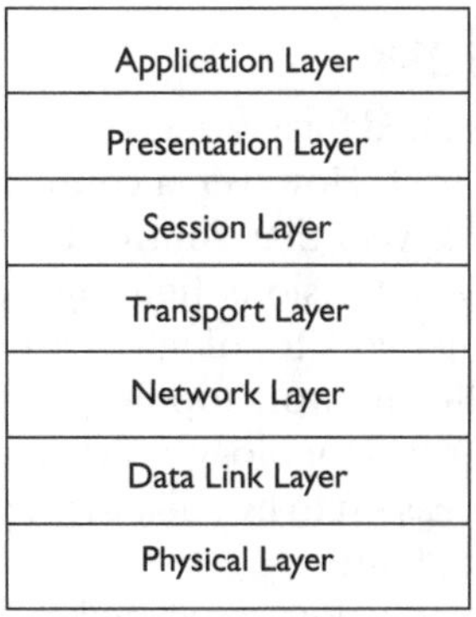

Figure 10-10
The Layers of the
Open Systems
Interconnect (OSI)
reference model

| Application Layer |
| Presentation Layer |
| Session Layer |
| Transport Layer |
| Network Layer |
| Data Link Layer |
| Physical Layer |

Here is a brief description of what each of the OSI model's layers defines.

- **Layer 7–Application layer**   This layer provides services to the software through which the user requests network services. The Application layer doesn't contain any applications, which means that PC application software isn't on this layer. In other words, programs like Microsoft Word or Corel's WordPerfect are not included in the specifications of this layer. However, software that interfaces with the activities of the network, such as browsers, FTP clients, and mail clients are.

- **Layer 6–Presentation**   This layer is concerned with data representation and code formatting, including ASCII, EBCDIC, compression, and encryption.

- **Layer 5–Session**   This layer establishes, maintains, and manages the communication session between computers.

- **Layer 4–Transport**   The functions defined on this layer provide for the reliable transmission of data segments as well as the disassembly and assembly of the data before and after transmission.

- **Layer 3–Network**   This is the layer on which routing is specified. The Network layer defines the processes used to route data across the network and the structure and use of logical addressing, meaning Internet Protocol (IP) addressing.

- **Layer 2–Data Link**   As its name suggests, this layer is concerned with the linkages and mechanisms used to move data about the network, including the specification about accessing the network.

- **Layer 1–Physical**   This layer defines the electrical and physical specifications for the networking media that carry the data bits across a network.

Chapter Review

Home networks are installed for a variety of reasons, including sharing devices, files, and a connection to the Internet. However, a control or home automation network includes the controllers and receivers that control the electrical and electronic devices in the home, including stereos, televisions, lighting, heating and cooling systems, and security.

The most common network topologies are bus, star, and ring. The bus topology is the most commonly installed network topology in business networks, but the star topology, installed as a hybrid star-bus topology, is far more common in home computer networks. The star topology is the easiest to install and provides the most fault tolerance—resistance to hardware or software failure.

The network technology most associated with the bus and star topologies is Ethernet, which is by far the most common network technology in use. Token Ring networks, which are installed on the ring topology, are more expensive to install.

The OSI reference model is a networking model that breaks the activities involved in transmitted data across a network into seven discrete layers. It is not emphasized on the HTI+ exam, but you should be familiar with the layers for reference purposes.

Questions

1. What type of network manages and monitors household appliances, heating and cooling systems, and audio and video systems?

   A. Computer network

   B. Integrated network

   C. Control network

   D. Hybrid network

2. Which of the following best describes the composition of a basic computer network?

   A. Multiple stand-alone computers in a single room

   B. Two computers connected by a communications wire for the purpose of sharing resources

   C. Two computers that can share the same removable media

   D. Multiple computers in a single room that each has a separate Internet connection

3. Which of the following is not a common network topology?

   A. Bus

   B. Ring

   C. Redundant

   D. Star

4. Which network topology is the easiest, least expensive, and most fault tolerant to install?

   A. Bus

   B. Ring

   C. Mesh

   D. Star

5. What are the essential components of a control network?

   A. Transmitters and receivers

   B. Transceivers

   C. Controllers and receivers

   D. Emitters and receivers

6. What is the term that describes the physical layout of a network?

   A. Schema

   B. Grid

   C. Plant

   D. Topology

7. Which of the common network topologies is based on a central "backbone" that runs the length of the network?

   A. Bus

   B. Ring

   C. Mesh

   D. Star

8. Which of the common network topologies involves the use of a central clustering device?

   A. Bus

   B. Ring

   C. Mesh

   D. Star

9. What is the standard specification for Ethernet networks?

   A. IEEE 802.2

   B. IEEE 802.3

   C. IEEE 1284

   D. IEEE 1394

PART III

10. What is the common name used for Layer 1 of the OSI model?

   A. Physical layer

   B. Network layer

   C. Transport layer

   D. Application layer

Answers

1. **C.** The world of home technology integration is also the world of home automation networks on which the electronic systems in the home can be integrated for control and management purposes. A home computer network typically doesn't include control of heating, lighting, etc. The other answers may be good descriptive terms, but they aren't used to name network types.

2. **B.** As few as two computers can make up a network, provided they are connected for communications and set up to share resources. None of the other choices would be a network.

3. **C.** I made this one up, actually. All of the other answers are valid topologies.

4. **D.** A star network is generally the least expensive to install because a line runs directly from each device to a central device. If one device fails, the others are unaffected. Bus, ring, and mesh topologies typically require additional hardware and software, and, in the case of mesh topology, a whole lot of additional cable.

5. **C.** Controllers and receivers are the terminal devices of a control network. Perhaps a case can be made for transmitters and receivers, but the purpose behind a control network is control.

6. **D.** The term topology is used to describe the physical layout of a network's media and nodes. A schema is a database plan and grid and plant are physical facility layout terms.

7. **A.** A bus network includes a backbone that runs the length of the network. A ring network also uses a central connecting cable, but it is referred to as the ring. Mesh and star topologies use direct connections to each node.

8. **D.** Regardless of whether it is used as a hybrid or a common star network, a central device is used to cluster the nodes to the network servers or backbone.

9. **B.** IEEE 802.2 defines the Data Link layer's sublayer functions, including MAC addressing. IEEE 1284 is a parallel cable standard. IEEE 1394 defines high-speed serial interfaces. This leaves IEEE 802.3 as defining Ethernet standards.

10. **A.** Layer 1 of the OSI model is the Physical layer. Layer 3 is the Network layer; Layer 4 is the Transport layer; and Layer 7 is the Application layer.

CHAPTER 11

Computer Network Hardware

In this chapter, you will learn about:
- Common home networking hardware
- Networking and networkable devices
- Network cable and wiring media

A home computer network isn't really all that different from any other type of computer network. The only difference that may exist is one of scale; a home network may have only a few computers and other devices connected together to support the data and networking requirements of the homeowners, whereas a network in a business may have dozens of computers and networked devices interconnected to it. The size of any network affects only the size and complexity of its physical layout, but in terms of hardware, cable and wiring, and communications devices, a network is a network.

In this chapter, I discuss the hardware components typically present in a home network and how they interconnect. In most cases, this involves computers, cable, network adapters, an Internet gateway, and perhaps a communication or connectivity device or two.

 NOTE Understand that when I use the term "home network" in this chapter, I'm referring to a home computer network or a home data network and not the telephone, lighting, heating, or security systems or networks.

Basic Network Components

As illustrated in Figure 11-1, a basic home network, whether for resource sharing or home automation, consists of a few primary components: computers, network adapters, cabling, and, if needed, some form of network clustering or connectivity device.

Computers

By definition, any network must interconnect at least two devices, whether they are desktop PCs, portable PCs, or computerized home automation controllers or receivers. Most

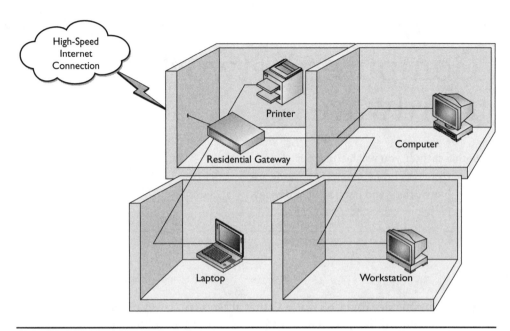

Figure 11-1   A simple home network using a communication service gateway device to share
a connection to a high-speed Internet service

PCs on the market today are network-ready and include either a built-in or preinstalled
network adapter, as shown in Figures 11-2 and 11-3.

Figure 11-2
A desktop
personal computer
with an installed
network adapter
being connected
to the network
media

Figure II-3   A notebook computer with a PC Card network adapter installed

Network Adapters

A network adapter, also commonly called a network interface card or NIC, is the device that, as its name suggests, connects a computer to a network. Technically, it is the NIC that is connected to the network and the PC is connected to the NIC. The PC interacts with the network and its resources through the NIC.

Desktop Computer Network Adapters

Network adapters come in a variety of styles. The most common is an expansion card, shown in Figure 11-4, which is installed in an expansion slot on the PC's motherboard. There are expansion card NICs for both wired and wireless networks. The NIC shown in Figure 11-4 is a wired network NIC.

A wireless NIC is installed in a computer in the same manner as a wired NIC. The difference is that the wireless NIC has an antenna on it (see Figure 11-5) that connects the NIC's transceiver to a wireless network access point (NAP) and the network.

Most of today's expansion card NICs, like those in Figures 11-4 and 11-5, are typically designed for installation in a PCI (Peripheral Components Interconnect) slot on a computer's motherboard (inside the PC's case). Older, or what are called "legacy" computers also provide one or more ISA (Industry Standard Architecture) interfaces, which is an

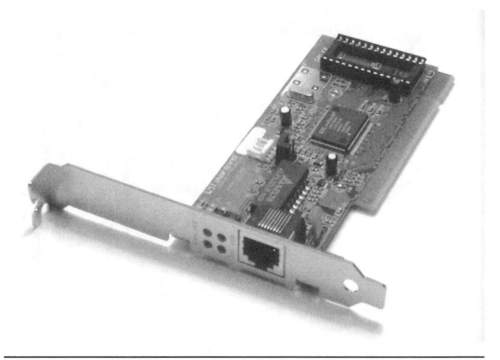

Figure 11-4   A PCI (Peripheral Components Interconnect) network interface card (NIC) expansion card

older interface type. There are also computers in use that provide EISA (Enhanced ISA) slots, a combination slot that can take either a legacy ISA card or an EISA card.

Portable PC Network Adapters

Portable PCs, such as notebook and laptop computers, typically use PC Card network adapters, such as the ones shown in Figures 11-3 and 11-6. Some portable PCs have a network adapter built into their motherboard, in which case, a connecting jack is available on either the case of the PC or its docking station. A PC docking station is a platform where a notebook PC can be mounted to gain additional ports, jacks, and often a network interface.

The NIC shown in Figure 11-6 is a PC card network adapter that uses a *dongle* to connect to the network media. The end of the dongle has a jack to receive the connector on the end of the network media. Many PC Card NICs, such as that shown earlier in Figure 11-3, have a media connection port built in.

Wireless Network Adapters

The network adapters or NICs discussed in the preceding sections are for use with a wired network, in which a physical wire or cable is used to interconnect computers and other devices to the network. As I will discuss later in the chapter, wireless networks are becoming

Figure 11-5
A wireless NIC
expansion card

*Photo courtesy of
Cisco Systems, Inc.*

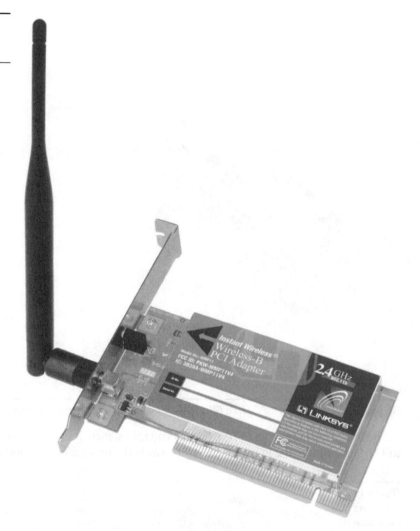

very popular and connecting a PC to a wireless network requires a wireless network adapter. A wireless NIC, such as the one shown earlier in Figure 11-5, is distinctive with its radio frequency (RF) antenna on the external part of the expansion card. Portable PCs can be configured for a wireless network using a PC Card type network adapter, such as the one shown in Figure 11-7. A portable PC equipped for wireless networking is free to roam anywhere within the range of the network's RF signal.

USB Network Adapters

Another way to attach a network adapter to a PC is through a USB (Universal Serial Bus) connector. There are a wide variety of these devices, but what they all have in common is that they can be hot-installed at anytime, whether the computer is running or not, to provide instant access to the network.

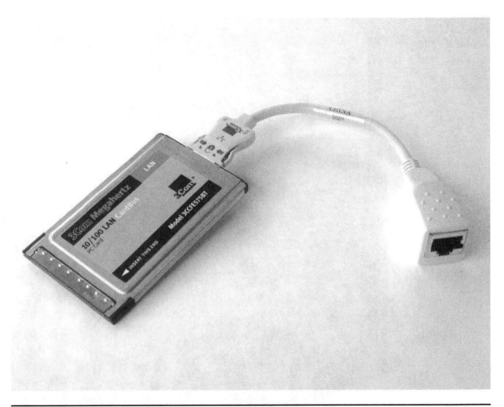

Figure 11-6 An Ethernet PC Card (PCMCIA) type network adapter and a dongle connector

The more common types of USB network adapters, such as those shown in Figures 11-8 and 11-9, connect to the PC through a USB port and have a jack to connect to the network

Figure 11-7
A wireless PC
Card network
adapter

*Photo courtesy of
Cisco Systems, Inc.*

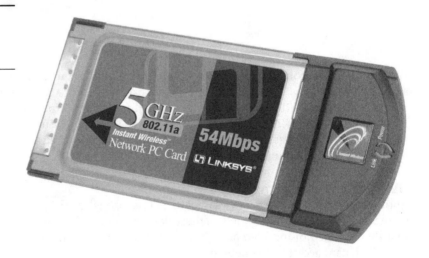

Figure 11-8
A USB network adapter that is connected to the PC using a USB cable

Photo courtesy of Cisco Systems, Inc.

media. Newer and more compact USB network adapters are now available that connect directly into the USB port (see Figure 11-10).

Figure 11-9
A wireless desktop USB network adapter

Photo courtesy of Cisco Systems, Inc.

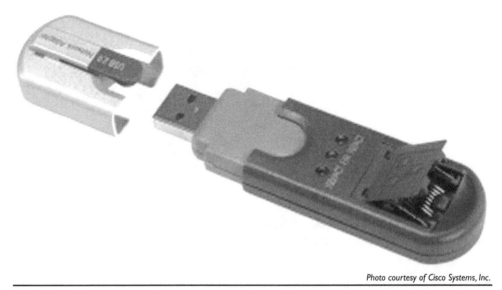

Photo courtesy of Cisco Systems, Inc.

Figure 11-10   A compact USB network adapter connects directly into the USB port on a PC.

Powerline and Phoneline Network Adapters

As I will discuss later in this chapter, network connections can also be made through power-line or phoneline wiring already installed in a home. These systems require special types of network adapters, such as the phoneline network adapter shown in Figure 11-11 and the powerline network adapter shown in Figure 11-12.

Network Media

A length of cabling that connects two communicating devices together is a *network medium*. For the plural reference it is *network media*. Cable, wire, and even wireless RF signals are all considered to be network media. This means that a network medium isn't necessarily a physical thing.

There are several factors to consider when choosing network media for a home network. They are listed here, in no particular order or priority:

- **New construction versus retrofit**   Just about any medium can be chosen in a new construction situation, but hardwired is best. It also depends on the homeowner's wishes and budget.

- **Existing network or new installation**   If an existing (and functioning) network is already in place with cable runs pulled throughout the house and the cable terminations remain in usable locations, there is little need to replace the existing network media. However, if the house is being remodeled extensively and the existing cable and its outlets will no longer be usable in a practical sense, then another medium should be considered.

- **Distance between network nodes**   As I will discuss shortly, most media types have effective distance limitations. For all practical purposes, the distance limits for most cable types shouldn't be a problem in most houses, but in larger houses, the length of the cable pulls may be an issue for each medium being considered.

- **Budget**   Each of the common network media types has its advantages and disadvantages that could translate into cost issues for a home network. The cost of the network hardware used with each medium can range from inexpensive to perhaps prohibitively expensive.

- **Homeowner's preferences**   Sometimes, if budget is not a concern, the medium choice may boil down to what the homeowner wishes to use. However, as a home automation professional, you should educate the user on the advantages and disadvantages of the alternative media types. Table 11-1 shows a comparison of the capabilities of the networking media most likely to be used in a residential setting.

Photo courtesy of Cisco Systems, Inc.

Figure 11-11   A PCI expansion card phoneline NIC

Figure 11-12
A powerline control (PLC) network adapter

Photo courtesy of NetGear, Inc.

Network Media Basics

Networks can be installed using either wired or wireless media. In a wired environment, new cabling, such as unshielded twisted-pair (UTP) Category 5 (Cat 5) wire can be installed in the walls or under the flooring. Another approach is to install wireless network access points and wireless network adapters in the networked computers to create a totally flexible and cable-less network. Existing wiring in the home, specifically the electrical wiring and the telephone wiring, can also be used to install a powerline or phoneline network.

Network media and their electrical and mechanical specifications are defined at the Physical layer of the OSI model. The OSI model's Layer 1 standards are actually developed by a variety of standards organizations, including the EIA/TIA (Electrical Industry Association/Telecommunications Industry Association), the IEEE, Underwriters Laboratories (UL), and others. The major standards governing the use of physical media in a network are discussed later in this chapter and in Chapter 4.

There are a few characteristics that should be considered for any network medium before it is chosen for installation and use. The primary considerations are as follows:

- **Attenuation** For nearly every media type, there is a distance at which a transmitted signal begins to weaken to the point that it may become incoherent. Several factors combine to degrade a signal, including impedance and resistance on wire transmissions and signal strength on wireless transmission, but every media type has an attenuation point. Because of attenuation, each media type specifies a maximum standard segment (cable run) length. For example, on twisted-pair

Table 11-1
Feature Comparison of Common Residential Network Media

Characteristic	Wire	Coaxial Cable	Wireless
Availability	Good	Good	Good
Expandability	Fair	Fair	Good
Transmission quality	Fair	Good	Fair
Security	Fair	Fair	Poor
Range	Good	Poor	Good
Environmental constraints	Fair	Good	Fair

copper cable, the maximum segment length is 100 meters (or 328 feet), which is the distance at which attenuation begins to degrade a transmitted signal on that medium. On wireless media, the effective communications range is essentially its attenuation point, which is affected by a variety of factors, including the materials and construction of the building and any radio frequency interference sources present.

- **Cancellation**   When two wires are placed too close to one another, there is a chance that their electromagnetic fields may cancel each other out. Generally, cancellation can be a good thing because it can help to control the signals being transmitted on the individual wires. However, too much cancellation can destroy the integrity of a signal being carried on either wire. For this reason, there are standards regarding how closely two cables can be placed and at what angle wires must cross each other.

- **Electromagnetic Interference (EMI)**   Virtually every electrical device emits electromagnetic waves that can cause interference and impair the signals of other devices. EMI can result when a wire is placed too close to electrical wiring or some electrical lighting fixtures, especially fluorescent fixtures. Electrical appliances, such as refrigerators, freezers, and even vacuum cleaners, can also create EMI. Too much EMI, regardless of its source, can lead to the bad kind of cancellation.

- **Radio Frequency Interference (RFI)**   Devices that broadcast wireless radio signals can cause interference with other wireless and wired transmissions. In a wireless transmission, RF signals that overlap or overpower a data transmission can scramble the signals (a condition called cancellation) to the point that the integrity of the original signal is destroyed. In the same manner that copper media absorbs EMI from nearby wires, the media can also absorb airborne RF signals.

Network Cabling Choices

In the home network environment, the network media typically used include a few choices not typically associated with business or industrial networking. The choices common to all computer networks are as follows:

- Thin coaxial cable (RG58)
- Category 5 (Cat 5) unshielded twisted-pair (UTP) wire
- Shielded twisted-pair (STP) wire
- Fiber optic
- Wireless RF

Other residential media choices, which are not typically associated with business networking (but, could be), are as follows:

- Powerline control (PLC)
- Phoneline

- Bluetooth
- HomeRF

Coaxial Cable   Thin coaxial cable, one of the oldest of the networking media standards, is the common name used to describe 50-ohm (impedance) RG58 coaxial cable. Other names used for RG58 cable include Thinnet, cheapernet, and 10Base2. RG58 coaxial cable is a thinner, more flexible product than what is called "full spec" coaxial cabling, or RG6 coaxial cabling, which is also called Thicknet and 10Base5.

RG6 cabling can also be used for networking, but would be very impractical in a home environment. This type of cable is more commonly used as a riser cable, to connect a rooftop receiver to a basement distribution system or the like.

There is only one primary connector type for RG58 coaxial cabling in a networking application: BNC connectors. Depending on whom you ask or believe, BNC stands for Bayonet Naval Connector, British Naval Connector, Bayonet Neill Concelman, or Bayonet Nut Connector—take your pick. Figure 11-13 shows a BNC T-connector that is commonly used in Bus daisy-chained networks.

CROSS-REFERENCE   Chapter 4 provides a more detailed look at the Ethernet cable specifications, including 10BaseT and other cable designations.

Powerline and Phoneline Media   Chapter 4 covers powerline and phoneline media in more detail, but here is a bit of a refresher.

The term "powerline media" refers to the electric lines inside the walls of a home that can be used as a low-cost alternative to installing Cat 5 cable. As explained in Chapter 4, there are three primary powerline standards available: CEBus, HomePlug, and X-10.

Phoneline media uses a home's telephone lines in much the same way that powerline media use the existing electrical lines in a home to transmit data. The primary standard for phoneline media is the Home PhoneLine Networking Association (HPNA)

Figure 11-13
A BNC
T-connector
is commonly in
networks using
coaxial cabling.

technology. Many vendors, including several also supporting powerline communications, are supporting this standard as well. HPNA currently operates at 10 Mbps and can coexist with DSL systems that may also be on the phone lines.

Wireless Network Media

To most technicians, the word "network" conjures up the physical components of a network and the means used to interconnect the networked devices. Essentially, a network is made up of any two devices connected together with some type of communications medium (cabling, wire, radio waves, and so on).

One of the very first decisions that must be made when designing a network of any kind is what media is to be used. One choice is to use network wiring or cabling and run it throughout the building to every location a PC or other networked device may be located at now or in the future. Another choice is to use a wireless medium. Wireless media require very little wiring and then typically only patch cords to connect the wireless network access point (NAP) to the residential gateway, but no new wiring in the walls, at least. However, each option has its pros and cons that should be carefully considered before choosing a networking solution. The primary wireless networking standards are as follows:

- **IEEE 802.11a**   This wireless networking standard defines a radio frequency technology in the 5-gigahertz (GHz) band that offers very high bandwidth (as much as 54 Mbps) over short distances, which makes it a good choice for home audio/video networks.

- **IEEE 802.11b**   This is the most common of the wireless networking standards in use today. Virtually every wireless network gateway, access point, or PC Card produced is based on one variation of 802.11b or another. This standard defines a 10 Mbps Ethernet network operating over a radio frequency technology in the 2.4 GHz band. In the place of hubs or other network connectivity devices, 802.11b systems use network access points (NAPs). Each computer is equipped with a wireless networking (802.11b) network adapter card, like the examples in Figures 11-5 and 11-7, earlier in the chapter.

- **IEEE 802.11g**   This wireless LAN standard is an extension of the 802.11b standard that increases 802.11b's data speeds from 11 Mbps to 54 Mbps using the same 2.4 GHz band. The 802.11g standard is backward-compatible so 802.11b access points can be upgraded to 802.11g through simple firmware upgrades.

- **Bluetooth**   Bluetooth is a radio frequency personal area networking (PAN) standard emerging from the cellular telephone industry. The benefit of Bluetooth, named after an ancient warrior king of Sweden, is that it is self-discovering and self-configuring among Bluetooth-capable devices, which means you can roam freely within a Bluetooth area and when you leave one server's range, another automatically picks you up. At the present, this is not a totally viable option for home networking, but as products are developed, its 10-meter range limit seems well-suited for most homes.

- **HomeRF** A radio frequency technology developed specifically for use in wireless home networking. The recently announced HomeRF 2.0 standard has received some strong support and products may soon be available, something that has hindered its adoption in the past.

Network Connectivity Devices

Once a computer has a network adapter installed, it is ready to connect to the network through the network media. The easiest way to share a communications link on a home network is through some form of a network connectivity device. While there are a wide variety of features and functions available on these devices, they basically boil down to a small number of choices: repeaters, hubs, bridges, and routers.

Repeater

Should it be necessary to install a network device at a distance that exceeds the maximum segment distance of a particular network medium, a repeater can be installed. A repeater merely regenerates the signal on the line and retransmits it so the signal is strong enough to be read by the distant device.

TIP Remember that the maximum segment length limit on a network medium includes all pieces of cabling between the signal source and the destination device.

Hub

In the same manner that a hub is a central distribution point for an airline's routes, a network hub serves as a clustering device that allows several devices to interconnect to the network and each other. In a home networking environment, a hub is used to cluster two or more PCs or peripheral devices to the residential gateway device. In a home network, a hub, like the one shown in Figure 11-14, can be used to connect several computers and peripheral devices together to, in effect, create a small peer-to-peer network.

Hubs are either passive or active. A passive hub is really just a pass along device in that it passes any signal it receives on any of its ports out to all of its ports. Active hubs are sometimes referred to as *smart* hubs They have some embedded firmware that allows them to make certain decisions about where a signal should be forwarded, stopping just short of performing bridging.

Hubs, as well as all networking devices, must be matched to the bandwidth speed of the network. If a network is running a 10-megabit per second (10 Mbps) Ethernet, then its hubs must be 10 Mbps hubs. However, if the network is moving from 10 Mbps to 100 Mbps one segment at a time or will in the future, there are speed-sensing hubs (called 10/100 hubs) that can automatically detect the line speed and set the speed accordingly.

In situations in which more connections are required than an existing hub can handle, two hubs can be daisy-chained to each other, an action that networkers call stacking. Because hub stacking is becoming more commonplace, many hubs now have a port available for just this purpose.

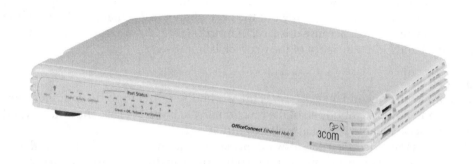

Photo courtesy of 3Com Corporation.

Figure 11-14 An eight-port Ethernet hub

Bridges and Switches

The essential function of a bridge is to interconnect two dissimilar network segments, such as an incoming DSL link and your local network. Bridging involves converting the incoming or outgoing signal so that the signal is in a form that can be used by a particular network segment. Bridges, and their more sophisticated and capable cousins, *network switches,* provide for multiple devices to connect and share the network bandwidth.

A switch is a hybrid device that combines the functions of an active hub with those of the bridge. On a home network, the function of a bridge or switch (see Figure 11-15) is essentially the same. However, on larger networks, these two devices have very discrete functions.

Photo courtesy of Cisco Systems, Inc.

Figure 11-15 An eight-part Ethernet switch

The primary difference between a bridge/switch and a hub is that a bridge or switch 1) determines the port on which a signal arrives and doesn't repeat the message to that port, and 2) sends the message only out the port where the destination address of the message can be reached. Because this level of functionality is more efficient than that of a hub, the bandwidth efficiency of the network is improved.

Routers

A router, like the one in Figure 11-16, is the workhorse of high-speed communication connections. Routers embody all of the functionality of hubs, bridges, and switches and perform a very valuable service as well—routing.

Routing is the process used to forward messages from the local (home) network to a remote network, such as the Internet. Much like the way that the postal service routes a letter from one city to the next and delivers it to a particular address, routing ensures that network messages reach their destination. The basis of routing is logical addressing, or what is referred to in the TCP/IP (Transmission Control Protocol/Internet Protocol) world of the Internet as IP addressing.

The objective of routing is to forward a message along the best path possible to reach its destination. In business local area networks (LANs), routing is used to send a message out the best path of several outbound choices. Because there typically is only a single inbound or outbound choice on a home network, routing is used to direct messages to the router port where a particular home network workstation is located. Yes, this is essentially what bridging and switching do, but routers perform a few other services, such as Network Address Translation (NAT) and security functions, which make them worth the investment.

 CROSS-REFERENCE See Chapter 12 for the details of IP addressing, routing, and Network Address Translation (NAT).

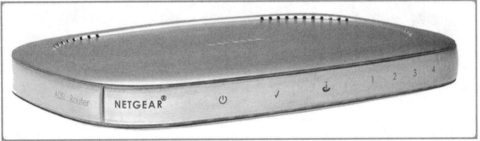

Figure 11-16   A wireless DSL Internet gateway router

Chapter Review

A home network consists of a few primary components: computers, network adapters, cabling, and typically a network clustering or connectivity device. A network interconnects two or more devices, including desktop PCs, portable PCs, or computerized home automation controllers or receivers.

A network adapter or network interface card (NIC) connects a computer to a network. The most common type of network adapter is an expansion card that is installed in an expansion slot on the PC's motherboard. Most of today's expansion card NICs are PCI (Peripheral Components Interconnect) expansion cards. Legacy computers may also support the ISA (Industry Standard Architecture) or the EISA (Enhanced ISA) expansion slots. Notebook and laptop computers commonly use PC Card network adapters. Some portable PCs have a network adapter built into their motherboard. A wireless NIC is distinctive with its radio frequency (RF) antenna on the external part of the expansion card. Portable PCs can be configured for a wireless network using a PC Card type network adapter. Another way to attach a network adapter to a PC is through a USB (Universal Serial Bus) connector. Network connections can also be made through existing powerline or phoneline wiring installed in a home. These systems require special types of network adapters.

The term "network media" refers to the cabling that connects two communicating devices together. Cable, wire, and even wireless RF signals are all considered to be network media. There are several factors to consider when choosing network media for a home network: new construction versus retrofit, existing network or new installation, distance between network nodes, budget, and the homeowner's preferences.

Network media and their electrical and mechanical specifications are defined at the physical layer of the OSI model. The primary standards for network media are the EIA/TIA (Electrical Industry Association/Telecommunications Industry Association), the IEEE, Underwriters Laboratories (UL), and others.

In the home network environment, the network media typically used includes a few choices not typically associated with business or industrial networking. The choices common to all computer networks are RG58 coaxial cable, Cat 5 UTP, fiber optic, and wireless RF. Cat 5 UTP wire is the most commonly used cabling on Ethernet networks.

Alternative media choices are powerline, phoneline, and coaxial cable. There are three primary standards for powerline technology: CEBus, HomePlug, and X-10.

Wireless networking effectively eliminates most of the network wiring. The primary wireless networking standards are IEEE 802.11a, IEEE 802.11b, IEEE 802.11g, Bluetooth, and HomeRF.

Network connectivity devices provide a means to share a communications link. The primary types of connectivity devices are repeaters, hubs, bridges, and routers. A repeater regenerates the signal on the line and retransmits it so the signal is strong enough to be read by a distant device. A network hub serves as a clustering device that allows several devices to interconnect to the network and each other.

A bridge interconnects two dissimilar network segments, such as an incoming DSL link and your local network. A switch is a hybrid device that combines the functions of an active hub with those of the bridge. A router combines the functionality of a hub, bridge, and switch and performs Internet routing.

Questions

1. The device installed in or connected to a PC that provides connection to a network's media is a

    A. Repeater

    B. Network adapter

    C. Hub

    D. Switch

2. The simple networking device that clusters networked devices and broadcasts an incoming signal to its multiple ports is a

    A. Repeater

    B. Hub

    C. Network adapter

    D. Router

3. The most commonly used network cabling for Ethernet networks is

    A. Cat 3

    B. Cat 5

    C. 10BaseF

    D. Cat 1

4. The maximum segment length of 10BaseT cabling is

    A. 50 yards

    B. 100 meters

    C. 185 meters

    D. 500 meters

5. Which of the following is not true regarding UTP cabling?

    A. Only 0.5 inch of untwisted wiring at each end of the cable

    B. No bends in the cable in excess of a 1.25-inch bend radius

    C. No more than 25 pounds of pull during installation

    D. The sheathing may be removed without introducing additional EMI impact.

6. Which of the following is not a type of powerline technology?

    A. CEBus

    B. HomePlug

    C. HPNA

    D. X-10

7. The connector type used for UTP cabling is

   A. BNC

   B. RJ-11

   C. RCA

   D. RJ-45

8. The expansion slot type used by most modern expansion card NICs is

   A. ISA

   B. EISA

   C. PCI

   D. USB

9. What type of coaxial cabling is commonly used in home networking installations?

   A. RG6

   B. RG58

   C. UTP

   D. STP

10. What is the wiring standard that governs the specification and connection for UTP cabling?

    A. EIA/TIA 232b

    B. EIA/TIA 568

    C. IEEE 802.3

    D. IEEE 802.11

Answers

1. **B.** A network adapter, or NIC, is typically installed inside a PC's case as an expansion card. A repeater is a cable attenuation device; hubs are used to cluster devices to the network backbone; and a terminal adapter is used to terminate an ISDN line.

2. **B.** Okay, this may seem like a trick question, but it's not. The key is clustering and multiple ports, both key characteristics of a hub.

3. **B.** Also called 10BaseT, Cat 5 is the most commonly used media. Cat 3 is also an Ethernet media, but Cat 5 has largely replaced it. There is no specification for 10BaseF and Cat 1 is used for audio systems only.

4. **B.** At 100 meters, attenuation begins to degrade the signal quality. Thinnet coaxial cable has a segment distance of 185 meters and Thicknet coaxial is at 500 meters. 50 meters is just a bad answer.

5. **D.** This is absolutely false. The other three answers are correct and you should remember them in the field and for the exam.

6. **C.** This is the standard for using home telephone lines for data networking. The other answers are all powerline standards.

7. **D.** BNC is the connector used with coaxial cabling; RJ-11 is the connector type on a standard telephone line; and RCA is an audio/video connector type.

8. **C.** PCI was introduced with the Pentium computer and has become the standard for expansion cards since then. ISA and EISA, while still supported on many computers, are disappearing more every year. USB may challenge PCI in the future and is an external connection type.

9. **B.** RG6 cabling is thick, hard to work with, and more expensive, all making it impractical for home use. UTP and STP are twisted-pair wiring and not a type of coaxial cable.

10. **B.** EIA/TIA 232 is a communications and cabling standard used with serial connections; IEEE 802.3 is the Ethernet standard; and IEEE 802.11 is a wireless Ethernet standard.

Computer Network Software

In this chapter, you will learn about:
- Network types
- Network operating systems
- Network protocols
- Network security measures
- Network addressing

The networking hardware discussed in Chapter 11 establishes the network in its physical sense, but without networking software, the network has no life. Networking software prepares and presents data to the media for transmission. At the other end of the media, software intercepts, formats, and presents the data to a computer for processing. When the response is ready, the software performs its tasks to deliver the data to the requesting PC and assists the PC to display the data for the user. Without several types of network software, none of that would happen.

In this chapter, we explore the elements of software that combine with the hardware to make a network function. I discuss protocols, the NOS (Network Operating System), and a series of networking utilities that can help you to test, debug, and troubleshoot a network, large or small.

Software and the Network

As networking has become more popular, even in the home, the software tools available have made the task of installing and configuring network software relatively easy. Network operating systems, such as Windows 2000, Windows XP, or Mac OS X, have made the task of configuring a network logically a fairly simple matter.

The general classifications of network software are as follows:

- **Network operating systems (NOS)** An NOS, on the whole, operates outside of the OSI model. Typically, an NOS is installed on a network server and used to manage and control the network resources. Most NOS packages provide their strongest support to the network at the Application layer. I'll talk again about the NOS when I discuss the client/server relationship later in this chapter. Some examples of NOS that can be used to manage a home network are Windows NT 4.0, Windows 2000 Professional, Windows XP Professional, Mac OS X, and Windows 2003, which is perhaps an overkill for a home network.

- **Network protocols** In the Internet environment, one group or suite of protocols is dominant, almost to the exclusion of any other protocol suite: Transmission Control Protocol/Internet Protocol or TCP/IP, as it is more commonly known. A protocol is a set of rules that must be obeyed by the parties in a communication, whether it is on the phone, across the fence, or over a network. Without protocols, or a set of rules, data transmission would be chaos.

  Included in the TCP/IP protocol suite are a group of utilities (software programs) that can be the network technician's best friend when a networked PC is having trouble communicating on the network.

- **Network security software** Arguably, this group of software is very important, especially in the days of "always on" network connections and the demonstrated skill level and number of evildoers out there on the Internet.

Network Operating Systems

The primary purpose of a network operating system (NOS) is to provide for centralized control and management of a network and its resources. In the early days of networking, nearly all networks were peer-to-peer arrangements, where every user was the administrator of his or her part of the network. But, as networks have grown, especially in size and their ability to interoperate, centralized administration of the network has become a virtual necessity.

Peer-to-Peer Networks

Each computer on a peer-to-peer network is directly connected to the computers before and after it in a daisy-chained fashion. The purpose of a peer-to-peer network, like any type of network, is to share resources. However, on a peer-to-peer network, the resources are owned and controlled by the individual users (owners) of the PCs that make up the network. Obviously, this arrangement requires some cooperation and sharing among the network users to succeed.

Figure 12-1 depicts a very simple two-computer peer-to-peer network structure. On this network, one user has a nifty new laser printer and the other controls the access to the Internet through a modem. If User1 wishes to allow User2 to access and use his or her laser printer, he or she must grant permission to User2 to do so. The same goes for User2 allowing User1 access to the Internet connection via the modem.

Peer-to-peer networks are very common in home networking situations because the PCs are in relatively close proximity and the number of computers is typically much fewer than 8 to 10. Above this range, the administration of the individual computers is more efficient if transferred to a centralized activity.

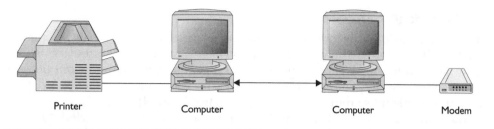

Figure 12-1 A two-computer peer-to-peer network sharing a printer and a modem

Commonly, a home peer-to-peer network is created by installing a network adapter in each PC and connecting the computers to one another using Cat 5 wire and RJ-45 connections (see Chapters 1 and 2 for information on these networking elements).

 TIP The EIA/TIA 568b cable (see Chapter 11) used to connect two network adapters directly is called a rolled cable, which means its receive and transmission lines are crossed over to directly interface to each other.

A peer-to-peer network doesn't require an NOS. Most client operating systems, such as Windows 9*x*, Windows NT Workstation, Windows 2000 Pro, Windows XP Pro, and Windows Me, all include features that support peer-to-peer networking and file, print, and other resource sharing.

Client/Server Networks

The type of network most commonly found in a business setting is a client/server network. The elements of this network include the network client, which formulates and sends requests to a server for information and the use of software or hardware, and the server, which interprets and responds to the requests from the clients. Just like in a restaurant, we are the clients and the server is, well, the server.

Client/server networks are built on a network structure that includes one or more centralized servers. In the context of client/server, a server is a piece of software that runs on a centralized hardware "server." We might have a fax server, an e-mail server, a database server, and most likely a web server on our network. In fact, as is the case on most networks, there is probably only a single computer on which all or at least most of the server software is running.

Ethernet networking is very popular on client/server networks. Understand that client/server networks are actually topology-independent. It really doesn't matter how the network is shaped or configured, as long as at any given time, clients can request services from servers.

Both the Mac OS and Windows Server operating systems include embedded support for client/server networking, including some advanced functions I'll discuss a bit later in this chapter. However, a full-blown NOS is often overkill for home networking requirements. There is no doubt that a full NOS will work, but there are the issues of tool-to-the-task and cost.

Network Protocols

A network protocol is a set of rules that govern the interactions between two communicating entities, regardless of whether they are two computers, modems, routers, or other hardware or software. When one modem dials up another, the transmissions between them are governed by a common protocol. The same goes for two computers on a peer-to-peer network or two routers on a wide area network (WAN).

The Transmission Control Protocol/Internet Protocol (TCP/IP) suite includes a collection of communications and networking protocols that can be used to initiate, facilitate, manage, maintain, and troubleshoot network communications, whether on a local area network (LAN) or a WAN.

The best way to understand the purpose and application of the TCP/IP protocols is by their function. Table 12-1 groups the TCP/IP protocols by their general function or when they are applied, and the OSI layer each operates on.

Here is a brief description of each of these protocols:

- **DNS:** The TCP/IP service used to convert human-friendly domain names (such as comptia.org) to their IP address equivalents (such as 10.0.100.20).

- **DHCP:** This protocol is used to automatically configure a networked PC each time the PC is booted (powered on or restarted). DHCP provides an IP address and other TCP/IP configuration data to enable a PC to connect and interact with its network.

- **FTP:** Used to transfer entire files from one computer to another over the Internet.

- **HTTP:** Defines how requests and response messages are formatted and transmitted and the actions web servers and browser software take in response to the commands included in the transmitted messages and files. S-HTTP (or HTTPS) is an extension of HTTP that provides for secure transmission of data.

Function	Protocol	OSI Layer
Application interface	Domain Name System (DNS) Dynamic Host Configuration Protocol (DHCP) File Transfer Protocol (FTP) Hypertext Transfer Protocol (HTTP) Internet Mail Access Protocol (IMAP) Post Office Protocol, ver. 3 (POP3) Simple Mail Transfer Protocol (SMTP)	Application and Presentation
Transmission of data	Transmission Control Protocol (TCP) User Datagram Protocol (UDP)	Transport
Addressing and delivery	Internet Protocol (IP) Internet Control Message Protocol (ICMP) Packet Internet Groper (PING) Trace Route (TRACERT)	Network

Table 12-1 The TCP/IP Protocols of a Home Network

- **ICMP**   Other protocols and devices that need to communicate with one another use this protocol.

- **IMAP**   A protocol that allows e-mail to be accessed and read on a mail server and optionally transferred to a mail client.

- **IP**   The workhorse protocol of the Internet, IP defines logical addressing (IP addresses) and how it is applied to networks and hosts across a network.

- **PING**   Used to verify that two network nodes are able to communicate with each other.

- **POP3**   A protocol used to move e-mail from a mail server to a mail client.

- **SMTP**   The protocol used to transfer e-mail messages between mail servers.

- **TCP**   A connection-oriented protocol that manages the transmission of data between two communicating stations. TCP includes processes that provide for reliable, guaranteed transmission and receipt of data between a source address and a destination address. TCP messages must be acknowledged as received before additional messages are sent.

- **TRACERT**   Used to determine the routing path used by messages to move across a network from a source address to a destination address.

- **UDP**   A connectionless protocol that transports messages across a network without mechanisms to provide for reliability or delivery guarantees. UDP messages are not acknowledged and are transmitted in a continuous stream.

Network Security

Security is perhaps the most important issue surrounding the use of networks. Security is a growing concern on all types of networks, whether they are small networks in homes and offices, or large international networks, such as the Internet.

Included in the TCP/IP protocol suite are a few utilities that help to create a secure environment for a home network. Most of the Internet gateways (modems, bridges, or routers) used with broadband communication services also provide services to help secure the devices attached to them. In addition, third-party software and hardware can be added to a home network to provide additional security.

TCP/IP Security

When a homeowner subscribes to an Internet service, the Internet service provider (ISP) provides the connection with an IP address. This address is assigned to the connection using DHCP and the IP address assigned will typically be different each time the user connects to the ISP's network. Dynamic addresses (those that change frequently) create a moving target for a network hacker looking to invade a home network. However, DHCP alone isn't enough to prevent an intrusion.

PART III

NAT

A home that has subscribed to either cable or DSL must use an Internet gateway device to connect to the service. Many of these devices have switching or routing capabilities. This is good news in terms of network security.

The Network Address Translation (NAT) protocol is supported by most of the Internet gateways used by cable and DSL services. Even most dialup connections are protected behind a router (at the ISP) that is running NAT services.

What NAT does is translate the IP address of a computer on its internal network into a generic one that is sent out over the external network. This way, anyone wishing to access a specific network computer has only the generic IP address issued by the NAT device and not the IP address of a particular computer.

Private IP Addresses

Within the grand scheme of IP addressing, three blocks of addresses are set aside for use on private networks (see Table 12-2). A private network is one where the networked devices are behind an Internet gateway (usually a router) and don't interact with the Internet directly. On the other hand, a public network is a network like the Internet, where all of the devices are able to communicate directly with one another, such as one router transmitting to another.

Because the Internet world has not converted to the much larger addresses of IP version 6, IP version 4 addresses (there was no real version 5) are now in short supply and as a result most Internet subscribers are issued only one or two IP addresses or are assigned an address through DHCP. Well, if a home network has four computers and a printer to address, using one IP address (and a dynamic one no less) just won't work. This problem is solved using NAT.

Using one of the private IP address blocks (see Table 12-2), each workstation and peripheral device on a home network can be assigned its own private network address. NAT, running on the Internet gateway, converts the private address to a generic public address that is broadcast to the external network. Don't worry—IP addressing and the address classes are covered a bit later in this chapter.

Access Lists

Another feature that may be available in the Internet gateway device is access lists. They are also called *access control lists* (ACLs). ACLs use a feature called *packet filtering* to scan the source and destination addresses included in network messages to determine if the sender has the authority or permission to send messages to the destination address—that is, if it can access the network at all.

Table 12-2	IP Address Class	Private IP Address Range
Private IP Address Blocks	Class A	10.0.0.0 to 10.255.255.255
	Class B	172.16.0.0 to 172.31.255.255
	Class C	192.168.0.0 to 192.162.255.255

When a packet-filtering device receives message packets from either an internal or an external source, it extracts the IP address of the sending station (source address) and compares it to an access control list created by the network administrator (the home-owner, in the HTI+ world). Depending on the action prescribed by the information on the list, the message is either permitted access in or out or denied access in or out.

Firewall

Internet gateways also provide basic firewall functions. A firewall works something like an access control list in that it performs packet filtering to deny access to a PC from external sources. However, on a firewall the filtering can occur on the type of application being accessed or the type of action requested, such as chat, e-mail, ftp, and so on.

Wireless Security

The primary security protocol on a wireless or 802.11b wireless gateway or access point is Wired Equivalent Privacy (WEP). Wireless (802.11b) gateways implement the WEP protocol to provide transmission security for wireless networks. WEP encrypts data sent between computers and other devices on a wireless LAN using either 40-bit or 128-bit encryption. Running WEP at all times on home networks running on a wireless plat-form ensures the security of the data transmissions.

Wireless networks shouldn't be operated without some type of security function in place. The most common type is encryption, which is what protocols such as WEP provide. WEP, or whatever security protocol is to be used, must be set up on the wireless router or gateway device. This setup varies by manufacturer, so reference the router's or gateway's documentation for the setup procedure.

Network Addressing

Addressing is a very important part of networking. Just as a house or building must have an address so that postal and package services and friends and relatives can find it, each node on a network must also have a unique address. In fact, on a network, most nodes actually have at least two addresses: a logical address and a physical address.

On every street in every town, each building, office, and house has a single mailing address that uniquely identifies it. In the same way, each node on a network must also be uniquely identified, and for just the same reason. In our society, even people can be identified in a number of different ways, including Social Security number, phone number, driver's license number, and home address.

A networked computer is also identified with a variety of physical and logical addresses, including its Media Access Control (MAC) address, Internet Protocol (IP) address, and per-haps a Uniform Resource Locator (URL). For example, a networked computer can have an IP address, such as 172.168.10.10, for use on IP networks, a MAC address, such as 00-A0-CC-34-0A-CE, for use on a local network, and a URL, such as http://www.rongilster.com, so people can find its web page.

Logical versus Physical Addressing

IP addresses are logical addresses because each address is created in a logical pattern that ties one network device to others on the same network. What this means is that it is safe to assume that a networked device with an IP address of 192.168.20.15 is logically located on the same segment of a network as the device with the IP address of 192.168.20.14. IP addresses tend to be assigned in a series, one at a time, in a logical pattern. On the other hand, physical addresses are random.

Physical Addresses

When a networking device is manufactured, it is assigned a physical address that is a universally unique identification number permanently embedded in its electronic circuitry. This number, known as a Media Access Control, or MAC, address is like a lifetime membership card to the networking club. On local networks, the MAC address is used to route messages to specific devices. In essence, a MAC address is the unique identifying number assigned to each network adapter or other networking device. MAC addresses are physical addresses.

A MAC address consists of a 48-bit or 6-byte hexadecimal number. It is represented in the form of six two-digit numbers separated by dashes. The first 24 bits (3 bytes) of the MAC address contain a code assigned by the IEEE (The Institute of Electrical and Electronics Engineers) to uniquely identify the manufacturer of the card, and the 24 bits (3 bytes) are a number uniquely assigned by the manufacturer. For example, a MAC address of 00-A0-CC-34-0A-CE includes a manufacturer ID number of 00-A0-CC and a serialized ID number of 34-0A-CE. The segments of this number are hexadecimal numbers, but their specific values aren't important, only their uniqueness.

Every networked computer has a MAC address—the address burned into its network adapter during manufacturing. On a Windows PC, the MAC address assigned to its network adapter can be displayed using the TCP/IP command IPCONFIG that should look something like the display shown in Figure 12-2. On this computer, the MAC address is listed as the Physical Address.

Logical (IP) Addresses

The most commonly used logical network address is what is called an IP address. It gets its name from the Internet Protocol (IP), which controls and manages logical addressing on TCP/IP networks, both small (like a home network) and large (like the Internet).

IP addresses are 32 bits long (the equivalent of 4 bytes) and are represented as four 8-bit segments, called octets, that are arranged into a dotted-decimal notation scheme, as in 100.100.100.100.

Figure 12-2

The display produced by the IPCONFIG command

```
0 Ethernet adapter :

        Description . . . . . . . . : Linksys LNE100TX Fast Ethernet Adapter
        Physical Address. . . . . . : 00-A0-CC-34-0A-CE
        DHCP Enabled. . . . . . . . : Yes
        IP Address. . . . . . . . . : 12.207.242.31
        Subnet Mask . . . . . . . . : 255.255.248.0
        Default Gateway . . . . . . : 12.207.240.1
        DHCP Server . . . . . . . . : 12.242.16.34
        Primary WINS Server . . . . :
        Secondary WINS Server . . . :
        Lease Obtained. . . . . . . : 08 18 03 5:00:16 PM
        Lease Expires . . . . . . . : 08 22 03 5:00:16 PM
```

NOTE The latest version of IP addressing to emerge is IP version 6 (IPv6), which provides a 128-bit address and supports a more complex numbering scheme than the currently popular IP version 4 (IPv4). IPv6 is backward compatible for IPv4, so don't worry too much about support for IPv6 in a home network.

Binary Address Representation

Although IP addresses are represented in decimal numbers for human readability purposes, computers and networking devices see these addresses as a series of binary bits. The binary number system uses only two values (0 and 1) to represent numbers in powers of 2.

Most people are accustomed to thinking and working in the decimal system, which is based on the number 10. To most people, the number 124 represents 100 + 20 + 4. To the computer, this number of 124 is 1111100, which is 64 (2^6) + 32 (2^5) + 16 (2^4) + 8 (2^3) + 4 (2^2) + 0 (2^1) + 0 (2^0). Each position in a binary number represents, right to left, a power of two beginning with 2^0 and increasing by one power of two as it moves left: 2^0, 2^1, 2^2, 2^3, 2^4, and so forth.

Perhaps we need a quick lesson in binary-to-decimal conversion. There are 8 bits in an octet, and each bit can only be a 1 or a 0. The highest binary number that can be expressed in an octet is 11111111. To convert this binary number to its decimal equivalent requires that we know the powers of two value of each position that has a 1, which in this case is all of them. The powers of two values for the 8 bits in an octet are

$$2^7\ 2^6\ 2^5\ 2^4\ 2^3\ 2^2\ 2^1\ 2^0$$

When a 1 is placed in one of the binary positions, it means that the value of that position adds into the decimal value being represented. A zero (0) in any position indicates that the value of that position is not added into the decimal value.

To convert a binary octet that has all 1s, use Table 12-3 as a guide to convert the values assigned to each position in an octet into the total decimal value being represented.

Using the information in Table 12-3, the binary number 11111111 converts into a decimal value by adding up the individual values of each position, as

$$128 + 64 + 32 + 16 + 8 + 4 + 2 + 1 = 255$$

This means that the largest decimal number that can be represented in an IP address octet is 255. This is important information for reasons I will discuss a bit later in this chapter. In the same manner, the decimal number 196 would be represented in an octet as 11000100 or

$$128 + 64 + 0 + 0 + 0 + 4 + 0 + 0 = 196$$

Binary Positional Value	2^7	2^6	2^5	2^4	2^3	2^2	2^1	2^0
Decimal Value	128	64	32	16	8	4	2	1

Table 12-3   The Decimal Values Assigned to Each Bit Position of an IP Address Octet

Table 12-4	Class	Value in the First Octet
IP Class Address Ranges	Class A	0–127
	Class B	128–191
	Class C	192–223

IP Address Classes

IP addresses are divided into five address classes; each is designated with a letter A to E. Classes D and E are not used for general IP addressing. Class D addresses are used for multi-casting (or broadcasting a message or an audio/video stream to a preset list of addresses) and Class E addresses are reserved for testing and future, reserved usage. Table 12-4 lists the IP address ranges included in Classes A, B, and C.

Using the ranges in Table 12-4, the address class of an IP address can be determined by the value in its first octet. For example, an address with 120 in the first octet is a Class A address; an address with 155 in the first octet is a Class B address; and an address with 220 in its first octet is a Class C address. As I discuss later in the chapter, knowing the address class of an IP address is key to setting subnet masks, if needed.

Networks and Hosts

The 32 bits and 4 octets of an IP address represent network and host IDs. The number of bits or octets used depends on the IP address class of the IP. Table 12-5 lists how each IP address class designates which octets are a part of which ID, network or host.

In the IP addressing scheme, every network is assigned a network address and every node, device, or interface (such as a switch, bridge, or router port) is assigned a host address. In Figure 12-2 shown earlier in the chapter, the IP address assigned to that computer was 12.207.232.21. Based on what we know to this point, we can assume that this is a Class A address and the network address is 12.0.0.0 (zeroes are used as placeholders) and the host ID portion is 207.232.21 on network 12.0.0.0.

Assigning Network Addresses

In a home networking situation, the Internet service provider (ISP), which provides the Internet connection, assigns one IP address to each subscriber. Typically, this address is a dynamic address and may be different each time a connection is made to the ISP's network. In some situations, such as in high-speed Internet connections, a static (permanent and unchanging) IP address may be assigned.

In a home network situation with, for example, four computers sharing the Internet connection, each of the computers must be assigned a unique IP address in order to

Table 12-5	Class	Octet1	Octet2	Octet3	Octet4
IP Address Class Network and Host Representation	Class A	Network	Host	Host	Host
	Class B	Host	Host	Network	Network
	Class C	Network	Network	Network	Host

communicate with the Internet gateway device (to which the IP address from the ISP is actually assigned). Typically, the address assigned by the ISP will be either a Class C address or a subnet equivalent (more on subnets later in the chapter). This may appear to present a problem, but the IP addressing specifications have made provisions for these situations through what are called *private addresses.*

Special Addresses

The IP address specifications set aside some addresses for use in special situations. These addresses fall into four categories:

- **Network addresses:** Any IP address where the host ID portion of the address is all zeroes is a network address and cannot be assigned to a host or node on a network.

- **Broadcast addresses:** Any IP address where the host ID portion of the address is all ones is a broadcast address and cannot be assigned to a host or node on a network. Broadcast addresses are used to send a variety of messages to all nodes on a network.

- **Loopback testing:** The address range 127.0.0.0 to 127.255.255.255 (the entire 127 address range) is reserved for loopback testing on any network. Loopback testing is used to test the connection and functionality of a network adapter.

- **Private network addresses:** Three address ranges have been set aside for use by private networks, those behind an Internet gateway device or those that don't connect to the Internet. Table 12-6 lists the private address ranges that have been reserved for this use. Each of the computers and networked devices on a home network is assigned an IP address from one of these ranges. The range that is used is actually a matter of choice in a home networking situation because each range has enough available addresses for virtually every home networking situation.

Subnet Masks

As mentioned earlier, an IP address has two parts: the network identification portion and the host identification portion. In order to route an address across a network, the network and host portions of the address must be separately identified. In most cases, if you know the address class, it's easy to separate the two portions.

The function of a subnet mask is to extract the network ID portion of an IP address. This function is performed, in the case of a home network, by the Internet gateway device to determine whether an IP address is on the local network or whether it must be routed outside the local network—to the Internet, for example.

Table 12-7 lists the default subnet masks for Class A, B, and C addresses.

Table 12-6 Private Addresses	IP Class	Address Range
	Class A	10.0. 0.0 through 10.255.255.255
	Class B	172.16.0.0 through 172.31.255.255
	Class C	192.168.0.0 through 192.168.255.255

Table 12-7	Address Class	Subnet Mask
Standard IP	A	255.0.0.0
Default Subnet	B	255.255.0.0
Masks	C	255.255.255.0

Without going into the Boolean algebraic functions that are used when a subnet mask is applied, the value 255 in an octet indicates the portion of the IP address that is used for the network ID. So, using the information in Table 12-7, a Class A address uses one octet, a Class B address uses two octets, and a Class C address uses three octets for the network ID.

Chapter Review

The software building blocks of a home network are the network operating system (NOS), the network protocols, and the network security software. The purpose of the NOS is to provide for centralized control and management of a network and its resources. Network protocols provide the rules and guidelines that govern the transmission of data between two communicating entities. Security features, whether implemented through software or features of the networking hardware, prevent unauthorized users from accessing the network as well as protect data transmission around wired and wireless networks.

The two types of network structures are peer-to-peer and client/server. Peer-to-peer is the most commonly used type for home networks. Star topology-based networks are also common.

TCP/IP is the most commonly used protocol suite on local area networks (LANs) and wide area networks (WANs). Included in this protocol suite are protocols that perform virtually every step in the process used to transmit data across a network, including DNS, DHCP, HTTP, POP3, PING, and TRACERT.

Network security is applied to a home network through several tools. First, the ISP provides some level of security. However, at the home network location, security must be applied through such tools as DHCP, NAT, private IP addresses, access lists, a firewall, and security protocols such as WEP (for wireless networks).

On TCP/IP networks, there are two types of addressing: logical and physical. An IP address is a logical address. Each network device has a universally unique MAC address embedded into its electronics during manufacturing. DNS is used to resolve domain names to their IP address equivalents.

An IP address is expressed in four 8-bit octets. IP addressing is divided into address classes A, B, and C. Within the address classes, a range of addresses have been set aside for use by private networks. An IP address is made up of network and host IDs. A subnet mask is used to extract the network ID from an IP address.

Questions

1. What type of network system software manages and controls a network's resources?

   A. Database management software

   B. Network protocols

   C. Network security software

   D. Network operating system

2. A specification of the rules and guidelines that govern the transmission of data between two communicating entities is called a

   A. Session

   B. Connection

   C. Protocol

   D. Handshake

3. Which two of the following are common network implementations in home networks?

   A. Mesh

   B. Peer-to-peer

   C. Star-based Ethernet

   D. Client/server

4. The protocol suite that provides the foundation for the Internet as well as most home and business networks is

   A. Banyan Vines

   B. TCP/IP

   C. Novell NetWare

   D. CSMA/CD

5. The protocol that is used to convert an IP address to a ghost IP address that hides its true identity and location is

   A. DNS

   B. TCP

   C. NAT

   D. PING

6. Which of the following IP addresses is not a private address?

   A. 10.220.0.115

   B. 172.32.10.1

   C. 192.162.0.253

   D. 172.31.254.250

7. The protocol that provides encrypted data transmissions for security on a wireless network is

   A. 802.11b

   B. WEP

   C. 802.11a

   D. WINIPCFG

8. What is the default Class C subnet mask?

   A. 255.0.0.0

   B. 255.255.0.0

   C. 127.0.0.0

   D. 255.255.255.0

9. Which of the following is a physical address?

   A. 00-0D-F3-23-A7-CC

   B. 124.100.15.4

   C. 255.255.255.0

   D. http://www.physaddr.info

10. What is the decimal equivalent of the binary number 11110011?

    A. 128

    B. 240

    C. 243

    D. 255

Answers

1. **D.** A network operating system (NOS) coordinates, manages, and controls connected network resources. Network protocols are the guidelines that control communications between two devices. Network security can be performed by an NOS, but it can also be performed by other elements of the network as well. Database management software is concerned only with managing a database.

2. **C.** Network protocols are the guidelines that control communications between two devices. Connections, sessions, and handshakes are all part of the functions controlled under a protocol's guidelines.

3. **B and C.** A mesh network, while highly reliable, would be overkill in a home network environment. A home network could be a client/server arrangement, and many are, but that is a functional network type rather than a physical characteristic.

4. **B.** TCP/IP was developed for the Internet although home, office, and other local area networks also use it as their network protocol suite. The others are individual protocols in the TCP/IP protocol suite.

5. **C.** Network Address Translation is a service performed by many Internet gateways that allows multiple internal network nodes to share a single IP address on the Internet. TCP is a transport protocol; DNS translates domain names into their associated IP addresses; and PING is used to test network node connectivity.

6. **B.** Each of the other addresses fall within the range of one of the three private IP address ranges.

7. **B.** Wired Equivalent Privacy provides, as its name implies, a level of privacy and security for transmitted data equivalent to that provided on wired networks. 802.11a and 802.11b are wireless Ethernet standards, and 802.3 is the wired Ethernet standard.

8. **D.** Remember that Class C (the third class) uses three octets to identify the network ID. The subnet masks 255.0.0.0 and 255.255.0.0 are Class A and B's subnet masks, respectively. The address 127.0.0.0 is a special IP address reserved for loopback testing.

9. **A.** A MAC (physical) address is distinctive in its format. Choice B is an IP (logical) address; choice C is the default subnet mask for Class C networks; and choice D is a URL.

10. **C.** Review the process described in this chapter for converting binary numbers to decimal numbers.

CHAPTER 13

Designing and Installing a Computer Network

In this chapter, you will learn about:
- Planning a home computer network
- Communication services
- Installing network cabling
- Terminating network cables
- Testing network wiring

In this chapter, we focus on the tasks performed to install a home computer network. At its most basic level, a home network may consist of only two computers that are connected using a standard parallel, serial, or EIA/TIA 568B cable, such as unshielded twisted-pair (UTP) wire. However, if the home computer network is also intended to provide a foundation for a home automation network, there are additional design and installation issues and tasks you must consider and perform.

Planning a Home Network

Whether you are planning a home network for yourself or a customer, you should perform a thorough study of just what the network is intended to provide. If the network is to be only a data network, its design is much less complicated and far easier to implement. Beyond a few decisions on its topology, technologies, and media, a home data network can be simply and easily installed. However, if a home network is meant to provide the infrastructure of a home automation network, the planning, design, and implementation steps take on added importance. Integrating several independent home systems requires not only an understanding of each of the systems to be integrated, but also how the integration best meets and serves the design and functional requirements of the home and its owners.

The major steps involved in planning and designing home automation networks are as follows:

1. **Identify the customer's current and future networking needs**   There is a network designer's adage about asking a ditch digger what he or she needs to do the job better. Because the ditch digger may have only a limited frame of reference, the answer is likely to be "a larger shovel." The point is that often you need to draw out what a customer really wants by listening first and then talking less about the whiz-bang equipment that's available and more about what the customer is saying about what he or she wants to have in his or her home when the job is done. A customer may say they want to have the porch light to be controlled by the home network, when what they really want is a new outside lighting system, something they didn't think could be automated.

2. **Conduct a project survey**   Are there any structural modifications needed to the home or building? How much of the existing equipment can be incorporated directly into the network? How much of existing equipment or systems need to be upgraded or replaced, or how much really needs to be completely replaced? A detailed project survey of the home should answer these and other questions. Look at the wiring layout and the types of wire used. List the current equipment and proposed future use.

3. **Outline the design project's scope of work—including equipment, budget, and timeline constraints**   Long before the actual work begins, a project scope, preliminary design, and budget must be developed and presented to the customer for approval. After the customer has approved it and signed off, this document provides the working scope of the job and outlines just what is to be included or not included, as the case may be.

4. **Develop preliminary design**   More than likely this document also contains your proposal, project detail, equipment list, and budget for the project as well. It is very important to get the customer to review, understand, and approve this document before work proceeds. This step concludes the preliminary phases of the project. No matter how small the job may seem, these four steps can help to keep a project on track, increase the work efficiency and effectiveness, as well as help reach consensus on just what the job is.

5. **Develop connectivity documentation**   This is the first stage of development for the actual network, assuming the decision was made in the preliminary stages concerning the use of wired versus wireless technologies for all or part of the network. The products of this step are the wiring diagrams, wireless coverage diagrams, schematics, equipment layouts, wiring closets, and the like.

The remaining steps, those involved with installing wire and equipment, testing, and trim out, are covered in more depth in the sections that follow.

Communication Services

Often, the customer has already made an important decision for his or her home network: the type of Internet connection the network will use. But, if this decision remains to be made, the choice boils down to availability, bandwidth, and cost.

For most customers, availability is the most critical. Not all Internet communication services are available in all areas and only the provider of each service can tell you if its service is available to the customer's home.

Internet Services

The primary Internet connectivity or communication services available to home users are

- **Cable** Taking advantage of the bandwidth of the coaxial cable used to carry television signals to homes, the cable industry also provides high-speed Internet connections over the same cable system. A cable Internet system is easily installed in a home that already has cable television service. One potential problem with cable Internet service is that it is a shared system, meaning television and Internet customers share the line and a busy line isn't able to provide the same speed as a lightly used line.

- **Dialup** This service type has now been in the marketplace for over ten years and is mature, tested, and reliable. Its speed is limited to 56 Kbps, which may not be enough to support more than a single user trying to download information at one time. If a dialup service is used, operating system–based features, such as Microsoft's Internet Connection Sharing (ICS), should be implemented.

- **DSL** DSL (Digital Subscriber Line) is a high-speed Internet service that is offered by the telephone company (Telco) over its existing copper POTS (Plain Old Telephone Service) lines. Only those homes that are connected to their local servicing central office (CO) using all copper lines have DSL services available to them. Another DSL limitation is distance. Because of the inherent attenuation issues of copper cable, DSL is not available to homes outside a certain distance from their closest CO. DSL is available in three flavors: Asymmetrical, Symmetrical, and ISDN over DSL. Asymmetrical DSL (ADSL) uses higher speeds for downloads and lower speeds for uploads, matching line speed to the amount of data being transmitted. A common offering of DSL is 128/384 Kbps, with the slower speed being the upload speed. Symmetrical DSL (SDSL) uses the same line speed for both upload and download and is better suited to web server support and business applications. ADSL is also much less expensive than SDSL. ISDN over DSL extends ISDN over the DSL system and has the capability to extend the distance limitations of DSL, but only at ISDN speeds.

- **ISDN** The ISDN (Integrated Services Digital Network) product available to home users is Basic Rate Interface (BRI) ISDN, which combines the two wires in a telephone link to transmit data at 128 Kbps. The total bandwidth on an

ISDN line is 144 Kbps, with the other 16 Kbps used for control and command signaling.

- **ISM** The Federal Communications Commission has set aside two bands of radio frequency (RF) spectrum for commercial and home use. The first of these is ISM (Industrial, Scientific, and Medical), which operates in the 2.4 GHz band. ISM is commonly sold as "wireless DSL" and requires a small 18-inch receiver dish placed on the home that has line of sight to the ISM transmitter. ISM is able to provide up to 90 Mbps, but is typically sold as 128 Kbps, 256 Kbps, and 768 Kbps data rates. One downside to ISM is that it operates in the same spectrum band as baby monitors, cordless phones, and emergency radios.

- **Satellite Internet** DirecTV, Hughes DirectWay, and other providers of satellite direct television services offer a high-speed Internet connection that either uses a telephone line for uploads and satellite transmission for downloads or provides two-way communications via a satellite. This service requires a small dish (see Figure 13-1) to be installed on the exterior of the home. This smaller dish is very similar to that used with ISM and UNII.

- **UNII** UNII (Uniform National Information Infrastructure) is very similar to ISM except that it operates at 5 GHz, which eliminates interference from the crowded band used for ISM. UNII is available in the same bandwidth increments as ISM and some larger increments as well. However, the cellular telephone industry has discovered the UNII band and it's fast becoming as cluttered as ISM.

Figure 13-1
A satellite
Internet dish
and receivers

Photo courtesy of
Pegasus Communications
Corporation.

Internet Gateways

Each of the various broadband services listed in the preceding section must provide some form of an interfacing device to convert its broadband signaling into baseband signaling for use on the internal network. Typically, the device providing the interface is supplied by the vendor with the service and also performs other services as well, but its primary function is to modulate the signal for interoperability.

> **NOTE** The telecommunications industry refers to the equipment that terminates the line or signal at the customer's premises as customer premise equipment (CPE). This includes the dish and receivers on wireless services. However, from the home wiring perspective, the CPE is known as the Network Interface Device (NID), which is also called the demarcation point or "demarc," for short.

Each of these interface devices, referred to as Internet gateways, is explained in Chapter 11, but briefly, here are the devices associated with each of the services listed in the previous section:

- **Cable** The Internet gateway provided by the cable service provider for its Internet services is a cable modem. Cable modems typically don't offer much more in the way of services. However, there are a wide variety of cable bridges, switches, and routers that can be used in place of a cable modem to gain several valuable control, security, and management functions.

- **Dialup** Nearly every computer has a modem either installed as an expansion card or built into the computer itself. Modems simply provide modulation services and not much more.

- **DSL** The Internet gateway used with DSL depends on the DSL in use. ADSL services use either a DSL modem or a bridge. These products are limited in their capabilities and services, much like a cable modem, but do typically offer multiple ports that allow multiple computers to share the service. SDSL services provide either a bridge or a router, with the router being the preferred device. A DSL router (see Figure 13-2) offers security, firewall, NAT, and other common router functions.

- **ISDN** The gateway device used with ISDN is called a terminal adapter and performs only ISDN reverse multiplexing services. Any additional services must be added through the installation of other network devices.

- **ISM/UNII/Satellite Internet** Like all broadband services, these wireless services require a wireless modem or bridge that is built into the receiver of the satellite service that produces a baseband signal usable to the internal network. Of course, there must also be an antenna as well.

Baseband versus Broadband

A distinction should be made between baseband and broadband transmission services. All high-speed Internet services are broadband services. This means they use a transmission

Figure 13-2

An SDSL router

Photo courtesy of Asante Technologies, Inc.

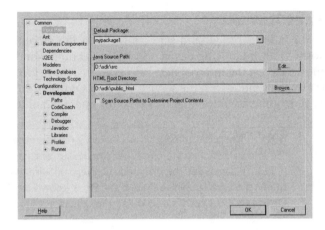

medium that is able to support a wide spectrum of transmitted signal frequencies. In other words, a broadband transmission service is able to carry multiple streams of audio, video, and data simultaneously. Each signal is carried over an individual, independent channel specific to the frequency of the signal.

Baseband is a networking technology that transmits its data over a single medium channel without frequency shifting. In practical terms, this means that a baseband network is able to transmit only one signal at a time. Ethernet is a baseband networking technology and it requires all of the nodes connected to the network medium to participate in every message sent over the network.

When you are looking for external networking services, such as Internet connectivity, you and the customer are looking for a broadband service.

Network Cabling

In a home network, the quality of the cable installation is far more important than the quality of the wire. Don't misunderstand: the quality of the cable is important, but how well the cable is installed can have a major impact on the performance of the network. It is critical that standard wiring practices and terminations be followed at all times.

New Construction

The type of network cable installed depends on the requirements the user defines for the network. The current cable standards, EIA/TIA 568 and 570, prescribe Cat 5 cabling (actually Cat 5e; the "e" means extended) for both data and voice networks. In a new construction situation, installing Cat 5e wire in the walls throughout the house, using a star topology (home runs), provides an infrastructure that should support the networking needs of the home for years to come. As a rule of thumb, each room in a home (those rooms where the home network is to be extended) should have at least two runs of Cat 5 cable—one each for voice and data.

Existing Structures

Retrofitting a home with Cat 5 wiring can prove to be a challenge. Pulling cable into existing walls, under floors, or over ceilings, while avoiding existing electrical wiring and fixtures and their interference problems, can be very difficult.

In these situations, the use of powerline, HomePNA (Home Phoneline Networking Alliance), or wireless systems should be seriously considered. The pros and cons of each type of medium needs to be discussed with the customers and the right mix of media selected to meet the client's needs. Of course, the primary consideration is still how well these systems can support both the data and automation network requirements.

 CROSS-REFERENCE See Chapter 5 for a discussion of the processes and best practices that should be used to install network cabling in a home, new or existing.

Cable Installation Standards

The primary concern for pulling cable into an existing, or new, structure is to spread the runs of the various cable types over as wide a space as possible. If it is absolutely necessary to cross cabling, there are standards and guidelines for the installation of low voltage cabling that cover overlap, separation, and crossing angles.

Here are the low-voltage cable installation guidelines you should follow:

- Use no more than 25 pounds of pull on the cable.

- Use at least 6-inches of separation between power and data cables.

- If a data cable crosses a power cable, it must do so at a 90-degree angle.

- A data cable should avoid fluorescent light fixtures.

- Cable sheathing can be stripped off not more than 1.25-inches from the connection end of the cable; 1-inch is recommended.

- UTP wire pairs should not be untwisted more than 0.5-inch; 0.375-inches is recommended.

- The bend radius of any network cable should not be more than 1-inch, but because some cable types are more sensitive than others, read the specifications of a cable before beginning installation.

When installing UTP cable, the total length of all cabling between a transmitting source and a terminating (receiving) device should not be more than 100 meters, which is a bit more than 300 feet. This doesn't mean just the longest run of cable between two points; it means all of the cable segments between two communicating devices. Actually, 95 meters is even better.

NOTE In North America, UTP is the most commonly used cable for low voltage (LV) installations. However, outside of North America, shielded twisted-pair (STP) and screened twisted-pair (ScTP) wiring is more common. As you read through this chapter and those that follow, please make the adjustment for your location and the cable types used in your area.

CROSS-REFERENCE Chapter 3 lists the recommended pre-wiring guidelines for low-voltage cabling.

RFI and EMI Interference

The purpose for the rules, standards, and guidelines of cable installation is to protect the cable and its electrical signals from external interference. Virtually anything electrical has the potential to generate sufficient interference to degrade the signal being carried in low-voltage cable. This is especially true when standard unshielded wire is used. UTP is highly susceptible to interference from any number of sources, including appliance motors, televisions, vacuum cleaners, AC power lines, nearby radio or cellular transmitters, and just about any other electrical source.

Contrary to common belief, interference on a UTP cable is cumulative. If a cable picks up interference at only two points along a long cable run, the effect can be cumulatively damaging. Each time the cable picks up additional voltage from an interference source, the risk also increases for damage to or loss of the signal quality.

Choosing the Cable

As discussed in Chapter 11, there are two basic networking cable types used in home network situations: twisted-pair and coaxial cable (RG6 or RG58). Some homeowners may choose to install fiber optic cabling, but typically the expense of using fiber optic cabling is prohibitive.

UTP/STP   Unshielded twisted-pair (UTP) cable is the lightest, most flexible, least expensive, and easiest to install of any of the popular physical network media. On the other hand, UTP is very vulnerable to interference and has attenuation issues as well, but for the most part, these issues can be overcome through proper use and installation. Unshielded twisted-pair (UTP) is the most commonly used cabling for networks because it is the easiest to install and maintain.

Inside a shielded twisted-pair (STP) cable, the wire pairs are wrapped in a copper or foil shield to help reduce EMI and RFI interference. The shielding makes STP more expensive than UTP wire, which is why it is not frequently used in home networking situations. However, if an existing home has more interference sources than can be easily avoided, STP may be the better choice of the twisted-pair pair.

Coaxial Cable   RG58 or RG6 coaxial cable is commonly found in many newer homes in the cable TV system that commonly has outlets in most of the rooms in the house. The primary differences between RG58 and RG6 are that RG58 has 100-ohm resistance and RG6 has 75-ohm resistance, and that RG6 has about twice the maximum distance of RG58, which is why RG6 is becoming more popular for networking purposes.

Coaxial cable has built-in features that make it more reliable than UTP, but it does cost more and is less forgiving to install. In existing home or retrofit situations, attempting to install new runs of coaxial cable may prove very difficult, if not virtually impossible. However, there are situations in which coaxial cable makes sense for a home network. In cases where network cabling must pass through, over, or under damp, wet, or extremely electrically noisy areas, coaxial cable is a better choice than either twisted-pair cable types. Of course, if the homeowner can afford it, fiber optic is even better, but on a cost-performance basis, coaxial cable is a good choice in these situations.

Cable Standards

Chapter 4 discusses the various electrical, wiring, and cable standards that apply to the structured wiring systems in a house, but here is a bit more on cable standards, especially in the context of designing and installing a computer network.

EIA/TIA 568

The EIA/TIA standards 568a and 568b are the most widely used cabling standards for computer network media. Included in these two standards are specifications and guidelines for six elements of computer network cabling:

- Backbone cabling
- Equipment rooms
- Entrance facilities
- Horizontal cabling
- Telecommunications closets
- Work areas

The 568 standard that directly affects home networking is the standard for horizontal cabling. This part of the standard covers the network media (cable, connectors, and so on) that run horizontally from the distribution facility or wiring closet to each of a network's nodes.

The 568 standard specifies that for each network location, there should be:

- At least two network connection outlets.
- A maximum distance of 90 meters (295 feet) for each cable segment of Cat 5 UTP cable in a horizontal run. Remember that Cat 5 cable itself is rated at 100 meters (328 feet). A cable segment is all of the cabling used to interconnect two communicating devices.
- Patch cords, cables used to interconnect two devices at a horizontal cross-connect, should not exceed 6 meters (19.6 feet) in length.
- Patch cords used to connect a computer to a wall outlet should not exceed 3 meters (9.8 feet).

- If the square footage of a building floor exceeds 1,000 square meters (over 10,000 square feet), or if any run of the horizontal cable exceeds 90 meters, another distribution facility should be added to the floor. Granted, this particular requirement is not likely to be a problem in most houses.

Distribution Panels, Cross-Connects, and Patch Panels

The primary distribution panel in an average house is the electrical panel. The electrical panel is the central point for the incoming electrical service and the service wiring of the home's electrical system. The electrical panel provides a central, single-point control and access unit for a home's electrical system.

In the same way, a single panel, closet, or center simplifies and centralizes the design, installation, and perhaps more importantly, the maintenance for the home's structured network cabling. The distribution panel should be centrally located in a house, but it is far more important that the distribution panel be central to the network to minimize the length of cable runs as much as possible. However, if the home has a natural or predesignated location for the distribution center, remember that cable is relatively inexpensive.

Figure 13-3 illustrates how a laundry room on the rear of a home can serve as the location for a central distribution facility for the network cable installed in the home.

Figure 13-3
A central point in the home should be chosen for the location of the home network's distribution panel.

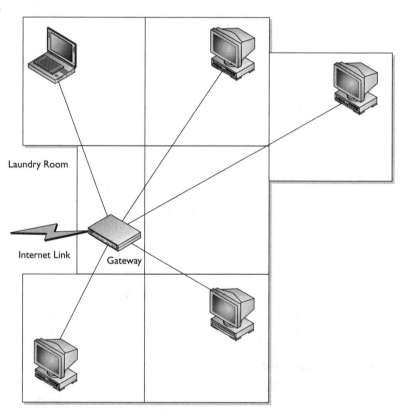

Laundry Room

Internet Link   Gateway

Figure 13-4 illustrates the physical components of a typical Ethernet network. The computers are connected into the jacks of a wall outlet using patch cords. The wall outlet is terminated with a punch down connection at a patch panel. The jack terminating the horizontal cable from the wall outlet is then interconnected into a hub, which provides connection to the network backbone.

In Figure 13-5, the patch cord that connects the patch panel to the hub creates what is called a *cross-connect*. Officially, a cross-connect is the connection made when the gap between a networked device's cabling is bridged to the network cabling. One of the most common methods of creating network cross-connects is to use a patch panel (see Figure 13-5). Each cable is terminated into a patch panel and then a patch cord is used to interconnect each port on the patch panel.

Cross-Connect Termination   Figure 13-4 shows horizontal cable runs coming into the distribution panel, but what if all of the horizontal cabling, say four UTP cables, must terminate at this point. You could install a 4-port hub before the patch panel to connect the runs to the network.

However, if at some point in the future, you or the customer needs to troubleshoot one of the cable runs, one of the first troubleshooting steps is to determine that the problem isn't the hub or one of its jacks. To do so, you'd have to disconnect one of the other runs and plug in the suspect cable. This is only a problem if none of the other workstations can be down while you test the lines.

PART III

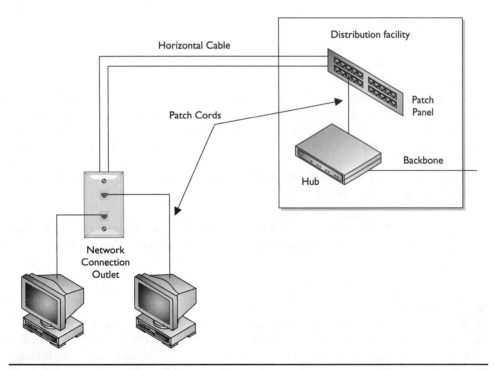

Figure 13-4   The components of a common Ethernet network

Figure 13-5

A patch panel is used to cross-connect horizontal cabling.

Photo courtesy of Signamax Connectivity Systems.

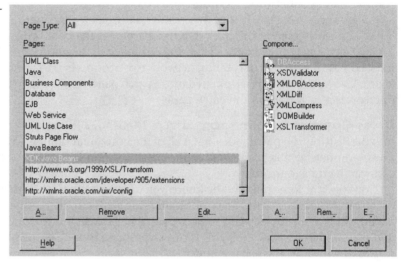

A better and recommended way to configure is to install a small patch panel that could be used as a distribution panel for telephone and audio wiring as well, eliminating the need for three central panels. Figure 13-5 shows a patch panel with 12 ports, but models are available with 4 to over 1,000 jacks, although 12 or 24-port patch panels are most commonly used in residential systems.

A cable run is attached to a patch panel jack by pushing each wire in the cable into a split tine using what is called a punch down or contact tool.

CROSS-REFERENCE See Chapters 3 and 4 for more information on EIA/TIA 568 standards and connecting network cable to a punch down jack.

Wall Outlets

Assuming a home network is using a wired installation, the cable plan must include wall jacks in those rooms where network access is to be provided. The type of jacks included on the outlet depends on exactly what service connections are to be supplied through the outlet. If the outlet is to provide a connection to the UTP horizontal cabling, then an

Figure 13-6
Wall outlets
can include
connections
for all the of
wired services
in a room.

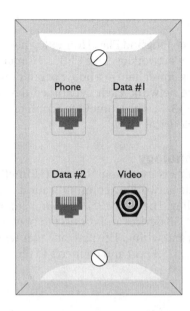

RJ-45 jack needs to be provided for each connection allowed in that outlet. However, if connections to other systems in the house are to be included on the outlet, the outlet could also include connection jacks for the telephones, video, audio, and television systems. Figure 13-6 illustrates a wall jack with two data network connections, a telephone connection, and a video connection.

Alternative Wired Solutions

The primary two choices for structured wiring alternatives are powerline and phone-line solutions, both of which are defined in Chapter 1. In the material that follows, we'll look at how these systems are connected to the wiring structure and the computer.

Powerline Technologies

There are three primary powerline technologies that can be used to network a home or extend the existing networks: CEBus, HomePlug, and X-10. X-10 is not useful as a structured-wiring network element and is better suited to on/off control and monitoring functions. I'll talk more about X-10 in Chapter 20.

CEBus

EIA and the Consumer Electronics Manufacturers Association (CEMA) developed CEBus (Consumer Electronics Bus) as a home communications standard over a decade ago. CEBus supports communication over 100V AC powerline, UTP, coaxial cable, and RF and IR signaling. The primary reason CEBus is not better known has been the lack of product development and the high cost of the few products that do exist. However, more CEBus products are becoming available.

HomePlug

Also known as Home Plug and Play, HomePlug has the most available products that can be used for computer networking. Like CEBus, HomePlug is primarily designed to transmit data over the existing power lines in a house or building. It operates as an Ethernet network.

On a HomePlug network, each networked device must connect into a HomePlug adapter (see Figure 13-7). The HomePlug adapter serves as the network adapter communicating over the electrical lines.

Phoneline Technology

The Home Phoneline Networking Alliance (HomePNA) has established a standard for devices that provide networking communication support over the existing phone lines in a house or building. The HomePNA network adapters can be found as PCI expansion cards and external USB devices and connect to network devices using standard telephone connectors (RJ-11) and wiring. The network adapter shown in Figure 13-8 connects to a computer through a USB port and connects to the HomePNA network using a standard phone cable and RJ-11 jack.

Figure 13-7
A HomePlug
outlet adapter
connects a
computer to
a powerline
network.

*Photo courtesy of
Cogency Semiconductor,
Inc.*

Figure 13-8
An example of a HomePNA USB phone line network adapter

Photo courtesy of 2Wire, Inc.

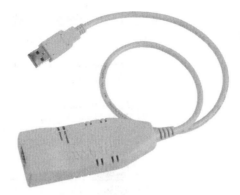

Configuring Network Clients

Perhaps the most important part of configuring a home network is the network configuration of each individual computer. Unless a computer is configured properly, it cannot communicate effectively across the network, regardless of whether it is connected on a peer-to-peer or a client/server network.

TCP/IP Configuration

Windows 2000 and XP have advanced network configuration to the point where it is almost automatic. If you are installing Windows 2000 or XP Professional or Windows XP Home on your home computers, there won't be much configuration for you to perform. The XP installation routine configures the computer to get its IP address configuration from DHCP and installs the appropriate protocols, services, and clients needed to communicate on a network.

On older Windows versions (Windows 9x and Windows NT Workstation), the network configuration must be done manually. The following steps detail the process you should use to configure Windows PCs in your home, and their NICs, to communicate on the network.

There are three ways to logically install a NIC: using the Add button on the Network window, using the Add New Hardware Wizard, or using the Plug and Play (PnP) functions of the PC. Assuming the NIC has been physically installed inside the computer case or attached to the appropriate external port, the steps used to configure a network adapter (NIC) so it is able to communicate with the network (using the Add button on the Network Properties window) are as follows:.

1. Access the Control Panel (Start | Settings | Control Panel). Find the Network icon and double-click it to open the Network properties window (see Figure 13-9).

   As shown in Figure 13-9, four networking components are configured on this window: adapters, protocols, clients, and services. Network services include specialized software that provides special capabilities, such as File and Printer Sharing for Microsoft Networks.

Figure 13-9
The Windows XP
Network
Properties
window

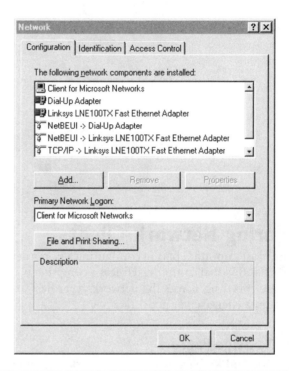

Network

Configuration | Identification | Access Control

The following network components are installed:

- Client for Microsoft Networks
- Dial-Up Adapter
- Linksys LNE100TX Fast Ethernet Adapter
- NetBEUI -> Dial-Up Adapter
- NetBEUI -> Linksys LNE100TX Fast Ethernet Adapter
- TCP/IP -> Linksys LNE100TX Fast Ethernet Adapter

[Add...] [Remove] [Properties]

Primary Network Logon:

Client for Microsoft Networks

[File and Print Sharing...]

Description

[OK] [Cancel]

TIP   For an alternative path to the Network window, right-click the Network Neighborhood or the My Network Places icon and choose Properties.

2. With the Configuration tab active, highlight the network adapter in the "The following network components are installed" box and click the Properties button.

   The adapter properties window opens with the Driver Type tab active. Assuming the NIC is a PCI card, the Driver Type tab should indicate an Enhanced mode (32-bit and 16-bit) NDIS (Network Device Interface Specification) driver for the NIC. The other choices listed are for network adapters that don't have 32-bit NDIS support or NICs requiring ODI (Open Data-Link Interface). Check the NIC's documentation if you are unsure which you have.

3. Choose the Bindings tab. The bindings should be preconfigured, but they can be modified. Binding means that two (or more) protocols have been associated. On an Ethernet network, the bindings reflect a binding of the NIC to the TCP/IP protocol stack.

TIP   Except for very rare instances, the Advanced tab is configured by the system and can be ignored.

4. On the Configuration tab, highlight the TCP/IP protocol for the network adapter in the installed components list. The entry should look something like TCP/IP <network adapter name>. Highlight this entry and click the Properties button to open the TCP/IP Properties window and select the IP Address tab, if necessary.

5. Choose the "Obtain an IP address automatically" option on the TCP/IP Properties window to have DHCP functions automatically configure the PC each time the PC is restarted. Otherwise, clear this option and enter the static (unchanging) IP address assigned to the PC into the box labeled "Specify an IP address" along with its subnet mask.

NOTE For security reasons, it's best for a home network to avoid using a static IP address.

TIP The DNS Configuration, WINS Configuration, and NetBIOS tabs are ignored during NIC configuration, unless your ISP has provided you information to enter. The IP address of the default gateway is entered on the Gateway tab. If you are using a cable or DSL modem, bridge, or router, refer to its manual to configure its functions, such as NAT, DHCP, ACLs, and more.

6. Click any and all Apply or OK buttons that appear. When asked to restart the system, do so.

Chapter Review

The process of planning and designing a home network, especially one that will be integrated into a home automation network, is an essential part of a successful project.

The primary choices for high-speed Internet connection services for most homes are cable Internet, DSL, and wireless ISM/UNII. Each of these services typically provides an Internet gateway device that is a modem, bridge, switch, or router.

Baseband communications use the full range of frequencies available on the medium to transmit, for example, Ethernet networking. Broadband communications, such as cable service, use individual and separate frequencies to transmit multiple messages simultaneously.

The primary cable choices for a home network are UTP or coaxial cable. Each has its advantages and disadvantages, but UTP is less expensive and easier to install and maintain. The EIA/TIA 568 standards provide the working specification for UTP cabling, including termination and cross-connection. Alternative network media choices include powerline (CEBus and X-10) and phoneline (HomePNA) technologies.

The computers connected to a TCP/IP network must be configured. Windows 2000 and Windows XP operating systems provide for automatic computer node configuration.

PART III

Questions

1. When installing data cabling, you encounter a situation in which you must cross over a power line. At what angle should the data cable cross the power cable?

   A. 30 degrees

   B. 45 degrees

   C. 90 degrees

   D. 180 degrees

2. What is the primary network cabling standard used in North America?

   A. RS 232

   B. EIA/TIA 432

   C. EIA/TIA 568

   D. IEC

3. After installing the wiring in a home network, you are running your data cable certification testing and fail the length test on the cable segment that runs to a far upstairs bedroom. In checking out the problem, you discover that the cable link is 295 feet long and there is a 20-foot patch cord connecting the computer to the wall outlet and a 15-foot patch cord connecting the patch panel to the Internet gateway. Which of the following is likely the cause of the problem?

   A. The link cable is too long.

   B. The home run cabling is too long.

   C. The patch cord at the computer is too long.

   D. The patch cord at the patch panel is too long.

4. Which of the following is not an Internet connection service commonly used in home networking situations?

   A. DSL

   B. ISM

   C. ISDN

   D. T-3

5. What Internet gateway device is generally used with an SDSL service?

   A. Modem

   B. Bridge

   C. Terminal adapter

   D. Router

6. Which of the following is true about broadband communications?

    A. Broadband and baseband are equivalent services.

    B. Broadband communications can carry only one signal at a time.

    C. Broadband communications can carry multiple signals at a time.

    D. Broadband communications are rarely used for home installations.

7. Which two of the following networking media are coaxial cabling types?

    A. RG6

    B. RG58

    C. UTP

    D. Existing electrical wiring

8. Which of the following technologies is not a powerline technology?

    A. HomePlug

    B. CEBus

    C. HomePNA

    D. X-10

9. Before a computer is able to communicate on an Ethernet network, it must first be configured with

    A. Microsoft Client for NetWare Networks

    B. Print and File Sharing

    C. TCP/IP

    D. IPX/SPX

10. What connector type is used to terminate a UTP cable?

    A. RS-232

    B. RJ-11

    C. RJ-45

    D. RG-45

Answers

1. **C.** A data cable must cross a power line at a 90-degree angle, no less and no more.

2. **C.** Let's hope you know this by now. You definitely need to know this for the exam. EIA/TIA 232 and EIA/TIA 432 are legacy cabling standards for serial connections. IEC is an international connection standard.

3. **B.** If you add up the lengths of the cables that make up the channel, the total comes to 335 feet. The specified total length for a Cat 5 channel is 328 feet. Remember that the channel length includes all cable segments used to connect a computer to its signal source. The cable link is only the portion between the patch panel and the wall outlet and it is at the maximum acceptable length.

4. **D.** DSL, ISM (wireless DSL), and ISDN are all common Internet connection services used with home networks. A T-3 communications line is a physical media technology that supplies bandwidth only.

5. **D.** A router is used with SDSL because it is assumed that because of its higher bandwidth and cost, it is installed for use in larger networking situations. The other devices listed are used with dialup/cable, cable/wireless, and ISDN, respectively.

6. **C.** Answers A and D are just false and answer B describes a characteristic of baseband communications.

7. **A and B.** RG6 and RG58 are types of coaxial cable. The other choices are commonly used in home networking situations.

8. **C.** HomePNA is a phoneline networking technology. The other choices are all powerline technologies.

9. **C.** None of the other choices are required for a computer to communicate over a TCP/IP or Ethernet network.

10. **C.** RS-232 is a legacy serial communications standard; an RJ-11 connector is used in telephone connections; and an RG-45, if it exists, would be a cabling standard.

Troubleshooting a Home Network

In this chapter, you will learn about:
- Troubleshooting network connections
- Troubleshooting network cabling
- Troubleshooting a network PC's configuration

Tracking down a problem on a network is often more of an issue of where to begin looking than it is resolving the problem. Often a network problem is easily remedied once you're able to pinpoint its source.

Networks, including home networks, bring together several layers of technology—cable, hardware, and software—all capable of causing or contributing to a network or a networked computer not performing properly.

In this chapter, we look at some of the ways you can diagnose and resolve problems on a network, including testing network cabling, a network connection, and a networked computer's configuration.

Be consistent: list problems then create solution checklists, or list each problem with its own checklist.

Troubleshooting Network Connections

Any number of things can go wrong with network connections, but generally, and especially in a home environment, once they are configured properly and working, network connections tend to continue to work until something is changed on the computer or its network. So, the first thing to check, if the network or a computer develops connection problems, is whether or not anything has changed recently.

Troubleshooting Dialup Connections

If a dialup connection fails to connect, there are five areas to check:

- Phone connections
- Modem problems

- Protocols
- Remote responses
- Telephone company or phone line problems
  - **Phone connection**   If there is no dial tone present, you should get an error message displayed on the computer to that effect. The sound produced by nearly all modems is there for the user to track the action of the connection (called a handshake, which is the activities involved with two modems negotiating the connection) as it is being made. The first of these sounds is the dial tone from the phone line. If the modem is not connecting and you don't hear a dial tone, there is likely a problem with the phone service, wall jack, the wire, the RJ-11 connector, or the connection between the connector and the wall jack. Of course, this assumes that you are getting a dial tone on all other phone connections.
  - **Modem problems**   If the modem is failing to complete the handshake with the modem at the other end and a timeout or connection failed message is displayed on the PC, it is likely that the modem is configured incorrectly in terms of its character length, start and stop bits, and speed. Check with the technical support people at the Internet Service Provider (ISP) to verify what the modem's settings should be. Depending on the modem, these settings can be made through software on the PC or may have to be made through toggle switches (DIP switches) on the modem. Set the modem configuration as required and retry the connection.
  - **Protocols**   Protocol problems are common with new modems and typically the modem's Transmission Control Protocol/Internet Protocol (TCP/IP) or another protocol has not been properly configured. Remember that dialup connections require the Point-to-Point Protocol (PPP). Verify that the proper TCP/IP protocols are enabled and that the proper bindings (protocols linked to one another) are set. If you aren't sure which protocols or bindings are required, contact the service provider's technical support for this information.
  - **Remote response**   The ISP network access server (NAS) to which you are attempting to connect may be down or having problems. The dialer may also be dialing an incorrect number or be configured improperly with other erroneous information. Before making any assumptions about why this may be happening, call the ISP's technical support people or have the customer call to verify these settings.
  - **Telephone company or phone line problems**   Static or crosstalk on the telephone line can cause a modem to disconnect frequently and, typically, very soon after completing a connection. Line noise can also cause so many data retransmissions that the connection's data speed can appear exceptionally slow. Another common problem is call-waiting being active on the modem line because the signaling that is sent to indicate a call is waiting will interrupt

the connection. If call-waiting is enabled on a line, you can temporarily suspend it by dialing *70 on the appropriate line before reattempting to dial out through the modem.

Troubleshooting a DSL or Cable Connection

The problems associated with a digital subscriber line (DSL) or cable connection are typically one of a set of common issues. DSL bridges and routers do have a few problems specific to them, just as cable modems have their unique problems. However, for the most part, connection issues for DSL and cable modems are very similar. The next few sections list the more common connection problems for these services and how to resolve them.

Common DSL and Cable Connection Problems

Here are the more common problems a customer could experience with a DSL connection:

- Authentication
- Link control
- Physical connection
- Sync
    - **Authentication**   If the connection fails to establish during a startup, the username and password being used to log onto the system or the configuration settings on the computer or Internet gateway may be erroneous. Understand that although DSL (and cable) are "always on" services, should the customer shut down (power off) his computer, then when the computer is powered on, a boot and sign on sequence occurs where these errors may appear.
    - **Link control**   If the connection link is established and then quickly dropped, the problem is likely one of configuration on the computer. Verify that the computer's settings match those indicated in the user documentation for the DSL or cable modem. If the computer's configuration is as it should be, contact the service provider for assistance.
    - **Physical connection**   If the connection is intermittent, there is something wrong with the physical connection. Verify the connections to the computer and Internet gateway and if they are properly connected, have the customer call the service provider.
    - **Sync**   To work properly, DSL and cable lines must be "in sync," or in synchronization, which means that the Internet gateway is connected and receiving a signal over the phone or cable line. In other words, the line must have a link established even if no data is being transmitted. Use the owner's manual for the Internet gateway to determine from the status light-emitting diodes (LEDs) on the device whether or not a link is established and the link is in sync. If the connection is not in sync, power off the computer and then

PART III

the Internet gateway device. Wait about 30 seconds and then power up the Internet gateway and then the computer. This should establish and sync-up the connection. If the problem persists, contact the service provider's technical support line.

DSL/Cable Troubleshooting Checklist

Before calling the technical support function or a service provider, here is a list of things to check so that you can be fairly confident of the source and nature of the problem:

1. Check the power connection on the Internet gateway device.

2. Check the cable/phone line connection on the Internet gateway device for snugness and to ensure that there are no free wires or cuts or breaks in the wiring connecting to the source.

3. Check the RJ-45 connection to the computer for snugness, free wires, or cuts or breaks in the patch cord.

4. Check the link lights on both the Internet gateway and the network adapter on the computer for activity and sync.

Troubleshooting Wireless Connections

If a computer equipped with a wireless network adapter is having a connection problem, the first step in troubleshooting the problem is to verify that the computer has recognized the wireless network adapter and that the appropriate device driver software has been properly installed. To troubleshoot this problem, follow these steps:

1. **Hardware check**   To check the network adapter and the device driver software, use the Windows Device Manager. If a red "x" or a yellow "i" icon is displayed next to the wireless network adapter's name instead of a small icon of a network card, you need to reinstall the network adapter and driver after checking the Hardware Compatibility List (HCL) for the Windows version running on the computer.

2. **Settings check**   If the network adapter and driver are properly installed, the next thing to check is the computer's network settings. Use the documentation for the network adapter and the network access point (NAP) to verify the settings for the adapter.

3. **Signal strength and link quality test**   The procedure used to check the signal strength and the link quality varies by manufacturer, so reference the device documentation for the process used for the specific network adapter and NAP in use. If moving the computer closer to the NAP eliminates this problem, this is definitely the issue.

4. **Renew IP configuration**   Under the heading of "if all else fails," use IPCONFIG to release and renew the Dynamic Host Configuration Protocol (DHCP) settings for the computer (see the following section for instructions on how to do this).

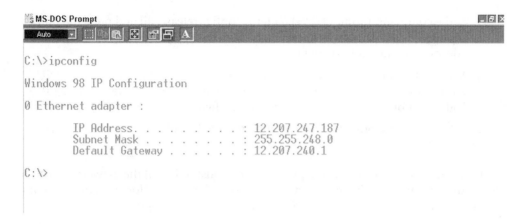

Figure 14-1   The output produced by the IPCONFIG command

Troubleshooting DHCP Problems

If after booting or restarting a networked PC, no network connection is present, a good place to begin your diagnosis is by running the IPCONFIG command. Figure 14-1 shows a sample of the output produced by this command. Notice the entry for "IP Address." In Figure 14-1, the IP address is fine, reflecting an address has been assigned to the PC by a DHCP server on the network, either locally or at the ISP.

Should a networked computer boot up and not find a DHCP server available, the computer will complete its boot cycle by using an Automatic Private IP Addressing (APIPA), which is a nonfunctioning IP address from a range reserved by Microsoft for just this purpose. When this happens, unless the PC requesting an IP address is able to get one, it will continue to poll for an IP address from the DHCP server after waiting increasingly longer wait periods. This process continues until the networked PC finally gets an IP address from a DHCP server.

The address provided by APIPA allows the PC (DHCP client) to automatically configure itself with an IP address from the range of 169.254.0.1 to 169.254.254.255 using a Class B subnet mask of 255.255.0.0. Understand that this IP address is merely a placeholder and cannot be used to access the network.

When a PC is unable to obtain an IP address from the DHCP server, check with the ISP to try to determine why this may be happening. The problem could very well be that the ISP's DHCP server is down. However, if the ISP indicates that there is no reason for a computer to not be able to get its IP configuration from its DHCP server, you should try releasing and renewing the DHCP "lease" using the following process (on Windows 98, Me, NT, 2000, and XP computers):

1. Click on the Start button and choose Run from the Start menu.

2. In the Open: box, enter "cmd" ("command" for Windows 98 and Me) and click OK. This will open a command prompt window.

3. At the command prompt (C:\>), enter ipconfig /release_all and press the Enter key. IPCONFIG will confirm the release with a display showing zeroes in the IP Address and Subnet Mask fields.

4. At the command prompt, enter ipconfig /renew_all and press Enter. IPCONFIG should confirm the renewal of the IP configuration data with values in the IP Address, Subnet Mask, and Default Gateway fields.

5. At the command prompt, enter exit and press the Enter key to close the command prompt window.

If this process fails to correct the problem, you must re-install the network adapter's device drivers and reconfigure the network protocols settings. Before retesting the connection, verify the network settings with the ISP's technical support.

Troubleshooting Network Connections

Another reason a PC may not be automatically configured by the network is that it no longer has a network connection or for some reason the network has stopped communicating with it. There are two TCP/IP utilities that can be used to make an initial diagnosis of this problem.

PING

The first is the PING utility. This command sends out a message that requests that a remote device with a specific IP Address or domain reply with a message (an echo). If this activity succeeds, you know the connection between the two devices is valid. The PING command also times this process. A slow response time could indicate congestion or perhaps a mechanical problem along the way. Figure 14-2 shows the output produced by the PING command.

NOTE The Domain Name System (DNS) is used to identify the IP Address of the domain name "osborne.com." This IP Address is then used by the PING command to send its messages.

However, if the PING command cannot find or doesn't receive a response from the destination address or domain entered, an error message will indicate that.

TraceRoute

The second command that you can use to determine if there is a path problem between two network devices is the TraceRoute utility. This traces and tracks the path used by a message to reach a remote destination IP Address by displaying each router or internetworking device the message passes through on its journey. The time used for each "hop" is also displayed to help diagnose possible bottlenecks on the network. Figure 14-3 shows the output produced by a TRACERT command.

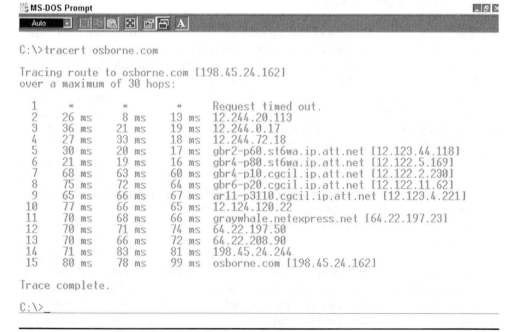

```
MS-DOS Prompt                                                      _ 🗗 ×
Auto                 🖻🖻  🖽  🖼🖨  A

C:\>ping osborne.com

Pinging osborne.com [198.45.24.162] with 32 bytes of data:

Reply from 198.45.24.162: bytes=32 time=71ms TTL=241
Reply from 198.45.24.162: bytes=32 time=78ms TTL=241
Reply from 198.45.24.162: bytes=32 time=86ms TTL=241
Reply from 198.45.24.162: bytes=32 time=78ms TTL=241

Ping statistics for 198.45.24.162:
    Packets: Sent = 4, Received = 4, Lost = 0 (0% loss),
Approximate round trip times in milli-seconds:
    Minimum = 71ms, Maximum =  86ms, Average =   78ms

C:\>_
```

Figure 14-2   The results of a PING command

```
MS-DOS Prompt                                                      _ 🗗 ×
Auto                 🖻🖻  🖽  🖼🖨  A

C:\>tracert osborne.com

Tracing route to osborne.com [198.45.24.162]
over a maximum of 30 hops:

  1     *         *         *      Request timed out.
  2    26 ms      8 ms     13 ms  12.244.20.113
  3    36 ms     21 ms     19 ms  12.244.0.17
  4    27 ms     33 ms     18 ms  12.244.72.18
  5    30 ms     20 ms     17 ms  gbr2-p60.st6wa.ip.att.net [12.123.44.118]
  6    21 ms     19 ms     16 ms  gbr4-p80.st6wa.ip.att.net [12.122.5.169]
  7    68 ms     63 ms     60 ms  gbr4-p10.cgcil.ip.att.net [12.122.2.230]
  8    75 ms     72 ms     64 ms  gbr6-p20.cgcil.ip.att.net [12.122.11.62]
  9    65 ms     66 ms     67 ms  ar11-p3110.cgcil.ip.att.net [12.123.4.221]
 10    77 ms     66 ms     65 ms  12.124.120.22
 11    70 ms     68 ms     66 ms  graywhale.netexpress.net [64.22.197.23]
 12    70 ms     71 ms     74 ms  64.22.197.50
 13    70 ms     66 ms     72 ms  64.22.208.90
 14    71 ms     83 ms     81 ms  198.45.24.244
 15    80 ms     78 ms     99 ms  osborne.com [198.45.24.162]

Trace complete.

C:\>
```

Figure 14-3   The display of the TRACERT command

PART III

TraceRoute is implemented on various systems as TRACEROUTE, TRACERT, or TRACE, with TRACERT used on Windows systems. This command displays the complete route from a source IP address to a destination IP address. TRACERT transmits probe packets one at a time to each router or switch on the path between the source and the destination. When an echo is received at the source, the round-trip time for that hop is displayed. TRACERT displays only two different events: the time (called time-to-live or TTL) was exceeded or the destination was unreachable. This information is very helpful in determining if there is a breakdown or bottleneck in a particular route.

Testing Network Wiring

The benefit that comes from planning a network before installing it is that you and the customer both know what to expect when you are done, right? The downside may be that by the same token both you and the customer know what to expect.

The only way you can assure yourself and demonstrate to the customer that the network's wiring and infrastructure supports the network to be installed on it is with a planned and formal test procedure that incorporates the Transmission Performance Specifications for Field-Testing of Unshielded Twisted-Pair Cabling Systems (TIA/EIA TSB-67 for short) and TSB-95, which provides additional test parameters for Cat 5 wiring.

Cable Certification Testing

A number of handheld devices are available to perform the tests prescribed in these two TSB standards. In fact, a variety of Cat 5 testers are available to perform what is called a certified test. By certifying the cable, the customer is assured that the network wiring is installed to specification and is ready to support any network-capable devices attached to the network. Certifying the cable also provides a benchmark for any future network or cable problems. However, Cat 5 testing devices can be quite expensive. Cable testing units include a master unit and a slave unit, which are attached to the ends of the cable segment being tested, and an auto-test function that measures the results of the test as either a pass or a fail.

Essentially, Cat 5 testing units perform two tests: a link test and a channel test. The link test measures the end-to-end connectivity of a cable segment and is typically run on the cable running from the distribution panel to a wall outlet. A channel test extends the link test to include devices attached to the cable segment.

A Cat 5 link (cable only) should not be more than 295 feet (90 meters) in length. A Cat 5 channel shouldn't be more than 328 feet (100 meters) in length. A link is a single cable run and a channel is all of the cable and connections between two communicating devices. The difference of 33 feet or 10 meters between a link and a channel represents the cables used to connect a computer or other device to a link. So what this boils down to is that the cable running between a patch panel and a wall jack can only be 90 meters in length and all of the cables used to complete the connection between a computer and a central device (such as a gateway or router) cannot exceed 100 meters in length.

EIA/TIA TSB Tests

The Telecommunications Industry Association/ Electronic Industries Alliance (TIA/EIA) TSB standards specify standard cable testing procedures. The standard TSB tests are

- **Attenuation test**   This test measures the attenuation affect on a signal transmitted on a cable. A series of frequencies up to 100 MHz is transmitted on each wire pair at one end of a link and the strength of the signal received at the other end of the cable is measured.

- **Length test**   As it sounds, this test measures the length of a cable segment. The test is set up to test both links and channels using what is called time domain reflectometry, or TDR technology. TDR emits a signal pulse and then calculates the length of the cable based on what is called nominal velocity of propagation (NVP). The result of this test is the distance to a reflection point on the cable. On a good cable, the distance displayed should be the length of the actual cable run. However, if there is a problem on the cable, such as a break, kink, short, or the like, the length test will return the distance to that problem.

- **Near-end crosstalk test (NEXT)**   This test places a test signal on one pair of wires and then measures all of the other wire pairs for signal presence to see how much crosstalk the cable is allowing. Crosstalk is electromagnetic signals on one wire being picked up by another wire.

- **Wire-map test**   This looks at each individual wire in the cable and whether or not it maps to the same pin at each end of the cable. This test is used to identify connector and pinning errors on a cable segment.

Any link that fails one of these tests should be replaced or, in the case of the length test, shortened. If a channel fails, you may need to test the patch cords used to connect the networked device to the link to decide if the problem is in the cable link or patch cords.

Wire testing should be performed in the pre-wire phase of a new construction project and then again before the network devices are attached.

If the network is to use powerline or phone line, any line problems should also be affecting the AC power or the telephone lines. If not, the problem is either with the media adapter or the patch cord used to connect a device to the adapter.

Simple Cable Testing Devices

It isn't totally necessary in every situation for the cable to be certified. Often, especially as part of a troubleshooting procedure, all that is needed is to a test for signal continuity, assuming the initial installation was properly tested. Whereas cable certification devices can cost thousands of dollars, quality cable testers range in capability from all-in-one devices to continuity testers and most are reasonably priced. For home automation networking, you should consider a multiple media tester, like the one shown in Figure 14-4.

Figure 14-4
A multiple media,
multiple function
LAN cable tester

*Photo courtesy of North
Hills Signal Processing.*

Configuring Network Computers

In a majority of situations, a network connection problem typically occurs when something has changed on a networked computer. This doesn't mean that cable, connector, service provider, and Internet gateway problems don't occur, only that these components of a network continue to work until changes are made.

When I say changes to a network computer, I don't only mean changes to the computer's networking configuration or equipment. Changes can include new software, new hardware, and the conflicts they may create. So, the Number 1 troubleshooting step when diagnosing a networked computer for connection problems is to determine if anything, and I mean anything, has changed on the computer and remove it to see if the problem goes away. Then you can deal with the issues being created and solve the larger issue of incompatibility.

Configuring a Windows Computer

When configuring a computer on a home network, you must check the installation of the network adapter and TCP/IP protocols and verify operations.

Checking the Network Adapter

Windows 2000 and XP use Plug-and-Play (PnP) technology to detect and configure an internal network interface card (NIC) installed in a Peripheral Components Interconnect (PCI) slot. However, before you get too far along with connecting a computer to the network, you should verify the NIC's settings. To do this, use these steps:

1. To open the properties window for the NIC, you have two navigation choices:

    a. Click the Start button and choose Settings from the Start menu and then Network and Dial-up Connections from the Settings menu.

   b. Right-click the My Network Places icon on the Desktop and choose Network and Dial-up Connections.
   Right-click the network connection that is or will be connected to the network to display the properties window for the NIC (see Figure 14-5).

2. In the panel labeled "Components checked are used by this connection," highlight Internet Protocol (TCP/IP), and then click the Properties button below the panel. The TCP/IP Properties window (see Figure 14-6) will open.

3. Verify that the Obtain an IP address and the Obtain DNS server address automatically are selected and if not, change the settings so that they are the only items with their radio buttons (a round option button) selected.

4. Click OK on this dialog box and the next window to configure the TCP/IP client. Windows 2000 computers must be restarted to set the configuration, but Windows XP computers don't require that step. The Windows 2000 computer will be assigned its IP configuration during the startup and the Windows XP computer gets the configuration after a few minutes. Use the IPCONFIG command (see "Troubleshooting DHCP Problems" earlier in the chapter) to verify the settings.

Figure 14-5
The NIC
Properties
Window on
a Windows 2000/
XP computer

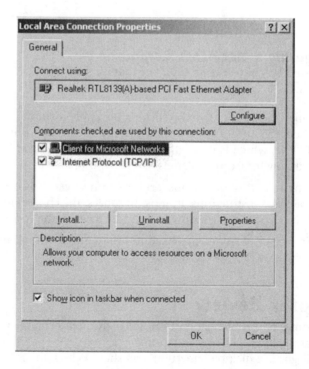

PART III

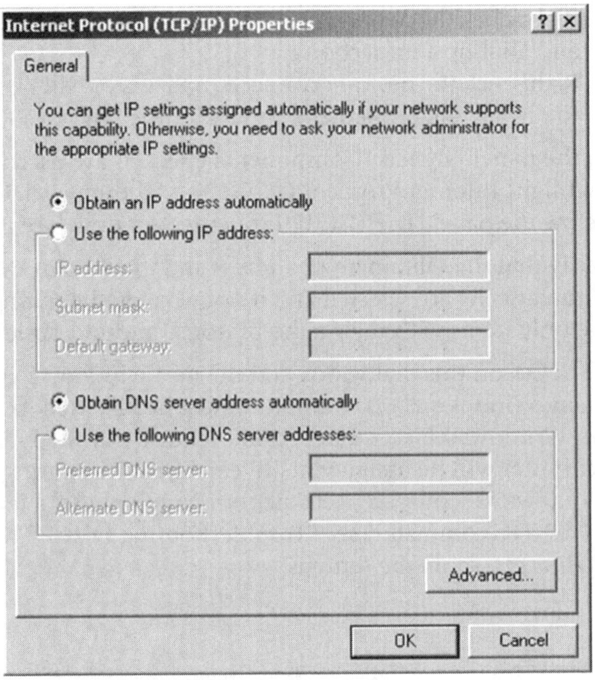

Figure 14-6

The Internet Protocol (TCP/IP) window on a Windows 2000/XP computer.

Configuring a Macintosh Computer

To enable a Macintosh computer, one that is running Mac OS 7 or later, use the following steps:

1. Open the Apple menu by clicking the apple icon on the top menu bar and choose Control Panels from the menu. From the Control Panels menu, choose TCP/IP, which is located near the bottom of the list. If the system opens a window for Control Panels, choose the TCP/IP icon.

2. On the TCP/IP dialog box, set the Connect via choice according to the Internet gateway's instructions. In most instances, the choice should be Using DHCP Server. Close the window and choose Save on the confirmation box.

3. Some Mac systems may need to restart at this point, and a message will be displayed indicating this.

Chapter Review

Most computer problems occur immediately after a change is made to the computer's hardware, software, or configuration.

To diagnose a dialup connection, you should check the following: the phone connection, the modem settings, the protocol configuration on the computer, the service provider's NAS, and if there are technical issues on the phone line.

To troubleshoot a DSL or cable connection, you should check the following: authentication, link control, the physical connection, and if the system has synchronized (is in sync). To diagnose a connection problem on a DSL or cable connection, check the power connection on the Internet gateway, the phone or cable connection to the Internet gateway, the RJ-45 connection to the computer and the Internet gateway, and the link lights on the Internet gateway and the network adapter, and verify the integrity of all cables.

To troubleshoot a wireless connection, perform a hardware check on the computer using the Device Manager to verify that the network adapter is properly installed and functioning, check the network settings on the computer, test the signal strength and the link quality between the computer and the NAP, and release and renew the IP configuration on the computer.

Many networked computer issues are related to the network configuration on the computer, especially in the DHCP settings. To check these settings, run the IPCONFIG command to display the IP configuration on the computer. A quick way to see if a computer is having DHCP problems is to run IPCONFIG; if the computer is assigned an IP in the range of 169.254.0.1 to 169.254.254.255, the DHCP is not functioning properly.

Two tools that you can use to check a computer's connection are the PING command to ping the Internet gateway and TRACERT to see if there is a routing issue between the home network and the service provider.

If you suspect the connection problem may be in the network media, you can run the TIA/EIA TSB-67 tests on the cable to check its attenuation, length, NEXT, and wire-mapping. Cable testing devices are generally inexpensive and readily available.

A common source for connection problems on a computer is its network configuration. The newer Windows systems (2000 and XP) virtually auto-configure themselves to a network, but you should check the network adapter's settings as part of your troubleshooting.

Questions

1. Which of the following is not likely the source of a modem connection problem?

   A. Modem

   B. Phone line

   C. Network adapter

   D. PPP protocol settings

2. Which of the following can cause a DSL/cable connection to fail because of username and password issues?

   A. Authentication

   B. Synchronization

   C. Link control

   D. Bad physical connection

3. What is one of the first things you should check to see if a physical connection, link, and sync have been established on a DSL/cable connection?

A. Temperature of the patch cord

B. Link/activity lights

C. Computer's TCP/IP settings

D. Service provider technical help

4. Of the following, which troubleshooting step is not performed on a computer using a wireless network adapter to connect to a network?

A. Hardware check

B. Setting check

C. Signal strength and link quality test

D. Renew DHCP configuration

5. What command can be used to verify the IP configuration on a computer?

A. PING

B. TRACERT

C. IPCONFIG

D. DNS

6. When a network computer cannot find a DHCP server, what service is used to assign the computer an IP address?

A. DNS

B. RARP

C. BOOTP

D. APIPA

7. Which TCP/IP command is used to verify the connection between two network devices?

A. TRACERT

B. DHCP

C. PING

D. IPCONFIG

8. What TCP/IP command is used to determine if a problem exists on the routing path between two network devices?

A. TRACERT

B. DHCP

C. PING

D. IPCONFIG

9. What is the cable testing standard for Cat 5 wiring?

    A. EIA/TIA 232

    B. EIA/TIA 568

    C. EIA/TIA TSB-67

    D. IEEE 802.3

10. Which is the technology used to check the length of a cable?

    A. Attenuation

    B. TDR

    C. NEXT

    D. Wire-map

Answers

1. **C.** A modem connects to a computer through its serial port and not a network adapter. The other choices can each contribute to a modem connection problem.

2. **A.** This step verifies the username and password of the link attempting to log into the DSL/cable service provider's network. The other choices, with the exception of a bad physical connection of course, are aspects of the link established between the Internet gateway and the ISP.

3. **B.** If there are no lights on or flashing on the Internet gateway, then something is seriously wrong with the connection. There could be something wrong with the TCP/IP settings, but the other choices are just silly.

4. **C.** All of the others are performed on the computer.

5. **C.** DNS is used to translate domain names into their IP address equivalents. (See questions 7 and 8 for PING and IPCONFIG.)

6. **D.** This service assigns a temporary IP address that allows the computer to complete its startup. RARP and DNS are used to look up IP addresses, and the computer uses BOOTP to request its DHCP information.

7. **C.** PING sends out an echo request message and if present or connected, the receiving station sends back an echo response.

8. **A.** TRACERT times the connection between each of the routers (hops) located on the path between two network devices.

9. **C.** This standard, along with TSB-95, establishes the testing procedures for Cat 5 wiring.

10. **B.** TDR emits a signal pulse and then calculates the length of the cable based on NVP.

PART IV

Audio/Video Systems

Distributed Audio System Basics

In this chapter, you will learn about:
- Audio concepts and basic terminology
- Different types of distributed audio systems
- Audio system hardware and components
- Different types of audio source equipment

The ability to have high-fidelity (Hi-Fi) music in every room of a home is no longer limited to the owners of million dollar mansions with unlimited budgets. With existing technology, the cost of installing a whole house audio system has fallen to the point where such a system can be a reality for virtually any homeowner.

Installing a distributed audio system, one that distributes audio throughout a house, allows the customer to virtually replicate his or her audio source equipment into every room of the house. The expense of actually installing Hi-Fi audio equipment in every room is prohibitive for most homeowners, but with a relatively modest investment in wiring, speakers, and controls, every room in the house can have radio and recorded music playback.

In this, and the next few, chapters, we look at the basics of a distributed audio systems, as well as a more detailed examination of the hardware and wiring, and installation procedures required, along with a few troubleshooting techniques.

Audio Systems Basics

Audio systems have a language all their own and when you help a homeowner choose the system and features that will work best for his or her needs and budget, you should be able to speak the language. The customer may have a number of questions about how one system may be a better choice than another or why one feature should be used over another, and with an understanding of audio system terminology and concepts, you will have the answers. On the other hand, the customer may be an audiophile that really knows his or her stuff or someone that knows the terms, but doesn't quite have the meanings down. In either case, being well-versed in audio systems is sure to contribute to the design and installation of a system that satisfies the customer's wishes, wants, and needs.

The audio terms and concepts you should know, at a minimum, are

- Sound characteristics
- Analog versus digital audio signals
- Line-level versus speaker-level
- Balanced versus unbalanced
- Electrical properties
- Surround sound

Sound Characteristics

Before you can understand audio systems, you need to first understand sound and how it is generated, heard, and transmitted. After all, what an audio system does is reproduce sound that has been recorded on some form of analog or digital media.

Sound is produced when an object creates vibrations in air, liquid, or something solid. I am going to deal with sound vibrations in the air first and discuss how sound is generated from a speaker later in the section titled "Speaker Basics."

Vibrating Air

When any object vibrates, it agitates the air around it, which makes the molecules in the air bounce around and a chain reaction starts. The moving molecules cause other air molecules to begin moving, and so on. This movement of the air molecules, which is caused by the originating vibration, is how sound moves through the air: one set of moving molecules causes others to move or vibrate. All of this vibration creates a pulsing wave of moving air molecules that travels through the air—something like ripples in a pond. The effect is a series of pulse waves with increased and decreased air pressure.

Your ears contain eardrums, which are thin membranes of skin. The eardrum catches the vibrating wave of air pressure and begins to vibrate. Your brain then interprets the vibrations of the eardrum into what we hear as sound.

A vibrating object creates a fluctuating wave of air pressure that moves through the air (or liquid or solids) to our ear, and our brain "hears" it as a voice, some music, or a whole range of other sounds. What causes one sound to be heard differently than another? Different sounds have different vibration patterns and air pressure fluctuations, which translate into a sound's frequency and amplitude.

Frequency and Amplitude

The frequency of a sound wave represents the number of times the air pressure of the wave fluctuates up and down in a certain period of time. Each fluctuation cycle (measured from the peak of one wave to the peak of the next wave, as shown in Figure 15-1) represents one sound wave and its wavelength.

How many waves occur in a set period of time, such as a second or a fraction of a second, represents the sound wave's frequency, or how frequent the sound wave fluctuates

Figure 15-1
The characteristics of a sound wave

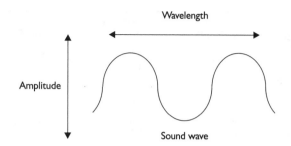

over time. As is illustrated in Figure 15-2, sound waves can have a higher frequency, meaning there are more waves in a time period, or a lower frequency, meaning there are less waves in a time period. High frequency sound waves are heard as higher-pitched sounds and low frequency sound waves are heard as lower-pitched sounds. The frequency of a sound wave is equivalent to the sound's pitch.

Another characteristic of sound waves is amplitude, which translates into how loud the sound is heard. The height of a sound wave, as shown in Figure 15-1, is its amplitude. The amplitude of a sound wave also represents the amount of air pressure in the wave. Higher amplitudes hit the eardrum harder and are heard as louder sounds.

Decibels

There is a relationship between the volume level a speaker produces and the amount of power an amplifier produces. The loudness of the sound coming from a speaker is a fairly subjective thing, with each listener having his or her version of what is too loud or not loud enough. In order to set how loud a speaker should be, a scale is used to determine a level that's acceptable to everyone and serves as a standard setting. For the sound produced by a speaker (and sound produced by just about anything), the measurement used is the decibel (dB).

A dB measures the intensity or the level of a sound. This logarithmic scale is able to represent a wide range of sound level measurements with relatively simple numbers. However, because decibel measurements are logarithmic, they can also be confusing; for example, 2.0 dB is not twice as loud as 1.0 dB. Table 15-1 shows the relationship of different dB levels to line voltage (signal strength), power (watts of amplifier output), and volume (the loudness of a speaker's output).

Figure 15-2
High frequency sound waves (top) have a higher pitch than low frequency sound waves (bottom).

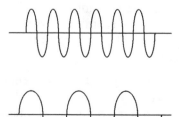

Table 15-1 The relationship of dB, Voltage, Power, and Volume in Sound Reproduction	dB Increase	Voltage Increase	Power Increase	Volume Increase
	3	1.4	2	1.2
	6	2.0	4	1.5
	10	3.2	10	2
	20	10.0	100	4
	40	100.0	10,000	16

Using the information in Table 15-1, to double the sound level produced by a speaker requires an increase of about three times the signal strength and a ten-fold increase in the amplifier output, which equates to a increase of 10 dB.

Analog versus Digital Sound

Recorded or broadcasted sounds are either analog or digital. The quality of a reproduced sound isn't necessarily affected by whether it is analog or digital. However, the quality of a recorded analog or digital sound and the fidelity of its reproduction are directly dependent on the equipment in use.

Analog Sound

Analog sound is sound that is transmitted or recorded in its natural state, which means it was originally created in sound-wave form. Phonograph records were manufactured to cause the phonograph needle to vibrate and reproduce the analog sound etched into the plastic or vinyl on the record.

Analog sound can also be recorded onto audiotape. The record heads present the characteristics of the sound as electromagnetic impulses stored on the tape. When the tape is played, the record heads pick up these impulses and translate them into frequency, pitch, and amplitude, which is heard as a representation of the original sound.

The quality of the sound reproduction, which is determined partly by the recording of the sound and partly by the quality of the playback device, is its fidelity. Hi-Fi sound reproduction reproduces a sound quality that represents a sound that is very similar to the original sound. Low-fidelity sound is a poor reproduction of the original sound.

Digital Sound

The quest of the recorded sound industry has always been to create recording and playback devices that are able to record and reproduce sounds that are a perfect reproduction of the original sound; this has led to the development of digital recording and playback technologies.

Converting Audio to Digital   Where analog recordings represent a sound by causing a pickup device to vibrate or emulate the vibrations of the original recording, digital recordings store a series of binary numbers that represent the characteristics of the original sound.

To do this, a sound wave is sliced into a number of samples, as illustrated in Figure 15-3. A piece of the sound is captured at different points along the wavelength. Each sample represents a different combination of frequency and amplitude in the sound, which can be converted to a numeric value and stored as a binary number on the recorded media.

Digital recordings and their playback mechanisms must be coordinated for the sampling rate (the number of samples taken per second of sound) and the sampling precision (the number of samples taken in a sound wave's vertical height).

The device used to convert an analog sound for digital recording is an analog-to-digital converter (ADC), which samples the sound and converts it to digital data. On the playback end, a digital-to-analog converter (DAC) is used to reconvert the digital values back into analog sound.

Sampling   Of course, the goal of a perfect reproduction would only be possible with 100-percent sampling; taking samples as often as tens of thousands per second can capture the sound quality at a level that fools most people's ears (and brains) into believing they are hearing the whole original sound.

Of course, the higher the sample rate and sampling precision are, the lower the probability a sampling error (or failure to capture the true original sound) will occur. The sampling rate standard for a music compact disc (CD) is generally 44,100 samples per second with a sampling precision of 65,536. Table 15-2 lists some of the standard sampling rates of digital recording media. As listed in Table 15-2, sampling rates are normally stated in kilohertz (kHz), or thousands of samples per second.

Line Level versus Speaker Level

A line-level audio signal is a signal with one to two volts (V) of amplitude that is used as the normal interface level of the audio components in a system. The line-level signal, which is also referred to as the pre-amp level, is the level (amplitude) of an audio signal before it is amplified to drive speakers.

A speaker-level audio signal is essentially a line-level signal that has been amplified to a higher voltage level to facilitate the transmission of the audio signals to a speaker and provide a reasonable level of volume at the speaker.

Unbalanced versus Balanced Audio

Essentially the difference between unbalanced and balanced audio devices, cables, and connectors is the same difference you see between home-use and professional systems.

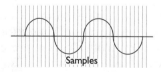

Samples

Figure 15-3   An analog sound wave is divided into a series of samples, which are used to digitally record the sound.

Table 15-2 Digital Recording Sampling Rates	Samples/Sec	Sampling Rate in kHz	Recording Media
	8,000	8 kHz	Digital telephony
	32,000	32 kHz	Extended play digital audio tape (DAT)
	37,800	37.8 kHz	CD-ROM/XA standard
	44,056	44.056 kHz	Video-embedded audio
	44,100	44.1 kHz	Stereo music CD and MP3
	48,000	48 kHz	Standard DAT
	96,000	96 kHz	DVD-Audio

Unbalanced Audio

Most audio devices found in homes include unbalanced audio inputs and outputs. This means that the audio signals produced by these devices, whether stereophonic (left and right) or monophonic (mono), are transmitted on a single conductor cable that has a single shield.

While unbalanced audio systems are adequate for most residential systems, they are best when used with shorter line-level signals because of their susceptibility to line noise and interference. Over long distances, unbalanced cables and connectors are probably not the better choice.

The connectors commonly used with unbalanced audio systems are RCA connectors, DIN connectors, ¼-inch (6.3 millimeter [mm]) connectors, and 3.5 mm connectors.

Balanced Audio

Balanced audio uses at least two conductors to transmit audio signals that are in opposite phase to each other to prevent cross-feed between the conductors while transmitting audio signals. The two wires are the live conductor, which carries a positive signal, and the return conductor, which carries an equal but opposite negative signal.

Balanced audio has the capability to resist external interference as the audio signal is carried over the wire, something an unbalanced link can't and doesn't do. The most common connector used with balanced audio systems is the Canon, or 3-pin XLR, connector.

Electrical Properties

There are certain electrical properties that are very important for getting the best performance from an audio system, including:

- **Resistance** Every conductor resists the flow of an electrical current through it to some extent, depending on the type of conductor and the conductor's physical characteristics. Some conductors offer less resistance and others more. Resistance, or the amount of resistive force in a conductor, is measured in ohms.

- **Capacitance** The characteristic of a circuit to store an electrical charge, or the potential difference between two closely spaced conductors in the circuit. The unit of measure for capacitance is a farad.

- **Inductance** The characteristic of a conductor or circuit that resists changes in the current. Inductance, which is measured in henrys, causes changes in the current on a circuit to occur after changes in voltage occur. Inductance increases with the frequency of the electrical current.

- **Impedance** Where resistance is the amount of opposing force on a direct current (DC) electrical flow, impedance is the resistance a circuit, wire, cable, or electrical device has to an alternating current (AC). Impedance measures the cumulative impact of both resistance and reactance in the conductor to an AC flow.

- **Reactance** The cumulative effect of capacitance and inductance on an AC electrical flow is reactance. Reactance, like inductance, varies with changes in the frequency in an electrical current. However, reactance decreases as the frequency increases.

Understanding Ohm's Law

Ohm's law, which is named for Georg Ohm, a nineteenth-century Bavarian mathematician, defines a relationship between power, voltage, current, and resistance. Ohm's law is the primary law electrical theory is based on.

What Ohm's law says is that when one volt is placed on a conductor, it has a resistance of one ohm and one ampere (amp) of current and with two volts you get two amps. However, if you have one volt with two ohms, you'll get one-half amp.

Technically, Ohm's law states that a steady increase in voltage should produce a constant and linear increase in current (amps) on a circuit that has constant resistance. However, it also says that a steady increase in resistance (ohms) will produce a nonlinearly weaker current (amps) on a circuit with constant voltage.

The formulas used to represent the relationships of voltage, current (amps), and resistance (ohms) are

$$V \text{ (voltage)} = I \text{ (current in amperes)} * R \text{ (resistance in ohms)}$$

or

$$I = V / R$$

or

$$R = V / I$$

The bottom line to all of this is that Volts = Amps * Resistance
Visit this web site for a handy Ohm's Law Calculator:
www.thelearningpit.com/elec/tools/ohms_calc/ohms_calc.asp

Surround Sound

A surround sound system is used to enhance the experience of watching a video presentation. The goal of a surround sound system is what the movie makers call "suspended disbelief," which means that the visual and audio images and sound come together to create an experience in which the viewer suspends her awareness of her surroundings for a time.

Surround Sound Systems

A true surround sound system incorporates several speakers that separate the sound by frequency as well as physically to literally surround the listener. There are systems called surround sound that include one, two, and three speakers, but a true surround sound system has five, six, or seven speakers.

An unofficial designation system for surround sound systems has been created by Dolby Digital sound systems that designates the number of channels, full-range and subrange, used in a particular system. Table 15-3 lists the three Dolby surround sound systems. Figure 15-4 illustrates the placement of the speakers in a 5.1 surround sound system.

A low frequency effects (LFE) speaker is a sub-woofer speaker that is used to reproduce the very lowest frequency sounds. LFE sounds are those that add impact to the sound used to emphasize certain actions in a film or video, such as a monster's footsteps, a bomb exploding, and the like.

The standard professional level surround sound is the 5.1 system, which Dolby specifies as including a 12 watt (W) root mean square (RMS) sub-woofer for the LFE channel, a 2W RMS center speaker, and four 2W RMS front and rear speakers. RMS is the measurement for the maximum amount of amplified sound signals the speaker is designed to

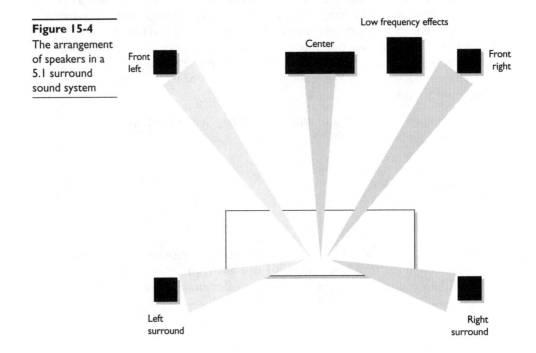

Figure 15-4

The arrangement of speakers in a 5.1 surround sound system

Low frequency effects

Center

Front left

Front right

Left surround

Right surround

System	Number of Full-Range Speakers	Number of Low Frequency Effects (LFE) Speakers	System Description
5.1	Five	One	Six channels (front left, front center, front right, left surround, right surround, and LFE)
6.1	Six	One	Seven channels (front left, front center, front right, left surround, right surround, rear surround, and LFE)
7.1	Seven	One	Eight channels (front left, front center, front right, left surround, right surround, rear surround (x2), and LFE)

Table 15-3   Dolby Digital Surround Sound System Designators

handle. More watts RMS means more power. A surround sound system also needs an amplifier with enough built-in channels to drive the system. Amplifiers are rated using a couple of different rating scales, but a 5.1 surround sound system requires an amplifier with 6 built-in amplified channels that produces a 50 to 20,000 Hertz (Hz) frequency response. The frequency response of an amplifier indicates the lowest and highest frequencies the amplifier is able to amplify and retransmit.

Surround Sound Formats
Although there are virtual surround sound systems, such as the Sound Retrieval System (SRS) and others, that need only two left and two right speakers and what are called psycho-acoustic effects that emulate true surround sound formats, they have not been developed to the point where they provide the same experience as a true surround sound format and the use of designated speakers.

Table 15-4 lists the most popular digital surround sound formats available.

Format	Systems	Channels	Media Supported
Dolby Surround Pro-Logic	5.1	Four	Hi-Fi, VHS, and stereo analog TV
Dolby Digital (AC-3)	5.1	Six	DVD video, Laserdisc, high-definition television (HDTV), digital broadcast satellite (DBS), and pay-per-view and video-on-demand movies
DTS Digital Surround	5.1	Six	PC and console games, DVD-Video, DVD-Audio, and DVD-ROM software
Dolby Digital EX	5.1/6.1/7.1	Six/seven	Extends 5.1 surround systems with rear surround channels
THX Surround EX	5.1/6.1/7.1	Six/seven	Extends 5.1 surround systems with rear surround channels
DTS Extended Surround (DTS-ES)	5.1/6.1/7.1	Six/seven	Extends 5.1 surround systems with rear surround channels

Table 15-4   Surround Sound Media Formats

PART IV

Distributed Audio Systems

Depending on whom you ask, a distributed, or multiroom, audio system installed as a part of new home construction or during a major renovation of the home may or may not add value to the home. Whether or not a distributed audio system, as illustrated in Figure 15-5, is an investment that increases the value of a home, it certainly increases the enjoyment and perhaps livability of the home for its occupants.

Regardless of the investment issue, a distributed audio system provides an infrastructure where the entire house can share the latest audio technologies, including CDs, AM and FM radio, Minidisc, satellite radio, hard disk drive systems, Internet music, and MP3 players. Depending on the investment made in the system, it is also possible for each room to control not only the local volume of the audio source, but also which source is distributed to that room.

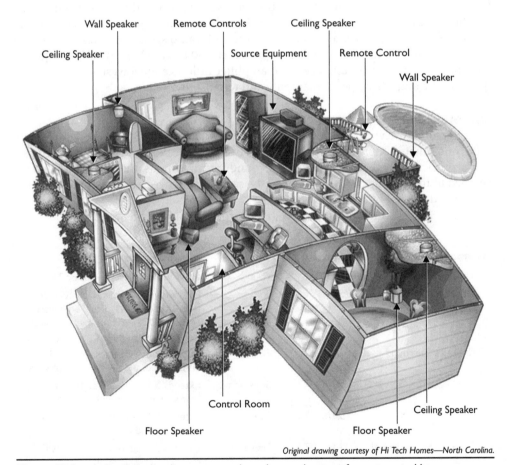

Original drawing courtesy of Hi Tech Homes—North Carolina.

Figure 15-5   A distributed audio system can be only one element of an automated home.

Centralization is the key concept of any distributed audio system. The system and its audio source devices are centrally located, either hidden away or on display, with only speakers and controllers placed in each room. In addition, it is possible for locally placed playback units in any one room to be connected into the system for local playback in that room or in other rooms as well.

Audio System Types

A distributed audio system can be classified by one of two major characteristics and typically it will actually be some combination of both. An audio system can be classified by the type of amplifier it uses or by the number of zones it supports.

Audio Amplifiers

There are two types of audio amplifiers from which to choose:

- Constant current amplifiers
- Constant voltage amplifiers

Constant Current Amplifiers   A constant current amplifier is able to support typically only one or two speakers because of its low impedance. The speakers must be directly connected to the amplifier and the minimum impedance load from the speakers cannot exceed the impedance load rating of the amplifier. A constant current amplifier can be used in a small, distributed audio system with several small speakers as long as the total impedance load of the speakers doesn't exceed that of the amplifier.

When using multiple speakers with a constant current amplifier, the speakers must be used in a "two times" configuration, which means one speaker, two speakers, four speakers, eight speakers, and so on. If more than one speaker is connected, the speakers must be configured in series or parallel connections. Figures 15-6 and 15-7 illustrate speaker configurations for a series configuration and a parallel configuration, respectively. Series connections are seldom used in a single-zone multiroom system, since it is typical to have individual stereo volume controls in each room. When more than one speaker is connected in a series, individual volume controls affect *all* speakers on the circuit, whereas parallel connections allow individual controls to be located between the

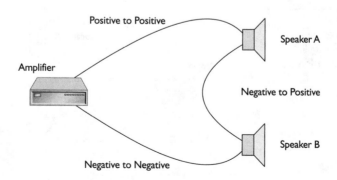

Figure 15-6
Speakers
configured
in a series

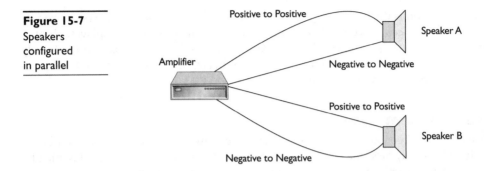

Figure 15-7
Speakers
configured
in parallel

amplifier and each pair of speakers. For this reason, most single zone music systems with more than one or two pairs of speakers on a single amplifier use some sort of impedance protection system or an amplifier capable of driving extremely low impedance loads.

NOTE See Chapter 16 for information on series and parallel configurations.

Constant Voltage Amplifiers Constant voltage amplifiers have a higher impedance output than constant current amplifiers, which allows them to support more speakers on longer runs of speaker wire. A constant voltage amplifier can support wire runs of up to several thousand feet, provided the speakers are mounted with line matching transformers that convert 8-ohm speakers to the higher impedance needed to match the speakers to the 70V output of the amplifier. Figure 15-8 illustrates a common configuration for speakers connected to a constant voltage amplifier.

NOTE Chapter 16 covers design and installation considerations for using a constant voltage amplifier.

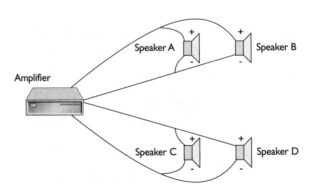

Figure 15-8
Speakers in a
series/parallel
configuration

Centralized versus Distributed Amplification

The sound signals sent to speakers from centralized source equipment (such as DVD players, CD players, AM and FM radio, and so on) typically must be amplified to overcome the electrical characteristics of the cable and to supply adequate volume at the speaker. In a home audio system, you have two choices for amplifying audio signals:

- Centralized amplification
- Distributed amplification

Centralized Amplification   Depending on the design of the audio system and the characteristics of the cabling, the source devices, and the speakers, a single amplifier may be able to supply enough amplification to drive all of the speakers in a home that are connected to the audio system. In general, the use of a single amplification source can limit the number of speakers in the system because as more speakers are added, which means more speaker cables and possibly local controls, the amount of amplification produced may prove to be inadequate to expand the system too much.

Distributed Amplification   Several distributed audio amplifiers are on the market, like the one shown in Figure 15-9, which have the capability to individually drive as many as eight channels (and soon more). In most situations, an eight-channel amplifier is able to distribute stereo sound (which requires two channels) to four areas, zones, or rooms of a home. These devices also include several advanced features that allow the system to be adapted to a wide-range of audio system requirements, including capabilities that allow the power output on individual channels, channels to be bridged to increase the power to a particular area, and the capability to assign a channel to multiple source devices.

NOTE   See Chapter 16 for information on audio system design.

Figure 15-9
An eight-channel distributed audio amplifier

Photo courtesy of Speakercraft.

PART IV

Audio Zones

Essentially, there are two general approaches to configuring a whole house audio system:

- Single zone
- Multiple zones

Single Zone Approach

In a single zone approach, all of the speakers in a house play the same sound supplied from a single source. The entire house is one large audio output zone. This has been a common approach to home audio systems, especially those simply added on in existing houses.

Multiple Zone Approach

In a multiple zone approach, you can select and listen to the audio from a different source in each room. In effect, an audio zone is an area of a home where all occupants hear the same sound. It is logical then that if the occupants of different parts of a house can hear different audio sources, the house has multiple audio zones.

In general, the capability to distribute different audio sources to different parts of a house requires multiple amplifiers/receivers, room controllers, source components, and speakers. A separate amp or receiver drives each zone. Some high-end amplifier/receivers include a separate second internal amplifier to drive a second zone. In fact, there are systems that include as many as six (or more) discrete amplifiers, a source distribution system, and a zone volume control, all built into a single piece of equipment designed especially for distributed audio systems.

Audio System Components

Just about any distributed audio system has certain essential components: speakers, controls, and amplifiers/receivers. Each of these components is typically purchased separately, but even so, they must be matched to one another electrically and performance-wise.

Audio Source Equipment

Without some equipment to receive or reproduce sound from radio transmissions or from a CD or tape, a distributed audio system doesn't have much purpose.

For most home audio systems, the audio source devices, so-called because they are the source of the audio signals sent to the speakers, are generally one of the following:

- **AM/FM tuner** This device receives AM/FM radio signals and amplifies them for distribution to speakers. For a single-zone audio system, a good quality AM/FM tuner/amplifier should be adequate to drive the system. For a multiple zone system, a remotely controlled AM/FM tuner, without an amplifier built in, is best when connected to amplifiers for each room.

- **CD/DVD player**   These digital devices read the digitally encoded data from the CD or DVD disc and convert it into analog audio signals. Most multiroom systems use a Multidisc changer capable of holding at least five or more discs so the owner doesn't have to access the centralized system each time he wants to hear a new selection.

- **Digital multiplex (DMX) cable music receiver**   This digital form of music transmission is carried to a home on the cable or satellite television signals. The cable or satellite receiver converts these signals to analog audio signals.

- **Minidisc player**   This recording format digitally records audio signals on a small magneto-optical disc encased in a protective cassette. The Minidisc player converts the digital signals to analog audio signals.

- **MP3 players**   Although usually associated with computers and the Internet, MP3 recorders and players store the digital audio signals of a CD or another MP3 device on a hard disk drive or a compact flash card for digital to audio playback.

- **Hard-drive-based music servers**   These relatively new components allow music tracks to be stored on a hard drive for instant access. The music files can originate from the owners' CDs or MP-3 files. It takes quite a bit of time to "burn" them into the hard drive, but there are services that will perform this task for a fee. They usually have a display that can be sent to a video display device and/or modulated so that the owner can use the local TV in each room to view the library of available music and access songs, albums, or play lists. Some music servers even have several zone outputs so different music zones can listen to different selections from the hard drive at the same time. Additionally, some of these devices can control high-capacity (200-400 disc) CD changers so the client can benefit from the convenience of the video display to access their entire library of recorded music. Some hard drive servers even allow playback of Internet radio stations!

- **Satellite radio tuners**   Two new subscription services (Sirius and XM radio) that were originally developed for the automotive market deliver commercial-free music and other formats in a digital format much like satellite TV. Tuners are starting to become available, as well as adapters that allow car units to be played in the home. Some multiroom systems manufacturers are starting to offers these satellite radio tuners built into their tuners, pre-amp/controllers, or multiroom receivers.

- **Tape players**   There are three types of audio tape players a customer may want in her home audio system:
  - **Audiocassette tape**   This source device is still widely used, even given the popularity of the CD. Sound is recorded as analog audio signals and playback merely reproduces the original audio.

- **DAT** DAT recorders and players are more common to professional systems, but this type of audio tape player records and reproduces very high-quality sound. DAT records audio signals digitally and in playback converts the digital signals to analog audio signals.

- **Reel-to-reel tape** The technology in use on reel-to-reel tape recorders and players is essentially the same as that used on the audiocassette. The difference is in the size of the tape and that it is wound on open reels.

Speaker Basics

Audio system speakers translate electrical signal representations of audio sounds back into the vibrations that create the sound waves we hear.

Speaker Anatomy

A speaker (I discuss the different types of speakers beginning with the next section) consists of the following major components:

- **Driver** This speaker component vibrates the cone (also known as the diaphragm) to create sound waves.

- **Cone/diaphragm/dome** The concave cone or diaphragm is typically paper, plastic, or a flexible metal. The cone is vibrated by the speaker's driver mechanism to create sound waves. Some speakers have a dome, which extends outward from the speaker assembly. Figure 15-10 shows the cone/diaphragm of a speaker.

- **Suspension/surround** The suspension or surround is a ring of flexible material that attaches the cone to the metal frame, called a basket, and allows it to move back and forth as it vibrates.

Figure 15-10
A speaker showing its cone, surround, and voice coil

- **Voice coil** Speakers have magnets at the bottom of the cone and at the top of the voice coil that, depending on the polarity of the power supplied from the voice coil, either attract or repel each other to move the cone in or out. By changing the polarity and amplitude of the voice coil (and its magnet), the magnet on the cone is pulled in or pushed out. Newer speaker models now include a dual voice coil (DVC) or twin voice coil (TVC) that allows both stereo channels to be played from a single speaker.

Frequency Range Speakers

Some speakers have specially adapted drivers that produce sound for a specific frequency range. The primary three frequency range speakers are

- **Woofers** This type of speaker has a larger driver than other speaker types and is designed to produce sounds in the low frequencies and pitch.

- **Tweeters** This type of speaker has a smaller driver and is designed to produce sounds in the highest frequency ranges.

- **Midrange** This type of speaker is designed to produce sounds in a range of frequencies that are between those produced by tweeters and woofers.

Many home audio and home theater speakers include speakers of all three types in one enclosure. To separate the sound to be produced by each speaker type, a device called a speaker crossover is used. There are two types of speaker crossovers: passive and active. Passive crossovers, like the one in Figure 15-11, which are the most commonly used, get their operating power from the audio signal passing through it. Active crossovers are electronic devices that separate the frequency ranges before the signal passes through an amplifier. Each frequency range signal then must be amplified separately before being passed on to the appropriate speaker.

Photo courtesy of AudioControl.

Figure 15-11 A passive speaker crossover that also include an equalizer.

Speaker Enclosures

Essentially, a speaker enclosure is a box that houses the speaker and crossover. However, a speaker enclosure can be an important part of the sound produced by the driver. The first function of a speaker enclosure, beyond holding all of the speaker's parts, is to absorb the vibrations the driver produces. Quality speaker enclosures are typically made of heavy wood panels, which are able to absorb the vibrations without vibrating itself.

There are four primary types of speaker enclosures:

- Sealed enclosures
- Bass reflex enclosures
- Dipole and bipole enclosures
- Bandpass enclosures

Sealed Speaker Enclosures   Sealed enclosures, which are also referred to as acoustic suspension enclosures, are the most commonly used type of speaker enclosures. A sealed enclosure is an air-tight box in which the air pressure inside the speaker box is used to assist in moving the speaker's driver to produce vibrations (sound waves). The speaker driver (or what most people call a speaker) is mounted to the enclosure and sealed so that no air can escape from inside. Figure 15-12 illustrates how a driver is mounted into a sealed enclosure.

Bass Reflex Speaker Enclosures   Where a sealed speaker enclosure uses its internal air pressure to push the driver back out when it moves inward, a bass reflex speaker enclosure allows the inward movement of the driver (as it moves in and out to create vibrations) to push the air in the enclosure out a port built into it. This type of enclosure is commonly used with woofers and subwoofers because the enclosure port allows the deepest sounds (lowest frequency sound waves) to escape. Higher frequencies are produced when the driver moves forward and lower frequencies are produced when the driver moves backward. Figure 15-13 illustrates a bass reflex speaker with a port built into the enclosure.

Figure 15-12
A cross-section of a sealed speaker enclosure

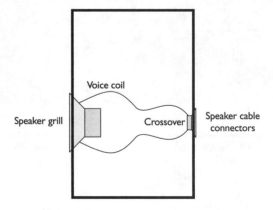

Figure 15-13
A bass reflex
speaker enclosure
has a port
through which
low frequency
waves can travel.

Dipole and Bipole Enclosures   Dipole and bipole speaker enclosures are designed to allow sound to generate both forward and backward from the enclosure. While most dipole and bipole speaker enclosures are square or rectangular, some are trapezoidal and even triangular with three or more surfaces on which speaker drivers are mounted at right angles. Figure 15-14 illustrates a common configuration of these types of enclosures.

Both dipole and bipole speaker enclosures generate equal amounts of sound from at least two of their sides, which are commonly referenced as their fronts and backs, although the sides could be adjacent (as shown in Figure 15-14). The difference between a dipole and a bipole enclosure is whether or not the front and back sounds are in phase.

Phase refers to the timing of two or more sound waves in relation to one another. For example, to enjoy stereo sound, the two stereo channels should be in phase so that you hear them at the same time. To produce sound from two or more speakers that is in phase, the speaker drivers must be synchronized in their movement, meaning that they must be moving in and out at the same time.

A dipole speaker produces equal amounts of sound forward and backward, but the two speaker drivers are not synchronized, which is referred to as being "out of phase."

Figure 15-14
Speaker drivers
in a bipole
speaker enclosure

*Photo courtesy of
Mordaunt-Short.*

A bipole speaker produces sound just like a dipole speaker does, but the two sound streams are produced in phase. Bipole speakers, because they are in phase, are commonly used in surround sound systems.

There are passive and active versions of bipole and dipole enclosures. A passive enclosure is very similar to a bass reflex enclosure except that a passive speaker driver is placed in the port. A passive driver doesn't have a voice coil (an active speaker does) and uses sound waves produced by another driver passing through it to generate sound. So, in a passive enclosure, the sound pushed back into the enclosure is used to produce additional sound through the passive driver.

Bandpass Enclosures   A bandpass enclosure is designed to allow only a single band of frequencies to exit the enclosure, such as bass frequencies. Common types of bandpass enclosures are the single and dual reflex bandpass enclosures. Bandpass enclosures have a single driver mounted in a rear interior sealed chamber and a front chamber that is ported with one or two (or more) passive reflex ports. Figure 15-15 illustrates the basic design of a dual bandpass enclosure.

Types of Speakers

The characteristics of the speakers to be installed depend on a number of factors. Primary among these are the type and capacity of the amplifier that the speakers will be connected to and whether the system is to be a surround-audio system or a two-channel stereo system. In addition, the space they will be located in, the type of listening that will be done, and aesthetics are all important when selecting speaker types.

There are eight standard types of speakers:

- **Bookshelf**   These speakers are smaller speakers designed to sit on shelves, stands, or other surfaces. Bookshelf speakers provide the maximum flexibility when designing a room's audio system.

- **Floor-standing/freestanding**   These speakers are larger, cabinet-mounted speakers that usually include one or more tweeters (treble speaker) and woofers (bass speakers). Figure 15-16 shows a floor-standing speaker.

- **In-ceiling**   These speakers are engineered to be built into a ceiling, with most of the speaker hidden inside the ceiling cavity. In-ceiling speakers come in many sizes and shapes. However, the most commonly used in-ceiling speaker design is the round "can" speaker like the one shown in Figure 15-17.

Figure 15-15
A single reflex bandpass enclosure

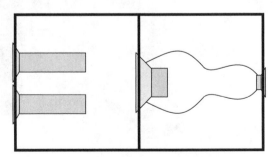

Figure 15-16

Floor-standing speakers with the grill removed (left) and the grill in-place (right)

Photo courtesy of Klipsch Audio Technologies.

- **In-wall** These speakers are designed to be built into a wall with most of the speaker hidden inside the wall. Like in-ceiling speakers, there are a variety of sizes and shapes available, but the most common are rectangular in shape. Figure 15-18 shows one example of an in-wall speaker.

Figure 15-17

An in-ceiling speaker

Photo courtesy of SpeakerCraft.

Figure 15-18
A back view of
in-wall speaker

*Photo courtesy of Klipsch
Audio Technologies.*

- **Outdoor** These speakers come in a wide variety of shapes and sizes that range from standard wall-mount, all-weather speakers to shapes that include rocks (see Figure 15-19), blocks, and other shapes meant to blend into a garden or patio setting.

Figure 15-19
An outdoor
speaker mounted
to an exterior
wall

*Photo courtesy of Klipsch
Audio Technologies.*

Figure 15-20

A sub-woofer speaker with its grill removed

Photo courtesy of Sonance.

- **Surround**   Surround sound systems are typically used in home theater setups and are usually a combination of special-purpose speakers, each supporting a different part of the audio signal.

- **Sub-woofer**   These speakers are designed to reproduce the lowest audio frequencies at a volume level that can be felt as well as heard. The "sound" of a sub-woofer is made up of frequency waves so large that it is often perceived more through vibrations felt in one's spinal column and skull than the manipulation of the eardrum. For this reason, some home theaters actually supplement the sub-woofer system with mechanical devices that cause the listener's chair or floor to actually shake. Figure 15-20 shows a freestanding sub-woofer with the grill cloth removed. Exact placement in the room is not critical, but sub-woofers are usually freestanding on the floor or hidden in a cupboard or closet and the sound disperses through cloth or vents.

- **Wireless**   Actually there aren't really any wireless speakers, but there are wireless speaker systems. A wireless speaker system uses an audio out transmitter and a remote receiver where the speakers are connected. The audio signal is transmitted using radio frequency (RF) signals to the receiver and on to and out of the speakers. As more devices in the home emit RF interference, the reliability and performance of wireless speakers becomes more compromised and inconsistent. This is probably why they are less popular than when they were first introduced about 15 years ago. Wireless speakers are typically not recommended except as a "last-ditch" solution in a multiroom audio system.

Figure 15-21
An invisible speaker assembly mounted on the backside of a wall's wallboard

Photo courtesy of Sound Advance Systems, Inc.

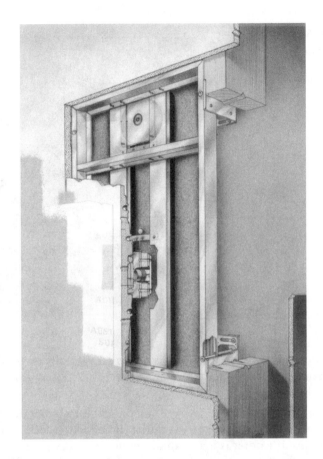

- **Invisible**   Just as they're called, these speakers are not visible. They are located behind the drywall and use the wall cavity to resonate the sound. There are two types of invisible speakers. Transducers are mounted inside a wall or ceiling cavity between wall studs or ceiling joists and use the drywall to transmit the sound to the room. The other kind of invisible speakers are mounted flush with the drywall or plaster wall (a hole is cut in the wall board of a wall or ceiling), have a mesh over them, and a thin layer of plaster is then applied to make them blend into the drywall. Figure 15-21 shows how one such speaker is attached to the back of a wall.

Local Controls

Regardless of whether the distributed audio system is in one or multiple zones, the objective is to control the centrally located equipment from any remote listening location. Much of the benefit of a distributed audio system is lost if the home's occupants must physically go to a central location to change the source device or the station, track, disc, or channel.

The best approach to controlling a distributed audio system is using distributed remote controls that transmit control signals back to the central equipment and allow the user to control the unit just as if she was standing right in front of it.

The most popular ways of controlling a distributed audio system are

- Local volume controls
- Control keypads
- Remote controls

Volume Controls

Volume controls come in several styles, including rotary dial, keypads with rocker switches, and push buttons. The type of volume controls used in home audio systems depends on the homeowner's preference and the number of zones the system supports. In a single zone multiroom system, it is advisable to have a volume control located in each room where speakers are installed to provide local volume control.

Sometimes designing sub-zones (individual rooms within a zone) make sense. An example might be a kitchen and breakfast nook that share an open air space. In this case, it might be desirable to have a zone keypad in the kitchen, with individual volume controls and speakers in both the kitchen and breakfast nook. It might make sense to play the speakers in one room area louder than the other, but it would never make sense to have two different music sources playing in the two rooms simultaneously.

Figure 15-22 shows a rotary volume control used to simply mute or turn up or down the volume of local speakers. Volume control can also be handled by stand-alone devices requiring manual operation or include infrared (IR) receivers that allow them to be controlled by a remote control device.

Control Keypads

Control keypads are available in a variety of styles. They can be used to simply mute or turn up or down the volume of local speakers or perform a full range of control functions, including controlling multiple source devices (when wired to a zone splitter device) as well as controlling their volume in a room.

Figure 15-22
A rotary
volume control

Keypads can be sold as part of a distributed audio system or be designed specifically to control the distributed audio system. They can also be of a generic nature and designed and programmed by the installer to control equipment (see Figure 15-23). Programming can be done at the keypad or on a computer and downloaded to the keypad. Follow the manufacturers documentation for setup and programming procedures.

Remote Controls

IR is the most commonly used technology for the remote control of audio components, including centrally located source devices controlled from a room or zone. IR control is most reliable when its signals are received by an in-room receiver, such as a keypad volume control, and transmitted directly over home run wires to the audio components using an IR repeater system.

An IR repeater system typically includes in-room IR receivers (see Figure 15-24) and a main system unit where the IR receiver is wired. The IR receiver converts the signal for transmission over the wire to the master system unit, which converts the transmitted signal back to IR and "flashes" an IR beam to the audio source device or remote speakers.

If coaxial cable has been placed in multiple rooms or zones, it can be used to send IR commands from remote locations to the central video system. IR signals are received remotely and converted for transmission over the coaxial cable. Special products must be used to extract and isolate the IR signal from the video signal on the coaxial if it is also being used to send a TV signal to that room.

NOTE I assume you realize that a signal extension system is only needed if situations where the device being controlled is not in the same room. In a single zone setup, where the entire home is one large listening zone, an IR extender can be used to control a centralized audio source device.

Figure 15-23
A touch screen audio system keypad control

Photo courtesy of Niles Audio Corporation.

Figure 15-24
An in-room IR receiver is connected to a central control device that controls source devices.

Multiple Device Controllers

If the design goal of the audio system is to have the capability of supplying a completely discrete sound stream to any room in the home, using multiple device controllers (see Figure 15-25) that are hard-wired over Cat 5e home run back to the centralized audio source equipment is recommended.

A multiple device controller is able to receive signals from IR remote controls and serve as a replacement device that consolidates the separate remote controls of the source devices. In-room multiple device controllers can be wall-mounted (Figure 15-25), handheld (Figure 15-26), or tabletop (Figure 15-27).

Another type of multiple room/multiple device system controllers are systems built on the A-BUS technology that transmits audio, IR, and source status signals over Cat 5e TP cable. The A-BUS input unit receives incoming audio signals, distributes them, and provides audio and source status signals to the system as well as receiving IR command signals through its enhanced keypad devices (see Figure 15-28).

Figure 15-25
An in-room audio systems controller that also has an IR receiver built in

Photo courtesy of Niles Audio Corp.

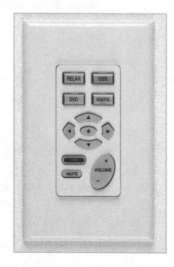

PART IV

Figure 15-26
A handheld
universal remote
control

*Photo courtesy of
Koninklijke Philips
Electronics N.V.*

Figure 15-27
A tabletop
multiple device
controller

*Photo courtesy of AMX
Corporation.*

Figure 15-28
An A-BUS
amplified keypad

*Photo courtesy of
Russound.*

A-BUS is a multiple room system that is able to control audio in four rooms and can be expanded in increments of four rooms by adding additional zone distribution hubs. A-BUS also provides support for connecting local source devices, such as portable players, for playback on local speakers.

Chapter Review

Sound is produced when an object creates vibrations in air, liquid, or something solid. Different sounds have different vibration patterns and air pressure fluctuations, which translates into a sound's frequency and amplitude. A dB measures the intensity or the level of a sound.

Recorded or broadcasted sounds are either analog or digital. Analog sound is in its natural state. A sound wave is sliced into a number of samples at different points on its wavelength. Each sample is converted to a numeric value and stored as a binary number or digital value. Analog sound is converted for digital recording with an ADC and a DAC is used to reconvert the digital values back into analog sound.

A line level audio signal has 1 to 2 V of amplitude and is used as the normal interface level between audio components. Speaker level audio is an amplified line level signal.

Unbalanced audio is transmitted on a single conductor cable that has a single shield. Balanced audio has at least two conductors, a live conductor and a return conductor, which are in opposite phase.

Resistance measures the physical opposition of a conductor to the flow of an electrical current through it. Resistance is measured in ohms. Capacitance measures the capability of a circuit to store an electrical charge. Capacitance is measured in farads. Inductance measures the resistance of a conductor to changes in current. Inductance is measured in henrys. Impedance is the resistance force a conductor has to an AC flow. Reactance measures the cumulative effect of capacitance and inductance on an AC flow.

A true surround sound system incorporates several speakers that separate the sound by frequency as well as physically literally surround the listener. A true surround sound system has five, six, or seven speakers. A LFE speaker is a sub-woofer speaker that is used to reproduce the very lowest frequency sounds. The standard professional level surround sound is the 5.1 system.

RMS is the measurement for the maximum amount of amplified sound signals the speaker is designed to handle. Frequency response of an amplifier indicates the lowest and highest frequencies the amplifier is able to amplify and retransmit.

A distributed audio system provides an infrastructure that allows an entire house to share audio technologies. It is possible for each room to control the local volume and source devices as well. Centralization is key to distributed audio.

There are two types of audio amplifiers from which to choose: constant current amplifiers and constant voltage amplifiers. A constant current amplifier supports only one or two speakers because of low impedance. A constant current amplifier is typically used in small, distributed audio systems with small speakers. Constant voltage amplifiers have a higher impedance output than constant current amplifiers and can support cable runs up to several thousand feet.

There are two choices that can be made for amplifying audio signals: centralized amplification and distributed amplification.

There are two general approaches to the configuration of a whole house audio system: single zone and multiple zones. In a single zone approach, all of the speakers in a house play the same sound from a single source. In the multiple zone approach, each room can select and listen to the audio from multiple zones.

For most home audio systems, the audio source devices are generally among the following: AM/FM tuner, CD/DVD player, DMX cable music receiver, Minidisc player, MP3 players, hard-drive based music servers, satellite radio tuners, and tape players.

Audio system speakers translate electrical signal representations of audio sounds back into the vibrations that create the sound waves we hear. A speaker consists of these major components: driver, cone or dome, suspension/surround, and voice coil. Some speakers have specially adapted drivers that produce sound for a specific frequency range. The primary three frequency range speakers are: woofers, tweeters, and midrange.

A crossover is used to separate the sound to be produced by each speaker. There are two types of speaker crossovers: passive and active. Passive crossovers get their operating power from the audio signal passing through it. Active crossovers are electronic devices that separate the frequency ranges before the signal passes through an amplifier.

A speaker enclosure houses the drivers and the crossover. It absorbs the vibrations the driver produces. The primary types of speaker enclosures are sealed enclosures, bass reflex enclosures, dipole and bipole enclosures, and bandpass enclosures.

The standard types of speakers are bookshelf, floor-standing, in-ceiling, in-wall, invisible, outdoor, surround, sub-woofer, and wireless.

The ways available for controlling a distributed audio system are local volume controls, control keypads, and remote controls.

Questions

1. Which two of the following are types of audio amplifiers?

   A. Current volume amplifier

   B. Constant current amplifier

   C. Constant volume amplifier

   D. Constant voltage amplifier

2. Which two of the following are configuration types for speaker wiring?

   A. Series

   B. Parallel

   C. Inline

   D. Discrete

3. What type of configuration is in use in a house when all rooms hear the same audio playback?

   A. Single zone

   B. Multizone

   C. Composite

   D. Aggregate

4. The audio source device that increases the amplitude of reproduced sound is called a(n)

   A. Tuner

   B. Radio

   C. Amplifier

   D. Amplitude modulator

5. What speaker system has become popular in home theater installations?

   A. Sealed enclosure

   B. In-wall or in-ceiling

   C. Stereo

   D. Surround

6. What type of speaker is designed to reproduce the lowest audio frequencies at a volume that can be heard?

   A. Bookshelf

   B. Tweeter

   C. Monitor

   D. Sub-woofer

7. Where should volume controls be located in a single-zone multiroom audio system?

   A. One central location only

   B. In each room where speakers are located

   C. For each speaker pair

   D. In all rooms of the home

8. Which of the following can be used to control a distributed audio system?

   A. Keypad

   B. Remote control

   C. Rotary volume control

   D. Multiple device control

   E. All of the above

PART IV

9. What type of wiring is typically used to connect a multiple device controller to centrally located source equipment?

   A. Speaker wire

   B. Cat 5e cable

   C. Coaxial cable

   D. Quad wire

10. Which of the following is an audio control system that transmits audio, IR, and source status signals over Cat 5e cable?

   A. A-BUS

   B. CEBus

   C. MP3

   D. PLC

Answers

1. **B and D.** The other two choices were made up.

2. **A and B.** A third possibility is in series in parallel, which combines the two correct choices. The other two choices do not apply to speaker wiring.

3. **A.** A multizone configuration allows each zone to control the different audio sources being heard.

4. **C.** Yes, that's the job of the amplifier. Often the signal strength of reproduced sound is not strong enough to drive the cone on the speakers to produce sound.

5. **D.** A surround sound system enhances the experience of watching a video.

6. **D.** Sub-woofer. Woofer would also be an acceptable answer.

7. **B.** If the goal of the system is to provide enjoyable audio to every room, then the occupants should be able to control the volume in any room with speakers. This is defeated if there is only one volume control in the home.

8. **E.** Any or all of these devices can be used to control a distributed audio system.

9. **B.** The multiple wire pairs provide flexibility for multiple devices in a room or zone.

10. **A.** None of the other choices would be acceptable audio control technologies. MP3 is a digital audio file format, anyway.

Designing and Installing Distributed Audio Systems

In this chapter, you will learn about:
- Designing and planning a distributed audio system
- Performing a rough-in installation of audio system components
- Performing the trim-out phase for the audio system
- Setting up the components, system, and testing

In a recent survey conducted by a home automation industry group, homeowners and people looking to buy a home responded that a whole-house audio system was either something they were planning to install or regarded as a plus when considering a new house. We are no longer limited to playing a radio very loud so it can be heard throughout the house (and possibly the neighborhood). Whole-house audio systems can be as sophisticated as the legendary system in Bill Gates' home, where the music played in each room is individualized to the room's occupant automatically, or as simple as the same audio output being played by all speakers placed in the ceilings or walls of each room of a home.

Planning, designing, and installing a whole-house audio system isn't really all that complicated, but there are some design considerations, pitfalls, and compatibility issues that must be included in the planning and design phases.

Like a computer network or a distributed video system, a distributed audio system can be retrofitted into a home. However, in new construction situations, with proper planning and the use of a structured wiring infrastructure, all three types of systems can be easily integrated. As the various audio system topics in this chapter are discussed, keep structured wiring and how the audio system can be combined into an integrated home system in mind.

Planning for a Distributed Audio System

The very first consideration when planning for a distributed audio system is whether the system is a retrofit, meaning if it is to be added to an existing structure or a new construction. In many ways, a retrofit installation is more difficult than a new construction installation. It is certainly much easier to wire an audio system into a house while it is being built than it is to run wire through existing and closed up walls, ceilings, or floors.

In a retrofit situation, or what the electricians call "old work," the most important project considerations are first where to place the distributed devices, such as speakers and controls, and then where and how to run cable to them from the centralized source devices.

Planning for Distributed Audio

Typically, at the start of any distributed audio installation project, whether for an existing or new structure, no real plan exists for what exactly is to be done. The homeowners may have some idea of what they desire, but not necessarily any idea of actually how it is to be accomplished. During the planning phase of the project, a number of issues must be considered, including:

- Will there be one or multiple audio sources?
- Are one or multiple audio zones desired?
- Will there be a single or a number of distributed controllers?
- Are local source devices to be integrated into the distributed audio system?
- Will the system include both interior and exterior devices?
- Should the planning provide for devices to be installed now and in the future?
- Are the source devices and speakers new or do they exist?
- Does the house's floor plan present any limitations or constraints to the design?
- What is the budget?

The last question in this list, which concerns the budget, may be the most important consideration of the entire project. How much the homeowners are willing to spend may influence some of the plan and design issues for you. You know how it goes: hi-tech tastes on a low-tech budget. Assuming that is not the case, the planning phase for an audio system needs to address each of the above issues and perhaps a few more. The simplest way to determine the answers to the remaining questions in the list is to ask the following two questions about each room in the home:

- Do you want to be able to listen to music in this room?
- Would you ever want to listen to something in this room that is different from what is playing in the rest of the house?

Laying Out the System

To a certain extent, the planning phase of a distributed audio project is the fact-gathering phase. It is virtually impossible to design a system for installation without collecting all of the facts about home use and the owners' desires that will impact the labor and materials required.

Start with a floor plan drawing and work with the customer to place the speakers, source equipment, and controllers in the rooms included in the system. For an existing house, the floor plan drawing may be something that must be created; in a new construction situation, a floor plan drawing is usually available. It is also very important that the length and width of the building and each of its rooms be obtained during this phase of the project. Figure 16-1 illustrates a sample floor plan with dimensions and the preliminary placement of the distribution panel and wall outlets indicated.

With the floor plan in hand and a concept of the customer's desires, you should be able to move on to the design phase of the project.

Designing a Distributed Audio System

During the design phase of the project, it's important to decide what components will be included in the system. For a residential distributed audio system, the following components must be considered:

- **Audio source units**   In most home situations, a CD- or DVD-player, preferably a multidisc changer, is the most common audio source device. AM/FM tuners are also common sources. However, with the emergence of digital audio, such as MP3 files or Internet radio from a computer, these options are becoming popular choices as well. The homeowner may also have legacy equipment, such as a cassette tape player, a reel-to-reel tape player, or even a phonograph or turntable.

- **Amplifier/Receiver**   Often combined into one device, the receiver portion receives AM/FM signals and the amplifier portion boosts the signal and distributes it to the speakers. In some cases, separate receiver and amplifier units provide for the best performance and flexibility in terms of adding additional source units and speakers to the system. In many cases, an existing amplifier/receiver

Figure 16-1

The floor plan of a building is a vital part of the planning for a distributed audio system.

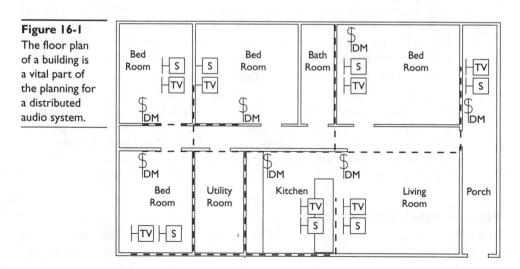

can be used only as an amplifier. In multiple zone applications, a multizone amplifier unit with multiple channels, equalization, and other features may provide the best results.

- **Distribution system** The cabling and impedance matching the distributed audio system must be carefully considered. If multiple rooms in a single-zone system are planned, the impedance matching capabilities of the distributed volume controls and speakers must be matched to the amplifier. The characteristics of the speaker wiring must also be considered.

 CROSS-REFERENCE See Chapters 1 and 15 for more information about speaker wiring.

- **Speakers** The choices in speakers vary from in-wall, ceiling, wall and surface mounted, and camouflaged "natural" shape speakers. The primary considerations for speakers are
  - **Physical appearance** The speakers should be consistent with a room's décor or style.
  - **Audio coverage (dispersion)** The speakers should provide the maximum audio coverage for their zone, with consideration given to the room's shape, size, and major features, such as a large chandelier, table, or the like.
  - **Acoustic sensitivity** Large rooms, such as family rooms, recreation rooms, or living rooms, can present an audio balance challenge, especially if the room's furniture, draperies, or carpeting absorbs sound, decreasing the volume that is heard. In smaller rooms, such as laundry rooms or bathrooms, the hard surfaces make the volume seem louder. Larger rooms may need additional or larger speakers and smaller spaces may need fewer or smaller speakers. Most manufacturers supply specifications about the sensitivity of each model of speakers they make, which is normally expressed as a number of decibels (dB)at 1 watt when measured at 1 meter from the speaker. This specification helps determine the best speaker or speaker set for a room and the amplifier requirements needed to drive the speakers in a room.
  - **Volume and keypad controls** The design of a distributed audio system must show the number and placements of the controls incorporated into the audio system, regardless of whether the controls are dedicated speaker volume controls or keypad controls that control the actions of several of a home's subsystems. Including the controls in the design will assure wire installation allows for these connections.

Fitting Sound to Rooms

In the design process, the speakers must be matched to the room size and the dB output desired for the room. The factors involved are the number of rooms and the number of speakers in each room. The power rating (in watts) of the amplifier must be sufficient to drive the speakers at the volume (in dB) desired for each space. The rule of thumb is that larger rooms need more power to produce acceptable sound levels. And for customers that like to play their music loud, even more power may be needed from the amplifier.

Speaker Sensitivity

Speaker or acoustic sensitivity ratings are available for nearly all quality speakers. Understand that a speaker sensitivity rating has almost nothing to do with sound quality, but everything to do with the amount of volume a speaker can produce from an input at a given power level.

The sensitivity rating of a speaker is stated as db/Wm, which translates to decibels per watt of power measured at 1 meter (about 3.3 feet) from the speaker. If a speaker has an acoustic sensitivity rating of 90 db/Wm, this means that the speaker produces 90 dB of sound from an input of 1 watt of power from the amplifier about 3 feet (1 meter) from the speaker.

 NOTE 90 db/Wm is a fairly average sensitivity rating for most speakers. A speaker with a rating of 87 or below is considered low sensitivity and a speaker with a 93 or higher sensitivity rating is considered high sensitivity.

What this means in terms of designing the sound system for a particular room or zone is that for an average amplifier that produces only a few watts of output power, speakers with higher sensitivity will be needed in areas where louder volumes are desired, such as in a home theater. The other way to address this issue is to drive low sensitivity speakers with more watts from the amplifier. However, be aware that the watts rating of amplifiers can also be a moving target. For example, on an inexpensive amplifier the potential watts-per-channel rating may coincide with the distortion level on each channel. Higher quality, and typically higher cost, amplifiers provide more accurate power ratings.

Acoustical Room Issues

Not every room is acoustically engineered—in fact, few rooms are. Sound produced by speakers in a room resonates around a room and the room's width and length can impact its quality, loudness, and clarity. The dimensions of a room affect the sound coming from a speaker in the same way that the sound from a pipe organ is affected by the diameter and length of each pipe.

A typical room has three physical features (a ceiling, a floor, and the walls), each producing a different audio frequency as sound resonates (bounces) around the room. Depending on where the speakers are located in a room, the sound produced will seem louder or softer due to the architectural features the sound encounters between the speaker and the listener.

The placement of speakers in a room is typically the only method available to you to improve the acoustics of any space, assuming that the ceiling, walls, floors, locations, and coverings cannot be changed.

PART IV

Acoustical Design Issues

To improve the acoustical quality of any room, there are a number of issues to consider in the design and placement of speakers in the room. These issues include:

- The dimensions of a room
- The placement of doors, windows, and other architectural features in the room
- The location of Heating, Ventilating, Air Conditioning (HVAC) vents and ducts
- The materials used in the wall, ceiling, and floor construction

Each of these issues should be considered when determining the location of the speakers in a room. Any of these issues can effect the quality of the sound a speaker produces by blocking the sound, vibrating because a speaker is placed to close to it, or absorbing too much of the sound.

Locating Speakers and Controls

The location of an audio system's speakers and controls are largely determined by the homeowners' desires and the room's décor.

The homeowners' desires should help determine where built-in or freestanding speakers are best for any given room. The homeowner should also help in the placement of controls as they know how the room will be laid out and used.

Built-In Speakers

Built-in speakers come with their very own set of limitations and problems. When designing the installation for built-in speakers, check with the manufacturer's appropriate baffle specifications so that you avoid a situation where there are too many or too few wall studs, hangers, or other construction features near the speakers.

Built-in speakers produce a conical audio pattern, which means that the sound produced can be heard very well directly under the speaker. However, when stereo sound is separated to two speakers, unless the speakers are placed in an overlapping pattern, the listener may hear one stereo channel louder than the other. Figure 16-2 illustrates this point. Although this illustration is somewhat exaggerated to make my point, in the shaded area the listener hears both stereo speakers equally. However, as the listener moves either left or right, the speaker on that side becomes dominant.

Built-in speakers are designed to be installed in walls or ceilings with the speaker grill flush with the wall or ceiling surface. They are designed to be installed in a wall or ceiling cavity, but it's a good idea to configure the cavity so the back of the speaker is covered to prevent insulation, dust, and other debris from getting inside the speaker. A simple solution is to fold a piece of cardboard from the speaker's carton and wedge it into the hole before installing the speaker. Some manufacturers now offer in-wall boxes (for new construction) or damping/isolation kits (for retrofit applications). Another consideration is to use weatherized speakers if the speakers will be exposed to a lot of humidity in the speaker cavity.

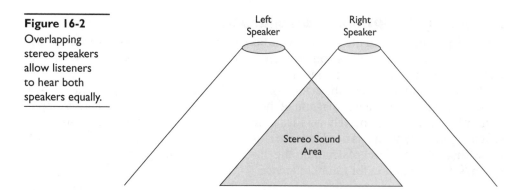

Figure 16-2
Overlapping stereo speakers allow listeners to hear both speakers equally.

Freestanding Speakers

Freestanding speakers have finished surfaces such as wood boxes or laminate surfaces for display and aesthetics. They can be placed on a stand, pedestal, bookshelf, or in a speaker cabinet. They can be mounted to walls, ceiling, or overhangs. In fact, speakers are typically designed and manufactured for a specific type of mounting. An in-wall (built-in) speaker would look and sound terrible mounted on a pedestal.

Placing Speakers Speakers should be placed in a room or zone where they produce the best stereo sound effects for the listener. The general guidelines for placing speakers in a room are

- **Separation** The speakers should provide left and right stereo separation when the listener is facing the main feature of a room. If there is no main feature, then the speakers should be placed facing the primary seating area. A room's main feature may be a fireplace, large window, or a television set or monitor. Speakers should not be placed any closer than 24-inches to any room boundary, including walls, corners, ceilings, or floors.

- **Zoning** A general practice used for speaker placement is to divide the room into three conceptual equal-sized listening zones. A speaker should be placed at the points where any two of the zones intersect, placing the speakers about the same distance from the room's corners and the main listening location. Speakers should not be placed too close to a room's corners to avoid what is called "doubling," which creates a booming sound in the audio. To avoid doubling, the speakers should be placed about one-quarter or one-third of the distance into the room away from a corner or wall.

- **Directionality** The ideal placement for freestanding speakers is to have the tweeters at approximately the same height as the listener's ears, as high frequencies tend to be more directional. Since this placement option is rarely available when using in-wall or ceiling speakers, many manufacturers now offer tweeters or mid-tweet baffles that are designed to pivot, allowing the installer to adjust the speaker to direct the high frequencies toward the listening position.

Designing Equipment Configuration

Before beginning to actually install an audio system (or an audio/video system), you should carefully plan how the source, distribution, and end devices are to be laid out and connected to the distribution wiring, as well as to each other.

The best way to document the layout, connections, and equipment placements in an audio system is to create a line diagram of the system. Figures 16-3 and 16-4 are examples of simple line drawings and very detailed drawings, respectively, of an audio visual (AV) system. Normally, all that is needed more closely matches Figure 16-3 than Figure 16-4, but with a sufficient level of detail on the diagram, the drawing can be included in the system's documentation for future reference.

Pre-Wiring

The standard for the wiring systems in residential settings is Telecommunications Industry Association/ Electronic Industries Alliance (TIA/EIA) 570A (see Chapter 4), which provides for both existing and most new technologies expected in the near future. This standard provides specification and standards for the primary cable runs of a distributed audio system.

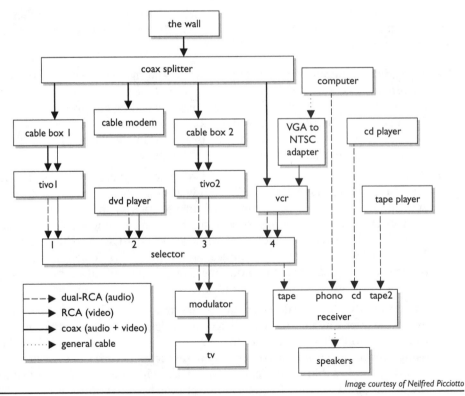

Image courtesy of Neilfred Picciotto

Figure 16-3   A simple AV system line diagram showing the general connections between the components of the system

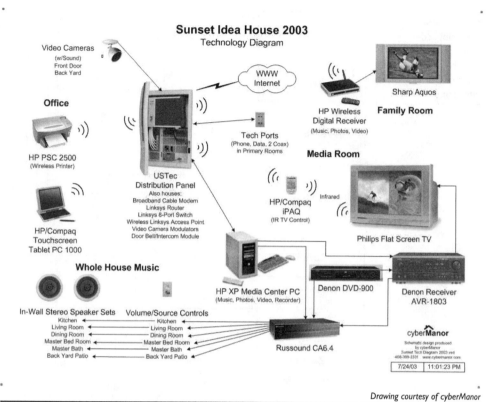

Sunset Idea House 2003
Technology Diagram

Drawing courtesy of cyberManor

Figure 16-4   A complete AV system line diagram that details each of the connections, the wiring run, and the components of the system

 CROSS-REFERENCE   See Chapter 4 for more information on TIA/EIA cabling standards.

A wiring plan for the distributed audio system should be developed with each of the three types of basic wire runs indicated on the plan. Figure 16-5 illustrates a very basic pre-wiring plan for 1) amplifier to distribution device, 2) distribution device to volume controls, and 3) volume controls to speakers.

There are four basic types of cable runs in a distributed audio system:

- **Amplifier to distribution device**   The source equipment is connected locally to the amplifier and it is then connected into the system's central distribution device. It is usually best to locate the distribution device as close to the amplifier as possible. The recommended cable support for the amplifier to distribution device is

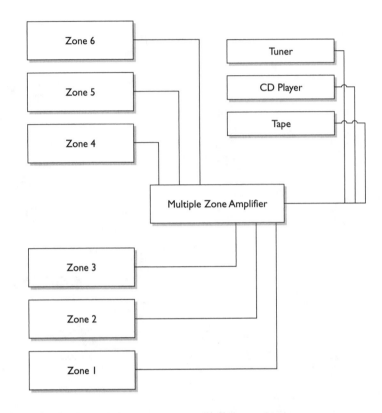

Figure 16-5
A distributed audio pre-wiring plan showing the paths of the cable runs

- **Three pairs (six conductors, usually 16- or 14-gauge) of speaker wire**   Four of the speaker wires' conductors connect and carry the left and right speaker signals from the amplifier to the distribution device. The remaining two conductors can optionally be used to carry direct current (DC) voltage to the distribution device for control applications.

- **One run of Cat 5e cable**   The four-pair Cat 5e cable provides support for such features as infrared (IR) extension, data communications, and video distribution.

 NOTE   Multiple cable runs should be planned into a room or zone to support situations where multiple system components are to be installed.

- **Distribution device to volume controls**   The cables in these runs connect the distribution device to the volume controls in each zone. The cables that should be included are

  - **Two pairs (four conductors) of speaker wire**   These wires carry the audio signals to the volume controls that will pass the signals to the speakers.

- **One run of Cat 5e cable** This cable provides for future expansion or a multiuse faceplate that could provide for a possible control keypad or IR reception for a remote control extension system. The cable can be used to support keypads, displays, amplified speakers, or IR extension systems. Many in-wall and ceiling speakers have knockouts that allow a remote IR sensor to be placed behind the speaker grill.

- **Volume controls to speakers** Wiring is required from the volume control to each speaker in a zone. The cabling in this run should include:

  - **One run of two-conductor speaker wire to each of the two speakers** These runs carry the audio signal from the volume control to each speaker.

  - **One run of four-conductor speaker wire to both of the speakers** Leave a two-foot loop of wire at the location of the first speaker, and then run the four-conductor cable to the other speaker's location. Four different colored wires allow for easy hookup and wire-pair matching at each speaker. Be sure you pay attention to the impedance of the system.

- **Local source to speakers** If the room has a CD, stereo, television, or another type of audio source component, the speaker wiring should loop from the volume control to the local source component and then on to the speaker. Both the four-conductor speaker wire and the Cat 5e cable should run from the volume control or keypad control and be connected to the outlet to be used by the local device. Figure 16-6 illustrates how a local source device is connected into a distributed audio system.

PART IV

Figure 16-6
Local audio source devices can be connected into a distributed audio system.

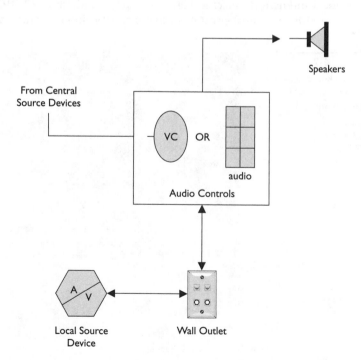

Cable Considerations

Typically, 16-gauge stranded twisted-pair (TP) wiring is used for an average length speaker run, with heavier wiring used for very long runs. The twist in the wire helps reduce the interference the cable could pick up.

There is a difference between real speaker cable and what is called interlink, or interconnect, cable. Speaker cable is designed to carry a powered signal, which means that it doesn't need much in the way of shielding to protect it from interference. Figure 16-7 shows an example of clear-jacketed speaker cable. Audio interconnect cables carry a line-level, nonpowered signal between two audio system devices and are susceptible to interference, therefore this type of audio cable requires shielding.

Choosing Speaker Wiring

There are several types of speaker wire on the market. The following terms are commonly used to describe speaker wire and its characteristics:

- **Cable Ratings**   The cable that meets the standards for a specific use is normally tested and rated for that use. For example, a cable designed for installation inside a wall, generally called plenum cable, carries a premise-wiring rating. Unfortunately, you can't assume that all speaker cable has a premise-wiring rating. Cable that has a premise-wiring rating complies with the National Electric Code (NEC) and National Fire Protection Agency (NFPA) standards, which provides you and your customer with the assurance that the cable meets the appropriate fire safety and electrical standards. Speaker cable that is installed inside a wall must meet all local and national electrical and fire safety standards as a high fire retardant wire. Premise rated speaker cable and wire carries either an Underwriters Laboratory

Figure 16-7
Clear-jacketed speaker cable provides no electrical shielding.

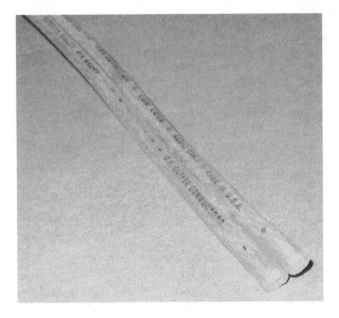

Speaker Wire Guidelines

When designing for the installation of speaker wire, there are a few guidelines you should observe:

- Speaker wire should be installed at least 2 feet from electrical wiring.

- If the speaker wire needs to cross an alternating current (AC) line, it should do so at a 90-degree angle.

- Always use full-run (continuous) lengths of cable when installing wiring in a wall or ceiling. If you absolutely cannot do so, two lengths of speaker wire should be joined using crimp connectors rather than wire nuts, but it is never recommended.

- Speaker wiring should be the last wiring you install. You should have already installed the electrical and data wiring, and should install the speaker wire directly after installing all HVAC and plumbing systems.

- In a new construction situation, the speaker wiring should be tested before and immediately after the dry wall is installed.

(UL) Class (CL) 3 or CL3R (riser) rating (see Figure 16-8). CL3 plenum cabling can be strung inside an HVAC duct, if needed, but the cable should not be installed on or near a dust-collecting electrostatic wire inside the duct.

- **Gauge** The wire gauge selected for a home AV system should be chosen based on its properties and the distance of the wiring runs. Speakers have low impedance (4 to 8 ohms); therefore, the resistance in the wiring is key to determining how much of the audio signal will reach the speaker. For example, a 100-foot run of 16-gauge TP wiring has a round-trip resistance of 0.8 ohms. When this wire is used with a 4-ohm speaker, 17 percent of the signal is lost to the resistance on the wire and only 83 percent of the sound signal actually reaches the speaker. The solution to this is to use heavier wire. The wire sizes typically used for home audio systems are 16 American Wire Gauge (AWG) or 14 AWG. They provide good compromises against signal loss, cost, and ease of installation. On top of that, the connectors on most audio devices are designed for these wiring sizes. Table 16-1 shows the

Figure 16-8
An illustration of a CL3-rated speaker cable

Original image courtesy of Canare Corp. of America.

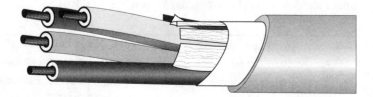

Speaker Ohms	Per cent of Db Loss	Power Loss	16 AWG Run	14 AWG Run
4	0.5	11	60 feet	100 feet
4	1.0	21	130 feet	210 feet
4	2.0	37	290 feet	460 feet
4	3.0	50	500 feet	790 feet
8	0.5	11	120 feet	190 feet
8	1.0	21	260 feet	410 feet
8	2.0	37	580 feet	930 feet
8	3.0	50	990 feet	1,580 feet

Table 16-1   Speaker Wire Power Loss Budget Table

power loss budget for 16 AWG and 14 AWG speaker wiring. Table 16-2 shows the gauge wire to be used based on the length of the run for virtually any home audio.

For virtually any home audio installation, 16 AWG or 14 AWG wire should work well for runs that are 100 feet or less. It is recommended that 12 AWG wire be used for runs in excess of 150 feet.

Design Issues

Here are some cable facts you should consider during the design phase:

- **Oxygen-free copper**   The best conductive copper for wiring and cabling is 99.99-percent oxygen free. Standard speaker wire cable is typically 99.90-percent oxygen free. If you wish to install the best cabling available, look for the code "OFC" (oxygen-free copper) printed on the cable's outer jacket.

- **Lower gauge/thicker cable**   A lot of speakers will work adequately with cable as small as 22-gauge wire. However, for longer cable runs, a thicker cable (with a lower gauge) extends the attenuation point of the wire. In terms of price and performance, at least 16-gauge wire should be used for the in-wall wiring for speakers.

- **High strand count/better performance**   When a higher number of strands are used in a wire, it creates a greater surface area. When a signal is transmitted across a wire, the electrons actually flow along the surface of the wire. So, more surface area means a better quality signal with less signal loss.

Table 16-2 Speaker Wire Gauge to Run Length	Wire Length to Speaker	Wire Gauge to Be Used
	50 to 100 feet	16-4 or 16-2 AWG speaker wire
	100 to 150 feet	14-4 or 14-2 AWG speaker wire
	Over 150 feet	12-4 or 12-2 AWG speaker wire

Audio System Rough-In

There are actually three different rough-in activities involved with a distributed audio system: wiring, speakers, and local room controls. Each of these rough-in activities has its own particulars, but in the end they all come together to provide the infrastructure of the audio system.

Rough-in is performed after the electrical cabling, plumbing, and HVAC rough-in has been completed and before the finished wall surface, typically drywall, is installed. Waiting until after the other rough-in work is completed prevents any of the other in-wall systems, such as running electrical wiring through the same holes of the audio wire, from interfering with the audio system's cabling.

Figure 16-9 illustrates the general concepts of rough-in for an audio system. Although this illustration simplifies this part of the project, it does show the parts of an audio system that are installed during the rough-in phase of the project.

Speaker Rough-in

During the design phase, either you or the customer (or both) have selected the size, shape, and brand of speakers and volume controls to be installed. When installing speakers and volume controls during a new construction project, you should install mounting brackets, if available, for any in-wall or in-ceiling, flush-mounted speakers and boxes for

PART IV

Figure 16-9
The primary components of a distributed audio

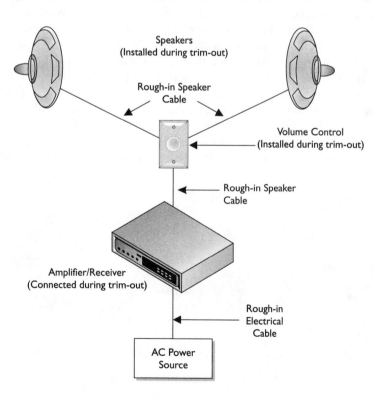

volume and keypad controls during the rough-in phase. Figure 16-10 shows the rough-in mounting bracket for a round in-ceiling speaker. Most speaker manufacturers sell rough-in kits separately for virtually all in-wall and surface mount audio speakers and controls.

Rough-in boxes for mounting volume controls or control keypads are available in a variety of types. These boxes and mounting brackets can be either single-gang or double-gang mountings, with open or backless boxes, to hold one or more control devices. Figure 16-11 shows two styles of rough-in mounting boxes for volume or keypad controls. In Figure 16-11, the box on the left is a single-gang backless box and the box on the right is an electrical box with a low-voltage mounting bracket attached to its side.

There are pros and cons to using rough-in kits. The benefits of rough-in mounting brackets include the early placement of speakers, resolving speaker mounting support issues, the fit of recessed speakers, and more accurate hole cutting when the drywall is installed. The primary disadvantages of using rough in kits are that they can lock in a device brand, size, and shape, permanently lock in the location of an audio system device, and the rough-in mounting's alignment is critical to the finished fit and alignment of a flush-mounted device.

In-wall and flush-mount speakers come in a variety of sizes and shapes. Typically, flush-mount ceiling speakers, like the one shown in Figure 16-12, require specific mountings to ensure fit and proper function, depending on their depth and circumference. If a mounting bracket isn't installed during rough-in, you have two choices: As illustrated in Figure 16-13, you can zigzag and loosely staple the wiring between a pair of studs that straddle the location of the speaker, or you can install a speaker that has mounting clips or clamps built in, like the speaker shown in Figure 16-14.If you choose to zigzag the wiring, you should photograph the wall prior to the drywall being installed over wiring so you later know where to make your cut in the drywall for installing the speaker.

Surface-mount or wall-mounted speakers require only that a standard J-box, mounting box, or mud ring, and of course the speaker cable, be installed so that the mounting bracket or foot on the speaker can be secured to the wall.

Whether or not a rough-in kit is used to locate a wall or ceiling speaker depends on the customer's wishes or your preferences. If the customer and you decide against using

Figure 16-10
A rough-in mounting bracket for a flush-mounted speaker

Photo courtesy of Crutchfield New Media, LLC.

Figure 16-11

Two styles of low-voltage boxes that can be installed during rough-in for later use for volume controls or keypads

Photos courtesy of Lamson & Sessions.

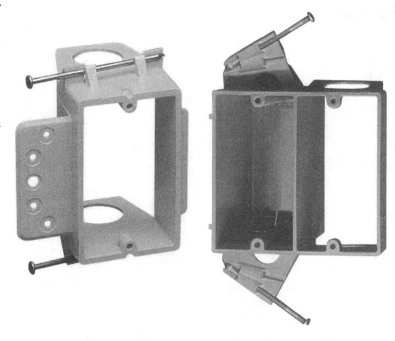

Figure 16-12

A flush-mounted ceiling speaker

Photo courtesy of Broan-NuTone, LLC.

Figure 16-13
Zigzag wiring between studs for future installation of speakers

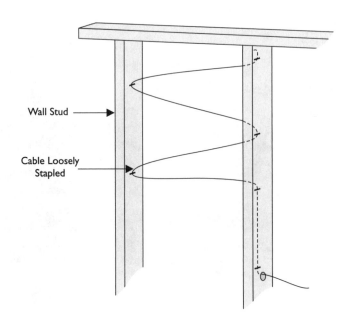

Wall Stud →

Cable Loosely Stapled

a rough-in mounting, remember that you will need to cut the drywall to accurately install the recessed speakers using the wiring installed during pre-wire in the locations documented by your pre-wire photographs.

Figure 16-14
A short depth recessed ceiling speaker

Photo courtesy of Niles Audio Corp.

Installing Audio Cable

In a new construction situation, the installation of audio cabling follows the general structured cable installation guidelines.

NOTE   As each cable is installed, it should be labeled according to the wiring diagram. Ensure that all of the cable that terminates at the central wiring distribution panel is labeled to ease the installation and connection of the distribution panel. The labels also help to facilitate wire testing and the trim-out and finish work yet to be accomplished.

CROSS-REFERENCE   See Chapters 5 and 6 for information on installing structured cable.

However, installing in-wall cable in what is called an "old work," or retrofit situation, rough-in is a bit trickier. The outlet boxes and cable must be installed behind existing walls without damaging the drywall surface.

Snaking in the Cable   Perhaps the hardest part of installing structured cabling in a retrofit situation is installing the cable inside the walls. Inside an existing wall there is likely electrical, telephone, and TV cabling, not to mention plumbing and perhaps wiring for other fixtures.

Depending on the home and its design, there are three options for installing audio cable (or any structured cable component):

- **Inside the walls**   This method requires that the cable be routed through the existing studs while avoiding electrical, plumbing, and other previously installed systems.

- **Through an attic**   Using this method, the audio cable can be run from the central distribution panel, which is referred to as an integrated service unit (ISU), to and through the top rail of the wall studs above the cavity in which the outlet box is or will be installed. Of course, using this method presumes a clear space exists above the main floor of the house in which to run the cable.

- **Under the floor**   Provided the house has either a basement or a crawl space in which to run the cables, the cables can be pulled through the footing rail of the wall studs and into the cavity in which the outlet box is installed.

Installing Cable in the Walls   Perhaps the most important task of installing audio cable in an existing wall is to first locate the wall studs and any plumbing lines that lay behind the drywall or other surface covering, such as lath and plaster. Most quality studfinders will locate wall studs as well as any metal behind the wall.

When all of the studs or pipes are located in the walls you plan to use to install the cable, you can plan the route for the audio cable. Always work with a whole-house diagram, rather than each room individually. Before you begin cutting access holes in the walls to run the cable, you should first check for obstructions or wiring in the space through which you plan on running cable. Once you have settled on the wire path, use either a drywall saw or a box cutter knife to cut away the drywall and expose the wall stud through which the cable will pass. Use a hand drill and a small drill bit to cut a hole in the wall in an out-of-the-way location that can be patched easily should the location prove unusable. A good practice is to use locations that are inconspicuous or can be hidden behind furniture or other objects.

Push a straightened-out wire coat hanger bent at an angle into the hole and fish around gently (there could be electrical wiring in there!) for any wires or pipes in the space where you plan on installing the audio cable. If you find fixtures in that location, adjust your wire plan accordingly.

Use a long-length drill bit to drill a wire path through the wall stud. A flexible shaft "flex-bit" is very handy in this application. Typically, the wire path should be at a slight downward slope because of the small opening in the wall through which the drill bit is inserted.

Push the cable through the wall opening and through the hole in the wall stud towards the next opening. Use the straightened coat hanger (with bent hook big enough to fit around the cable) to pull the wire to the wall opening. Drill the next hole, insert the cable, and pull it to the wall opening, repeating the steps until the cable is installed throughout the room or the house.

Special Installations   Not all walls have wood studs. In some newer construction, sheet metal studs may be used for a house's framing. In these cases, after drilling a hole for the cable, insert a plastic grommet before inserting the cable through the stud to protect the cable from the sharp edges of the metal.

When passing through a metal stud or ceiling joist, the NEC requires that the cable be no closer than 1.25-inches to the edge of the stud or joist and a protective plate that is at least 1/16 of an inch thick must be installed to protect the cable from nails or screws.

Remember that speaker wire should be installed separately from all other wire and should be at least 1-foot away from any other wiring, including other structured cable and electrical wire and any light fixtures in the walls or ceilings.

Volume Control Rough-In

In both new construction and retrofit situations, outlet boxes of sufficient depth to mount the volume control units must be installed in the walls where the volume controls are to be located. Follow the guidelines described in Chapter 3 to place the boxes in the walls and pull cable to them.

The speaker wiring should run to the volume control and then to the speakers to be controlled with a loop at the volume control location. Figure 16-15 shows an example of a local volume control device. In a multiple zone application, the speaker wire is usually left in a continuous loop to the speakers since the audio signal comes directly from the distribution equipment, and the Cat 5 cable is used to connect the local keypad to the system's zone control preamp at the main system location. Although many brands specify specific cables for their zone control keypads, most brands now offer compatibility with Cat 5 cable.

Local Source Rough-In

If the customer wishes to use the speakers in a room or zone for local AV sources in addition to the whole house system, some switching method, either manual or automatic, must be designed into the system. If local sources are designed into the system, the design must reflect that the speaker wiring go to the source switch before going to the speakers. If a local volume control is also included, it is wired before the source switch.

Testing the Cable

After the cabling is installed, a cable verification test should be performed. This testing determines if nails, screws, or any other sharp items in the wall may have damaged the

Figure 16-15

A remote speaker volume control

Photo courtesy of Niles Audio Corp.

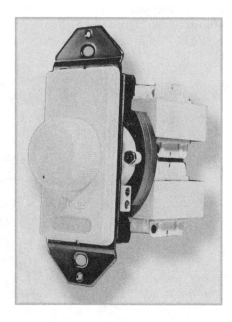

cable during installation. For any unterminated cable , such as speaker wire, the testing procedure should test for any opens or shorts in the speaker cable and the continuity of each conductor in the wire.

CROSS-REFERENCE   See Chapter I for more information on wire basics and wire testing procedures.

Audio System Trim-Out

As is the case in any trim-out operation, the cables are terminated and tested. In the trim-out phase of a distributed audio installation, each of the speakers, speaker jack wall plates, volume controls, and keypads are installed. Follow specific manufacturers' instructions for installation of these devices.

CROSS-REFERENCE   Chapter 2 details the audio connectors and when each is used.

In addition to the connectors detailed in Chapter 2, some speakers require spade-type connectors (illustrated in Figure 16-16). Spade connectors are crimp-on connectors that are easily installed.

Figure 16-16
An audio cable
terminated
with spade
connectors

*Photo courtesy of
Monster Cable Products,
Inc.*

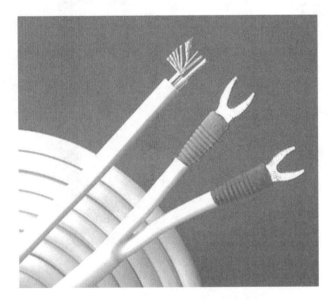

Audio System Setup and Testing

After all devices are trimmed out, install the components and hook up all equipment per documentation. Be sure to follow the line diagram of equipment hookup developed during the design phase. If any changes are made on site, be sure to record them on the line diagram so that final documentation of the system hookup is completed.

All control keypads need to be setup and programmed if necessary. This may include programming through setup software and learning the IR codes needed to control the equipment. Follow the manufacturers' documentation for setting up and programming.

Now test the system in every zone. Be sure to test each volume control in each location and make sure every speaker has output and sounds good. On the control keypads, test and verify every button performs as set up and programmed.

Chapter Review

The first consideration when planning a distributed audio system is whether the system is a retrofit or new construction. During the planning phase of the project, a number of issues must be considered, including single or multiple audio sources, zones or controllers, local source devices, future devices, the limitations of the floor plan, and the budget.

Begin the design with a floor plan and work with the customer to place the speakers, source equipment, and controllers into the rooms. During the design phase of the project, the decisions on the components to be included are made.

Speakers must be matched to the room size and the dB output desired. The factors involved are the number of rooms and the number of speakers in each room. The rule of thumb is that larger rooms need more power to produce acceptable sound levels. An average amplifier produces only a few watts of output power and the speakers may need higher sensitivity where louder volumes are desired. The placement of speakers in a room is typically the only method available to you to improve the acoustics of any space, assuming that the ceiling, walls, floors, locations, and coverings cannot be changed.

To improve the acoustical quality of any room, a number of issues should be considered in the design and placement of speakers in the room, including the dimensions of a room, the placement of doors and windows, the location of HVAC features, and the wall, ceiling, and floor materials and construction. Speakers should be placed in a room or zone where they produce the best sound applying certain principles: separation, zoning, and directionality.

The standard for the wiring systems in residential settings is TIA/EIA 570A, which provides specification and standards for the primary cable runs of a distributed audio system. There are four basic cable run types in a distributed audio system: amplifier to distribution device, distribution device to volume controls, volume controls to speakers, and local source to speakers. Several types of speaker wire are available. Cable rating and gauge are the terms commonly used to describe speaker wire and its characteristics.

Three rough-in activities are involved when installing a distributed audio system: wiring, installing speakers, and establishing local room controls. In a new construction situation, the installation of audio cabling follows the general structured cable installation guidelines. After installing the cable, it should be tested to determine if nails, screws, or any other sharp items in the wall have damaged it during installation.

During the trim-out operation, cables are terminated and tested and the speakers, wall plates, volume controls, and keypads are installed. After the connection devices are trimmed out, the components are installed and hooked up. Next, all controls are set up and programmed. Finally, the system is tested in every zone.

Questions

1. Which of the following is not a distributed audio system design consideration?

   A. Single or multiple audio sources

   B. Brand and model of source devices

   C. New or existing source units or speakers

   D. Budget

2. What is the purpose of an amplifier in a distributed audio system?

   A. Signal amplification

   B. Volume control

   C. Impedance matching

   D. Stereo sound balancing

3. What is the standard for residential structured wiring for audio?

   A. TIA/EIA 568A

   B. TIA/EIA 568B

   C. TIA/EIA 570A

   D. TIA/EIA 232

4. Which of the following is not a basic cable run in a distributed audio system?

   A. Amplifier to distribution device

   B. AC power wiring for source units

   C. Distribution device to volume controls

   D. Volume controls to speakers

5. By what factor should the amplifier's output be increased to affect a 10 dB increase in speaker output?

   A. Two

   B. Three

   C. Five

   D. Ten

6. During which phase of an audio installation project is the wiring installed?

   A. Planning

   B. Rough-in

   C. Trim-out

   D. Testing

7. What is the acoustic sensitivity rating of an average speaker?

   A. 80 dB/Wm

   B. 87 dB/Wm

   C. 90 dB/Wm

   D. 93 dB/Wm

8. What is the purpose for testing an audio cable at the end of the rough-in phase?

   A. Check for proper termination

   B. Check for shorts in the wire

   C. Check for wire continuity

   D. All of the above

9. What rating should an audio cable have to be installed in an HVAC duct?

   A. 22 AWG

   B. Premise wiring

   C. Plenum rating

   D. No specific rating required

10. Which of the following are included as rough-in activities when installing a distributed audio system?

    A. Wiring

    B. Installing speakers

    C. Establishing local room controls

    D. All of the above

Answers

1. **B.** During the planning phase, only the power requirements and impedance issues are important. The other choices are important, but perhaps budget is the most important consideration.

2. **A.** Most amplifiers don't perform the other actions listed.

3. **C.** TIA/EIA 568 standards cover Cat 5 wiring and 232 is a serial connection standard.

4. **B.** AC wiring is not included in structured wiring systems.

5. **A.** The amplifier's output in watts must be increased by a factor of two to achieve an increase of 10 db.

6. **B.** Wiring is pulled into the walls during the audio rough-in phase along with the installation of speaker brackets and boxes. Planning and testing are self-explanatory, and during trim-out the wire is terminated.

7. **C.** A rating of 87 dB/Wm or below is considered low sensitivity and a rating of 93 dB/Wm or higher is considered high sensitivity.

8. **D.** These are the primary tests that should be performed on newly installed and terminated cabling.

9. **C.** This rating describes a cable that is fire-rated for use in ducts and commercial applications.

10. **D.** Each of the activities included in answers A, B, and C are performed as rough-in activities for a distributed audio system.

Distributed Video Basics

In this chapter, you will learn about:

- Video signal transmissions
- Video standards
- Internet media
- Televisions and video monitors
- Personal video recorders (PVRs)
- Media servers

One of the truly daunting parts of writing a book on technology, let alone an emerging technology such as home audio video (AV), is that the technologies included are changing as fast as this book is written. Okay, it may not be as bad as that, but home AV technologies are fast moving targets. So, this chapter takes a look at some of the currently available AV recording, storage, and distribution devices.

Much of the material in this chapter is background information. However, that doesn't mean you don't need to know it. In fact, if you are new to distributed video, it is recommended that you read this chapter.

Transmitting Video Signals

Video signals are broadcast in either an analog or a digital format. Analog signals are broadcast through the air and received by a home's TV antenna. However, analog signals can also be transmitted to a home over a cable system. Digital video signals are typically not broadcast but transmitted over a cable system between a source device and a video display device. High-definition television (HDTV) is the closest an on-air analog broadcast system comes to reproducing the quality of a digital video signal because HDTV transmits a signal with more lines of resolution than the standard analog broadcast.

Analog video signals are radio frequency (RF) signals regardless of whether they are transmitted through the air or carried on a cable system. Broadcast, or "over the air," video signals are limited to licensed broadcasters, who are typically VHS broadcasters licensed by the Federal Communications Commission (FCC) to do so. Unlicensed, or "cable," operators transmit their video signals using dedicated broadcasting methods, such as microwave and cable transmissions.

Baseband Versus Broadband

There are two basic types of transmitted radio frequency (RF) signal formats used to carry video signals: baseband and broadband.

Baseband

Baseband communications use the entire transmission medium to carry a single frequency or composite signal in original, unmodulated form. There are three types of baseband signals:

- **Composite** This signal format transmits the complete video signal, including its picture (luminance), color (chrominance), and signal-blanking and synchronization pulses.

- **Component** This signal format uses three conductors to carry five separate frequency bands (one each for red, green, and blue, also know as RGB, and one each for luminance and chrominance. Component baseband is rarely used, except in very high-end video systems.

- **S-Video** This signal format, which is also known as Y/C video, super video, and separate video, transmits the luminance and chrominance signals separately, which improves the picture clarity. The Y (luminance) signal carries the brightness information and the C (chrominance) signal carries the color information.

Two baseband cables are required to transmit the video and audio source signals in a television broadcast. Figure 17-1 illustrates how broadband RF signals are received by an

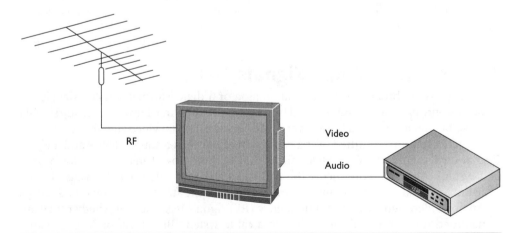

Figure 17-1 On-air baseband TV reception

antennae and passed to a TV receiver, which splits the audio and video into separate baseband signals for other devices.

Broadband

Broadband communications transmit multiple signals using a separate frequency for each one. The most common broadband video system is the cable television system, which transmits its broadband RF signals over coaxial cable. Broadband coaxial cable, which is commonly referred to as Community Access Television (CATV), is capable of transmitting 130 analog (RF) channel transmissions, and in some cases even more. Table 17-1 lists the standard channel allocations for broadband RF. Each channel carries both the audio and video signals of the transmission.

Modulation

The video device used to convert baseband to RF (broadband) signals is a modulator (more on modulators and other video devices later in the chapter). However, not all video signals require modulation. The analog video signals received by a home antenna and those transmitted over cable television service are RF signals and don't required modulation for transmission or playback.

Two objectives must be designed into the cabling (typically coaxial cabling) used to carry RF signals in a home's distributed video system: the signal strength must be sufficient to provide a quality signal to the display or playback device, and that radio and electrical interference must be minimized or eliminated. The best way to make these assurances in a video distribution signal is through the use of high-quality RG6 cable and connectors.

Video cabling is only able to transmit RF signals from point A to point B. They cannot be used in parallel to transmit signals in a one-to-many arrangement because the receiving end of the cable expects to receive only a single 75-ohm signal. In situations where a

Band	Frequencies	Broadcast Channels	CATV (Cable) Channels
Very High Frequency (VHF) Low Band	54 – 84 MHz	2 – 6	2 – 6
Frequency Modulation (FM) Radio	88 – 108 MHz		
CATV Mid Band	120 – 170 MHz		14 – 22
VHF High Band	174 – 212 MHz	7 – 13	7 – 13
CATV Super Band	216 – 296 MHz		23 – 36
CATV Hyper Band	300 – 468 MHz		37 – 64
CATV Extended Hyper Band	468 – 820 MHz		65 - 121
Ultra High Frequency (UHF) Band	470 – 806 MHz	14 – 69	

Table 17-1   RF Broadcast and CATV Bands

single RF video source is to be transmitted to more than one end device, a splitter (see Figure 17-2) must be used. A splitter is a device that takes in a single 75-ohm RF signal and outputs two or more separate 75-ohm signals. The most common type of splitter used is a passive splitter, which does nothing to enhance the strength of the split signals.

Another RF signal device that can be used in a distributed video system is a combiner, which is, in effect, the mirror opposite of a splitter. A combiner combines two (or more) incoming RF signals into a single combined broadband signal, as long as the two incoming signal lines don't share any common channels. A combiner can be used to combine cable television service with the signals from a digital satellite system passed through a modulator to change their channel modulations so there is no overlap with the cable channels.

Video Signal Loss

As the video signal is distributed throughout a home's video system, the signal strength suffers loss (meaning a loss of signal strength) as it passes through splitters, combiners, and connectors. As a result, the signal strength that reaches the display device may not be sufficient to provide a quality picture or sound, especially on systems where the video signal is being distributed to multiple displays.

 NOTE   Video signal strength is measured in decibels (dB), and most televisions require a signal between 0 dB and 12 dB, although most will operate with -4 dB to 15 dB.

To maximize signal strength, focus the antenna or satellite by using either a compass to point it in the appropriate direction of the broadcast source or the signal strength indicator that is sometimes built into the receiver. If you are not sure of the provider's transmission location, give them a telephone call.

For a strong enough signal where no amplifier is required you must have 0 dB signal off of an off-air antenna (ultra high frequency, or UHF, and very high frequency , or VHF). The digital satellite signal (DSS) level should be between -55 dB and -35 dB. Always

Figure 17-2
A one-line to two-line RF cable splitter with a distribution center mounting

Photo courtesy of Channel Vision.

use 75-ohm resistor terminators at any unused jack to prevent signals from traveling back up the line and causing ghosts. If direct current (DC) power or infrared (IR) signals are being sent over coaxial cable, use a DC blocking capacitor.

There are several places on a video line where signal loss can occur, but the most significant locations are:

- **Connectors**   Signal is lost wherever a connection is made. This is where most signal strength is lost in a typical residence.

- **Wiring**   Signal is lost as it travels through the coaxial cable. This loss is dependent on the length of the wire (the average is 3 dB to 6 dB of signal loss per 100 feet), the type of wire, and the frequency of the signal being carried. Losses are greater at higher frequencies; the greatest loss occurs at channel 13 in a VHF system or channel 83 in a UHF/VHF system.

- **Splitters**   Line splitters split the signal into two, three, four, or eight separate lines. Splitters divide the input signal equally, providing the same amount of signal at each output of the splitter. When a splitter is inserted in the line, the signal in each branch leg will be less. The quality of the splitter used does have an impact on the amount of loss incurred with the splitter. The losses that occur with average quality splitters are:

    - **Two-way splitter**   3.5 to 4 dB loss
    - **Three-way splitter**   3.5 dB loss
    - **Four-way splitter**   6.5 to 8 dB loss
    - **Eight-way splitter**   10 to 12 dB loss

The signal sent to each branch of the system is equal to the signal sent into the splitter minus the loss induced by the splitter. For example, an input of 30 dB into a three-way splitter delivers a signal of 26.5 dB to each branch of the system (30 dB minus a 3.5 dB loss).

Figure 17-3 illustrates this phenomenon. As illustrated, the incoming video line signal has signal strength of 15 dBmV (decibels per millivolt on a 75-ohm line). Each splitter or combiner device through which the signal passes causes signal loss in varying amounts (see Table 17-2). In Figure 17-3, an 8-way splitter causes a loss of -12 dBmV, reducing the signal to only 3 dBmV. A cable run of 100 feet introduces additional loss of -4 dBmV, leaving the cable with a negative gain or virtually no signal strength.

Figure 17-3

Signal loss on a video distribution system

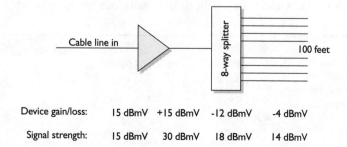

Device gain/loss:	15 dBmV	+15 dBmV	-12 dBmV	-4 dBmV
Signal strength:	15 dBmV	30 dBmV	18 dBmV	14 dBmV

Table 17-2	Device	General Signal Loss
General Signal Loss of Video Distribution Devices	2-way splitter/combiner	-4.0 dBmV
	3-way splitter/combiner	-6.5 dBmV
	4-way splitter/combiner	-8.0 dBmV
	8-way splitter/combiner	-12.0 dBmV
	100 feet RG6 cable	-4.0 dBmV

Signal loss can also be caused by the length of the cable over which it is transmitted. Table 17-3 lists the common signal loss (measured in decibels per each 100 feet of cable length) on the two standard coaxial cable types used in residential video systems.

Amplification

To overcome the loss of signal on the distributed video line, an amplifier should be added to the system. The purpose of the amplifier is to add sufficient gain to the signal to compensate for the signal loss on the line. Amplifiers also stop signals from radiating outside the house. To properly size an amplifier, the amount of loss accumulated on the distributed line must be added up (per the specifications of each device).

When choosing an amplifier, the four main considerations are the frequencies and number of channels to be received; the total distribution system losses (the losses caused by cable, splitters, and connectors); available input signals (the signal levels fed to the distribution amplifier input); and the output capability of the distribution amplifier (the maximum signal the amplifier can deliver without overloading). An amplifier has three primary inputs and outputs:

- **Input level** The video signal coming in
- **Gain** The amplification of the video signal
- **Output level** The video signal going out

Remember that the amplification of the input signal plus any gain added to the signal equals the signal strength of the output signal. The "input plus gain" of a signal needs to be greater than the total loss the signal suffers on the distribution system. However, the output level of the signal can never be greater than the output capability of the amplifier. Some amplifiers have a variable gain adjustment, which can be very useful in some applications. An attenuator/tilt compensator may need to be added to decrease the am-

Table 17-3	Frequency	RG59	RG6
Maximum Attenuation (dB Loss Per 100 feet)	55 MHz	2.06 dB	1.60 dB
	270 MHz	4.47 dB	3.50 dB
	400 MHz	5.48 dB	4.30 dB
	750 MHz	7.62 dB	6 dB
	1 GHz	8.87 dB	7 dB

plification of the lower frequency signals that are amplified much easier than the higher frequencies. Also, the FCC limits a signal to no more than 15.5 dBmv at any outlet.

In most installations, an isolation amplifier can be used to provide enough gain to compensate for the loss suffered by signals as they travel through the cabling and devices of a distributed audio system.. As illustrated in Figure 17-4, an isolation amplifier (labeled "AMP") is installed on the primary antenna or cable input line. This amplifier increases the gain on the line sufficiently high enough to withstand the loss introduced by the devices between it and the terminal device. However, an isolation amplifier is rarely needed, though in situations where the incoming signal is too weak to withstand passes through the distribution devices without additional amplification, it is an easy solution to the problem.

Another approach, and a more common solution, is the inclusion of a main system amplifier in the video distribution system. An amplifier with a variable output level (gain) is best, but a fixed output amplifier can be used, if it is able to provide sufficient gain to offset any loss in incoming signals. The amount of gain required from an amplifier is calculated by adding up the signal loss on the input side (before the amplifier) to the loss on the output side (after the amplifier).

An amplifier only converts an incoming signal, regardless of its source, into a signal that has increased amplitude, or signal strength, to ensure delivery and quality playback on any connected devices. Most common amplifiers have the capability to increase the gain (volume) potential of a signal from 0 MHz to 400 MHz, with somewhere around 100 MHz as typical.

Gain refers to the percentage of signal strength or performance when the input signal is compared to an amplifier's output signal. There are actually two types of gain associated with video systems. The first is the amplification of the audio signal that accompanies a video signal, which increases the volume potential for the playback. The second type of video gain refers to how much light (projected image) is reflected by a projection screen. As a screen is able to reflect more light, it produces a better quality image.

Receivers

Many systems combine the functions of an amplifier and a receiver, but these two devices perform completely separate functions. Most video receivers have an amplifier built-in. Very high-end systems may choose to use a separate amplifier, claiming that the receiver's circuitry can add noise in the form of a buzzing sound to the audio. However, this is true

Figure 17-4
An amplifier is added to the video circuit to overcome signal loss.

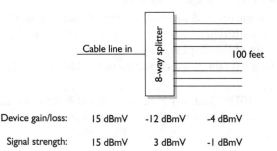

Cable line in   8-way splitter   100 feet

Device gain/loss:	15 dBmV	-12 dBmV	-4 dBmV
Signal strength:	15 dBmV	3 dBmV	-1 dBmV

PART IV

only on the very low-end units. Good quality receivers, not necessarily the most expensive ones, don't have this problem.

A receiver is an AV device that receives signals that are broadcast through the air and converts them to a form for viewing or listening presentation. There are receivers designed to receive and convert radio, satellite, cable, or microwave transmissions. A video receiver in its most common form is an ordinary television set and includes a complete AV system with a receiver, an amplifier, speakers, a display screen, an antenna, a tuning control, and volume controls.

An AV receiver is essentially an audio device that is included in a system to receive, convert, and coordinate the audio part of video playback. However, it should include support for all of the audio and video inputs that are planned to be used (and then some) and have the capability to pass video signals directly to a video display device.

Video Signal Formats

There are a variety of video signal formats in use in video distribution systems as well as on computers. The primary video signal formats are: RGB, component, S-Video, and composite.

Video signals are either optical or electronic. Optical signals originate from a camera or a scanner, and electronic signals originate from a computer's graphics card. Regardless of how a video signal originates, it is made up of electric impulses that represent the intensity of each of three primary colors—red, green, and blue (RGB)—and the vertical and horizontal synchronization of each picture frame.

The RGB encoding tells the display mechanism at the receiving end how to re-create each picture element (pixel) of the original image. It is assumed that the final image has red, green, or blue colors in it. The video signal indicates how much, or the intensity, of each color used in each pixel. The intensity of each of these three colors, when combined by the human eye, determines the final color displayed.

If you look at the display of your television set, assuming it has a Cathode Ray Tube (CRT)—more on this later in the section "Video Screen Formats"—using a magnifying glass, you should see either a dot pattern or a pattern of lines. In either of these display methods, an electron beam is used to energize colored phosphor, which coats the glass on the face of the CRT's tube either in patterns of dots or stripes.

Processing Video Signals

Regardless of the method used to create the display on the CRT, how the signal is processed, stored, or transmitted can have more to do with the quality of the displayed picture than the capability of the display device itself.

Table 17-4 lists the most common of the video signal formats in use.

 NOTE   You may have noticed that Red/Green/Blue (RGB) is not listed in Table 17-4. RGB is not a video standard. It is a standard for computer monitors.

Signal Format	Description
RGBHV	RGB with Horizontal and Vertical sync.
RGBS (RGB)	RGB with composite sync
RGsB (SoG)	Aka Sync on Green, RGB with a sync signal sent on the green single, like composite video.
YCrCb	Component video, a black and white composite video signal that includes Luminance (Y) brightness information and composite sync, and two signals that carry matrixed color information (Chrominance) for Red and Blue (Cr and Cb) that can be removed from the Y signal to yield the green information.
S-Video (Y-C)	Black and white composite video that contains Y brightness and composite sync information. The composite C (chrominance) contains all of the color information. S-Video is also referred to as SVHS.
Composite video	The one composite video signal contains all of the information on brightness, color, and synchronization.
TV/CATV	Composite video and audio modulated to allow multiple signals to share a common transmission medium, such as terrestrial aerial, cable TV, or satellite.

Table 17-4   Video Signal Formats

To combine the color information and the brightness and synchronization (timing) information, both must be coded. There are three primary coding schemes, also referred to as broadcast standards, in use:

- **National Television System Committee (NTSC)**   The NTSC developed the first color television coding system in 1953. It uses a fixed resolution of 525 horizontal lines and a variable number of vertical lines, depending on the electronics or format in use. NTSC displays 30 frames per second. NTSC is also a type of television signal that can be recorded by various tape recording formats, including VHS, 3/4-inch, and U-matic.

- **Phase Alternation by Line (PAL)**   This European improvement over NTSC was released in 1967. PAL uses 625 horizontal lines, which also make up its vertical resolution. It produces a more consistent tint, but at 25 frames per second.

- **Systeme Electronique Couleur Avec Memoire (SECAM)**   This encoding method was introduced in France in 1967 and, like PAL, uses 625 lines of resolution and displays 25 frames per second.

These three-color encoding standards are incompatible with one another. However, most modern television sets are multistandard and can decode a video signal encoded with any of these schemes. Table 17-5 provides a sampling of the countries using these three-color standards.

The most common of the video signal formats in use is S-Video. Virtually all AV amplifiers support S-Video, but only a few include higher-level formats such as component or RGBHV. If higher-level signal formats are all that is available, the signal can be converted to a lower-level signal for one or more devices. For example, an incoming RGB signal can

Table 17-5	Country	Encoding Standard
Video Color Encoding Methods Used Around the World	Canada	NTSC
	Chile	NTSC
	China	PAL
	Egypt	SECAM
	France	SECAM
	Japan	NTSC
	Mexico	NTSC
	Russia	SECAM
	United Kingdom	PAL
	USA	NTSC

be converted to S-Video for distribution throughout a home. Remember that there is no advantage or picture quality improvements gained by converting a signal to a higher-level format such as S-Video to RGB.

Television Video Formats

When the primary video types and broadcast standards are applied to the primary television formats, a variety of speeds, resolutions, and tape and disc record times result. Table 17-6 lists the various television, tape, and disc formats available.

Format	Broadcast Standard	Max Time (Minutes)	Media
VHS	NTSC	480	T-160
	PAL	600	E-300
	SECAM	600	E-300
SuperVHS	NTSC	480	ST-160
	PAL	480	SE-240
Digital VHS (D-VHS) and Digital Video Computing (DVC)	NTSC	60	MiniDV cassette
	PAL	180	DVC
Video 8	NTSC	240	P6-120
	PAL	180	P5-90
Hi-8	SECAM	180	P5-90
	NTSC	240	P6-120ME
	PAL	180	P5-90ME
LaserDisc	NTSC	60	Constant Linear Velocity (CLV)
	PAL	72	CLV
DVD	NTSC	Varies	Dual Layer (8.6 GB)

Table 17-6   Common Video Formats

Distributed Video Terminology

The following list includes the more important video system terms you should know when specifying, selecting, and interfacing with video systems:

- **Interface scan**   A display format where the displayed image is separated into two passes: the first pass scans the odd-numbered horizontal lines (1, 3, 5, and so on) and the second pass scans the even-numbered lines.

- **Progressive scan**   A display format that displays each horizontal lines of an image in a single pass at typically 24, 30, or 60 frames per second (fps).

- **National Television Standards Committee (NTSC)**   The signal format used to broadcast standard (non-HDTV) television.

- **Standard Definition Television (SDTV)**   The standard interlace scan TV display using 460 by 480 pixels. Also referred to as 480i.

- **Advanced Television Standards Committee (ATSC)**   The signal format used to broadcast HDTV.

- **Enhanced Definition Television (EDTV)**   A progressive scan format that supports 460 by 480 pixels (standard TV) and 720 by 480 pixels (widescreen). Also referred to as 480p (480 vertical lines using progressive scan) and 720p.

- **High Definition Television (HDTV)**   A display format that supports either 1280 by 720 pixels for progressive scan or 1920 by 1080 pixels for interlace scan. Also referred to as 1080i and 8-level Vestigial Sideband(8-VSB), which is the radio frequency broadcasting format used for HDTV.

- **ATSC (Advanced Television Standards Committee)**   The signal format used to broadcast HDTV.

Common Video Signals

For a home theatre installation, the video receiver should support the three primary video signal formats: component video, S-Video, and composite video. However, it is not common for an audio receiver to include jacks for all three input types. Sometimes there is a problem in that a receiver that does support these three signals may not include support for HDTV or progressive scan digital versatile disc or digital video disk (DVD) signals.

HDTV and Digital TV   HDTV is one of the digital television standards defined by the ATSC. Digital TV (DTV) transmits using binary data (using positive and negative electrical impulses to represent ones and zeroes, just like a computer uses) to encode its images and audio. Standard analog TV signals use waveforms, frequencies, and amplitudes to transmit images and audio. In addition to the actual images and audio, the digital data of the DTV signal includes information that defines the resolution, aspect ratio, refresh rate (how often the image is scanned), and the type of scanning in use (interface versus progressive).

HDTV can be delivered to a home using one of the following four methods:

- **Broadcast digital satellite** Companies like the DISH Network and DIRECTV offer HDTV to customers that have upgraded their satellite dishes and receivers for DTV signals. The satellite dish needs to be a dual-Low Noise Block Feedhorn (LNBF) to receive both HDTV and standard programming. Remember that standard digital satellite signals are not necessarily the same as DTV.

- **Over the air (OTA) broadcasting** A DTV antenna and a DTV receiver are required to receive OTA broadcast DTV signals. OTA DTV uses 8-VSB modulation.

- **Recorded media** HDTV programming that can be recorded on Digital VHS videotapes, DVDs, or high-definition PVRs. Playing back DTV from either a VHS or DVD source device may require replacing or upgrading the device.

- **Terrestrial cable** Cable television companies now offer HDTV channels that typically require a Quadrature Amplitude Modulation (QAM) set-top box to decode the DTV signals. QAM is the modulation method used to transmit DTV signals over a cable.

Video Bandwidth When choosing a video receiver it is very important to consider its bandwidth (MHz). Table 17-7 lists the bandwidth required by the common home video system components.

Emerging Home Audio Video Standards

Up to now, this book has discussed the separate and distinct standards that have been brought together to create a home AV system. Largely, a home AV system that meets or exceeds a customer's requirements is the result of the designer and the installer acting together as system integrators.

Device	Bandwidth Required
Standard DVD	7 MHz
Progressive scan DVD	14 MHz
Progressive scan to 4:3 compression devices	18 MHz
720p HDTV	22 MHz or 37 MHz
1080i HDTV	37 MHz

Table 17-7 Bandwidth Requirements of Video System Devices

Home AV Interoperability (HAVi)

Several leading consumer electronics and computer manufacturers are seeing the potential of integrating a variety of technologies in the home and as a result have developed the Home Audio/Visual Interoperability (HAVi) standard. The HAVi standard defines how home entertainment and communication devices interface and interact, including home PCs and single controller devices, such as TV sets, home appliances, radios, stereos, and more.

The primary difference between the HAVi standard and the general networking and interoperability guidelines now used is that HAVi uses the IEEE 1394 (FireWire or i.Link) standard as its interconnecting medium. Another big difference is that a HAVi network doesn't require a computer to interact.

For example, consider a home where the TV and telephone system have been integrated using a HAVi 1394 connection. When the telephone rings, the TV is programmed to automatically mute itself and switch to pick up the incoming video-telephone signal. Or, on another occasion, when a television show uses a word you don't recognize, you speak the word into a nearby microphone, which feeds the sound to an Internet browser-based audio to text dictionary lookup program that searches for the word and displays its meaning in the corner of the TV screen. You may even rig up the TV to serve first as a monitor to display the image captured by a security camera and then as a communication device between you and someone at the front door. At least these examples are within the goals of the HAVi initiative. The HAVi standard promises brand independence and interoperability, hot Plug and Play, and the ability to use some legacy devices that can be easily upgraded as required.

The HAVi specification is made up of a set of application programming interfaces (APIs) and interface software ("middleware") that can automatically detect entering or leaving devices on the network, manage their networking functions, and ensure their interoperability. HAVi relies on other home networking standards, such as Jini and Universal Plug and Play (UPnP), for its platform neutrality.

Jini

Unlike many Internet standards or products, the letters in the name Jini don't stand for anything. Jini is not an acronym; it is derived from the Arabic word for magician and pronounced as "DJEE-nee."

Jini was developed by Sun Microsystems as an architecture to help users create what Sun calls "spontaneous networking." It enables peripheral devices, such as printers, storage devices, speakers, and even computers, to be added to a network and become instantly available to everyone on the network. When a device is added to a network, every user is notified of its availability.

Jini is an extension of the Java programming language and is intended to provide the extension that allows a network to appear as one large computer, in application. Where HAVi has a consumer electronics focus, Jini is not limited to only consumer electronics and also extends to the computer and digital worlds, as well.

Versatile Home Network (VHN)

The Video Electronics Standards Association (VESA) establishes and supports industry-wide interface standards for personal computers, workstations, and other computing environments with an emphasis on interoperability and the display of information. In the late 1990s, VESA began working on a standard for home AV device interoperability, which they called the VESA Home Network (VHN) standard. VESA later combined with the Consumer Electronics Association (CEA) and renamed the standard the Versatile Home Network (VHN).

The VHN standard also uses IEEE 1394 as its backbone architecture on Cat 5 UTP cabling. Actually, it specifies the IEEE 1394b standard, a longer distance version of IEEE 1394. VHN uses the networking concept of IP subnetting to create its "zones." Because it uses the standard Internet Protocol (IP) technologies, non-IEEE 1394 devices can be used to create subnets for other home automation technologies, such as X10, CEBus, and others. Another benefit of an IP-based network is that it interfaces to the Internet very easily.

The idea behind the VHN standard is that the creation of a home network will become even more of a Plug and Play affair than it already is. Figure 17-5 illustrates the concept of a VHN.

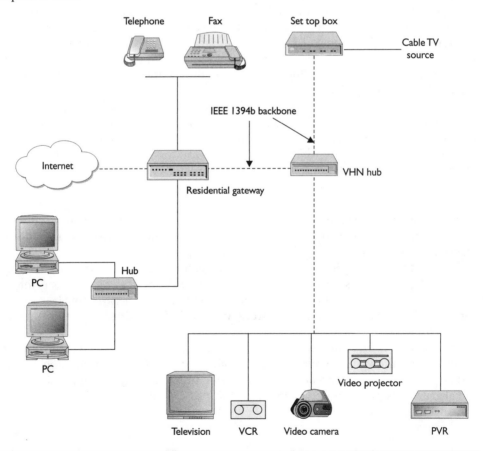

Figure 17-5   An example of a VHN that integrates both IEEE 1394b and IP networking.

Universal Plug and Play (UPnP)

The underlying standard for most home networking architectures, including HAVi and VHN, is UPnP, a Microsoft tool that provides discovery functions to dynamic network environments, like those we've been discussing. UPnP uses a series of IP-compatible protocols to provide services that discover and configure new devices added or removed from a network.

Internet Media

More and more the Internet is becoming a source of digital media. In the recent past, we've seen the tussles of Napster and KaZaA with the recording industry and copyright issues. However, with the emergence of pay-per-download sites, such as Apple's iTunes.com (www.apple.com/music/store) and BuyMusic.com (www.buymusic.com), and free-to-listen sites, such as Lycos Rhapsody (http://music.lycos.com/rhapsody) and Yahoo! Launch (launch.yahoo.com), you can download and enjoy music and video without risking heavy fines, being hauled into court, or going to jail.

On some "jukebox" sites, you can create a play list and listen to your favorite music via a streaming audio feed in much the same way you would listen to the radio, which is something else you can do online. The Internet is a very broad range receiver and allows you to listen to radio stations around the globe or those created especially for the Internet.

The number of video sources on the Internet is also growing. Sites such as MovieFlix.com (www.movieflix.com) and InternetMovies.com (www.internetmovies.com) allow you to open a streaming download of a movie and watch it on your desktop. Of course, the problem with watching a streaming download is that you can't save it to disk. If you want to watch the movie again or stop it and finish watching it later, you'd have to pay and download the movie again.

This problem is being solved by web sites such as MovieLink.com (www.movielink .com) that will sell or rent a (24-hour) license for a movie and allow you to download and store it on your computer for later viewing. It can't be that long before you'll be able to direct the stream to your PVR.

Streaming Media Types

Way back in 1995, before streaming technologies had come along, to play back an A/V file, the entire file had to be downloaded and stored before the playback could begin. At the data transfer speeds available at that time, a ten-minute video clip could take anywhere from two minutes to two hours to download.

With the advent of streaming media technologies, the content in an AV file can begin its playback as it is being downloaded and before the entire file is downloaded. Of course, heavy traffic on the Internet or an interruption in the connection can cause the sound or picture to break up or hesitate, but that's the price we pay for convenience.

There are actually two types of media streaming:

- **True streaming** This is the type of streaming described above. Playback of the AV content begins after only a portion of the file is received and it is continuous while the remainder of the file is received. True streaming is commonly used for longer AV files.

- **Progressive streaming**   Before the playback of a file begins, a significant portion of its contents must be received. This streaming method is common for short media pieces of 15 seconds or less and allows users to save the file to their hard drives for later viewing.

If you were to download a movie file from a pay-per-view site on the Internet, most likely the movie would be streamed to you using true streaming. However, if you were renting the movie for a period of time, the file would be streamed to you progressively so you could save it to disk.

Streaming media can include virtually any AV content that can be recorded, including text, recorded video or audio, still images, and live radio or television broadcasts. All of these media types can be consolidated into a single streaming file, provided the originator and the receiver each have the sufficient bandwidth to support it.

There are three major proprietary and distinct streaming technologies in use on the Internet: RealNetworks (RealMedia), Apple QuickTime, and Windows Media. At one time, to play back a file created for a particular media player, you needed to use that specific player. This is not the case anymore; with the exception of QuickTime, the players now play back each other's technologies.

Streaming Media File Formats

The most common streaming media file formats in use on the Internet are those that match up with the three most common streaming media players:

- **RealMedia**   The two primary file types used are RAM and RPM
  - RA   RealAudio clip
  - RAM   RealMedia file
  - RM   RealVideo and RealFlash clips
  - RPM   RealMedia plug-in file
- **QuickTime**
  - MOV   QuickTime movie file
  - QT, QTL, and QTM   QuickTime AV files
  - QTV and QTVR   QuickTime virtual reality movie files
- **Windows Media**
  - ASF   Windows Media Advanced Streaming Format file
  - AVI   Windows Media AV Interleaved file
  - WMA   Windows Media audio file
  - WMV   Windows Media AV file
  - WMX   Windows Media play list file

There are a few other open standard media file formats in use, with likely more to come, but for now the more popular ones are:

- **MPEG-2**   This media type is used commonly in digital TV, interactive graphics, and interactive multimedia. Don't confuse MP3 files with MPEG-3. MP3 files are actually MPEG-2 Layer 3 files.

- **MPEG-7**   This is an emerging standard that will allow users to search for audio and video files by their content.

- **Multipurpose Internet Mail Extension (MIME)**   There are several MIME file types, but only two AV file types: audio and video.

Video Receivers, Televisions, and Monitors

If the customer wishes to configure and install a home theatre or just merely connect her television set to the audio/video/computer-integrated network, there's more to it than just plugging the TV into the network.

Along with any decisions to be made about the wiring, speaker placement, seating arrangements, and the like, there are a number of video system issues that must be considered, including screen formats, amplifiers and receivers, sound formats, DVD or CD capabilities, and the display device itself. Once you have a clear understanding of the customer's vision, you can work through these issues to design and implement the customer's dream system.

Video Screen Formats

One of the primary considerations when choosing a video display device is aspect ratio. Occasionally when you watch a movie on television, or a rented DVD or video, the image is centered vertically on the screen and the top and bottom portions of the screen are black boxes. The black areas are called letterboxes and are the result of a video signal that is set for a different aspect ratio than your television or monitor supports. In this case, the video is playing back in widescreen and not full screen.

Aspect Ratio

The aspect ratio of any display device, including televisions and monitors, states the number of picture elements (pixels) used horizontally and vertically to form the displayed image. For example, most display devices are set for an aspect ratio of 4:3, or four to three. This means that for every four horizontal pixels used in the display, three vertical pixels are used. Another way to think about this is that the image is displayed about 1.33 times wider than it is tall. Widescreen video is set for a 16:9 aspect ratio, which is why it doesn't always exactly fit on a home television set. The 4:3 aspect ratio has the early standard for the movie industry.

When television became popular in the 1950s, it too adopted the 4:3 aspect ration, so it could show movies in their standard form. To compete with television, the movie industry began creating different screen formats, especially those that provided a wider or larger image display, such as CinemaScope and Panavision. Today the recognized standards of the movie industry are 1.85:1, which is called Academy Flat, and 2.35:1, which is called Anamorphic Scope. These standards are often translated into a standard aspect ratio of 16:9, or 16 units of width for each 9 units of height.

Three methods are used to fit the motion picture's 16:9 aspect ratio onto the television's 4:3:

- **Letterbox** When a 16:9 picture is fitted onto a 4:3 television frame, the result is black bars at the top and bottom of the displayed picture. This reduces the displayed image to what can be likened to a mail slot or a letterbox. This is a common effect from DVDs.

- **Pan and scan** This method produces a full-screen display at the cost of picture quality. The image is created by panning and scanning left to right in order to fit the entire picture on the display. This method is common with VHS tapes and movies shown on broadcast television.

- **Movie compression** This method forces the 16:9 image into the 4:3 display and produces images that are taller and thinner in appearance than intended.

Of course, the solution to the incompatibility between 16:9 and 4:3 is to display the image on a display device that can handle the widescreen aspect ratio of the movie.

Resolution

A display characteristic closely related to the aspect ratio is resolution that defines the number of pixels used to produce the displayed image. As more pixels are used to display an image, the image quality improves.

The resolution of the displayed image on a television or monitor can be the result of any one, two, or all of the following factors:

- **Transmission quality** The extent to which the resolution of the original picture when it is broadcasted or stored (like on a DVD) is retained has a direct bearing on the resolution of the displayed image.

- **Recording quality** The resolution used to capture live or art-based images can impact the resolution that can be produced by the display device during playback.

- Displayed resolution The resolution that a display device is capable of producing is the final link in the picture quality of a displayed image.

Nearly all display devices produce an image by electrifying clusters of RGB dots. Just like the images in a black and white newspaper are made up of dots of black printed on a white background, where the number and separation of the dots causes the human eye and brain to form a picture using shades of black and gray, a television uses illuminated RGB dots (see Figure 17-6) that the human eye and brain can make into images.

Most conventional television sets and computer monitors use a picture tube that is a Cathode Ray Tube (CRT). A CRT produces an image by illuminating color dots with an electron beam, as illustrated in Figure 17-7. The intensity used to illuminate a pixel and its proximity to other pixels causes the human eye to assign a color or shade to that area

Figure 17-6
A color display picture element (pixel) is made up of red, green, and blue dots.

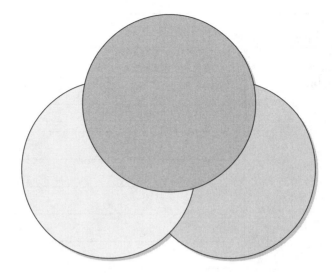

of the screen. It is the number of pixels horizontally and vertically used to create the displayed image that defines a display's resolution.

 NOTE Although the CRT is used to explain the concepts of displaying an image, these characteristics also apply to other display types, including liquid crystal display (LCD) and plasma. Display types are discussed later in the section "Video Display Devices."

The CRT and virtually all other display types must refresh the display constantly to keep each pixel illuminated (the brightness of an illuminated pixel begins to fade almost immediately) and to accommodate changes in the image, like the motion in a motion picture. To refresh the screen, the electron gun sweeps (scans) the screen in a left to right, top to bottom pattern, sometimes in multiple zones of the screen simultaneously. Figure 17-8 illustrates a common scan pattern for a CRT display device.

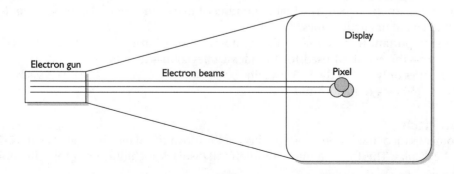

Figure 17-7   An electron beam is used to illuminate picture elements (pixels) on a CRT's display.

Figure 17-8
The scan pattern used by a conventional CRT display

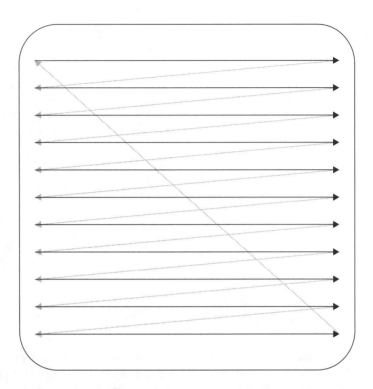

The common resolutions for television, recorded, or broadcast images use 525 horizontal scan lines (top to bottom) on the display screen. The resolution of the display is stated as the number of pixels available on each horizontal scan line. The most common advertised horizontal resolutions for television sets are 240, 425, 500, with some even higher. The number of scan lines on the display establishes the vertical resolution for the display, typically 525 scan lines. So, for an average television set, the resolution could be 500 by 525, or 500 horizontal pixels and 525 vertical pixel rows (scan lines).

Of course, the size of the display and the size of each pixel has a direct bearing on the number of pixels that will fit on each horizontal line and the number of scan lines that can be fit onto the screen. The higher number of pixels, the better the display can deal with diagonal or circular lines.

It is important to note that a display doesn't use all of its scan lines in the NTSC standard—the standard used for broadcast television—to produce an image. There picture uses only 480 of the 525 scan lines, and each line has only 440 pixels visible, to create a 480 by 440 picture grid.

Dot Pitch
Another factor of resolution is the dot pitch, or the proximity of the pixels (see Figure 17-9), on the display. This factor applies to virtually all displays, including rear projection units as well.

Figure 17-9
Dot pitch
measures the
space between
picture elements.

Dot pitch

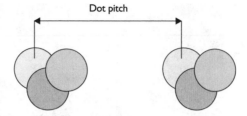

Video Display Devices

Video display devices, or terminal devices that can reproduce video images, and typically audio sound, from either an amplified digital or analog signal, are available in a variety of types and sizes, with a variety of capabilities.

The most common video display device types are:

- CRT
- Flat panel
- Projection

NOTE   CRT displays, actually standard television sets, are discussed in the preceding section.

Flat Panel Displays

It wasn't that long ago that hanging a television screen on a wall like a piece of art was considered science fiction. However, with the development of flat panel technology, a variety of displays are available that can be hung on the wall or placed on a narrow table. It is no longer necessary to assign floor space solely to a television. Flat panel screens, like the one shown in Figure 17-10 can be set on furniture, hung on the wall, ceiling, or placed just about anywhere.

Flat panel display devices are currently available using two primary display technologies: advanced liquid crystal display (LCD) and plasma.

LCD Displays   LCD screens use positive and negative voltage to rotate the polarization of the crystals to either pass or block light through the crystal. The crystals form the pixels used to produce the displayed image. LCD televisions are backlighted and the crystals reflect and manipulate the light. LCD displays are available in sizes that range from 6 inches, measured diagonally, to 45 inches (and soon larger, we're sure).

Plasma Displays   Plasma displays have been in use for a number of years in point-of-sale monochrome displays and other similar uses. However, using a plasma display as a television monitor, as in Plasmavision, is a relatively new use of this technology.

The technology of a color plasma display is very similar to that used in a conventional CRT (discussed earlier in the section "Video Display Devices"). The display consists of

PART IV

Figure 17-10
A flat panel
television display

*Photo courtesy of Sony
Electronics, Inc.*

an array of RGB cells (pixels). An electrical current reacts with the cells that contain gas in its plasma state that is conductive to produce light in an RGB color. Unlike LCDs, plasma displays produce their own light source and are not backlighted. Plasma screens are available in sizes that run from 30 inches to more than 60 inches.

The advantages of a plasma television display are:

- **Higher resolution**   Compared to standard, and even some DTV sets, a plasma display uses 1024 by 1024 pixels to display its images.

- **Wide aspect ratio**   Plasma displays have a 16:9 aspect ratio.

- **Flat screen**   A CRT screen is curved and can distort an image along the side edges and in the corners. This is eliminated on a flat screen and the picture can also be viewed from wide angles as well.

Plasma Displays Versus LCDs   LCDs seem to have an edge in terms of quality and reliability over plasma displays. The most commonly cited advantages of LCD over plasma are:

- LCDs produce an image that is crisper and brighter than a plasma display.

- LCDs don't have a burn-in effect, like a plasma display does, where the phosphors used to produce an image etch the glass covering of the display and produce ghost-like images.

- Using today's technology, LCDs have a longer life of approximately 50,000 hours versus approximately 30,000 hours for a plasma display.

- LCD televisions weigh 10 to 15 percent less than a plasma television of the same size.

- LCD displays are more readable in daylight, though plasma displays have a brighter display in a darkened room.

Video Projection Systems

One of the options available for a home theatre system, meaning beyond a standard television set or an LCD or plasma television, is a video projection system (see Figure 17-11). These devices project the images transmitted to them on a screen or virtually any flat surface.

The most common types of video projectors use one of two technologies:

- **Digital light processing (DLP)** A DLP projector directs light through a rotating RGB filter onto a digital micro-mirror device (DMD) chip that reflects the colored light out of the projector's lens and onto a screen. The DMD chip is covered with more than 900,000 micro-mirrors, each producing one pixel of the displayed image.

- **LCD technology** An LCD projector uses three LCD glass panels, one each for red, green, and blue, to project the image transmitted to the projector. The light that is passing through the color glass panels is controlled using LCD technology and the opening and closing of the liquid crystals.

DLP and LCD projectors are typically front or forward projectors and both are commonly used as ceiling-mounted projection systems. The major difference between LCD and DLP projectors is color adjustment. Because an LCD project uses separate controls for RGB, its brightness, color, and contrast can be adjusted at the color channel level. This adjustment process can take quite a bit of time: four hours or so. An LCD projector typically produces a brighter display. On the other hand, the color settings on a DLP projector are essentially fixed in place and require minimal or no adjustment.

PART IV

Figure 17-11
A video projector is used to project a television image on a screen.

Photo courtesy of ViewSonic Corp.

Personal Video Recorders

For most downloaded AV files, once you have them stored on a computer hard drive, it is a simple matter of opening them to play them again. However, what about storing live television or radio for later playback? Well, there are two ways to go: use a PVR or convert a personal computer (PC) into a digital video recording device.

In order to pass an AV file intact between one device and another, the AV content has to have been recorded in a digital format. This can take place on a computer, digital video camera, or a digital video recorder (DVR).

Adding a PVR device to a home network allows a homeowner to expand the capabilities of a traditional video system. Products are now available that incorporate live Internet streaming, video archiving, and format translation directly into the network (see Figure 17-12). In other words, having an integrated PVR function on the network is like having an AV studio with an IP address.

Other PVR devices such as ReplayTV and TiVo can record up to 80 hours of television in digital format. PVRs can be stand-alone devices, like the ReplayTV shown in Figure 17-13, or they can be built into set-top devices, such as a digital broadcast satellite (DBS) receiver.

Some other features of PVRs are:

- **Share recorded programs**   Two PVRs can share recorded content room to room as a streaming file, as a file transfer, or as a file transfer over the Internet.

- **Digital audio output**   Connects the PVR sound output into a sound system.

- **Instant replay**   Jumps back in seven-second intervals to replay a missed segment.

PC-Based PVR

A home computer can also be used as a PVR by installing a PVR expansion card into the computer. Products like the one shown in Figure 17-14, enable a user to watch TV on a PC and to record from a cable or antenna television feed or stereo FM radio, as well as other digital video sources.

Figure 17-12
An IP-addressable
DVR that can be
added into a
home network

*Photo courtesy of
Digital Rapids Corp.*

Figure 17-13
A personal video
recorder (PVR)

*Photo courtesy
of TiVo, Inc.*

Media Servers

In the context of home automation, a media server refers to any network computer or network device that uses UPnP to recognize and connect to any consumer electronic (CE) device and supports any AV content produced by the CE device. In the UPnP world, devices like VCRs, CD players, DVD players, audiotape players, digital cameras, digital camcorders, radios, PVRs, televisions, set top boxes, and, of course, a computer, can all be a media server.

A media server acts as a go-between to mitigate the various file formats used by the different AV devices and provides a compatible format to each device wishing to access media files. The functions performed by a media server include:

- Identifying the media content provided to clients on the home network
- Processing requests for media content from networked devices and negotiating a common transfer protocol and file format
- Controlling the transfer of media content to target devices

Figure 17-14
A TV PVR
expansion card
converts a
desktop PC into
a personal video
recorder.

*Photo courtesy of
AverMedia Technologies,
Inc.*

The term media server is commonly used in connection with Voice over IP (VoIP) functions, and in instances where a customer wishes to install VoIP functions on a home network, a media server function must be present on the network. VoIP media servers are normally created with the installation of the VoIP control software.

Chapter Review

Video signals are broadcast in either an analog or a digital format. Analog signals are RF signals that are broadcasted through the air and received by a home TV antenna or transmitted over a cable system. Digital video signals are transmitted over a cable system.

Broadband coaxial cable is capable of transmitting 130 analog channels; baseband video cable is capable of carrying only a single video or an audio transmission. The video device used to convert baseband to broadband signals is a modulator.

In situations where a single RF video source is to be transmitted to more than one end-device, a splitter is used. Another RF signal device used in a distributed video system is a combiner, which combines two (or more) incoming RF signals into a single broadband signal.

Splitters, combiners, and even connectors can impact the video signal's strength. An amplifier is used to compensate for the signal loss on the line. An isolation amplifier can be installed on the incoming line to provide sufficiently high enough gain. A main system amplifier with a variable output level may also be used. An amplifier increases the gain of the incoming signal.

A receiver is an AV device that receives broadcasted signals and converts them for viewing or listening. The most common video receiver is a television set.

There are a variety of video signal formats in use in video distribution systems as well as on computers. The primary video signal formats are: RGB, component, S-Video, and composite. The three primary coding schemes or broadcast standards are: NTSC, PAL, and SECAM. The most common video signal format is S-Video, which is supported by virtually all AV amplifiers.

HDTV is one of the digital television standards defined by the ATSC. Digital TV transmits using binary data (using positive and negative electrical impulses to represent ones and zeroes, just like a computer uses) to encode its images and audio. HDTV can be delivered to a home using one of the following four methods: broadcast digital satellite, over the air broadcasting, recorded media, and terrestrial cable.

Several new AV standards are emerging, including HAVi, IEEE 1394, Jini, VHN, and UPnP. In addition, Internet-ready devices can support two types of media streaming: true streaming and progressive streaming. The primary streaming media formats are RealMedia, QuickTime, and Windows Media. Other open standard file formats also used for Internet media are MPEG-2, MPEG-7, and MIME.

The primary considerations when choosing a video display device are aspect ratio, resolution, and dot pitch. Different methods are used to display incompatible aspect ratios: letterbox, pan and scan, and movie compression. Resolution is the number of pixels used to produce a displayed image. It is the result of three factors: transmission quality, recording quality, and display resolution. Dot pitch is the proximity of the pixels on a display. The most common video display device types are CRT, flat panel, and projection.

Storing live television or radio for later playback can be accomplished using a PVR. A media server refers to any networked computer that connects to any consumer electronic device.

Questions

1. Which of the following standards makes a network appear to be a single computer?

   A. VHN

   B. HAVi

   C. Jini

   D. UPnP

2. What is the backbone architecture used with the VHN standard?

   A. IEEE 1284

   B. IEEE 802.3

   C. IEEE 1394b

   D. IEEE 802.15

3. What is the underlying discovery function in HAVi and VHN?

   A. UPnP

   B. IEEE 1394

   C. True streaming

   D. IP

4. What type of file is an AV file where playback can begin prior to the entire file being received?

   A. Digital

   B. Streaming

   C. Analog

   D. Progressive

5. What differentiates a progressive streaming file from a true streaming file?

   A. A significant portion of the file must be received before playback begins.

   B. Only a small portion of the file must be received before playback begins.

   C. All of the file must be received before playback can begin.

   D. There is no substantial difference between a progressive and a true streaming file.

6. Which two of the following are technologies used with flat panel displays?

   A. CRT

   B. DLT

   C. Plasma

   D. LCD

7. Which of the following aspect ratios produces the widest displayed image?

   A. 4:3

   B. 1.33:1

   C. 16:9

   D. The aspect ratio doesn't affect the width of the display.

8. What video display characteristic most affects the clarity of the displayed image?

   A. Aspect ratio

   B. RGB

   C. Resolution

   D. Refresh rate

9. What is the common name for a device that records from a digital television feed preset by a user?

   A. Digital object recorder

   B. Video cassette recorder

   C. Personal video recorder

   D. Personal object recorder

10. What is the device or service that coordinates and supports the AV content produced by UPnP CE devices on a home network?

   A. VoIP server

   B. Media server

   C. Media client

   D. UPnP server

Answers

1. **C.** This Sun Microsystems protocol creates seamlessness for the network for all devices. VHN and HAVi are home AV network standards and UPnP is a device discovery and configuration protocol commonly used with CE.

2. **C.** Remember that the b version of IEEE 1394 is a faster, more robust version. The other choices are printer and Ethernet networking standards.

3. **A.** UPnP is commonly used in most home AV standards.

4. **B.** Of course it may be digital, but that has nothing to do with its playback format. It could be progressive, but it must first be streaming. Analog files aren't streamed.

5. **A.** As opposed to a streaming video file, more of a progressive streaming file must be buffered (received) before its playback can begin.

6. **C, D.** CRT is the picture tube in a conventional television and DLP is the technology used in one type of a projection television.

7. **C.** The standard aspect ratio for widescreen displays is 16.9. 4:3 and 1.33:1 are equivalent aspect ratios. Choice D is absolutely false.

8. **C.** The higher the resolution capability on a display, the better the picture quality is likely to be, subject to the resolution of the original image. None of the other choices have much to do with the clarity of the displayed image.

9. **C.** PVRs are also called digital video recorders (DVRs).

10. **B.** A media server is also a central component of a VoIP network.

Designing and Installing Distributed Video Systems

In this chapter, you will learn about:

- Designing and planning a distributed video system
- Performing a rough-in installation
- Performing a trim-out installation
- Configuring and connecting the components of a distributed video system

A distributed video system is a network of video source and display devices that are interconnected through a house's structured wiring and a centralized service panel or facility. What a distributed video system can do is allow the output signals produced by a DVD, video cassette recorder (VCR), personal video recorder (PVR), satellite or cable TV, or any other video playback device to be viewed in any room of the house that is connected to the system. No longer will each room need its own VCR, DVD, or receiver in order for multiple viewers in multiple rooms to view the same programs.

Often, a key element of a complete distributed home video system is one or more security surveillance cameras and the associated video monitors. However, that part of a video system is covered in Chapter 35.

Designing a Distributed Video System

The design of a distributed video system should be developed using a systematic approach intended to identify the customers' objectives and the equipment, cabling, and controls needed to achieve their goals.

Your role in this process, besides that of the designer, is to guide your customers through the maze of choices in equipment, layout, function, and installation to create a distributed video system that meets or exceeds their wishes, while remaining within or below their budget.

Performing the design steps in a certain sequence is the best way to complete the design phase to everyone's satisfaction. The major steps of the design phase should be

1. Identifying and designating the distribution points

2. Planning the layout of each room or zone

3. Deciding on the control system to be used in each room or zone

4. Planning for the centralization of the source equipment

Each of these design phase activities is outlined in the sections that follow.

Designate the Distribution Points

The decision of whether or not any particular room in a house is wired into a whole house distributed video system is strictly that of the homeowner. If the customer wishes to have the bathrooms, laundry rooms, or storage rooms, in addition to the living room, family room, bedrooms, and other living spaces, included in the system, then so be it. However, you should point out that each room should be considered on a cost-benefit basis. In most situations, only the living room, family room, den, one or more bedrooms, and perhaps a home theater or home office are included in a distributed video system. However, the choice is up to the customer.

In a structured wiring environment, the potential distribution points are based on the wiring and where the video system is or will be installed. Where the video system is able to connect to the wiring can, in many situations, predetermine its design and potential distribution among separate rooms or zones.

Essentially, each area of a house that shares a common video signal belongs to the same video zone as any other area also receiving that signal. If the video distribution system is to provide the capability for each room to select its own source device or signal, then each room is potentially a separate zone. Whether a distributed video system is to support one, two, or multiple zones is a key decision that must be made early on in the design phase of the project.

Lay Out Each Room

Unlike a distributed audio system, which should complement the video system, the primary choices for each room are where the video cable will terminate at a wall jack and if a control system or extender is to be installed, what kind is to be installed and, if applicable, where it is to be located. In most situations, these issues are usually considered during the planning of the structured wiring.

 CROSS-REFERENCE See Chapter 6 for more information on structured wiring design.

The ideal situation is to place the video connection in proximity to the video display device. For example, if a standard television in a bedroom is to be connected to the system, then the video connector should be on the wall, behind, or close to the side of the TV set.

Decide on the Control System

One of the most important decisions to be made with designing a distributed video system is the type of controls to be installed in each zone. If all zones are to receive the same video signal, then perhaps only on/off and volume controls are needed in each room for the audio. However, if the intent is that each room can choose its audio source device or video signal, then more sophisticated controls are necessary.

On most zone video display devices, the volume control is part of the same device, like it is on a television set or a computer. However, if a stand-alone video monitor or display device that lacks volume controls is used and the audio portion is to be fed to speakers in the room, the audio portion of the signal must be controlled separately. Video system controls that can be mounted on a wall or other room surface range from relatively simple volume controls to sophisticated LCD touch screen panels and multiple device controllers.

Local Control

The on/off function on any video display device physically located in a zone can be easily controlled from a local handheld remote control or on the device itself. This allows for local control of the display device (on/off/source/channel). It also allows for control of the audio if the audio comes directly from a display device such as speakers built into the television. When the audio of the local video display device has been integrated into an audio system, it can be controlled manually with a volume control.

Volume controls are typically rheostat controls that look very much like the dimmer dials used with lighting systems (see Figure 18-1). The idea is simple: turn the dial to turn up or turn down the volume. Most rotary dial volume controls have 8 to 12 volume level settings and an on/off position as well.

 CROSS-REFERENCE See Chapter 15 for more information on audio control.

Multiple Device Control

If the customer wishes to be able to control a centralized source device from a zone, some form of remote controller is necessary. Multifunction controllers, on the low-end, are all-in-one handheld remote controls like the one shown in Figure 18-2. These devices can be easily programmed to control multiple source devices, provided line-of-sight between the control and each device is possible.

Figure 18-1
A wall-mounted volume control to control the audio portion of a distributed video system

Photo courtesy of Niles Audio.

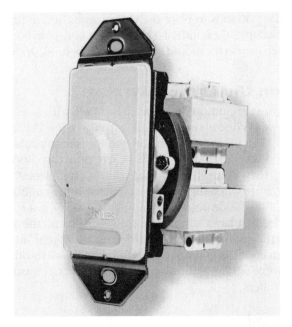

The technology of handheld and hands-free remotes is evolving quickly. For example, the remote shown in Figure 18-3 can be operated as a handheld remote control, or as a hands-free remote using voice-activated commands.

Figure 18-2
An all-in-one remote control unit

Photo courtesy of Intrigue Technologies, Inc.

Figure 18-3

An Invoca remote control that can be used as either a handheld or a hands-free remote

Photo courtesy of Brookstone Company, Inc.

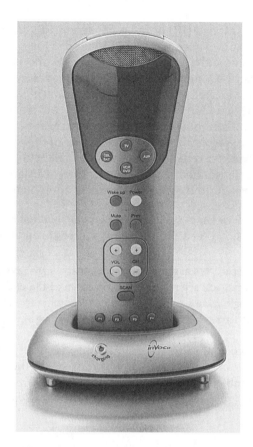

PART IV

Controlling a Centralized System

Regardless if the home video system is in one or multiple zones, the key to ease-of-use is the ability to control the centrally located equipment from any remote listening or viewing location. The best approach to controlling a home audio visual (AV) system is through the use of distributed remote controls that transmit control signals back to the central equipment as if the user were standing right in front of it.

The most popular ways of controlling a connected AV system from a zone are

- **Wired infrared (IR)**   Wired IR is considered to be the most foolproof way to control remote devices. It incorporates an IR receiver placed in a remote location, such as a master bedroom, which is then wired to an IR emitter that has line-of-sight to the equipment being controlled, such as a CD player in the the family room.

CROSS-REFERENCE   See Chapter 17 for more information on IR control.

- **Wireless infrared (IR) or radio frequency (RF)** Wireless is generally considered a single zone solution, but this method is the easiest and least expensive to implement and use. How this approach works is that the IR beam or radio frequency (RF) signal produced by the wireless remote control is received by a receiver located either in the same room (in the case of IR, it requires line-of-sight) or within a 100-foot range and converted into either a RF signal or a powerline control (PLC) signal that is transmitted to a base station attached to the device being controlled. An example of this system is shown in Figure 18-4. This device converts IR signals from a handheld remote control into RF signals that are transmitted to the receiver, where the signals are converted back into IR and "flashed" to operate the electronic equipment.

IR and RF extender systems are also available that translate the control signal for transmission over a PLC system to a receiver connected to the central equipment.

NOTE We assume you realize that a signal extension system is only needed when you are not in the same room as the equipment being controlled. In a single zone setup, where the entire home is one large listening zone, an IR or RF signal may need assistance reaching your single set of AV equipment.

- **IR over coaxial cable** If coaxial cable has been placed in multiple rooms or zones, it can be used to send IR commands to the central video system. The coaxial cable must be home run back to the AV equipment for this to work.

Figure 18-4
The PowerMid IR Extender System converts IR signals into RF for transmission to a base station.

Photo courtesy of X-10 Wireless Technology, Inc.

- **Discrete controllers in multiple zones**   If the design goal of the AV system is to supply a completely discrete set of sight and sound streams to every room in the home, a controller can be set up to communicate with and control the centralized AV equipment. This discrete controller can be hard-wired back to the equipment or communicate by RF to a base unit back at the equipment location that communicates with the AV equipment (see Figure 18-5), using one of two basic methods:

  - Direct home-run wiring from the controller to the central AV equipment using Cat 5 wiring.

  - IR controllers communicating to a base station device connected via home-run wiring or RF to the central AV equipment.

In either case, the discrete room controller must either be able to receive the signals from original equipment remote controls or be a replacement device that consolidates as many of the separate remote controls as possible. These devices can be handheld (see Figure 18-5), wall-mounted, or tabletop (see Figure 18-6).

Centralizing the Sources

For new construction or in remodel projects where it's easier to run cable from each zone back to the centralized A/V equipment, the use of direct and dedicated cable runs is definitely preferred over other signal transmission schemes. IR or RF signals can be converted by in-zone receivers and transmitted over the wire back to the centralized equipment.

Select the location of the central equipment and the wiring panel associated with it. All of the cables from the different rooms or zones should terminate here along with the wiring from all external sources (cable, telephone, satellite, antenna, and the like) that provide the video signals that are to be distributed throughout the house.

Figure 18-5
A handheld remote control device that can control up to nine discrete devices using IR signals

Photo courtesy of Philex Electronic, Ltd.

PART IV

Figure 18-6   A tabletop touch screen AV controller

NOTE   Since most locations will include structured wiring and a structured wiring distribution panel, the video or audio cabling should eventually terminate at the distribution panel, where it can be connected to the cabling that distributes it throughout the house.

The location of the equipment should meet the homeowners' design, accessibility, and usage needs. Many homeowners wish to display their equipment in a nice rack arrangement in a prominent location. Others may place this equipment in a closet, utility room, or another out-of-view location. Of course, the homeowner could also hide some from view and display the really cool pieces, kind of like electronic artwork.

Depending on your customer's desires and budget, the equipment found in the central hub location may include the following.

- AV controller
- Cable TV converter
- CD player/burner

- Digital satellite system (DSS) receiver
- DVD player/burner
- Internet gateway
- PVR
- VCR
- Digital media storage device
- Video distribution panel

CROSS-REFERENCE See Chapter 16 for more information on audio video components.

Installing Video Cable

Video distribution transmits RF signals over physical cable, which is typically shielded coaxial cable. A coaxial cable is able to carry more than 130 standard channel frequencies and a major part of delivering a quality signal to produce a quality image is keeping the video signal in the cable and other signals that might interfere outside the cable. Each channel transmitted on the coaxial cable has both video and audio components, and with MPEG Transport Streams (MTS) encoding in use, each channel can also carry stereo sound.

A coaxial cable is able to carry many channels and their signals at the same time. However, baseband signals, like those produced on a VCR or DVD player, require an entire cable for each channel. So, transmitting the entire baseband AV output from a VCR player requires two coaxial cables or a coaxial cable and separate audio cables.

For the best results, use quality RG6 coaxial cable (or a wireless RF system) to distribute video signals throughout a home. Depending on the design of the system, each room included in the distributed video system should have at least one cable connection jack. In rooms where there may be one or more video sources, additional jacks should be installed.

Another design consideration is the load on the video cabling. Remember that 6 decibels (db) of signal is lost for each 100 feet of RG6 cable. If the number of devices and the cable run lengths add up to too much attenuation, you may want to consider designing in a video amplifier. Also remember that if you use splitters or combiners (typically a hybrid single device), as shown in Figure 18-7, there is also loss when the signal passes through that device as well.

CROSS-REFERENCE See Chapter 17 for more information on video signal loss and calculation.

Figure 18-7
A video signal
splitter/combiner

*Photo courtesy of
Channel Vision.*

The cables that work best with different video applications are

- **Coaxial**   This cable is the standard used for cable television connections. It is typically terminated with a barrel Bayonet Neill Concellman (BNC) connector, but it can also be terminated with an RCA connector. Although other applications are in development, coaxial cable is used primarily for antenna and cable inputs.

- **Component (also called digital component)**   The newest of the cable and connector types that provides the best picture quality. The video signal is separated into three separate signals (Y, R-Y, B-Y, where Y represents black and white luminance, R represents red, and B represents blue) and results in better color and clarity. The connection for a component cable has three plugs, one for each color component. Make sure the colors are matched to the device jack colors.

- **Composite**   A standard video signal format that contains the color, brightness, and synchronization information. Virtually all VCRs and other legacy video equipment have composite video input or output. The jacks and plugs used for composite video are RCA connectors. This signaling and connection format is distinctive in that it uses three wires for connections: a yellow jack for video, a white jack for left-side audio, and a red jack for right-side audio.

- **S-Video**   The signal is split into two color groups: Chrominance and Luminance. Chrominance carries color information and Luminance carries brightness and lighting information. S-Video is used primarily to transmit video signals to a television from a VCR or game device. The pin configuration on the jack and plug on a S-Video connection prevent the connection from being made incorrectly.

- **Video Port (VPort)**   This connector is primarily used to connect video game devices that have an RCA VPort connector that carries a composite video signal. It was originally designed to host the Microsoft Xbox video gaming device on RCA televisions.

- **Digital Video Interface (DVI)**   This interface connector provides connections for both analog and digital monitors on a single cable. Each of the three DVI configurations is designed to accommodate either analog (DVI-A), digital (DVI-D), or integrated (DVI-I) signals. When a DVI connector and port are used, a digital signal sent to an analog monitor is converted to an analog signal. If the monitor is a digital monitor, like a flat panel display, no conversion is performed.

- **High-Definition Multimedia Interface (HDMI)**   An improvement over the DVI interface, HDMI supports either RGB or YCbCr digital video at rates well above the 2.2 Gbps required by high-definition television (HDTV). HDMI also supports up to eight channels of digital audio.

Rough-In Cable Installation

During the rough-in phase of construction, the outlet boxes are mounted and cabling is installed in the walls while the walls are still open. From the outlet boxes, the video and audio cables are run to the location of the central panel. It isn't absolutely necessary to install the central distribution panel during rough-in, but it can be a good idea, especially if the panel is to be flush-mounted on a wall. Of course, this presumes that a floor plan and wire layout has been created and approved by the customer before you begin the installation of the rough-in items.

Rough-in work is generally done right after the electricians, plumbers, and Heating, Ventilating, Air Conditioning (HVAC) technicians complete their rough-in work and before the wallboard (drywall) is installed. Working after the electricians, plumbers, and other technicians allows you to install the cable so that it has the minimum distance and clearance from electrical wiring and any other objects inside the walls. Table 18-1 lists the minimum distances that AV cabling should be from the other fixtures in the house.

 NOTE   Remember that if the video cable must cross an electrical cable, it should do so at a 90-degree angle.

Table 18-1	Fixture	Minimum Distance
Cable Minimum Distances for Rough-In	AC electrical cable	6 inches
	Motors and motor wiring	12 inches
	Fluorescent lighting and wiring	24 inches

Passing Through Studs

The structured wiring being installed, which includes the video and audio cabling, can be an inch or more in diameter. To pass the cable through the wall studs, a hole at least 1/8-inch larger should be drilled through each stud along the cable path. Remember the general cable installation guidelines (see Chapter 1) and keep the structured wire bundle the proper distances from the electrical and other wiring that should already be installed. The same process applies even if only a single cable is being installed. Generally, the path for the AV cable can follow the path used by the electricians for the electrical cabling, keeping the proper distances, of course.

Outlet Boxes

A wide variety of low voltage mounting brackets and outlet boxes are available for use, as illustrated in Figure 18-8. The primary issue when selecting outlet boxes for structured wiring, including video and audio cables, is the bend radius of the cable. Coaxial and Cat 5 cable cannot be bent sharply, which may create a problem for inserting the cable into a standard electrical outlet box. For this reason, open back outlet boxes and mud rings, like those shown in Figures 18-8 and 18-9, or standard electrical outlet boxes, commonly called J-boxes, with the backs removed should be used. The common practice for home wiring systems is the use of blue or metallic boxes for electrical systems and orange nonmetallic boxes for structured wiring.

Photo courtesy of Lamson & Sessions.

Figure 18-8   A variety of outlet boxes are available to choose from for use with structured wiring.

Figure 18-9
An open-back
outlet box
protects
structured wiring
from sharp bends.

*Photo courtesy of
Lamson & Sessions.*

It may be necessary to adjust the locations of the structured wiring outlet boxes from the original plans in order to avoid the electrical wiring and other in-wall systems. However, new dual voltage outlet boxes and add-on single and dual gang boxes that accommodate both electrical and low voltage cabling are available. These boxes allow for a common placement of both electrical and structured wiring outlets.

Install the outlet box so that the front edge of it will be inside the hole the drywall installers will cut around the box. The box shouldn't extend so far out from the stud that it extends beyond the dry wall, but it shouldn't be so far back that it ends up behind the dry wall either. Check with the dry wall installers, if possible, or the contractor to determine the correct distance the box should extend beyond the stud. Typically this measurement should be either 1/4 or 3/8 of an inch. The box should be placed at the same height from the floor as the electrical outlet boxes, if for no other reason than aesthetics.

Most outlet boxes can be nailed or screwed to an adjacent stud using either the nails already on the box, like those in Figure 18-10, or through the holes provided on the box.

Trim-Out Installation

The trim-out phase of a distributed video system installation project is when the system begins to take shape. Trim-out is when the finish work of the project is done, which includes terminating, testing, and making the connections. This phase of the project has three primary steps:

- Terminating the cable and installing the face plates on the outlet boxes or mud rings
- Testing the cable system
- Configuring and connecting the central video distribution panel and the distributed video sources

PART IV

Figure 18-10
A structured
wiring outlet
box attached
to a wall stud

*Photo courtesy of
Lamson & Sessions.*

Terminating the Video Cable

Terminating the video cable at the outlet box or mud ring involves attaching the cable to
the connectors on the back of the wall outlet jack. If coaxial cable is used, then the raw
cable must be terminated with a male F connector and then connected to the female
connector on the back of the wall outlet. If twisted-pair (TP) cable is in use, the back of
the wall outlet will have a 110 punchdown block. See Chapter 2 for more information
on coaxial and TP connectors.

The wall outlet used should reflect the systems in its vicinity. For example, if only a
television set is in the room, the wall outlet needs to support only an F connector for
video distribution. However, if the room also has one or more computer, speakers, and
other end devices, a multiple-jack outlet, like the one shown in Figure 18-11, would support the existing requirements and possibly help to future-proof the room.

Trim Out the Central Distribution Panel

As discussed in Chapter 5, the central distribution panel is the key component of a structured wiring scheme. Each of the video cable runs should terminate and interconnect to
the cables connecting to the source devices at the distribution panel.

The procedure for connecting the cable runs to the distribution panel is much the
same as that for connecting each of the jacks in the wall outlets and uses the same tools.
TP cabling is attached to a 110 block on the panel and coaxial cabling is attached using F
connectors. It is usually possible for the distribution panel itself to be purchased separately from its enclosure.

A structured wiring or structured media distribution panel interconnects the cabling
that runs to rooms with the cabling running from the source devices. The panel shown
in Figure 18-12 includes interconnects for TP and coaxial cable as well as room for line
support devices, like an impedance amplifier or line converter.

Figure 18-11

A multiuse modular outlet that includes two TP, an S-Video, a BNC barrel, and two F connector jacks

Photo courtesy of SmartHome, Inc.

PART IV

Testing the System

The first part of testing the system is performing a thorough visual inspection of the wall outlets and the connections at the distribution panel. If anything looks wrong, even slightly wrong, it should be examined very closely and when in doubt, either repaired or replaced.

Figure 18-12

A structured media distribution panel

Photo courtesy of Channel Vision.

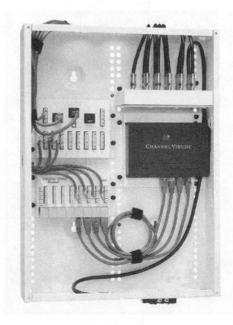

To test the video cabling system, you should use a cable tester to check the unshielded twisted-pair (UTP) and coaxial cables for bad connections and cable continuity. The next level of testing involves dynamic testing of the cabling using a structured wiring test device, like the one shown in Figure 18-13, to perform the Telecommunications Industry Association / Electronic Industries Alliance (TIA/EIA) TSB-67 tests on TP cabling and the TIA/EIA 570 tests for coaxial cabling.

 CROSS-REFERENCE See Chapter 1 for more information on wire basics and wire testing procedures and Chapter 4 for information on cable and test standards for structure wiring systems.

Equipment Hookup

In general the steps used to connect the video source equipment together and into the distribution system should be performed in a specific sequence. Although the steps in the following list are fairly general (and a particular video system may require some additional or specialized steps), the steps you should perform are

Figure 18-13
A structured
cable tester

*Photo courtesy of
Megger/Avo Multi-AMP
Corp.*

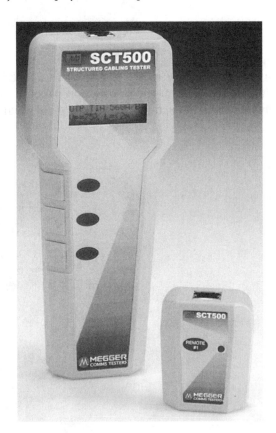

1. Remove the components from their boxes in the order you wish to install them. Set aside the product warranty, user guides, and other documents, along with the original remote control, for later use.

2. Set the component in the location it will occupy permanently.

3. Study the component's owner's manual. Make a note of any special hookup instructions required for the device (unplanned connectors, equipment cords, and the like), but don't hook up the equipment just yet.

   • If the video components (cable receiver, digital broadcast satellite (DBS) receiver, DVD-player, videotape player, and so on) are from a single manufacturer, which is somewhat unusual, follow the instructions in the manufacturer's documentation very closely, using the specified cables and connectors as prescribed.

   • However, if the equipment is from several different manufacturers, verify the connector jacks on the backs of the devices and that the devices have common connections between them before beginning to cable the devices together. It is a good idea to "dry run" the system before actually beginning to connect the components together with their cables, just to verify that you have the correct cables and connectors required.

4. Connect the video components together and install a small television set on each of the output lines (one at a time) that will supply distributed video throughout the home. Check the video picture and correct any problems at the device, following the troubleshooting guides in the device documentation.

5. If the video devices are performing as they should, connect the video output or source lines into the distribution panel and connect to the video splitter or amplifier.

6. Retest the system using the small television set at each of the distribution outlets that terminates the video distribution cabling. Once it is verified that the outlets are working, hook up the video devices in each room, working with one device and one room at a time. If there are any problems in the distributed video signal received at the outlets, the problem is likely in the outlet or the cabling it terminates. The cable should be tested using the appropriate equipment and in accordance to the specification of the splitter, amplifier, or end device to which it connects.

 CROSS-REFERENCE   See Chapter 16 for more information on testing distributed audio/video cabling.

Figure 18-14 illustrates the connections typically made in a distributed video system.

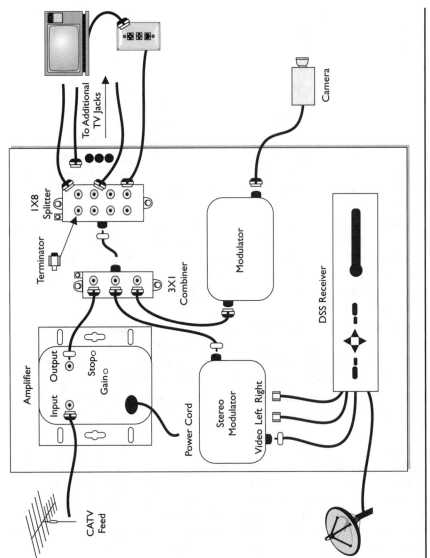

Figure 18-14   The connections made in a video system

Chapter Review

There are a variety of video signal formats in use in video distribution systems as well as on computers. The primary video signal formats are: RGB, component, S-Video, and composite. Video signals are either optical or electronic. Optical signals originate from a camera or a scanner and electronic signals originate from a computer's graphics card.

The common video signal formats are: CATV, composite video, RGBHV, RGBS, RGsB, S-Video, and YCrCb. The three primary broadcast standards are: NTSC, PAL, and SECAM. The best signal format is RGBHV, but it isn't available in all locations. The most common video signal format is composite, which CATV is part of.

The design phase for a distributed video system involves designating the rooms to be included, laying out the locations for the wall outlets, and deciding on the type of controller for each room or zone.

Each area that shares a common video signal is in the same video zone. Whether a distributed video system is to support one, two, or multiple zones is a key decision that must be made early on in the design phase of the project. The video wall connector should be placed in proximity to the video display device. Video controls range from relatively simple volume controls to LCD touch screen panels and multiple device controllers.

The common controller types are: wireless IR or RF, dedicated device controllers, extended IR or RF controllers, and IR over coaxial cable.

Video distribution transmits RF signals over physical cable, which is typically shielded coaxial cable. A coaxial cable is able to carry more than 130 standard channel frequencies and a major part of delivering a quality signal to produce a quality image is keeping the video signal in the cable and other signals outside the cable. Baseband signals, like those produced on a VCR or DVD player, require an entire cable for each channel. So, transmitting the entire baseband AV output from a VCR player requires two coaxial cables.

RG6 coaxial cable is the best choice for distributing video signals throughout a home, but other cable media can be used, including: coaxial, component, composite, DVI, HDMI, S-Video, and TP.

In the rough-in phase of construction, the outlet boxes and cabling are installed in the walls after the electricians, plumbers, and HVAC technicians complete their rough-in work and before the wallboard (drywall) is installed. The structured wiring is installed to pass through the wall studs.

A wide variety of low voltage mounting brackets and outlet boxes are available for use with structured video cabling. The common practice for home wiring systems is the use of blue or metallic boxes for electrical systems and orange nonmetallic boxes for structured wiring.

Install the outlet box so that the front edge of it will be inside the hole the drywall installers will cut around the box. The box should be placed at the same height from the floor as the electrical outlet boxes, if for no other reason than aesthetics.

During the trim-out phase of a distributed video system installation, the finish work of the project is done, which includes termination, testing, and making the connections. If a room has one or more computer, speakers, and other end devices, a multiple-jack outlet should be used to support the existing requirements and to help future-proof the room.

A key component of a structured wiring scheme is the central distribution panel, which is where each of the zone cable runs terminate and connect into the source devices. The procedure for connecting the cable runs to the distribution panel is much the same as that for connecting each of the jacks in the wall outlets and uses the same tools.

The first part of the testing system is a thorough visual inspection of the wall outlets and the connections at the distribution panel. To test the video cabling system, a cable tester should be used to check the UTP and coaxial cables for bad connection and cable continuity.

Questions

1. Composite video and audio that is modulated to allow multiple signals to share a common transmission medium best describes which video signal format?

    A. RGBHV

    B. YCrCb

    C. RGsB

    D. CATV

2. Which of the following is not a standard television coding system?

    A. NTSC

    B. ATSC

    C. PAL

    D. SECAM

3. What is the term applied to an area in a house where everyone receives the same video signal?

    A. Room

    B. Video area

    C. Zone

    D. Theatre

4. If a homeowner desires to control a centralized source unit using an IR remote control from a remote area of the house, what device should be considered?

    A. RF remote control

    B. IR extender

    C. RF extender

    D. Voice controlled remote

5. What is the number of AV channels a coaxial cable is capable of carrying?

   A. 1

   B. 16

   C. 130

   D. 256

6. What is the db signal loss per 100 feet from RG6 coaxial cable?

   A. 1

   B. 2

   C. 4

   D. 6

7. Which of the standard video formats splits the image coding into two groups, one for luminance and one for chrominance?

   A. S-Video

   B. Composite

   C. Component

   D. DVI-D

8. When is the rough-in phase of a structured wiring project performed?

   A. Before the electrical, HVAC, and plumbing is installed

   B. Before the wall studs are erected

   C. Before the drywall is installed

   D. After the drywall is installed

9. What is the minimum distance away from an AC cable that a structured media cable should be installed?

   A. 3 inches

   B. 6 inches

   C. 12 inches

   D. 24 inches

10. During which of the following phases of a structured wiring project should the cable be terminated and tested?

   A. Prewire

   B. Rough-in

   C. Trim-out

   D. Finish

Answers

1. **D.** This is the signal format used with cable television. The other choices are all standard video signal formats that are used with computer monitors and other such displays.

2. **B.** This is the standards group that deals with HDTV standards. The other choices are transmission and signal formatting standards.

3. **C.** A home can have one or multiple zones. It can have multiple and overlapping audio and video zones.

4. **B.** Another choice would be IR over coaxial cable using wall outlet mounted IR receivers that are cabled back to the source unit.

5. **C.** This is why coaxial cable is a common choice for video systems.

6. **D.** Additional signal loss occurs if splitters or combiners are used.

7. **A.** Most of the other video standards use a single channel to transmit color and brightness information.

8. **C.** It's best to wait until after the electrical wiring is installed so you can avoid installing structured media cable too close to other wiring.

9. **B.** More is always better, but in a wall that may be difficult. Also remember that if the media cable must cross the electrical wiring, it should do so at a 90-degree angle.

10. **C.** Prior to this phase the surfaces of the walls are not finished and the connectors and plates would be exposed to possible damage. However, continuity testing should be performed in the rough-in phase and then again in the trim-out.

Troubleshooting Audio Systems

In this chapter, you will learn about the following:
- Common audio cable and system problems
- Troubleshooting audio cable

There may be nothing worse for a homeowner than to fire up his or her distributed audio system to play a favorite recording of Mozart or the Rolling Stones and hear static, hum, or buzz drowning out their dulcet tones, or, even worse, nothing at all.

A distributed audio system typically involves more than source devices, cable, and speakers. In many systems, there can also be selectors, volume controls, and remote controls, and each can introduce problems into the system.

This chapter looks at the most common problems a distributed audio system can develop and the processes and devices used to diagnose and troubleshoot audio problems.

Diagnosing Audio System Problems

A distributed audio system is a series of audio devices that are connected to one another over structured wiring. The parts of the distributed audio system that can cause audio performance problems are all of the components (including the speakers) and the cabling that connects the speakers and controls to the source devices. So, when you get a call that there is a problem with the audio system, gather as much information as possible and be sure to listen and analyze what the homeowners are saying. For example, if they say there is no sound or an improperly functioning control device, the obvious place to start tracking down the problem is by checking the source devices. Start with checking the components, the connections, and the parts of the system related or connected to the structured wiring system—oh, and check the power too!

Review the audio system configuration and identify all equipment components and how they are connected. The line diagram completed earlier in the project is an excellent reference for this information. Use a structured step-by-step troubleshooting process that includes at least these steps:

CROSS-REFERENCE See Chapter 16 for information and examples of an audio system line diagram.

1. Identify the problem

2. Start troubleshooting at the audio source

3. Use a methodical approach

4. Eliminate components one at a time as the source of the problem

5. Refer to the manufacturer's documentation for troubleshooting suggestions specific to a particular component.

The detail steps performed within this framework should include most of these steps:

- Ruling out the obvious
- Checking all connecting cables
- Checking all control devices inline with the suspected components
- Checking that the connection is the correct type for the equipment in use

Rule Out the Obvious

As obvious as it may seem, make sure that all of the connections are secure and fit properly, including the alternating current (AC) connection on the amplifier and any other source devices related to the problem. Make sure all components have power, especially if they are powered through a surge protector.

Check the speakers to make sure that all of the connections are secure. See if only one or both of the stereo speakers are not working. If only one is not working, check the connections throughout the distributed audio system that deliver the signal to that channel. If both speakers are not working, check the connections on both channels throughout the system and look closely at the connections from the source equipment.

Also check the volume controls, both at the source and in the affected room or zone. a room or zone volume control can't increase the volume if the source device's volume is set low. Another quick test of the audio is to plug a portable speaker directly into the source device. If the sound is available from the portable speaker, then the problem is likely in one or more of the distributed audio cables or speakers.

Check the Cable

As is the case with all distributed cabling systems, there is a short list of cable problem causes, including:

- A broken connector caused by someone tripping over a connector cable
- Corroded connections caused by too much moisture in a wall or room

- Stretched or broken conductors caused by too much pull tension during installation

- An audio cable that was damaged during installation

Your diagnostics should be organized to identify and isolate these common problems.

In most cases, the best way to test audio or video cables is to test the input or output levels of the cable with a signal from one of the system devices on the cable. For example, to check the cable connecting a CD-player, play a CD and test the cable at the speaker terminations where it connects to a volume control or the speakers. By far the most common audio video cable problem is an open circuit, which most commonly occurs at the cable ends.

Cable Properties

The three properties that should be tested, usually with a good quality multimeter, on an audio cable (or any cable for that matter) are:

- **Capacitance** Cable capacitance is a common problem on audio lines that are more than 100 feet or 30 meters in length. If the capacitance is too high, it may interfere with systems that have high impedance. Use a handheld multimeter or a cable test device to determine the capacitance of the cable. If the capacitance is too high for the device to which it is connected, consider replacing the cable with one that is rated at less than 100 picofarads per foot pF/ft).

- **Inductance** High inductance can affect audio by changing the tone of the sound during transmission. Inductance can vary depending on the cables are installed and whether they are coiled or looped. A coiled up cable will typically have higher inductance than an uncoiled cable. The best way to correct inductance is to ensure that the length of the cable between two devices is appropriate and without unnecessary loops or coils. Some systems also have inductor circuits built-in to block certain frequencies in an audio signal; for example, the crossover in a woofer may "roll-off" higher frequency sounds. If the audio is distorted in this situation, the problem may be in the crossover and not the cable.

- **Resistance (impedance)** Depending on the needs of a specific audio system, if the resistance is too high, the audio signal may be decreased in quality, especially at the speakers. Impedance is how much a cable impacts the flow of current through the wire and is measured in ohms. Systems are either high impedance or low impedance, but low impedance systems are typically in the range of 150-ohms to 800-ohms and high impedance is generally in the range of a few kilo-ohms to tens of kilo-ohms. Residential systems are typically low impedance devices and the rule of thumb is to assume output impedance at around 1 kilo-ohm (K-ohm). The speakers and other distributed components of an audio system should be matched for resistance and impedance.

To troubleshoot the audio visual (AV) system for resistance, perform these checks:

- Check all connectors and connections for improper installation, loose shielding, stray strands, or damage.

- Check the cable for continuity using a volt-ohm meter (VOM) or multimeter.
- Check any cables that terminate at the distribution panel from the end of the cable terminated at a wall outlet. The resistance of the cable should be close to that of the terminator or the device connecting to the outlet.
- If RG6 cable is installed, use a multimeter or VOM to check the resistance between the center conductor and the shielding in the cable. If the resistance is below 100 K-ohms, it is likely that the cable has a short in it at some point and should be replaced.

Cable Verification

If you suspect that a problem may exist in the distributed audio cabling, you should perform the same cable tests you performed to test and verify the cable during trim-out:

- Visually inspect the terminations at the distribution panel, at the source device, and at the outlets. Depending on the type of cable in use, check to see that the connector or jack is properly attached.
  - **Coaxial cabling** Is the connector's wire mesh inserted around the outer channel of the connector body? Is the center conductor wire extending the proper distance (about ¼-inch) beyond the front of the connector? If the connector is a crimp-on type, is the connector tightly crimped to the cable? Is the screw-on collar (on an F-type connector) properly aligned and tightly connected?
  - **Speaker wire** Are the wire conductors in contact when they connect to the outlet jack (a condition that may exist if too much insulation was stripped from the wire)? Are the jacks securely fastened to the conductors?
  - **Twisted-pair (TP)** If RCA or mini-plug jacks are in use, is the wire pair insulation preventing the two conductors from touching at the jack. If a balanced interface is in use, is the connection providing a ground line?
  - **Commercial audio cabling** When using a manufactured audio cable set, are the connectors firmly attached to the cable without breaks, cracks, or splits between the connector plug or jack and the cable?
- If the connector jacks and plugs are good, next test the cable for its transmission properties.
  - **Digital versus analog** Verify which interface format is in use. In most systems, the format will be either be analog or the more common standard digital signal formats used in residences, Audio Engineering Society/ European Broadcast Union (AES/EBU), which recommends shielded TP cable. Verify that an analog device is not connected at the source or in a room or zone. AES/EBU does not convert digital signals back to analog.
  - **Coaxial cable** The cable should carry 75-ohms of impedance, which can be verified with a multimeter. Check the cable for continuity as well.

- **Speaker wire**   Most speaker wire (also called zip wire) fails to meet the requirements for in-wall cabling specified in the building and electrical codes. Distributed audio wire should have a Class 2 or 3 fire insulation rating, and clear insulation speaker wire doesn't. There are commercial audio cables that do meet the codes, but not many do. If standard two-conductor, clear-insulation speaker wire is installed in the walls of a home, your first recommendation is that it should be replaced. Secondly, it must carry 4-ohms to 8-ohms of impedance and can be verified with a multimeter.

- **TP**   Shielded TP (STP) cable should carry from 100-ohms to 120-ohms of impedance if connected to a digital interface. TP cable used for analog audio transmission should carry 45-ohms to 70-ohms of impedance. Verify that an analog device isn't connected to a digital device. If it is, you may have found the problem. Verify continuity, impedance, and perhaps even run a wiremap test on the cable.

 CROSS-REFERENCE   Chapter 9 provides information on how to perform the cable tests referenced in this section.

Ground Loops

Another common problem that is typically attributed to cabling is a ground loop that can create a humming noise in the audio playback. A ground loop is caused when two or more AC powered devices that are connected to the electrical system on two different outlets in two different rooms are linked to one another with an audio cable and part of the AC power flows over the cable.

Solving ground loops is not an easy task because there are no absolute grounding systems. Solving this problem may require assistance from an electrician to balance the grounding of the outlets in use or, if an unbalanced line is in use, the installation of a balanced audio interface.

Check the Controls

Distributed volume controls and selector controls can and do go bad, but not often. In most cases, if a volume control is not properly responding to changes in its setting, the problem is either the connection or the volume control itself.

Remove the control from its outlet, assuming it is not a remote control, and check its connections carefully. Also check the wiring where it comes into the outlet box or structured wiring bracket. If the wire is bent or kinked that could very well be the issue. If the connections appear to be proper, replace the control with a new one. If this solves the problem, then the control was bad. However, if the problem persists, then you should check the cabling both before and after the control.

Balanced Versus Unbalanced

Beyond the obvious, such as the source device being unplugged, AC power can cause audio problems, especially if the speaker interface is unbalanced. There are two types of audio interfaces used in audio systems: unbalanced and balanced.

Unbalanced Interface

An unbalanced interface is typically installed on a single conductor shielded wire, such as a solid core conductor cable like coaxial cable. The shielding around the wire serves to ground not only the cable, but also the two devices connected to it, typically an amplifier and a speaker, but could also include a microphone or other audio source device. Unbalanced cabling is typically terminated with RCA or mini-plug connectors.

The problem with an unbalanced interface, especially one of some run length, is that it is very susceptible to picking up what is called ground loop interference that can add hum or buzz to the audio playback by a speaker.

Ground loop interference is a common characteristic of shielded copper wire. Removing the cause, the cable's shielding, isn't the way to solve it. However, it can be removed with an isolation transformer. While all systems that use an unbalanced interface are likely to have ground loop interference problems, on smaller systems, it's typically not much of a problem. However, in a high-end system that includes some professional level audio or video equipment, either the cabling should be replaced or an isolation transformer installed.

Balanced Interface

Professional and better audio devices are connected using balanced cabling, constructed to minimize the amount of interference they pick up. A balanced cable has the built-in capability to pass along the audio signal and filter out interference.

A balanced cable includes two 24-gauge conductors to carry signals plus a grounding wire. Several manufacturers produce a variety of balanced cabling. Balanced cabling is typically terminated with an XLR connector. The balance in this type of audio cable is achieved by maintaining the impedance of the two signal lines equal to that of the ground. However, balanced audio also works on ungrounded cabling as well with the right equipment.

Chapter Review

The obvious place to begin diagnosing distributed audio problems is checking the source devices. Make sure that all of the connections are secure and fit properly, including the AC connection on the amplifier and any other source devices related to the problem. Check the volume controls, both at the source and in the affected room or zone. If sound is available from a portable speaker connected to the source device, the problem is likely in one or more of the distributed audio cables.

There is a short list of cable problem causes, including: a broken connector, corroded connections, stretched or broken conductors or damaged cable. Your diagnostics should be organized to identify and isolate these common problems.

The three properties that should be tested on an audio cable (or any cable for that matter) are: capacitance, inductance, and resistance (impedance). To determine if a problem may exist in the distributed audio cabling, test and verify the cable using the same tests used during trim-out. Visually inspect the terminations at the distribution panel, at the source device, and at the outlets. Test the cable for its transmission properties.

A ground loop can create a humming noise in the audio playback. A ground loop is caused when two or more AC powered devices that are connected to the electrical system on two different outlets in two different rooms are linked to one another with an audio cable and part of the AC power flows over the cable.

If a volume control is not properly responding, the problem is either the connection or the volume control itself. Remove the control from its outlet and check its connections carefully. Check the wiring where it enters the outlet box for bends and kinks. If the connections are proper, replace the control with a new one. If the problem persists, check the cabling both before and after the control.

There are two types of audio interfaces used in audio systems: unbalanced and balanced. An unbalanced interface is typically installed on a single conductor shielded wire, such as a solid core conductor cable like coaxial cable. An unbalanced interface is very susceptible to ground loop interference and can add hum or buzz to the audio playback by a speaker.

A balanced cable has the built-in capability to pass along the audio signal and filter out interference. A balanced cable includes two conductors and a grounding line.

Questions

1. When diagnosing an audio system problem, what should be the first area to check?

   A. Structured wiring

   B. Volume controls

   C. Connections

   D. Source devices

2. Which of the following is not a common cable problem?

   A. Broken connector

   B. Corroded connection

   C. Cable quality too high

   D. Stretched or broken conductors

3. Which of the following can impact the performance of an audio system?

   A. Capacitance

   B. Inductance

   C. Resistance

   D. Cable length

E. All of the above

4. What is the rule of thumb for residential audio system impedance (resistance)?

    A. 4-ohms

    B. 20-ohms

    C. 1 kilo-ohm

    D. 20 kilo-ohms

5. Which of the following can cause audio cable problems at the connector?

    A. Insulation material

    B. Stranded versus solid wire conductors

    C. Conductor wires in contact

    D. Ground loop

6. Which of the following is a digital audio standard?

    A. AES/EBU

    B. IEEE

    C. NEC

    D. S/PDIF

7. What impedance should a coaxial cable used in a distributed audio system carry?

    A. 15-ohms

    B. 50-ohms

    C. 75-ohms

    D. 100-ohms

8. Which of the following cable types is least likely to meet the building and electrical codes for fire safety?

    A. STP

    B. Coaxial

    C. Speaker wire (zip wire)

    D. UTP

9. Two AC power devices that are connected to AC power in two different rooms and are linked by an audio cable are likely to cause what audio system problem?

    A. Feedback

    B. White noise

    C. Ground loop

    D. Clipping

10. An unbalanced audio interface is typically installed on what type of cable?

   A. Solid core, single conductor cable

   B. Stranded speaker wire

   C. UTP

   D. STP

Answers

1. **D.** If a source device is not connected, powered, or has improper settings, it is likely the cause of at least one audio system problem.

2. **C.** I'm not sure if this is entirely possible, but about the only problem it can cause is cost. The other issues listed are all common cable problems.

3. **E.** Actually, just about anything at all relating to an audio system can, if only in a small way, can cause some problem. But these choices are the causes, either alone or in combination, of many audio system problems.

4. **C.** Most systems will range a bit lower than 1 kilo-ohm, but that is the standard rule of thumb.

5. **C.** If the insulation has been stripped too far back on the conductors so that they make contact at the connector, the audio signals are being shorted out.

6. **A.** This standard does not convert digital audio signals back to analog and, as a result, the standard is not compatible with standard analog audio devices.

7. **C.** Coaxial cabling is commonly used in unbalanced audio that has longer run lengths.

8. **C.** Commonly available speaker wire typically has transparent insulation doesn't carry the NEC/UL fire safety ratings for in-wall installation.

9. **C.** A ground loop condition can add buzz to the audio signal.

10. **A.** The lack of a grounding conductor is the key characteristic of an unbalanced cable.

Troubleshooting Video Systems

In this chapter, you will learn about:
- Common cable-related distributed video problems
- Troubleshooting video cabling and distribution systems

Regardless of the actual source of a problem, a homeowner who can't watch the big game, the latest episode of "24," his favorite talk show, or whatever show he wants is experiencing a video system problem. With all of the connection and distribution points involved in a distributed video system, tracking down the source of the problem can be daunting.

In a structured wiring environment, tracking down the cause of a problem (assuming that the problem is cable- and distribution-related) is eased a bit because access points to all of the cable home runs are available for testing, as are all of the distribution and interconnection points.

This chapter extends the information from Chapters 9 and 19 to focus on the cabling and connection problems that can affect the performance of a distributed video system and the troubleshooting steps that can be used to identify a problem source.

Diagnosing Distributed Video Problems

As is the case with other distributed media systems, most of distributed video problems can be traced to cabling. How the cable was installed, how it was terminated, and how it is connected into the equipment distributing the signals to different rooms or zones of a home all can have an effect on the quality of the video seen on that big, expense high-definition TV (HDTV) plasma display.

As with all problems reported by the customer, you should listen, look, and analyze the situation (see Chapter 9 for more details on this process) before beginning your diagnostics. Once you have a clear understanding of what the customer "sees" as the problem, you can begin your diagnostics to isolate the cause and apply a remedy.

Rule Out the Obvious

As I've said a few times already in this book, before you begin performing cable tests, or worse, check out all possible systems that are related to the problem, and even those that aren't, check for things such as unplugged alternating current (AC) cords, poorly mounted connections, and the like. In a majority of cases, especially in those where the system has been in place for more than 30 to 90 days, it is likely that the cause is external to the cabling and its termination and something fairly simple.

Check the Cable

Video systems are generally installed over coaxial cabling, either RG59 or RG6 (or using their newest nomenclatures, Series 59 or Series 6). However, some distributed video systems are being installed on twisted-pair (TP) cabling as well. In any of these cases, how the cable was installed and terminated should be the first check in your diagnostics.

Coaxial Cable

As illustrated in Figure 20-1, coaxial cable actually has two conductors: the center, solid-core copper conductor and the shield placed around the dielectric insulating material and the inner conductor. The center conductor is the primary signal carrier of the cable, and the shield provides a return path for the signal ground. When a coaxial cable is terminated, if attention isn't paid to both conductors, the quality of the transmitted signal can be affected.

Cable Shielding   The shield can be one of several materials, but typically it is wire mesh, foil, or both (including two of one or both). Each of these different shield types is designed to resist certain kinds of radio frequency interference (RFI) and Electromagnetic Interference (EMI). A foil shield is primarily used to deflect RFI from the cable. Foil shields have a thin drain wire that allows the foil to be connected to the outer channel of an F-type or BNC connector. A wire-mesh or braid shield, which is usually made of tinned copper, is used to ward off EMI from the center conductor. In high-quality cables, both shields may be installed. In either case, the shield must be in contact with the metal body of the connectors to perform its task.

Center Conductor   The center conductor can also be a source of cable performance issues. If the center conductor extends too far from the connector, it can easily be bent or

Figure 20-1
The layers of
a coaxial cable

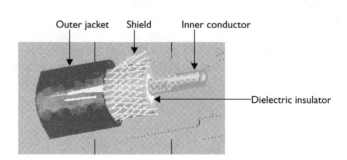

Outer jacket   Shield   Inner conductor

Dielectric insulator

pushed to the side when the connector jack is attached to the connector plug. If the center conductor isn't extended far enough out from the connector, the conductor may not meet the conductor on the other half of the connector. Notice the center conductor extending beyond the connector body in Figure 20-2.

Cable Properties   The performance of a coaxial cable in a video system is determined by the properties of the cabling installed. The primary properties that can affect the performance of a coaxial video cable are

- **Frequency**   As the frequency of the signal transmitted over a coaxial cable increases, the greater the affect the cable's capacitance and conductive resistance have on the signal.

- **Interference**   RFI and EMI can distort the signal if the cable is not properly shielded against them. Crosstalk is a type of interference that occurs when cables that are run adjacent aren't properly shielded and pick up signals from one another, which can distort the signal on either or both cables.

- **Length**   The longer a signal travels through a cable, the more its quality decreases. All copper cabling is susceptible to attenuation, which is caused by an electrical signal being affected by the materials of the cable as the signal travels through the cable. Each series of coaxial cable has a specific maximum cable segment length. For example, RG6 coaxial cabling has a rating to about 200 meters.

- **Specifications**   The four primary properties included in a manufacturer's cable specifications are

  - **Attenuation**   This is perhaps the most important specification for a coaxial cable and is stated in the number of decibels (dB) of signal loss that occurs beyond a fixed length (typically around 30 meters or 100 feet) for different signal frequencies. An example of an attenuation specification is -2.2dB/100 feet @ 100 MHz, which means that a transmitted signal will lose 2.2 decibels per 100 feet of run length. In addition, the attenuation rating of a cable also changes as the run length of the cable increases. In effect, attenuation gradually decreases the quality of the signal as the signal travels over the line, which can impact the display produced by a signal transmitted over an extended length run.

  - **Capacitance**   Capacitance measures a cable's capability to take an electrical charge, hold the charge, and then discharge. In a coaxial cable, capacitance

Figure 20-2
A coaxial cable terminated with an F-type connector

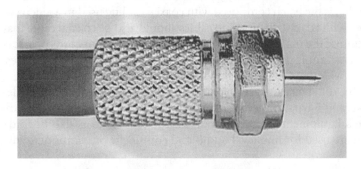

PART IV

indicates how well a cable can hold a change in its dielectric insulator to offset the potential difference between the conductors, which on a coaxial cable is the center conductor wire and its shielding. One video condition that can be affected by a cable with an improper capacitance is the black-to-white transition of the video signal, which might be displayed with a gray transition between the black and white. The capacitance of a coaxial cable is measured in picofarads per foot (pF/ft), or one-trillionth of a farad.

- **Impendence** This rating determines the amount of signal flow the cable supports. A possible source for system performance issues is unmatched impedance, which can cause the signal to be reflected back up the cable instead of on to its destination. Reflection signals can also be caused by improper termination. Coaxial cable typically has 75-ohm impedance.

- **Resistance** A cable's resistance rating defines how resistive the cable is to signal flow. A cable with a very high resistance impairs the amplitude of a signal and converts the lost voltage to heat. The materials used in the cable and their dimensions, as well as the temperature of the area in which the cable is installed, determine a cable's resistance. A cable's resistance is stated in ohms per 1,000 feet (305 meters).

- **Temperature** Heat can affect the performance of a cable, which can also make troubleshooting difficult. In areas such as walls, ceilings, and equipment racks that may not be properly ventilated to prevent heat buildup, cables can be subject to higher heat. Special cabling types are available for installation in locations where heat may be a problem.

Terminations The different types of connectors used with coaxial cabling can impact the quality of the signal transmitted because they may create an impedance mismatch on the line. For example, a BNC connector has 75-ohm impedance, which matches that of the typical coaxial cable. However, an RCA connector typically has between 35- and 55-ohm impedance. This doesn't mean that an RCA connector should not be used with coaxial cable, it just depends on the system being supported. Some systems include a 25-ohm resistor on the incoming cable jack.

Not all video connectors use crimp-style attachments. Many styles of connectors must be soldered into place, which creates another failure point for the cable. Improperly applied soldering can create problems with continuity, impedance, and resistance of a cable.

Another potential problem area that actually extends beyond the scope of structured cabling is the patch cords used with coaxial cabling used in a video system. The patch cords used with coaxial distribution cables should also be coaxial cable that matches the specification of the main distribution cable. The equipment cords provided with video devices by the manufacturer are good for use only directly between devices and aren't designed or provided for use as patch cords between the distribution cable and the device.

The difference between a patch cord and an equipment cord boils down to connectors. BNC and F-type connectors are used with coaxial cabling on both distribution and patch cords. Equipment cords commonly have RCA connectors, like the cord shown in Figure 20-3, and are used for line-level audio and composite or component video interfaces.

Figure 20-3
A video
equipment cord
terminated with
RCA connectors

*Photo courtesy of
Canare Corporation
of America.*

Twisted-Pair Audio Cables

Unshielded twisted-pair (UTP) cable can be a less expensive alternative to coaxial cable for a distributed video system. Cat 5 or better (meaning Cat 5e, Cat 6, or Cat 7) can be used to distribute video signals if it's properly installed and terminated.

Using UTP cable for a video system requires that one pair of wires is used for each signal. Or in other words, up to four video system signals can be transmitted on a UTP cable, one signal per wire pair.

Attenuation   One specification of UTP cabling that can be an issue for a video system is attenuation. If a system is performing poorly, and UTP cabling is in use for distributing the video signal, attenuation could be the problem. Table 20-1 compares the dB/100 feet loss of coaxial and UTP cabling.

To offset the dramatic attenuation differences shown in Table 20-1, video baluns (transformers) should be placed between BNC connectors (coaxial cable) and RJ-45 connectors (UTP cable).

A video balun, besides providing an interface between the two termination types, converts the UTP line from unbalanced to balanced (see Chapter 19 for more on video baluns and their use with UTP cable).

Common UTP Video Problems   Perhaps the most common problem for video systems installed on UTP cable is color separation. For example, light colored lines or the edges of light-colored objects appear to have a red or purple tinge to them. This is caused by the number of twists per inch of the wire pairs inside the Cat 5e cable. If the twists-per-inch of one wire pair, carrying one part of the video signal, is tighter than on another wire pair, the signals arrive at slightly different times, especially on long cable runs. This problem is more noticeable on high-resolution systems.

If the customer is complaining of this problem from a video system installed on UTP cable, you may need to install a video graphics array (VGA) to UTP adapter to correct the

Table 20-1
A DeciBels per
100 Feet for
Common Cabling

MHz	RG6	RG59	Cat 5
1	0.2	0.4	1.8
10	0.6	1.4	5.8
50	1.4	3.3	11.0
100	2.0	4.9	19.3
400	4.3	11.2	42.0

PART IV

RGB conversion and signal timing. This device uses a potentiometer to adjust the skew of the signal timing.

Cable Testing

The cable tests recommended in Chapter 9 are the same procedures used when performing diagnostics on coaxial or UTP cabling in a video distribution system. However, the following few sections provide a brief overview of these tests and their use in diagnosing and troubleshooting a distributed video system.

Coaxial Cable Tests

The primary tests that should be performed on coaxial cabling as part of your diagnostics are

- Test the cable for 75-ohm impedance
- Test for continuity on both the center conductor and the shield
- Test for attenuation
- Test for cable length

If there are other tests that are required by your company, city, county, state, or federal regulations, you may want to repeat them at this time just to verify that none of the cable's characteristics have been changed.

Testing Guidelines

When testing coaxial cabling, follow these guidelines:

1. Perform a visual inspection and verify the correct cabling is installed, the connectors are the appropriate type, the terminations are correct, the patch or equipment cords are appropriate, and you don't see any visible cable damage.

2. Start your tests at the central distribution panel or the demarcation point of the video system, such as the cable television network interface device (NID).

3. If you suspect that the problem may be attenuation on a very long run of cable, add a repeater to the link as near to the middle of the cable as you can. If the problem continues, the repeater may not be necessary.

4. If you suspect a particular device or system is causing the problem, after eliminating the cable as the source of the problem, remove that device from the system, if possible, and retest.

5. Connect each modulator or video hub directly to a television set to verify the device is working properly.

Coaxial Cable Test Tools

When testing coaxial cabling as a part of your diagnostics, certain tests are used to answer certain questions. Table 20-2 lists the troubleshooting questions and the test you can use to provide answers.

Question	Test Tools
Which cable is this?	Documentation, tone generator/probe
Is the cable run wired correctly?	Multimeter
Is the cable too long?	Multimeter, time domain reflectometer (TDR)
Is the impedance correct?	Multimeter, certification test set
Is there too much interference on the line?	Certification test set

Table 20-2   Coaxial Cable Diagnostic Testing Tools

CROSS-REFERENCE   See Chapter 9 for more information on the use of a multimeter and the TDR test on structured wiring cable systems.

Troubleshooting Video Problems

Many video system performance problems are less directly related to the cable than they are to the overall system configuration. Table 20-3 lists several common video system problems, their causes, and what you should consider to resolve each problem.

Problem	Cause	Possible Solution
Dark bars on video display	AC power interference	Move cable at least 18 inches from AC power lines.
Modulated signals not displaying on monitor	Cable TV box may not pass modulated signals	Add splitter in front of cable box and install high-pass filter to modulated line.
Modulated signals ghosting	Inadequate shielding on coaxial cable	Replace existing cable with cable that has appropriate shielding.
No picture on TV	Coaxial cable problem	Perform a signal strength test on each cable segment. Test before and after each cable run, including testing before and after the cable demarc, splitter, amplifier, distribution panel, the patch cord to the TV.
No picture on some channels	Insufficient cable bandwidth	Replace RG59 cabling with RG6 and verify capacity of video splitters, if any. Also the problem may be that the TV set's tuner is not capable of displaying certain channels.
Rolling lines or patterns on many television channels	Signal strength is too high	Add a line attenuator to reduce signal amplitude.
Static or snow on some channels	Problem coaxial cable run	Damaged cable or broken connector.
Snowy (static) picture on all channels	Signal interruption between TV and modulator	Check connection at each end of cable. Verify modulator settings.

Table 20-3   Common Video Power and Cable Issues

PART IV

The SCART Connector

In European countries, the connector used to connect televisions, VCRs, and set-top boxes is the SCART (Syndicat des Constructeurs d'Appareils Radiorécepteurs et Téléviseurs) connector, which is illustrated in Figure 20-4. This connector, which is also called a Peritel connector, is used to terminate input lines, output lines, and lines that do both. The SCART connector is a 21-pin block that is a crimp on connector type.

Figure 20-4
A SCART connector is used with TV systems

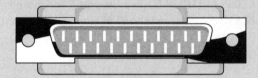

Many brands of television sets, those manufactured for sale in both the United States and Europe, have a SCART connector on them.

Chapter Review

How the cabling is installed, terminated, and connected can effect the quality of the video display.

Before you start testing, check out all possible systems that may be related to the problem, such as unplugged AC cords, poorly mounted connections, and the like. If the system has been in place for more than 30 to 90 days, the problem is likely caused by external devices.

Video systems are generally installed over coaxial cabling, either RG59 or RG6, but distributed video systems are installed on TP cabling. How the cable was installed and terminated should be the first check in your diagnostics.

Coaxial cable actually has two conductors: the center, solid-core copper conductor and the shield placed around the dielectric insulating material and the inner conductor. The center conductor is the primary signal carrier of the cable, and the shield provides a return path for the signal ground. When a coaxial cable is terminated, if attention isn't paid to both conductors, the quality of the transmitted signal can be affected.

The performance of a coaxial cable in a video system is determined by the properties of the cabling installed. The primary properties that can affect the performance of a coaxial video cable are: frequency, interference, length, specifications (which includes attenuation, capacitance, and impendence), resistance, and temperature.

The different types of connectors used with coaxial cabling can impact the quality of the signal transmitted because they may create an impedance mismatch on the line. Many styles of connectors must be soldered into place. Improperly applied soldering can create problems with continuity, impedance, and resistance of a cable.

UTP cable can be a less expensive alternative to coaxial cable for a distributed video system. Cat 5 or better (meaning Cat 5e, Cat 6, or Cat 7) can be used to distribute video signals if it's properly installed and terminated. One specification of UTP cabling that can be an issue for a video system is attenuation. If a system is performing poorly, and UTP cabling is in use for distributing the video signal, attenuation could be the problem. A video balun, besides providing an interface between the two termination types, converts the UTP line from unbalanced to balanced.

The cable tests used during trim-out should be used when performing diagnostics on video cabling. The primary tests that should be performed on coaxial cabling as a part of your diagnostics are: test the cable for 75-ohm impedance, test for continuity on both the center conductor and the shield, test for attenuation, and test for cable length.

Questions

1. Which of the following is not recommended for distributing video signals in a structured wiring environment?

   A. RG59

   B. RG6

   C. Speaker wire

   D. UTP

2. In a coaxial cable, which layer carries the signal to ground current?

   A. Center conductor

   B. Dielectric insulation

   C. Shielding

   D. Outer jacket

3. Which type of coaxial cable shielding is used to resist RFI?

   A. Foil

   B. Dielectric

   C. Wire mesh

   D. Wire braid

4. Which of the following coaxial cable problems could create a continuity problem on a video distribution run?

   A. Cable pierced by a staple

   B. Center conductor not extended far enough

   C. Center conductor extended too far

   D. Wire mesh not in contract with the connector body

   E. All of the above

PART IV

5. Which of a cable's properties limits the distance a cable is able to successfully carry a transmitted signal?

A. Attenuation

B. Capacitance

C. Frequency

D. Resistance

6. What is the normal impedance level of a coaxial cable terminated with a BNC connector?

A. 35-ohms

B. 55-ohms

C. 75-ohms

D. 120-ohms

7. When UTP cabling is used for distributing video signals, which of the following is true about the cable configuration?

A. One signal per single wire

B. One signal per wire pair

C. One signal per cable (four pairs)

D. Two signals per wire pair

8. True or False. The dB loss per 100 feet of UTP cable is typically less than that with either RG6 or RG59 coaxial cable?

A. True

B. False

9. Which of the following is a test that may not be performed on coaxial cabling during troubleshooting?

A. Attenuation

B. Crosstalk

C. Impedance

D. Continuity

10. When troubleshooting a coaxial cable for length, what testing tool should be utilized?

A. Cable certification set

B. Time domain reflectometer

C. Tone generator/probe

D. Wiremap tester

Answers

1. **C.** Speaker wire is not rated for in-wall installation, nor is it robust enough to carry the frequencies required for video transmissions. The other choices are used for video systems.

2. **C.** Whether the shielding is foil or wire mesh or braid, it is used to provide a return for the signal to ground current.

3. **A.** The foil shield resists RFI and the wire mesh or braid shield resists EMI. The dielectric insulator is used to provide capacitance.

4. **E.** Any one of these conditions could cause continuity problems on a coaxial cable.

5. **A.** On every copper cable, including UTP, there is a distance point at which the signal strength begins losing power.

6. **C.** UTP cable is typically in the range of 35- to 55-ohms.

7. **B.** Up to four signal paths can be provided by a single run of Cat 5 or better UTP cable.

8. **B.** The attenuation on a UTP cable can be on the order of two or more times greater.

9. **B.** Unless you believe that there are two coaxial cables carrying high frequencies that are placed too close together, this would not typically be a problem with coaxial cable.

10. **B.** TDR is the most commonly used test for testing copper (and fiber optic) cabling length.

V

Home Lighting Management Systems

CHAPTER 21

Home Lighting Basics

In this chapter, you will learn about:
- Light and lighting terminology
- Lighting loads and types
- Lighting fixtures

In a typical home, to turn a light fixture either on or off, you must be in the same room and access either a wall or lamp switch. However, through a home lighting control system, it's possible to turn lights on or off from another room or perhaps even another town.

When designing a lighting system for a home, you have more to deal with than just how to turn light fixtures on or off. To properly design a lighting system, you must consider a number of issues, including the following:

- Where to place the lights
- What kind of lights should be used and how many
- Where to put the switches, what type of switches should be used, and what lights are controlled by what switches
- What lights are to be controlled remotely

Lighting systems have some very basic operational components: light, light sources, light fixtures, and lighting controls. These basic components, when used in the right combinations and programmed well, can provide a system of lighting that serves the needs of a home's occupants.

This chapter covers lighting basics and fixture types. Although I mention a few of the devices typically included in a lighting system, Chapter 22 covers that area in more detail.

Light

Perhaps the first topic we should discuss is *light*, which is obviously a central part of a lighting system. The word *light* has over 30 different meanings in an English dictionary, but in the context of a home's lighting system, *light* takes on only a few meanings:

- The illumination that enables us to see
- A device that produces illumination
- The illumination from the sun

In the daylight hours, we depend on the sun and its light rays to provide illumination. However, after sundown, artificial light sources must be used. In designing a home's lighting system, the trick is to place the light sources and the correct level of illumination in the right places.

What Is Light?

Visible light, which means the light that you can see, is only one band in the electromagnetic spectrum that has radio waves at one extreme and gamma rays at the other extreme. Visible light is about in the middle of the electromagnetic spectrum—right between infrared (IR) waves and ultra violet (UV) waves.

Although it may sound like a contradiction, we can't actually *see* visible light; we can see only reflections of light waves from objects, but not the actual light source. What this means is that you can't actually see light before it hits an object and is reflected back into your eye. Without going into the astrophysics of lighting and luminescence and the history and evolution of modern lighting devices, let's just agree that the design of a lighting system must take into consideration how light is reflected to achieve desired results.

Light Waves

Light reflects from objects in waves of energy that can travel through virtually any space, including a vacuum. A light wave has the same properties of any electromagnetic wave, including wavelength and frequency. Visible light has a wavelength between 400 nanometers (nano means one-billionth) and 700 nanometers (nm). The full spectrum of electromagnetic light (see Figure 21-1) ranges from gamma rays (at 1 nm) to radio waves (in meters and centimeters). The frequency, or the number of waves per second, is measured as hertz (Hz). It is the frequency of visible light that we see as color. For example, the light we see as red has a frequency of 430 trillion hertz (teraHz) and the light we see as violet has a frequency of 750 teraHz. Between these two frequencies exist the other primary colors (orange, yellow, green, blue) each at a different frequency.

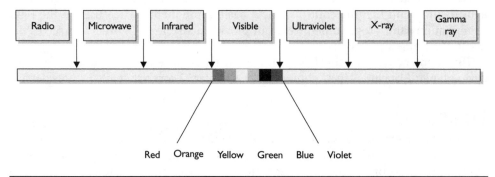

Figure 21-1   The electromagnetic spectrum showing the colors (frequencies) of visible light

Generating Light

Producing light involves applying a charge to the atoms of a material to energize their electrons. The energized electronics emit photons, which are the particles that produce the light we see. The photons produced from different materials, which means different types of atoms, have a particular frequency. The frequency of the photon determines the color of its light. For example, the sodium atoms in a sodium vapor light produce photons of a frequency that falls in the yellow light spectrum.

The most common way to energize atoms to produce light is with heat, which is the action behind incandescence, as in an incandescent lamp. Applying enough heat to a material creates photons on every color spectrum that merge together to create what is called white light, or colorless light. For example, in an ordinary 100-watt lamp, an inner metallic strip is heated using electricity to generate light.

White light, or colorless light, is the light produced by the sun. With just our naked eye, we can't see the colors that combine to create its colorlessness, but if the light shines through a glass of water or a prism, we can see its various color frequencies.

Light and Color

To create colored light, we have two choices: color by addition and color by subtraction. Here's how they work:

- **Color by addition**   If you pass white light through a colored filter, such as a colored glass or piece of cellophane, the resulting light becomes the color of the filter. This works on the same principles we learned in grade school about mixing different paint or crayon colors together—red and blue make violet, blue and green make cyan, and green and red make yellow (see Figure 21-2). This is the same principle used by computer monitors to create colors on their screens.

Figure 21-2
Red, green, and blue colors can be combined to create other colors, including white.

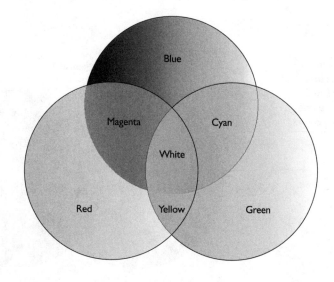

- **Color by subtraction**   Absorbing certain frequencies of a light beam—in other words, removing one or more colors—is another way to create light of a particular color. The resulting light will have only the frequencies of the light that weren't removed. Again, without getting too scientific here, this is how paint and ink work. Paint and ink are engineered to absorb all or part of some light frequencies and reflect back only the remaining light, which results in the colors we see. When you look at a wall and see green, the paint on the wall has absorbed the red and blue frequencies, so all you see is green. Figure 21-3 illustrates that when color is removed from a visible color, another color is produced, including black (the effect of removing all color frequencies).

The bottom line on light and color is that an object can create light by emitting the frequency of a certain color or it can absorb light frequencies to reflect a certain color.

Light and Objects

When light shines on any object, the light interacting with the object's surface will do one of four things:

- **Absorption**   The object absorbs the light or certain frequencies of the light, such as from a painted wall or a color photograph.
- **Transparency**   The light passes through the object without changing, such as light through a windowpane.
- **Refraction**   The light passes through the object, but is divided into its separate frequencies.
- **Reflection**   The light bounces back or is scattered by the object.

More than one of these actions can occur when light strikes an object.

Figure 21-3
Colors change when paint or other colors are designed to absorb one or more colors.

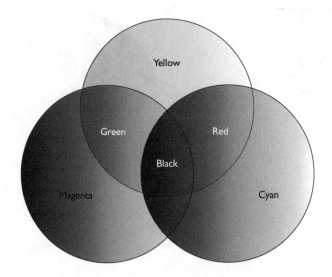

Lighting Characteristics

Light is measured in a variety of standard measurements. The light produced by lighting fixtures is measured using the following:

- **Foot-candles**   This is the measurement of the amount of light that reaches a particular object. Foot-candles are commonly used to measure the amount of light hitting a video screen. A foot-candle is the equivalent of one lumen per square foot. For example, most rooms and areas of a home, such as the bathrooms, kitchen, hall, and living spaces, should have 35 foot-candles of light for general lighting. In areas where task lighting is needed, 70 foot-candles of lighting should be available.

- **Lumens**   The amount of visible light produced by a light source. The exact definition of a lumen is very technical but, in general, the more lumens a light source produces, the better.

- **Wattage**   In the context of lighting, wattage (or watts) measures the amount of electricity a lighting source uses and not the amount of light it produces. In most cases, a higher wattage lamp produces more light because it uses more power to produce light, but not always.

Light Sources

The primary light sources in home lighting, besides the sun, are incandescent lamps, fluorescent tubes and lamps, and halogen and Xenon lamps. The type of lighting source (lamp or tube) used in a lighting fixture can make a huge difference in the lighting level and color in a room or zone.

For example, in a screw base lighting fixture, such as a table or floor lamp, the light produced by a 100-watt incandescent lamp is much different than the light produced by a 75-watt compact fluorescent lamp, besides the obvious difference in wattage.

Incandescent Lamps

Incandescent lamps, or what are commonly called, simply, light bulbs, are not complex devices. The primary components of a lamp are its two metal contacts, which are attached to two wires and a thin metal (commonly tungsten) filament. The whole assembly is enclosed inside a glass bulb that is filled with an inert gas such as argon. When the bulb is screwed into a socket and the power is switched on, an electrical current flows through the wires and the filament, which heats up to about 4,000 degrees Fahrenheit (or about 2,200 degrees Centigrade) and emits light. Incandescent lamps emit what is called warm light.

Lamps are rated by the amount of light (measured in watts) they produce in a certain period of time. Lamps with more power have larger filaments and, in turn, a higher watt rating. A three-way bulb actually has two different filaments on two separate circuits, each producing a different wattage. The socket for a three-way lamp has three positions to select each of the two circuits, or both at the same time.

Fluorescent Lights

A fluorescent light has a low-pressure mercury vapor inside and, when ionized, emits ultraviolet (UV) light. UV light can be harmful to humans, so the inside of the light's glass tube is coated with phosphor, which converts the UV light into visible light. Inside the fluorescent tube are electrodes at each end that excite the mercury in the tube into a vapor that emits UV light. The legacy fluorescent tube emits what is called *cold light*.

Fluorescent Tube Markings

If fluorescent lighting is included in a lighting design, it's important to use the right fluorescent tubes or bulbs for the job. To know you have the correct lights, you should be able to decode the markings on the tube (see Figure 21-4).

If you find a fluorescent tube marked with something like F40T12CW/IS or F30T8 RS, here's how to decode it:

- The "F" indicates a fluorescent lamp, which you probably already knew.
- The next two digits (40 or 30 in this case) indicate the wattage.
- The "T" indicates a tube type lamp.
- The next number represents the tube's diameter in eighths of an inch. For example, 12 means 12/8 (twelve-eighths) or 1.5 inches and 8 means 8/8 (eight-eighths) or 1-inch in diameter.
- The remaining letters represent the characteristics of the lamp. Some of the more common markings are
  - CW   Cool-White, the type of light emitted by the lamp
  - IS   Instant Start, the type of fixture ballast for which the lamp is designed
  - RS   Rapid Start, another type of ballast
- A fluorescent lamp may also have HO (High Output) or VHO (Very High Output) either before or after its coding to indicate its ballast type. Understand that a VHO lamp requires a special fixture with a specific connector set.

Figure 21-4
Standard
fluorescent
light tubes

*Photo courtesy of
General Electric Lighting.*

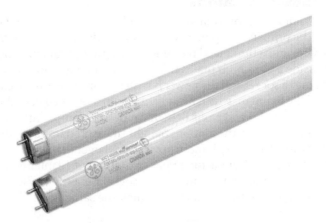

Figure 21-5

A compact
fluorescent lamp

*Photo courtesy of
General Electric Lighting.*

Compact Fluorescent Bulbs

The latest development in fluorescent bulbs is the compact fluorescent bulb (see Figure 21-5) that is a screw-in replacement for an incandescent bulb and fits in most standard light fixtures. In comparison to an ordinary lamp, the compact fluorescent bulb has a longer life (as much as 10,000 hours), uses less energy, produces less heat, and emits a warmer light.

Halogen Lamps

Incandescent lamps aren't very efficient, and they only last up to about 1,000 hours of normal use. On top of that, most of the energy produced by an ordinary lamp is heat. The tungsten filament of a halogen lamp is encased inside a quartz enclosure filled with halogen gas, which enables it to produce a brighter light. However, like the incandescent bulb, the halogen lamp also produces a lot of heat. Because of its design and elements, a halogen lamp (see Figure 21-6) can outlast a regular lamp. Some halogen-type lamps are filled with Xenon gas, which produces a brighter and whiter light.

Figure 21-6

A halogen lamp
can be a good
choice for task or
showcase lighting.

PART V

Lighting Load

There are actually two types of lighting load that can be calculated: circuit lighting load and lighting load. A circuit lighting load is the total electrical draw placed on an electrical circuit breaker in the central electrical panel. A circuit lighting load typically includes the multiple lighting loads in one or more rooms. For example, in the electrical panel, circuit breaker #4 could be connected to the kitchen ceiling, kitchen sink area, and the kitchen island area lighting loads.

A lighting load, as opposed to a circuit lighting load, is the total electrical draw from all of the fixtures controlled by a single lighting switch or control. For example, a kitchen wall switch may control the 6 ceiling fixtures in the kitchen. One of the more important outcomes of a lighting design is the determination of the lighting loads. The lighting load of a room or zone is the total wattage requirement (energy consumption) of all of the fixtures in that area. For example, if a kitchen has four ceiling-mounted recessed light fixtures, each with a 100-watt lamp, the total potential lighting load for that room is 400 watts. If a dimmer control (see Chapter 22) is installed, when the dimmer is set to 50 per cent (one-half brightness), the lighting load for the room is reduced to 200 watts. The total or maximum lighting load of a room is a key consideration when deciding on the best lighting control to use.

 NOTE A standard rule of thumb that can be used to estimate the lighting load of any space is to multiply the square footage by 3 watts.

Estimating Lighting Loads

To estimate the energy consumption or wattage requirements for a room, use these two guidelines:

- For general lighting requirements, multiply the total square footage of the living space by 3 watts of lighting load per square foot. For example, in a 120 square foot room, the general lighting load for the room is estimated at 360 watts.

- If fluorescent lighting is being considered, the lighting load estimation factor can be reduced to 2.5 watts per square foot for general lighting and to 1.5 for ambient lighting. For task lighting, an estimation factor of 4.0 watts per square foot should be used.

CROSS-REFERENCE Chapter 22 covers the importance of lighting load on the lighting control in detail.

An important part of designing a home lighting system is to reduce or minimize the amount of energy and the peak energy consumption, in the form of electricity, of the lighting fixtures and their lamps and bulbs.

Lighting Types

There are essentially three types of lighting used in most homes:

- General or ambient lighting
- Task lighting
- Accent lighting

General and Ambient Lighting

General lighting is used to replace sunlight in open living areas. It is the lighting type that provides illumination to enable occupants of a room or space to see the objects in a room and walk about safely. General lighting, which is also called ambient or mood lighting (see Figure 21-7), can also be used to show a room and its contents in their "best light."

The types of lamps or light fixtures typically used to provide general lighting are chandeliers, wall and ceiling-mounted fixtures, recessed or track lighting for indoor spaces, and exterior lamps and other light fixtures for outside walkways and patios.

Task Lighting

Task lighting is what it sounds like—lighting specifically designed for close work, such as reading, cooking, hobbies, games, sewing, and the like (see Figure 21-8). The objective for task lighting is to provide the proper amount of light to illuminate the task area, reduce glare and shadow, and to relieve eyestrain.

Task lighting is typically provided using recessed or track lighting, pendant lamps, or portable (table or adjustable arm) lamps.

Accent Lighting

In most instances, accent lighting is used as a part of a room's overall décor to spotlight interior artwork, plants, draperies, or other room features (see Figure 21-9). Accent lighting can also be used outdoors to highlight exterior landscaping features. To provide the proper level of light and to draw interest to the lighted feature, the lighting level used should be at least three times higher than any of the general lighting in that area.

Typically, recessed, track, or floor, ground, or wall-mounted fixtures are used as accent lighting.

PART V

Photo courtesy of LiteTouch, Inc.

Figure 21-7 An example of general or ambient lighting in a room

Photo courtesy of LiteTouch, Inc.

Figure 21-8 Task lighting is used to reduce glare and shadows.

Photo courtesy of American Fluorescent.

Figure 21-9   Accent lighting can be used to spotlight specific room or landscaping features.

Lighting Fixtures

A wide variety of lighting fixture types can be used to provide the type of lighting desired: ceiling-mounted, chandelier, pendant, portable, recessed, track, under-counter, and wall-mounted. Here's a description of each of these fixtures types:

- **Ceiling-mounted fixtures**   Ceiling fixtures, like those in Figure 21-10, are used to provide general or ambient lighting in spaces such as hallways, bedrooms, kitchens, bathrooms, laundry rooms, and the like.

- **Wall-mounted fixtures**   To state the obvious, these fixtures are mounted to walls and include light-bars and sconces (shown in Figure 21-11). Wall-mounted fixtures are used to provide general lighting, but can be used to provide task lighting in some areas, such as above a bathroom mirror.

- **Chandeliers**   Although a chandelier is actually a ceiling-mounted fixture, I am listing it separately because in most cases, it is much more expensive than other lighting fixtures in a house and is chosen for its appearance as much as its ability to provide general or task lighting. Chandeliers, like the one shown in Figure 21-12, come in a wide variety of sizes, shapes, and designs and are commonly used in foyers, living rooms, and dining rooms with higher ceilings. Chandeliers can provide ambient lighting or through pendant-style elements, task lighting over

Photo courtesy of LiteTouch, Inc.

Figure 21-10   Ceiling-mounted lighting fixtures provide ambient lighting.

tables, pianos, and the like. If a chandelier is to be a part of the lighting control system, its typically high wattage should be taken into account.

- **Pendant fixtures**   This is another ceiling-mounted fixture that can be used for either task or general lighting, or both. Pendant fixtures, shown in Figure 21-13, can be used over cooking areas, tables, and work areas or, if fitted with a globe or shade, as a part of a room's general lighting.

Photo courtesy of LiteTouch, Inc.

Figure 21-11   Wall-mounted fixtures provide general lighting.

Photo courtesy of LiteTouch, Inc.

Figure 21-12   An example of a chandelier light fixture

- **Portable fixtures**   Table lamps, floor lamps, torchieres (a type of floor lamp that directs its light upward from an inverted cone shade or reflective bowl), adjustable task lighting, and special-purpose lamps, such as art or piano lamps, are all considered to be portable lighting fixtures. Portable fixtures are used to provide general, task, and accent lighting.

- **Recessed lighting**   Recessed lighting utilizes ceiling-mounted fixtures to provide general, accent, and task lighting inconspicuously. Recessed lighting can be used virtually anywhere inside a home, but is common in areas with low ceilings.

- **Track lighting**   This fixture type allows flexibility by providing adjustable lighting scenes in a room. Most track lighting fixtures can be swiveled or rotated to adjust the areas being illuminated. Track lighting fixtures are available with built-in or external converters (to convert household AC power to DC power for the lamp), which impacts the shape and wattage of the fixture, something that must be considered when track lighting is included in a design.

- **Under-cabinet fixtures**   These fixtures can be used to add accent lighting under a shelf or task lighting under a cabinet, such as in a kitchen. There are various types of fixtures with fluorescents, track lighting, and halogen or Xenon mini-lights.

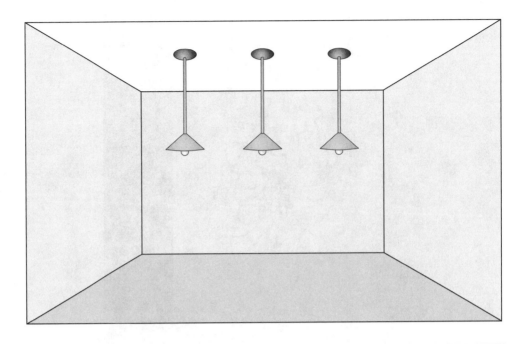

Figure 21-13   Pendant fixtures provide task lighting.

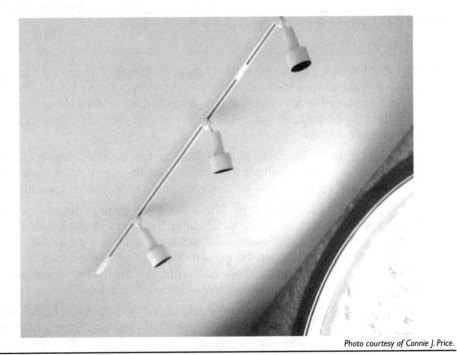

Photo courtesy of Connie J. Price.

Figure 21-14   An example of a track lighting fixture

Chapter Review

Lighting systems have some very basic operational components: light, light sources, and lighting controls. In the context of lighting systems, light is illumination, an illumination device, and sunlight. The primary home lighting sources are incandescent lamps, fluorescent tubes and bulbs, and halogen lamps. Lamps are rated by the amount of watts they produce in a certain period of time. A fluorescent light has a low-pressure mercury vapor inside and when ionized, emits ultraviolet (UV) light that is filtered through phosphor. The fluorescent tube emits cold light. The tungsten filament of a halogen lamp is encased inside a quartz enclosure filled with halogen gas. This enables it to produce a brighter light.

Light is measured in a variety of standard measurements, including foot-candles, lumens, and wattage. The lighting system must be designed to provide the minimum light needed (measured in foot-candles, lumens, or wattage).

The lighting load for each room or zone must be determined before selecting the lighting controls. To estimate the energy consumption (lighting load) of a room or zone, multiply the total square footage by 3 watts to yield the lighting load per square foot for the space. There are essentially three types of lighting used in most homes: general or ambient lighting, task lighting, and accent lighting. General lighting replaces sunlight in open living areas. Task lighting provides the proper amount of light to illuminate the task area, reduce glare and shadow, and to relieve eyestrain. Accent lighting is used as a part of a room's overall décor to spotlight interior artwork, plants, draperies, or other room features.

A wide variety of lighting fixtures can be used to provide the type of lighting desired: ceiling-mounted, chandelier, pendant, portable, recessed, track, under-counter, and wall-mounted.

Questions

1. Which of the following is not a commonly used lighting source for home lighting systems?

   A. Incandescent bulbs

   B. Fluorescent tubes

   C. Mercury vapor lamps

   D. Halogen lamps

2. What is the meaning of the "T12" in the fluorescent tube marking of F40T12CW?

   A. A tube 12 inches long.

   B. A tube 1.5 inches in diameter.

   C. The tube requires a terminated ballast of 12V AC.

   D. It is a manufacturer's identity code.

3. What is the life expectancy for a compact fluorescent lamp?

   A. 200 hours

   B. 2,500 hours

   C. 10,000 hours

   D. Unlimited

4. What is the measurement used to measure the amount of light that reaches an illuminated object?

   A. Foot-candle

   B. Lumen

   C. Watt

   D. Voltage

5. What is the measurement used to measure the amount of electricity used by a lighting source?

   A. Foot-candle

   B. Lumen

   C. Watt

   D. Voltage

6. What is the factor used to estimate general lighting loads?

   A. 1.5 watts per square foot

   B. 2.0 watts per square foot

   C. 3.0 watts per square foot

   D. 4.0 watts per square foot

7. Which of the following is not a type of residential lighting?

   A. Spotlight

   B. Ambient

   C. Task

   D. Accent

8. What ceiling or wall-mounted lighting fixture type is used to provide adjustable lighting scenes in a room?

   A. Track

   B. Pendant

   C. Vanity

   D. Chandelier

9. Calculating the lighting load for a particular space is important for choosing which of the following?

   A. Lighting fixtures

   B. Lighting sources

   C. Lighting controls

   D. Sky lights

10. What material is used to filter UV light to create visible light on a fluorescent lamp?

    A. Halogen

    B. Mercury

    C. Phosphor

    D. Tungsten

Answers

1. **C.** Mercury vapor lamps are commonly used for exterior lighting, but virtually never as an interior lamp as the other choices are.

2. **B.** The number, which is typically either 8 or 12, represents the number of eighths of an inch in the tube's diameter. The "T" indicates tubes.

3. **C.** The standard incandescent bulb has a life as long as 1,000 hours.

4. **A.** Lumens measure the amount of visible light produced by a lighting source. Watts measure the amount of power used by a lighting source. Voltage is not a lighting measurement.

5. **C.** Lumens measure the amount of visible light produced by a lighting source. Watts measure the amount of power used by a lighting source. Voltage is not a lighting measurement.

6. **C.** The other factors are used for fluorescent as well as task and accent lighting.

7. **A.** A spotlight is a type of accent lighting; ambient lighting is the general lighting in a room; and task lighting is used in work areas.

8. **A.** Track lighting can be repositioned, rotated, or swiveled to create a new lighting scene when desired.

9. **C.** Lighting fixtures and lighting sources contribute to the lighting load and determine the energy consumption specified by the lighting load. A skylight should be considered when determining the lighting level in a space, but isn't a part of the lighting load calculation. Lighting loads are very important to the selection of the appropriate lighting controls.

10. **C.** The color of the phosphor provides the color of the light produced by the lamp.

CHAPTER 22

Home Lighting Devices

In this chapter, you will learn about:
- Lighting fixtures and devices
- Lighting controls
- Wire run and wireless lighting control
- Powerline controls

A lighting system in a home is created from the combination of lighting fixtures chosen to provide the desired amounts of light in each room or area of the home. The previous chapter provided an overview of the basics of lighting and lighting system elements. This chapter takes the next step and details the fixtures and luminaries that can be incorporated into a residential lighting system.

Lighting Fixtures

Lighting fixtures are known by a variety of names, including lamps, chandeliers, pendants, tracks, luminaires, and others. Each of these fixtures is designed to produce visible light, each with its own specific use and purpose. A light fixture, such as a lamp, is first and foremost an electrical device that produces visible light. Secondarily, a light fixture can also be considered as a piece of furniture or part of a room's décor that holds light bulbs or other light source devices.

You will often see some light fixtures referred to as a luminaire. The term luminaire refers to all of the components of a light fixture, including its light source, the features used to distribute or diffuse the light, to mount the light fixture to a surface, and the features used to protect the light source.

In Chapter 21, I listed the most common of the lighting fixture types, but we now need to discuss the components that make up each type of fixture and where and how each is best applied.

Architectural Luminaires

Built-in lighting systems are referred to as architectural luminaires. In most cases, a luminaire is a constructed feature that encloses a fluorescent fixture with one or more linear (meaning tube type) lamps. Architectural luminaires are most commonly attached to a wall or ceiling with a shielding board or structural feature used to hide the fixture.

Architecture Luminaire Types

Architectural luminaires are used to add ambient lighting accents to rooms with light-colored walls and ceilings and to provide task lighting in kitchens and baths. Here are some common examples of architectural luminaires:

1. **Coves**   The light from a cove luminaire is directed up. Cove luminaires, as shown in Figure 22-1, are commonly used in rooms with high ceilings or above the cabinets in a kitchen.

2. **Soffits**   A soffit luminaire directs its light down. Soffits are commonly used to provide ambient lighting in rooms with low ceilings or to provide task lighting for a counter or work area table.

3. **Valances**   A valance luminaire directs its light both up and down. Valances are used to provide ambient lighting, but can also be used for washing a wall with light. Typically, valance lighting is used above windows and doors.

Luminaire Lighting

The lighting effect and the direction of the light produced by a luminaire can be controlled through the use of baffles, louvers, and diffusers. The purpose and use for each of these features is

- **Baffles**   Baffles are either parallel slats or a crosshatched grid placed over the light source to block direct views of the lighting source. Figure 22-2 shows a

Figure 22-1
Cove lighting creates lighting effects and provides general lighting.

Photo courtesy of Connie J. Price.

Figure 22-2
A fluorescent fixture with a grid of baffles installed

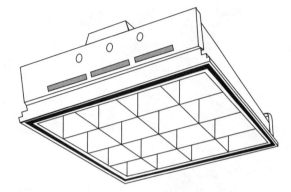

fluorescent fixture with baffles installed. Baffles are available in a variety of sizes and spacing.

- **Diffusers**   A diffuser serves two purposes: to completely block views of the light source and to spread or scatter the light in an even pattern in all directions. Figure 22-3 shows a compact fluorescent light fixture covered with a plastic diffuser.

- **Louvers**   Louvers, also called egg crates, are a cross-hatched grid work of cells (see Figure 22-4) that block direct views of the lighting source and concentrate the light into a narrower pattern in the direction the fixture is pointed.

Recessed Downlight Fixtures

The recessed lighting fixtures that are the most commonly used in homes are primarily downlights installed in ceilings. Two types of recessed downlights are available: round recessed downlights (see Figure 22-5), also called cans and high-hats, and square or rectangle recessed downlights (see Figure 22-6), also known as troffers. However, there are troffer styles that can also be surface-mounted as well.

PART V

Figure 22-3
A compact fluorescent fixture with a diffuser

Photo courtesy of Ronfell Lighting.

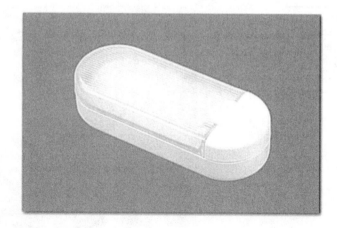

Figure 22-4
A louvered cover
for a fluorescent
light fixture

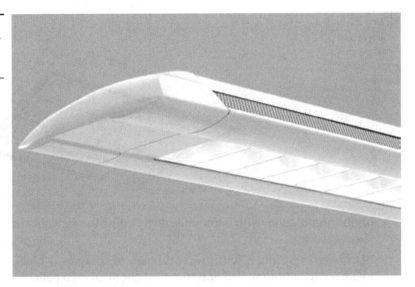

Round downlights can be incandescent, halogen, or compact fluorescent. Square downlights, typically larger than the round downlights, are usually linear (tube) fluorescent or halogen lamps.

Downlights are best used for all lighting types, but are most typically used for wall-wash and ambient lighting applications. If positioned properly, a downlight or group of downlights can also create task lighting.

NOTE When installing a recessed downlight in an insulated ceiling, the lighting fixture has been approved for this type of installation. The IC (insulated ceiling) marking should be on the lighting fixture in plain sight.

Figure 22-5
An adjustable
round recessed
downlight

*Photo courtesy of
Electric Lighting, Inc.*

Figure 22-6
A recessed troffer-style downlight

Photo courtesy of Amerillum Corporation.

Ceiling and Wall-Mounted Fixtures

Many of the same fixtures that can be used in architectural or recessed installations will also work for surface mounting on a ceiling or wall. Ceiling-mounted lighting fixtures, like the one shown in Figure 22-7, are available in a wide variety of shapes and sizes to fulfill not only the lighting requirements of a space, but to add to the room's décor as well.

Ceiling fixtures can be classified as chandelier, flush-mounted, close to ceiling, pendant, and spotlight, each with its own purpose and best use. Linear or circline fluorescent fixtures, incandescent fixtures (even with compact fluorescent lamps), pendant fixtures, and track lighting provide for ambient lighting, and in some instances, task lighting in

Figure 22-7
A spotlight ceiling-mounted light fixture provides task lighting.

Photo courtesy of Access Lighting, Inc.

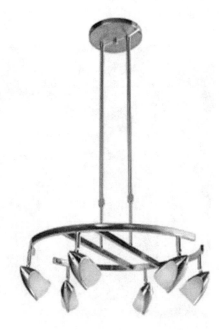

PART V

a room. Linear fluorescent fixtures can provide good light levels for laundry rooms, bathrooms, garages, kitchens, and the like, which require ambient lighting that nears the level of task lighting. Incandescent fixtures are commonly used for general lighting in all areas of a home. Pendant and track lighting fixtures are more commonly used to provide task lighting to a specific area.

Wall-mounted Fixtures

The name of this type of lighting fixture basically explains the application and placement of these fixtures. Wall-mounted fixtures include wall sconces, vanity lighting, track lighting, and spotlights:

- **Wall sconces**   These fixtures are designed to use either incandescent or compact fluorescent lamps. Sconces are used in hallways, living rooms, bedrooms, and rooms with low ceilings to provide accent and ambient lighting.

- **Vanity lighting**   Vanity lighting is applied in bathrooms and occasionally bedrooms to provide task lighting. Typically, vanity lighting is placed either on the sides or above a bathroom mirror. Figure 22-8 depicts a bathroom that uses both overhead and side-mounted vanity lighting.

- **Track lighting**   In wall-mounted placements, track lighting can use either incandescent or halogen lamps to provide flexible accent and task lighting. Figure 22-9 shows track lighting installed in a hallway.

- **Spotlights**   Spotlights can be used to provide wall-wash, general, and task lighting. The light should be positioned to prevent direct view of the light source, as this type of lighting is typically high-output. Figure 22-9 illustrates track lighting used as spot lighting.

Figure 22-8
A bathroom with vanity lighting both above and to the side of the vanity mirrors

Photo courtesy of Connie J. Price.

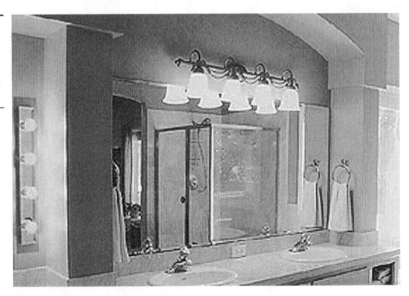

Figure 22-9
Tracking lighting placed to spotlight wall locations for future art pieces

Photo courtesy of Connie J. Price.

Daylight Considerations

One lighting source that should not be overlooked when considering the lighting sources for a room or zone is daylight—the natural sunlight that comes in through any windows, skylights, or the like.

Chapter 23 details how you should incorporate daylight into a lighting scheme. However, we should discuss the ways that the amount of daylight entering a room can be controlled, especially in special-purpose rooms like home theaters and home offices.

Daylighting

Daylighting is a lighting design technique that uses artificial light and natural daylight to maintain a certain level of lighting in a room or zone. Daylighting requires the use of photocell and timer controls, both are discussed later in the chapter. However, in summary, the photocell controls sense the amount of light present in a certain area and turns on artificial light fixtures to bring the lighting to a certain level or to turn off artificial lighting when the daylight entering the area is sufficient to supply the lighting level desired. Timers can be used in conjunction with photocells to either turn on or turn off the artificial lighting on a preset schedule, when the daylight levels in a room are predictable, such as a room that only gets morning light or afternoon light.

Window Treatments

An often-overlooked way to control the lighting in a room is window coverings and UV filters. Window coverings include draperies, blinds, shades, and the like. UV (ultraviolet) filters are typically films that are placed on the interior of the windows to block UV rays and reduce the temperature of the energy generated by sunlight passing through the window glass.

Window Coverings   In the context of home technology integration, the focus should be on the automation of window coverings, which can be integrated into the lighting controls as a part of a lighting scene. For example, if the homeowner wishes to be able to darken a room so he or she can show the digital pictures or video of his or her vacation using a digital projector, it is conceivable that they want one, a ceiling-mounted screen to descend; two, the room lights to automatically dim; and three, the light-blocking window shades or draperies to automatically close. All of this should happen at the touch of a button on a local control station or on a remote control.

There are a variety of motorized and controllable window shades (including UV filtering shades), draperies rods, and horizontal and vertical blinds that can be controlled as a stand-alone system or integrated into either a lighting control system or a home automation control system. These are discussed further in Chapter 42.

UV Filters   UV window filters are available as either window shades, special drapery materials, or as a glued on window film. Window films are typically dyed polyester opaque film that is installed either permanently or temporarily on a window's interior surface using a low-tack adhesive. Window films filter out high temperature, UV rays, and its color controls the amount of sunlight entering a room.

Exterior Lighting

Lighting installed on the exterior of a home serves a variety of purposes, perhaps the most important being:

- **Leisure**   Exterior leisure spaces, such as patios, sports courts, and play yards can be lighted to make them usable at night.

- **Landscaping**   Lighting that highlights the décor of a home's landscaping can add to the visual attractiveness of the home during dark hours. Trees, large bushes, and yard art can be illuminated to make them visible at night.

UV Light

Ultraviolet (UV) radiation is one of the parts of the sun's light spectrum. UV light is invisible, but it can have a damaging effect on people, fabric, and even plants. Overexposure to UV light can cause sunburn, and if the exposure is over a long term, it can even cause skin cancer, eye cataracts, and damage to the human immune system. In a home, the UV light coming through a window can fade or damage fabric, carpets, furniture, and even artwork.

- **Security**   Security lighting is used to illuminate the exterior of a home to create a visual deterrent to crime or it can take the form of detection devices, such as passive infrared or other motion detection systems that turn on exterior lighting when someone enters a certain area.

- **Safety**   Pathways and driveways can be lighted to provide for safe passage of people in and around a property and to illuminate a pathway or a doorway to show its direction or location. In rural areas, safety lighting can also include roadway lighting in front or near a home.

The type of exterior lighting fixture used in each of the above situations varies primarily with the application and the size of the area to be illuminated:

- **Large area lighting**   The most effective lighting for large areas is PAR (parabolic aluminized reflector) lamps, which can be incandescent, halogen, or High-Intensity Discharge (HID) tubes. To conserve energy, motion detectors or photocells that turn on the lights only when someone enters the area or during nighttime hours should be used.

- **Porch and entry lighting**   Because this area is small and the lighting is used primarily as general lighting, a wall-mounted, post-top, or architectural luminaire will supply the illumination needed.

- **Landscape and walkway lighting**   The choices for walkway and landscape lighting include both wired and no-wire solutions. Solar-powered lighting doesn't require wiring and usually includes photocells to turn the lamps on or off depending on sunlight or the lack thereof. Floodlights can also be installed to wash a walkway to highlight landscaping features.

- **Leisure area lighting**   Wall-mounted fixtures designed for exterior use can be used to provide both general and task lighting for exterior settings.

Lighting Fixture Components

The primary components of a lighting fixture is its electrical wiring, its light source receptacle, its housing, and its diffuser. The components of a light fixture are designed together for use in a particular application and to produce a specific range of light.

Light Fixture Wiring

In order to produce light, a lighting fixture must have an electrical source. The electrical power required by the fixture to produce light can come through a direct interconnection into a home's electrical wiring, from a plug-in connection to an electrical outlet, or from a battery. For use as a part of a home lighting system, we will consider only the first two of these power sources, as battery-powered lighting fixtures are not typically included as part of an integrated lighting system.

Hard-Wired Lighting Fixtures   Nearly all lighting fixtures, and especially those that are ceiling or wall-mounted fixtures, are hard-wired into the electrical system (see

Figure 22-10). By hard-wired we mean that they are directly connected to the household electrical system using the wires provided by the fixture's manufacturer.

Outlet Plugs Freestanding lamps and those fixtures designed to be portable are generally not constructed for hard-wiring installation and use a two- or three-prong plug that is inserted in a standard AC receptacle table and floor lamps, some under-counter fluorescent or halogen lights, and portable task lighting are generally outlet plug type fixtures.

Light Socket or Receptacle

Regardless of the type of lighting to be used, each has a built-in receptacle, socket, or a pair of sockets (like in a fluorescent fixture) where the bulb, tube, or light source is installed. Incandescent light fixtures have a threaded socket that the light bulb is screwed into. Fluorescent fixtures have a pair of sockets where a fluorescent tube is installed by placing the pins on the ends of the tube into the slots on the socket and twisting the tube to lock it into place. Halogen and other high-intensity fixtures have a two-contact socket into where the lamp is pushed.

Figure 22-10
The hard-wire installation of a ceiling-mounted light fixture

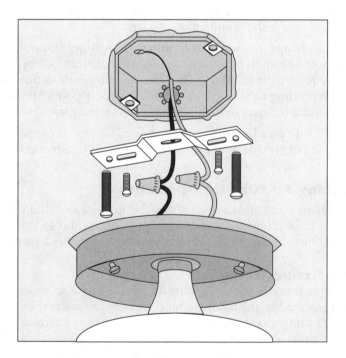

Figure 22-11
The globe on
this light fixture
diffuses the light
produced by
the fixture's
light source.

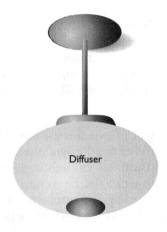

Diffuser

Diffusers and Shades

Nearly all light fixtures include a cover or what is called a diffuser. A diffuser, like the globe on the light fixture shown in Figure 22-11, is an opaque or translucent glass, plastic, acrylic, or perhaps alabaster piece that performs two functions: to shield the light source and to spread or scatter the light in an even pattern in all directions.

Diffused lighting produces less shadowing than direct lighting because the light doesn't come from any definite direction. In addition to a diffuser that is a part of a light fixture, a white or light colored wall could also produce diffused light.

A lampshade may seem like it could be a diffuser as well, but the purpose for a lampshade on a table or floor lamp or perhaps a wall or ceiling-mounted fixture is to shade the light source and protect your eyes from a direct view of the light source. In most cases, lampshades are used to direct light either down or up and although some light may be diffused through the cloth, plastic, or glass of the shade, its purpose is not the same as a diffuser.

Lighting Controls

Lighting controls, depending on the type in use, are used to lower a room's light levels to conserve energy and extend the life of a light source, change the ambient lighting in a room, set the light level of task lighting, and to create a variety of lighting scenes at the touch of one button for each space.

As briefly discussed in Chapter 21, there are a variety of lighting controls that can be used in a home. Lighting controls range from the common toggle on/off switch to new wireless in-room and whole-house controls.

In-Room Controls

The most common in-room lighting control is still the two-position on-off switch, but technology no longer limits the choice to this basic light control. A variety of new controls are available that not only control room lighting, but also provide flexibility and in many cases, reduce energy costs. The most common of the in-room lighting controls are

- **Dimmers:** This type of switch is used to reduce the voltage flowing to a lighting fixture that in turn reduces the light produced by the fixture. Dimmers are usually associated with incandescent lighting, but with a dimming ballast installed, fluorescent lighting can also be controlled using a dimmer. Dimmer switches are available in a variety of control types: rotary (shown in Figure 22-12), slide (shown in Figure 22-13), or touch styles (see Figure 22-14).

- **Motion and occupancy detectors**   Not only do motion detector controls provide convenience for a person entering a room, but they also help save energy by turning off lighting in unoccupied rooms. Different types of motion detector controllers (an example is shown in Figure 22-15) are available, including fully automatic and manual on automatic off. Motion and occupancy sensors use two different technologies: passive infrared (PIR) and ultrasonic. PIR sensors detect changes in energy generated by occupants entering or moving about in a space. Ultrasonic sensors send out high-frequency sound waves that bounce off objects in the space. Moving objects in the space change the frequency of the wave, which is interpreted as somebody being in the room and the lights are turned on or stay on for a preset amount of time.

Figure 22-12
A rotary-style
dimmer control

Figure 22-13
A slide switch
dimmer control

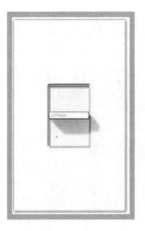

- **Photocells** Photocells, also called photoelectric cells and electric eyes, are small devices that can be mounted on a ceiling (see Figure 22-16), wall, along a driveway, or just about anywhere. A photocell senses changes in lighting levels and sends a signal to a central controller that interprets the signal as a need for turning on lighting fixtures in a room or zone. Some photocells also include the signal processing and can be used to directly control a lighting fixture directly wired to it.

- **Switches** The everyday on-off light switch is convenient and is still preferred by some homeowners for home resale purposes. Beyond the two-position up or down toggle switch, there are variations that replace the toggle with a two-position rocker or a push-button and some that include an indicator light that glows when the lighting is on.

Figure 22-14
A touch switch
dimmer control

Figure 22-15
A motion
detector sensor

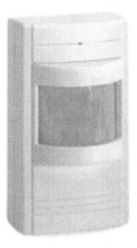

- **Timers** Timers can be electronic interval timers or some form of a rotary control. Timers are best applied in rooms that are infrequently occupied or with lighting that is used only for short periods, such as the lighting in bathrooms, closets, and pantries.

Automated Lighting Controls

The primary component of a centralized whole-house automated lighting control system is the keypad interfaces placed throughout the home. With keypads the walls are cleaned up since a single-gang keypad can control up to nine different lights or scenes. Keypads, like the one shown in Figure 22-17, allow a room's lighting to be controlled by the touch of a button to create preferred lighting in a room. Each preset lighting variation or combination in a room or area is called a lighting scene.

Lighting control keypads can be in-wall devices (Figure 22-17), handheld devices (Figure 22-18), or tabletop touch-screen units (Figure 22-19).

Figure 22-16
A photocell, like
this model, can
be mounted on
a ceiling or wall.

*Photo courtesy of
Leviton Manufacturing
Company, Inc.*

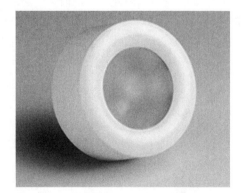

Figure 22-17
Two configurations of a multi-function keypad lighting control

Photo courtesy of Smarthome, Inc.

Figure 22-18
A handheld X-10 lighting system remote control uses RF signals to communicate to a base receiver

Figure 22-19
A tabletop touch-
screen system
controller

*Photo courtesy of
AMX Corporation.*

Wireless Lighting Controls

Wireless lighting controls (those that don't require new wire to be installed) provide the ability to control the lighting of an occupied room, as well as in other rooms, to set or change lighting scenes easily.

The most popular wireless lighting control systems use either radio frequency (RF) signaling or powerline carrier (PLC) technology. RF signals require radio wave transmitters and receivers. PLC actually does work on wires but we list it here under wireless since it requires no special/new wiring. PLC transmits and receives its signals over the AC wiring in a home.

Wireless control systems require the installation of "smart" switches. With RF control, if wall-mounted keypads are to be used, the wiring for keypads must be done during the pre-wire phase of construction or retrofitted.

Powerline Lighting Controls

PLC systems use the AC wiring of a home to communicate signals to a lighting control system. PLC system remote controls use RF technology to communicate to a PLC receiver device, such as a light switch, lamp module, or appliance module. Some PLC systems

Figure 22-20
A PLC
transceiver
module

also offer a portable keypad that can be plugged into any AC outlet and sends signals to control the lights connected to the PLC system. PLC systems can be configured to control dimmers, light switches, and even ceiling fan switches.

The primary components of a PLC system are

- **Light switches**   PLC light switches look just like a standard light switch and are wired into the electrical system using a nearly exact procedure. The difference between a PLC light switch and an ordinary light switch is that the wiring is used for signal transmission rather than opening and closing the circuit to the lighting fixture.

- **Lamp controls**   Lamp control modules either plug directly into an AC outlet or can be inserted into the lamp to control a lamp. There are two types of plug-in modules, dimmer and screw-in. Lamp controls are used to reduce or raise the AC power to a lamp, which dims or brightens the lamp. Dimmer modules are controlled using an RF dimmer or keypad.

  - **Plug-in lamp controls:** This type of PLC lamp control is plugged into an AC outlet and the lamp to be controlled is then plugged into an AC outlet on the face of the control module (see Figure 22-21).

  - **Screw-in or bayonet lamp controls:** This type of PLC lamp control (see Figure 22-22) is either screwed or inserted and twist-locked into the lamp socket of the light fixture. The light bulb or lamp is then screwed or inserted into the control. The control is operated using a remote control to dim and turn off the lamp.

Figure 22-21
A PLC plug-in lamp control module

Photo courtesy of Smarthome, Inc.

- **Appliance controls**   Appliance control modules plug directly into an AC outlet. They control like a relay and can only turn the device plugged into them on or off. They cannot dim like a lamp module. They come either with a two-prong plug or a three-prong plug with ground.

- **Room keypads**   PLC room controls commonly have buttons that allow for individual device control and preset lighting scenes. Figure 22-17, earlier in the chapter, shows examples of room keypads.

- **Whole house controllers**   This type of controller allows for programming of devices by time and situation and allows for setup of scenes. When combined with keypad buttons, it gives remote and scene control throughout the house. It is a larger and smarter version of a PLC room keypad that is capable of controlling the lighting throughout a house from any room.

Figure 22-22
A PLC screw-in lamp control module

Photo courtesy of Smarthome, Inc.

Figure 22-23
A PLC lighting
keypad controller

*Photo courtesy of
Smarthome, Inc.*

PLC System Mapping   In a PLC lighting control system, a combination of codes is used to address the individual remote controls, transceivers, and modules. The addressing scheme uses a combination of codes, a house code and a unit code, to address as many as 256 devices on a system. An alphabetic letter, such as the letters A to P, commonly represents the house code and the unit code is a number, like the numbers 1 to 16.

The house and unit codes are typically set on a device by turning the house and unit code wheels with a small screwdriver. Only devices with the same house code will communicate with one another, so if you are installing a PLC lighting control system, be sure to set the house and unit codes, which can be assigned sequentially, before installing the devices.

 NOTE   The default house code on most systems is "A." It is recommended that "A" not be used to avoid any possibility of the next-door neighbor turning on or off the lights.

Wireless RF Controls

In addition to PLC wireless controls, there are also RF lighting control transceivers that interpret the RF signal for transmission over twisted-pair wire and some that transmit directly to an RF receiver connected to the lighting system controller. One such system is the Lutron RadioRA system that includes the following RF devices in its basic package, as illustrated in Figure 22-25:

- **Wall-mounted master control**   This control allows for preset lighting scenes or the control of individual lamps. Wall-mounted controls in one room can be used to turn on lighting in other rooms or throughout the house.

PART V

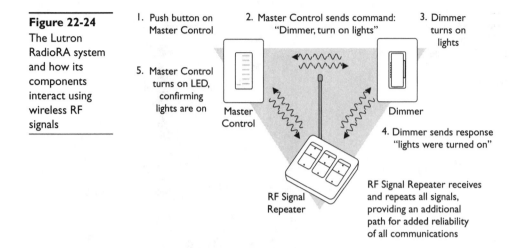

Figure 22-24
The Lutron RadioRA system and how its components interact using wireless RF signals

1. Push button on Master Control

2. Master Control sends command: "Dimmer, turn on lights"

3. Dimmer turns on lights

5. Master Control turns on LED, confirming lights are on

Master Control

Dimmer

4. Dimmer sends response "lights were turned on"

RF Signal Repeater

RF Signal Repeater receives and repeats all signals, providing an additional path for added reliability of all communications

- **Dimmer controls**   Dimmers are controlled by a master control module that directs the dimmer to turn on, dim, brighten, or turn off one or more lights in a room or area.

- **RF signal repeater**   In large homes, or in systems that wish to have a larger RF range, an RF repeater receives and retransmits the signals of the lighting control system. A signal repeater enables such optional features as car controls (to turn on the lights from within a car pulling into the driveway) or exterior lighting controls.

- **Tabletop controls**   Remote control devices can be used to activate room or area lighting scenes or to turn on or off lighting throughout a home.

- **Entry master controls**   Allows the lighting system to be controlled from outside at an entryway into the home.

Wired Lighting Controls

Wired lighting control systems are essentially what they sound like—lighting controls connected to lighting fixtures or controllers by electrical wiring or networking cable.

Standard Lighting Controls

Perhaps the most basic of wired lighting controls is the standard on/off toggle switch or dimmer controls found in virtually every home. The switch or dimmer is wired directly in-line with the lamp or fixture it controls. The most common controls found in standard lighting control systems are

- **On/Off switches**   The traditional type of lighting control used in virtually all homes. This control is simply a two-position or toggle switch that either turns on or turns off the electricity flowing to a light fixture.

- **Rotary dimmer controls**   The most common type of dimmer control found in homes, this control uses a push-on/push-off switch that can be rotated to change the lighting level of a room.

- **Slider dimmer controls**   A variation on the rotary dimmer, these controls have a slider switch that allows the lighting level of a room to be set manually.

- **Timer controls**   These controls incorporate a clock or timer to complete or break the electrical circuit to any light fixtures attached to the device. These controls can be either separate or built-in devices.

- **Touch dimmer controls**   Using either a one-button control or a keypad, the lighting level in a room can be changed.

Automated Lighting Controls

A more advanced approach to wired lighting control systems are those that connect room controllers and modules using low-voltage cabling, such as coaxial or twisted-pair cable. Basically, this type of system consists of room control stations that are connected over structured wiring to a central lighting system controller that receives and transmits signals to carry out the commands requested by the control stations to and from the controllers connected to light fixtures. The central controller device in a digital lighting control system is either a proprietary microprocessor-based controller or a networked PC running specialized lighting control software.

Automated lighting controls can either be centralized or distributed. What is meant by centralized is that all the lighting loads controlled are wired to a central control panel for control. In a distributed system, the control switch or device is located locally in the area of the lighting being controlled, such as the wall switch. In some spaces, such as a home theater, having the master control unit local simplifies the cabling.

CROSS-REFERENCE   Chapters 23 and 24 also cover lighting system topics, including information on lighting system design and installation.

Chapter Review

Lighting fixtures are known by a variety of names, including lamps, chandeliers, pendants, tracks, luminaires, and others, with each designed for a specific use and purpose. A light fixture is an electrical device that produces visible light. Light fixtures are also referred to as luminaires.

Built-in lighting systems are referred to as architectural luminaires, which are constructed features that enclose a lighting fixture. Architectural luminaires are most commonly attached to a wall or ceiling with a shielding board or structural feature used to hide the fixture. Common examples of architectural luminaires are coves, soffits, and valances.

The lighting effect of a luminaire can be controlled through the use of baffles, louvers, and diffusers.

Recessed lighting fixtures are primarily installed in ceilings. Two types of recessed lights are available: round recessed downlights and square or rectangle recessed downlights. Round downlights can be incandescent, halogen, or compact fluorescent. Square downlights are usually linear fluorescent or halogen lamps.

Ceiling fixtures can be classified as chandelier, flush-mounted, close to ceiling, pendant, and spotlight. Linear or circline fluorescent fixtures, incandescent fixtures, pendant fixtures, and track lighting provide for ambient and task lighting. Linear fluorescent fixtures provide light for laundry rooms, bathrooms, garages, and kitchens. Incandescent fixtures are used for general lighting. Pendant and track lighting fixtures are used to provide task lighting. Wall-mounted fixtures include wall sconces, vanity lighting, track lighting, and spotlights.

Daylighting is a lighting design technique that uses artificial light and natural daylight to maintain a certain level of lighting in a room or zone. Daylighting requires the use of photocell and timer controls. Window coverings and UV filters can be used to control the amount of sunlight that enters a room.

Lighting installed on the exterior of a home serves a variety of purposes, including: leisure, landscaping, security, and safety. The exterior lighting fixture types used for these types of lighting are: large area lighting; entry lighting, landscape lighting, walkway lighting, and leisure area lighting.

Lighting controls are used to lower a room's light levels to conserve energy and extend the life of a light source, change the ambient lighting in a room, set the light level of task lighting, and to create a variety of lighting scenes. A variety of lighting controls are used to control room lighting: dimmers, motion and occupancy detectors, photocells, switches, and timers.

The primary components of a centralized whole-house automated lighting control system are keypad interfaces placed throughout the home. Keypads allow a room's lighting to be controlled by the touch of a button. Lighting control keypads can be in-wall devices, handheld, or tabletop units.

Wireless lighting controls provide the ability to control the lighting of an occupied room, as well as in other rooms, to set or change lighting scenes easily. Wireless lighting control systems use RF or PLC technology. PLC systems use AC wiring to communicate signals to a lighting control system. PLC systems can be configured to control dimmers, light switches, and even ceiling fan switches. The primary components of a PLC system are: lamp controls, room keypads, and whole house controllers.

RF lighting control transceivers interpret signals and transmit them over twisted-pair wire or directly to an RF receiver at the lighting system controller.

The most common controls found in standard lighting control systems are: on/off switches, dimmer controls, and timer controls.

An advanced approach to lighting control systems connects room controllers and modules over low-voltage cabling. The central controller device is a proprietary microprocessor-based controller or a networked PC running specialized lighting control software. Automated lighting controls can either be centralized or distributed.

Questions

1. What is the lighting system technique that uses artificial light to augment natural light levels in a room or area called?

    A. Downlighting

    B. Daylighting

    C. Skylighting

    D. Sunlighting

2. In order to block sunlight from a room with windows, which of the following lighting control features could be used as a part of an automated lighting control system?

    A. Motorized draperies or shades

    B. Block-out window inserts

    C. Photo-sensitive glass

    D. UV filters

3. Which of the following is not a purpose for exterior lighting?

    A. Landscaping

    B. Growth lighting for exterior plants

    C. Safety

    D. Security

4. Which of the following is not a type of dimming control?

    A. On/Off

    B. Rotary

    C. Slide

    D. Touch

5. What technology is commonly used to detect when someone enters a room?

    A. Photocell

    B. PIR

    C. RF

    D. Time clock

6. PLC systems are applications of which communications technology?

    A. RS-232

    B. RS-422

    C. HomePNA

    D. X-10

7. What are the two types of PLC lamp controls?

   A. Automatic

   B. Bayonet

   C. Dimmer

   D. Relay

8. Up to how many devices can a PLC system address using a combination of home codes and unit codes?

   A. 8

   B. 64

   C. 128

   D. 256

9. What type of cable are wired lighting control system keypads typically installed on?

   A. High-voltage wiring

   B. Low-voltage wiring

   C. HVAC wiring

   D. Telephone wiring

10. A lighting control system where the devices in a room are controlled by devices located in that room is said to be

   A. Centralized

   B. Decentralized

   C. Distributed

   D. Isolated

Answers

1. **B.** Downlighting is a type of lighting installation where the lamps are ceiling mounted or luminaires; skylighting is a window treatment; and sunlighting is neither.

2. **A and D.** Block-out window inserts and photo-sensitive glass are not part of an automated lighting control system—one requires manual installation and the other is a chemical reaction to sunlight.

3. **B.** Okay, so it was a bit obvious, but I wanted you to remember the purposes for exterior lighting and cause you to reflect on how exterior lighting can be included in a lighting control system.

4. **A.** Rotary, slide, and touch controls are all types of dimming controls. An on/off switch can only turn a lamp on or off.

5. **B.** Passive infrared technology (PIR) is the most commonly used technology in motion and occupancy detectors. Ultrasonic sensors in another technology that is used in this type of device.

6. **D.** X-10 is a communications technology that transmits signals over AC power lines. CEBus is another AC powerline technology, though most systems available are based on the X-10 technology. RS-232 and 422 are types of serial data communications and HomePNA is used primarily for data networking.

7. **C** and **D**. In order for a PLC system to be automatic, some type of sensor must be used. Bayonet is one of the types of screw-in dimming controls, but the general types of PLC lamp controls are dimmers and relays.

8. **D.** Given that each home code typically can address up to 16 unit codes, only 16 home codes are required to address up to 256 devices from a central lighting controller.

9. **B.** LV wiring, meaning the type of cabling used in a structured wiring system— coaxial and UTP—are typically used for wiring automated centralized lighting control systems.

10. **B.** A centralized system is controlled through a single system controller in which local controllers are distributed and a decentralized system controls the lighting from within a room or zone. I guess it could be isolated, but that's not a lighting control system term.

Designing a Home Lighting Control System

In this chapter, you will learn about:

- The types of loads to be controlled
- Lighting loads
- Lighting scenes
- Lighting zones
- Exterior lighting

Designing a whole house lighting system involves more than selecting the lighting for each individual room. Each room of a house can have several levels of lighting requirements. At different times a room's occupants may desire a room to have ambient lighting or task lighting. The lighting system must be able to accommodate either lighting type easily. You must also consider how the lighting is to be provided and the type of light to be used.

In this chapter, you look at the various issues that must be considered when designing a lighting system for a room as well as an entire house.

Designing a Home Lighting System

Like the design process used for all systems in a home technology integration project, a systematic approach is necessary when designing a home lighting system. The use of a step-by-step approach ensures that the system is complete and addresses the needs and requirements of the homeowners.

The steps that should be used to design a home lighting system are as follows:

1. Identify the lighting loads to be controlled by each lighting control station.

2. Identify the lighting type associated with each load.

3. Calculate wattage requirements of each lighting circuit.

4. Determine the type of control devices to be used.

5. Determine the locations of the lighting controls and lay out their wiring loops.

6. Determine the lighting scenes to be programmed into each room or zone.

7. Plan and program the layout of the control switches.

Lighting Loads

As I discussed in Chapter 21, a lighting load is the amount of energy consumed to provide a certain level of illumination in a space. Knowing the lighting load of a house and its rooms and ensuring that the load doesn't exceed the electrical power available to each space are essential parts of any lighting system design.

Types of Loads

On the electrical side of lighting, there are two types of loads that must be considered: inductive loads and resistive loads.

- **Inductive load**   An inductive load is created by electrical devices that have moving parts, from devices with motors like power drills, fans, and vacuum cleaners to devices that include transformers, such as a fluorescent light fixture.

- **Resistive load**   A resistive load provides resistance to the flow of electrical current. Devices that create resistive loads include electric heaters, electric stoves, and even irons, but in the context of lighting loads, incandescent and halogen lamps create resistive loads.

The primary reason you should know the type of load a lighting device produces is that it allows you to match lighting controls to the type of load created by the fixture being controlled. Inductive load devices should not be controlled with resistive load controllers, and *vice versa*. Table 23-1 lists the common lighting types, their load type, and the type of controller typically matched to them.

Calculating Lighting Load

Prior to the pre-wire phase of a home's construction, the lighting loads must be determined based on your understanding of the customer's lighting requirements and desires.

The number of lighting fixtures on each of the lighting loads is used to determine the number of electrical circuits required to support the lighting requirements of a space.

Lighting Type	Load Type	Controller Type
Incandescent	Resistive	Incandescent dimmer.
Fluorescent	Inductive	Relay or special fluorescent dimmer; lighting fixture may require dimmable ballast.
High intensity discharge (HID)	Inductive	Relay or special HID dimmer; fixture may require dimmable ballast.
Low voltage	Inductive	Low voltage dimmer.
Quartz halogen	Resistive	Incandescent dimmer.

Table 23-1   Lighting Types, Loads, and Controllers

Some estimate must be made as to the type and number of lighting fixtures to be used to accomplish the lighting requirements. Once this has been decided, it is possible to estimate the total lighting load for each circuit, room, and the entire house. For example, an incandescent load with three fixtures with 75-watt lamps each equals a total load of 225 watts. This information is needed when designing the control requirements and layout of the total lighting system.

The lighting loads are calculated slightly different from incandescent and fluorescent and HID lighting. Incandescent lighting loads are calculated as the wattage of all of the lamps connected to a single control, such as a switch, dimmer, or keypad.

When calculating the lighting load for a control connected to fluorescent or HID lamps, the power required by the ballasts may need to be factored in. Magnetic ballasts, whether for fluorescent or HID fixtures, use an additional 15 percent of power over and above the power requirements of the lamps, which means that the total wattage requirement for a lighting circuit needs to be multiplied by a factor of 1.15. However, if electronic ballasts are used, no additional wattage needs to be included.

Table 23-2 shows the lighting loads in a kitchen that has three incandescent fixtures of 100 watts each, two fluorescent fixtures with 40-watt lamps, and three under-counter fixtures with HID lamps of 60 watts each. Assume here that each lighting type is connected to a dedicated control.

Volt-Amps, Watts, Lumens

The measurements used when designing a lighting system are volts, amperes, watts, and lumens. However, which of these measurements is used depends on what is being measured. These electrical and lighting measurements are discussed in the following sections.

Volt-Amps

Volt-amps, or voltage-amperes (VA), are commonly stated as kilo (1,000) volt-amps (KVA). VA represents the value of an AC circuit's current (A) times its voltage (V). VA is just one way to define the electrical power requirements of a lighting fixture and its lamp. On resistive circuits, such as a circuit with incandescent lighting fixtures, the VA requirement can also be referred to as the apparent power requirement and stated as watts.

Watts

Watts are calculated using Ohm's law, which computes watts as equal to the voltage times the amps on a circuit. All lamps use electricity to produce light and the amount of electricity required is stated in watts (W). One watt is the equivalent of 1 volt-amp. See Chapter 15 for more information about Ohm's law.

Lighting type	Watts/Lamp	Number of Lamps	Lighting Load
Incandescent	100	3	300 watts
Fluorescent	40	2	80 watts
HID	60	3	180 watts
Total lighting load			560 watts

Table 23-2 An Example of the Lighting Load Calculation in One Room of a Home

Lighting lamps are all rated in watts, especially incandescent lamps. The wattage rating on a lamp indicates the amount of power the lamp uses to operate efficiently. On fluorescent fixtures, the lamps or tubes use electrical power, but because the fluorescent lights require a ballast to start up, its wattage (typically rated in amps) must be included in the power requirements of the fixture.

Lumens

Different lamps produce differing amounts of light. However, as the amount of light produced increases, so does the amount of power consumed to do so. For example, a 100-watt incandescent light bulb produces more light than a 60-watt bulb and requires 40 more watts of power to do so. Because of this, many people believe that the wattage rating on the bulb is a statement of how much light the bulb produces. To a certain extent this is comparatively true, but not exactly.

The amount of light produced by a lamp is measured in lumens. Lumens are typically stated as lumens per watt (LPW) on the packaging of a lamp. LPW indicates the number of lumens produced for each watt of power used and is, in effect, a measure of the lamp's efficiency in converting power to light. Because some lamp types are more efficient than others, the LPW varies by lamp type. Incandescent lamps are generally rated in the 17–20 LPW range and fluorescent and high-output lamps can produce as much as 90 LPW.

Designing Room Lighting

Many countries around the world have standards for recommended levels of light for different types and uses of spaces. Of course there are a number of factors that must be considered when determining the level of light for any particular space. Rooms can require different light for a variety of activities. For example, a room that needs task lighting for detailed activities requires more light than a room that needs only ambient lighting. Other criteria for the amount of light a room requires are the preferences of the occupants and if the lighting levels are to be incorporated into a room's décor.

In new construction situations, the lighting designer may need to work closely with the architect to achieve a balance between the basic lighting requirements of an area and any artistic uses of lighting.

Fitting the Light to the Room

When designing the lighting levels for a space, you must consider the color of the light, the shape of a room and its contents, and the size and dimensions of the room.

Light Color

Light produced by lighting fixtures has color, which can be used to accent the décor and design of a room and its contents. In a lighted room, the color on any surface is produced as a combination of the color of the surface and the color of the light hitting that surface.

The light produced by a lamp in a light fixture can literally change the perceived color of the walls and objects of a room. Color can also affect the mood of a room's occupants. Bright and varied color in a room can create a mood of happiness, but monotone and dark colors and gloomy light can cause the opposite effect. Different room and lighting colors produce different effects—red is warm and blue or green is cold.

Objects in a Room

The angle at which light strikes an object can alter the perception of its size or shape by creating glares or shadows. Of course, this issue is difficult to predict for a home that may not be built or furnished yet, but if these issues are important to the homeowners, adjustable lighting should be considered.

Room Size and Dimensions

Light can be used to change the perception of a room's size or volume, or to highlight a room's design elements to make them more attention grabbing.

Different lighting levels and styles can be included in a room's lighting plan to enhance a room's features. For example, illuminating a ceiling can create the illusion of a high ceiling, and low lighting on a structural feature can make it appear smaller or closer. Lighting can also be used to create a virtual pathway through a room or between rooms. For example, when the rear of a pathway is more brightly lit than its entrance, visitors are drawn to the rear by the lighting.

Identifying Lighting Needs

Lighting is easily the least expensive decorating option available to homeowners, at least compared to the cost of remodeling and home decorating. This is a good reason for the lighting design to focus on complementing the lifestyle of the homeowners.

One very important consideration when identifying lighting needs and loads is the amount of sunlight available to light a room during the day. If a room doesn't directly receive much sunlight, it may require day lighting as well as nighttime lighting.

Identify Room Lighting Needs

The lighting design for a room should take into account how a room is to be used, the mood or atmosphere desired, and any room décor or contents that are to be highlighted. Another consideration is the color of the walls, ceiling, and floor coverings. Dark colors absorb light and light colors reflect light, and the lighting design should reflect this.

Rooms planned for multiple uses or activities may require multipurpose, adjustable, or perhaps multiple lighting types to provide the desired and recommended lighting for each activity. The recommendations for the common rooms of a house are as follows:

- **Bathroom**   The lighting in a bathroom should be evenly distributed and as shadow-free as possible. Vanity lighting and recessed wall-mounted or ceiling-mounted fixtures are most commonly used in this space.

- **Bedrooms**   Bedrooms typically require adjustable lighting along with task lighting. Ceiling-mounted or wall-mounted fixtures, controlled with a dimmer control, can be used for general lighting and task lighting supplied through table lamps or wall sconces can provide the task lighting.

- **Dining room**   Depending on the homeowners' plans for how a dining room will be used, the lighting can include general, accent, and task lighting to provide the appropriate lighting levels for entertaining, family gatherings, and perhaps homework, hobbies, or games.

- **Hallways and entrances**   Entrances typically use a single, large ceiling-mounted lighting fixture, such as a chandelier, to provide general lighting. Hallways should be lighted every 8 to 10 feet for safety reasons, typically using recessed ceiling-mounted or wall-mounted sconces. Track lighting can also be used, especially if art or other objects are to be accent lighted.

- **Living or family rooms**   These rooms typically are multipurpose rooms. General lighting should be included for entertainment or watching TV; task lighting should be provided for reading and other close or detailed activities; and, if desired, accent lighting should be included to accent or highlight plants, art, or architectural features of the room.

- **Kitchen**   Kitchens are work areas, but can also be gathering places. So, both general and task lighting is commonly installed in this area. Under-counter and ceiling-mounted task lighting is also commonly used in kitchen. If desired, cove or soffit luminaires can also be included to provide room accent lighting.

Lighting Scenes

A lighting scene is the preset combination of lighting levels for load(s) configured to provide the lighting appropriate for a particular activity or purpose. Lighting scenes can be manually adjusted using one or more dimmers or lighting controls. However, lighting scenes are typically associated with automatic controls and are one of the key benefits of lighting control.

Multiple lighting scenes can be defined for a single room or area. Different combinations of lighting level settings on the lighting fixtures in a room can be defined to create one or more ambient lighting levels, one or more task lighting patterns, and one or more accent lighting patterns. Selecting the desired lighting scene is then as easy as pressing a button on a keypad or a touch screen controller. For example, the keypad controller shown in Figure 23-1 has been programmed with four lighting selection.

Lighting Zones

A lighting zone can include one room, multiple rooms, open floor areas, hallways, stairways, exterior areas, and any combination of these areas. A lighting zone is an area of a house for which a lighting scene is established. When selected, a lighting scene illuminates a lighting zone. Likewise, a lighting zone can have many possible lighting scenes defined for it, but only one can be in use at a time.

When designing lighting scenes in lighting zones, the dimensions, shape, contents, and colors of the zone must be considered. If any part of a lighting zone prevents the desired lighting effect from being achieved, it may be necessary to divide the zone into multiple lighting zones.

Figure 23-1
A four-function
keypad lighting
control station

*Photo courtesy of
Smarthome, Inc.*

Lighting Controls

There are essentially two types of lighting controls that can be installed in a home: dimming and switching. Each of these control types can achieve the goal of controlling the lighting level in a room, zone, or home, but they do it in slightly different ways.

Dimming Controls

Dimming controls changes the amount of light emitted by a lamp from none to the lamp's full capability. Dimming controls are typically more expensive than switching controls, but they provide more cost saving and a less abrupt transition from one light level to another. Another advantage to a dimming controls is that they are more easily re-adjusted should the lighting requirements of a room, zone, or home change.

A variety of dimming control types is available, including rotary, slide, and touch controls. Manual rotary dimmers, like the one shown in Figure 23-2, are available for either incandescent or fluorescent lamps, although a fluorescent lamp also requires a dimmable ballast (more on this later in the chapter).

Figure 23-2
A rotary
dimmer switch
for controlling
incandescent
lamps

PART V

Figure 23-3
A standard
two-position
switching control

Switching Controls

A basic single-lamp switching control has two settings: the lamp is either on or off. More lamps, such as in a typical two-lamp fixture, can have both lamps on or both lamps off and there are no intermediate settings between on and off for any of the lamps.

Two-position light switches, like the one shown in Figure 23-3, are the most common lighting control used in a home.

Controlling Electrical Flow

One of the basic principles underlying a lighting control system is that what is actually being controlled is the electricity flowing to light fixtures. Dimming controls reduce or increase the amount of voltage flowing to a fixture, thereby decreasing or increasing the amount of light the fixture's lamp produces. Switching controls either turn on or turn off the power flowing to the fixture, turning the lamp on or off.

Exterior Lighting

Lighting zones and lighting scenes aren't just interior lighting areas. The exterior of a home and its landscaping, leisure areas, work spaces, and play areas can be designated as lighting zones in which safety, security, ambient, and accent lighting scenes can be defined.

The various types of exterior lighting scenes that can be created are as follows:

- **Landscape lighting** Standard and specialized lighting fixtures can be used to create a variety of lighting effects for a home's exterior, especially with landscaping and gardens. Lighting can be used to create general moonlighting effects, focal points, uplights on trees, and spotlights on sculpture or other objects. The basic types of landscape lighting are

  - **Backlighting** This type of lighting creates a backdrop of light that creates a visual depth in the dark.

- **Downlighting**   This type of lighting effect is used to replace the sun and natural lighting on fixtures, walls, or gardens. The lighting fixtures can be mounted to walls, in taller trees, or mounted on elevated ground.

- **Moonlighting**   This is a form of downlighting that uses lighting fixtures suspended in trees or mounted on higher objects to create a soft, diffused light that emulates the effects of moonlight.

- **Uplighting**   This type of lighting effect is used to produce large shadows and to illuminate a tree, statue, or other object. The typical placement for an uplighting fixture is on or near the ground.

- **Safety lighting**   A very important reason to include exterior lighting in a lighting design is safety. Safety lighting provides a lighted pathway on steps, sidewalks, walkways, and around potentially hazardous landscaping or objects. Safety lighting is down-pointing and positioned so that it is glare-free to avoid shining into anyone's eyes.

- **Security lighting**   Lighting spread evenly around buildings and their immediate surroundings, especially doorways and ground floor access points, can serve as a deterrent to prowlers or other intruders. Eliminating shadows is the primary objective of security lighting. Photocells and motion-detectors can add to the effectiveness of security lighting.

Chapter Review

A lighting load is the amount of energy consumed to provide a certain level of illumination in a space. The two types of loads that must be considered are inductive loads and resistive loads. Electrical devices with moving parts create an inductive load. A resistive load provides resistance to the flow of electrical current. Lighting load is determined by the amount of wattage used by the lamps connected to a single control. Volt-amps, or voltage-amperes (VA), measure the value of an AC circuit's current (A) times its voltage (V). On resistive circuits, the VA requirement is the apparent power requirement and stated as watts. Watts are equal to the voltage times the amps on a circuit. The wattage rating of a lamp indicates the amount of power the lamp uses to operate efficiently. The light produced by a lamp is measured in lumens. Lumens per watt (LPW) indicate the number of lumens produced for each watt of power.

Light produced by lighting fixtures has color, which can be used to accent the décor and design of a room and its contents. Color can also affect the mood of a room's occupants. Light can be used to change the perception of a room's size or volume, or to highlight a room's decor.

Rooms planned for multiple uses or activities may require multipurpose, adjustable, or perhaps multiple lighting types to provide the desired and recommended lighting for each activity. Lighting scenes are preset combinations of lighting levels that provide lighting for a variety of activities. Lighting scenes are typically associated with automatic controls.

PART V

A lighting zone is an area where a lighting scene is established. If any part of a lighting zone prevents the desired lighting effect from being achieved, it may be necessary to divide the zone into multiple lighting zones.

The various types of exterior lighting scenes that can be created are landscape lighting, safety lighting, and security lighting. The basic types of landscape lighting are backlighting, downlighting, moonlighting, and uplighting.

Questions

1. The total wattage required by a lighting circuit controlled by a single control is the

   A. Lumens

   B. Lighting level

   C. Lighting load

   D. Power factor

2. A resistive load is defined as

   A. A load created by electrical devices with moving parts

   B. The type of load created by electric stoves and irons

   C. The load created by drills and vacuum cleaners

   D. The type of load created by a fluorescent fixture and its ballast

3. If a room's lighting scheme includes three incandescent ceiling lights at 100 watts each on one control and five fluorescent lamps at 40 watts each in fixtures using electronic ballasts on a second control, what is the combined lighting load of these two circuits?

   A. 300 watts

   B. 400 watts

   C. 500 watts

   D. 575 watts

4. A watt is equivalent to a

   A. Foot candle

   B. Volt-amp

   C. Lumen

   D. KVA

5. Which of the following is not a design consideration for lighting scenes?

   A. Light color

   B. Color of the lighting fixture

   C. Room objects

   D. Room size

6. Which type of lighting is most appropriate for a bathroom?

   A. Sconce

   B. Chandelier

   C. Vanity

   D. Ambient

7. Which of the following best describes a lighting scene?

   A. A preset combination of lighting levels each designed for a certain activity

   B. The area covered by a preset lighting set

   C. One or more rooms for which lighting is defined

   D. Multiple lighting zones

8. Which of the following is not typically a type of exterior lighting?

   A. Backlighting

   B. Safety lighting

   C. Security lighting

   D. Ambient lighting

9. A programmed keypad controller is generally associated with what type of lighting control system?

   A. Single scene

   B. Single zone

   C. Automated/automatic

   D. Single room

10. The LPW rating for incandescent lighting is in the range of

   A. 1–4

   B. 17–20

   C. 60–100

   D. 1,000–1,500

Answers

1. **C.** Lumens measure the light produced by a lamp; lighting levels is a generic term not really specific to anything much; and power factors relate to the efficiency of lamps.

2. **C.** The other choices describe inductive loads.

3. **C.** The lighting load on the incandescent circuit is calculated as 3 times 100 for 300 watts and the lighting load on the fluorescent circuit is calculated as 5 times 40 for 200 watts. Because magnetic ballasts are not in use, no increase is made for the ballasts. So, the total is 500 watts.

4. **B.** Foot-candles measure the amount of light needed to illuminate a 1-foot square that is 1 foot from a light source and a lumen measures the intensity of that light. KVA refers to kilo-volt-amp.

5. **B.** The customer may have a preference, but it hardly matters to the lighting scene.

6. **C.** Another choice would be task lighting. None of the other choices are common in bathrooms.

7. **A.** Lighting scenes are used to preset certain lighting patterns, typically matched to certain activities, for a room.

8. **D.** Exterior lighting is rarely there to provide ambient lighting.

9. **C.** Manual systems, including single scene, zone, and room settings, use dimmers and slide controls.

10. **B.** LPW provides an indication to the brightness of a lamp.

Installing a Home Lighting Control System

In this chapter, you will learn about:
- Installing PLC lighting control system
- Installing wired lighting control system
- Installing wireless lighting control system
- Programming Control Options
- NEC compliance in lighting systems

A residential lighting control system provides a homeowner with the ability to control the lighting in a room or zone and to set a variety of lighting scenes in each area. Whenever home technology integration or home automation is discussed, lighting control is almost always included in the conversation. Lighting controls not only provide for better task lighting, they also can be used to "set the scene" through their ability to control the lighting levels in a given area or an entire house. On top of these benefits, a lighting control system can also save homeowners money by reducing energy costs and increasing lamp life.

This chapter covers the installation of the different types of lighting control systems, including the different types of lighting controls, the devices used in setting them up, and NEC compliance.

Power Line Control System Devices

A PLC lighting control system can be a very simple affair, consisting of few plug-in modules and a handheld remote control, or it can be a very complex whole-house system that is controlled by a home automation controller or PC-based home control software. The way a PLC system works is that control commands are sent over the electrical wiring and the appropriate controlled switches or devices respond and execute the command received. An example of coding is in X-10 technology, each of the controlled devices is given a code that consists of a letter (A-P) and a number (1-16). An example would be the kitchen sink light is coded D-4 and the kitchen counter lights are D-5. The command "D-4 ON" would turn on the kitchen sink light. The command "D ALL OFF" would turn off both the kitchen sink light and the kitchen counter lights. The following sections describe the various devices that may be used in a PLC system. The devices that can be used in a PLC lighting control system are

- **Switches** A PLC light switch replaces a standard light switch and is used to either stop, start, reduce or increase the amount of electrical power flowing to a lamp. There are essentially two types of PLC switches:
  - **Dimmer** A PLC dimmer works virtually the same as a manually operated dimmer, except that the dim/bright setting is activated through a signal transmitted over the PLC lines. Some models of dimmer switches allow for dim/bright control to happen at the switch. A common form of a PLC dimmer switch is a rocker switch where pressing the rocker down dims the lamp, as shown in Figure 24-1.
  - **Relay** A PLC relay is essentially an on-off switch that is used to complete or interrupt a power circuit to a device and is used to turn on or turn off a lamp.
- **Plug-in modules** This type of PLC module connects to the electrical wiring of a home through a room outlet by plugging into the electrical system like any other electrical appliance. The device you wish to control, such as a lamp or fan, is then plugged into the PLC module.
  - **Dimmer** PLC lamp modules that plug into an electrical outlet are used to provide dimmer control of table lamps and other lamps that can be plugged into an AC outlet on the module.
  - **Relay** PLC appliance modules can be used to control the on/off functions of lamps and other electrical devices. They do not allow for dim/bright control. Figure 24-2 shows a PLC plug-in relay module.
- **Hard-wired modules** This type of PLC lighting control module is directly installed and connected to the AC wiring of a home.

Figure 24-1
A PLC dimmer
rocker switch

Photo courtesy of
Smarthome, Inc.

Figure 24-2
A PLC plug-in
relay module
can be used to
control lamps
and electrical
appliances.

*Photo courtesy of
Smarthome, Inc.*

- **Dimmer**   Hard-wired PLC dimmers are switches that offer remote control of dim/bright/on/off of lighting. Figure 24-3 shows a hard-wired PLC dimmer control and Figure 24-4 shows a hard-wired PLC dimmer control installed in an outlet box.

- **Relay**   Hard-wired PLC relay modules can be used to control the on/off functions of lamps and other electrical devices. They do not allow for dim/bright control.

- **Controlled Outlet**   Hard-wired electrical receptacles offer either one or two PLC-enabled and remotely controlled AC outlets in a duplex device. Relay devices are also available that are installed directly into the AC system without the need to replace existing light switches. Figure 24-4 illustrates a controlled outlet.

PART V

Figure 24-3
A PLC hard-
wired lighting
module that
can be used to
control dimming
and on/off
functions of a
lamp/lighting load

*Photo courtesy of
Smarthome, Inc.*

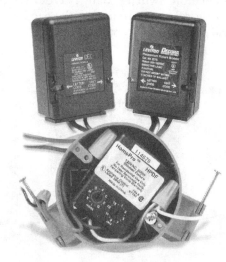

Figure 24-4
A PLC controlled
outlet installed
in an outlet box

*Photo courtesy of
Smarthome, Inc.*

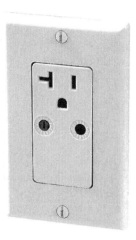

- **Control Devices**
    - **Plug-in Controller**   PLC plug-in interfaces and controllers can be used to control any device controlled by PLC such as switches, plug-in modules, hard-wired modules and controlled outlets.

    - **Wireless Handheld Remote**   PLC wireless remote controls use radio frequency (RF) signals to control both plug-in and hard-wired PLC modules. A handheld remote control communicates to a remote control transceiver module that is connected to the home's AC lines by plugging into an outlet. It receives the RF signal and converts it to a PLC signal and sends the desired control command out over the electrical wiring.

    - **Wired Remote Control Switch**   PLC control signals can be sent from hard-wired control switches that transmit PLC control commands. See Figure 24-5.

    - **Wireless Remote Switch**   Many PLC devices are remote control-enabled to allow the on/off and dimmer functions to be controlled remotely through a handheld or tabletop remote control.

Figure 24-5
A PLC handheld
remote control
and plug-in
wireless
base unit

*Photo courtesy of
Smarthome, Inc.*

Figure 24-6
A PLC lighting
controller unit

*Photo courtesy of
Smarthome, Inc.*

- **System Controller**   PLC controllers are available that provide the capability to program control of the lighting in a single room, zone, or a whole house. Programming can usually be done to control several lighting loads at a time, by time of day, day of week, sunrise/sunset, or an input to the system.

Wired Lighting Control System Devices

A wired lighting control system can be a very simple affair, consisting of a local wall-mounted controller or it can be a very complex whole-house system that is integrated into a programmable controller. How a wired lighting control system works is that each lighting load is wired back to a control module that regulates the electrical power to the load. The following sections describe the various devices that may be used in a wired lighting control system, but the emphasis is on a more robust system.

The devices that can be used in a wired lighting control system are

- System controller
- System enclosure
- Modules
  - Relay module
  - Dimmer module
  - Circuit breaker module
  - Relay Input/Output module
- Control station
- Sensors

Lighting System Controller

Also referred to as the master unit or CPU, the system controller includes the micropro-cessor, clock, and operating memory of the lighting control system. A particular brand

PART V

of lighting control system may require multiple controllers—one for each zone—or the system controller may be capable of controlling multiple zones. The system controller, see Figure 24-7, typically has a user interface that consists of a keypad (or keyboard) and display (small window or full size monitor) through which the controller is programmed, controlled, and diagnosed. Or the controller has the option for connection from a computer for downloading and uploading of programming.

Many lighting control systems are available with a complete control panel, like the one shown in Figure 24-7. These systems typically include all of the features required by an average-sized home, but in larger homes, the fully integrated control system may need to be assembled from a robust controller and optional modules and components to get the correct mix of device controllers, breakers, and power.

System Enclosure

Depending on the system, the enclosure cabinet will accommodate a varying number of control modules. The size of the enclosures and the quantity needed should be chosen based on the number of control modules to be placed inside the enclosures. The number of control modules is determined by the number and type of lighting loads to be controlled. Many models of enclosures are available to accommodate anywhere from one to six different lighting control or power modules and up to 48 relays or 30 dimmers, with some even larger. For example, the enclosure shown in Figure 24-8 can be configured with a large number of both relays and dimmer controls. Common features of lighting control enclosures are locking doors, internal venting fans, internal power supply, and optional flush-mounting kits.

Modules

Modules are installed inside the enclosures and lighting loads controlled are connected to the appropriate type of module. Power is fed to the enclosure and then to each of the

Controlling Fluorescent Lamps

In many situations, switching controls are used to regulate fluorescent lamps. However, dimmable electronic fluorescent ballasts are available that allow the illumination produced by a fluorescent lamp to range from as low as two percent of its capability to a full 100 percent illumination.

Dimmable fluorescent ballasts vary in how much they are able to dim a fluorescent lamp. Ballasts are available with dimming ranges that range from 100 percent to less than 20 percent, less than 10 percent, less than 5 percent, and less than 1 percent. How much dimming is required by the lighting design will determine which dimmable ballast should be installed. One note though, as the dimming range increases, so does the cost of the ballast.

Figure 24-7

A lighting control system controller

Photo courtesy of LiteTouch, Inc.

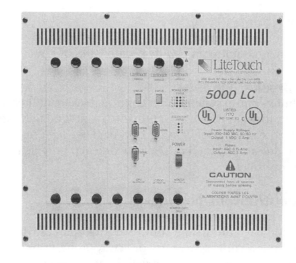

modules and then on to the individual lighting loads. The type of lighting load determines the type of module needed. See Chapter 23 for detailed discussion on lighting load types.

Relay Modules

Relay modules control the ON/OFF of a variety of loads including light fixtures, fans, proprietary two-wire and virtually all three-wire devices such as fluorescent, incandescent, and other types of low-voltage lighting.

Figure 24-8

A compact lighting system central control unit can be outfitted with several dimmer and relay modules to control a whole-house lighting system.

Photo courtesy of LiteTouch, Inc.

PART V

Dimmer Modules

Dimmer modules control the ON/OFF/DIMMING of incandescent light fixtures. Some dimmer modules can handle certain types of low-voltage lighting.

Circuit Breaker Modules

Some lighting control systems offer controllable circuit breaker modules or panels (see Figure 24-9) that can be preset to provide circuit-level lighting control, such as security lighting, landscape or pool lighting, or other large lighting groups. In some systems, the breaker modules and panels can be networked to provide for additional zones under a common controller.

Relay Input/Output Modules

Relay I/O modules are used on lighting control systems for low voltage input and output signals to and from the system controller. Examples of what might be on a relay input module include security system or a driveway probe. Examples of what might be on a relay output module include a motorized shade or garage door opener. Typically, the relay modules of a lighting control system can be interconnected on a common high-speed data link that allows them to share input and output among themselves and with the controller unit. In some systems, the relay modules have independent processors that allow them to function with or without the controller online.

Control Stations

Control stations, like the one shown in Figure 24-11, are placed in the individual rooms and allow the occupants to control the lighting loads/lamps in the room, or around the house, individually and by scene control. Since each of the control buttons is designed in programming, they can do simple ON/OFF control, dimming control (see Figure 24-10), scene control or can even be programmed to control outside systems connected to the

Figure 24-9

A relay module that is mounted in the central lighting control unit

Photo courtesy of LiteTouch, Inc.

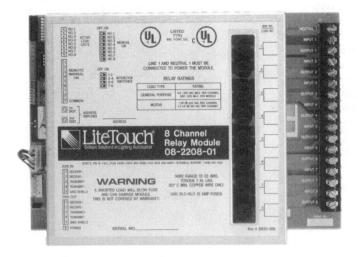

Figure 24-10

A dimmer control module

Photo courtesy of LiteTouch, Inc.

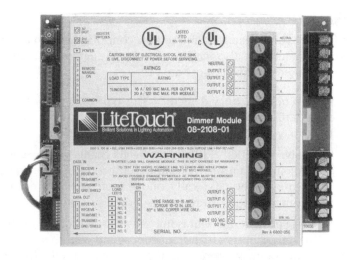

lighting control system such as a whole-house music system. Many manufacturers offer custom engraving on the lighting control's buttons to mark each button with the scene or zone it controls.

Figure 24-11

A multifunction remote station lighting control unit

Photo courtesy of LiteTouch, Inc.

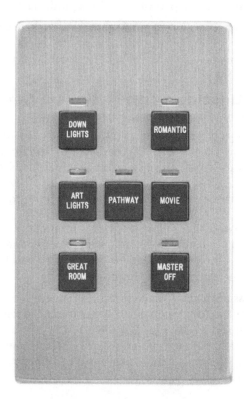

Sensors

In addition to control stations and remote controls placed in a room or zone, the lighting control system can also include sensors that detect occupancy and daylight levels. The sensors used for this purpose are

- **Motion or occupancy detector** This type of detector senses when someone enters a room or when there is movement or activity within its scanning range. The two types of motion or occupancy detectors are

  - **Passive IR (PIR)** PIR sensors detect changes in the energy radiating from occupants in a room. Like all IR sensors, PIR sensors require a line of sight to work properly. Typically, one or more sensors are placed in a room to encompass its doorway and the primary activity areas.

  - **Active ultrasonic** Ultrasonic sensors work something like sound wave radar. The sensor emits a high-frequency sound wave that is reflected off of an object in the room. Movement in the room changes the frequency of the reflected sound wave, which is interpreted as somebody entering the monitored space. A signal is transmitted to the controller, which then turns on the lights.

  There are sensors available that incorporate both PIR and ultrasonic technologies to detect occupancy or movement in a space. Most have settings that can be adjusted to ignore pets or vibrations produced by the HVAC system.

- **Photo sensors** This type of sensor detects the level of natural light in a room or zone. Typically, a photo sensor is used to detect the need for additional artificial light to augment natural daylight to maintain a certain level of lighting in a space.

Wireless Lighting Control System Devices

A wireless lighting control system can be a very simple affair, consisting of a small wall-mounted controller or it can be a very complex whole-house system that integrates remote wireless switches and control devices into a programmable controller. The following sections describe the various devices that may be used in a wireless lighting control system.

The devices that can be used in a wireless lighting control system are

- **System controller** The system control unit is essentially the same type of unit as is used in a hard-wired system with the exception of wireless RF communications that allow the system to receive and send signals for control anywhere inside or nearby the exterior of the home.

- **Wireless switches** Wireless lighting system switches are hard-wired to the electrical and can be operated either locally or remotely using RF signals. They transmit and receive signals via RF to/from a base station or the system controller. They should not be confused with PLC wireless remote control switches. Wireless lighting system switches, like those of a hard-wired or PLC system are either dimmers or relay-type controls.

- **Dimmer switches**   Wireless dimmer controls are either a part of a whole-house wireless lighting system or they can be stand-alone devices that control only one or two individual lamps. Stand-alone wireless dimmers require a receiver unit be installed in the lamps to be controlled by the dimmer; when the dimmer is operated manually, it transmits an RF signal to the lamp receiver that dims or brightens the lamp.

- **Relay switches**   Like other relay light switches, a wireless relay switch (see Figure 24-12) controls the on/off functions of a lighting load/lamp. Like wireless dimmer switches, there are devices that are intended for use as a part of a whole-house system and stand-alone devices, which require a receiver to be installed on the lamp.

- **Remote control station**   Typically, a wireless lighting system station, which provides the same functions as hard-wired control stations, also serves as a signal extender to ensure the signal strength throughout a home.

- **Sensors**   Wireless occupancy sensors or motion detectors transmit their event or alarm signals using RF transmission rather than requiring hard-wired connections.

Programming Control Options

The most powerful benefit of a lighting control system is the extensive automated or logical control that can be programmed, including scheduling, scenes, and what-if situations. Programming can enhance the simple control, safety, security, and energy savings of a home.

Scheduling Programming

A scheduling program turns lighting on, off, down, or up based on a preset daily time schedule or day of the week or calendar date. This approach to lighting control is intended to avoid lighting areas during daylight hours or during periods when a home is not occupied. In many systems, each zone can be programmed with a different lighting schedule according to the lighting needs of the homeowners. The program can often be set up to

PART V

Figure 24-12
A wireless relay switch and lamp receiver

Photo courtesy of Smarthome, Inc.

know the latitude and longitude of the location and so figure out sunrise and sunset and then schedules can be made based on this information such as landscape lights on at sunset.

Scenes

Virtually all lighting control systems have the ability to control a number of different lighting scenes, often in more than one lighting zone. Creating a preset lighting scene, which the press of a single button on a local control station, will ultimately activate, involves first and foremost some detail planning.

Depending on the lighting control system in use, a lighting scene is created with either a top-down or a bottom-up approach. In the top-down approach, the lighting scene function, such as "movie," is created first. Then the lighting devices to be controlled in the scene are added and finally the dimmer level of each lighting fixture included in the scene is set, typically as a percentage of its maximum lighting level. In a bottom-up approach, the various lighting levels for each lighting device are created and given some form of an identity, such as "ceiling lights—50%," "sconces—25%," or "lamps—10%." This creates a sort of menu from which the lighting events desired for a particular scene can be added together to create the scene.

What-if Situations

Based on input, lighting control commands are executed in what-if situations. The input can be from known information such as "Security System in NIGHTTIME mode." An example would be "If Security armed in NIGHTIME, landscape lights OFF." What-if questions can be combined to have complex decisions made regarding lighting control. These compound what-if questions are a form of Boolean logic. An example would be "If dark AND security armed in Away Mode THEN turn on living room lights." You would repeat this command with the same what-if question to have them turned off at 10:15 pm, or if it is Friday or Saturday, turn them off at 11:20 pm.

Occupancy Sensor Input for Lighting Control

When a sensor placed in a room or zone detects that someone has entered a room, a signal is sent to the lighting system controller and it takes the necessary action to turn the lighting on in that space. Occupancy control systems are more energy efficient because lighting is provided only when a room is occupied. If the sensor determines the room is not occupied or that there hasn't been any activity in the room for a certain time, the controller can then turn off the lights. The type and placement of the sensor used is the key to how well this type of lighting control approach works.

Daylighting Sensor Input for Lighting Control

Daylighting sensors attempt to use the natural daylight in a room to determine the amount of artificial light that should be added to produce a certain preset amount of lighting in the room. Daylighting systems, which are also called daylight harvesting systems, can be used with either dimming or switching controls. However, the availability of dimming controls for fluorescent lamps has made this type of system very popular in commercial settings and more recently in homes.

Boolean Logic

In the 1800s, a mathematician by the name of George Boole developed a correlation between mathematics and logic called Boolean algebra, which is based on combinations of true and false or on or off conditions.

Boolean algebra, which is more commonly referred to as Boolean logic these days, is the mathematical principles used in computer logic. Boolean logic creates logical relationships between entities using three primary comparison operators (OR, AND, and NOT) to determine if a logical comparison is true or false.

The OR operator returns true if any entity in a set meets the conditions of the logical comparison. For example, if the conditional test of "Is a Girl" is applied to a set of children made up of two boys and one girl, the result is true because one entity in the set actually is a girl. The fact that two of the children are boys is irrelevant and because the girl is a girl the set satisfies the test, which is applied sort of like "if this one is a girl, or that one is a girl, or the other one is a girl," then Is a Girl is true. In a lighting situation, the test might actually be something like, "If Night OR Morning, then ..." This test would return true if either of the preset values Night or Morning were true themselves.

The Boolean AND operator tests for all entities of a set meeting a logical condition. If we were to apply the test of "Is a Girl" to the same group of children (two boys and one girl) using the AND operator, the result would be false. In order to satisfy the conditions of the test, all three of the children would have to be girls. This test is applied as "if this one is a girl, and that one is a girl, and the other one is a girl, then Is a Girl is true, otherwise Is a Girl is false. An example of how the AND operator is used in a lighting control program might be something like, "if Day-Light AND < 1700, then ..." In this case, if the variable DayLight is true and it's earlier than 5:00 pm, then the test returns a true and performs whatever action is indicated by the "then" statement.

The Boolean NOT operator reverses the test by being true only if the result is false. Huh? Okay, bear with me on this one. If we test for "Is NOT a Girl" on each of the children, we would get two trues and one false. As convoluted as it may sound, when this test is applied to the children, we are actually testing for "Is a Boy," because the NOT operator reverses the test. So, when we test "Is NOT a Girl" on a boy, the result is true because he is not a girl. An example of how this could be used in a lighting program is "If NOT Activated, then ...," which would return true only when the system is not activated.

Without becoming too complicated, Boolean NOT logic also can be used to reverse OR and AND comparisons as well. For example," NOT Girl OR Boy" would return a true only if all of the children were girls or boys, which is effectively the same as testing "Girl AND Boy." In the same way, "NOT Girl AND Boy" returns a true if the set includes both girls and boys—or the equivalent of "Girl OR Boy." As you can see, NOT logic is probably best used when testing a single value.

Daylighting systems use photoelectric sensors to detect the lighting level in a room or space. When the lighting is too high, the controller dims or turns off light fixtures to lower the ambient light. When the lighting is too low, the controller turns on or up the lighting in the room to bring the light up to the desired level. In a large area, more than one sensor may be required to prevent uneven lighting.

Lighting System Standards and Guidelines

A licensed electrician must perform electrical work. You need to work with the project electrician on the layout and installation of the lighting control system. Remember to plan for electrical power for the controller and discuss if a generator will be in the home and if yes, what lighting loads (and the system controller) should be on it. The wiring for the remote control stations is usually low voltage wiring and in most areas does not need to be done by a licensed electrician.

In any case, you should be aware of the national, state, and local electrical codes and regulations that apply to the installation of a lighting control system and any wiring required to support it.

NEC

The National Electric Code (NEC) is the generally accepted basis for almost all state and local electrical codes. However, some areas may exceed the requirements of the NEC and require higher quality materials or more stringent cable management requirements. Be sure to know what is practiced in your area.

The general requirement by the NEC is for a minimum of 14 AWG circuit wiring protected by a 15-amp circuit breaker or fuse. There are some exceptions to this requirement, such as the wiring for doorbells and a few other low-voltage systems, but by and large, 14-gauge wiring is the standard. However, there is a trend in home construction to install 12-gauge wiring on 20-amp circuits, which has become a standard in some locales.

If given a choice, you should prefer the heavier 12-gauge wiring and the 20-amp circuit breaker. This larger wiring will provide the lighting system with brighter lights, better energy efficiency, and far fewer tripped circuit breakers or blown fuses.

Some other areas where the NEC has requirements that impact a lighting system are in the areas of the height (from the floor) for wall switches, outlets, and connectors and its specifications for acceptable light fixtures and switches. See Chapter 4 for more details on codes and Chapter 23 for more information on these requirements.

Chapters 4 and 5 of the NEC detail the requirements for low-voltage lighting systems (including lighting control systems), and particularly in Article 411 of the NEC. Residential lighting and lighting control systems come under the requirements specified in Article 411 and UL (Underwriters Laboratories) 2108 and the components installed in these systems must comply with the requirements of these regulations.

The primary issues to consider when installing a lighting control system to comply with the NEC regulations are that the lighting control panel must not be placed in close proximity of the home's main electrical panel and any relays installed in the lighting control panel must be protected by a circuit breaker or fuse. Be sure that all components of the lighting control system conform to NEC Section 110-10 and Article 411 regulations and any applicable UL, CSA, or other fire safety testing authority guidelines. All elements of the total control system must be considered and be matched to the circuit and its over-current protection devices (circuit breakers or fuses). The NEC refers to this rating as a component short-circuit rating (SCCR). Remember that if any one component in the entire system doesn't comply with the applicable regulations, the entire system is not in compliance.

Installation Safety

Your safety and that of your customer are the intent of the NEC and the other electrical and fire safety regulations that govern the components and installation of lighting control systems. To ensure a safe and effective installation, here are some guidelines you should follow:

1. Ensure that all devices to be installed are matched to the voltage level of the circuit to which they are to be attached.

2. Turn off the power supply of the control system and turn off the electrical supply on its circuit and the main electrical panel before you begin installation.

3. Test all newly installed wiring for continuity prior to connecting it into the lighting control panel.

Completing the Installation

The following steps should be used to complete the installation of a lighting control system:

1. Power up system control panel, following the manufacturer's instructions.

2. Install all local control devices and test locally room by room.

3. Test remote control devices.

4. Program preset lighting scenes and set local station functions. Test all scene settings to ensure they are properly set.

5. If scheduling and what-if situations programming are in use, test and observe these functions during complete cycles.

Chapter Review

PLC lighting control uses the electrical wiring to send command signals to control switches and devices. In X-10 technology, each device is coded by a letter (A-P) and a number (1-16). The PLC devices typically used are switches, plug-in modules, hard-wired modules, and control devices.

A hard-wired lighting control system can consisting of local wall-mounted controllers or be a whole-house system integrated into a programmable controller. How a wired lighting control system works is that each lighting load is wired back to a control module that regulates the electrical power to the load. The devices that can be included in hard-wired lighting system are a system controller, several types of special purpose modules, remote stations, and sensors.

The lighting system controller includes the microprocessor, clock, and operating memory. Multi-zone systems may have a single controller or require multiple controllers. The system controller typically has a user interface that consists of a keypad or keyboard and a display. The various types of lighting control modules that can be installed in a wired lighting control system include relay modules, dimmer modules, circuit breaker modules, and relay I/O modules.

Control stations in the individual rooms allow occupants to control the lighting loads/lamps in the room, or around the house, individually and by scene control. In addition to simple ON/OFF and dimming control, some control stations can be programmed to control outside systems.

Sensors can be used to detect occupancy and daylight levels. The sensors used for this purpose are motion or occupancy detectors and photo sensors.

A wireless lighting control system provides the same functionality as PLC and hard-wired systems, with the exception that the control of the lighting control switches and devices is by RF communications. The devices used in a wireless lighting control system, include system controllers, wireless control switches, relay modules, remote stations, and sensors.

The most powerful benefit of a lighting control system is the extensive automated or logical control that can be programmed to provide scheduling, lighting scenes, and what-if situations. Scheduling programs turn lighting on, off, down, or up using a preset time or day schedule. Programmed lighting control commands are executed in what-if situations, where time, day, and sensor inputs are tested to determine the activation of certain lighting scenes.

A licensed electrician must perform electrical work. Work with the project electrician on the layout and installation of the lighting control system. You should plan for electrical power for the controller and, if a generator is part of the electrical system, which lighting loads and devices should be on it. You should be aware of the national, state, and local electrical codes and regulations that apply to the installation of a lighting control system and any wiring required.

The National Electric Code (NEC) is the generally accepted basis for almost all state and local electrical codes. Some areas may exceed the requirements of the NEC and require higher quality materials or more stringent cable management requirements. The general requirement by the NEC is for a minimum of 14 AWG circuit wiring protected by a 15-amp circuit breaker or fuse. Residential lighting and lighting control systems are specified in NEC Article 411 and UL (Underwriters Laboratories) 2108.

To ensure a safe and effective installation: ensure that all devices to be installed are matched to the voltage level of the circuit where they are to be attached; turn off the power supply of the control system and turn off the electrical supply on its circuit and the main electrical panel before you begin installation; and test all newly installed wiring for continuity prior to connecting it into the lighting control panel.

Questions

1. What two types of lighting controls are generally used in most residential lighting control systems?

   A. Dimming

   B. Inductive

   C. Photo cell

   D. Switching

2. What is the type of lighting control that has the ability to range the amount of light emitted by a lamp from off to the lamp's full capability?

   A. Dimming

   B. Inductive

   C. Photo cell

   D. Switching

3. True or False: A switching control has the ability to lower a lamp to 50 percent of its lighting capability.

   A. True

   B. False

4. What type of lighting control sensor involves the use of IR sensors?

   A. Daylighting

   B. Occupant-sensing

   C. Scheduling

   D. Preset

5. What type of technology uses AC power lines to transmit lighting control system signals?

   A. Bus

   B. Data networking

   C. Wireless

   D. PLC

6. What type of lighting control system uses motion detectors placed in certain areas to turn on or off the lighting in an area?

   A. Scheduling

   B. Occupant-sensing

   C. Daylighting

   D. Exterior

7. What type of lighting control system uses artificial lighting to enhance the natural lighting in a room or zone?

   A. Scheduling

   B. Occupant-sensing

   C. Daylighting

   D. Exterior

8. What device is the primary unit of a lighting control system?

   A. Remote station

   B. Relay module

   C. Breaker module

   D. System controller

9. Which part of the NEC specifies the requirements for lighting control systems?

   A. Article 411

   B. Section 110-10

   C. UL 2108

   D. SCCR

10. What communications technology do wireless lighting control systems use?

   A. IR

   B. PLC

   C. RF

   D. HomePNA

Answers

1. **A** and **D**. Lighting control systems have the option of either dimming the lamp of a fixture or switching it on or off.

2. **A**. The only other choice available that makes any sense at all is switching, and it has only on or off settings.

3. **B** (False). Switching controls are all or nothing devices.

4. **B**. Motion or occupancy detectors are used to turn on the lighting of a room when a room is occupied or someone enters the room.

5. **D**. PLC technology is implemented as either X-10 or CEBus. The other choices do not apply in this case.

6. **B**. Scheduling systems use preset time schedules and daylighting use photocells to determine the level of daylight in a room. Exterior systems may use any motion

detectors to turn on lighting, but they then become occupant-sensing systems as well.

7. **C.** Photocells are used to enhance the daylight or natural lighting of a room to maintain certain lighting levels.

8. **D.** The other choices are optional devices in any lighting control system, but the system needs a controller unit.

9. **A.** Actually, NEC Chapters 4 and 5 are the general references, but Article 411 is specific to lighting controls.

10. **C.** You may see some PLC systems referred to as "wireless," but in their case, the wireless refers to either "no-new-wires" or the use of an IR remote control to activate a dimmer or control module.

CHAPTER 25

Troubleshooting and Maintaining Lighting Control Systems

In this chapter, you will learn about:
- Maintenance activities for a lighting control system
- Diagnostic and troubleshooting procedures for a lighting control system
- Troubleshooting power line control (PLC) control devices in a lighting control system

Unfortunately, lighting control systems are rarely "set-'em-and-forget-'em" affairs. There are certain services and tasks required to maintain the system, including its lamps, remote controls, and programming.

This chapter focuses on the maintenance tasks and services you should perform on a customer's lighting control system to keep a home's lighting system working as designed, and the procedures used to troubleshoot and diagnose a lighting control system with an emphasis on systems installed on PLC technology.

Maintaining a Lighting Control System

The maintenance activities for a lighting control system primarily involve ensuring the lighting levels and control desired by the homeowner are maintained. The purpose of the lighting control system is to provide the type, mix, and level of lighting the system was designed to produce, all controlled easily. However, there are a number of factors that can contribute to a lighting system failing to perform as expected.

In the context of home technology integration and home automation certifications, the maintenance activities for a lighting control system are

- Preventive maintenance
- Control changes
- Manufacturer upgrades
- Troubleshooting and diagnostics

Preventive Maintenance

A preventive maintenance plan should be developed and regularly executed for all control systems in an automated home, including the lighting control system. The purpose of a preventive maintenance plan is to maintain the system in proper working order and to prevent or detect problems early on.

At minimum, preventive maintenance should be performed on the lighting control system once a year. Every task in the maintenance plan must be completed and a written record indicating what was done and who did it produced.

The maintenance plan should include, at minimum, the following activities:

- Checking all connections and visible wiring
- Cleaning the control panels and keypad controls
- Cleaning any fans and motors in the control panel
- Verifying the lighting load of each circuit
- Applying any control changes or lighting adjustments desired by the homeowner
- Creating a backup of the control panel programming
- Updating the system's maintenance log

Check Connections

The connections at the lighting system control panel should be checked and verified for proper contact. This check should include both a visual check and an electrical check using a multimeter to ensure electrical continuity and voltage for each line in the system.

You should also visually inspect the condition of the exposed wiring for deterioration of the insulation or conductors. If a problem is found, the problem and your recommended solution should be brought to the attention of the homeowner.

Cleaning

The interior of the control panel should be cleaned to remove any dust or other debris that may have accumulated. Avoid using a standard vacuum cleaner to prevent the introduction of high levels of static electricity to the controller's circuits. Use either a special-purpose vacuum cleaner (the type recommended for cleaning the inside of computers works best) or a can of compressed air to clean the inside of the control panel.

The exterior of the control panel should also be cleaned. First, use a nonstatic cloth (such as the 3M Electronics Cleaning Cloth) to remove any dust on the exterior of the controller and the keypad, if one is present. Use a nonsudsing cleaner to clean the exterior of the controller. In most cases, the manufacturer's documentation should indicate the acceptable cleaning solutions that can be used. These same procedures should be used to clean the keypad, dimming, and switch controls throughout the home.

Check Fans

If the lighting control system has a cooling fan, verify that the fan is working properly. The fan should be cleaned regularly to ensure proper airflow to the circuits inside the controller. Use compressed air to blow away any dust collected on the fan's blades. Avoid using any liquids to clean the fan. Also clean the exterior and interior grills, if any, of the fan assembly.

Check Lighting Loads

It is possible that the homeowner may have replaced an original lamp with one that is outside the designed operating limits of a lighting circuit and inadvertently increased the lighting load of the circuit. If the current lighting load of a circuit is outside the operating tolerances, this situation should be explained to the homeowner and the lamp should be replaced with one that brings the circuit into its designed load.

Check with the homeowners to see if they wish to have any or all of the lamps in the home replaced. If they so desire, replace the lamps, retaining any good lamps as spares for the homeowner.

Control Changes

The homeowner may wish to change one or more lighting scene or control level of the lighting system. If so, make the necessary programming changes and thoroughly test the system to the homeowner's satisfaction.

Also check with the manufacturer for any controller or system upgrades that can be applied. You should understand the affects of any upgrades to the system and make a recommendation to the homeowner on whether or not the upgrade should be applied. Some manufacturers issue accumulative upgrades that allow some upgrade levels to be skipped and others issue incremental upgrades that must be applied in every case. After applying any system upgrades, retest the system thoroughly to ensure it's functioning properly.

 NOTE Many manufacturers issue maintenance bulletins with recommended upgrades. Another good place to find information about upgrades to the system is the manufacturer's web site.

Back Up the Controller

Regardless of whether programming changes are made or not, a backup of the controller's programming should be created. In some cases, this may be only a print out of the programming statements or commands. In other cases, it may be possible to create a backup to a removable media (such as a diskette), especially if the controller is programmed from a PC.

A copy of the backup should be kept at the home and another copy should be stored in the project folder off premises.

Maintaining Maintenance Logs

The importance of maintaining a maintenance log that records all maintenance activities is not often realized until some point in the future when a problem arises that can be traced back to a maintenance action performed in the past. The most common types of troubleshooting problems are those caused when another problem is fixed. Maintaining a maintenance log that records every action, repair, upgrade, and even preventive maintenance provides another technician with a history of the types of actions a system has required.

Table 25-1 illustrates an example of a simple maintenance log form and the types of information that should be recorded.

Troubleshooting Lighting Control Systems

Before beginning any other diagnostic or troubleshooting activities, your first action should be to debrief the homeowner on the nature of the problem he or she is experiencing with the lighting system. Especially in an integrated system environment, a problem may be showing up as a lighting issue when, in fact, it could be a problem with another subsystem or the structured wiring. After gaining a full understanding of the problem from the homeowner, you can begin your activities to isolate the problem and repair it.

Debriefing the Homeowner

Feedback from the homeowner is maybe the best way to learn about performance problems on a newly installed lighting control system. Debrief the homeowner to learn if the lighting scenes are still effective; if scheduled lighting scene changes occur when they should; if there are problems with lighting levels in any room, zone, or on a particular fixture; and if the lamp life on a particular fixture or lighting group is less than it should be.

Troubleshooting Lighting Controls

When a problem is identified with a distributed or stand-alone relay or dimmer switch, the best place to start your investigation is at the switch in question. You'll use a different repair approach on hard-wired switches, stand-alone switches, or PLC switches.

Troubleshooting Hard-Wired Switches

Hard-wired lighting controls generally have one of two problems if they aren't working correctly: the switch itself is faulty or a problem has developed with its wiring. If the switch is bad, it should be replaced, but never assume that is the only problem. The switch failing

Date	Activity	Technician	Comments
1/5	Clean controller interior	HH	Dust heavy; should clean more frequently
1/5	Clean controller exterior	HH	Dusty; clean more frequently
1/5	Check wire contracts	HH	Normal
1/5	Continuity check	HH	Normal
1/5	Backup controller	HH	Copy to HO; copy to office

Table 25-1   Sample Preventive Maintenance Log

could very well be caused by a problem on the alternating current (AC) wiring, such as a short or open circuit. So, check the switch for scorch marks or other causes for its failure, and also verify the characteristics of the AC connections using a multimeter.

Relay switching controls, like those controlling an incandescent lamp, have relatively simple problems and are generally easy to troubleshoot—for example, problems such as a broken toggle switch, no power, or bad wiring. However, dimmer controls can be a bit harder to troubleshoot.

One reason dimmer controls can be harder to troubleshoot is that there are several different types. Further, they have more internal parts to go bad. Table 25-2 lists some of the more common problems that dimming controls may have.

Troubleshooting Stand-alone Lighting Controls

Stand-alone controls that control only a single lamp or multiple lamps connected to a common lighting circuit are much like hard-wired controls in terms of what areas should be diagnosed for a problem. There are three major areas you should investigate, and all

Problem	Diagnostic	Troubleshooting
Lamp remains off	Is power available to the dimmer?	Verify the AC connection before checking the dimmer control.
	Is the circuit breaker tripped or the fuse blown in the electrical panel?	
	Is a rotary dimmer or push-button control connected to AC power?	
	Is only one dimmer in a room not working?	If shorting around the dimmer powers the lamp, change out the dimmer control.
Lamp remains on	Does the lamp remain on after disconnecting the neutral wire?	The dimmer's thyristor is likely bad. Replace the dimmer control.
Lamps flicker	Are the incandescent lamps flickering and the lighting cannot be controlled up or down?	The dimmer is bad and should be replaced.
Lamps flicker at some adjustment levels	Is there an electronic transformer on the circuit?	A dimmer for incandescent lamps cannot be connected to a leading-edge transformer. The dimmable ballast cannot be connected to a failing-edge transformer.
Dimmer range is limited	Does the dial turn the full distance without adjusting the lamp to its full range?	Change Min or Max setting on dimmer.
Other dimmer performance problems	Is the impedance on the lighting cable 25 kilo-ohms?	Test the impedance on the lines linking the dimmer to the fixtures.

Table 25-2   Troubleshooting Dimmer Controls

PART V

three should be checked each time, even if you think the problem is obvious: the control, the wiring, and the lamp or lamps being controlled.

Troubleshooting PLC Lighting Controls

A common problem with PLC controls is that the device coding for one or more control modules is incorrect. Each PLC device is identified to the system with a unique unit code that is typically set using one or two dials located on the device. Figure 25-1 illustrates the unit coding dials on a PLC control module. Most PLC devices have both a house code and a unit code. In larger homes, each zone can be coded to a different house code, with each unit within the zone numbered serially.

Another common problem with PLC systems can be the phase of the electrical current on the AC lines. The electrical phase, especially if different electrical phases are present on a home's wiring, can cause problems for lighting control systems that use PLC to communicate with controlled switches/devices. If some devices in a power line lighting control system work and others don't, the nonworking devices could be on a different phase of the house wiring from those connected to the control unit that serves the signal.

Another common problem with power line systems is that voltage spikes on the AC lines can independently trigger modules. If this is a common occurrence in a home, a spike suppressor or phase filter should be installed on each phase at the main electrical panel.

The problem of modules operating independently can also be caused by power dips (short sags in the voltage) or brownouts (longer sags in the voltage). Many power line lamp modules include a local control feature that allows the module to be turned on or off using the switch on the lamp or device connected to it. The local control feature operates by sensing changes in the voltage level, either up or down, and a sag or spike can cause the module to turn on or off. If this problem occurs frequently, the local control option

Figure 25-1
The unit code dials on a PLC control device

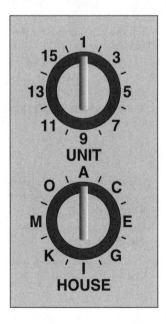

AC Power and Phase Shifts

When the AC power in a home produces two different currents from its main electrical panel, the different currents are said to be in different phases. Several factors can cause phase shifts, such as inductance, reactance, resistance, and so on, but at some point the electrical system is carrying electrical power waves that are identical in every respect, except for their timing.

Figure 25-2 illustrates two electrical currents that are in different phases. Current A and Current B are identical, but Current A peaks and troughs at different times from Current B. If power line devices are on different phases, the receiving station may not properly interpret the command signals transmitted across the AC wiring. The effect is very similar to attenuation on a copper data cable when the signal attempts to move between phases.

A cure for phase shifts is the installation of a phase coupler at the electrical panel.

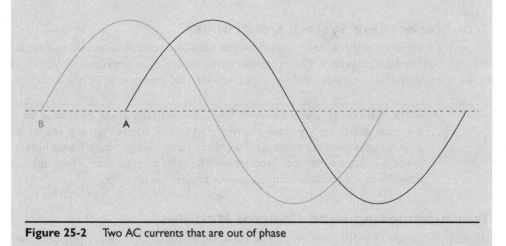

Figure 25-2   Two AC currents that are out of phase

should be defeated or the modules replaced with modules that don't have this feature. Of course, another option is to provide backup power at the main electrical panel.

Power line systems are also susceptible to line noise on the AC circuits. Many TV sets generate electrical noise and dump it onto the AC lines. If you suspect that a television or other appliance is affecting the power line control, plug the problem device into a line filter to isolate it from the AC circuits.

Hard-wired intercom systems that transmit over house wiring can block power line signals if they are left in transmit or talk mode. If this problem exists in a home, there are limited possibilities for resolving the issue. Try changing the lighting control system to a different phase of the electrical system or install phase couplers on the electrical panel.

PART V

However, these changes may not solve the problem. Unfortunately, installing a wireless intercom is not an answer either. For some reason, PLC controllers and wireless intercoms cannot both work in the same house.

Here is a list of things to avoid when using power line controlled switches and control modules:

- **Lamp modules** Don't use a lamp module to control appliances, fans, fluorescent lamps, any incandescent lamp greater than 300 watts, or any lamp that has a built-in dimmer.

- **Grounded modules** Always use a grounded module when controlling a grounded device.

- **Wall switch modules** Don't use a dimmer wall switch module to control fans, appliances, fluorescent lamps, and any lamp less than 60 watts or incandescent lamp with more than 500 watts. Don't use a dimmer wall switch module to control an outlet into which somebody may plug an appliance, fan, or vacuum cleaner. Relay wall switches are available for controlling these types of loads.

Troubleshooting System Controllers

If a problem develops with the system controller of a lighting control system, in most cases the problem is related to power: The AC power to the enclosure is interrupted, AC power to the controller is interrupted, or the controller's internal power supply has failed.

NOTE Of course, a problem with a system controller could be related to programming, but every make and model of lighting control systems has fairly unique command sets; there is no way I can really address those issues here. If you suspect a controller problem may lie in its configuration, check the manufacturer's documentation and your programming setup.

Troubleshooting Load Control Modules

If a relay or dimmer module is failing or performing erratically, check the power source to the module or replace the module itself. However, if you suspect the module is a malfunctioning zone control, check the data line connections and check for continuity and impedance to ensure they conform to the manufacturer's specifications. Also, verify the ground connection for the main power supply to the enclosure.

Verify the connecting cables between the modules mounted in the lighting control system's enclosure. If the ambient room temperature where the enclosure is located is warm, make sure the enclosure's exhaust fan is properly functioning and clean. The modules may be overheating, which may cause them to fail or function intermittently.

Common Lamp Problems

Some problems are common to all lamps. Table 25-3 lists a few of the most common of these problems.

Problem	Diagnostic	Resolution
Lamps flickering	How long have the lamps been installed?	A lamp must burn in for around 100 hours before it will produce initial lumens (full light). This includes fluorescent lamps, which should be burned in before dimming.
	Is the line voltage constant?	Test the line voltage to the lamp and to the lighting control for constant current.
	Is the HVAC blowing air across the lamp?	Change the direction of airflow away from the lamp, so that the temperature of the lamp remains constant.

Table 25-3   Common Problems with Lighting System Lamps

Incandescent Lamps

Incandescent lamps are fairly easy to troubleshoot because the problem is typically one of only a few possibilities: the lamp is burned out, the glass bulb of the lamp is cracked or broken, or the lamp is not getting electricity. Table 25-4 lists common problems with incandescent lamps that you should eliminate when troubleshooting a lighting system with this type of lamp.

The most common problem with incandescent lamps is burnout. While every bulb has an average life rating, all this means is that half of a batch of lamps last longer than the average and half do not. Table 25-5 lists the average life ratings for common incandescent lamp bulbs.

Problem	Diagnostic	Resolution
No light from lamp	Is the lamp burned out or defective?	Replace lamp.
	Is the lamp properly seated in its socket?	Remove the lamp and check the socket for good metal-to-metal contact; reseat the lamp.
Short lamp life	Is the voltage supply too high?	Check circuit to correct over voltage situation.
	Is the lamp subject to vibrations or sudden jarring?	Replace with compact fluorescent or rough-duty lamp.
Lamp bulb has deposits	Is the lamp cracked?	Check for moisture around the lamp and correct; replace lamp with silicone-coated lamp.
Lamp bulb blistering or bulging	Is the operating temperature too high?	Check the wattage of the lamp and match it to the fixture; replace the lamp.
Lamp in recessed fixture burns out too quickly	Does the lamp conform to manufacturer's recommendations?	Recessed fixtures build up heat; too high a wattage or the wrong type of lamp may cause failure sooner than expected.
Lamps brighten or dim when other fixtures are turned on or off	Is the AC power neutral connection properly wired?	Check the neutral connection in the main electrical panel or any sub panels.

Table 25-4   Troubleshooting Incandescent Lamps

PART V

Table 25-5	Wattage	Average Life (Hours)	Minimum Lumen Output
Incandescent Lamp Average Life and Lumen Output Ratings	100	750	1670
	75	750	1150
	60	1000	840
	40	1500	440

Fluorescent Lamps

Fluorescent lamps and fixtures have more components that can fail. Troubleshooting a fluorescent lamp or fixture is a bit more complicated than it is with an incandescent lamp, as evidenced by the length of Table 25-6. The good news is that there are several common failures, and they are the easiest to resolve. Table 25-6 lists common problems with fluorescent lighting systems.

Problem	Diagnostic	Resolution
Lamps do not start or start slowly	Are the lamps properly aligned in their sockets?	Reseat the lamps in their sockets.
	Are the sockets cracked or broken?	Replace the fixture.
	Is the fixture defective?	Install a good lamp to determine if problem is the lamp or fixture.
	Is the ballast defective?	Replace the ballast.
Good lamps are not lighting	Is the manual reset on starter pressed?	Press reset button on the starter.
	Is the starter defective?	Replace the starter.
	Is the ballast defective?	Replace the ballast.
	Are the lamp and ballast compatible?	Check the labels of the lamp and ballast and replace the lamp with a compatible lamp.
	Is the lamp dirty?	Clean the lamps and ballasts.
	Is the line voltage correct?	Check the line voltage and make necessary repairs.
	Is the fixture wiring correct?	Compare the wiring against the wiring diagram on the ballast's label and correct as needed.
	Is the ballast working properly?	Replace the ballast.
Lamp has short life	Is the lamp burned out?	Replace the lamp; some lamps fail earlier than others. If problem continues, check the line voltage.
	Are the ballast and lamp compatible?	High-output (HO) lamps and very high-output (VHO) ballasts (or vice versa) are not compatible; replace lamp with correct type.

Table 25-6 Troubleshooting Fluorescent Lamps

The ballast can often be the cause of a problem in a fluorescent fixture, especially in dimmable fixtures. If the lamps in a problem fixture work in another fixture, then the problem is likely either the ballast or starter, or it's power-related. If the problem is the ballast, it should be replaced. Table 25-7 lists a few problems specific to a failing ballast.

Troubleshooting HID Lighting

High-Intensity Discharge (HID) lighting is a general term used to describe any lamp that uses a gas-filled arc tube that operates at much higher vacuum conditions than those used in fluorescent lamps. HID lamps are named by the type of gas contained in their arc tube, such as metal halide, mercury vapor, and high-pressure sodium lamps.

Troubleshooting an HID lamp is very much like troubleshooting fluorescent lamps. Most of the problems, beyond burned out lamps or failed ballasts, are related to power and grounding issues. HID lamps must be matched to the ballast in use to prevent lamp or ballast failure. Another common problem is the use of the wrong lamp in a fixture. For example, metal halide and high-pressure sodium lamps are physically interchangeable, but cannot be interchanged electrically.

If an HID lamp fails immediately after being installed, check the impedance on the AC line. HID lamps are negative impedance devices and require a current-limiting ballast. HID ballasts provide an HID lamp with three functions: the proper starting voltage, the proper operating voltage, and conditioning the current for a particular type of HID lamp. If an HID lamp is not working properly, the problem is either the lamp or the ballast, or both.

Problem	Diagnostic	Resolution
Ballast cycles continuously	Is the line voltage correct?	Check the line voltage.
	Are the lamps good?	Replace lamps to isolate the problem as a ballast problem.
	Is insulation covering part or the entire fixture?	Make sure that the ceiling or wall insulation isn't covering part of the fixture, especially the ballast. Too much heat causes the ballast's thermal protector to cycle.
	Are fixtures mounted to the ceiling designed for that use?	Some fixtures require air space for cooling purposes. Replace the fixture with one designed for ceiling mounting.
Lamp starts too slowly	Is the ballast a rapid-start or instant-start type?	Replace rapid-start ballast with a compatible instant-start ballast.
Lamp will not start	Is the ambient temperature below 50 degrees Fahrenheit?	Many ballast require a minimum starting temperature of 50 degrees Fahrenheit or higher.
Lamps are noisy	Is the ballast securely mounted?	Check the ballast mounting and other loose fixture components that may be vibrating.
	Is the sound rating of the ballast appropriate?	Check the sound rating of the ballast and either replace it or mount it remotely to the fixture.

Table 25-7   Troubleshooting Fluorescent Lamp Ballast Problems

Lighting Control System Maintenance Plans

In order to maintain a lighting control system in top working order, there are certain activities that should be performed as a part of a regular periodic preventive maintenance program. Whether the person performing these activities is you or the customer isn't as relevant as the fact that they are performed, and performed regularly.

Lamp Disposal

State and federal regulations govern the methods that can be used to dispose of lamps and ballasts removed from a lighting system. Fluorescent and HID lamps contain mercury and ballasts contain polychlorinated biphenyls (PCBs), two potentially hazardous waste materials.

The U.S. Environmental Protection Agency (EPA) controls the disposal of fluorescent and HID lamps under the Resource Conversation and Recovery Act (RCRA), which treats these lamps as hazardous waste. As such, these lamps must be disposed of in hazardous waste landfills or recycled. Under the RCRA, they cannot be dumped in a general solid waste landfill or burned. However, recently some newer, and more expensive, lamps have been designed to meet the requirements of the EPA and can be disposed of as general trash.

Prior to 1979, magnetic ballasts contained PCBs, which are also considered hazardous material. A magnetic ballast has a service life of around 25 years, so many are still in service. Many newer magnetic ballasts are now manufactured without PCBs and are labeled as "No PCBs." However, without that marking, you must assume the ballast contains PCB and must be handled according to the EPA regulations.

Chapter Review

Feedback from the homeowner may be the best way to learn about performance problems on a newly installed lighting control system. Debrief the homeowner to learn if the lighting scenes are still effective; if scheduled lighting scene changes occur when they should; if there is a problem with lighting levels in any room, zone, or on a particular fixture; and if the lamp life on a particular fixture or lighting group is less than it should be.

The maintenance activities of a lighting control system primarily involve ensuring the lighting levels and control desired by the homeowner are maintained. The maintenance activities are: performing preventive maintenance, applying control changes, applying manufacturer upgrades, and performing troubleshooting and diagnostics.

A preventive maintenance plan should be developed and regularly executed for the lighting control system. The purpose of a preventive maintenance plan is to maintain the system in proper working order and to prevent or detect problems before they become major. At minimum, preventive maintenance should be performed on the lighting control system once a year.

A backup should be made of the lighting system controller's programming each time preventive maintenance is performed. One copy of the backup should be kept at the home and another copy should be stored in the project folder off premises.

The importance of maintaining a maintenance log that records all maintenance activities is not often realized until some point in the future when a problem arises that can be traced back to a maintenance action performed in the past.

Hard-wired lighting controls generally have one of two problems: the switch itself is faulty or a problem has developed with its wiring. Relay switching controls, like those controlling an incandescent lamp, have relatively simple problems (broken toggle switch, no power, or bad wiring) and are generally easy to troubleshoot.

A common problem with PLC controls is that the device coding for one or more control modules is incorrect. Each PLC device is identified to the system with a unique unit code that is typically set using one or two dials located on the device. Another common problem with PLC systems can be the phase of the electrical current on the AC lines.

If a problem develops with the system controller of a lighting control system, in most cases, it's related to power: the AC power to the enclosure is interrupted, AC power to the controller is interrupted, or the controller's internal power supply has failed. If a relay or dimmer module is failing or performing erratically, check the power source to the module or replace the module itself.

In order to maintain a lighting control system in top working order, certain activities need to be performed as a part of a regular periodic preventive maintenance program.

Questions

1. When you are troubleshooting a power line lighting control system, the modules on one electrical circuit are working properly, but the modules on a second electrical circuit work intermittently, if at all. What electrical issue may be causing this problem?

   A. Faulty wall outlet modules

   B. Line noise on all circuits

   C. Different electrical phases on separate circuits

   D. Faulty lamp modules

2. What record should be maintained for an installed home system?

   A. A detail of installation activities

   B. A log that lists repair actions only

   C. A log that lists maintenance activities only

   D. A log that lists all maintenance and repair activities

3. Which of the following should be included in a comprehensive preventive maintenance program for a lighting control system?

   A. Clean fans

   B. Apply manufacturer upgrades

   C. Verify lighting loads

   D. Identify new or replacement systems now available that could be installed

4. What action should be taken before beginning any diagnostic or troubleshooting activities?

   A. Retest the system

   B. Disconnect all controls

   C. Debrief homeowner

   D. Apply all manufacturer upgrades

5. What should be verified or reset when a single PLC control module is not functioning properly?

   A. House code

   B. Unit code

   C. PLC device model number

   D. PLC device serial code

   E. A and B

   F. A and D

6. What electrical activities on AC lines can independently cause modules to activate on a PLC lighting control system?

   A. Voltage spikes

   B. Voltage sags

   C. Brownouts

   D. Electrical noise

   E. All of the above

7. If you suspect a zone load control module or zone control is failing, which of the following should you troubleshoot?

   A. The AC power connections to the control

   B. The connections to devices and controls connected to the control module

   C. The data line connections before and after the zone control

   D. Replace the control unit

8. What is likely the problem when a dimmable fluorescent lamp is exhibiting intermittent problems?

   A. Lamp

   B. Fixture

   C. AC power

   D. Ballast

   E. A or D

   F. A or C

9. If a problem is isolated to a lighting system controller, what are likely the primary issues?

   A. Power

   B. Data connections

   C. Programming

   D. Revision level

10. What is the best source of information regarding upgrades and revisions to a lighting system controller?

   A. Trade magazines

   B. Product bulletins

   C. Troubleshooting logs

   D. Manufacturer's web site

Answers

1. **C.** PLC signals can suffer attenuation when attempting to bridge electrical phases.

2. **D.** Maintaining a maintenance and repair record of all actions performed on a system can reduce the guesswork when troubleshooting a system.

3. **A, B,** and **C.** When performing maintenance, it may not be the appropriate time to upsell a customer on newer models or systems.

4. **C.** If some time has passed since the last maintenance or repair activity, the information the homeowner has about the system's performance and any needed repairs, corrections, or upgrades can be critical to tracking down any reported problems.

5. **E.** Many PLC devices have both a house code and a unit code. Even if the PLC device has only a unit code, it must be assigned uniquely within the system or house.

6. **E.** Any abnormal electrical events can cause PLC devices to activate independently or cause PLC command signals to be lost due to attenuation.

7. **A.** The first troubleshooting step should be to check the AC power connections and, if a DC transformer is in use, the DC power connections.

8. **E.** Problems with fluorescent lamps are typically either the lamp or the ballast. However, when the problem is with a dimmable fluorescent lamp, the first place to begin your troubleshooting is with the ballast.

9. **A.** Power is often the contributing factor to a system controller problem.

10. **D.** The manufacturer's web site can provide troubleshooting and upgrade information about a device.

VI

Telecommunications

CHAPTER 26

Home Communication System Basics

In this chapter, you will learn about:
- Home telecommunication system characteristics
- Telephone operations and fundamentals
- Intercom operations and fundamentals
- Telephone and network integration
- Telecommunication system service options

For those of us old enough to remember rotary dial telephones and dialing without an area code (to really date ourselves), the telephone and telephone service has drastically changed over the past couple of decades. In this chapter, we discuss telecommunications systems for the home, including telephone and intercom systems, their functions, operations, and characteristics. We also discuss the possibilities of integrating a home telecommunications system into control and data networks.

Telecommunications Basics

In most cases, a home telephone and telecommunications system is limited to RJ-11 outlet jacks (Figure 26-1) in one or two rooms of a home that is more than seven to ten years in age or in just about every room of a newer home. The telephone outlet jack can be used for local and long distance calling, to support a fax machine, as a part of a cable or direct satellite TV system, or to support a dial-up modem connection for either a single computer or a computer network. Actually, when you think about it, that little telephone jack really has quite a bit of capability, which is generally underutilized in most homes.

The Telephone System

Most people take the telephone system for granted and get very used to the idea that, for the most part, it always works. Before you can begin designing a home telecommunications system, you should have some understanding of how this system works and its various components.

Figure 26-1
An RJ-11 jack
faceplate

*Photo courtesy of
Belkin Corporation.*

The telephone network consists of two network layers: the Plain Old Telephone System (POTS) and the Public Switched Telephone Network (PSTN). POTS service consists of the wiring and cabling that connects a house to the local telephone company switching system at the telephone company's network interface device (NID) on the side of the house. PSTN includes the switching system and all of the equipment and transmission lines used to carry the voice signals to the house by the phone company.

The Connection to the Central Office

The line that runs back to the telephone company or the telephone service provider (aka the Telco) terminates at a house in what is called the demarc. The demarc (short for demarcation point) is a terminating device that connects the wires in the Telco bundle to the home. In many respects, the demarc is very much like a network's patch panel (see Chapters 11 and 13) in that it interconnects the telephone wiring in the home to the Telco's cabling and switching systems.

Demarcation Point   The demarc device is typically located on an outside wall of a home or in an easily accessed location, such as inside a garage or basement. The official name for the telephone demarc is a Network Interface Device (NID), and it is commonly a gray plastic or metal box with a snap-tight cover (see Figure 26-2).

As shown in Figure 26-2, an NID has two sections, the panel of connections on the right side of the box are accessible by the homeowner or their contractors for testing and connection purposes, and the panel of connections on the left has an inside cover and is accessible only by Telco personnel. The owner-accessible panel, Figure 26-3 gives a zoomed-in view, has four to six screw connectors that connect the Telco's incoming lines (the connections made in the Telco-accessible panel) to the short piece of telephone cables that are plugged into the RJ-11 jacks. When the RJ-11 plug is removed from the jack, the line (and service) from the Telco is disconnected. However, if a phone is plugged

Figure 26-2
A Network Interface Device (NID) showing both the Telco-only side (left panel) and the owner-access side (right panel) connections

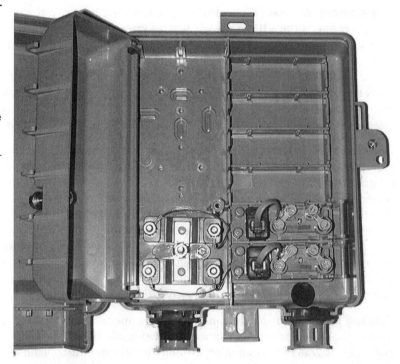

into this jack and works during a service test, any problem with the phone system in the house is being caused by the inside wiring, not by the Telco service.

The demarc is where the Telco's lines and system meet the telephone lines of the homeowner. The Telco owns the lines up to the demarc (and most times the demarc itself), but no further. Beyond the demarc, everything belongs and is the responsibility of the homeowner. However, especially on new homes, some homeowners are choosing to install their own NIDs, which aren't expensive. Installing and owning the demarc allows for more flexibility for expanding the telephone system inside the home, better quality connections at the demarc, the ability to complete the inside wiring (to the demarc) even before the telephone service is installed, and perhaps the best reason, the homeowner can put the demarc wherever they wish. However, the Telco's responsibility ends at the terminator on their cable, which may be a good reason to let them install their NID.

Figure 26-3
A close-up of the owner-accessible panel in an NID

The Central Office   The wiring that connects a house to the telephone network actually connects the NID to the wiring and intermediate devices that lead back to the nearest switching center for the Telco, called a central office (CO). Figure 26-4 illustrates the basics of the connections that link a house to the CO.

The Telco's CO is a switching station that routes calls (including signals on DSL and ISDN services) to the location of the number being called. A CO handles all of the telephone traffic in a particular area. In smaller towns, the CO handles all calls and in larger areas, the CO handles a certain area of a city, county, or a specific area code.

Cabling and Entrance Bridges   If we look at the cabling used to provide a telephone service connection to a residence and start at the CO, in older situations, copper cabling with tens or even hundreds of wire pairs and, in newer lines, fiber optic cabling is used to distribute "dial-tone" (analog telephone services) to every home. In areas where the telephone cabling is installed underground, a device called an entrance bridge is located in the yards of each or every two, three, or more houses. This device is about 2 to 3 feet tall and about 8 inches square (see Figure 26-5) and is where 50 pairs of wiring comes up from underground to be interconnected into houses. On occasion, larger boxes that are about 4 or 5 feet tall and 2 feet wide are also located in neighborhoods that serve as intermediary bridges that distribute wiring to the entrance bridges.

Analog Lines   Analog telephone systems operate using voice and sound signals. Analog phone equipment is designed to interpret audible signals (of the number dialed) and route each call to its destination to build a temporary virtual circuit where the caller and the called can speak over their own private circuit. This circuit is torn down after the call is disconnected. Analog telephone lines support modem connections made by computers, as well as most of the voice transmissions over the Telco system.

Digital Lines   Digital telephone circuits convert sound waves into digital (binary) signals for transmission to the other end of the connection where another telephone, modem, or even a television, converts the digital signals back to audible tones. The primary difference to the telephone user is clarity, because the digital system is able to remove any distortion in the signal. In addition, more features can be carried over the digital line than over an analog line.

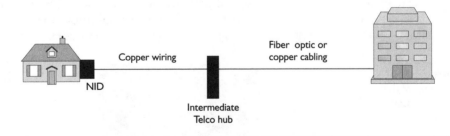

Figure 26-4   Telco lines connect a house to the Central Office for telephone service.

Figure 26-5
An entrance
bridge is used
to distribute
telephone system
wiring to individual
houses.

By installing the proper switching and bridging equipment, existing telephone wiring can also be used to transmit digital data, such as with Digital Subscriber Lines (DSL), Integrated Systems Digital Network (ISDN), and frame relay services. Digital services use the existing copper and fiber optic cabling to transmit digital (binary) data rather than analog (audible) signals.

DSL is able to transmit data only over copper wiring and so it is available only to those houses that have only copper lines connecting them to the CO. Even if only copper wiring connects the home to the CO, DSL is a distance-limited service and may not be available to every home. The wire distance used to determine DSL service availability is the length of the wire itself. Table 26-1 lists the various flavors of DSL and the standard wire distance limitations for each.

ISDN and other digital transmission services can operate over both copper and fiber optic, so they are generally available to most homes, without wire distance limitations. However, ISDN requires that the residential terminating equipment match the type of ISDN switching used at the CO. The most common types of ISDN switching are AT&T 5ESS, Northern Telecom (NT) DMS-100, and National (ANSI) ISDN-1.

PART VI

Table 26-1		
DSL Wire Length Limitations	144 Kbps ISDN over DSL (IDSL)	37,000 feet
	256 Kbps Symmetrical DSL (SDSL)	17,000 feet
	384 Kbps SDSL	17,000 feet
	768 Kbps SDSL	12,000 feet
	1.1 Mbps SDSL	10,000 feet
	1.5 Mbps / 384 Kbps Symmetrical DSL (SDSL)	12,000 feet

Dialing Systems

To place either a local call or a long-distance call requires a number of elements to be available:

- A telephone key set
- A dial-tone sound
- Telephone bandwidth
- Telephone number

Telephone Key Sets   A telephone, or what is also commonly called a key set, has four primary parts:

- **Hook switch**   This is the part of the phone that opens and closes the circuit loop that tells the phone's circuitry whether the phone is on hook (circuit open) or off hook (circuit closed). When the phone's handset is lifted (or the speaker phone button is depressed), the circuitry of the phone detects that the loop is closed and plays the dial tone sound or passes sound through it.

- **Keypad or rotary dial**   On older phones, a rotary dial was used to emit pulses, with 0 to 9 pulses representing the numbers 0 to 9. Newer phones are almost all touchtone that emit a recorded sound at a certain frequency for each number pressed on the keypad. For example, as you dial the numbers in a phone number, the phone emits a stream of combined frequency tones, the combination represents each number on the keypad.

- **Microphone**   A microphone is located in what is most commonly called the mouthpiece of a telephone's handset. The microphone converts the sound it picks up into sound samples that are transmitted to the telephone system.

- **Speaker**   The speaker in the handset of a telephone key set is a small 8-ohm speaker that plays back the audible signals transmitted to or played by the phone circuitry.

Dial Tone   The dial tone, as well as the tones representing the numbers dialed and several other common dialing sounds, such as busy, off-hook, and others, are recorded sounds embedded on a chip on the telephone's circuitry.

All of the tones produced by a telephone are a combination of two frequencies. For example, combining a 350-hertz tone with a 440-hertz tone creates the dial tone and the busy signal is a combination of a 480-hertz tone and a 620-hertz tone that is cycled on and off.

System Bandwidth   The public telephone system limits transmitted sounds to not less than 400 hertz and not more than around 3,000 hertz. Any sounds with frequencies below 400 hertz or above 3,000 hertz are discarded and this is why a person may sound completely different over the phone than in person, where you can receive the full range of their voice's frequencies.

The telephone key set also limits the bandwidth requirement of voice communications by transmitting sound samples rather than the entire sound it receives. A concentrator circuit works with the telephone's microphone to create 8,000 samples per second of the sound it hears and transmits the sound samples across the public telephone system for playback by the speaker at the other end's handset.

Telephone Number Digits   Like the physical address of a networked computer (see Chapter 12) or the address of a home, a telephone number is a unique address for a destination circuit. Each part of a telephone number has meaning, from a country code used to dial an international call, the area code, the prefix, and the line number. For example, in the number 509-555-1212, the 509 is the area code, the 555 is the prefix, and the 1212 is the line number.

- **Area code**   Area codes in the United States are regulated and assigned by the Federal Communications Commission (FCC) to designate a specific geographic region that could be a part of a city or state. For example, 509 is the area code for Eastern Washington State. Each area code can address 7,920,000 prefix and line number combinations. In the United States, only around 215 area codes are in use out of the 680 usable areas.

- **Prefix**   At one time, the prefix represented a specific switch (at the CO) where a particular telephone is connected. However, since automated switches have been in use, phone numbers, included the prefix are now portable under a method called local number portability (LNP).

- **Line number**   The CO switch identifies a specific line using the last four digits of a telephone number.

Caller Identity   Most newer telephone key sets are able to display the identity (the phone number and the name the phone number is registered to) of the calling party either on the phone itself or on a satellite caller ID box.

The technology used to provide caller ID isn't new, in fact it is the same used by modems to set up a connection—frequency shift keying (FSK). This technology uses certain tone frequencies to represent binary digits, such as 1,200 hertz for a one and 2,200 hertz for a zero, and the telephone or caller ID box converts these to ASCII characters for display.

Wireless Telephones

To this point, we have been discussing telephones in general, so most of this information applies to the standard wire-connected telephone and key sets. However, it is common for today's homes to include one or many cordless or wireless telephones, either in addition to or in replacement of standard telephones.

Cordless Telephones

A cordless telephone, like the one shown in Figure 26-6, allows a user to talk through the telephone's handset without being tethered to the telephone's base unit. As far as

Figure 26-6
A cordless phone
has two parts:
a base and a
handset, which is
portable and not
attached to the
base with a cord.

*Photo courtesy of
Siemens Information
and Communication
Mobile, LLC.*

functionality goes, cordless phones have essentially the same features offered by a standard or corded telephone.

RF Functions Cordless telephones combine the functions of a standard telephone with those of radio frequency (RF) transmitter/receiver. The base of a common cordless phone is wired into the telephone system just like a standard telephone. However, the base communicates to the handset using RF communications and a frequency modulation (FM) signal. The handset receives the FM radio signal and converts it back to an audio signal and is sent to the handset's speaker. The microphone on the handset performs an opposite action, translating the audio signals into FM radio signals for transmission to the base unit that converts the RF signals to voice signals for transmission through the telephone wiring.

The handset and base of a cordless telephone use a pair of different frequencies, one for incoming signals and one for outgoing signals. A frequency pair that is used this way is referred to as a duplex frequency. For example, the base unit may use 44 MHz to transmit and 49 MHz to receive, which is reversed on the handset where 49 MHZ is used to transmit and 44 MHz is used for the receiver.

Operational Issues A cordless telephone does have a few operational issues that a standard telephone doesn't have:

- **Range limitations** The operating frequency (RF band) of a cordless telephone has a direct impact on the operating range of the handset or the distance the handset can be from the base and continue to work properly. Table 26-2 lists the operating ranges for the more common frequencies used on cordless telephones.

Table 26-2	Band	Operating Range (Upper Limit)
Conservative operating ranges for cordless telephone RF Bands	49 MHz	250 feet (75 meters)
	900 MHz	1,500 feet (450 meters)
	2.4 GHz	2,000 feet (600 meters)
	5.8 GHz	2,000 feet (600 meters)

- **Sound reproduction** The sound quality of a cordless phone's handset is affected by a variety of things, including distance and interference created by obstructions, such as walls, or electrical appliances.

- **Security issues** Because a cordless phone transmits using RF signals on common radio frequency bands, the transmitted signals can be intercepted by other RF devices, including other cordless phones that operate on the same band, baby monitors, radio scanners, and the like.

The performance issues of a cordless phone are the result of the phone's design and features, primarily the phone's RF band, whether the phone is analog or digital, and the number of channels it has available.

Inexpensive cordless phones are commonly analog devices that are generally electrically noisier, susceptible to interference, and more easily intercepted by other RF devices. Digital cordless phones provide a better sound quality and, because they also use digital spread spectrum (DSS) signaling, they are generally more secure than an analog phone. DSS uses several frequencies to transmit signals between the base and the handset and this makes it very hard for another device to intercept an entire conversation.

RF frequency bands can be divided into several channels and the more channels available, the better chance the base unit is able to find a channel pair that is relatively free from interference. Typically, a 49MHz cordless telephone has from 10 to 25 channels available; a low-end 900 MHz phone has from 20 to 60 channels; and higher-end 900 MHz, 2.4 GHz, and 5.8 GHz phones have as many as 100 channels.

Residential Telephone Systems

If the homeowner desires only a single telephone line with multiple extensions without any added features, beyond those provided by the Telco, once the wiring and the phone jack outlets are installed during pre-wire, chances are that the house has everything it needs to fulfill this requirement.

However, if the homeowner wishes to have multiple phone lines accessible throughout the house, careful consideration must be given to exactly what features the homeowner is looking for and if a telephone system will meet their needs.

There are several advantages to a telephone system over the standard telephone service found in most homes. These advantages include:

- **Call routing** An automatic call distribution (ACD) allows callers to select the direct line to a member of the household or leave a voice message for a specific user.

- **Multiple phone line accessibility**   All phones have access to the phone lines connected to the phone system and allow for the automatic selection of the next available line—no current conversations can be interrupted by someone else in the home picking up the phone on the same line.

- **Intercom capabilities**   All phones, and even a door bell station, can be intercom stations and can be called from other phones in the house. Also, phones can be put on "private mode" so the room is not interrupted with the telephone ringing.

- **Expandability**   Phone systems are typically based on an expandable base unit to which additional features or telephones can be added or upgraded as the homeowners' needs change.

- **Fax/Modem connections**   A phone system can provide connections for a fax or modem without tying up a voice line.

- **Voice and data integration**   Many phone systems include the ability to integrate high-speed voice and data communications using computer telephony integration (CTI).

- **Voice messaging**   Phone systems commonly have the ability to record outgoing announcements for each household member and record incoming voice messages in separate voice message boxes.

KSU-Based Systems

A KSU is a central device that provides the switching and control services for the entire network of key sets on a telephone system. In some cases, the KSU may also be referred to as a Public Branch Exchange (PBX) or a computerized PBX (C-PBX). Regardless, a KSU provides additional or advanced features to standard telephone sets, including such features as call forwarding, extension dialing, voice mail, music on hold, and more. The fact that a KSU must be configured in a star topology is considered a drawback to many, but structured wiring provides "star" topology, and a phone system can easily be installed on structured wiring. Most KSU-based systems may require proprietary or specially configured key sets that add to the overall cost of the system.

KSU systems provide many "business" functions as well, including auto-attendant that answers the phone with a recording and allows the caller to select an extension from a recorded menu, such as "For Ron, press 1; for Connie, press 2," and so on.

KSU-based systems also offer a wide range of optional features as well, including:

- Automatic routing for fax calls to a fax machine
- Toll restriction that prevents certain users from placing certain outgoing toll or long-distance calls
- PC-accessible call and activity reporting
- Call-waiting
- Music on Hold from an external music source
- Three-party teleconferencing

- Do not disturb function that blocks incoming calls (internal and external) from ringing on a blocked extension

- Call pickup that allows calls on one extension to be picked up on another extension when put on hold

- The ability to connect a door phone or an intercom station to talk with visitors on any extension phone

- Interface to relay devices or AC outlets that allow home lights, appliances, and other devices to be turned on and off through the telephone

KSU-Less Systems

Another type of KSU system, at least in terms of functionality, is the KSU-less system. KSU-less systems are relatively low-cost options for residential phone systems with two to seven telephone lines. The primary attractiveness to a KSU-less telephone system, beyond its features that is, is that it can work with nearly any ordinary phone, including both rotary dial and touch-tone. However, to realize all of the features of the system, a central unit or specialized telephone stations may be required. KSU-less systems typically provide all, or at least the majority, of the features of a KSU-based system, but commonly at a much lower cost.

Digital Systems

Digital telephone systems are key systems like KSU-based systems and rely on a central processor for many of their functions. Digital key systems, also like a KSU system, allow the telephone system to share multiple CO lines across a number of key stations. Figure 26-7 shows the central unit and samples of the digital key stations for one residential and small business system.

Figure 26-7
A digital telephone system with a digital PBX, key station, and cordless phone

Photo courtesy of Panasonic USA.

Because they have what amounts to a computer at their core, digital telephone systems are programmable, typically through a graphical user interface that can be accessed either by attaching a monitor to the central unit or connecting the central unit to a data network.

One of the downsides to a digital telephone system is that they require the use of special digital telephone key sets and any existing fax machines and modems must continue to use separate analog phone lines. On the other hand, however, the digital phones are feature-rich, including such features as:

- **Automatic Call Distribution (ACD)** Callers can use a hierarchy of voice prompts and menu choices to route themselves to the proper phone.

- **Computer Telephony Integration (CTI)** This feature supports the integration of some telephone functions with those of a computer network. A common CTI feature is the routing of voice mail into a user's e-mail mailbox.

- **Incoming and outgoing call logs** Digital systems have the ability to store Calling Line Identification (CLID) information and prepare listings reporting call, time, and date information.

- **Intercom** Most digital systems provide intercom functions for station-to-station communications.

- **Integrated Voice Response (IVR)** This feature is less important for residential use, but can come in handy for home offices. IVR allows the voice response of information retrieved from a computer file or database. If you've ever called a credit card company for your balance, you were likely using IVR.

- **Programmable key set buttons** Each key station on the system can be customized to the needs of the user.

- **Speakerphone** Digital phones provide high-quality audio, which facilitates hands-free conversations, teleconferencing, and background music playback, all with volume control.

- **Speech recognition** This feature allows callers to use voice commands to navigate through ACD menu choices.

IP Telephone Systems

Internet Protocol (IP) telephone systems operate over the cabling and computers of a data network. Residential IP telephone systems replace the existing residential gateway with one (see Figure 26-8) that provides both the RJ-45 network connections required by the data network and RJ-11 connections used to provide phone service to IP telephone key stations.

The benefits of an IP telephone system are several, including cost-effective access through phones anywhere in the world that are connected to the Internet, and the fact that the system is relatively easy to install. The drawbacks of an IP telephone system primarily have to do with the performance. Sometimes there is a delay in the speaking, and clarity is not as consistently good as on a standard phone line. Also, signals can be lost more easily than on standard phone lines.

IP telephones use a technology called Voice over IP (VoIP) to transmit telephone calls over a data network in the same way that data messages are sent over the network. VoIP

Figure 26-8
An IP telephone
system residential
gateway

*Photo courtesy of
Mediatrix Telecom, Inc.*

converts voice samples into network packets that are transmitted over both the local in-home network and the Internet.

VoIP uses coder/decoder (codec) circuitry to convert audio signals into compressed digital format for transmission and back to voice signals at the receiving station for playback. Two primary protocols are used by VoIP to transmit voice signals:

- **H.323** This is the international communications standard that specifies real-time, interactive teleconferencing, data sharing, and IP telephony.

- **Session Initiation Protocol (SIP)** This protocol, developed by the Internet Engineering Task Force (IETF) is a streamlined version of the H.323 protocols designed specifically to support IP telephone services. Because it is not a complete suite of protocols like H.323, SIP employs other protocols, such as the Media Gateway Control Protocol (MGCP), to establish gateway connections to the PSTN.

The primary ways VoIP can be used across the PSTN is in computer to telephone, telephone to computer, and telephone to telephone calling.

- **Computer to telephone** This calling method allows a user to call any telephone connected to the PSTN from a computer, using the computer's speakers and microphone to communicate.

- **Telephone to computer** This calling method allows a call to be placed across the network from a telephone to a computer. The computer user has the ability to answer the call by activating a software function or allowing the computer to answer the call, play an outgoing announcement, and record a voice message.

- **Telephone to telephone** This calling method is the one that employs the methodology and technology that can be used on a home network to place calls through the residential gateway to a PSTN-connected telephone.

Intercom Systems

There are two general categories of intercom systems that can be installed in a home: wired and wireless. There are two ways to implement an intercom system in a home: through the telephone system or through the installation of an independent, stand-alone wall-mounted intercom system.

Telephone-Based Intercom Newer key stations and analog telephones feature intercom and speaker-phone capabilities that allow the telephone to be used to call room-to-room, typically with the press of a single button, and talk with someone in another location in the house with a totally hands-free conversation.

Stand-alone Intercom Systems   We refer to these systems as independent only to differentiate them from telephone-based intercom systems. This type of intercom system consists of master units, remote controls, speakers, and now even displays that are typically wall-mounted devices placed at the mouth-level of the average person.

There are a variety of stand-alone intercom systems available:

- **Doorbell intercom**   This type of intercom system includes a doorbell for visitors to ring the standard phones in the house with a unique ring-ring to identify it is the doorbell intercom and not an incoming phone call. When a phone is answered in the house, the connection becomes a two-way voice intercom that allows the homeowner to speak with the visitor. Some systems also include the ability to remotely open or unlock a door.

- **Voice-only intercom**   This is the type of intercom system that is implemented on a telephone system and on low-end intercom systems. Low-end voice intercom systems typically only support half-duplex (two-way communication, but only one way at a time) conversations where the user must push a button to speak or announce. Voice-only intercom systems implemented on KSU, KSU-less, or digital telephone systems generally support full duplex (two-way communications, two ways at the same time) conversations.

- **Voice/radio intercom**   These systems represent the mid-range in cost and capability in intercom systems. Many limit voice communications to half-duplex, but more full-duplex systems are now available. The master unit of a voice/radio intercom includes an AM/FM radio that can be played throughout the system. Some newer models also include playback units for audiocassettes or CDs.

- **Video intercom systems**   Video intercom systems are primarily used to identify someone at a doorway or other secured areas. These systems incorporate a voice intercom and video capture and display and are available with a single built-in, wide-angle camera or have the ability to connect to multiple external cameras. The video image can be one-way, where only the master unit inside the house has a video screen, or two-way, where both the inside and outside devices have displays.

Chapter Review

The telephone network consists of two network layers: the Plain Old Telephone System (POTS) and the Public Switched Telephone Network (PSTN). POTS refers to the wiring and cabling connecting a house or building to the local CO. The PSTN includes CO and the equipment and transmission lines that carry voice signals to a destination.

The Telco's POTS line, which terminates at a house at the demarcation point (demarc) or Network Interface Device (NID), is a terminating device that interconnects Telco wiring to a home's telephone wiring. The demarc is commonly located on an outside wall of the house. The Telco owns the lines up to the demarc (and most times the demarc itself), but all internal telephone wiring is the responsibility of the homeowner. The POTS lines connect a house to the Telco's central office (CO) or switching facility. The CO routes calls to the CO and switching associated with the number being called.

Analog telephone systems transmit voice and audio signals. Analog telephone lines also provide support for modem connections made by computers. Digital services use the existing copper and fiber optic cabling to transmit digital (binary) data rather than analog (voice) signals. Digital services include DSL and ISDN.

A telephone set has four primary parts: hook switch, keypad or rotary dial, microphone, and speaker. Combining two audible frequencies creates the tones produced by a telephone. For example, combining a 350-hertz tone with a 440-hertz tone creates the dial tone.

The telephone system transmits sounds between 400 hertz and 3,000 hertz. Sounds below or above this range are discarded and this is why people sound different on the phone than in person. Telephone key sets transmit sound by creating 8,000 sound samples per second.

Each part of a telephone number has meaning. A telephone number typically consists of an area code, a prefix, and a line number. Caller ID uses frequency shift keying (FSK) to transmit ASCII caller identification information.

A cordless telephone includes a stationary base unit and a portable (unwired) handset. Cordless telephones combine a standard telephone with a radio frequency (RF) transmitter/receiver. The cordless phone base communicates to the handset using RF communications and a frequency modulation (FM) signal.

There are three primary types of residential home telephone systems: KSU-based systems, KSU-less systems, and digital key systems. A KSU is a central device that provides the switching and control services for the entire telephone system. KSU-less systems are relatively low-cost options for residential phone systems with two to seven telephone lines and work with standard telephones. Digital key systems rely on a central processor for their functions and provide advanced features.

Common features for residential telephone systems are: Automatic Call Distribution (ACD), Computer Telephony Integration (CTI), intercom capability, programmable key set buttons, speaker-phone compatibility, and speech recognition.

Internet Protocol (IP) telephone systems operate over the cabling and computers of a data network. Residential IP telephone systems replace the existing residential gateway with one that provides both RJ-45 network connections and RJ-11 connections to IP telephone key stations.

IP telephones use a technology called Voice over IP (VoIP) to transmit telephone calls over a data network in the same way that data messages are sent over the network. VoIP converts voice samples into network packets that are transmitted over the local in-home network and the Internet. VoIP uses coder/decoder (codec) circuitry to convert audio signals into compressed digital format for transmission and back to voice signals at the receiving station for playback. VoIP provides support for computer to telephone, telephone to computer, and telephone to telephone calling.

Three general types of intercom system can be used in a home setting: doorbell intercoms, stand-alone voice intercom systems, and intercoms integrated into phone systems.

PART VI

Questions

1. What connecting jack and plug standard is used for telephone system wall outlets and key sets?

   A. RJ-232

   B. RJ-45

   C. RJ-32

   D. RJ-11

2. What is the name applied to the cabling used to connect a house to its local CO?

   A. PTSN

   B. POTS

   C. PSTN

   D. ISDN

3. What is the common name for the device used to terminate the CO line to a house?

   A. POTS

   B. PSTN

   C. Telco

   D. Demarc

4. What Telco device is used to distribute CO line wiring to individual houses or buildings?

   A. Multiplexer

   B. Entrance bridge

   C. Line splitter

   D. NID

5. Which type of telephone system transmits a telephone call as audible signals?

   A. Analog

   B. Digital

   C. KSU

   D. KSU-less

6. What is a high-speed broadband service that transmits over existing POTS lines?

   A. POTS

   B. PSTN

   C. DSL

   D. H.323

7. What are the frequency ranges transmitted by telephone systems?

   A. 0 to 10,000 hertz

   B. 400 to 3.000 hertz

   C. 1,000 to 8,000 hertz

   D. 2,000 to 10,000 hertz

8. What is the technology used to transmit caller identification information?

   A. PSTN

   B. DSL

   C. H.323

   D. FSK

9. What technology do cordless phones use to transmit between the handset and the base unit?

   A. IR

   B. RF

   C. IVR

   D. DSL

10. What digital key system feature allows for the integration of voice and data features and functions?

   A. ACD

   B. CLID

   C. CTI

   D. IVR

Answers

1. **D.** RJ-11. An RJ-45 jack is used to connect twisted-pair wiring; the other choices don't exist.

2. **B.** POTS. The Plain Old Telephone System describes the analog wiring and service used to connect a CO to the demarc of a house. PSTN is the Public Switch Telephone Network that includes the switching systems of a Telco; ISDN is the Integrated Services Digital Network, which is a digital data system; and PTSN is not a Telco abbreviation.

3. **D.** Demarc. Demarc is short for demarcation point, which is also called a Network Interface Device (NID). POTS and PSTN are the different network layers of the telephone network and Telco is a short-form of telephone company.

4. **B.** Entrance bridge. An entrance bridge is a 2- to 3-foot tall device where the underground cable is distributed to individual buildings.

5. **A.** Analog. Analog systems transmit signals in their native form without converting them into digital format. KSU and KSU-less systems are types of facility-based telephone systems.

6. **C.** DSL. Digital Subscriber Line (DSL) service uses existing POTS lines to carry digital broadband signals. H.323 is an IP telephony standard.

7. **B.** 400 to 3,000 hertz. This is the reason why people sound different over the telephone than in person.

8. **D.** FSK. Frequency shift keying uses different frequencies to transmit binary-encoded ASCII data to a telephone set.

9. **B.** RF. Radio frequency technology is used to connect the handset to the base of a cordless phone. IR (infrared) is not used for this purpose; IVR is a key system feature; and DSL is a POTS broadband technology.

10. **C.** CTI. Computer Telephony Integration provides the ability for voice mail messages to be saved as e-mail messages. ACD, CLID, and IVR are other key system features.

Designing and Installing a Home Telephone System

In this chapter, you will learn about:
- Residential telephone design considerations
- Standard phone line installation hardware and termination points
- Telephone system installation hardware and termination points
- Intercom installation

The primary considerations when designing a residential telephone and telecommunications system are meeting the client's needs and integrating the telephone system and its wiring into the structured wiring, data network, control system, and other whole house systems.

In this chapter, we discuss design considerations and installation activities for the structured wiring installation for both standard phone lines and a phone system.

Residential Telephone Systems Design

The design process for a residential telephone system using structured wiring must address the inclusion and placement of the telecommunication wiring schemes, outlet boxes, wire termination, jacks, punchdown blocks, patch panels, wire identification and labeling, and, of course, the telephone key sets (specialized phones designed to work with the key system unit).

 CROSS-REFERENCE   See Chapters 5 and 6 for more information on structured wiring.

Wiring Schemes

Telephone system wiring is typically installed using one of two schemes: series wiring or star (also know as home run) wiring. The star wiring scheme is the basis of a structured

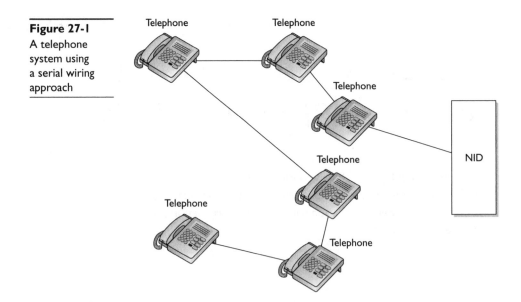

Figure 27-1
A telephone system using a serial wiring approach

wiring approach and is always recommended for new construction or complete retrofit installations. Unfortunately, series wiring is common in older existing homes.

Series Wiring

Before 1980, series wiring was the standard wiring scheme used by telephone companies to install residential telephone service. The series-wiring scheme is also referred to as daisy chain wiring because the wiring is installed by running wires from one contact to the next. However, in situations where the telephone wiring must be reconfigured to accommodate more central office (CO) lines or more than three or four extension telephones, series wiring can be very restrictive.

Perhaps the best way to plan for a new telephone system around series wiring is to insert a punchdown block or patch panel at a point that creates separate runs to each room or zone of the house. Figure 27-1 shows a simplified drawing of series wiring in a house. In this case, the telephones (perhaps more than would be normally found in a home, but included to make the point) are wired in a daisy chain from the single connection in the network interface device (NID). Figure 27-2 shows a possible rework for the telephone system incorporating a Key Service Unit (KSU) phone system.

 CROSS-REFERENCE   See Chapter 26 for more information on KSU systems.

Star Wiring

A star wiring approach (see Figure 27-3) for a residential telecommunications system runs telephone wiring from each phone jack in the rooms of a house to a central point that is

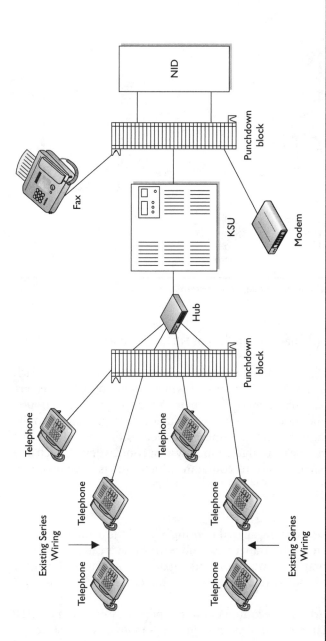

Figure 27-2   A series wiring system reconfigured into a star wiring approach

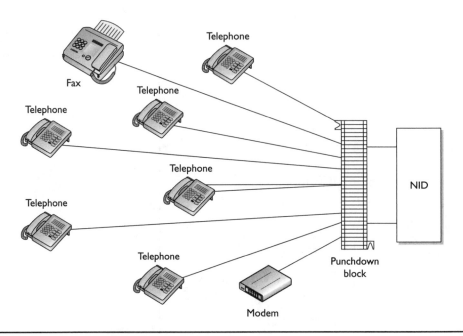

Figure 27-3   A basic star-wiring scheme for a telephone system

usually located near the demarc (demarcation point) or NID where the line or lines from the Telco's CO arrive at the house.

Running a separate run of four-pair Cat 5 unshielded twisted-pair (UTP) wire to each telephone outlet jack provides flexibility in terms of which incoming CO lines are linked to which phones. In situations where only a single CO line comes into a house, the choices may be to make some outlets only intercom stations and give access to the CO line to others. However, should more CO lines be added to the system at some point, using a punchdown block or a central telephone system control device, such as a KSU or digital control unit, makes it easy to configure which outlets have access to which CO lines as necessary.

Horizontal Wiring

Because the wiring inside a house, meaning all of the wiring beyond the demarc, is the responsibility of the homeowner, it is important to use only wiring that is category verified and carries a Underwriters Laboratories, Inc. (UL) marking on its outer jacket. Category verified wiring meets or exceeds industry fire, electrical, and materials specifications and also meets local building codes.

The current industry standards and recommendations specify a minimum of UTP Category 3 wiring for residential voice applications, although many new construction installations now use Cat 5e wiring in its place. Category 3 cable consists of four twisted pairs of 100-ohm, light gauge (typically 22 or 24 AWG copper wiring), as does Cat 5e.

Standard Phone Line Installation

Installing a residential telephone system in a new construction situation involves installing four basic elements: structured wiring, outlet jacks, punchdown or distribution blocks, and phone devices.

Telephone Wiring

When working with the wiring installed by the telephone company, you may find one or more of the following wire and cable types:

- **25-pair cable** This is a gray-, beige-, or pink-jacketed cable that contains 25 pairs of twisted wire, as shown in Figure 27-4. Although this large of a cable is unusual in residential situations, some older large homes have been known to have a 25-pair cable connected to the demarc using an RJ-21 50-pin connector, commonly called an Amp (short for Amphenol) Champ. RJ-21 connectors are used to connect this size cable to punchdown blocks and other types of distribution panels.

- **Satin cord** So called for its silver coating, this flat cable has 4 untwisted 26 gauge wires, has either RJ-11 (shown in Figure 27-5) or RJ-45 jacks, and is used to connect a wall outlet to a telephone set.

- **Station wire** Many existing residential telephone systems use station wire, which consists of 4 24-gauge solid-core wires (see Figure 27-6) that are twisted together into 2 wire pairs—1 consisting of red and green wires and 1 consisting of yellow and black wires. This type of wire is also called plain old telephone service (POTS) wire. Newer types of station wire is made up of blue and orange wires banded with white in which one pair is blue/white and orange/white and the other pair is white/orange and white/blue.

Figure 27-4
A 25-pair UTP cable cut-away to show the internal wire-pairs

PART VI

Figure 27-5
A terminated
satin cord

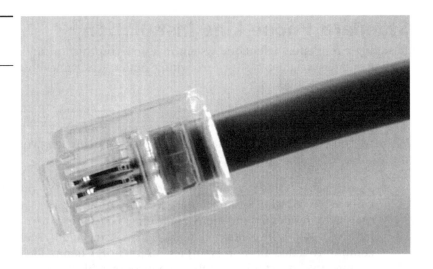

Structured Wiring for Standard Telephone System

Chapters 5 and 6 detail the requirements for installing structured wiring. However, as far as support for a telephone system in the structured wiring goes, there are some product specifications and handling issues you will need to consider.

Standard Phone Outlet Wiring

Four-pair UTP Cat 3 minimum wiring (Cat 5e recommended for future-proofing) should be installed between a location near where the demarc can be easily reached. The wire pairs provide the capability to connect up to a combination of four phone, digital subscriber line (DSL), fax, or modem lines to inline locations in the house, as illustrated in Figure 27-7.

Cable

If a structured wiring installation is to support only a telephone system, only a four-conductor cable, such as station wire, is required and category-rated cabling isn't needed. However, installing Cat 5e cable to each outlet of the telephone system helps to future-proof the system. If structured wiring is being installed to support audio, control, video, and other whole-house applications, it may be better to install composite cable that

Figure 27-6
A piece of station
wire, stripped to
show its internal
wires

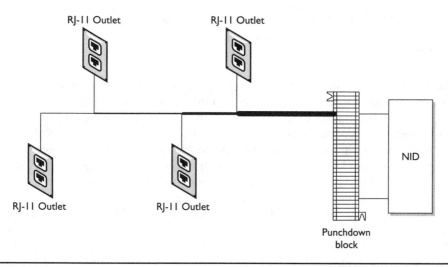

Figure 27-7   Cat 5e wiring installed to provide connections to four outlets

includes all of the various wire types needed to support each of a home's subsystems, as well as provides for future cable requirements.

The wire elements included in common composite cables are typically two or more runs of either Cat 5e or Cat 3 UTP and one or more runs of coaxial cable. Figure 27-8 illustrates the makeup of one type of residential structured wiring cable.

In most instances, installers choose to use one of the Cat 5e cabling in a composite cable for voice delivery and the other Cat 5e for data networking.

Punchdown/Distribution Blocks

Structured wiring concepts involve a central distribution point that serves as both the center of the star topology and a single testing, maintenance, and configuration location. A cable interface, patch panel, or punchdown block, also called a cross-connect block, is typically used as the distribution point in structured telephone wiring installations. If a structured pre-wiring system is in use in the home, then the telephone lines will terminate in the central service unit of that system.

PART VI

Figure 27-8
Composite
structured wiring
cable with two
runs each of
Cat 5e and
coaxial cable

CROSS-REFERENCE See Chapter 7 for information on the different types of distribution panel connectors.

Distribution Panels There are several models of telephone system distribution panels made especially for, and incorporated into, residential telephone systems. Residential phone distribution modules simplify the wiring for a home telephone system because they include features such as already in-place bridging for up to 4 CO lines to 12 or as many as 48 telephone outlets, 110-style punchdown or RJ-style connectors in and out, and wall-mount kits. Most of these systems also satisfy the requirements for home distribution devices as required by the Electronic Industries Alliance/Telecommunications Industry Association (EIA/TIA) 568 and 570 wiring standards.

For many residential installations, an RJ-11 patch panel makes more sense than using a punchdown patch panel to create the cross-connect between the CO line entrance cables and the Cat 3 or Cat 5 cable runs to the RJ-11 outlets. Most homeowners are not technical and should the need arise to talk a customer through a line change for testing purposes, it is much easier to explain how to move an RJ-11 jack than a punchdown or pole and screw connection.

A home patch panel, such as the one shown in Figure 27-9, incorporates 110-type punchdown connectors that link a CO line to distributed RJ-style connectors are connected to

Figure 27-9
The two sides of a Cat 5 patch panel showing the IDC connections on the back and either RJ-11 or RJ-45 connectors on the front

Photo courtesy of Signamax Connectivity Systems.

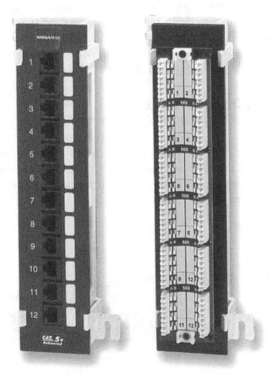

the cabling that runs to the outlets. There are also patch panels available that have RJ-style connectors for both incoming and outgoing connections.

Connecting to the Demarc

Once the pre-wire stage is completed and the horizontal wiring is pulled into where the central distribution panel is located, the next step in completing the telephone system wiring is to bridge the demarcation point to the outlet wiring runs. As we discussed above, this bridge is created using either a distribution panel or a patch panel.

Demarc to Patch Panel   The simplest way to connect the demarc point or the NID into the distribution point is to terminate a single run of Cat 5 wire with an RJ-11 jack and plug it into the customer-access side of the NID. A single run of Cat 3 or Cat 5 wire accommodates up to four incoming CO lines. The four pairs of wire in the Cat 3/5 wire are then terminated into the distribution panel, which for this discussion is an RJ-11 patch panel with 110-type punchdown blocks.

For testing purposes, it is always best to terminate the wiring from the demarc/NID at standard phone jacks at the phone system location. This allows for testing of each phone line inside of the house before the phone system. If there is a problem with one or more phone lines, this rules out the phone system as the cause of the problem.

 NOTE   It is always advisable, especially if there is a phone system or security system, to run the cable of each phone line from the NID through a surge suppressor before connecting it into the distribution panel. Many structured wiring panels have built-in surge suppressors to protect alternating current (AC) electrical outlets, coaxial cable outlets, and RJ-11 outlets.

Distribution Panel to Outlets   The cable installed during pre-wire for the telephone outlets should be terminated with the appropriate RJ-style outlets in the rooms of the house and into the distribution panel so that each outlet is bridged to the appropriate CO line, per the homeowner's wishes.

Depending on the type of telephone system you are installing, the outlet jacks can be a standard telephone (RJ-11) or an RJ-45 outlet that supports a KSU/telephone system or an IP-based telephone system. Since RJ-11 jacks fit in both RJ-11 and RJ-45 outlets it is advisable to always install RJ-45 outlets to accommodate both standard phone and future phone systems.

Outlet jacks are typically color-coded and are either a 66- or a 110-punchdown connector; the 66-type is more common with telephone equipment and the 110-type is more common with networking devices. If the outlet is a standard phone jack, the red and green pins are used to enable line one and if a second line is being connected to the jack, line two is connected to the yellow and black pins. If you are using a data jack (RJ-45), the blue colored pins are connected for line one and the orange pins are used for line two, if needed.

Telephone to Outlet   If the phone cords aren't already terminated or you decide not to purchase already terminated cords, you may need to terminate the cords with RJ-11

Signal	Cat 3/5 Wire Color	RJ-11/12 6-Pin	RJ-11 4-Pin
Line three (Tip)	White/green	1	
Line two (Tip)	White/orange	2	1
Line one (Tip)	White/blue	3	2
Line one (Ring)	Blue/white	4	3
Line two (Ring)	Orange/white	5	4
Line three (Ring)	Green/white	6	

Table 27-1 RJ-11 (4-Pin Plug) and RJ-11/12 (6-Pin Plug) Pinouts for Station Wire Connections

plugs. A variety of manufacturers now make self-terminating jacks for RJ-11 and RJ-45 outlets that eliminate the need for wire striping, untwisting wires, and the use of a punch-down tool.

Table 27-1 lists the pinouts for RJ-style plugs typically used to terminate Cat 3 or Cat 5 cable. Figure 27-10 compares 4-pin RJ-11 and 6-pin RJ-11/12 jacks.

NOTE The terms "Tip" and "Ring" are used in telephony to indicate the pins and wires that carry positive and negative voltage. These terms come from the old switchboard plug-in where the positive voltage was connected to the tip of the plug and the negative voltage was connected to a slip ring that was around the plug.

Telephone Outlets

Communications outlets are placed at the same height as the electrical outlets in a room, but no closer than one foot from an electrical outlet horizontally. If a room has a wall phone, its outlet should be mounted at about eye level, between 48 and 52 inches, on a wall. Wall phones require special outlet wall plates to support the physical phone on the wall.

Modular Jacks Modular jacks are common in older and most existing homes. This type of jack is surface mounted and provides connections for up to two communication lines on a single jack. Figure 27-11 shows the common modular jack design.

Figure 27-10
A 4-pin (left) and a 6-pin (right) version of the RJ-11 plug

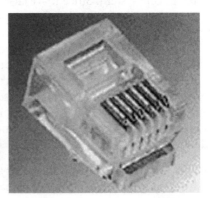

Figure 27-11
A modular RJ-11
telephone jack

Outlet Wall Plates and Jacks   Flush-mounted wall outlet jacks, like the one shown in Figure 27-12, are more common in today's newer homes. Wall jacks are available with one, two, and up to six jack configurations.

Typically, each of the individual jacks in a wall jack has either a 110-type connector or a RJ-11/12 style connector to receive and terminate the incoming telephone wiring.

Installing a KSU Telephone System

An alternative to installing a standard telephone system, in which many services, such as voicemail, caller ID, and call-waiting are provided as subscribed services by the telephone company (Telco), is installing a KSU system. A KSU-based telephone system has its own separate controller (the KSU itself) that can independently provide many of the same Telco subscriber services to specialized and/or standard telephones in the home.

Figure 27-12
A surface-
mounted RJ-11
wall jack

PART VI

The features typically provided by a residential KSU system include the capability to connect to standard telephones (and not proprietary key stations like many business KSU systems), voice-messaging (voicemail), station-to-station intercom support, auto-attendant, music-on-hold, caller ID, and in many cases, support for a door intercom.

Not every home needs or can afford a KSU telephone system, but in those homes with several phone lines and multiple extensions that desire these features and perhaps a few more, a KSU may be a very good value.

Installing the KSU

The KSU or controller of a KSU system (see Figure 27-13) should be treated like any central control unit and placed in a central location within the home, very near where the telephone line wire runs terminate. The commonly used method for connecting the KSU to the cable homeruns that are linked to the telephone outlets throughout a home is to terminate the cable runs into a 66-type punchdown block that bridges the cable runs to patch cords (also called pigtails) to the KSU using 25- or 50-pin Telco-type connectors (see Figure 27-14).

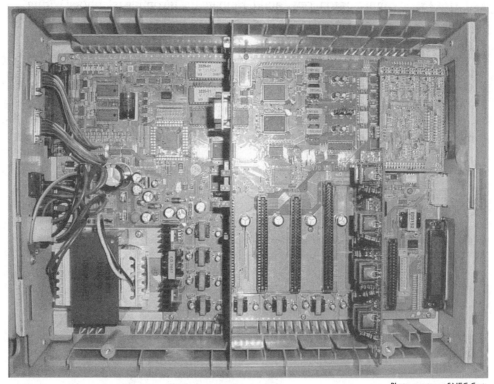

Photo courtesy of NEC Corp.

Figure 27-13　A KSU for a residential telephone system

Figure 27-14
A 25-pin Telco connector is used to connect the internal phone wiring to a KSU.

The KSU should also be located fairly close to the connection for the Telco lines entering the home. In most cases, KSUs have RJ-11 jacks to connect to as many as eight incoming phone lines. The KSU should have a clean AC power source, preferably with a surge suppressor installed inline between the KSU's power supply and the AC outlet.

Programming

In most cases, a KSU telephone system is preprogrammed for most of its basic functions for a certain number of stations. However, some adjustments may be required to set the clock, program speed dials, or add additional phones or features. Depending on the changes required, the programming manuals for the system should detail the process used to affect these changes. Some KSUs can be programmed through a system phone, or they provide an interface for connecting to a computer system or a terminal; in this case, changes are entered through software on the KSU. In other cases, some form of user interface, such as a liquid crystal display (LCD) and a keyboard, may be included on the KSU itself.

Planning for KSU Programming

The homeowners decide which features should be configured on the KSU system. Prior to beginning any programming changes or station configuration, you should summarize the system's features on a worksheet that details the number of telephones to be installed and the features available to each telephone. Table 27-2 shows a portion of a sample worksheet that could be used to record the KSU system's features the homeowners desire.

Unit	Feature	Yes	Comments
Table 27-2 A KSU Features Worksheet Example			
Master Unit (KSU)			
	Auto-attendant		
	Automatic Call Distributor (ACD)		
	Caller ID		
	Direct Inward Dialing (DID)		
	Hunt group (rollover)		
	Unified messaging		
Station 1			
	Do Not Disturb (DND)		
	Intercom		
	One-Number dialing (speed-dialing)		
	Speakerphone		
Station 2			
	Do Not Disturb (DND)		

Programming Key Sets

If proprietary key sets (telephones) are installed along with the KSU, you will likely need to do some programming to set up each key set. In these instances, do this programming on each key set, following the procedures outlined in the system documentation.

If standard telephones are to be connected to the KSU, you may need to do some programming on the KSU unit as well as through the telephone, using the specialized buttons and the standard touch-tone buttons of the telephone.

Labeling Key Sets

KSU systems that require proprietary key sets (telephones) typically have a preprinted faceplate with labeling for the features supported by the system. On standard telephones connected to a KSU, some labeling will be required to mark the keys that activate certain functions. If multiple key presses are required to activate or deactivate a feature, a phone card or an instruction sheet should be made up for each station. Labeling the functions on the telephone or key set helps minimize the training required for the homeowner and extend its effectiveness.

Installing an Intercom

An intercom can provide a home's occupants with the convenience of being able to speak to each another without having to share the same space or shout at each other. Intercom systems are fairly common in new upscale homes and are a feature homeowners generally like.

There are three basic types of intercom systems:

- **Independent intercoms** These types of intercom systems are not interconnected into another system, although they may use existing wiring in a home to communicate. Independent intercoms can be installed using three forms of communications:

- **HomePNA intercoms**   These types of independent intercoms communicate through a home's existing telephone wires and the users speak through standard telephone handsets. The intercom action is started by pressing a certain sequence of keys or the number of a special station number on a standard telephone. These systems, like the doorway system shown in Figure 27-15, allow a person arriving at a home's doorway to place a telephone call into the home and ring the phones with a unique ring. This provides both security and convenience to homeowners.

- **PLC intercoms**   These types of intercoms communicate over AC electrical lines and operate in a similar fashion to HomePNA intercoms. However, PLC intercoms can cause potential problems with other PLC systems, such as lighting controls and PLC-based computer networks. For this reason, this type of intercom system isn't recommended if other PLC systems are in use.

- **Wireless intercoms**   Wireless independent intercom systems are essentially room-to-room systems, such as baby monitors and tabletop or wall-mounted units. These units use ultra high frequency (UHF) or very high frequency (VHF) radio frequency (RF) signaling and work on the same principles as a walkie-talkie. Some wireless intercoms also offer the capability to encrypt transmission to prevent exterior interception. Keep in mind that many intercoms advertised as "wireless" are, in fact, PLC systems.

- **Stand-alone intercoms**   Stand-alone intercoms are self-contained systems that communicate over their own dedicated wiring. These types of systems have been, and still are, somewhat popular in homes. In addition to allowing a home's occupants to communicate room-to-room, they also include doorway units and master unit options that can include a radio receiver and a tape or a CD player that plays music throughout the intercom system stations. Figure 27-16 shows a fully featured stand-alone intercom master unit.

Figure 27-15

A doorway
telephone
intercom unit

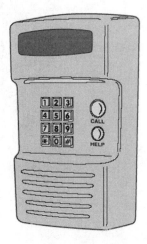

Figure 27-16
A stand-alone
intercom master
unit with a CD
player

*Photo courtesy
of Broan-Nutone.*

 NOTE Some homeowners prefer to use standard telephones throughout their home and install a stand-alone intercom system.

- **Telephone-based intercoms** Using the existing or standard telephone wiring and standard phones in a home, a doorbell intercom unit, like the one shown in Figure 27-17, can be installed to enable the doorbell unit to ring a unique ring throughout the home on standard telephones and provide intercom service between the door and the telephones.

Figure 27-17
A door intercom
that connects
into a home's
telephone system

*Photo courtesy
of LocalPlex.*

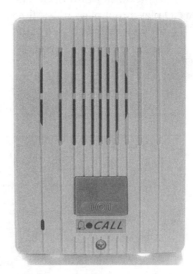

Chapter Review

The design process for residential telephone systems includes telecommunication wiring schemes, outlet boxes, wire termination, jacks, punchdown blocks, patch panels, wire identification and labeling, and telephone key sets. Telephone wiring is installed using either series wiring or star/home run wiring, but star/home run wiring is preferred.

The telephone wiring inside a home is the responsibility of the homeowner. It is important to use only category verified wiring that meets or exceeds industry, fire, electrical, and materials specifications and standards, and local building codes. Current industry standards specify a minimum of UTP Cat 3 wiring. However, most new construction installs Cat 5e wiring.

There are four basic elements to a home telephone system: structured wiring, outlet jacks, punchdown or distribution blocks, and phone devices. Wiring installed by the telephone company can include 25-pair cable, satin cord, or four-conductor station wire.

Structured wiring support for a telephone system must address standard phone outlet wiring, structured wiring cable, punchdown/distribution blocks, and connections to the demarc.

Modular jacks are common in most existing homes. This type of jack is surface mounted and provides connection for up to two communication lines on a single jack. Flush-mounted wall outlet jacks are more common in newer homes.

A KSU-based telephone system has its own separate controller that provides many of the same Telco subscriber services to the telephones in the home. The features provided by a residential KSU system include the capability to connect to standard telephones, voice-messaging (voicemail), station-to-station intercom support, auto-attendant, music-on-hold, caller ID, and, in many cases, support for a door intercom. A KSU telephone system is preprogrammed with its basic functions. To add additional phones or features, some adjustments may be required to the KSU's programming. Prior to beginning any programming or station configuration changes, you should summarize the system's features on a worksheet that documents the number of telephones to be installed and the features available to each telephone. A worksheet should be used to record the KSU system's features desired by the homeowners.

There are three basic types of intercom systems: independent intercoms, stand-alone, and telephone-based intercoms. The most common types of independent intercoms are: HomePNA intercoms, PLC intercoms, and wireless intercoms. Stand-alone intercoms are self-contained systems that communicate over dedicated wiring. Telephone-based intercoms allow for intercom service between the doorbell and the house telephones.

Questions

1. Under a structured wiring approach, telephone systems should be installed using what wiring scheme?

   A. Series

   B. Bus

    C. Ring

    D. Star

2. What device is placed at the center of the structured wiring for a telephone system?

    A. RJ-11 outlet

    B. Distribution panel

    C. Demarc

    D. Telephone key set

3. Virtually all household wiring standards require the use of what type of wiring?

    A. Cat 3

    B. UL Category verified

    C. Riser

    D. Plenum

4. A type of telephone system that is implemented on a central control unit that supports standard telephones or proprietary phones is a/an:

    A. Intercom

    B. KSU

    C. Telco

    D. Wireless

5. Which of the following is not a type of intercom system?

    A. Stand-alone

    B. Independent

    C. Telephone-based

    D. KSU

6. Which of the following should be done before making any programming changes to a KSU system? (There may be more than one answer.)

    A. Complete features worksheet

    B. Interview homeowners

    C. Program telephone

    D. Remove default programming

7. What cable is typically used to connect a telephone key set to a wall outlet?

    A. Station wire

    B. Coaxial cable

C. Satin cord

D. Zip wire

8. Which of the following is not a type of outlet jack commonly associated with telephone connections?

A. F-type

B. Modular

C. Face plate

D. Inline

9. What do the terms Tip and Ring refer to?

A. Incoming signal and bell

B. Positive and negative

C. Ring and busy tones

D. Dial and busy tones

10. How many phone lines can be supported by a single run of Cat 3 or Cat 5 cable?

A. Two

B. Three

C. Four

D. Six

Answers

1. **D.** Structured wiring is installed using a star topology. The other choices listed can be used for data networks, but aren't recommended for residential wiring.

2. **B.** The other choices listed should be configured as satellites from the distribution panel.

3. **B.** Category verified cable has been tested and certified to meet residential cable standards. The other choices listed represent residential cable types or characteristics.

4. **B.** A KSU is a central controller device that supports the functions of the telephone units connected to it.

5. **D.** A KSU is a type of telephone system. The other choices are all types of intercoms.

6. **A and B.** Prior to making any programming changes to a KSU, you should interview the homeowners and record their desires on a KSU system worksheet that includes the features of the master unit and each of the telephones.

7. **C.** This flexible pre-configured wire is the common standard for outlet-to-station connections. Station wire, if used, is used for horizontal cabling; coaxial cable is rarely used in voice applications (although it could be); and zip wire is absolutely not voice system wiring.

8. **A.** F-type connectors are associated with coaxial cabling. Inline, though not mentioned in the chapter, is used to connect two RJ-11 connectors together.

9. **B.** At one time, these terms may have had other purposes, but today they represent only positive and negative voltage.

10. **C.** A four-pair UTP cable is able to support as many as four phone lines.

Troubleshooting a Home Communication System

In this chapter, you will learn about:
- Common voice communication system problems
- Troubleshooting telephone system problems
- Communication system troubleshooting tools
- Testing communications cabling

Of all of the various systems in a home, the one that people can't seem to live without is the telephone system. So when problems develop, even minor problems can seem like an emergency. Your ability to diagnose, troubleshoot, isolate, and resolve a problem on a home's communication system becomes extremely important to restoring the home's ability to communicate with the outside world.

This chapter is focused on identifying the problems common to home communication systems and the methods and tools used to resolve these problems quickly and efficiently. The good news is that in a structured wiring environment, many of the processes used are the same used to troubleshoot wiring and connection problems for most of the other systems in a home. As a home technology integration professional, you must know which troubleshooting process is used to identify and isolate each type of problem.

Wiring Issues

The telephone company's responsibility for problems on a home communication system ends at the demarcation point or network interface device (NID), which is where the telephone company's lines terminate at the home. Beyond the NID, the wiring that provides telephone service throughout a home is considered to be customer premise inside wiring (CPIW) by the phone company. The homeowner is responsible for any problems that occur with the CPIW, unless the homeowner purchases wire maintenance services from the telephone company and even then there are limits to what the telephone company will service.

NID Wiring

Basic telephone wiring is a four-wire cable that actually consists of two pairs of wire. As shown in Figure 28-1, the wires in the incoming telephone wiring connected into the NID are green, red, black, and yellow. The green and red wires are treated as one pair and the black and yellow wires are treated as another pair. Each pair of wires carries the tip and ring signals used by a telephone to connect and communicate. As shown (Figure 28-1), the green wire is the tip wire in pair one and the black wire is the tip wire in pair two. The red and yellow wires provide the ring link in each pair, respectively.

The NID is usually located on an outside wall of the house. At the NID (see Figure 28-2), each incoming line uses one of the two pairs in the telephone cable and if only a single line is entering the home, by telephone company standards, the red and green wires are connected to the point where the CPIW attaches to the NID. If a second line is provided, then the yellow and black wires are also connected. However, when connecting a second line, the black wire is treated as if it were green and the yellow wire as if it were red. If more than two lines are entering the home, the incoming wiring is likely to be Cat 3 cable with its four wire pairs. See Table 28-1 for color-coding of wiring.

One wiring problem you might run into inside the NID is that in situations where the red or the green wires have become damaged, the black and yellow wires may have been used to replace them instead of installing a new run of quad wire back to the distribution point. If you encounter this, and a second line is being installed, the phone company will need to replace their service line with a good four-wire cable.

Cat 5 and the NID

When Cat 5 wiring is connected to an NID, there are no red, green, yellow, and black wires to use, only blue, orange, green, and brown. If one or more lines in a home are having connection problems, the problem may be wiring inconsistencies at the NID.

Each of the four wire pairs in a Cat 5 cable can be used to replace the green and red (tip and ring) wires required for the connection. Table 28-1 lists the wire color replacement convention when using Cat 5 in place of quad wire. As you can see, the white striped wire in each pair replaces the "green" wire (tip) in the telephone convention and the solid color wire in the pair replaces the "red" wire (ring).

 NOTE A good way to remember the order that the Cat 5 colors should be used for multiple telephone lines is to remember that the colors go from sky to earth: blue sky, then orange sunset, green trees, and brown dirt.

Figure 28-1
The wires in
a four-strand
telephone wire
(quad wire)

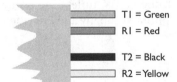

T1 = Green
R1 = Red
T2 = Black
R2 = Yellow

Figure 28-2
In the NID, each incoming telephone line is connected separately.

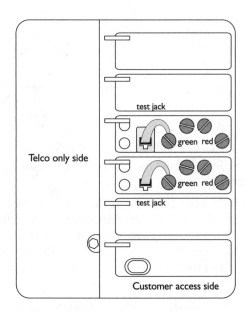

The order and assignment of the Cat 5 wire pairs listed in Table 28-1 should be used throughout the home communications system. It is very important to use the same wiring scheme throughout a system to ensure conformity and consistency, since this can eliminate at least one potential problem when you have to troubleshoot the system.

Troubleshooting the NID

If a telephone line is dead on all inside telephones as well as at the structured wiring distribution panel, the problem could very well be with the incoming telephone line. To troubleshoot the connections in the NID, follow these steps:

1. Locate the test jack (Figure 28-3) for the incoming line in question inside the NID.

2. Ensure the RJ-11 plug connected to the green wire's setscrew is inserted into the jack securely.

PART VI

Table 28-1
Quad Wire to Cat 5 Conversion Conventions

Cat 5 Wire Color	Quad Wire Color	Function
White-Blue	Green	Line 1 Tip
Blue	Red	Line 1 Ring
White-Orange	Black	Line 2 Tip
Orange	Yellow	Line 2 Ring
White-Green	N/A	Line 3 Tip
Green	N/A	Line 3 Ring
White-Brown	N/A	Line 4 Tip
Brown	N/A	Line 4 Ring

Figure 28-3
Each incoming telephone line connection in the NID has a test jack.

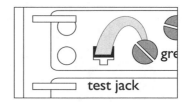

3. You should remove and reinsert the plug into the test jack and recheck the problem telephone line to see if the problem wasn't just a problem with the connection at the test jack.

4. If the problem persists, remove the plug and connect a good telephone handset directly into the test jack. Removing the plug disconnects that line from the CPIW. When you insert a plug connected to the handset, the line is now connected directly to the telephone company's distribution system. If the line is still dead (no dial tone) then the problem is on the telephone company's lines and they should be notified of the problem.

5. However, if plugging directly into the test jack yields a dial tone, try calling a working telephone number to make sure there are no other problems on the telephone line.

6. If the line is working normally, then the problem is with the CPIW and you need to troubleshoot the structured wiring connected to the communications system (more on this later in the chapter).

Inside Wiring Issues

If a telephone line is working at the NID, but not inside the home, the problem is most likely a wiring problem somewhere between the NID and the structured wiring panel or the telephone outlets (assuming you've already checked the handset and the telephone patch cord connecting it to the outlet).

The best way to troubleshoot exactly where the problem may be is to connect a handset to each connection point along the cable path. When you find the point where there is no dial tone on the phone, you can then begin to determine why that link is not working. Some common problems on the faulty link to look for are

- **Loose setscrew**   Check any terminal strips or setscrew connections to ensure they are tightened down. You should check the NID for this condition as well.

- **Reversed wires**   The wires in a wire pair may be reversed or two pairs may be reversed or a split pair condition may exist.

- **Faulty termination**   Verify that the plug and jacks are securely attached to the cable. Check the wire pinout used in an RJ-11 or RJ-45 jack and plug. Replace the termination with the correct pinout, if needed.

- **Wire damage**   If some telephone jacks have phone service but others don't, the problem may be a damaged cable where only one or two wire pairs are shorting to each other because the cable has been cut or pierced. To verify this condition, you should run length, TDR, and wire map tests (discussed later in the chapter).

Interference and Noise

If a homeowner is complaining about hum, static, or that conversations on one of a home's telephone lines can be heard on another, the issue is likely in the wiring somewhere.

Here are some common wire issues that can create noise on a telephone line:

- If the outer jacket of a cable is cut and even a small hole is opened, static or crackling may be heard on the phone lines attached to that cable. If even a small amount of moisture enters the cable, it can create a low-level short between two or more pairs, which may be heard on the line as static, snapping, or crackling.

- If there are any loose or poorly done splices (heaven forbid!), taps, or loose connections between the distribution panel and an outlet, users may hear static, buzzing, or a hum on the line. If there are any splices or taps in the line, they should be removed and any loose connections repaired or replaced.

- If the users complain of a loud hum on a line, the problem is likely a connection made to a grounded line. The connection should be redone avoiding the ground. You will need to retrace the wiring back to the main electrical panel to identify the circuits connected to the main's ground then reconnect the telephone wiring to avoid a connection to these circuits.

- If the outlet has a line splitter installed and a fax machine, answering machine, or even another telephone is sharing the line, it can add noise to the line when they are in use. If the other equipment has permanent needs, additional lines should be installed to service them.

- The telephone patch cords that come with telephone sets are also called line cords, but they aren't always the best quality. A faulty or poor quality line cord can create noise on the line at the handset.

- EMI and RFI can be a problem for communication systems that are installed on UTP. If all other troubleshooting tests fail to identify the source of noise on a line, verify the placement of the UTP cable and ensure that it is installed per the EIA/TIA guidelines regarding other electrical equipment and AC power lines.

Connector Issues

When a second phone line is added to an existing telephone system, the outlet jacks and wiring blocks are commonly overlooked. If the original installation didn't provide wiring blocks and jacks that were pre-wired for two or more lines, the wiring connecting the second line to the outlet is virtually dead-ended. Whenever installing new wiring, be sure to terminate all wires and connections.

If a phone line isn't working for only a single outlet or handset, check the termination of the home-run cable at the wiring block or structured wiring panel and into the jack. An RJ-11 plug will connect into an RJ-45 jack. So, verify that the RJ-45 jack has been terminated for a telephone connection and not a data network connection. Use Table 28-1 from earlier in the chapter and the information in Chapter 13 to differentiate these connections.

HomePNA Issues

If a Home Phoneline Networking Alliance (HomePNA) networking system is installed on telephone circuits that are still in use for voice communications, problems with line noise on the circuit can greatly affect the performance of both the data network and the telephone system.

In addition to correcting the interference and noise issues listed earlier in the chapter, you may also need to install a low-pass filter between the computers and their HomePNA connections.

Cable Testing

The cable conditions that can impact the performance of a home communications system are the same as those that can affect all other systems connected to the structured wiring system.

Common Wire Faults

The more common cable faults that can affect the telephone system are

- **Crossed pair** This condition occurs when a wire pair is connected to different pins on each end of a cable run. For example, if wire pair 2 is connected to pins 4 and 5 on one end of the cable and pins 7 and 8 on the other end.

- **Improper impedance** Although a connector terminating a Cat 5 cable appears to be attached correctly, the connector may not measure at 100 ohms, which is the normal impedance for Cat 5 cable. If the connector and the cable have different impedance, signal reflections can occur. Another problem that can affect the impedance of a cable is a very sharp bend or kink in the cable causing the cable to not test out at 100 ohms.

- **Open circuit** This condition is caused when a cable pair doesn't have continuity between the ends of a cable. This is the most common problem with copper cabling.

- **Reversed pair** This condition occurs when the tip and ring wires of a telephone line are reversed at the termination of one end of the cable. For example, if one of the wires in pair 2 is connected to pin 1 on one end of the cable and pin 2 on the other end, and the other wire in the wire pair is connected between pins 2 on one end and pin 1 on the other end, the telephone signals will be transmitted or received improperly.

- **Short circuit** If two of more conductors in a cable are in contact (metal to metal), it creates a short circuit, which is like a roadblock for signals traveling on the cable pairs affected.

Working Safe

A telephone circuit carries electrical currents in various voltages that are also present in any connectors and terminal screws. If the phone line you are working on is connected through to the NID and a call comes in on that line, you could get an electrical shock.

Here are some tips for working safely on a telephone circuit:

- Ensure that the cable you are working on is not connected directly or indirectly to the NID. If you cannot disconnect the cable from the NID, set the handset portion of the telephone so it is not in its cradle, which busies out the phone.

- Use screwdrivers that have insulated handles

- Don't touch bare conductor wires or screw terminals with your hands or body

- I hope this one is obvious, but don't work on a telephone circuit during a lightning storm.

Wire Testing Tools

When testing UTP cabling used for a communications system, the tools used are essentially the same used for testing UTP in a data network (see Chapter 14). The following list provides an overview of the testing tools most often used to troubleshoot the cables in a communications system:

- **Cable certification testers**   This tool can be used to verify that a cable meets the performance standards specified in TIA/EIA TSB-67, the test standard for network cable. The tests performed by a certification tester are impedance, length, attenuation, wire map, and near-end crosstalk (NEXT).

- **Multimeter**   Whether analog or digital, a multimeter measures voltage, current (amps), and resistance (ohms) on copper wiring. If used with a shorting device, a multimeter can also test for continuity. Performing an ohms test with a multimeter is one way to identify an open circuit on a cable.

- **Telephone test set**   This tool is used to simulate the functions of a telephone system and to perform circuit diagnostics and perform standard telephone cable testing.

- **Time Domain Reflectometry (TDR) testers**   A TDR test is performed to identify any problems or defects on a cable and its termination, but TDR tests are most commonly used to measure cable length or pinpoint the location of a problem on a cable.

- **Wire map tester**   This tool, also called a pair scanner, is used to test for opens, shorts, crossed pairs, split pairs, and reversed pairs on a UTP cable.

 CROSS-REFERENCE   Chapters 9 and 14 cover structured wiring and data network cable testing in more detail.

Chapter Review

The telephone company's responsibility for problems on a home communication system ends at the demarcation point or network interface device (NID) of a home. Beyond the NID, the telephone wiring is customer premise inside wiring (CPIW), and is the responsibility of the homeowner.

Basic telephone wiring is a four-wire cable (also called quad wire) that has green, red, black, and yellow wire. The green and red wires are treated as one pair and the black and yellow wires are treated as another pair. Each pair of wires carries the tip and ring signals used by a telephone to connect and communicate. The four wire pairs of a Cat 5 cable can be used for the tip and ring wires of the telephone connection.

If a telephone line is dead on all inside telephones as well as at the structured wiring distribution panel, the problem could very well be with the incoming telephone line. If a telephone line is working at the NID, but not inside the home, the problem is most likely a wiring problem somewhere between the NID and the structured wiring panel and the telephone outlets. Some common problems on the faulty link you may want to look for include: loose setscrew, reversed wires, faulty termination, and wire damage. Many common wire faults can create noise on a telephone line.

The common cable faults that can affect the telephone system include: crossed pair, improper impedance, open circuit, reversed pair, and short circuit.

The testing tools that should be used to troubleshoot the cabling of a communications system include: cable certification tester, multimeter, telephone test set, TDR tester, and wire map tester.

Questions

1. At what point do the telephone company's responsibilities end for the telephone wiring of a home?

   A. Distribution panel

   B. Network interface device

   C. Telephone handset

   D. Telephone outlet

2. What are the two functions associated with the wires of a telephone circuit?

   A. Dial tone

   B. Ring

   C. Caller ID

   D. Tip

3. If Cat 5 wiring is used to distribute telephone service throughout a home, what is the basic color of the wire pair used to replace the wires used for Line 1?

   A. Blue

   B. Orange

   C. Green

   D. Brown

4. After determining that a telephone line is dead on all circuits inside a home, what should be checked to determine if there is a problem with the incoming telephone line?

   A. Distribution panel

   B. NID

   C. Inside cable

   D. None of the above; only the telephone company can make this determination.

5. Which of the following would be the prime suspect when no interior handsets are able to get a dial tone?

   A. Damaged wiring

   B. Faulty termination

   C. Loose test jack or connection in the NID

   D. Reversed wires

6. Which of the following can be a cause of static or other noise on a telephone line?

   A. Cat 5 cabling

   B. Spliced cabling

   C. RJ-45 connectors

   D. Low-pass filters

7. What is the condition created when the conductors of a wire pair are connected to different pins of a terminator at each end of a cable?

   A. Crossed pair

   B. Open circuit

   C. Reversed pair

   D. Short circuit

8. Cat 5 cabling should have 100 ohms of impedance. When used in a communications system, how much impedance should the terminations of a Cat 5 cable have?

   A. 50 ohms

   B. 75 ohms

   C. 100 ohms

   D. 150 ohms

9. What testing device is most commonly used to measure voltage, current, and resistance?

   A. Cable certification tester

   B. Multimeter

   C. TDR

   D. Wire map

10. Which testing device is commonly used to test for opens, shorts, crossed pairs, split pairs, and reversed pairs on a UTP cable?

   A. Cable certification tester

   B. Multimeter

   C. TDR

   D. Wire map

Answers

1. **B.** This device is also called the demarcation point, or demarc for short. The other devices listed are all interior devices, which are the responsibility of the homeowner.

2. **B and D.** These functions are used to complete the circuit on a telephone line.

3. **A.** The order of the wires used for Lines 1 through 4 of a telephone system is blue, orange, green, and brown.

4. **B.** The incoming line can be checked using the test jack inside the NID.

5. **C.** If the plug in the test jack isn't properly seated or wires aren't secure on the connection terminals, the line may be interrupted before it can enter the home.

6. **B.** In a structured wiring system, there are no spliced wires, but if in an existing system, the wire is spliced or tapped, a bad connection can cause noise on the line.

7. **A.** The signals on the telephone line would not be properly received or transmitted.

8. **C.** The impedance must match on the cable and its terminations.

9. **B.** The other devices listed are used for higher-level and more complicated testing procedures.

10. **D.** A wire map tester is used to test wire pairs on category UTP cable.

PART VII

HVAC and Water Management

HVAC Controls

29

In this chapter, you will learn about:

- HVAC control equipment
- Installing HVAC controls
- Maintaining and troubleshooting HVAC controls

Heating, Ventilation, Air Conditioning (HVAC) includes the equipment, ducting, and vents that either collectively or separately provide heat, ventilation, or cooling to a home. As indicated by its name, an HVAC system provides three basic environmental services: heating, cooling, and air handling, ventilation, and air quality. Home automation can extend to include controlling a home's HVAC system. This includes automating the function of the thermostat either on a whole-house or zone basis.

HVAC systems with thermostat control use standardized electrical signals to communicate with external thermostats. It's that part of HVAC systems this chapter addresses.

Residential HVAC

There are several types of heating and air conditioning systems found in homes, but the primary types are forced air, baseboard and convection, hydronic, and evaporative cooling systems.

Forced Air Systems

Forced air systems use a circulating blower to move heated or cooled air into the rooms of a house (see Figure 29-1). There are two very general types of forced air systems: constant air volume (CAV) and variable air volume (VAV).

CAV Systems

CAV systems supply a constant flow of air to the whole house. The central terminal-reheat unit heats or cools its flow of air to heat or cool the coldest or warmest zone in the house. Each zone, an area of a house equipped with a zone terminal-reheat unit and controlled by a zone thermostat, then adjusts the temperature of the central forced airflow to meet its specific heating or cooling needs. These types of CAV systems are also referred to as single-duct systems, and are the most common type of HVAC found in existing homes.

Figure 29-1
A forced air
system circulates
heated or cooled
air to change
a room's
temperature.

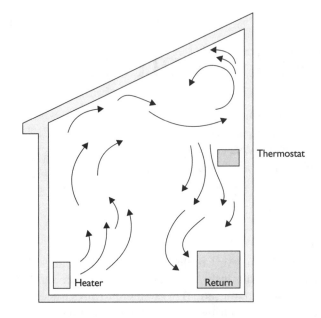

Thermostat

Heater

Return

 NOTE A terminal-reheat unit maintains a comfortable temperature in a zone by reheating or cooling the airflow to the temperature set on a zone thermostat.

In most cases, the airflow into the zone has been partially cooled or heated to a general setting by the central air-handling device. Dual-duct CAV systems supply both cool and warm air, each in its own ducting, to a mixing chamber in each zone. The zone thermostat controls the temperature of the air leaving the mixing chamber by managing the amount of warm and cold air allowed to enter the mixing chamber. This type of CAV system eliminates the need for terminal-reheat units in each zone.

VAV Systems

VAV systems supply air that is heated or cooled to a constant temperature to each HVAC zone. Each VAV zone is controlled by a thermostat that uses a damper to regulate the temperature in each room by controlling the amount of cool or warm air allowed to flow into the zone. Typically, the damper is not closed all the way, which allows some fresh airflow into each zone.

VAV systems offer a number of advantages over CAV systems, including that they cost less to purchase and install, their operating costs are typically lower, and because only those areas requiring heating or cooling receive air, they are more energy-efficient than CAV systems. However, on the downside, VAV systems don't provide much variability and flexibility when heating or cooling selected zones in a house, because there is only a single air supply and no local zone equipment.

VAV systems also do very little to balance both ventilation and temperature control, and because they generally reduce the volume of heated or cooled air flowing into any particular zone, air quality can be compromised.

Baseboard and Convection Systems

Baseboard devices installed along the baseboards of a wall, typically under a window, can provide heat by either using an internal electric heating element or the flow of air or water to a baseboard or freestanding register from a central gas or oil-fired furnace.

These units can be controlled using several methods. The most common are

- An on/off switch on the unit
- A thermostat controlling one or more local units
- A thermostat controlling the central heating device

Figure 29-2 shows an example of an electric baseboard heating unit.

Although some baseboard, and most in-wall heating, units include air blowers, most baseboard units use convection to heat a room. Convection heating uses the natural phenomenon of heated air rising: when the rising heated air comes into contact with the cooler temperatures of the window surface, the heat is forced outward from the window into the room.

Convection system electric baseboard units or water-flow registers are placed on the floor against the bottom edge of a wall centered under a window in the outside wall of a room. Most convection devices use either an internal electric heating element or a gas-flame heating chamber to heat a room until the room air temperature matches that of an in-room thermostat or a thermostat built into the convection unit itself.

Another type of local heating device is an in-wall electric heating unit, like the one shown in Figure 29-3. These units are either self-contained devices that include an electric heating element, a blower, and a built-in thermostat, or are gas-fired heating chambers that reheat the airflow from a central heating system.

Those electric baseboard or heating chamber devices that are locally controlled using an in-room or in-zone on/off switch can be connected into a home control system and centrally controlled using relay switches. In those units that are controlled using a room

Figure 29-2

An electric baseboard heating unit

Photo courtesy of Cadet Manufacturing.

Figure 29-3
An in-wall
electric
heating unit

*Photo courtesy of
Cadet Manufacturing.*

thermostat, the thermostat is typically limited to turning the unit on or off according to its temperature settings. The units that are connected to a centralized control system through a thermostat interface can be controlled remotely.

Hydronic Systems

The term hydronic has recently replaced the term hot water when describing heating systems that use boiler-heated water to provide convection and radiant heating in rooms, floors, ceilings, and even walkways, patios, and driveways.

Hydronic baseboard heating is commonly found in houses built over the past 30 years or so, especially in those areas with colder winters. Well-known for its efficiency and low-operating cost, hot-water heating is also making a comeback largely because of improved and more efficient oil- and gas-fired boiler systems.

Hydronic Baseboard Heating

Hydronic heat uses hot water that is heated in a boiler or some form of a water heater to transfer heat into a room or zone. For room hydronic systems, hot water is circulated through heating elements that have long, thin aluminum-finned radiators; these radiators have largely replaced the tall cast-iron radiators of the past.

The length of the radiator in a particular room is determined by how quickly heat dissipates from a room and the amount of heat required to maintain a comfortable range in that room. The room radiators are incorporated into a continuous loop of copper pipe that loops from room to room. Like other convection heating systems, hydronic baseboard units are placed beneath windows.

Hydronic systems offer several advantages: they are quiet, provide constant warmth, and are fuel-efficient. However, controlling individual zones requires a separate piping and pumping system for each zone. Even with a separate hydronic system for each zone, hydronic systems are either on or off.

In hydronic systems, a boiler heats the water, which circulates through the piping throughout a zone or the entire house. A separate pipe returns the cooling water back to the boiler or water heater. The water is circulated through the system by a circulating pump.

Hydronic Radiant Heating

Another form of hydronic heating gaining in popularity is radiant heating that is embedded or installed inside room floors, patios, driveways, walkways, and other exterior areas where the heat can be used to melt snow or ice.

To install radiant floor heating, the hydronic piping system is either attached to the underside of a floor or embedded in a concrete slab, as illustrated in Figure 29-4. Hot water or some other type of liquid running through the piping heats the flooring or concrete surface, providing warm floors and clear and frost-free exterior passageways.

Radiant heating can be zoned to separate rooms or hallways. Using multiple boilers provides more specific settings and control. How the boilers are fueled can vary from natural gas, to fuel oil, to electricity, and even to solar energy to either directly or indirectly heat the water.

Radiant floor heating takes a long time to heat up so it is not a likely candidate for automated control by temperature. A simple on/off remote control makes sense in situations where the home is a vacation home and not always occupied. One benefit to radiant floor heating is it removes the decorative limitations of radiators, vents, outlets, and return vents of other types of room heating.

Figure 29-4
Radiant heating coils installed in a home's flooring

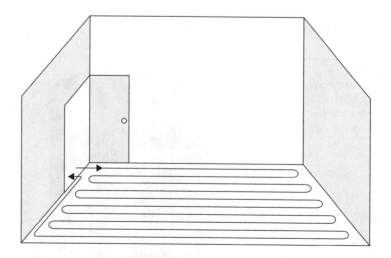

Central Heating Units

Heating systems are typically defined by their central units, which are typically referred to as furnaces. The common central heating units are

- **Electric furnace**   Inside an electric furnace are resistance wires that heat up when a current passes through them. A circulating fan passes cooler air from inside the house over the heated wires to heat the air and return it into the rooms of the house. Because no exhaust gases are produced, electric heating systems don't require venting or chimneys.

- **Electric heat pump**   Many people confuse a heat pump, shown in Figure 29-5, with an air conditioning system because both are exterior devices and their appearances are very similar. Heat pumps use a specific piping system to extract heat from outdoor air, even at very cold temperatures. The heat is then transferred to a coil located inside the house. A blower then blows air over the coil, which warms the air before it is circulated into the heating zones.

- **Gas furnace**   This type of heating unit is actually a heat exchanger that transfers heat into a home. Natural or propane gas is mixed with air brought in from outside and fired inside a heat exchanger. The exhaust gases travel through the heat exchanger and exit the home through a vent pipe or chimney. A fan circulates cooler air from inside the home over the heat exchanger. The heated air is then circulated through the home's ductwork into the rooms. Some newer gas furnace models have multiple heat exchangers that improve the heat exchange efficiency and heat the circulating air faster.

- **Oil furnace**   The operating principle of an oil furnace is very much like that of a gas furnace. The obvious difference is that fuel oil is used instead of gas vapor. Because the oil is liquid, it must first be converted into a vapor-like mist and mixed with air before it can be burned.

Figure 29-5
An electric heat pump unit is placed outside a home.

Evaporative Cooling

- An older, but still effective, cooling system is evaporative cooling, which is also called swamp cooling by some HVAC people. Evaporative cooling works on the two principles of water evaporation and the relative humidity of the air. The first principle is that when moisture is added to air that has less than 100-percent relative humidity, the temperature of the air is lowered. The second principle is that the lower the relative humidity of the air, the greater the temperature drop will be when moisture is added to the air.

- In the western United States and other dry-climate areas around the world, evaporative cooling can provide an energy-efficient alternative; it uses one-fourth less energy than compressor-based air conditioning systems.

There are three basic types of evaporative cooling systems:

- **Direct evaporative cooling** Direct evaporative cooling devices are commonly referred to as swamp coolers because they provide the same cooling effect as a breeze blowing across a swamp, lake, or another body of water. This type of evaporative cooling simply adds moisture to a moving airflow to increase its humidity and thereby lower the temperature of the airflow. However, direct evaporative cooling requires a moving air source with air that is drier than the space being cooled. Commonly, outside air is forced through a constantly wet fiber or corrugated pad by an inner air turbine that also pushes the moistened air into a space displacing drier indoor air. To ensure that the pad stays wet, a recirculating pump pours more water onto the pad than it can evaporate. The excess water flows into a sump to be recirculated. The system replaces any water that evaporates using an automatic valve to refill the sump to a preset depth. Direct evaporative cooling systems are either on or off systems that can be controlled directly or by using a relay switch on a central home system controller.

- **Indirect evaporative cooling** Indirect evaporative cooling systems are commonly used in larger commercial applications, but there is no reason this type of system can't be installed on a large home. Like a direct evaporative system, indirect systems use water evaporation to cool air. However, an indirect system does not increase the humidity of the inside air. Rather, it separates the wet side of the process from the dry air used to cool a space. A direct evaporative process is used to cool air or water on one side of a heat-exchanging surface, such as plastic plates or tubes. The heat exchanger transfers the cooling to an air stream that is used to cool a space. Indirect evaporative cooling systems are used either as complete cooling systems or to supplement a compressor-based air conditioning system. These systems are essentially on/off systems and, as a result, can be controlled directly or by using a relay switch on a home system controller.

- **Two-stage evaporative cooling** This type of evaporative cooling system uses both direct and indirect evaporative cooling to cool an airflow. In effect, the air flowing into the two-stage unit is cooled using the direct evaporative method.

The cooled air is then passed through an indirect cooling system before flowing into a space.

HVAC Controls

The primary control in a HVAC system is a room thermostat. In some installations, a house may have only a single thermostat for the entire house, but in most new installations, each room or zone of a house will have a separate thermostat.

Thermostats

When selecting a thermostat for a home HVAC system, the first rule is that it must be compatible with the HVAC system. That may sound obvious, but not all thermostats are compatible with all systems.

The more common types of thermostats are

- **220V baseboard thermostat**   This type of thermostat is different than nearly all other types because it has to be mounted to an in-wall high-voltage (220V) outlet box. It is not commonly installed in new homes and is typically being replaced.

- **Digital thermostats**   Also known as electronic thermostats, this type of thermostat features a digital temperature and set point (the point at which the HVAC system is activated) display. At the low-end price range, digital thermostats are typically mechanical thermostats with a digital display. A digital thermostat draws its operating power (for the display) from one or more batteries or from the 24V HVAC line. Other common features are the auto-changeover switch in the HVAC system between heating and cooling, capability to work with heat pump systems, and capability to be wired to an external control device, such as a motion sensor, timer, or computer-based control system.

- **Mechanical thermostat**   Mechanical thermostats are available for heating-only control as well as heating and cooling control. Some models include setback timers, but they typically don't include an auto-changeover feature. In general, mechanical thermostats are not compatible with heat pump systems.

- **Programmable thermostat**   This type of digital thermostat allows users to preset heating and cooling changes with a built-in clock (time and day of the week) using a keypad. When the conditions programmed into the thermostat are met, such as either the temperature or clock time, the thermostat activates the HVAC system.

- **Remote control thermostat**   Remote control thermostats are digital thermostats that can be adjusted, programmed, or activated remotely. These thermostats allow the user to change the current set point or heating/cooling mode using a remote control device. The commands sent to the thermostat can be transferred over dedicated wiring from the controller to the thermostat or over the home's existing AC power lines using power line technology.

Other features that are available on some thermostat models are

- **Heating/cooling anticipator** Because thermostats, both mechanical and electronic, aren't always located in the same room as that receiving heat, the room can actually be overheated by the time the temperature at the thermostat reaches the set point. A heating or cooling anticipator is an adjustable setting inside the thermostat that turns off the HVAC system at a point that anticipates the desired condition, turning off the heating or cooling system early. A heat anticipator is one way to compensate for a less-than-perfect thermostat location.

- **Remote temperature sensor** In many houses, the thermostat is not placed in the best possible location, but in an adequate location where it can be easily accessed. By placing a temperature sensor in a location where it can sense the desired room or zone temperature readings accurately, the thermostat may better serve the heating and cooling needs of the homeowner, so its placement isn't as critical. A remote temperature sensor, like the one shown in Figure 29-6, can be used to trigger the set point on a thermostat; this way, the homeowners don't have to rely on the thermostat's built-in thermometer. Remote sensors can be connected to the thermostat directly using thermostat wire or using power line technology.

Control Thermostats

Powerline communication (PLC) thermostats are remote control thermostats that allow the user to change the current set point or heating/cooling mode using a remote control

Figure 29-6
An indoor remote temperature sensor

Photo courtesy of Residential Control Systems, Inc.

device. The commands sent to the thermostat are transferred over the home's existing alternating current (AC) power lines using PLC technology.

There are two basic types of PLC-compatible thermostats:

- **One-way** This type of remote control thermostat carries commands to the thermostat, but doesn't have the capability to carry any feedback back to an X10 remote control device. Some one-way control thermostats are compatible with telephone responder units that also allow the thermostat to be controlled remotely through a telephone, though they are only one-way with no feedback.

- **Two-way** This type of remote control thermostat has the same capabilities as a one-way device but it is also able to transmit information, including the temperature, set point settings, and current mode, back to the controlling device.

Other types of remote control thermostats are currently available, including Electronic Industries Alliance (EIA)-232 and EIA-485 devices. These devices use serial interfaces to provide a reliable high-speed connection that is directly compatible with computers (EIA-232) or can be networked with other sensor and control devices (EIA-485).

HVAC Zones

Creating HVAC zones in a house can save energy as well as better serve the heating and cooling needs of different areas of the house. Many people confuse zones with independent systems where each area has a separate HVAC system. Zoning a house involves the design and installation of a series of airflow dampers that control the ambient temperature separately from other zones or areas of the house using a single HVAC system.

A single zone system or, in other words, a single HVAC system doesn't require damper systems; the whole house is a single zone with one ambient heating and cooling environment. A multizone HVAC system has at least two airflow dampers, with each damper managing the airflow into one specific zone and independently controlled by a thermostat.

Zoning is recommended in homes that have any of the following characteristics:

- Multiple levels or floors
- A widespread design, such as homes with separate building wings or large ranch-style layouts
- Rooms with large window surfaces
- Large open architecture areas with vaulted or cathedral ceilings, an atrium, or a solarium
- Living space in a finished basement or attic
- Rooms with exposed concrete flooring (such as in a basement)
- An indoor swimming pool or spa
- Earth-shelter houses that have only one or two exterior walls

HVAC Zone Controllers

A standard HVAC system typically has a single thermostat that controls the heating and cooling for an entire house. A zone control system connects two or more thermostats to a single HVAC system. The thermostats aren't the zone controllers; rather, there is a master zone control device that is connected to the thermostats in each zone, the HVAC system, and each airflow damper.

The master zone controller reacts to the set points of the zone thermostats and opens or closes the dampers, which are located inside the source HVAC ducts leading to each zone. In their normal state, the dampers are open, but the controller can shut them to close off the flow of heating or cooling to a zone.

The zone thermostat operates normally to call for heating or cooling according to its set points. However, the zone thermostat signals actually go to the master zone controller that controls the HVAC system and adjusts the dampers according to the zone settings.

The criteria for selecting a zone controller, such as the unit shown in Figure 29-7, are the number of zones, the type of HVAC system in use, and the size of the house. The size of the house is especially important, as is if the house has more than one story or levels, such as a two-story, three-story, or a tri-level house. In these situations, the master zone control unit should include a thermal equalization capability that balances the ambient temperature of the different levels.

HVAC Zone Design

HVAC zoning is very difficult to add to an existing HVAC system, so for the most part, zoning is a new construction application. Not many home automation firms take on the job of designing the actual HVAC system, the ductwork, or the location of the airflow registers, so leave this part of the job to the HVAC and mechanical engineering people.

Figure 29-7
An HVAC zone control unit

Photo courtesy of Residential Control Systems, Inc.

PART VII

Once the HVAC system is designed, the design of the HVAC zoning can be done using the following steps:

1. **Establish the number of zones.** Typically, a two- (or more) story house has at least two zones, but the goal is to establish HVAC zones that are roughly the same size in area. The zones shouldn't be too small because they will be difficult to control, or too large because they may be subject to cold or hot spots. A zone should be created for each separate climatic environment the homeowner desires, typically defined by the activities of the area. For example, a family room where the occupants may be more active can be slightly cooler than a living room where the occupants are less active.

2. **Adjust the HVAC duct plan to fit the zone design.** Ductwork must be designed so that each zone is a separate branch of the main HVAC duct system. The damper for each zone will be installed just after a zone's ducts branch from the main duct. The volume of the ductwork branches may need to be increased to handle an increased airflow volume. Work with the HVAC specialists to design the volume of the ductwork for a system that is open all the time. Each duct in the system should be able to handle the entire airflow volume of the HVAC system. This allows the system to function normally, even when a damper is closed, without putting too much back pressure on the HVAC system and possibly damaging it. The general rule-of-thumb for increasing the size of the ductwork is to add an additional 25 percent of volume for every two zones on the system. For example, a two-zone system should be increased 25 percent; a four-zone system should be increased 50 percent; and so on.

3. **Establish the location of the dampers and thermostats.** During the pre-wire stage, run two-conductor thermostat wire to the damper locations and five to seven conductor thermostat wire to the thermostat locations. If you are using remote temperature sensors with the system, that wiring must be installed as well.

Zoning Hydronic Systems

Hydronic systems are generally zoned by default, but if you wish to be able to turn the heat on or off in different areas of a home, control valves must be installed in the hydronic piping in the same way that dampers are installed in the air ducts of a forced air system.

Hydronic valves (see Figure 29-8) are motorized to open and close according to the commands of the master zone controller. They open and close the flow of water through the hydronic system.

Locating a Thermostat

For the best results, a thermostat should be located on an inside wall in an area that is frequently occupied. The thermostat should be at least 18 inches from any outside walls and at least 5 feet above the floor. It should also be placed in an area with freely circulating average temperature air. A thermostat should not be located in any of the following areas:

- On an outside wall

- In direct sunlight or near any heat produced by any closely placed appliances

- Near or in line with a heating or air conditioner vent, a stairwell, or an outside door

- Near any device that produces electrical interference

NOTE Some thermostats are "power-stealing" units. This type of thermostat takes power from the "W" (see Table 29-1 later in the chapter) heat connection running from the HVAC system. If multiple zone control units are also being installed, don't connect a power stealing unit or an older style mechanical or anticipator type thermostat to the controller. Neither of these thermostats will work properly with an HVAC control unit.

Wiring a Thermostat

The wiring used to connect a thermostat to the HVAC systems must be no less than 20-gauge wire, and for wire runs longer than 100 feet, 18-gauge wire is highly recommended. Thermostat wiring is different from other wire, such as Cat 3 or 5, audio/video, or speaker wiring. Thermostat wiring has two to seven conductors (see Figure 29-9) of solid core wiring with the color-coding for a seven-wire cable consisting of white, red, green, blue, yellow, brown, and orange. Most HVAC central unit controls, which the thermostat wire connects to, use from five to seven conductors. However, in new construction situations, installing seven-conductor thermostat wire adds to the future proofing of the house.

Standard HVAC Thermostat   Typically, the HVAC technicians install the wiring for a central-system thermostat at the time the HVAC systems are installed. The wiring for the thermostat normally is either two- or four-conductor wiring to support either 24V or 120V systems, depending on the needs of the HVAC system and the thermostat planned into the HVAC system. If the plan is for the home system technician to install a standard thermostat, you will need to follow the thermostat manufacturer's wiring diagram. Figure 29-10 shows an example of a wiring diagram for a typical nonautomated, or noncommunicating, thermostat.

Figure 29-8
A hydronic
motorized value

*Photo courtesy of
Invensys Building
Systems, PLC.*

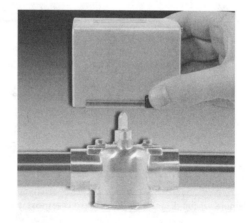

Figure 29-9
Examples of
stwo- and five-
conductor
thermostat wiring

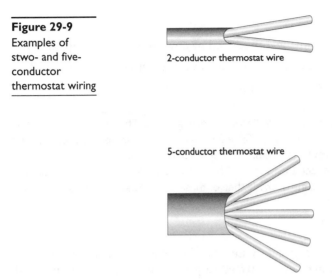

2-conductor thermostat wire

5-conductor thermostat wire

When connecting the thermostat wire to the thermostat terminals (see Figure 29-11), strip about ¼-inch of the insulation at the end of each conductor. On most standard thermostats, the terminals are marked with either stickers or embossed letters in the thermostat's plastic that indicate which wire color should be connected to which terminal. Wrap the exposed end of the conductor wire clockwise around the terminal screw. The manufacturer's wiring diagram and documentation should also have these details.

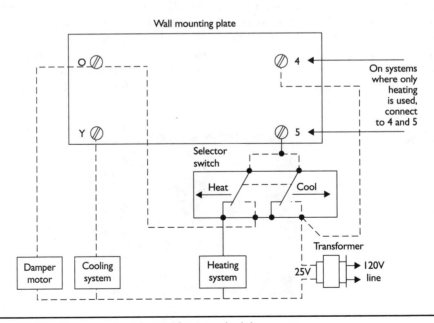

Figure 29-10   A sample wiring diagram for a standard thermostat

Figure 29-11
Installing the
wiring on a
standard
thermostat
device

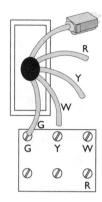

 NOTE   Of course, you already know that regardless of the type of wiring in
use for the thermostat, you should turn off the power at the AC circuit breaker
panel before beginning to attach the wire to the thermostat.

Remote Controlled Communicating Thermostat   It is more likely that if
the system installation plans for a home include the home technology technicians installing a thermostat, the thermostat is one that can be remotely controlled by some form
of remote control unit and is able to communicate with a central home system control
unit either with radio frequency (RF) or PLC signals.

The basic wiring for a remotely controlled thermostat is typically very similar to that
of a standard thermostat. However, additional installation steps are usually required to
accommodate its communications functions.

If the thermostat uses RF signals to communicate to a receiver module located near
the HVAC equipment or a home system controller, follow the manufacturer's guidelines
for range and placement in a room. For example, most manufacturers recommend that
an RF thermostat be place at least five feet from the floor and not behind a door or other
large object in a room.

If the thermostat uses PLC signals to communicate to a home system control unit, at
least two devices must be installed and possibly three. This includes one or more wall
display units and a control module that serves as an interface between the display units
and either the HVAC system (see Figure 29-12) or the home system control unit, and
possibly a separate communications module for remote control access. Figure 29-13
shows the modules of a three-part PLC thermostat system.

Figure 29-12
An illustration
of the general
installation of a
PLC thermostat

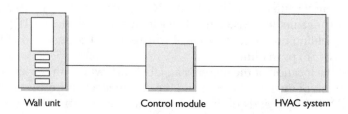

Wall unit   Control module   HVAC system

PART VII

Figure 29-13
The components of a PLC remote control thermostat system, with the controller (left), thermostat (center), and the PLC module (right)

Photo courtesy of Smarthome, Inc.

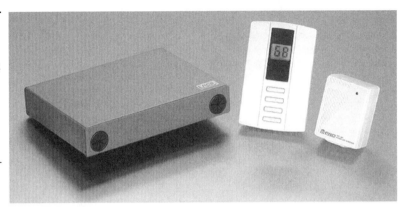

Rough-In   If the HVAC wiring is going in before the HVAC system, meaning the central HVAC system, first identify the location of the HVAC system. In most houses, the HVAC system is either in a basement, garage, or utility closet. To help with interfacing to the HVAC system, install a low-voltage box on a stud near where the HVAC system will sit. Locate the outlet box so that it is accessible for wiring and hookup. One idea is to place it one foot above the floor (measured to the center of the box). You should leave eight to ten feet of thermostat wire available to later wire the thermostat to the HVAC control.

At the spot where each thermostat will be installed during trim out, leave about one foot of wire slack to connect to the thermostat. During trim out and before the thermostat is attached to the wall and connected to the wire, be sure to seal around the hole the wire is passed through to avoid cold or warm air from the wall effecting the performance of the thermostat.

When pre-wiring for the HVAC control, run the wire from the thermostat and route it by the HVAC system unit (in an outlet box with an eight to ten foot loop) and on to the home control unit. It is a good idea to always prewire for HVAC control, even if not desired initially by the homeowner. By installing the wiring now, it is easy to add HVAC control in the future.

HVAC systems have two levels of wiring: line voltage and low voltage. Line voltage wiring supplies power to the components of the HVAC system, including its condenser, fan, furnace, or boiler. An electrician typically installs line voltage lines. Low voltage wiring for an HVAC system includes the thermostats, zone controls, any relay or control modules, and the control wiring for the system.

Typically, the wire installed for the HVAC control links should be a shielded wire with conductors of not less than American Wire Gauge (AWG) 14. Many local electrical codes require that control wiring be twisted as pairs and referenced to a particular wire type and manufacturer, such as Belden 8760 (single shielded twisted pair) or 8770 (three-conductor shielded twisted resistance temperature devices [RTD] cable). In addition to the shielding on the cable, control wiring should be installed at least a distance of 12 inches from power lines.

At the location of the thermostat, label each wire with the letter code assigned to the terminals of the HVAC system and the thermostat using cable marking tape or masking tape. Label both ends of the cable to ensure conformity. Table 29-1 lists the terminal

Terminal Designation	Wire Color	Application
B	Blue or orange	Switch reversing valve on heat pump to heat
C	Blue, brown, or black	Transformer common
E	Blue, pink, gray, or tan	Heat pump emergency heat relay (not commonly used)
G	Green	Furnace fan
L	Blue, brown, tan, or gray	Service indicator light
O	Orange	Switch reversing valve on heat pump to cool
R	Red	Transformer–hot lead
T	Tan or gray	Outdoor anticipator reset
W	White	Heat
X	Blue, brown, or black	Transformer common
Y	Yellow	Cooling compressor

Table 29-1　Commonly Used HVAC Terminal Codes

codes most commonly used in the more popular heating systems. Not every system will have every one of the codes included in Table 29-1 and, in some cases, they may substitute or reassign a wire color or terminal code to another function. Be sure to review the system wiring documentation before labeling the wires to ensure the wires are properly labeled at each end.

 NOTE　Heat pumps have two stages of heating and cooling, while standard gas or electric HVAC systems have only a single stage of heating or cooling.

Chapter Review

The primary types of air systems are forced air, baseboard and convection, hydronic, and evaporative cooling systems. Forced air systems use a circulating blower to move heated or cooled air into the rooms of a house. The two types of forced air systems are CAV and VAV. CAV systems supply a constant flow of air. VAV systems supply heated or cooled air at a constant temperature.

Baseboard heating devices provide heat using an internal electric heating element, or the flow of air or water to a baseboard element. Baseboard units use convection heating.

In-wall electric heating units are either self-contained devices that include an electric heating element, a blower, and a built-in thermostat, or gas-fired heating chambers that reheat an airflow from a central heating system. Electric baseboard or heating chamber devices are either locally controlled or connected to a home control system.

Hydronic heat uses hot water that is heated in a boiler or some form of a water heater to transfer heat into a room or zone. The advantage of a hydronic system is it is fuel efficient. Another form of hydronic heating gaining popularity is radiant heating embedded in floors, patios, and other areas.

PART VII

The common central heating units are: electric furnaces, electric heat pumps, gas furnaces, and oil furnaces.

Evaporative cooling works on the principles of water evaporation and relative humidity: Adding moisture to drier air lowers the air temperature. The three types of evaporative cooling systems are: direct evaporative cooling, indirect evaporative cooling, and two-stage evaporative cooling.

The common types of thermostats are: baseboard thermostats, digital thermostats, mechanical thermostats, programmable thermostats, remote control thermostats, heating/cooling anticipators, and remote temperature sensors.

Power line thermostats allow the current set point or heating/cooling mode to be changed through a remote control device. The two basic types of PLC-compatible thermostats are one-way and two-way devices.

HVAC zones save energy and better serve the heating and cooling needs of a home's residents. Zoning a house involves the design and installation of a series of airflow dampers that control the ambient temperature separately from other zones, or areas, of the house using a single HVAC system. A single zone HVAC system doesn't require damper systems. A multizone HVAC system has at least two airflow dampers where each damper independently controlled by a thermostat. A zone thermostat communicates with the HVAC system and adjusts the dampers according to the zone settings.

A thermostat should be located on an inside wall at least 18 inches from any outside walls and at least 5 feet above the floor in an area that is frequently occupied. The wiring of an HVAC system should be no less than 20 AWG for runs less than 100 feet; 18 AWG wire is recommended for runs longer than 100 feet. Thermostat wiring has two to seven conductors of solid core wiring and the color coding of a seven-wire cable is white, red, green, blue, yellow, brown, and orange.

The wiring for a remotely controlled thermostat is very similar to that of a standard thermostat. However, additional installation steps are required to accommodate its communications functions.

HVAC systems have two levels of wiring: line voltage and low voltage. An electrician typically installs line voltage lines. Low voltage wiring includes the thermostats, zone controls, any relay or control modules, and the control wiring for the system.

Questions

1. Which of the following is not a type of HVAC system discussed in this chapter?

   A. Forced air

   B. Forced hot water

   C. Hydronic

   D. Convection

2. What are the two types of forced air HVAC systems?

   A. CAV

   B. Hydronic

C. VAV

D. CAT

3. A CAV forced air system is also known as a

A. Multizone system

B. Single-zone system

C. Single-duct system

D. Multiduct system

4. A heating system that takes advantage of the natural phenomenon that heated air rises and reacts to cooler surfaces to circulate is called

A. Forced air

B. Induction

C. Convection

D. Zoning

5. Which type of system uses heated water circulating through pipes to heat a room?

A. Forced air

B. Heat pump

C. Hydronic

D. Convection

6. Which of the following is not a common type of fuel used with central HVAC units?

A. Electricity

B. Fuel oil

C. Heat pump

D. Natural gas

7. What type of thermostat includes digital displays and the capability to be preset with user-created HVAC settings?

A. Mechanical

B. Programmable

C. Remote control

D. Digital

8. What is the maximum number of conductors typically available in thermostat wiring?

A. Two

B. Four

C. Five

D. Seven

9. The wire used for HVAC controls should be what type?

   A. Shielded AWG 14 single conductor wire

   B. Shielded AWG 12 2 or more conductor wire

   C. Unshielded AWG 14 single conductor wire

   D. Shielded AWG 14 2 or more twisted conductor wire

10. What are the areas of an HVAC system that has been separated with a series of airflow dampers that control the ambient temperature of each area separately from the other areas called?

    A. HVAC zones

    B. HVAC hot spots

    C. HVAC controls

    D. HVAC subsystems

Answers

1. **B.** Nor will you find this system discussed in any HVAC book. All of the other choices are common types of HVAC systems.

2. **A and C.** Constant air volume (CAV) and variable air volume (VAV) are the two types of forced air systems.

3. **C.** There are multiduct CAV systems, but they are most commonly called single-duct.

4. **C.** The heated air from any HVAC system rises—a natural physical phenomenon—and convection heating is built around that principle.

5. **C.** Okay, some convection systems are hot water systems. However, all hydronic systems use hot water.

6. **C.** The "fuel" of a heat pump system is actually electricity, even though its heating process is a heat transfer.

7. **B.** A digital thermostat does have a digital display, but not all digital thermostats are programmable and not all remote control thermostats are digital. Mechanical thermostats are neither.

8. **D.** Although many HVAC systems use five-conductor wire, using seven-conductor wire provides future proofing for the system.

9. **D.** National and local electrical codes recommend shielded twisted conductor wiring of at least 14 AWG.

10. **A.** None of the other answers really apply to this definition.

CHAPTER 30

Water Management Systems

In this chapter, you will learn about:
- Water management system design
- Water management devices and usage
- Control of a water management system
- Water management system programming
- The different heating and cooling technologies of water management systems

A modern home has many water systems that people take for granted, including water heating and yard sprinkler systems. Few people actually consider that there are several operational and cost-saving benefits that can be gained by installing a water management system to manage and control these systems.

Water management control systems use the same existing and emerging technologies as many other parts of a home automation system, such as those used to control lighting, heating, and air conditioning, and other energy and utility-based systems in a home.

In this chapter, we take a look at the ways in which various parts of a home's water system can be managed and controlled to conserve water and to provide both energy and cost savings to the homeowners.

Residential Water Management Systems

The primary water systems that can be considered when designing a residential water management system are water heating, sprinkler systems, watering systems, and pools, spas, and hot tubs. Many of the everyday uses of water in a home, such as drinking water, cold-water laundry, and perhaps washing the car, don't require water to be heated. Heating water can be a major expense and area of energy consumption to many homeowners—and this doesn't even include systems like a hydronic (hot water) radiant heating system (see Chapter 29). In addition to heating water, another major use of water in many households, and its associated expense, is the use of a yard sprinkler system or watering plants.

It stands to reason, therefore, that by using a water management system to control the functions of heating water and its use in large-volume use applications there should be energy and cost savings to be gained.

Water management systems are comprised of a variety of subsystems. The subsystems most commonly included in a home system environment are

- Water heaters
- Interior irrigation systems
- Exterior sprinkler systems

Water Management System Devices

The list of devices that are common to a water management system in a home isn't actually very long. In fact, for most homes, the list is limited to a water heater and perhaps the outside sprinkler system. However, many newer homes are including a variety of other water-related devices that can be designed into the water management system.

Water Heating Systems

After the Heating, Ventilating, Air Conditioning (HVAC) system, the water heater is the next largest energy consumer in a home. Controlling a water heater can reduce the amount of time water is actually being heated without the homeowners ever having to do without hot water. In fact, some systems even allow the homeowners to use a telephone to call ahead and start up the water heater. Table 30-1 compares the features of an automated water management system with a home without one.

In addition to the features listed in Table 30-1, some water management systems can also provide such features as remote control of water heaters, showers, and tubs using either remote control or voice control, scald protection, and control of the system through a PC, telephone, or handheld or tabletop remote control.

Water Heater Types   There are actually several types of water heaters that can be used in a home. The most common types are storage water heaters, which are the most prevalent and are often referred to as conventional water heaters. Storage water heaters use a variety of fuel types or energy sources, such as natural gas, propane, electricity, and

Home with Water Heater Controls	Home Without Water Heater
Automated shower controls with preset water temperatures	Mix hot and cold water manually
Virtually unlimited hot water	Runs out of hot water
Heats water only on demand or on schedule	Water heated everyday around the clock, whether it is needed or not
Water heaters are on only when house is occupied	Water heaters always on

Table 30-1   Advantages of a Water Management System

oil, to heat water held in its tank that typically has a capacity of 20 to 80 gallons (75 to 303 liters). Heated water is drawn from the top of the tank whenever a hot water tap is opened and cold water flows into the bottom of the tank to keep the tank full. Storage water tanks are continuously heating the water in the tank to the temperature set on its heating control. One of the drawbacks to a storage water heater is its standby heat loss that results in energy use to keep the water at a constant temperature.

Other types of water heaters that are less often used in homes are

- Demand water heaters
- Heat pump water heaters
- Tankless water heaters
- Indirect water heaters
- Solar water heaters

Sprinkler and Irrigation Systems

Sprinkler and irrigation systems can be used both inside and outside a home. Although sprinkler systems are more commonly associated with exterior landscape irrigation, they can also be used as part of a fire alarm system, although this application is rarely found in residences.

Irrigation systems inside the home can be used to maintain a regular watering schedule or plan for home's interior plants.

Interior Irrigation Systems   Interior plants can be an important part of a home's interior design, not only for their aesthetics, but also for their contribution to the home's air quality. However, the downside of interior plants, especially if there are a fair number of them, is that watering can be the most time-consuming part of houseplant care. Because of this, and the desire of homeowners to decorate with live plants, automated precision micro-irrigation (APM) systems have emerged.

APM systems can be used to irrigate a variety of residential plants and plantings, including interior planter boxes, freestanding plants, and hanging planters (see Figure 30-1). APM systems can also be used to irrigate exterior plants as well, such as in exterior planter boxes, patio plant containers, hanging planters, and entrance and walkway areas.

An APM system uses low-pressure lines, high-integrity fittings, and adjustable emitters to supply water to a home's plants on very short, but frequent watering cycles. These systems can be fully automated using stand-alone controllers or incorporated into home management systems for automated or remote control activation.

APM uses cross-linked polyethylene (PEX) tubing that is placed inside the walls or through joists during new construction or remodeling. The water pressure on the tubing is never high, which helps to alleviate the worry of a tube breaking inside a wall and the damage that would cause. The APM system uses frequent, short 10 to 20 second pulses of moisture to provide water to each plant.

APM controllers, to which the tubing is attached, use solenoid valves that open and close to send water to the various watering stations on the system. In use, an APM system

PART VII

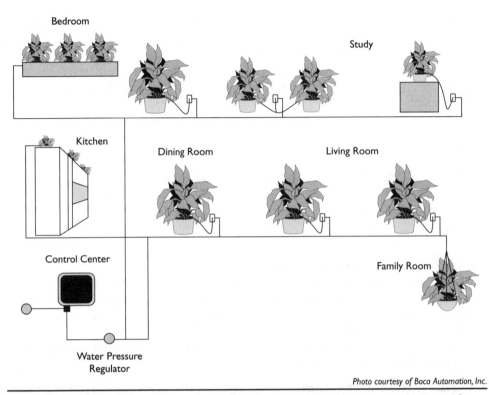

Photo courtesy of Boca Automation, Inc.

Figure 30-1 A stand-alone APM system installed into a home provides automated irrigation for houseplants.

operates very much like a home's distributed audio or video system. The major difference, of course, is that water is being distributed and not electrical impulses.

Exterior Sprinkler Systems Automating the control of a landscape sprinkler or irrigation system has several benefits, not the least of which is conserving water. There are several automatic sprinkler controllers on the market that accept relay and PLC signaling to control their on/off and cycle functions. Several home management systems can be configured to use signals to control watering schedules, zone watering, run-on protection, and the integration of weather sensors that detect wind, freezing temperatures, or rain, like the integrated system shown in Figure 30-2, to cancel or temporarily suspend watering.

Figure 30-3 shows an automated sprinkler controller that replaces a standard electronic sprinkler timer. The automated sprinkler controller receives scheduled PLC transmissions from a home management system relay and reacts to turn the sprinklers on and off, zone by zone or the whole system. Most of the automated sprinkler controllers include features that automatically turn off the system should the signal to do so not be received, such as in the event that the home management system fails. Some units will also work with a PLC remote control unit.

Figure 30-2
A weather-sensor can be used to detect rain, wind, freezing temperatures, and wind conditions to suspend a sprinkler system's operation.

Photo courtesy of Rain Bird Corp.

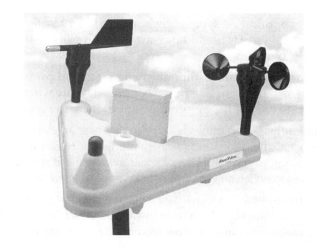

Water Management System Components

Depending on its scope, a water management system can include a variety of control valves, sensors, relays, solenoids, and other types of actuators, which carry out the actions dictated by the control system.

The most common components of a water management system are

- **Actuator**   An actuator is a device used to open or close a valve. Actuators are commonly found on control valves that can be remotely controlled.

- **Control valves**   Basically, a control valve is either a manual or automatic valve that is used to control or enhance the flow of water (in this case) at a given point. Commonly, in residential settings, control valves are associated with

Figure 30-3
Two models of automated sprinkler control units

Photo courtesy of RCI Automation, LLC.

water purification systems, hydronic boilers, or water heaters. In these systems, a control valve is used to increase water pressure or to stop or start the flow of water, or both.

- **Relays** Relays are commonly used to start and control the pumps of the water system. Pump start and pump control relays are wired to water system control units to control the on/off functions of the water pumps.

- **Solenoids** A solenoid is a device that uses an electrical current to create a magnetic field to either release a plunger or retract it. A solenoid valve, which is common to several forms of water management systems, opens and closes the valve gate when an electrical signal is applied to create the electromagnetic charge.

- **Water pumps** In water-based heating systems and in irrigation systems, water is moved through the system by pumps, which are typically sized to produce the gallons per minute flow required by the water system and its functions.

- **Heaters** Beyond the water heater used to heat water for general use, a water system may also include heaters to warm water at the tap (instant hot-water systems) or for other uses. Water heating units are typically electric or gas-fired, using a heating element immersed in a water holding tank that directly heats the water.

Water Management Design Considerations

The water systems that can be included in a water management system typically are the big three: water heaters; pools, spas, and hot tubs; and sprinkler/watering systems. The first two are management system candidates because they involve the heating of water that involves the use of electric or gas energy. Sprinkler and watering systems, if not managed, can pump out a large volume of water, often more than really needs to be applied.

Several stand-alone control systems are available to satisfy the desires of customers to reduce their water and energy bills. Control systems can provide not only time of day, day of week, and range of days on and off functions, but also flow volume and water temperature control.

General Design Considerations

Residential water systems can be installed as either stand-alone systems with their own discrete system controller or integrated into a home system controller. When a residential water system is integrated into a home automation controller, the interface is typically made through an available control unit relay or an add-on relay module.

The type of general water management system desired is perhaps the first issue that must be addressed in designing the system. The basic types of water management systems are

- **Zoned** Just like the lighting, HVAC, and audio video systems, the water management system can be divided into zones. A water management zone is one where the demand patterns and volume is very much the same and can be managed as a single entity. For example, if one area of the home has bathrooms attached or adjacent to bedrooms, the demand pattern for hot water is likely to be the same. However, if one of the bathrooms has a larger demand for water, hot or cold, it may be necessary to create a separate zone for that room and install separate supply systems for it. An obvious water management scheme would be to design separate water management zones for interior and exterior water systems.

- **Remote access** A remote access water management system may actually encompass any other types of water management schemes. Regardless of whether a house's water management system is zoned, scene-based, or timed, the customer may have a desire to access the control system remotely, either from within the home or from a remote location. The key issues are to identify the particular systems for which remote access is desired and determine the nature of the remote access and the type of control desired.

- **Scene-based** Typically, water management system scenes, or subsystems, are specific water applications or treatments within a water management zone. One scene design may define the systems required to operate a fountain in a large foyer or on a patio; another scene may control the irrigation for houseplants throughout the house; another may direct hot water on demand to one particular bathroom during certain hours of the day; and yet another may control the filters, lights, and temperature of an in-ground pool. Defining water management zones may provide general system management, but a water management scene defines the specific actions required within a zone. Yes, in many cases, a zone and a scene may be coincident.

Obviously, the generic water management system types can overlap and commonly do. It is entirely possible for a timed or remote access system to be designed in either a zoned or scene-based arrangement. However, each of these system types should be considered to provide the best overall design possible.

The overriding assumption throughout all of the general water management system types is that a networked water management and control system is used to manage, control, and monitor the system.

Water Management System Programming Considerations

Four levels of water management system configurations can be applied when configuring or programming the system: seasonal presets, and time-of-day, zone, and conditional programming.

Seasonal Presets Certain systems in a home are needed and not needed depending on the month, season, or weather. For example, in those locations where freezing temperatures are common during the winter months of the year, the management system can be programmed with a present month and day to turn off the landscaping sprinkler system until the month and day when the threat of freezing temperatures has passed. In this situation, the water management system could be preset to cease operating the yard sprinklers on November 15th and begin operating them again on March 15th.

Seasonal presets can also be used to manage the home's systems, including the water management system, during periods when the homeowners are scheduled to be away from the home for extended periods. For example, if the homeowners know they will be away at their beach, mountain, or winter place during a particular season, the management system can be preset for this and shutdown or slowdown certain systems until a preset return date.

Time-of-Day Programming   Time-of-day control of the water management system is a very commonly applied control method. Whether the control is installed as a water flow timer on an outside water faucet to control the water flow to a single hose, an electronic sprinkler system timer (see Figure 30-4), or installed as a part of a whole-house management system, the principle is the same.

The demand for water, and especially hot water, varies throughout the day. In fact, there are times during the day, such as between midnight and early morning, when there is little in the way of hot water demand, but there is a demand for cold water to run the

Figure 30-4

A stand-alone electronic landscaping sprinkler system timer provides time-of-day (and day-of-week) programming to control when yard sprinklers operate.

Photo courtesy of The Toro Co.

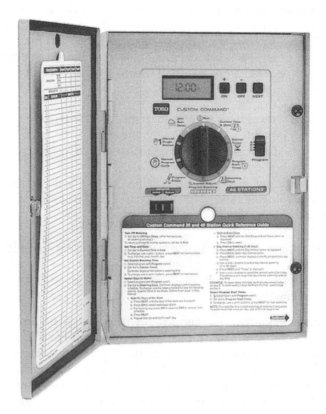

landscaping sprinkler system. A timed system can turn on or off certain parts of the water system to save energy and converse water.

Time-of-day programming is a basic feature of home automation controllers, including water management system controllers. This feature is also used to control when the hydronic HVAC system operates, when the water heater is on or off, and when the outside yard sprinklers run.

Zone Programming   The control and management of water systems in a specific zone, such as when a water heater dedicated to one particular zone is on or off, allows the water management system in one particular area of a home to function independently of any other defined water management zones. One reason a zoned approach may need to be taken when designing a residential water system is that the water pressure to the home may not be sufficient to provide adequate pressure to all zones at the same time.

If zone programming is desired in a home's water management system, the choice for an automated home controller or a water management system controller dictates that it provide multiple zone contacts and presets.

Conditional Programming   Another type of programming that can be used to control when water systems operate in one or more locations of a home uses a variety of sensors and preset actions or conditions. One example of conditional programming is a leak detector that can detect a leak in a pipe, fitting, or storage tank, like the device shown in Figure 30-5, and shut off the flow of water to that area of the house or the entire water system, depending on its placement. Another example of conditional programming is shutting off the water heaters when a preset "Vacation" condition triggers.

Figure 30-5
A wireless water leak detector is able to detect a change in the water pressure and close its valve to stop water flow.

Photo courtesy of Dynaquip Controls.

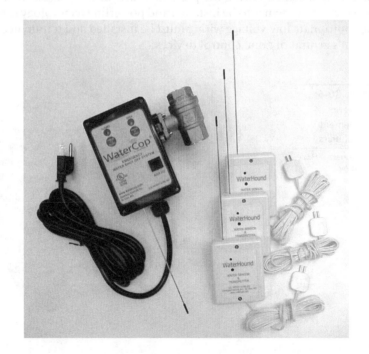

A home control system can save the homeowner money, confusion, and frustration by replacing stand-alone systems for water systems, HVAC, and the like.

Many automated sprinkler control units include an interface for temperature, rain, snow, and other weather conditions in which the customer may not want the yard sprinklers to run temporarily. The water management system, using feedback from either the weather sensor or the sprinkler control unit, could then skip one or more days until the situation improves. This same principle can also be applied to the HVAC and other systems in the home.

Connecting to the Management System

In most water management systems, no special wiring is required, especially if control units are installed directly to the device being controlled. Those systems that require wiring can be connected to a home system control unit using low-voltage wiring, either as a part of the structured wiring or as stand-alone wiring. Many water management systems are "wireless," meaning no new wiring is required to install them, and use PLC technology (like the units shown in Figure 30-6) that communicates over existing alternating current (AC) power lines.

For those systems that are not PLC-compatible or when this type of system isn't desired, thermostat wire can be used to connect a system's components and controls for low-voltage connectivity, and, if desired, Cat 5e wiring can be used for both communications and low-voltage signaling.

A water management system must be preplanned into a home so that its control wiring can be installed during the pre-wire phase of the project. If an automated home management system is to be installed and powerline technology is not to be used, then the appropriate low-voltage wiring must be installed and terminated as required for the system's central or zone control devices.

Figure 30-6
PLC water
management
control units

*Photo courtesy of Home
Controls, Inc.*

Chapter Review

Residential water systems include the control and monitoring of water flow and the on/off functions of water heaters, sprinkler systems, irrigation systems, and pools, spas, and hot tubs. Water management systems are comprised of a variety of subsystems: water heaters, interior irrigation systems, and exterior sprinkler systems.

The most common type of water heater used in homes is a storage water heater. Other types of water heaters, although less often used in homes, are demand water heaters, heat pump water heaters, tankless water heaters, indirect water heaters, and solar water heaters.

Sprinkler and irrigation systems can be used both inside and outside a home. APM systems are used to irrigate residential plants and exterior plants. Automatic sprinkler controllers control the on/off and cycle functions of sprinkler and irrigation systems. A water management system commonly includes control valves, sensors, relays, solenoids, and actuators. Residential water systems are either stand-alone systems or integrated into a home system controller.

There are three basic types of water management system designs: zoned, remote access, or scene-based. These general water management system types assume a networked water management and control system is used to manage, control, and monitor the system. Water management system can be configured with seasonal presets, and time-of-day, zone, or conditional programming.

In most water management systems, no special wiring is required, especially if control units are installed directly to the device being controlled. Some systems use PLC technology that communicates over existing AC power lines. A water management system must be preplanned into a home so that its control wiring can be installed during the pre-wire phase of the project.

Questions

1. Which of the following is not typically integrated into a water management system?

    A. Water heater

    B. Sprinkler system

    C. Heat pump

    D. Water faucets

2. What type of water management system incorporates controls that turn water systems on and off based on the time of day?

    A. Timed

    B. Zoned

    C. Remote access

    D. Scene-based

3. Typically, the HVAC system is a home's largest energy consumer. What home system is the second largest energy consumer?

    A. Air conditioning

    B. Sprinkler system

    C. Water heater

    D. Lighting

4. An APM system would be integrated into a home to provide what function?

    A. Control pools and spas

    B. Monitor a hydronic system

    C. Control landscaping sprinklers

    D. Irrigate houseplants

5. What component can be used to open, close, or enhance the flow of water?

    A. Control valve

    B. Relay

    C. Solenoid

    D. Mixing pump

6. Which of the following is not a common type of water management system subsystem?

    A. Water heaters

    B. Interior irrigation systems

    C. Exterior sprinkler systems

    D. Tap water systems

7. "Wireless" water management controls most typically use what communications technology?

    A. RF

    B. PLC

    C. IR

    D. Ethernet networking

8. Which two of the following are general types of water management system control configurations?

    A. Integrated

    B. Stand-alone

C. Interior

D. Exterior

9. What are the primary reasons for installing a home control system in a home?

   A. Save money

   B. Replacing stand-alone systems

   C. Centralizing controls

   D. Establishing HVAC, lighting, and water management zones

   E. All of the above

10. The most commonly used type of home water heater is

   A. Demand water heater

   B. Heat pump water heater

   C. Tankless water heater

   D. Storage tank heater

Answers

1. **D.** The remaining choices are types of systems that are commonly integrated into a water management system. Outside water faucets can be, but are not commonly, incorporated under a water management system's control.

2. **A.** Remote access systems are those that can be controlled from outside the system, and scene-based systems are commonly used to control water devices within a zone.

3. **C.** After the HVAC system, which includes the AC, the water heater consumes the most energy. The sprinkler system uses very little in the way of electrical or gas utilities (energy), and the lighting system may very well be third on the list.

4. **D.** Automated precision micro-irrigation (APM) systems can be used to automatically water inside and outside houseplants. The other choices are systems that can be controlled under a water management system.

5. **A.** Either acting on a signal from a thermostat, a control unit, or a home management system controller, a control valve starts or stops the flow of water, gas, or fuels. Relays are used to redirect control and communication signals; solenoids do open and close a flow, but cannot enhance the flow; and pumps are strictly flow enhancers.

6. **D.** The other systems are commonly included in water management systems.

7. **B.** Several types of PLC water management controllers are available.

8. **A** and **B.** Water management systems can be either stand-alone, meaning self-contained and independent of a home control system, or integrated into a home control system.

9. **E.** These are some of the primary benefits of installing a home control system, but this list is far from complete.

10. **D.** The storage tank type of water heater is by far the most common type installed in homes.

PART VIII

Security System Basics

Security System Basics

In this chapter, you will learn about:
- Residential security systems types
- Security system devices
- External security services

Numerous studies have shown consistently that the homes with the most risk of crime typically have the least protection. And in a significant percentage of these homes, there is no protection or warning systems installed, beyond door locks and fencing, that is. Those homes that do have some type of protective system, commonly have some form of burglar alarm, but even this is only common in more expensive homes.

Of course, protection is the main purpose of a security system. However, the primary benefit of a residential security system is not necessarily protection, but rather the peace-of-mind that comes from having a security system installed.

The type and technology of a residential security system should be fitted to the home, lifestyles, and the level of protection desired by the homeowners. In this chapter, we look at security system basics, including the various types of systems available, their components, the communications technologies they employ, and a few of the external services that can be used for monitoring.

Residential Security Systems

A home security system provides protection at two levels: interior and perimeter. Interior protection includes the detection of, and an alarm for, events inside the home, including:

- Someone moving about inside
- Someone breaking into a cabinet, cupboard, or the like
- Smoke, fire, or carbon monoxide gases
- Environment sensors

Perimeter protection provides detection of, and an alarm for, events such as:

- A door opening
- A window breaking
- Someone in the yard
- Unauthorized access to the property

Reactive Vs Proactive Security

Traditional security systems are "reactive" in that they react to an intruder and sound an alarm. This alarm usually scares the intruders away, warning them that they have been detected and that the local authorities are probably already on the way. But the alarm is in response to the intruder already being in the home and jeopardizes the safety of the occupants.

By integrating a security system with home control, the system can be "proactive" in that it will increase the safety of the occupants by lighting the way outside when the smoke alarm goes off or lighting the walkway when they arrive home late at night. It can deter the potential intruder from selecting the home to break into as the home can have the "lived-in look" when the homeowners are away.

Interior Protection

The function of interior detection is to protect a home's occupants and contents from intruders and keep them safe. The primary features of interior security include:

- **Access control**   A process that allows or denies access, or entry, to the home itself or to a particular area. Typically, access control systems require the entry of codes, the use of a key, an access card, a proximity card, or a physiological characteristic of a person, such as hand or thumbprint. Access control can be as simple as a mechanical lock and key or as sophisticated as biometrics (which is an access control method that uses fingerprints, retinal scans, and the like).

- **Intrusion detection**   The opening of a door, a window breaking, a shock or vibration on a surface, or even a motion in a secured area can create a notification or an event that triggers an alarm to sound or sends an intrusion alert message to an external security monitoring service that then contacts the local police and fire departments.

- **Smoke, fire, and dangerous gas detection**   Independent or integrated sensors can detect smoke, the heat from a smokeless fire, and even carbon monoxide or radon gases and sound a built-in alarm, send an alarm signal to a central security system controller, or relay a message to an external security monitoring service.

- **Panic buttons**   Though they are not found in all security systems, a panic or emergency alert feature can be a desired feature for some customers. Typically, a centrally or conveniently placed button or a special sequence of digits on the telephone or alarm keypad can be used to sound an alarm or to transmit an emergency request to the monitoring service to dispatch the local emergency services or the police department.

- **Environment sensors**   Optional temperature and humidity sensors can be installed to monitor the environment. Low temperature sensors can detect when the heat goes too low and notify the monitoring service or indicated parties prior to the pipes freezing and bursting. Humidity and temperature sensors help maintain the correct environment for wine cellars and cigar rooms. Flood or water sensors can detect when water is at a level it shouldn't be, such as what occurs when a sump pump fails or a pipe breaks in the basement.

Perimeter Protection and Detection

The primary purpose of perimeter protection is detecting intruders in the area around a home before they attempt to enter it. In addition, exterior detection can make it a safer place for the homeowners and their guests when it is interfaced with the outside lighting. The primary features of perimeter protection and detection are

- **Access control**   Gates or an entryway onto the property can be secured and entry granted to only those people the homeowners allow to enter through a remote control or remote switch or those people who know the security code or have an access card.

- **Intruder detection**   If intruders enter the secured space around a house, the system should detect their presence and perform a variety of optional security functions, such as signaling the lighting system to turn on the exterior lighting after dark, sounding an alarm, alerting the homeowner, or contacting a monitoring service after hours.

- **Glass breakage detection**   Because double-paned glass is common on most new homes, sensors should also be placed on the exterior windowpane to detect an intruder attempting to enter the home by breaking through a window.

- **Screen breakage detection**   By placing a sensor on the screen frame or using special screen woven for security detection, an alarm signal can be sent to the security system if the frame is removed or the screening cut.

Security System Components

Many residential security systems come with a certain number of features and components, such as hard-wired systems with a control panel, an RJ-31x interface, multiple zone inputs, and a keypad controller and wireless systems that include a control panel, sounder (alarm), keypad, window or door contacts, and a remote control. Different manufacturers offer different systems, packaged with what they believe to be the most commonly used features, components, and devices. However, it is virtually impossible for a manufacturer or reseller to know exactly which features and devices a specific house requires for its security system installation. This is why most of the components needed are offered as options.

Regardless of whether of not a system is a wireless or hard-wired system, and most of the newest systems can be adapted to include both, the most commonly used components are available for use with either type of system. The most commonly used security system components and features include:

- **Security control panel** This central device in the security system serves as both a command center and a distribution point for the devices and features connected to or managed by the system. Choosing a security control panel for a home means choosing one that has the capacity to support the number and type of devices to be installed and one that supplies the feature set that's both desired by the homeowner and required by the security system design. Hard-wired control panels are typically enclosed in a cabinet and installed near a home's central distribution panel. Figure 31-1 shows a power line control (PLC) wireless control panel.

- **Keypads** Virtually every residential security system includes a keypad (see Figure 31-2), the homeowner's primary interface and input device for entering setup parameters and setting security system features on or off. Many hard-wired systems also provide a computer connection and control software that allows these functions to be performed from a PC terminal. Many keypad models also provide wireless remote access through a PLC relay, a handheld remote control, or a key fob control.

- **Sensors** There are a variety of sensors that can be installed as a part of a home security system; each designed to detect a different event. Table 31-1 lists the more common sensors used in home systems and their functions.

Figure 31-1

A PLC wireless security system control panel

Photo courtesy of Smarthome, Inc.

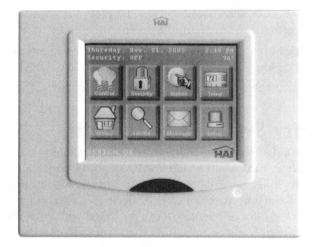

Figure 31-2

A residential
security system
keypad

*Photo courtesy of GE
Interlogix.*

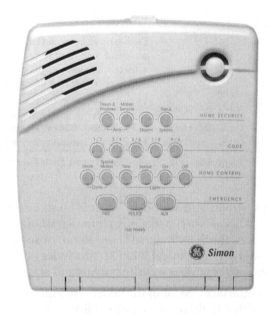

Sensor Type	Function
Water/flood sensor	Detects the presence of water in an area where it shouldn't be. Used for such things as spa overflow, pipes breaking, and sump pumps failing.
Low temperature sensor	Detects when the temperature goes below a preset temperature.
Humidity sensor	Detects when the humidity goes outside of a preset range.
Natural gas sensor	Detects the presence of natural gas in the air
Carbon monoxide (CO) sensor	Detects the presence of a higher than normal level of CO in the air.
Contact sensor	Detects the opening or closing of a window or door in opposition to its normal state, either Normally Open (NO) or Normally Closed (NC).
Glass-break sensor	Detects the sound of shattering or breaking glass.
IR beam sensor	Detects when the line of an IR beam is broken.
Floor mat sensor	Detects the pressure on a thin surface. Often placed below the carpet on steps to detect someone coming upstairs.
Shock/vibration sensor	Detects the presence of natural gas in the air.
Heat sensor	Detects rapid changes in an area's temperature using a metal strip that either melts or changes shape when exposed to higher than normal temperatures. Many smoke detectors have heat sensors built in.

Table 31-1   Residential Security System Sensors and Their Functions

Sensor Type	Function
Motion sensor	Uses passive infrared (PIR) technology to detect movement in an area. Sensitivity can be adjusted to only detect objects over a certain size and weight or the lens can be masked out to not see pets below a certain sight line.
Smoke detector	Uses an ionization chamber or a photoelectric cell to detect the presence of smoke in the air. Smoke detectors typically have an internal alarm as well as a relay to send an alarm signal to the central unit. See Figure 31-3.

Table 31-1   Residential Security System Sensors and Their Functions *(continued)*

- **Alarms, sirens, and sounders**   Nearly all security systems include some means to alert a home's occupants of an intruder, smoke, or other security event. In most cases, this is an internal siren, alarm, or sounder circuit that activates an external sounding device. Table 31-2 includes the most commonly used terminology regarding security systems and alarms.

- **RJ-31x interface**   Most of the better residential security systems include an RJ-31x jack that facilitates a specialized feature on a standard telephone line called line seizure. The RJ-31x interface is used when a security event triggers a call to be placed to a homeowner's remote telephone number, cell phone, or pager, or to a security monitoring service. By seizing the phone line, the security system is able to disconnect any calls on the line and use the phone line to make its security notification call.

- **Hard-wired sensor converter**   This device is used to adapt existing sensors, such as a door or window contact into a wireless device.

- **Cameras and monitors**   Security cameras and monitors can be part of a security surveillance system.

Figure 31-3

A cut-away view of the internal components of a residential smoke detector and alarm device

Photo courtesy of GE Interlogix.

Security System Feature	Devices Used to Implement the Feature
Perimeter detection	Sensors, such as contact sensors, placed on exterior doors and windows that activate an alarm.
Interior detection	Sensors, such as motion detectors and smoke detectors, placed in the interior of a home excluding windows and doors.
Silent alarm	An alarm that notifies a monitoring service that an alarm event has occurred but there is no alarm sounded in the home to alert the intruder.
Local alarm	A siren or bell that is sounded in or outside of a home with no other notification made.
Silent/audible alarm	A switching feature on security systems that allows the alarm to be silent when a home is unoccupied, but sounds a siren or bell when occupants are in the home.
Digital dialer	An electronic device that uses an RJ-31x connection grabs the phone line to place a telephone call to a monitoring service and then verifies the connection and sends an alarm activation message.
Line seizure	An RJ-31x connection is used to capture and hold a telephone line until an alarm call can be made and completed. When it seizes the line, it hangs up any phone connection already in progress.

Table 31-2   Common Security Features and Devices

NOTE   Surveillance systems, including cameras and monitors, are covered in Chapter 35.

Security System Connections

Residential security systems use two means to link their sensors, detectors, and alarms to the control unit: radio frequency (RF) signals and wire or cable runs. Wireless RF-based systems don't require unit-to-unit wiring and typically provide the most flexibility during installation but do require ongoing maintenance because the detection devices operate on batteries. Hard-wired systems must be pre-planned so that the appropriate cabling can be installed during the pre-wire phase of a new construction or a remodeling project.

Hard-wired systems generally offer a better quality signal than a wireless system, provided the cabling used is installed to specification. However, as wireless technology continues to improve—for example, as a larger number of communication channels are added—wireless systems are proving to be much more reliable.

Another difference between wireless and hard-wired systems is the initial cost factors. Wired system components are generally less expensive than the wireless versions, but part of the cost savings realized with a hard-wired system is eaten up with the cost of the cabling and its installation. Over time, the wired system usually lasts longer because the components do not include the advanced technology that is present in wireless systems.

Hard-Wired Security Systems

In many residential situations, a hard-wired security system has some advantage over a wireless one. A hard-wired system directly and physically connects the components of the system—the contacts, sensors, and so forth—to the main unit with a cable or wire. The primary benefit of the hard-wired approach is that unlike a wireless system, the hard-wired system is significantly less sensitive to electromagnetic and radio frequency interferences, especially if the system's wiring was properly installed.

Hard-wired systems are made up of a main security control panel, like the one shown in Figure 31-4, which is connected to the system's contacts, sensors, alarms, keypads, and other devices with home run wires. Understand that the illustration in Figure 31-4 is highly simplified and that the controller unit is typically centrally located with the devices wired into it attached to home run wiring and located throughout a home.

Hard-wired systems are certainly easier to install during a new construction project, but they can also be retrofitted to a home provided there is open wire run space in an attic, basement, or crawl space.

Wiring a Hard-Wired Security System

In general, hard-wired security systems recommend the use of 2-conductor or 4-conductor cabling that should be planned along with the structured wiring plan during the

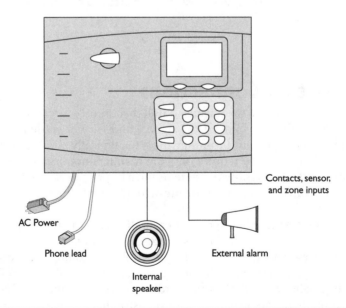

Figure 31-4   An illustration of the control panel and wiring leads of a hard-wired security system

Security System Component	Wire Recommendation
Keypads	Standard: 22 AWG 4-conductor stranded
	Advanced (with voice pick-up and playback): 2 runs of 18 AWG 2-conductor shielded stranded
Internal and external alarms, speakers, and sound devices	18 AWG 2-conductor copper wire
AC power connections	18 AWG 2-conductor copper wire
Motion sensors, glass break detectors	22 AWG 4-conductor copper wire
Door and window contact sensors	22 AWG 2-conductor copper wire
Fire alarm connections, smoke detectors and heat detectors	FPLP (fire power limited plenum) cable or FPL (fire power limited) cable: 18 AWG 4-conductor
Ground connection	14 AWG 1-conductor copper wire
RJ-31X console	22 AWG 4-conductor copper wire minimum, CAT 3 or CAT 5 preferred
Wireless sensors	Any of the above sensors but RF communications and batteries power them, so no wiring is required
Video monitors and video capture devices	RG-6 coaxial cable

Table 31-3   Wire and Cable Guidelines for Hard-Wired Security Systems

design phase and installed during the pre-wire phase of the project. However, there are wiring guidelines (minimum cable recommendations) for use with different security system components. Table 31-3 lists the more commonly used components and the recommended wiring or cabling to connect them into a hard-wired security system.

Wireless Security Systems

Depending on how technically you define the term wireless, wireless security systems can be either completely wireless RF-based systems, powerline (PLC such as X-10) technology systems, or both.

"Wireless" Wireless Systems

Wireless security systems typically provide the same functions as hard-wired systems, especially with the expanded RF range (around 600 feet) of some newer products. Essentially, a wireless system requires only that a main control unit, like the one shown in Figure 31-5, be connected to an AC power source and the system is ready to use. Of course, sensors, detectors, and other devices need to be installed where appropriate, but these operate on self-contained batteries. The main benefit of a wireless system is that no wiring is required.

Wireless systems allow for flexibility when defining multiple wireless security zones and some systems can also be connected into an existing wired security system to extend the original system or replace the wired system control unit.

Figure 31-5
A wireless main unit needs only to be plugged in to activate the system

Photo courtesy of General Electric Interlogix.

NOTE See Chapter 32 for more information on designing security zones.

NOTE One consideration about using wireless devices is that the detectors and sensors are typically battery operated, which means that although these devices normally have a long battery life, the batteries do need to be replaced on a regular schedule, such as every six months.

External Security Services

Some security systems can be programmed to call a phone number (residence, friend, cell phone) when the system goes into alarm, but this does not notify or dispatch the police. This system depends upon someone answering the call at the time it is received, listening to the message, and responding immediately.

Some homeowners prefer to have someone outside the home monitoring their home security system because it gives them the assurance that there is always somebody to summon help when there is a break-in or an emergency. This involves a recurring monthly fee. For these homeowners, there are two basic types of external security services available:

- Alarm monitoring
- Remote viewing monitoring

Alarm Monitoring Services

Alarm monitoring services are usually connected to a home through an RJ-31x connection that places a call to the service's monitoring system and communicates digitally, whenever the security system is breached and an alarm event is triggered, regardless if an alarm sounds in the home or not. The connection to the monitoring company can also be through a cell phone or long-range radio. Some security systems allow for the monitoring service staff to "listen-in" through the security keypads in the home. The security system may even provide two-way voice communication between the monitoring service staff and the occupants of the home.

Some companies will work with the installer and the homeowner to design a security system that best provides the security level desired and then contract for the alarm monitoring services for that system. Most, if not all, city and county police and sheriff departments no longer provide alarm monitoring and security review services and only respond to calls from security monitoring services. Many municipalities also have a policy of charging the homeowner for repeat false security alarm calls.

The upside to alarm monitoring services is that they are always there—24/7—and are to respond immediately. The downside is that because they are off-site, and especially in cases when the homeowner is away from home, they can dispatch the police or fire department to investigate the cause of an alarm. Should the problem be caused by something other than an intruder, such as a branch blown through a window or an alarm caused by an electrical fault, the homeowner can be charged a fine for a false alarm.

Remote Viewing Monitoring Services

Another type of residential security services is remote access monitoring services, which use surveillance cameras and microphones to monitor a home's interior and exterior for unauthorized access or presence.

 NOTE See Chapter 35 for more information about the types of service provide by monitoring services.

Chapter Review

A home security system can be either "reactive" or be interfaced to a home control system and be "proactive." A security system provides protection on two levels: interior and perimeter. Interior protection systems include detecting and sounding alarms in response to events inside and outside a home. The function of interior detection is to protect a home's occupants and contents from intruders. The purpose of exterior or perimeter protection is detecting intruders in the area around a home before they attempt to enter the house.

A residential security system links to its sensors, detectors, alarms, and control units using either radio frequency (RF) signals or wire or cable runs. Wireless RF-based systems don't require unit-to-unit wiring. Wireless security systems can be completely wireless RF-based systems or interfaced to wired systems. Hard-wired systems must be preplanned so that the appropriate cabling can be installed during the pre-wire phase of a new construction or a remodeling project.

A hard-wired system directly and physically connects the components of the system—the contacts, sensors, and so forth—to the main unit with a cable or wire. The primary benefit of the hard-wired approach is, unlike a wireless system, a hard-wired system is significantly less sensitive to electromagnetic and RF interferences, especially if the system's wiring is properly installed to avoid interference sources.

Common devices and features of a residential security system include a control panel, a RJ-31x interface, multiple zone inputs, alarms, window or door contacts, a remote control, and a keypad controller. An important feature on systems that support alarm monitoring is an RJ-31x interface.

Two basic types of external security services are available: alarm monitoring and remote video monitoring.

Questions

1. Which of the following is not a common feature of a residential interior security system?

   A. Access control

   B. Intrusion detection

   C. Perimeter intrusion detection

   D. Smoke or fire detection

2. What communications technology is used by a truly wireless system?

   A. PLC

   B. HomePNA

   C. Cat 5e

   D. RF

3. A security system integrated into a home system controller is said to be

   A. Intrusive

   B. Preventive

   C. Proactive

   D. Reactive

4. What type of alarm only notifies a monitoring service that an alarm event has occurred?

   A. Silent alarm

   B. Local alarm

   C. Digital alarm

   D. Zone alarm

5. What device is used as the homeowner's primary interface to a security system?

   A. Control panel

   B. Keypad

   C. Remote control

   D. Personal computer

6. What is the specialized connection used in security systems to seize a telephone line for purposes of notifying an alarm monitoring service of a security breach?

   A. RJ-11

   B. RJ-12

   C. RJ-31

   D. RG-6

7. What type of sensor is used to detect the opening or closing of a door or window?

   A. CO sensor

   B. Glass-break sensor

   C. Contact sensor

   D. PIR sensor

8. If a homeowner wishes to have an outside party take action on security and alarm events that are triggered, the type of firm contracted would be a

   A. Remote monitoring service

   B. Alarm monitoring service

   C. Remote alarm management service

   D. Alarm security service

9. Which of the following is not a form of a security system's interior protection?

   A. Someone moving about inside a home

   B. Someone breaking into a cabinet, cupboard, or the like

   C. Smoke, fire, or carbon monoxide gases

   D. A door opening

10. Which of the following is not a protection provided in a perimeter security system?

   A. Access control

   B. Smoke, fire, or carbon monoxide gases

   C. Glass breakage detection

   D. Screen breakage detection

Answers

1. **C.** Interior systems, which should be obvious from its name, include all security measures placed inside a home. The other choices are all typically included in an interior security system.

2. **D.** Radio frequency (RF) signals are used by wireless systems to communicate. X-10, which is a form of wireless system, uses existing powerlines to communicate; Cat 5e is a networking cable standard; and HomePNA (Home Phoneline Networking Alliance) is a standard for communications over interior telephone lines.

3. **C.** Security systems that are integrated into a home automation control system provide proactive security.

4. **A.** This alarm doesn't sound an alarm locally, but notifies the monitoring services. An audible alarm can also notify services although it also sounds an alarm. A local alarm sounds a siren or bell without notification action. The term digital alarm is erroneous; a digital dialer is the mechanism used to notify the monitoring service.

5. **B.** Regardless of the system type, hard-wired or wireless, the homeowner's interface to a security system is primarily through a keypad. However, a PC can be used with most hard-wired control panels and a remote control can be used to activate or de-activate the alarm system.

6. **C.** Actually, the connection is an RJ-31x. RJ-11 and RJ-12 are one-and two-line telephone line connectors and RG-6 is a coaxial cabling standard.

7. **C.** This sensor detects that it has been either opened or closed, depending on whether it is set to Normally Open (NO) or Normally Closed (NC). A CO sensor detects carbon monoxide gas; a glass-break sensor detects the sound of breaking glass; and a PIR (passive infrared) sensor is a motion detector.

8. **B.** A remote monitoring service performs video surveillance on a property and the other choices are just plays on words.

9. **D.** Detecting an exterior door opening is a part of a perimeter security system.

10. **B.** Smoke, fire, and CO detectors and alarm systems are classified as components of an interior security system.

CHAPTER 32

Designing a Home Security System

In this chapter, you will learn about:
- Design issues for a home security system
- Planning the structured wiring for a home security system
- Lighting interfaced to the security system

The basic idea behind the inclusion of a home security system is to protect the home's occupants and their belongings. The design of a home security system must secure any possible point of entry into a home, detect any breach in that security, and notify and alarm the home's occupants and any desired outsiders such as monitoring services or family and friends should there be a breach of security. When the security system interfaces with a home control system it adds safety and gives the homeowners and occupants peace of mind.

The residential security system technology must fit the requirements of the homeowners, as well as their budget. This chapter focuses on the issues you need to considered when designing a home security system and using security lighting systems, and a look at some options that can make the system more effective.

Design Considerations for a Home Security System

The first consideration when designing a home security system is whether the home is a new construction or an existing house. The options in a new construction situation are numerous since you have more flexibility in planning and installing a structured wiring environment. In an existing home, the choices are more challenging and may be more limited.

Deciding What Should Be Secured

In many cases, homeowners aren't sure exactly what they wish to have included in a home security system; they just want their home secured and to feel safe. Considering that most customers also have a limited budget for this type of project, it is important to identify the minimum protections they should consider installing as well as options to further enhance the system.

Based on the recommendations of the security services industry and several police and fire department checklists, the questions listed in Table 32-1 should provide the information you need to determine the must-haves and the could-haves of a home security system.

Interview the homeowners to identify how much interior and exterior detection and protection they desire. Review the floor plans and be sure to discuss the following items:

- Doors—all entry doors as well as and doors to separate areas of the house.
- Windows and/or screens to be protected.
- Interior motion sensor locations.
- Fire protection. Has an electrician installed it? Is it interfaced to security system? Be sure to follow local codes.
- Environment considerations—wine cellar, pool, spa, basement, low temperature areas.
- Keypads at main entry points, plus the master bedroom.
- Exterior motion detection and actions.
- Desire to interface with home control of lighting and Heating, Ventilating, Air Conditioning (HVAC).

In addition, be sure to discuss how many security access codes the homeowners would like and if they want to be able to secure a portion of the house while using the rest of it (this is called partitioning in security jargon). The results of this interview will help determine the security panel and components you will use.

Security System Technologies

In new construction situations, wired security systems are the first choice. They are easy to install during the pre-wire stage and are cost-effective over wireless technology components. However, wireless systems can be easily retrofitted into an existing home, though wiring is an option if the attic, crawlspace and basement allow for retrofit wiring.

Other technologies, such as infrared (IR), ultrasonic, electromagnetic induction, and digital signal processors (DSP) are used in the sensors and detectors that can be incorporated into the system. However, the most important consideration when designing a security system is the technology that is to be used to interconnect the components of the system, wired or wireless.

Security Zones

An important element in the design of a security system is the planning of the security zones and how the security system's components are to be placed in each zone. A security system zone includes the adjacent areas of a home that will be reported together

Situation	Possible Solutions
Do all the exterior doors have deadbolt locks?	Automatic door locks and (NC) contacts
Are all the exterior doors lighted?	Security lighting
Are all the exterior doors visible to the street or sidewalk?	Security lighting
Is the main entrance to the home convenient to the main activity areas or bedrooms in the home?	Door intercom and keypad, remote control of automatic door locks, camera at the main entrance
Does the garage door have an automatic door opener?	NC contacts and automatic door opener
Do all windows have locks?	Window locks and NC contacts
Are all windows in plain sight and not hidden by shrubbery or trees?	Window locks, contact sensors, security screen wiring, security lighting
Is exterior lighting installed to illuminate all sides of the home?	Security lighting
Are motion detectors installed to control the exterior lighting?	Motion detectors and security lighting
Are smoke detectors installed in the hallways, bedrooms, stairways, basement, and garage?	Smoke detectors
Is a carbon monoxide detector installed in or near the bedrooms and near the furnace?	Carbon monoxide detectors
Are the smoke or carbon monoxide detectors hard-wired or battery powered?	Hard-wired detectors
Is at least one telephone available on every floor of the house for emergency use?	Installation of additional telephone outlets
Are keys to the house hidden near the main or secondary entrances?	Doorway keypads

Table 32-1   Security Issues and Solutions

when an alarm occurs. Each zone in a home can have a different number of doors and windows, and can include different contents of the room or rooms. A security zone may be a single room, multiple rooms, open areas, or the exterior of the home.

The zoning of a home should be based on the floor plan or layout of the home, the requirements of the homeowners, and the capabilities of the selected security system. For example, the zoning plan illustrated in Figure 32-1 creates five zones, each of which has different needs and requirements. Table 32-2 lists these five zones and their security needs.

Beyond the planning shown in Figure 32-1 and Table 32-2, additional information must be included, such as:

- Most fire safety laws and building codes require smoke detectors in all sleeping areas, hallways, kitchens, and on each level of a home.

- Four of the bedroom windows are located on the street side of the home.

- The two doors leading to the patio and the family room door leading to the porch are glass sliding doors.

PART VIII

Figure 32-1
An example of a
zone layout plan

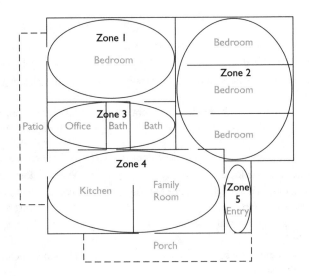

Security Component Planning

The owners of the home illustrated in Figure 32-1 have expressed a desire for the security system, when it's enabled, to detect doors and windows being opened, glass breaking on street-side windows and sliding doors, a person entering through the main doorway or the home office, and a vehicle on the driveway. In addition, they are considering install-ing security cameras on the exterior of the home and security lighting on the front and street sides of the home. Table 32-3 summarizes the components required to provide this level of security by zone.

Defining the zones and sensors to be included helps you outline the specifications for selecting the security control panel. Most panels come with a standard number of zones, such as eight, and the panel can be expanded to add more zones. When designing which devices will be on what zones it is important to look at each of the device's power requirements and the maximum power that can be supplied by the security panel. It may be necessary to add additional power sources to feed all of the powered devices. Consult the manufacturer's documentation for details.

Zone	Rooms	Outside Doors	Windows	Contents
1	Master bedroom	1	4	TV, jewelry, art
2	Bedrooms	0	6	TVs, collectibles
3	Office, baths	0	1	Computer, office equipment
4	Kitchen, family room	2	4	Microwave, appliances, home entertainment center
5	Entry	1	2	Art

Table 32-2   The Zone Plan for the Layout Shown in Figure 32-1

| | Zone | | | | | | |
Component	1	2	3	4	5	Exterior	Total
	Master Bedroom	Bedrooms	Office & Baths	Kitchen & Family Room	Entry		
Cameras	0	0	0	0	0	2	2
Door Contacts	1	0	0	2	1	0	4
Glass Break Detectors	1	0	0	1	0	0	2
Driveway Sensor	0	0	0	0	0	1	1
Motion Sensors	0	0	1	0	1	0	2
Smoke Detectors	1	3	1	1	0	0	6
Window Contacts	4	6	1	4	2	0	17

Table 32-3   Security System Component Planning

If the security system design includes either interior or exterior surveillance cameras or motion detectors, consider their placement carefully to ensure they can "see" the areas they are intended to view.

 CROSS-REFERENCE   See Chapter 31 for more on the functions and use of security system components and devices and Chapter 35 for more on video surveillance systems.

Security Systems and Structured Wiring
The next step in the design of the security system is to plan the cable requirements for the system. If the plan is to install home run wiring to each of the security system components, the structured wiring plan must be adapted to include these cable runs.

Security System Wiring
In a structured wiring environment, wiring is terminated at the security system's master unit, or panel, from each sensor, keypad, contact, smoke or heat detector, or alarm sounding device. The wiring, like all structured wiring, is installed in a star topology with a home run between the security system control panel and each device.

Be sure to include the security wiring on the structured wiring chart or make a separate chart for it.

Hard-Wired Systems
The wiring installed to connect each component to the security system control unit should be home runs between the security panel and each of the security devices. Looping, that is installing several devices, such as window or screen contacts, on a single loop of wire in

series, should be minimized, if possible. Any security device that will be used to trigger the action of another home system device, such as a door contact or motion detector signaling a room's lights be powered on, must be wired separately and individually.

Table 32-4 lists the more commonly used security system components and the wire type recommended for each device.

Wireless Systems

Wireless security systems communicate with RF signaling that is typically in the range of 300 to 900 megahertz (MHz). In many situations, a combination of wireless and wired devices may prove to be a more reliable design, depending on the distance from the wireless device to the base unit (range) or the necessity to install wireless devices to eliminate the need to pull wiring into the walls of a home. Be sure to read and follow the specifications of the manufacturer's products when installing wireless devices to ensure good performance. Also be sure to note battery replacement is recommended annually.

RJ-31X Connections

If the security system is to include a telephone link for calling out, such as to the home-owners cell phone or a security monitoring service ,when an alarm condition occurs, the design should consider whether a single phone line connection or multiple line connections are best for the home.

Security System Component	Wire Recommendation
Keypads	Standard: 22 AWG 4-conductor stranded
	Advanced, with voice pick-up and playback: 2 runs of 18 AWG 2-conductor shielded stranded
Internal and external alarms, speakers, and sound devices	18 AWG 2-conductor copper wire
AC power connections	18 AWG 2-conductor copper wire
Motion sensors, glass break detectors	22 AWG 4-conductor copper wire
Door and window contact sensors	22 AWG 2-conductor copper wire
Fire alarm connections, smoke detectors, and heat detectors	Fire power limited plenum (FPLP) cable or fire power limited (FPL) cable: 18 AWG four-conductor
Ground connection	14 AWG 1-conductor copper wire
RJ-31X console	22 AWG 4-conductor copper wire minimum, Cat 3 or Cat 5 preferred
Wireless sensors	Any of the above sensors but with radio frequency (RF) communications and batteries to power them so no wiring is required

Table 32-4 Wire Recommendation for Various Security System Devices

In the event of a security event (break-in, fire, and so on), the system can call out on a standard phone line; or by using an RJ-31x phone jack, it has the capability to seize the telephone line and hang up any phone call in progress, preventing any disruption from interfering with the automated telephone alert process.

CROSS-REFERENCE Chapter 27 provides information on attaching RJ-type jacks and plugs, and Chapter 31 discusses the use of the RJ-31x jack in a security system in more detail.

Lighting Interfaced to the Security System

Security lighting has been proven to prevent intrusions, to deter malicious activity, and to enhance the aesthetics of a home. By interfacing with a home control system the lights can be programmed to go on when an alarm sounds, blink when a fire alarm sounds, and even turn on and off while the homeowners are away to make the house look occupied. All of this can be linked to the time of day so it only occurs when it is dark. Many security systems today have some form of lighting control built into them for just these reasons, and act as the home control system.

The design goal for a security lighting system should be to light the areas of a home's exterior, especially those close to the home, that would, without lighting, be shadowed or dark. Motion detectors can be used to turn on lighting around the home should movement be detected. These same outdoor motion sensors can also be set up to sound a simple chime inside the home to alert the occupants that someone is outside.

When designing lighting control for security purposes, consider the following:

- **Accent lighting** downlights, coach lights, landscape lighting
- **Security lighting** flood lights
- **Interior lighting** kitchen lights, living room lights, bedroom lights for a "lived-in" look

Make a list of the lighting loads to be controlled, and be sure to communicate with the electrician that these loads will be controlled by the security/home control system, so no timers or daylight sensors are needed.

The best way to provide good lighting and vision in exterior areas is to install medium intensity, nonglare lighting fixtures that are aimed downward or shielded. For exterior lighting, three types of lamps can be used:

- **Halogen** Halogen lamps are commonly used as floodlights or landscaping lights because they provide a bright white or near-white light. Halogen lamps can be used to brightly light an area in connection with a motion detector sensing movement in its monitoring area.

- **High-Intensity Discharge (HID)**   HID lamps include mercury vapor, metal halide, high-pressure sodium, and fluorescent lamps. With the exception of fluorescent lamps, HID lamps require a warm-up period before reaching their full brightness. For this reason, HID lamps should not be used in situations where the security system requires instant-on lighting. HID lamps are better used as general lighting to constantly light an area, such as landscape or accent lighting.

- **Incandescent**   High wattage incandescent lamps can be used in just about any security lighting situation. However, because of their relatively limited life, they can be prone to burn out and defeat the purpose of the security lighting system if they are not properly maintained with a regular group replacement scheme.

If security lighting is being included in the security system design solely to provide lighting for exterior surveillance cameras, consider using cameras that include IR lighting capabilities that allow the camera to virtually see in the dark.

Chapter Review

An important element in the design of a security system is planning the security zones and how the security system's components are to be placed in each zone. A security zone may be a single room, multiple rooms, open areas, or the exterior of the home. The zoning of a home should be based on the floorplan or layout of the home and the requirements of the homeowners.

The design of the security system should include a plan for the system's cable requirements. Structured wiring is installed in a star topology with a home run from the security system master unit to each device. Wireless security systems communicate with RF signaling. A combination of wireless and wired devices may prove to be more reliable.

If the security system is to include an RJ-31x jack to provide the system with a telephone link, the system will have the capability to seize a telephone line to place an automated telephone alert.

Security lighting has been proven to prevent intrusions, to deter malicious activity, and to enhance the aesthetics of a home. The design goal should be to light areas along a home's exterior that are in the shadows or dark. Motion detectors can be used to turn on lighting around the home should movement be detected. In addition, lighting should be identified and controlled to give the home the "lived-in" look.

Questions

1. Which of the following questions may not be asked during a design interview with a homeowner?

   A. Do all exterior doors have deadbolt locks?

   B. What are the homeowners' occupations?

   C. Do all the windows have locks?

   D. Are the smoke or carbon monoxide detectors hard-wired or battery powered?

2. Which type of wiring provides the best solution for a security system being installed as a part of a new home construction project?

A. PLC

B. Wireless

C. Structured wiring

D. Daisy-chain

3. What is the primary characteristic of a security zone?

A. It contains only one type of security system device.

B. It includes adjacent areas that have the same security requirements.

C. It is easily reached with home run wiring.

D. It is frequently occupied or used.

4. Fire safety and building codes require smoke detectors be placed in which areas of a home?

A. Near or in bedrooms

B. Hallways

C. Stairways

D. Kitchens

E. All of the above

5. The design of a security system can impact which other home automation designs or plans?

A. Lighting

B. Structured wiring

C. Telephone

D. Data network

E. All of the above

6. Which type of security system sensors or contacts can be wired in series on a loop?

A. Door contacts

B. Window or screen contacts

C. Cameras

D. Motion sensors

7. In general, what is the recommended cabling for window and door contacts and sensors in a home security system?

A. 14 AWG 1-conductor copper wire

B. 22 AWG 2-conductor copper wire

  C. Cat 5e

  D. RG6

8. What type of connection is used to link a security system to the telephone interface to allow for line seizure?

  A. BNC

  B. RJ-11

  C. RJ-31X

  D. RJ-45

9. Which of the following lamp types is/are commonly used for brightly illuminating the exterior area in a security lighting system?

  A. Halogen

  B. HID

  C. Incandescent

  D. IR

  E. All of the above

10. Which of the following lighting system characteristics should be included in the design of a security lighting system?

  A. Medium intensity

  B. Non-glare

  C. Downward

  D. Shielded

  E. All of the above

  F. None of the above

Answers

1. **B.** Although this information could be important in a small way to the design, it really has no bearing on the need to secure the home. If this were important to the design, the homeowner would certainly volunteer it. The other choices are questions you should likely ask.

2. **C.** Daisy chaining is a no-no, PLC and wireless can be incorporated into a security system, and structured wiring is typically the best way to go.

3. **B.** This answer just about says it all.

4. **E.** Be sure you verify these requirements with the local fire department or building code authority.

5. E. In a home technology integration environment, any system design can impact any or all other system designs.

6. B. Window or screen sensors can be wired in a series-connected loop. All other security system devices should be wired in parallel with individual home runs.

7. B. These devices require only two-conductor wire.

8. C. This is a special-purpose connector that provides an interface between the security system and the telephone system.

9. A, B, and C. IR lighting is used to allow security cameras to see in the dark, but it won't work to light up the exterior area of a home.

10. E. These are the lamp and fixture characteristics that provide the best exterior lighting.

Installing a Home Security System

In this chapter, you will learn about:
- Wiring and installing home security sensors, contacts, and keypads
- Configuring the security system control panel
- Testing a home security system

The activities involved with the installation of a home security system are about the sensors and contacts. In order for the home security system to perform and protect the residence and its occupants, they must be carefully placed to do their job properly. If a window contact doesn't contact correctly or an opened door blocks a motion sensor, the security system won't be able to perform as it should and detect an intruder, defeating the purpose of the entire system.

This chapter focuses on the steps used to install and test the sensors, contacts, keypads, and control panel of a home security system. The focus is on installing hard-wired systems, but some information about the installation of a wireless system is included as well.

Video surveillance and home access systems can also be integrated into a home security system and are covered in Chapters 35 and 36, respectively.

Installing a Home Security System

A hard-wired security system requires very little after-installation maintenance and provides the assurance that if a sensor or contact trips, the system master or control panel will receive a signal, which may not always be true of a wireless system. However, a wireless security system is easier to install in a retrofit situation, but it also has some placement and operational issues that are discussed later in the chapter.

Component Wiring and Installation

Installing security system components as part of a new construction project allows the cabling required for the sensors, contacts, and keypads to be placed in a room or zone to be installed along with the structured wiring system. However, if the system is being installed in an existing home, wiring must be pulled through the existing walls, floor, or ceiling. Remember, the right wire type needs to be installed for each specific type of device.

The minimum wiring requirements for each of the more common security system components are detailed in the following sections. See Chapter 32 for a summary of the wiring requirements of a security system and its components.

Security System Control Panel

The system control panel, also referred to as an alarm system or a master unit, is where all the wiring of a security system's sensors and contacts terminates. The system control panel should be placed in the same area as the structured wiring distribution panel or, if that is not possible, in a centrally located and convenient location that is not easily accessible from the outside (do not place it in the garage). A closet or the mechanical room are both good locations.

The only specific electrical wiring for the system control panel itself is access to an electrical outlet for the AC power transformer. The wire used should be 4-conductor 22-gauge copper cable from the control panel to the transformer.

Keypads

Security system keypads, like the one shown in Figure 33-1, can be wall-mounted or recessed units that provide a user interface to the security system to control a single zone or the whole-house system.

Security system keypads require a 4-conductor 22-gauge copper cable. Two of the wires carry power from the control panel to the keypad, and the other two wires are used to transmit signals between the keypad and the control panel.

Figure 33-1
A security system keypad is used to control the security settings for a zone.

Photo courtesy of Honeywell International Inc.

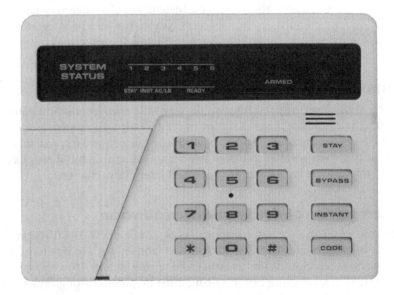

Door and Window Contacts

Door and window contacts are passive switches and don't require separate power from the system control panel. To connect a door or window contact to the control panel, use 2-conductor 22-gauge unshielded copper cable. Door and window contacts can be wired in series in a loop, with the wiring from the last contact looping back to the first contact. In this configuration, a signal from any of the contacts in the loop will be transmitted back to the control panel from the first unit in the loop. Figure 33-2 illustrates how window contacts can be wired in series on a single loop of wire.

Door and window contacts are available in a variety of styles, including the most commonly used ones known as recessed switches that are inserted in holes drilled in the door or window and its framing (see Figure 33-3), surface-mount switches (see Figure 33-5), and roller-ball styles that operate by compressing and releasing a roller-ball (see Figure 33-4).

Figure 33-5 shows how a surface-mount window contact works. When the window is closed, a magnet in the part mounted on the window closes the switch into its normally closed (NC) position. When the window is opened, the magnet moves away from the spring-loaded switch inside the frame-mounted part and a trip signal is generated. A door contact operates in the same way; the only difference being that the magnet part moves away from the switch part when the door is opened.

To allow for a window to be open and still provide security protection, a second magnet can be mounted in the window frame to detect contact while the window is in the open position. This allows for the window to be in two positions, closed and open to this distance, and either location provides a NC (normally closed) contact.

Glass Break Sensors

The two common types of glass break sensors are acoustic (sound) and vibration (shock). Which type is better for a particular installation depends on the type of glass (plate glass, tempered glass, or laminated glass) in the window, door, or relight pane.

Figure 33-2
A diagram showing window and glass break sensors wired in a series loop

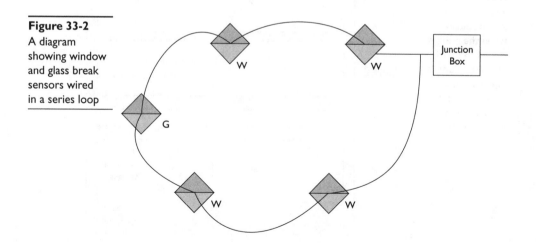

Figure 33-3
A roller-ball style door and window contact switch

Photo courtesy of Honeywell International Inc.

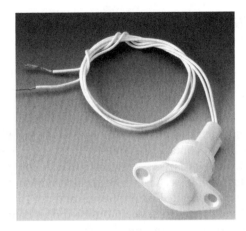

Acoustic Glass Break Detectors   Acoustic detectors are tuned to only pick up the sound of breaking glass and this prevents them from generating a trip signal for any other sounds. Acoustic glass break detectors are placed on a wall or ceiling near the windows to be monitored. Typically, a single acoustic sensor (see Figure 33-6) is able to monitor all the windows of a medium-sized room.

One challenge to installing acoustic glass break sensors is testing them. Instead of actually breaking a window to see if the sensor is working, several sensor manufacturers also sell glass break detector testers that make the sound of glass breaking—a much better way to test these units.

Figure 33-4
Part A of this illustration shows a recessed roller switch compressed when the door is closed. In Part B, when the door is opened, the ball is released and a signal is sent by the switch.

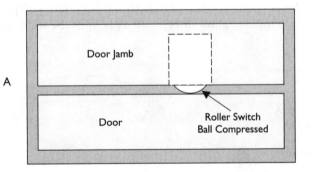

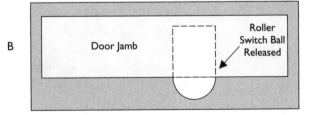

Figure 33-5
The operation of
a window contact
switch

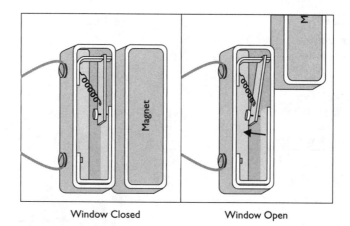

Window Closed　　　　Window Open

Acoustic sensors, also called active sensors, require power from the control panel plus two conductors for signaling; so 4-conductor 22-gauge copper wiring is required. If the sensor has a tampering relay and the homeowner wishes to connect it to the control panel, six conductors are needed.

Vibration Glass Break Detectors　Vibration glass break detectors, also called passive detectors, are place directly on the glass or on the window frame very close to the window. If an intruder knocks or taps on the glass or breaks it, the vibration is sensed and a trip signal is generated.

Vibration detectors, see Figure 33-7, are passive devices that don't require power from the control panel. Two-conductor 22-gauge wire is used to connect the detector to the control panel.

Figure 33-6
An acoustic glass
break detector
"hears" the
sound of breaking
glass and signals
the alarm system.

Photo courtesy of FBII.

Figure 33-7
A vibration glass break detector is mounted on a windowpane to sense vibrations from knocks, taps, or hits on a window.

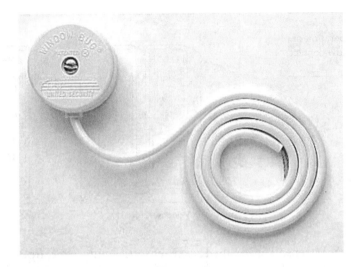

When deciding the type of glass break detector to install, be sure to consider if power is available to drive the acoustic sensors. When strategically placed, acoustic sensors can cover more than one window at a time but with vibration detectors there needs to be one installed on every window to be protected.

Motion Sensors

Two technologies are used in motion sensors: passive IR (PIR) or active ultrasound. Regardless of the technology used, the wiring requirements are the same. The most important issue when installing a motion sensor is placement in the room. If the purpose of the sensor is to detect someone entering the room, the sensor cannot be placed so that an opening door blocks the sensor. The sensor should be placed so that it monitors the areas of a room where the homeowners have the most concern. The recommended height of a motion sensor is 7-feet above the floor.

A common cause of false alarms for standard PIR motion detectors are small children or household pets entering a room and the detector signaling a security event. Many PIR units are available with horizontal scan "pet alleys" that prevent movement by short or small children or pets from triggering an alarm. Adaptive units such as PIR/Microwave sensors self-adjust to the room and its environment and other sensors are designed to be pet-smart with horizontal bands of the scan range set aside for pets and small children. Some units even attempt to estimate the weight of a scanned object and suppress the alarm for moving objects that are estimated to weigh less than 80 pounds.

Motion sensors, like the one shown in Figure 33-8, require a minimum of four conductors between the control panel and the sensor: two to carry 12V DC power from the control panel and two to carry the trip (motion detected) signal. Some motion detectors also have additional contacts to detect attempts to tamper with the sensor and to report self-diagnostics to a control panel. Although these additional tamper monitoring terminals are generally not connected in home systems, if the homeowner wishes to include

Figure 33-8

A motion sensor detects movement in a room.

Photo courtesy of Honeywell International Inc.

these functions in the security system, use add two additional conductors in the cable to connect the sensor to the control panel.

Smoke, Fire, and CO Detectors

Smoke, fire and carbon monoxide (CO) sensors are surface-mount devices that are installed on the ceiling or above doorways in hallways near bedrooms, kitchens (close to cooking areas), stairways, garages, mechanical rooms, and near furnaces and boilers.

Smoke, fire and CO detectors require a 4-conductor 18-gauge unshielded fire-rated cable and can be wired in series (daisy-chained) with the wire terminating at the control panel connected to the first sensor, which is then wired to the second sensor, and so on. If more than five sensors are to be installed in series, they should be split up into separate series of four units to make troubleshooting easier, should it be necessary later.

Sirens

Most residential security systems use what are called speaker sirens. The siren (sounding) unit is a module located in the security system control panel that is connected to the siren speaker using 2-conductor 18-gauge copper cable. The siren speaker is a passive device that doesn't require power, much like a standard audio speaker but does require a heavier gauge cable than the sensors so that the sound signal is not lost as it travels over the cable.

Speaker sirens are available in two general styles, horn or surface-mount. Horn-style speaker sirens are typically used for exterior applications or placed in an out-of-the-way location, like an attic or a garage. Surface mount speakers (see Figure 33-9) are like small audio speakers that can be mounted in a room or another interior location.

Low Temperature Sensors

There are two types of low-temperature sensors: those that have a mechanical switch, also called a "freezestat," and those that use a length of tubing that acts as an averaging sensor. In either case, when the temperature falls below a certain level, for example 39 degrees Fahrenheit or 41 degrees Fahrenheit (both common settings), the sensor sounds

Figure 33-9
A surface-mount speaker siren.

Photo courtesy of Ademco.

an audible signal, if desired, and transmits a signal to a security system controller. Some devices are hardwired and send signals through a relay and others connect using an RJ-12 connection to structured wiring.

Water Detectors

These types of sensors or detectors are also called leak detectors, and what they do is detect water leaks by monitoring for water pooling in a certain area or any detectable change in the water pressure in a pipe or tube. Nearly all water detector sensors can be connected to a home security network through either an interface module or via a relay connection on the sensor.

Humidity Sensors

Humidity sensors monitor the moisture content of the air inside a home or enclosed area. Most of the better humidity sensors have a high setting and a low setting that signals when the humidity gets too low or too high. Other humidity sensors have only a single set point and either signal when the humidity is either too low or too high, but not both. Those humidity sensors that can be interfaced to a home security control system are able to connect to any system that recognizes relay signals or dry contact switches, such as PLC and other powerline technologies.

Telephone Interface Connections

Most security control panels have a relay connection that is used to seize a telephone line to transmit an alarm signal, message, or voice recording to a home security monitoring service or telephone numbers programmed in the system.

The security system control panel should be the first device on the telephone wiring in the home. This means that the RJ-31X jack on the control panel or an add-on telephone module (see Figure 33-10) should be connected directly from the NID and before the telephone distribution module of the structured wiring system. The wiring from

Figure 33-10
A telephone
interface module
with an RJ-31X
jack.

*Photo courtesy of
ChannelVision.*

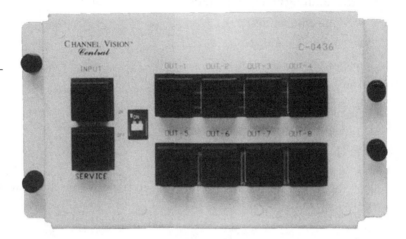

the NID to the security control panel and between the security control panel and the telephone system panel should be Cat 5e cable.

Configuring the Security System Control Panel

The process and detailed steps used to configure the security system control panel for a home security system vary by manufacturer. Most systems have a proprietary configuration process that is tied to the particular modules that are included in the standard configuration of the control panel. When installing and configuring a home security system control panel, follow the manufacturer's documentation to set up and configure the system.

Perform an interview with the homeowner about the security system to get the information necessary for system setup and user codes. Using the worksheets usually provided by the manufacturer, identify the information required. The installer can complete much of this information prior to the interview, so just get the homeowner's approval and a few more details to help speed the process along.

When setting up an alarm system, the modules and functions that usually must be configured to ensure the proper operation of the security system are:

- Hardware and Devices
  - Control panel install and power up
  - Telephone connection
  - Keypad hookups
  - Sensor interfaces
  - Fire alarm interfaces
  - Sounder outputs

- Programming and Configuration (where applicable)
  - Zone type setups
  - User codes and setups
  - Entry/exit delays
  - Panic modes
  - Digital communicator setup
  - Alarm verification process setup
  - Home control setups
  - Remote telephone control

Again, be sure to follow the specifics for setup outlined in the manufacturer's documentation.

Home Security System Testing

The installation of a home security system isn't finished until the entire system has been completely tested and any necessary adjustments are made and retested. The testing process essentially boils down to triggering trip alerts on each installed component of the system. This means that every sensor, contact, and detector must be tested by forcing the condition it was installed to monitor: opening windows and doors and entering rooms or areas outside the home monitored by motion detectors. The complete security system should be tested, including any video surveillance (Chapter 34) or home access (Chapter 35) systems that are installed and attached to the security system control panel.

The testing should start with the testing of the components in each of the rooms in a single zone and after one zone is completely tested, proceed to the next zone. It is recommended that the first room and zone tested should be the one nearest the security system control panel. Be sure to use a zone list or wire chart to check off every device tested.

Cable Tests

During pre-wire or prior to device installation be sure to conduct cable or wire testing. You should perform the standard structured wiring cable tests, including continuity and impedance. This should be done at pre-wire so as to catch any problems that can easily be remedied while the walls are open. Testing can also be done at trim-out prior to the installation of devices to confirm all the wiring is good and if a problem exists, it would be with the devices being installed.

 CROSS-REFERENCE Chapters 8 and 9 detail the testing procedures for structured wiring.

Detector Tests

After installation, hookup and setup programming of all devices, perform the following testing steps in each room:

1. Set the exit timer to its lowest setting. Security systems usually have at least two settings that allow a variable amount of time before the system arms or disarms to give the homeowners time to enter the home and disarm the system or exit the home after arming the system.

2. Centrally arm the system, as it would be when the homeowners were to leave the home.

3. Allow the exit delay time to lapse.

4. Open each protected door and window or enter a space monitored by a motion sensor to cause a trip signal and verify the alarm is triggered.

5. Also test each smoke and CO sensor located in each room or zone by pressing the test button on each. If the expected alarm isn't activated, continue to troubleshoot and test the sensor, control panel, and the alarm until all three are working properly, then move onto the next sensor.

6. On most systems, you'll need to reset the system after testing each contact, sensor, or zone.

7. After completing the testing in all zones, repeat the testing with at least one sensor in each zone with the customer observing the test.

8. Remember to reset the exit time setting to the desired time before leaving.

After completing the detector testing, test all of the user codes and any other unique system setup areas. Finally, orient the customer to the system and train the customer on the system's normal operations.

Documentation on use of the security system should be given to the homeowners for reference. Documentation of the security wiring and zones should be kept in the security control panel. Documentation of system setup should also be given to the homeowner for safekeeping away from the panel and not readily accessible to others. Finally, be sure to keep documentation in the project folder of the security system setup, programming, testing, digital communicator, and ongoing maintenance and service of the system.

Security and Fire Alarm Testing Regulations

Many countries, states and provinces, counties, and cities have regulations or guidelines, in addition to the home security industry's guidelines, on how frequently a home security system must be tested. Ensure the customer is aware of the regulations and guidelines. Table 33-1 lists the guidelines listed in the National Fire Protection Agency's (NFPA) standard #72. In addition to the NFPA, testing guidelines for home security systems are developed and published by the Security Industry Association (SIA), Underwriters Laboratories (UL), American National Standards Institute (ANSI), Canadian Standards

System Component	Testing Frequency
Monitored control panel components	Annually
Unmonitored control panel components	Semi-annually
Control panel diagnostic services	Annually
Control panel/Telephone interface	Annually
Smoke and CO detectors	Annually
Door and window sensors	Annually
Sirens, sounding devices, and strobe lights	Annually

Table 33-1   Recommended Security System Testing Frequencies

Association (CSA), and the National Burglar and Fire Alarms Association (NBFAA), as well as standards organizations and police and fire associations around the world.

Included in Table 33-1 are testing frequencies of monitored and unmonitored control panel components. A monitored component is one that the control panel has circuitry to monitor and display an alert should the component begin to fail, even intermittently. Unmonitored components are those for which a failure is not alerted. For example, a security keypad near a back door of a home may be an unmonitored component of a security system. If the keypad malfunctions, the homeowner knows the device should be repaired or replaced, but the security system may not display a notice or signal the component failure. However, the security system should alert the homeowner if a monitored component such as a door contact or a motion sensor fail to respond to monitoring signals.

Also explain to the homeowners that they should review the alarm ordinance in effect in their city, county, or state or province, and that they may be required to get a permit or license for their home security system before it will be recognized as a legal system by that authority. As a billable service to your clients, you may identify this information and process the necessary paperwork for them.

Chapter Review

Installing security system components as part of a new construction project allows the cabling required for the sensors, contacts, and keypads to be placed in a room or zone to be installed along with or as part of the structured wiring system. If the system is installed in an existing home, wiring must be pulled through the existing walls, floor, or ceiling.

The system control panel terminates the wiring from all sensors or contacts. The system control panel should be placed in the same area as the structured wiring distribution panel or a protected area, not in the garage. The system control panel usually requires electrical wiring to an AC outlet for the plug-in power transformer.

Door and window contacts are passive switches and don't require separate power from the system control panel. Door and window contacts are available in a variety of styles, including recessed switches, surface-mount switches, and roller-ball styles.

The two common types of glass break sensors are acoustic and vibration. The type that should be used for a particular installation depends on the type of glass used. Acoustic detectors are tuned to only pick up the sound of breaking glass in a medium sized room. Vibration glass break detectors are placed directly on the glass or the window frame of every window being protected.

Security system keypads are wall-mounted or recessed units that provide user interface to the security system to control a single zone or the whole-house system.

Motion sensors are either passive IR (PIR) or active ultrasound. The recommended height of a motion sensor is 7-feet above the floor.

Most residential security systems use speaker sirens that are activated by the control panel sending audio signals. Speaker sirens have two styles, horn or surface-mount.

Smoke, fire, and carbon monoxide (CO) sensors are surface-mount devices installed on ceilings or above doorways in hallways near bedrooms, kitchens (close to cooking areas), stairways, garages, and near furnaces and boilers. Smoke and fire detectors must be installed with fire-rated wiring.

Environmental monitoring sensors, which include low temperature sensors, water or moisture detectors, and humidity sensors, can be integrated into a security system to prevent conditions from harming the home or its contents.

Security control panels use a relay connection inside an RJ-31 telephone jack to seize a telephone line and transmit an alarm signal, message, or voice recording to a home security monitoring service or programmed phone numbers. The security system control panel should be the first device on the telephone system.

The process and detailed steps used to configure the security system control panel for a home security system varies by manufacturer, and a proprietary configuration process is used to configure the control panel. When installing and configuring a home security system control panel, follow the manufacturer's documentation to set up and configure the system.

The installation of a home security system can be considered finished when the entire system has been completely tested and any necessary adjustments are made and retested. The testing process involves triggering trip alerts on each installed component of the system. Testing should begin with cable or wire testing and continue by testing the sensors and contacts in each room or zone. Documentation should be done of wiring and zones and kept inside the security panel. Documentation of setup should be given to the homeowner for safekeeping and all documentation should be kept in the installation company's project folder.

Many countries, states and provinces, counties, and cities have regulations or guidelines concerning the frequency for home security system testing. Homeowners should be made aware of any alarm ordinances in effect in their city, county, or state or province.

Questions

1. In a home security system, where do home runs to zone sensors and contacts terminate?

   A. Security system control panel

   B. Home automation controller

   C. Keypad

   D. Wiring distribution panel

2. Which of the following is not a passive device?

   A. Door contact

   B. PIR motion detector

   C. Vibration glass break sensor

   D. Window contact

3. Which type of glass break sensor is typically mounted directly to the glass of a window or door?

   A. Acoustic

   B. Vibration

   C. PIR

   D. All of the above

4. At what height should a wall-mounted motion detector be installed?

   A. 4 feet

   B. 5 feet

   C. 7 feet

   D. Even with light switches and keypads

5. On some sensors, there are tamper sensors and self-diagnostic relays. When these options are wired, what wire/cable should be used to completely wire a motion sensor?

   A. 4-conductor 22-gauge unshielded copper wire

   B. Two runs of 4-conductor 22-gauge unshielded copper wire

   C. Cat 5e

   D. None of the above; motion sensors are passive devices.

6. A speaker siren is a self-contained device that generates its own audible sounds.

   A. True

   B. False

7. Which of the following is not a recommended location for a smoke detector?

   A. Bedrooms

   B. Hallways near bedrooms

   C. Kitchen

   D. Bathroom

8. What connector type is used to connect a security system control panel to a telephone interface?

   A. RJ-11

   B. RJ-21X

    C. RJ-31X

    D. RJ-45

9. Which of the following standards organizations issues guidelines for the frequency of home security system component testing?

    A. ANSI

    B. CSA

    C. NFPA

    D. UL

    E. All of the above

10. Which of the following security system elements should be checked and tested at least semi-annually?

    A. Monitored control panel components

    B. Unmonitored control panel components

    C. Smoke and CO detectors

    D. Door and window sensors

Answers

1. **A.** The home run wiring of the security system could be routed through the structured wiring distribution panel or the home automation controller, but this approach would complicate the home's wiring unnecessarily. Keypads only serve as user interfaces and zone controls in a security system.

2. **B.** PIR motion detector is the only active (powered) device.

3. **B.** PIR is not a type of glass break sensor and acoustic sensors are typically mounted where they can listen and monitor all of the windows in a room.

4. **C.** This height allows the sensor to scan the full-height of any person entering or occupying a room.

5. **B.** Six conductors are required to complete the wiring of a sensor with tamper detection.

6. **B.** Speaker sirens receive audio signals from a siren module installed in the security system control panel.

7. **D.** It is not necessary to install a smoke detector here. The other choices are locations in which a smoke detector should be installed.

8. **D.** A telephone interface module with an RJ-31X jack facilitates line seizure and the ability to place a security alert on a telephone line.

9. **E.** All of these organizations, plus several others, create testing frequency standards for fire and intruder alarms systems.

10. **B.** The other security system components should be tested annually.

34

Troubleshooting and Maintaining a Home Security System

In this chapter, you will learn about:
- Preventing false alarms
- Troubleshooting home security systems
- Maintaining a home security system

In order for a home security system to function properly, it must be properly maintained. Even more than most other home systems, a security system is one that the homeowner must be able to depend upon. For the most part, a security system is rarely activated, and most homeowners hope it is actually never needed. However, if or when an intruder attempts to gain access to a home, the security system must function properly.

The key to a reliable security system is regular preventive maintenance and testing, and these procedures are the focus of this chapter.

False Alarms

The single most important issue for a homeowner and a home security system is false alarms and preventing them. However, on some systems, there can be a fine balance between a system that provides immediate detection and activation in the event of a home security breach and one that sets off frequent and costly false alarms. In many cities and counties, false alarms are not only embarrassing for the homeowner, but they can also be expensive.

In an effort to deter false alarms, especially for alarms systems monitored where emergency services are called, many communities have passed ordinances that levy escalating fines for multiple false alarm offenders to offset the cost to the community for providing these response services. The solution is to prevent false alarms with a well-defined and regularly performed maintenance and testing program.

There are many causes for false alarms, including:

- User errors
- Power or battery problems
- Ill-fitted, misaligned, or improperly placed sensors and contacts
- Malfunctioning detection devices
- Sensors not configured for pets or children
- Heating, Ventilating, Air Conditioning (HVAC) vents or air drafts that cause light objects to move

User Errors

More than two-thirds of all false alarms are caused by user errors that can include operating the system improperly and forgetting the access codes. Another major reason for a sudden rash of false alarms from a system can be caused by changes to the home, such as guests visiting, the addition of a new family member or pet, or remodeling doors, floors, windows, or ceilings.

The homeowner should train the new family member or houseguest on the use of the security system. In addition, the homeowner may contact his security system provider whenever these or other changes occur to the home. He should also contact the security system provider and request a "visitor" user code be set up when keys are given to outsiders or he plans to put the house up for sale.

Some municipalities require a home security system be inspected and tested by a certified (licensed) technician no less than once a year, with some requiring semi-annual inspections and testing. During the annual or semi-annual inspection, maintenance, and testing, the homeowner should be given a fresh orientation to the system, with emphasis placed on any user-error caused false alarms since the last visit.

The user should also be advised on how to prevent future false alarms. This includes what to check before activating the alarm system, including locking all protected doors and windows and keeping pets, plants, balloons, holiday decorations, and the like out of the scanning field of a motion detector or sensor.

Power or Battery Issues

A security sensor or contact that is intermittently reporting false alarms (also called positives) may have power or continuity issues caused by cable or wire problems. Passive security devices receive power from their primary wiring from the security control panel. Active security devices require an independent power source that is typically supplied through a power supply or battery. A device with faulty wiring or an active device with the wrong type of battery installed may cause false positive signals to be transmitted to the security system controller.

Misaligned Sensors or Contacts

A window or door contact that is even slightly misaligned may generate a false alarm even if the window or door is closed and locked. A window or door that is not completely closed and locked in the position where its contact was aligned can create this situation. This problem can also be caused by a window or door warping or otherwise changing its fit. All doors and windows should be closed completely and locked before the alarm system is activated.

Motion sensors can generate false alarms if they are in view of outdoor activities that could trigger them. Be sure the line-of-sight of a motion sensor is clear of any unwanted motion.

Sensors and detectors can also generate false alarms if they are placed too closely to some normal activities in a home. For example, if a smoke detector is located directly above a stove after a kitchen remodeling, it can generate false smoke alarms.

Malfunctioning Detection Devices

Detection devices have been known to fail over time. When they do fail, they can stop functioning completely or function intermittently and cause random false alarms. Hopefully these are caught during routine maintenance checking. Replace the device in question and this should rectify the false alarm problem. It is a good rule to replace carbon monoxide detectors every three to four years as their performance deteriorates over time.

Pets and Children

Motion sensors can be configured to avoid signaling an alarm event for small children and pets. If this setting is overlooked during installation or incorrectly set originally or incorrectly reset by the homeowner, the sensor can generate a false alarm. When installing motion sensors with adjustable viewing, be sure to set these up per the manufacturer's instructions and test extensively from all angles of view of the motion sensor.

Moving Objects

If the placement of motion sensors does not take into consideration the location of HVAC vents or ceiling or room fans, the movement of an object, such as a houseplant or curtain, may set off an alarm from a motion detector. Or perhaps the motion detector was not properly aligned to avoid these objects during its installation. In either case, the motion sensor could be generating false alarms that may not be easily resolved if the cause isn't happening during an investigation. Watch out for helium balloons often given as a greeting of "Happy Birthday" or "Get Well Soon" as these rise and fall with the change of temperature in a room and are an unwanted easy target for a motion sensor.

Lost Setup on the Security System Controller

The security system panel is programmed to know the types and names of the security zones. In addition, it is programmed to know all of the user codes and other system setup variables. If any of this information is lost in the memory of the system, false alarms can easily occur as zone types and setups usually default to factory settings. If this is the problem, it usually will be revealed at the keypad because programmed names no longer appear. A prolonged loss of power may be the cause if the battery life is exhausted. To correct this, restore power to the system and reprogram it or download a saved setup of the programming. Many systems now have remote access capabilities and the security system provider can phone the home and download this information.

Troubleshooting a Home Security System

When troubleshooting a home security system, you must first determine whether the problem is being caused by one of the four major areas of a security system:

- Contacts, sensors, or detectors
- The security system controller
- The wiring
- The interface to the telephone system

One of the better ways to pinpoint a fault on a home security system is to completely retest the system using the same procedure used during the trim out of the system (see Chapter 33). Once you have isolated the room or zone where the problem is occurring, you can then begin to focus on the security devices in that area.

Troubleshooting Contacts, Sensors, and Detectors

If you suspect that a home security system problem is being caused by a contact or sensor, you should check the alignment, fit, cleanliness, and wiring of the device to ensure that they haven't changed since installation.

NOTE A quick way to check the wiring connecting any contact, sensor, or detector device to a control panel or system controller is to replace it with a known-good device. If the known-good device fails, the problem is likely in the wiring; otherwise, if the known-good device works as it should, the problem is the failure of the original device.

Door and Window Contacts

The alignment of the two halves of a door or window contact sensor is crucial to its proper operation. If the contacts do not line up properly (see Chapters 31, 32, and 33), the electromagnetic functions of the sensor may not work properly. The misalignment of door and window contacts can be caused by the door or window becoming warped or sagging on its hinges or frame. The contacts may have been bent, moved, or knocked off by a hit or struck with some force. These conditions should be easily spotted with a visual inspection. The remedies are to realign, reinstall, or replace the contact to its correct position.

As a part of a visual inspection, check the contacts for corrosion and cleanliness. If the contact has been subjected to moisture, it is possible the contact face has become corroded or perhaps even shorted out. The contacts should be cleaned using denatured alcohol (isopropyl alcohol) and a lint-free cloth in any case and retested.

If you or your company did not install the security system, you should also check that the contacts are wired properly. Normally Closed (NC) contacts are typically wired in series, and Normally Open (NO) contacts are typically wired in parallel. Also verify that the wiring to each contact is correctly attached using proper wiring methods, and that the appropriate wire types were installed.

To test NC contacts wired in series, the contacts should be tested in sequence, starting with all but the first contact disconnected from the wiring. After each contact is tested (and all is well), the next contact in line should be added back to the system and tested, until all contacts are reconnected and tested. Any defective contacts should be replaced.

Motion Sensors

The first step in troubleshooting a motion sensor is to verify its line-of-sight or scanning field. Objects such as curtains, draperies, art, or plants may be moving because of airflow in the room. The airflow may be from a window that is regularly open or even an HVAC system vent. Perhaps the swing of a door into the room was overlooked during installation and is blocking the view of the sensor or the sensor is set too high or too low to properly detect unusual motion in its room.

If the scanning field of the sensor is unobstructed and properly set, the next thing to check is the power. If the sensor is an active device, verify that its power light-emitting diode (LED) is on. If the power indicator is not on, check the device's power source, especially if the device uses an alternating current/direct current (AC/DC) converter, to ensure it is snugly plugged into an AC outlet. (Some AC/DC converters are too heavy for the AC connectors and can fall out of the socket.)

If the device is a passive device where it gets its power from its wiring, check the wiring and verify that it conforms to the device's documentation. If the wiring is correct, check the accessory connections on the system controller using a multimeter to verify a connection of 12 to 18 volts to match the power requirements of the device.

If the wiring checks out, it is likely the device has failed, regardless of whether it is passive or active, and should be replaced.

Smoke, Fire, and CO Detectors

The quickest way to troubleshoot a smoke, fire, or carbon monoxide (CO) detector or alarm is to first determine how the device is powered. If the detector is battery-powered, change the battery and test the device; if it works, the battery was dead. However, if the detector fails to work regardless of its power source (assuming the power source is good), it may be that the photoelectric circuits (the detectors) have failed or have been damaged. In either case, this means the detector should be replaced.

If a smoke, fire, or CO detector is giving false alarms, the activities in its room or area may be the cause rather than the device itself having a problem. For example, CO detectors can generate an alarm from some common household products, such as hair spray,

spray air deodorizers, bleach, paint, glue, nail polish and nail polish remover, dirty baby diapers, cigarette smoke, or even the nitroglycerin in heart medication—any product that may give off a vapor or contains CO gas. Carbon dioxide (CO_2) detectors also deteriorate over time and should be replaced every three to four years. A smoke detector placed too close to a normal activity that could produce some smoke, such as cooking, can also generate an alarm.

In these cases, the location of the detector may be the problem. However, if this is not the case, check the device wiring, and if all is well, replace the device.

Troubleshooting Keypad Controls and Wiring

If a security system fails to respond to the commands made through a keypad controller, the first suspect should be the wiring connecting the keypad to the system controller. The wiring should be tested for continuity, and the wire terminations on the keypad and at the control panel should be checked and verified.

If the wiring proves to be okay, the problem could be that the control panel or keypad has failed, but the problem may also be in the configuration or programming of the security system. If the keypad can be replaced successfully with a known-good device, then the keypad was the problem. However, if this is not the case, the system should be reprogrammed for that keypad, or reprogrammed by restoring a backup of the controller or by reentering the original (and tested) configuration.

Troubleshooting RJ-31X Connections

If a security system fails to connect to a telephone line to place an outbound call to a security monitoring system or to emergency services in a security event, the RJ-31X connections of the system should be tested and diagnosed.

To troubleshoot a system's RJ-31X interface, follow these steps:

1. Verify the installation and validity of the wiring to the security system controller and the telephone system to the RJ-31X jack, as well as the cabling and termination to the jack.

2. Check the continuity of telephone line wiring. If an open circuit or damaged contact exists, track it down, repair it, and retest the RJ-31X interface.

3. If the RJ-31X interface still has problems, check the RJ-31X jack and plug carefully. An RJ-31X jack has shorting bars that cross terminals 1 to 4 and 5 to 8. When the plug is inserted in the RJ-31X jack, the contact wires are lifted away from the shorting bars and make contact with the tip and ring circuits leading to the security system. Should the jack or plug become damaged, it is possible that the contact wires are not making the proper contacts to the security system or the phone. Visually inspect the jack and plug for damage and replace either or both if necessary.

4. To completely test the RJ-31X interface, cause a security event on the control panel and verify that the security system has seized the line and the interior lines cannot access the phone line.

Preventive Maintenance

A regular periodic program of preventive maintenance can assure the homeowners that their security system is properly functioning and reliable. The frequency of the preventive maintenance program should never be less than at least once annually, with quarterly or semi-annual programs at the discretion of the homeowners. However, the more complex the security system, the more frequently it should be checked.

While there aren't any disadvantages to frequent preventive maintenance checks to a homeowner, other than perhaps the cost, the advantages are

- Prevention of false alarms
- Fewer service or problem calls
- Desired changes implemented when needed
- Reliability of the system
- Manufacturer's upgrades applied regularly
- Developing or potentials problems corrected before they cause the system to fail

Periodic Testing

To be in compliance with National Fire Protection Association (NFPA) 72 guidelines, a home security system must be tested at least once per year. A certified system tester must perform the annual test, but the homeowner should know how to test the system and perform a test every 30 days (which is the requirement of some local security system ordinances).

Homeowner Testing

The testing procedure performed by the homeowner should include the following tests:

- **Arm and disarm the system**   Every person with a key to the home should perform this test.
- **Fail all exterior ingress points**   Test each window and outside door contacts and motion sensors. The homeowner should alert the monitoring service before the testing begins and when it is complete.
- **Test smoke and CO detectors**   Press the test buttons on all of these devices.

Preventive Maintenance Testing

The testing performed as a part of a preventive maintenance check should approximate the testing performed during the original acceptance tests (see Chapters 32 and 33). If a local emergency services authority, such as the police department, monitors the system, they may require the system to be recertified each year and a "Certificate of Completion," a NFPA form prescribed in NFPA 72, issued (although this is primarily for fire alarm systems, some communities also use it for security systems in general). Figure 34-1 shows

Fire alarm Certificate of Completion

Business Name _____   Installation Company _____

Business Address _____   Company Address _____

telephone Number_____   Telephone Number _____

Supplier_____   Business License Number _____

1. Type(s) of System or Service

NFPA 72, Chapter 3 - Local
If alarm is transmitted to location(s) off premises, list where signal is received:
Address: _____
Telephone: _____

NFPA 72, Chapter 3 - Emergency Voice/ Alarm Service
Quantity of voice/ alarm channels: _____ Single _____ Multiple _____
Quantity of speakers installed: _____ Quantity of speaker zones_____
Quantity of telephones or telephone jacks included in system: _____

NFPA 72, chapter 5 - Auxiliary
Indicate type of connection:
    Local energy   Shunt   Parallel telephone
Location of telephone numbers for receipt of signals: _____

NFPA 72, chapter 5 - Remote Station
Alarm: _____
Supervisory: _____

NFPA 72, chapter 5 - Proprietary
If alarms are transmitted to a public fire service communications center or other, indicate and telephone
numbers of the organization receiving alarm:
Address: _____ Telephone _____
Indicate how alarm is retransmitted: _____

NFPA 72, chapter 5 - Central Station
Prime Contractor: _____ Central station location _____

Means of transmission of signals from the protected premises to the central station:
    McCulloh   Multiplex   One-way radio
    Digital alarm communicator   Two-way radio   other
Means of transmission of alarms to the public fire service communications center:
(a) _____

Figure 34-1   The Certificate of Completion prescribed by NFPA 72

the first page of the NFPA 72 Certificate of Completion. In some communities, the local fire or police service may reinspect the system, but only if a Certificate of Completion has been issued by the installing or recertifying contractor.

Chapter Review

The prevention of false positives or false alarms should be one of the primary purposes of a regular maintenance and testing procedure. There are many causes for false alarms, including user errors, power or battery problems, misaligned or improperly placed sensors and contacts, sensors not configured for pets or children, malfunctioning detection devices, HVAC vents or air drafts that cause light objects to move, and setup configurations lost in the security panel. Most false alarms are caused by user errors and changes made to the home. Some municipalities require a home security system to be inspected and tested by a certified (licensed) technician no less than once a year, with some requiring semi-annual inspections and testing.

A security sensor or contact that is intermittently reporting false alarms may have power or continuity issues caused by cable or wire problems. A window or door contact that is even slightly misaligned may generate a false alarm even if the window or door is closed and locked. All doors and windows should be closed completely and locked before the alarm system is activated. Sensors and detectors incorrectly placed can also cause false alarms. Motion sensors should be configured to avoid alarm signals for small children and pets. The placement of objects in a secured room should take into consideration the location of HVAC vents or room fans.

When troubleshooting a home security system, you must first determine whether the problem is being caused by one of the four major areas of a security system: contacts, sensors, or detectors; the security system controller; wiring; or the interface to the telephone system.

A regular periodic program of preventive maintenance can assure the homeowners that their security system is properly functioning and reliable. The frequency of the preventive maintenance program should never be less than at least once annually, with quarterly or semi-annual programs at the discretion of the homeowner.

The advantages of periodic preventive maintenance on a home security system are: prevention of false alarms, fewer service or problem calls, desired changes implemented when needed; reliability of the system, manufacturer's upgrades applied regularly, and potentials problems corrected before they cause the system to fail.

In compliance with NFPA 72 guidelines, a home security system must be tested at least once per year. If a local emergency services authority, such as the police or fire department, monitors the system, they may require the system to be recertified each year and a "Certificate of Completion" issued.

Questions

1. What is the primary performance and maintenance issue with a home security system?

    A. Corroding window contacts

    B. False alarms

    C. Dead batteries

    D. System programming

2. What is the cause of more than two-thirds of home security system false alarms?

    A. Faulty wiring

    B. Misaligned contacts

    C. System programming

    D. User error

3. Which of the following could be the cause of window or door contact generating false positives?

    A. Misalignment

    B. Corrosion

    C. Change in the shape or fit of the door or window

    D. Damage to the contact

    E. All of the above

4. Which one of the following is most likely the problem when a motion detector that is otherwise functioning properly does not sense someone entering the room where it is located?

    A. The lighting level is too low

    B. The opening door blocks the scanning field

    C. The sensor is set too high or too low

    D. Too many objects are in the room

5. Which of the following should be included in the troubleshooting process for a security system controller?

    A. Reload the controller's backup

    B. Apply all manufacturer's upgrades

    C. Test the system

    D. Disconnect all zone devices before troubleshooting the system controller

6. When troubleshooting NC contacts wired in series, what procedure should be used?

A. Test all contacts in the series

B. Disconnect all but the first contact and add the contacts back to the system one at a time

C. Disconnect all but the last contact and add the contacts back to the system one at a time

D. NC contacts should be wired in parallel

7. Which of the following is a good troubleshooting technique for a suspected faulty contact or sensor?

A. Disconnect the suspected device and retest the system

B. Disconnect all but the suspected device and retest the system

C. Replace the suspected device with a known-good device and retest

D. Replace the suspected device immediately

8. When performing a visual inspection of contacts and sensors, which of the following should you be looking for?

A. Corrosion

B. Cleanliness

C. Alignment

D. Wiring

E. All of the above

9. What is the national standard that governs the installation and testing of fire alarm systems?

A. NEC 72

B. IEEE 72

C. NFPA 72

D. EIA/TIA 72

10. When troubleshooting an RJ-31X connection, which of the following steps should be performed?

A. Check jack and plug for damage

B. Check continuity of wiring to security system controller

C. Check continuity of wiring to telephone system

D. Cause a security event from the control panel and verify the interior line has been seized by the system

E. All of the above

F. None of the above

Answers

1. **B.** False alarms can be embarrassing and costly for a homeowner.

2. **D.** Improper training is likely the underlying reason behind the number of user errors resulting in false alarms.

3. **E.** All of these are possible causes for any security device to generate a false positive.

4. **B.** The opening door blocks the scanning field. Improper placement of a motion sensor can defeat its function.

5. **C.** Before any other action is taken, the system should be retested completely to ensure that the reported problem is not caused by another underlying problem.

6. **B.** Disconnect all but the first contact and add the contacts back to the system one at a time. However, if the devices are wired in parallel, they can be tested individually.

7. **C.** Replace the suspected device with a known-good device and retest. Replacing a suspected device with a known-good device is a quick way of identifying or eliminating a device as a problem.

8. **E.** All of these choices should be included when visually inspecting security devices.

9. **C.** Many communities use this standard as the local standard as well.

10. **E.** All of these steps should be included when troubleshooting an RJ-31X connection.

Home Security Surveillance Systems

In this chapter, you will learn about:
- Surveillance system basics and design considerations
- Surveillance system components and devices
- Surveillance systems video formats and standards
- Installing a surveillance system

Typically added as an extension of a home security alarm system, a security surveillance system adds the ability for homeowners, or their surveillance monitoring service, to visually monitor their home's exterior and interior spaces. When used in conjunction with a security alarm system, the homeowner is able to visually scan an area where an alarm has sounded to determine if the problem is in fact a threat or if it is a false alarm. Surveillance systems can also be used in less threatening situations, such as seeing who is ringing the front doorbell, who is knocking on the door, or how the baby is doing in the nursery.

 CROSS-REFERENCE See Chapter 31 for more information on security alarm systems.

In the world of home technology integration, surveillance systems are comprised of cabling, cameras, mounts, monitors, and control systems. In this chapter, we look at each of these devices as well as their standards.

Surveillance System Basics

Video surveillance equipment is a natural extension of home security. However, it isn't necessary to have a home security system to install video surveillance cameras and equipment.

A video surveillance system uses the same technology used to distribute video images throughout a house, where modulators are used to send video signals from a source such as a VCR or DVD player to any number of televisions. The primary difference between a video surveillance system and a cable or satellite television system is merely the source of the video images. In a security surveillance system, the image source is one or more cameras placed around the interior or exterior of a home.

The general technology that is used in video surveillance systems is referred to as closed-circuit television, or CCTV systems. Because the links in a residential video surveillance system run only between a local camera to a monitor or recording device, the loop is considered a closed loop, or a closed circuit.

Video Surveillance Devices

The primary components of a video surveillance system are

- Video camera
- Video monitor
- Video switchers
- Cabling and connectors

Video Cameras

A video surveillance system can include a wide variety of camera types, including cameras that range in style, focal length, interior versus exterior use, and certainly price, which we won't be discussing here.

Camera Styles   The type or style of camera used in a home security system depends on its location and the range of view desired. There are five basic camera styles to choose from:

- **Board camera**   Board cameras are designed to be used as hidden cameras and to be placed inside household objects, such as walls, books, or other objects where they can be camouflaged. Board cameras are not typically protected for exterior use. Figure 35-1 shows an example of a board camera, also known as a pinhole camera.

- **Box camera**   This type of camera gets its name from its shape (see Figure 35-2). The box casing is weatherproof and allows the camera to be mounted on exterior surfaces. Some box models include zoom capabilities.

- **Bullet camera**   This type of camera (see figure 35-3) gets it name from its elongated shape. Bullet cameras are commonly used on building exteriors in both home and commercial security systems.

Figure 35-1   A board camera is typically hidden away out of view.

Figure 35-2   A rearview of a box-style security camera showing its connectors

PART VIII

Figure 35-3   A bullet-style security camera

- **pDome camera**   Dome cameras are common in stores, casinos, and other commercial installations. Dome cameras are typically capable of pivoting to provide a 360-degree pan view of an area. Dome cameras can be retrofitted into an existing home, but are easier to install during new construction. Figure 35-4 shows an example of a dome camera.

Photo courtesy of JVC Professional Products Company.

Figure 35-4   A dome camera, which observes an area with a 360-degree sweep, is typically mounted on a ceiling.

- **PTZ (pan, tilt, and zoom) camera**   Pan means moving side to side; tilt means moving up and down; and zoom means getting closer to an image and magnifying it. PTZ cameras (shown in Figure 35-5) provide the most flexibility for security cameras. These cameras can be controlled through a manual control, such as a joystick controller or computer software. Some dome cameras have PTZ capabilities, and PTZ bases can be used as mounts for nearly all camera types.

Although they're only an adaptation of board cameras, another category of cameras you commonly see listed is hidden cameras. These devices are built into such objects as smoke alarms, motion detectors, clocks, exit signs, and the like. Some hidden cameras are also referred to as nanny cams because of their capability to observe household workers and occupants.

Choosing a Security Camera   Once the types of cameras to be used inside and outside a home are selected, the characteristics of these particular cameras must be considered. The four primary features that should be considered for a home surveillance system include the camera's focal length, light sensitivity rating, lines of resolution, and if it's color or black and white.

- **Focal length**   The focal length of a camera is the distance (in millimeters) from the lens to the point where the image is in focus. The most common focal range on security cameras is 3.6 millimeters (mm), which typically provides a full view of a room if the camera is mounted in a corner near the ceiling. A longer focal length, such as 6.0mm, provides a greater magnification of images, such as faces, hands, and the like, at a distance.

Figure 35-5   A PTZ camera can be controlled to move up and down, side to side, and to produce a closer view.

- **Light sensitivity**   The light sensitivity of a camera is measured in lux (lumens). One lux is the equivalent of the amount of light produced by one candle measured at a distance of one meter. The lux rating on a camera indicates the minimum of light the camera needs to capture images clearly. Those cameras that have a lux rating of less than 1.0 are capable of capturing images in very dim light. While there are some 0 lux cameras, most security cameras are in the range of 0.1 to 0.8, where less (the lower lux rating) is more (it can capture photo in low light).

- **Lines of resolution**   This characteristic measures the number of horizontal lines used to represent the images a camera captures. For example, a standard television set typically has 300 lines of resolution, but video monitors often support many more (800 lines is common). Higher resolution on a camera means that images at a distance are more easily recognizable. A camera that produces a higher number of lines of resolution translates to a better image on the monitor (providing the monitor is capable of reproducing the resolution of the camera). The normal range available is between 300 and 600 lines. However, the better the resolution, the more expensive the camera.

- **Color**   Another consideration for choosing a camera is if it's black and white or color. For most installations, black and white is probably adequate, but some homeowners may wish to install (and pay for) color cameras.

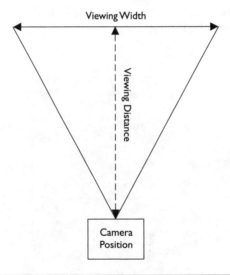

Figure 35-6   Measuring the viewing distance and the viewing depth

How to Calculate Focal Length

If you wish to have more detail through the lens of a security camera and wish to look for something beyond a 3.6 mm focal length, here's how to go about it (remember, you're insisting on this!):

1. Measure the viewing width, the distance between the points you wish to be the left and right extremes of the image viewed. This means measure how wide a field of view you wish to capture. Figure 35-6 illustrates how this is done.

2. From the center of the line between the right and left edges of view, measure the point where the camera lens will be mounted. Figure 35-6 illustrates how the viewing distance is measured.

3. Depending on the camera and its format —it should be 1/3-inch, 1/2-inch, or 2/3-inch (also referred to as 1/3 chip, 1/2 chip, and 2/3 chip)—a factor that corresponds to the format is used to adjust for either the horizontal range or the vertical range of the lens. Table 35-1 lists the various horizontal and vertical factors for the common security camera formats.

4. The formula used for calculating focal length is one of the following, depending on whether you wish to use vertical or horizontal adjustment:

   ```
   Focal length (f) = v * (Viewing distance / Viewing width)
   ```

   or

   ```
   Focal length (f) = h * (Viewing distance / Viewing width)
   ```

5. So, assuming we wish to emphasize the horizontal view of a 1/3-inch format camera and our measurements (in millimeters) are a 380 mm viewing width and an 1800 mm viewing distance, the calculation for the focal length is:

   ```
   f = 3.6 * (1800 / 380) = 3.6 * (4.8) = 17.3 mm
   ```

6. The result of 17.3 mm is the focal length desired. Security camera lens are available with focal lengths that typically range from 1.9 mm to 25 mm. The closest lens size to the desired focal length is a 16 mm (f16) lens, but you could move up to an f25 if you wish to improve the viewing range.

Factor	1/3-inch format	1/2-inch format	2/3-inch format
Horizontal (h)	3.6	4.8	6.6
Vertical (v)	4.8	6.4	8.8

Table 35-1   Focal Length Calculation Horizontal and Vertical Multipliers

PART VIII

Image Capture Formats

Not all cameras are alike. What separates cameras and their capabilities more than any other characteristic is how they capture an image (or in this case video images). The most common camera types used for surveillance purposes are black and white analog cameras, primarily because of their relatively low cost. However, black and white and even color digital cameras are becoming popular for surveillance use as well.

The most common types of cameras used for security surveillance purposes are

- Analog cameras
- Digital cameras
- Infrared cameras

Analog Cameras   Analog cameras use the RS-170 television standard to capture and transmit images as analog signals, and a synchronization pulse supplied by the camera. The transmitted image is created through a sampling process that captures a set number of frames per second (fps) and the position of each feature in a particular frame is determined by the timing between its signal and the synchronizing pulse. A feature called a frame grabber interprets the analog signals and resamples the video images into pixels that are transmitted to the video display device. Analog cameras produce 8-bit resolution, which is able to represent only 256 grayscale shades.

Although commonly referred to as a digital device, another analog image capture device is a CCD (charge coupled device) chip. A CCD chip is light sensitive and captures images in grayscale. Color CCDs uses a RGBG (red, green, blue, and green) mask to provide color images to the display device (the second green is used to create contrast on the image). CCDs are typically connected directly to an analog-to-digital converter (ADC), which provides a digital representation of the captured images.

Digital cameras   A digital camera is really an analog camera that has an ADC built in. Because the analog image is converted to digital pixel coding inside the camera, the quality of the signal is improved and the image accuracy is better than on an analog camera.

Digital cameras use a progressive-scan mode to capture images that produce larger image sizes, higher frame rates, and better resolution. Digital cameras are able to produce higher than 8-bit resolutions; 10-bit cameras can produce 1024 grayscale shades; and 12-bit cameras can produce 4096 grayscale shades of resolution. Digital color cameras use 24-bit resolution or the combination of 8-bits each for red, green, and blue color channels.

The connection between the digital camera and the display devices is commonly one of the following formats:

- **IEEE 1394**   Also known as FireWire and iLINK, this link competes with USB (Universal Serial Bus) for ease of use and data transfer speed.

- **Parallel interface**   The most common parallel formats used with digital video cameras are TTL (transistor-to-transistor logic), EIA/TIA (RS) 422, or LVDS (EIA/TIA [RS] 644) signaling formats.

   - Parallel TTL (through-the-lens) can only be used with very short cable runs (less than 15 feet) and works best with a TTL-capable monitor and requires a TTL-to-TTL cable.

 NOTE   Don't confuse TTL (through-the-lens) focusing and light metering capabilities on a camera with TTL (transistor-to-transistor logic) signaling.

   - EIA/TIA-422 is a differential serial interface that provides greater distances and faster data speeds than the more common EIA/TIA-232 serial interface. LVDS (low-voltage differential signaling) is a gigabit high-speed low-voltage, low-amplitude signaling format for copper wiring.

   - USB (Universal Serial Bus)   A high-speed serial interface.

Table 35-2 lists the specifications for each of the above cable standards.

Infrared (IR) Cameras   Infrared (IR) cameras use IR light to illuminate the field of view and an analog CCD chip for image capture. In dim or dark lighting conditions, the IR illuminators enhance low-light visibility and allow the CCD to capture images in black and white at low resolution.

IP Cameras   Although not technically a type of image capture, IP (Internet Protocol) cameras use any image capture technology and have the built-in capability to connect to and communicate over a network running the TCP/IP protocols. Figure 35-7 shows a rearview of an IP-compatible surveillance camera and its RJ-45 connector.

IP cameras have a built-in network adapter, network connectors, and circuitry to support network communications. Connecting an IP camera to a home network allows captured images to be transferred across the data network and be displayed on computer monitors or stored as digital files on networked storage devices.

Interface	Conductors	Cable Requirement
IEEE 1394	4, 6, or 9	Double Shielded 20 - 28 AWG
Parallel	16 or 18	Shielded 22 - 30 AWG
USB	4	Shielded 20 - 28 AWG

Table 35-2   Camera Interface Cabling Standards

Figure 35-7
An IP camera
includes a
network jack

Photo courtesy of Veo.

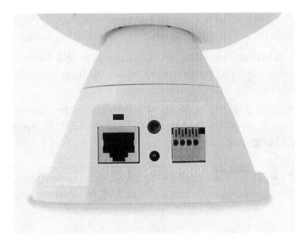

Wireless Cameras   There are several types of wireless cameras that can be connected into a home surveillance system:

- **IP wireless cameras**   These type of wireless cameras are designed to connect into wireless Ethernet data networks using the 802.11 wireless networking standards.

- **ISM (Industry, Science, and Medical) wireless cameras**   ISM cameras transmit images using the 2.4 GHz radio frequency (RF) band, which is the same band used by many home wireless products, such as cordless telephones.

- **PLC "wireless" cameras**   PLC cameras are wireless only in the sense that they require no new wiring. They operate over the existing electrical lines.

Wireless cameras require a compatible receiver or base unit connected to a computer or a television monitor. In terms of reliability, wired camera systems continue to be more reliable due to potential interference problems with wireless transmitted video signals.

Truly wireless systems either have a wireless transmitter built into the camera itself or connect to a wireless transmission unit or they use a wireless balun-style transmitter (see Figure 35-8). A wireless receiver must be connected to a switcher or monitor. The downside of this type of wireless system is that it typically uses the 2.4 GHz RF band, is the same band used by many other wireless systems in a home, including cordless telephones, baby monitors, and the like.

Audio-Capable Cameras   Several surveillance camera models include built-in microphones to pick up sounds from the immediate surrounding areas. Adding audio to the video images captured by the surveillance camera can provide input on activities that may be out of the camera's range, such as directly beneath the camera.

Figure 35-8

A wireless video transmission set connects into the video system for transmitting video signals.

Photo courtesy of Silent Witness Enterprises, Ltd.

Cameras that include audio capabilities use triple RCA composite audio/video cabling and connectors.

Cross-reference   See Chapter 15 for more information about audio cabling and connectors.

Camera Power Sources

Virtually all CCTV video cameras use either 120V AC or 24V AC power sources.

- **120V AC**   Common household AC power is a common power source for video cameras. 120V AC cameras typically come with a 6- to 10-foot power cord, so the camera must have an AC power outlet within that distance.

- **24V AC**   Most commercial security systems use this voltage, which is usually provided through an external plug-in low-voltage power adapter or power supply that can be some distance from the camera. The power source can be connected to the camera using 18- or 20-gauge speaker wire or using what is called Siamese wire. Siamese wire has a power cable and a coaxial cable inside a single outer jacket. Using a central power source, all wiring can be run up to 350 feet to a central location. However, typically a 24V AC power supply is not provided with the camera and must be purchased separately.

Figure 35-9

A stand-alone television monitor can be integrated into a surveillance system.

Photo courtesy of JVC Professional Products Group.

Video Monitors

Essentially, stand-alone video monitors used with video surveillance systems are television sets (see Figure 35-9) that are designed specifically for use as a security system monitor or have a video-in jack to connect directly to a camera or a modulation unit.

- **Security system monitors** Typically, specialized security system monitors are sold as a part of a complete security system or as an option or extra to a brand-name line of security products designed to work together. These monitors typically have their controls on a front panel and multiple input and output jacks on the back. They typically range in size from 5.5-inches to 13-inches diagonally measured. Some security system monitors also have the capability to display two to four different camera inputs simultaneously using a split-screen technique (see Figure 35-10).

- **Video-in TVs** Any television that has a video-in jack compatible with the cabling and connectors of a particular video camera can be used as a video surveillance monitor. In cases where the TV is unable to connect directly to

Camera A   H Split   V Split   Corner   Fade   Camera B

Figure 35-10 The various combinations available from a split-screen system with two camera inputs (cameras A and B).

a video camera, because of signaling differences primarily, a video signal modulator can be used to convert the signal to a standard TV format (a TV channel) that can be displayed on the monitor.

- **Computer monitors** Video camera signals can also be displayed on a computer monitor if the computer is equipped with the proper interface device or expansion card. IP cameras transmit video images in a format that can be immediately displayed on a computer monitor using video display software. Other signal formats, such as CCTV, CATV (community antenna TV), or NTSC (National Television Standards Committee) must be modulated before they can be displayed on a computer monitor using a external or internal interface device (see Figure 35-11).

Modulators

Modulators are devices that convert a video signal from one format to another. In the context of a home video surveillance system, a modulator converts the baseband video signal from the camera into one that is compatible with one or more VHF (very high frequency) or UHF (ultra high frequency) television channels and broadcasts the video image on that channel.

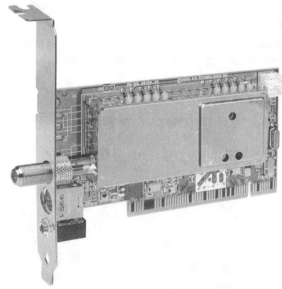

Photo courtesy of ATI Technologies, Inc.

Figure 35-11   A video interface card provides a computer with the ability to receive TV signals.

If the homeowner wishes to display the video from a security camera on a specific channel of a television set, a modulator will be needed between the camera and the TV to convert the signal accordingly.

To display a video image, a display device must receive a video signal formatted for the particular signal configuration it displays. Devices with the capability to display a selection of multiple video signal channels (such as a TV) separate the incoming signals based on their modulation. Transmitted video signals are modulated (converted) for a particular channel. When you change the channel on a TV set, you are telling the receiver to display those signals modulated for the channel you want to see.

In a home system, especially one with multiple video source devices, each device must be modulated to a particular channel so it can be displayed on a TV monitor or a computer monitor. To do this, the video signals must be passed through a device called (what else?) a modulator. For a home system, a range of different modulators is available:

- **Single channel modulators** This type of modulator converts the incoming video signal (from one or more selectable sources) to the format of a single TV channel, typically channel 3 or 4. A good example is a VCR or DVD player. Figure 35-12 shows a single channel modulator.

- **Multiple channel modulators** This type of modulator accepts multiple input sources and modulates each video input to unique selectable output channels. This type of modulator, shown in Figure 35-13, allows you to select which source device is displayed on which TV channel.

- **Micro modulators** This type of modulator is used with digital video capture devices for display on computer monitors or digital TVs.

Figure 35-12
A distribution panel mountable single channel modulator

Photo courtesy of ChannelVision.

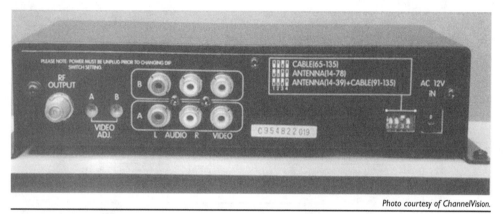

Photo courtesy of ChannelVision.

Figure 35-13 A multiple channel video modulator

Video Switchers and Multiplexers

If a home's video surveillance system requires more than one camera, whether the cameras are interior or exterior, some form of switching is typically required. A video switcher sequences between multiple cameras to permit viewing or recording from the full-screen display from each camera, one at a time.

Switchers There are several types of switchers to choose from for a surveillance system, depending on the number of cameras and the needs of the homeowner:

- **Alarming switcher** This type of switcher can be connected to a motion detector or an alarm device and when an alarm signal is detected on that channel, the switcher stops any sequencing and locks onto the camera associated with the alarm. The switcher can also automatically connect the selected camera to a recording device when the alarm signal is detected.

- **Bridging sequential switcher** This type of switcher supports two outputs, but typically has multiple inputs. A bridging switcher is able to display two cameras on separate monitors and on some models even sequence multiple cameras on either monitor. Figure 35-14 illustrates the connections used with a bridging switcher.

- **Homing switcher** This type of switcher has only one output connection, but can support multiple inputs. This switcher can display or record one camera or multiple cameras in a rotating sequence. Figure 35-15 illustrates the connections used to connect a homing switcher to multiple cameras.

- **Sequential switcher** This type of switcher automatically switches between multiple cameras or video recorders with the capability to record a variable amount of delay between the switching from one unit to the next.

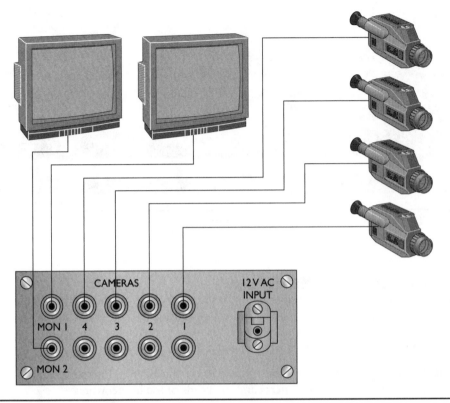

Figure 35-14   The connections used to connect a bridging switcher to multiple devices

Quadrant Switchers2   Another type of specialized video switcher is a quadrant-switcher (quad-switcher) that allows the viewing or recording of up to four cameras on the same screen at one time. If the video signal is recorded, the recorded image is also in quadrant format. Figure 35-16 shows a Pelco monitor that has an integrated quad-switcher built in, and Figure 35-17 illustrates the connections made with a stand-alone quad-switcher.

Multiplexers   There are two types of multiplexers used in video surveillance systems: simplex and duplex. A multiplexer is able to mix and match devices together for display, recording, or playback. It can display one camera on a monitor while another camera is being recorded on a video recorder.

A simplex multiplexer can display one camera while recording all other cameras and a duplex multiplexer is able to display one or more live cameras while recording all other cameras and even displaying playback from a second video recorder.

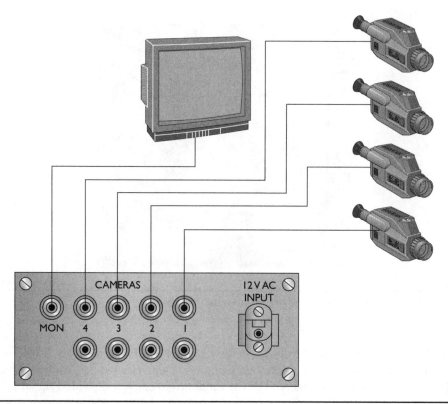

Figure 35-15   The connection pattern used to connect a homing switcher to four cameras and a monitor

Cabling and Connectors

Most surveillance systems available on the market are wired systems that use the same standard cabling used in structured wiring schemes. However, there are wireless systems where the camera sends its video signals to a base station using RF signaling. This base station then displays the image or transmits the video signal over wire to the monitor.

Standard Cabling

For most of the connections needed in a video surveillance system, such as from a camera to a monitor, RG6 coaxial cable can be used, provided none of the individual cable runs are more than 200 feet. For distances longer than 200 feet, RG59 coaxial cable, called surveillance video cable, should be used, even though it now is not normally used in home video installations.

Figure 35-16 A security monitor with an integrated quad-switcher

Twisted-pair cabling can be used provided a video balun, a device that converts the coaxial cable-compatible signal into one compatible with twisted-pair cabling. A video balun must be installed at each end of the cable run to convert the video signal to and from traveling on the twisted-pair cabling. Figure 35-18 shows a sample of a video balun. Note that one end of the balun has an RJ-45 jack and the other end has a push-on F-type connector.

Most security camera kits come with a length of cable for installation, but in a structured cabling environment, the cabling for the surveillance system should be installed during the pre-wire process. If coaxial cable is used, an adapter cable, like the one shown in Figure 35-19, may be required to connect F-type connectors to the camera that may support only an RCA, parallel, or s-video connector. If Cat 5e cabling is used, a balun must be installed at each end of the cable.

NOTE Some video security systems use proprietary or special cabling that provides both video transmission from and electrical power to the camera. On these types of systems, the cabling is connected to a single system distribution box that connects into the house AC system.

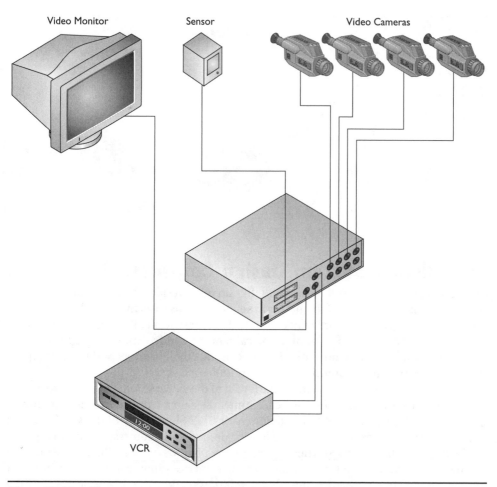

Figure 35-17   The connections used with a stand-alone quadrant-switcher

Figure 35-1

A video balun is
used to interface
coaxial signals to
twisted-pair cable.

*Photo courtesy
of Almex Ltd.*

Figure 35-19
A coaxial (S-video) to composite (dual RCA) conversion cable

Photo courtesy of TriangleCables.com

Surveillance System Design Considerations

The design of a video surveillance system, like all other residential surveillance systems, must first satisfy the needs of the homeowner and, in this case, involve what the homeowners wish to watch or record inside or outside of their home. Table 35-3 shows a sample of a worksheet used for planning the cameras of a video surveillance system. The worksheet should include not only the cameras, but the monitors and support equipment, such as switchers, multiplexers, and modulators, as well.

Perhaps the biggest consideration is the layout of the viewing zones, the areas to be covered by the video cameras. In essence, each camera sets up a separate zone for the surveillance system. Are the cameras to be stationary or PTZ? Should any of the viewing zones overlap? Are there areas where a camera may be desired in the futures? It's these considerations that must be addressed when laying out the plan for the surveillance system.

The next question then is where to place the cameras. What features of the home or exterior should be watched? Gates, doors, windows, and other entry points into the home are the primary targets. If vandalism is a problem, then those areas of the property that are most accessible to vandals should be included. Another consideration is the direction that people (invited or uninvited) face when entering a certain space.

Interior cameras are typically placed either in a ceiling corner of a room or on the ceiling of a passageway. In any case, be sure to include the main entrances and exits from a room or areas in the camera's view.

Exterior cameras should be weatherproof and if placed in unlighted areas should also include an IR illumination source.

Location	Mount	Type	Lens	Wiring
Front Door	Wall	Weatherproof	3.6mm	Cat5e
Rear Door	Wall	Weatherproof	3.6 mm	Cat5e
Entry	Ceiling	Dome	Standard	Cat 5e
Office		Modulator – 4 channel		Coaxial
Office		Splitter – 4 channel		Composite
Office		Monitor – 15-inch		Composite

Table 35-3   Video System Planning Worksheet

Chapter Review

A video surveillance system uses modulators to transmit and convert video signals from source devices to the system's monitors. The technology used in video surveillance systems is CCTV systems.

The primary components of a video surveillance system are: video cameras, video monitors, video modulators and switchers, and cabling and connectors.

Home security system cameras are available in five basic styles: board cameras, box cameras, bullet cameras, dome cameras, and PTZ cameras. The characteristics that should be considered for a surveillance camera are focal length, light sensitivity, lines of resolution, and color or black and white. The most common types of cameras used for security surveillance purposes are: analog cameras, digital cameras, and infrared cameras. IP cameras have the built-in capability to connect to and communicate over a network running the TCP/IP protocols.

Several types of wireless cameras can be connected into a home surveillance system: IP wireless cameras, ISM wireless cameras, and PLC cameras. Several surveillance camera models include a built-in microphone to pick up sounds from the immediate area around the camera. Virtually all CCTV video cameras use either 120V AC or 24V AC power sources. TV monitors are commonly used with video surveillance systems: security system monitors, video-in TVs, and computer monitors.

For most video surveillance connections, RG6 coaxial cable is used and RG59 can also be used. UTP cabling can be used with a video balun.

The first design consideration of a video surveillance system is the layout of the viewing zones. The next consideration is where to place the cameras. What features of the home or exterior should be watched? Gates, doors, windows, and other entry points into the home are the primary targets. If vandalism is a problem, then those areas of the property that are most accessible to vandals should be included. Another consideration is the direction that people (invited or uninvited) face when entering a certain space.

PART VIII

Interior cameras are typically placed either in a ceiling corner of a room or on the ceiling of a passageway. Exterior cameras should be weatherproof and if placed in unlighted areas should also include an IR illumination source.

Questions

1. What is the general technology used in residential video surveillance systems?

   A. CATV

   B. HDTV

   C. CCTV

   D. FM

2. Which of the following is not a primary component of a video surveillance system?

   A. Cameras

   B. Monitors

   C. Sound systems

   D. Switchers

3. Which of the following surveillance camera types is able to pivot, move up and down, and in and out under remote control?

   A. Board camera

   B. Box camera

   C. Bullet camera

   D. PTZ camera

4. Which of the following is not a primary consideration when choosing a video camera for a surveillance system?

   A. Mounting style

   B. Focal length

   C. Light sensitivity

   D. Lines of resolution

5. Which of the following surveillance camera types is able to provide illumination in darkened areas?

   A. Analog

   B. Digital

   C. IR

   D. RF

6. Analog cameras, such as CCDs, convert analog signals to digital signals using which device?

   A. DAC

   B. DSP

   C. CCD

   D. ADC

7. Which of the following is not a common connection type supported by a digital surveillance camera?

   A. IEEE 1394

   B. EIA/TIA-422

   C. USB

   D. RJ-45

8. What are the two voltages most common to residential surveillance systems?

   A. 12V DC

   B. 24V DC

   C. 24V AC

   D. 120V AC

9. What device is typically required in order to display multiple cameras on a single monitor?

   A. Switcher

   B. Modulator

   C. Multiplexer

   D. Hub

10. What is the cabling type most commonly used with video surveillance systems?

    A. RG-6

    B. RG-59

    C. UTP

    D. Fiber optic

Answers

1. **C.** Closed-circuit television (CCTV) is used primarily for security purposes. CATV is cable television; HDTV is high-definition television; and FM modulation is used with some wireless systems, but typically still within the CCTV system.

2. **C.** Not that sound systems couldn't be included in a surveillance system, but our focus here is video surveillance. The other choices are all components of a video surveillance system.

3. **D.** Pan, tilt, and zoom cameras are able to be repositioned under remote control. The other choices are typically stationary cameras, unless they are mounted on a PTZ mounting.

4. **A.** If all other features of a camera are desired, the mounting style can be adapted to. However, if the camera application (dome, PTZ, and so on) is not appropriate for the intended use, the other features hardly matter.

5. **C.** Infrared illumination cameras can use IR light to illuminate an area so that the camera can "see" in the dark.

6. **D.** Analog-to-digital converters do just what their name says they do. The other devices are a digital-to-analog converter (DAC), a digital sound processor (DSP), and a charge-coupled device (CCD), which is an image capture device used in video cameras.

7. **D.** By using a balun, a coaxial BNC adapter can be converted to an RJ-45 to send signals over twisted-pair wiring. The other choices are all fairly common camera connector types.

8. **C** and **D.** Most cameras operate on AC current whether plugged directly into a household current (120V AC) or into an external power supply (24V AC).

9. **A.** Switchers, well, switch. They switch between cameras, monitors, and video recorders either manually or automatically.

10. **A.** RG-6 coaxial cabling is the same coaxial cable used in structured wiring.

36

Home Access Control Systems

In this chapter, you will learn about:

- Access control devices and their applications
- Installing and wiring access control systems

Burglars and other intruders gain access to a home in a variety of ways. However, according to published statistics, 65 percent of them gain access to a home through one of a home's doors. Only 6 percent of these uninvited evildoers gain access through an unlocked door, but more than 60 percent of illegal entries occur while a home is occupied. These statistics indicate that some type of access control system is needed to secure the doors of the average home to alert the homeowner or monitoring service of an entry attempt.

Access control systems include several features that are typically included in many residential security systems. However, home access security can be installed without the need for a whole-house security system. This chapter covers those devices and systems that can be installed solely to provide access control security to a home.

 CROSS-REFERENCE See Chapter 31 for more information about residential security system basics.

Access Control Systems

A home access control system can be very simple and involve only such things as standard door locks. It can also be very complex and include the latest biometric devices straight out of the James Bond world. The level of complexity required for any home depends on two issues: the level of security required by the homeowners and their budget.

An access control system is any combination of devices that secure a home and prevent or detect an unauthorized entry through a door, window, or other exterior feature that can be used to gain access to a home. For the majority of homeowners, the access control system in use is limited only to a key-locking door handle and perhaps a deadbolt lock on the front and maybe the rear doors of the home. Often, sliding glass doors and the like are secured only with a toggle lock that is really not all that burglar-proof. Adding additional access control security to any home can only make it safer.

Access Control System Components

Residential access control systems consist of a variety of devices that can be used to gain access to a secured home. The devices that are most commonly considered for a home's access control system are

- Card readers
- Door locks
- Driveway loops
- Keypads
- Proximity card scanners
- Motorized gates

Card Reader Systems

Card reader systems scan coding on a credit card- or smaller-sized plastic or laminated card to unlock or open a door. While this technology is fairly commonplace in the business world, only a few types of card reader systems have been adapted for residential use. While newer card reader systems support the use of keychain cards in place of the credit card– sized cards, the plastic card is still the most common form of key card in use.

Most basic card readers only read a number from each card and transfer it to the card reader's control unit or to the security system controller for processing by either the standard software or custom programming, respectively. More sophisticated systems offer the capability to create customized software, using C-language programming or a Windows-based interface on the card reader controller.

Depending on the type of card system in use, the need and the complexity of the actions that can be programmed into the system vary from very simple read-only features to Smart Card systems that can be used to activate a wide range of home security and automation actions. As the capabilities of the system increase, the level of programming required to customize the system also increases. Some manufacturers of the more sophisticated systems offer a variety of preprogrammed modules and templates that can be downloaded from the Internet or obtained on a disk as a means to simplifying this process.

The most common card reader systems used in residential applications are

- Barcode readers
- Magnetic stripe readers
- Proximity card readers
- Wiegand proximity card readers

Figure 36-1

The wiring configuration of a PLC card reader connected to an electric door strike

Photo courtesy of Smarthome, Inc.

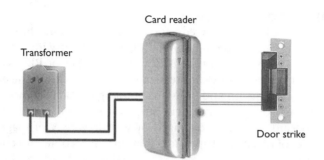

Card Reader Wiring

Depending on the type of card the card reader is designed to scan, the wiring or connectors will vary. Card readers that are designed to interface with computer equipment directly will have either a 9-pin DB connector (DB-9) or an RF-45 plug. Some include a six or more position screw terminal strip to which the ground, power, and relay wires are connected. Powerline communications (PLC)-compatible card readers must be wired to a transformer that provides both the electrical power and the connection to the alternating current (AC) powerlines. Figure 36-1 illustrates the wiring required for a PLC card reader.

Barcode Readers

The technology of a barcode reader is quite similar to the readers used in the checkout stands at most supermarkets and chain stores. The primary difference between the home security barcode reader and the ones at the store is that in home systems, the barcode is swiped through a reader and not scanned.

The barcode encoded information, which is typically either a card number or a personal identification number (PIN), is printed on a plastic credit card sized card or on a paper card that has been laminated to prevent wear.

Actually, the reader reads the white (or dark gray) spaces of the barcode and not the black stripes (see Figure 36-2). The thickness of the white area represents a number or an alphabetic character that is then transmitted to a control unit and either verified (and the door is unlocked) or rejected. Some systems do include the capability to signal an erroneous read as well.

Figure 36-2

An example of barcode, similar to what is found on barcode reader access control system cards

Magnetic Stripe Readers

On the back of virtually all credit and automatic teller machine (ATM) cards is a black or reddish-brown stripe that is permanently magnetized with information, and in the case of home access security cards, it is a card number or PIN. When the card is passed through a magnetic stripe card reader, the reader picks up the electromagnetic fields of the stored information and translates it to digital data for processing.

There are two types of magnetic stripe cards: low coercivity and high coercivity. Low coercivity cards are easily damaged by a wide variety of magnetic sources, including other types of magnetic stripe cards that they may come into contact with in a wallet or purse. High coercivity cards are less easily damaged and are able to hold their information even when in contact with low-grade magnetic sources.

 NOTE Coercivity is the strength of a magnetic field required to reverse the polarity on a magnetic medium.

High coercivity cards are more reliable because they are more resistant to common magnetic forces. However, the reliability of any magnetic stripe card depends on the magnetic film tape used on the card. The magnetic force that can erase a magnetic stripe card is coercive force, which is measured in Oersteds. A standard bankcard has a coercivity of around 300 Oersteds, which is low coercivity. At this level, a magnetic stripe card can be damaged by other cards in the same wallet or by the magnetic clasp on a purse. Card systems using magnetic materials with coercivity ratings of 2,100 to 4,000 Oersteds are less susceptible to being erased or damaged. When the card is swiped through the reader (see Figure 36-3), the magnetic stripe reader scans the magnetic stripe on the back of a card, translates the information, and then either transmits the information to a control unit that issues a signal to one of its relays or processes the information and sends a signal out one of its onboard relays. The relay where the approved signal is sent is attached to an electronic lock that releases and the door can then be opened. Unauthorized or damaged cards are rejected by a signal sent back to the card reader.

Figure 36-3
A magnetic stripe reader can be a stand-alone device like this one or built into another device.

Photo courtesy of Scan Technology, Inc.

Magnetic stripe readers are not a good option in areas where dust, dirt, heavy rains, or fog are a problem. Dust and moisture can cause the stripe reader to misread or fail altogether.

Proximity Card Readers

Unlike magnetic stripe card readers or barcode card readers, a proximity card reader doesn't require a card to be inserted into the reader. When a proximity card is held near (in the proximity) the card reader, from two inches to six feet from the reader, the reader is able to detect the information on the card and capture it for processing.

Proximity cards and readers use low-frequency radio signals to communicate. A proximity card has a passive radio frequency (RF) transmitter embedded in it that continuously transmits its information. When the card is within range of the card reader, the information is received, processed, and verified, and signals are passed to the appropriate relay to open or unlock a door or gate. Passive devices do not require a battery to operate.

Many proximity card reader models also include a keypad like the one shown in Figure 36-4. On systems that require two levels of security, the keypad is used to enter a PIN after the card is scanned. On other systems, the keypad can be used in lieu of the card reader.

The primary benefit of a proximity card reader is convenience to the user. Another benefit is that they are also good for either indoor or outdoor use. The downside is that metal objects nearby can cause interference and the scanner in the reader can be damaged if the card is bent or flexed when it's being scanned. However, the convenience of the system and its longevity—typically longer than contact readers like the magnetic stripe or barcode readers—outweighs the potential problems.

Wiegand Proximity Card Readers

Wiegand cards have special electromagnetic wires embedded in them in a specific pattern that is unique to each card. Like a standard proximity card reader, the cards and readers communicate using low-frequency radio waves. Because of this, they are virtually impossible to counterfeit. Another benefit to this type of card and reader is that they

Figure 36-4

A proximity card reader with a keypad

Photo courtesy of HID Corp.

Figure 36-5
A Wiegand
keychain sized
"pocket tag"
proximity card

*Photo courtesy
of HID Corp.*

operate in extreme weather and environmental conditions, something not all other card reader types can do.

The Wiegand technology permits the "card" to be reduced to the size of a coin, key fob, small card, and other convenient sizes, like the keychain size shown in Figure 36-5.

 NOTE One more bit about access cards: every card, regardless of the type, is manufactured with a unique facility or site code. This code differentiates one user's cards from another and prevents one user's card from working with another user's reader.

Keypads

Keypad access control systems require a user to enter a multiple-digit code to gain access. Keypad units (see Figure 36-6) typically have a 10-digit number pad where the user can punch in her pass code.

Keypad systems are a good low-cost option in low-risk situations. This system is safe as long as the code stays secret. However, resetting the numerical code is simple using access directly on the keypad through an administrative number code.

Figure 36-6
A keypad access
control unit

*Photo courtesy of Kenny
International.*

Keypad Wiring

The wiring requirements for a keypad access control device depend on the devices the keypad will control, such as an electric door strike, or the other systems the keypad is to be connected to. If the keypad and a door strike are from the same manufacturer, it is likely that documentation details the wiring requirements of the two devices. However, if the keypad is to be used as a stand-alone key entry device that reports to a security system controller, the wiring, while fairly standard, may be a bit involved.

In every case, study the manufacturer's documentation before beginning the installation of the keypad, which should normally happen during the trim-out phase. Some keypad devices may include a user interface connection on the internal circuit board that accepts a strip connector with up to 12 wire positions. Study the wiring diagrams if this is the wiring approach to be used to connect the keypad for remote trigger, panic, or other relay outputs or inputs.

On basic keypad devices, electrical wiring no larger than 16 AWG should be used to connect the keypad to its power source and a door strike, if used. Either unshielded twisted-pair (UTP) or shielded twisted-pair (STP) wiring is used to connect the keypad to the home security system controller for relay signals out or in.

Keypad Programming

Keypad systems can be programmed for several features, including settings that allow entry only during certain hours of the day, eliminating unauthorized access during set periods of the day or night. Programming a keypad system can be done a number of ways. The most common method to program the functions of a keypad system is to press the keys in certain sequences, according to the manufacturer's documentation. Uploading a keypad's program from the system controller or downloading the program from the system controller is another common way to program some keypads. In many cases, a computer-based programming interface is used to create keypad programming on the system control unit and then uploaded to each keypad.

Electronic Key Systems

An electronic key system (see Figure 36-7) works essentially like a regular lock and key. It has an electronic key that is inserted into a reader to either permit or deny access through a door. A reader can be set up to allow certain keys entry into some areas and other readers can be set up to not allow access to others.

The advantage of an electronic key system is that a home's locks don't have to be rekeyed should a key be lost or stolen. Instead, the system can be easily reprogrammed to make the lost key inoperable.

Spare or new keys are typically assigned a pass-code number using a separate device called a key programming unit and the electronic cylinder or door lock unit can be programmed for additional key numbers or pass-codes using a lock programming unit that attaches to a personal computer. New programming is loaded to the cylinder unit through a special key attached to a cord on the lock programming unit.

Figure 36-8
An electronic key
that is used with
an electronic
door lock system

*Photo courtesy
of Intellikey Corp.*

Electric Door Lock Systems

Electric door lock systems are typically used in conjunction with an authorization device, such as a card reader, electronic key, or keypad. This type of access control device can be used to limit both entry and exit through a door. A card reader and other authorization systems send signals to an access control panel or directly to a connected device, such as an electric door lock. These signals, if received on the appropriate relay, instruct the lock to release the door.

Electric door locks consist of a number of components, including electric strike plates, magnetic locks, drop bolts, and electric locksets. However, not every door will work with an electric door lock and the door lock system needs to be fitted to the door, doorknob, and latch in each case.

A wide variety of products fall within the general category of electric locks, including remote control deadbolts, push-button and keypad door locks, and electric door strikes that can be used to upgrade an existing mechanical door lock.

Remote Control Deadbolts

A remote control deadbolt, see Figure 36-8, works essentially the same way a manually operated deadbolt does. The difference is that remote control deadbolts can be locked or unlocked using a multiple-function infrared (IR) remote control in addition to allow for manual operations.

Push-Button/Keypad Door Locks

Push-button and keypad door lock systems are keyless locks that can be unlocked by entering a code number sequence by pressing buttons or keys on the face of the door lock. As shown in Figure 36-9, the face of this type of lock system has a keypad. The keypad is used to both operate the door lock and enter programming commands.

Figure 36-7
An IR-remote
control deadbolt

Figure 36-9

A keypad deadbolt or door lock eliminates the need for a mechanical key.

Photo courtesy of Weiser Lock.

There are mechanical and electronic versions of this type of door lock system. A mechanical (nonelectric) push-button lock (see Figure 36-10) requires its buttons be pressed in a certain sequence.

One or more AA batteries are typically used to power an electronic keypad door lock. These devices, like the one shown in Figure 36-10, electrically retract the locking mechanism in the door latch when the correct sequence of keys is pressed. Programming, which typically means entering or changing the number set and sequence, is accomplished through the keypad.

Figure 36-10

A mechanical push-button door lock

Electric Door Strikes

Electric door strikes are available in a variety of styles to fit a variety of door materials and should be chosen based on the type of door in use. All electric door strikes, like the one shown in Figure 36-11, work essentially the same way: when an electrical charge is sent to the door strike, the locking mechanism releases to unlock the door. The door strike can be operated from a central security control unit acting on a command from a keypad to send a charge to the strike through a relay or a simple push-button release, like those used in many apartment houses and secured entries.

Several door lock system manufacturers also offer electric door strikes that are compatible with their standard door locks. Electric strikes operate on either 12- or 24-volt direct current (DC) or on AC power. Most electric strikes include a fail secure feature that keeps the door locked should the power source fail.

The installation of an electric door strike is performed much like the installation of a standard nonelectrical door strike in that the strike is installed into the door frame or on a wall in line with the door's latching mechanism. The primary difference between an electrical strike and a nonelectrical strike is cabling.

The wire size installed to carry electrical signals to the strike varies by manufacturer, but one thing nearly all manufacturers agree upon is that the wiring must be plenum-rated. In most cases, the connector used is a two- or three-position snap-fit jack (see Figure 36-12) and plug that terminates the wiring of the strikes electronic module and the plenum cable, respectively.

Biometric Access Control Systems

Biometric access control systems use a feature of the users' bodies to verify their identities, such as fingerprints, facial features, and even retinal patterns. For residential systems,

Figure 36-11
An electric door strike provides remote door lock control.

Photo courtesy of Rutherford Controls International Corp.

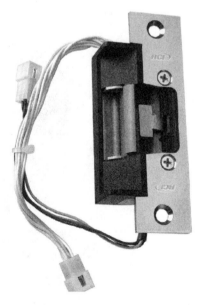

Figure 36-12
A wire-to-wire
connector of the
type commonly
used with wiring
for door strikes
and other access
control devices

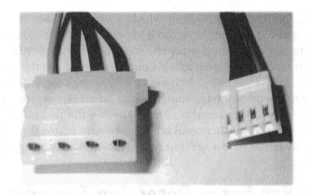

the most commonly used biometric system is one that uses fingerprints to control access. These systems, like the one shown in Figure 36-13, typically have an IR finger well into which the user places her finger and the reader scans her fingerprint and matches the pattern entered during setup.

The advantage of biometric access control systems should be obvious. There are no keys, cards, or codes to lose or forget. The homeowners carry their security devices with them at all times—right on the tips of their fingers, on their faces, or in their eyes.

The wiring required for a biometric access control system depends on the application. Biometric units produce a low-voltage charge to signal a pass condition, meaning the biometric scan produced a valid match. If the unit is to operate an electric door strike or other electric locking system, a relay module is required. However, if the signal is to be transmitted to a home security system controller, typically no additional modules are required for the biometric unit.

Wiring for biometric units can vary, but for the most part, four to six conductors of UTP wiring is required. Many units feature either RJ-45 or RJ-12 jacks for connecting to a network or a communications system. Electrical power is most commonly provided through a power-converting transformer plugged into an AC outlet near the device.

Figure 36-13
A fingerprint
biometric access
control system

Photo courtesy of
Precise Biometrics.

Programming a biometric unit, which is typically done through its keypad or interface, involves training the unit to record and recognize the hands, fingers, eyes, or other anatomical features of authorized users. Some additional programming may be required if the unit is to take more than a single output function. As the programming methods vary by model, follow the unit's documentation for the programming process used.

Some high-end biometric units also record an exportable log file that can be accessed through a network or serial interface. The log file records all successful and, perhaps more importantly, unsuccessful attempts to gain access through the lock controlled by the unit. Whether or not the unit records a log file is a programming option.

Driveway Entry Detection Systems

If a home has a gated driveway, all of the access control systems discussed above can be used to control access through the gate. However, for homes without gated driveways but with a long driveway, the homeowners may wish to install a system that detects and reports a pedestrian, cyclist, or car entering the driveway. Driveway detectors can also be used to activate lighting systems along the driveway after dark. The signal from the driveway detector can be used to turn on entry and interior lighting.

There are a variety of driveway detection and monitoring systems available:

- Induction loop systems
- Metal detection systems
- Motion detection systems

Induction loop systems

This type of system is installed with loops of special cable placed under the driveway and uses a very similar technology to that used to detect cars on a street to trigger the traffic lights. As illustrated in Figure 36-14, the buried cable is induction cable that emits an electromagnetic field that has a fixed frequency. As a vehicle enters the induction cable's field, the vehicle's electromagnetic field interacts with that of the cable and changes the frequency of the inductive field. The control unit detects this frequency change and a relay is activated. Most driveway loop systems allow the sensitivity of the system to be set

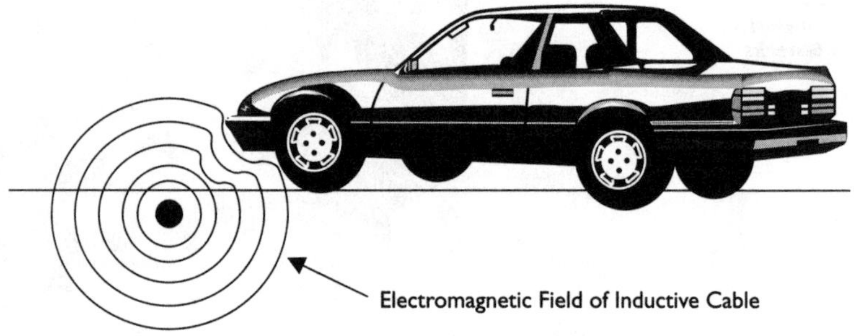

Figure 36-14
A car entering the electromagnetic field of a buried induction cable of a driveway loop system causes an alarm event.

Electromagnetic Field of Inductive Cable

between high and low sensitivity, but it should not be set higher than necessary to detect vehicles entering the driveway so that vehicles passing by on the road do not trigger the control unit.

Typically, the induction cable is installed under the concrete or paving material of a driveway in a rectangular or quadratic shape. Depending on the area and length of the driveway, multiple runs of the inductive cabling may need to be placed in the loop slot where the cable is laid. More cable is needed for smaller circumference loops than for larger loops. The cable should be laid far enough away from the street so it doesn't false trip when a car on the road drives by the driveway.

Metal Detection systems

This type of system uses sensors that detect large metallic objects moving past, which can include steel-toed boots or other metallic objects such as an automobile that pass close to the sensor. These systems are typically installed as a wired system, with one or more sensors (see Figure 36-15) buried or placed on the ground's surface along the side of the driveway, and then hardwired into a control unit that can then be connected to a home system. The control unit is then wired into the home system controller or home security system controller through its screw post connections, which are shown in Figure 36-15.

Motion and Entrance Detection Systems

Exterior motion detectors and IR-beam detectors use passive infrared (PIR) to detect when an object enters a driveway or another exterior space. These systems are intended to provide a homeowner with early detection of an intruder.

Exterior Motion Detectors

Exterior motion detectors use the same basic technology as interior motion detectors. A PIR beam or sweep constantly scans a fixed area and signals a security event should the beam be interrupted. Some systems can be adjusted to detect only larger moving objects and can be configured with "pet alleys" to avoid signaling an alarm for pets and wild

Figure 36-15
The sensor, cable, and controller of a driveway metal detection system

Photo courtesy of Mier Products, Inc.

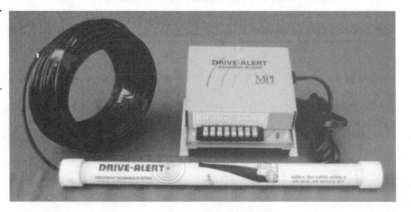

animals. Although several types of exterior motion detectors are available, many are wireless systems with ranges of up to 1,000 feet. Many exterior motion detector devices are incorporated into exterior security lighting fixtures, like the one illustrated in Figure 36-16.

Beam Entrance Detectors

A beam detector transmits a continuous IR beam, referred to as an IR laser beam in some models, between two stations, across a driveway, a garage entrance, a walkway, or whatever exterior feature the homeowner wishes to monitor. As illustrated in Figure 36-17, an IR beam detector requires two IR transceivers be placed in direct line of sight of each other across a monitored pathway or driveway. When an object, meaning a person, animal, or vehicle, breaks the IR beam, a signal is generated from the controlling transceiver. This signal travels to a controller device that then communicates it on to the subsystem control to which it's connected.

Each transceiver requires its own power source. Typically, transceivers are powered through a 12V DC current from an AC power transformer. One or both of the IR transceivers are wired into a device controller. The controller is then connected to a PLC control module or with UTP cable and either an RJ-12 or RJ-45 connector to the home control system.

Motorized Security Gates

In a home that is set back from a street and has a lengthy driveway, a barrier that prevents access to the driveway can provide both security and, in many cases, aesthetics as well. A remote control motorized security gate provides security by allowing only users with the proper remote access control device or keypad code open the gate for entry.

A motorized gate is equipped with a two-directional motor system that is used to open and close the gate upon receiving a signal. When the device controller receives a signal, it activates the gate motor, which performs the action opposite of the action last performed. What this means is that if the last action the gate performed was to open the gate, the next action will be to close the gate, much in the same way a garage door opener operates. Motorized gate systems are available as swing gate, slider gate, and lift gate systems.

Access through a motorized security gate is gained commonly through a remote control device, much like a garage door remote control, or through a keypad or card reader located on the side of the driveway. Although, the gate can be closed using a remote control

Figure 36-16
An exterior security lighting fixture with a built-in motion detector

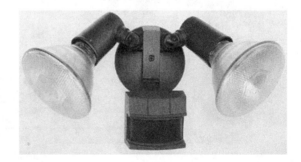

Figure 36-17
An IR beam
detects someone
entering an area.

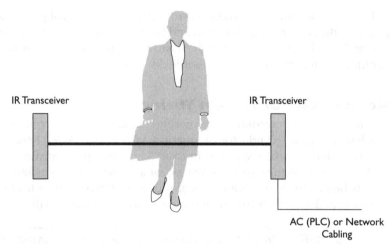

IR Transceiver

IR Transceiver

AC (PLC) or Network
Cabling

or other access control device, including telephone-based systems, most systems can be configured to automatically close after a preset period of time, typically 30 to 60 seconds.

In a typical scenario, as a vehicle approaches the security gate, the driver uses an access control device to send a signal to the gate control device that activates the motor to open the gate. On a high-end system, inductor loops can be embedded under the driveway as outer and inner loops. As the vehicle moves through the gate, it passes from the outer loop to the inner loop, which creates a signal to keep the gate open. After both loops are cleared, a timer in the control unit controls when the motor is activated to close the gate. When a vehicle approaches the gate to exit the property, the inner loop signals the controller to open the gate and the gate is held open until the vehicle clears the outer loop.

Access Control System Installation Considerations

The primary installation issues for an access control system are wiring and the effective placement of the detection and control devices. The manufacturer's recommendations for the type of wire to be used, placement of the sensors, inductive cables, and so on, should be followed to ensure an effective and functional installation.

Access Control Panels

The central point of most access control systems is a control panel. The reader, scanners, card slots, driveway systems, and other access control devices connect to the control panel as input devices and the door locks and door releases connect as output devices. In addition, the output can be wired as an input to a security system. Sometimes detection devices such as an exterior motion detector are wired directly to a security panel. The security system can sound an alarm or trigger an output such as notifying the lighting system to turn on the driveway and entry lights if it is dark.

PART VIII

In some preconfigured access control systems, the control panel (see Figure 36-18) performs the authentication process and in others, the control panel serves as a bridging device that redirects signals through relays to activate preset actions, such as through the lighting system, security system, door locks, and so on.

Access Control System Wiring

The most commonly recommended wiring standard for access control systems is RS-485, which requires 2 to 6 conductor 24 American Wire Gauge (AWG) twisted-pair cable. However, the cable properties specified in RS-485 are more than satisfied by Cat 5e cable.

When planning the structured wiring for a home that is to include an access control system, be sure to include homeruns of additional Cat 5e cabling to connect the system's detection and locking devices to the access control panel and to the home control unit.

 NOTE Wiring for access control systems varies by manufacturer and, in some cases, even between models. Be sure to follow the manufacturer's documentation and recommendations when wiring an access control device. Remember, no matter what, you should always follow the standard electrical and low-voltage wiring guidelines and codes applicable to a home's location.

Figure 36-18
A security system control panel

Photo courtesy of Amtel Security Systems, Inc.

Chapter Review

An access control system is any combination of devices that secure a home and prevent or detect an unauthorized entry through a door, window, or other exterior feature that can be used to gain access to a home.

Residential access control systems consist of a variety of devices used to gain access to a home, including card readers, door locks, driveway loops, keypads, proximity card scanners, and motorized gates.

Card reader systems read coding on a credit card- or smaller-sized plastic or laminated cards to unlock or open a door to a home. A basic card reader reads a number from the card and transfers it to a control unit or security system controller.

A barcode reader is similar to the devices used in the checkout stands at supermarkets. Barcode encoded information is printed on a plastic or paper card.

A magnetic stripe reader reads the information stored on a black or reddish-brown magnetic stripe placed on a plastic card. There are two types of magnetic stripe cards: low coercivity and high coercivity.

Proximity systems read information from a card held near the card reader using low-frequency radio signals. Wiegand cards are a type of proximity readers that have special electromagnetic wires embedded in them in a specific pattern, unique to each card.

Keypad access control systems require the entry of a multiple-digit code sequence.

An electronic key system works much like a regular lock and key, except that electronic keys are inserted into an electronic reader.

Electric door lock systems are typically used in conjunction with an authorization device, such as a card reader, electronic key, or keypad. This type of access control device can be used to limit both entry and exit through a door. A wide variety of products fall in the general category of electric locks, including remote control deadbolts, push-button and keypad door locks, and electric door strikes that can be used to upgrade existing mechanical door locks.

A remote control deadbolt works much like a manually operated deadbolt, except that a remote control deadbolt can be locked or unlocked through an IR remote control.

Push-button and keypad door lock systems are keyless locks that can be unlocked by entering a code number sequence by pressing buttons or keys on the face of the door lock.

Electric door strikes lock or unlock a door acting on a command from a charge sent to the strike through a relay or a simple push-button release.

Biometric access control systems use a feature of the users' bodies to verify their identities, such as fingerprints, facial features, and even retinal patterns. For residential systems, the most commonly used biometric system is one that uses fingerprints to control access.

There are a variety of driveway detection and monitoring systems available: induction loop systems, metal detection systems, and motion detection systems.

An induction loop system installs loops of special cable under a driveway. The induction cable emits an electromagnetic field that interacts with anything that changes the frequency of the inductive field.

Metal detectors use sensors to detect large metallic objects moving past.

Exterior motion detectors emit a PIR beam or sweep that constantly scans a fixed area and signals a security event should the beam be interrupted. Beam detectors transmit a

PART VIII

continuous IR beam between two stations and when an object breaks the IR beam, a signal is generated from the controlling transceiver.

A motorized gate is equipped with a two-directional motor system that is used to open and close the gate upon receiving a signal. Motorized gate systems are available as swing gate, slider gate, and lift gate systems.

The primary installation issues for an access control system are wiring and the effective placement of the detection and control devices. The manufacturer's recommendations for the placement of the sensors, inductive cables, and so on, should be followed to ensure an effective and functional installation.

The central point of most access control systems is a control panel. The reader, scanners, card slots, driveway systems, and other access control devices connect to the control panel as input devices and the door locks and door releases connect as output devices.

The most commonly recommended wiring standard for an access control system is RS-485, which specifies 4 to 6 conductor 24 AWG twisted-pair cable. The cable properties specified for RS-485 cabling are more than satisfied by Cat 5e cable.

Questions

1. Access control systems are used primarily for what purpose?

   A. Intrusion detection and alarm

   B. Remote monitoring services

   C. Preventing unauthorized entry

   D. Securing windows

2. Which of the following is not typically part of a home's access control system?

   A. Card reader

   B. Interior motion detector

   C. Electric door lock

   D. Keypad

3. Which of the following types of readers do not require a card or key be inserted or swiped?

   A. Barcode

   B. Magnetic stripe

   C. Proximity cards

   D. Electronic key

4. What type of card system uses embedded wires arranged in a unique pattern?

   A. Proximity

   B. Magnetic stripe

   C. Barcode

   D. Wiegand

5. What technology is used with proximity card systems?

   A. Barcode

   B. Magnetic stripe

   C. RF

   D. IR

6. What is the drawback to using keypad access control systems?

   A. Length of the numerical code

   B. Limited number of codes

   C. Unauthorized person learning code

   D. Weather

7. Which of the following is the physical feature most commonly used for residential biometric access control systems?

   A. Facial features

   B. Fingerprint

   C. Retinal scan

   D. Ear scan

8. What type of system uses cables installed under the driveway to detect a car entering the driveway?

   A. Induction loop systems

   B. Metal detection system

   C. Motion detection systems

   D. Visual detection systems

9. What cable type can be used in place of the recommended RS-485 cabling for an access control system?

   A. Cat 3

   B. Cat 5e

   C. Coaxial cable

   D. Quad wire

10. What device is used to bridge and control the sensors and detection systems of an access control system to door locks and other entry security devices?

    A. Bridge

    B. Central switch

    C. Control panel

    D. Hub

Answers

1. **C.** Interior and exterior security systems incorporate the other choices, but an access control system is used to control the entry into a home.

2. **B.** Access control systems are focused solely on alerting the homeowner to a visitor's presence and the control of access to the home.

3. **C.** These systems use RF signals that can be detected from a short distance of the reader. The other choices require a card or key be inserted or swiped through a reader.

4. **D.** Because the pattern of wires in a card is essentially manufactured into the card, they are virtually impossible to counterfeit.

5. **C.** Proximity cards use passive low-frequency radio frequency technology to communicate.

6. **C.** As long as the code number to be entered on the keypad is secret, the system remains secure. None of the other choices are typically much of a problem.

7. **B.** Although the other choices, well, perhaps with the exception of an ear scan, can be used, the equipment is prohibitively expensive for residential applications. As far as I know, there are no ear scan systems.

8. **A.** As a car drives over the induction loop, the frequency of the electromagnetic field changes, which is detected by the system's controller. The other choices listed are generally above-ground systems.

9. **B.** Cat 5e wiring, which is typically used for structured wiring anyway, can be used to connect access control sensors and detection systems to the access control panel.

10. **C.** In most access control systems, the microprocessor and processing capabilities exist in the control panel, which performs authentication and authorization functions.

PART IX

Home Technology Integration

Defining Users Needs and Desires

In this chapter, you will learn about:
- Identifying a customer's current and future needs
- Developing a preliminary design
- Defining a project's scope, budget, and timeline
- Preparing a proposal

A potential customer may not actually know what he or she (or they) really wants from a home automation project, at least not in detail. He may know that he wants a home theatre, music and TV throughout the house, a security system, and perhaps a door lock he can remotely control (an access control system). However, he doesn't know what is involved specifically to implement his vision. And that's where you, the home technology integration professional, come in.

This chapter provides an overview of the steps you should perform to fully understand the customer's desires and needs, today and into the future, how to organize and document these desires and needs, how to prepare and present a proposal.

Identify the Client's Needs

After an initial conversation with the customer where you actively listen more than you talk, you should have an idea of what the customer wishes to accomplish in a home technology integration project. Active listening means that you provide feedback to the speaker and work to gain an understanding of what's being said. Be sure to request a floor plan of the customer's home. If a floor plan is not available, tour the home and sketch one out. In an existing home or one already under construction, you should do a site survey and walk-through anyway, if for no other reason than to acquaint yourself with the workplace and its conditions.

Typically, if the project involves new construction, a floor plan, in the form of a blueprint, should be available from the builder. However, in remodel or retrofit projects, you will most likely need to create one. Keep in mind that the dimensions of the rooms, walls, and features of the home are important, not only for planning purposes, but for budgeting as well. The amount of time you spend discussing the project and its design objectives really depends on its scope and inclusions.

Your task is to work backwards from the customer's stated needs to identify alternative approaches and perhaps better solutions. The process you should use is detailed in the following steps:

1. Identify the customer's stated and hidden needs, ensuring that no critical need is missed or forgotten in the conceptual design. When discussing all the possibilities, be sure to cover every one of the subsystems you offer, such as:

- Structured wiring

- Computer networking

- Distributed audio and video distribution

- Home theatre

- Lighting management

- Telecommunications

- Heating, Ventilating, Air Conditioning (HVAC) and water management

- Security protection system

- Home access control systems

- Home control system

- Other automated devices

To help keep track of the customer's desires and needs, create worksheets for each of the subsystems to accurately and consistently record the discussion and decisions. Table 37-1 is a sample worksheet for the audio distribution system.

Table 37-1 shows a sample of a worksheet developed for an audio subsystem portion of a home automation project. Creating worksheets for each subsystem, rather than one large worksheet for the entire project, is a good way to focus the

Zone #	Room	Placement	Speakers	Volume Control (VC) What does V/C stand for?	Keypad	Special Instructions
1	Kitchen	Ceiling	Round Model #	VC with IR input	Keypad	Keypad by pantry
1	Dining Room	Ceiling	Round Model #	VC	NONE	Controlled by keypad in kitchen
2	Living Room	Wall	Rectangle Model #	None	Keypad	Integrate with home theatre
3	Deck	Surface mount bracket under eave	Outdoors Model #	VC	Keypad	V/C and Keypad located by slider door to deck

Table 37-1 Design Planning Worksheet for a Home Technology Project

discussion with the homeowner on each subsystem. The detail in the worksheet for each subsystem should provide good input when preparing a design proposal.

2. Tie every alternative approach back to a need identified by the customer.

3. Prepare a conceptual design for the project that identifies your understanding of the customer's current and future desires and provide a factual basis for your system specifications. The format of the conceptual design can be the worksheets you design, a drawing, a narrative, or all three. Figure 37-1 illustrates a drawing of conceptual design.

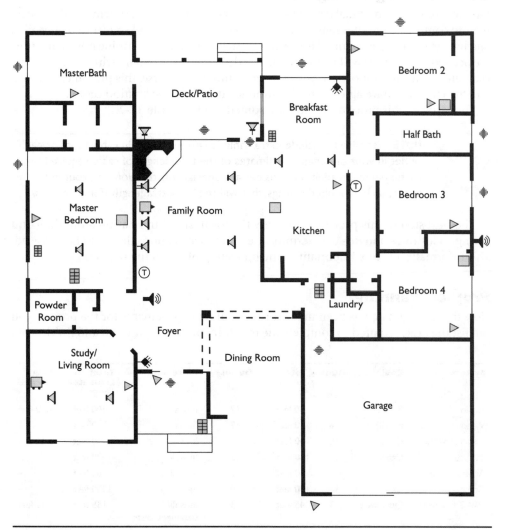

Figure 37-1   Floor plan with conceptual design of devices and locations

NOTE Consumer Electronics Design and Installation Association (CEDIA) has adopted and published a set of planning icons it hopes will become accepted industry wide for planning and design purposes. While the number of icons are far too numerous to list here, Figure 37-1 illustrates how they are used.

4. Discuss the conceptual design with the customer, highlighting how the design addresses their current and future needs. After making any necessary adjustments, obtain their approval to move forward with the project proposal.

Consolidating Wiring Requirements

Working from the conceptual design (see Figure 37-1), list the major systems (audio, video, remote controls, computer network, security, HVAC control, and so on) to be installed and list the wiring type required for each. For each cable type, determine how many runs are needed, where they will be installed, and develop a preliminary wiring plan and an estimate of the amount of each wiring type required. Of course, this presumes that you and the customer have agreed on a location for the cable distribution center.

The result of this process should look something like Table 37-2.

NOTE Be sure to include extra cable length for rough-in cable loops at each outlet in your preliminary estimates of the total length of cable required for each system. In addition, consider any special construction or layout in the home, such as vaulted ceilings, that will require extra length tfor wire runs.

The next step in this process is to verify the local, state, and national building and wiring codes and standards to determine the cable specifications that must be followed. This information is very important to the budgeting phase of the project.

Project Planning

Now that an estimate has been made for the cabling requirements for the project, you can list the tasks required to complete the rough-in, pre-wire, trim-out, and finish work

System	Cable	Runs	Total Length	Outlets	Placement	Total Estimated Length	Total Needed
Audio	RG-58	6	50 feet	12	In-wall	300 feet	660 feet
Video	RG-58	6	60 feet	12	In-wall	360 feet	–
Data Network	Cat 5e	10	100 feet	10	In-wall	1000 feet	3980 feet
Security	Cat 5e	16	120 feet	12	In-wall	1920 feet	–
Access Control	Cat 5e	2	30 feet	2	In-wall	60 feet	–
Communications	Cat 5e	10	100 feet	10	In-wall	1000 feet	–
HVAC Controls	Quad wire	3	45 feet	3	In-wall/ basement joists	135 feet	135 feet

Table 37-2   A Preliminary Wiring Estimate

for the entire system. As part of this process, you should list the tasks to be performed in their chronological sequence (you may need to coordinate with the builder or contractor to learn their schedules and sequences).

The project planning should include all tasks, including customer training, follow-up, coordination, approval, inspections, and so on. Leaving out a pacing item could lead to a later misunderstanding between you and the customer, especially if a third-party begins to pace the project. You heard it here first: the most important part of any project is your communications with the customer.

You should then cost out the wiring, outlets and faceplates, controls, control panels, networking devices, and labor required to complete the project as conceptualized. This information allows you to prepare a budget.

Preparing a Proposal

Your proposal to the customer for the work to be performed creates a working contract in the customer's mind. So, anything that is important to the success of the project should be included in the proposal. This means that any and all tasks to be performed should be listed; all equipment and devices should be listed; all prices should be firm (with language to cover changes or additions to the original plan); all timelines should be reasonable and doable; and any potential obstacles to meeting the timeline should be listed, such as contractor delays, material delays, inspection delays, and the like.

The project budget should be developed so that it reflects the cost of each system to be installed. This information allows the customer to answer two questions: are you the contractor of choice (in a competitive situation) and does she really want to install all of the systems on her wish list?

When presenting the proposal to the client, also share a finalized drawing or diagram of the project and its scope of work. Clearly identify wire runs, outlet placement, and cable distribution and consolidation points. An incomplete proposal with vague drawings creates a situation where the project's objectives are "in the eye of the beholder." The proposal should detail exactly what will happen, when it will happen, and how much it will cost the customer.

On the other hand, be cautious about including too much information. There is no need to include the appropriate building codes and cable specification sheets, unless you believe it is important to provide the customer with this information in a competitive situation. It is a fine line between sharing your concepts and giving them away. Consider which documentation for the project you want to give to the customer at the time of proposal as you have not been awarded the contract yet. You don't want your hard work designing the system to be used by others who might be able to outbid you, installing your system at a lower price since they didn't do the design work.

Be sure your proposal is dated (you may end up presenting several versions to the customer before you reach a final agreement) and includes a Signed Acceptance Agreement that clearly outlines the payment terms and what happens if they are not followed.

Present the proposal to the customer in person and review it in detail. Explain why you made the decisions about the system and components based on previous conversation(s).

Sending it to the customer through the mail or e-mail and then discussing it over the telephone or by e-mail creates the opportunity for the customer to misinterpret technical information and, most important, not understand how your bid represents a quality installation. By meeting in person you can answer questions directly, get a much better sense for the customer's thoughts, and, hopefully, close the sale.

Chapter Review

In your initial conversation with the customer, listen carefully to learn what the customer wishes to accomplish in his home technology integration project. Request a floor plan of the customer's home, but if one is not available, tour the home and create one. You should do a site survey to acquaint yourself with the workplace and its conditions. The dimensions of the rooms, walls, and features of the home are important for planning and budgeting purposes.

The steps in the initial phases of the project planning process are: identifying the customer's current and future needs, and preparing and presenting a conceptual project design. After the customer has approved the conceptual design, develop the formal project planning. The project phases should include consolidating the structured wiring requirements and developing a project plan and budget that addresses each phase and task of the project.

To consolidate the cable requirements, work from the conceptual design and list the major systems to be installed and the cabling required by each. You should first gain approval from the customer on a location for the cable distribution center.

You will need to verify local, state, and national building and wiring codes and standards for the cabling to be installed. This information is important for budgeting the project. List the tasks required to complete the rough-in, pre-wire, trim-out, and finish work for the entire system in a chronological sequence.

Cost out the materials required to complete the job as designed and prepare a project budget. The project budget should reflect the cost of each major system to enable the customer to make decisions regarding the feasibility of the project.

The project proposal should include all the information that is important to the success of the project: all the tasks to be performed; firm prices; reasonable and doable timelines; and potential obstacles to completing the project as scheduled. Include a finalized drawing of the project. You should present the proposal to the customer in person.

Questions

1. What should be your approach for learning a potential customer's needs and vision in your initial meeting with a customer regarding an HTI project?

   A. Present a list of the latest and greatest system alternatives to educate the customer.

   B. Listen carefully and actively to the customer's needs and requirements, and then prepare a conceptual design.

    C. Listen to the customer's stated requirements and then discuss all newer and state-of-the-art system approaches.

    D. Politely listen to the customer and then prepare a conceptual design that includes the systems you believe are best for the customer's situation.

2. Which of the following should be performed during your initial visit with the customer?

    A. Preliminary design

    B. Conceptual design

    C. Site survey and/or blueprint review

    D. Budget preparation

3. Of the following, whom should you consult during an installation project in a new construction situation?

    A. Builder

    B. Customer

    C. Building inspector

    D. Electrician

    E. All of the above

4. What customer needs should be addressed in the development of a conceptual design? (There may be more than one answer.)

    A. Stated needs

    B. Hidden needs

    C. Unspoken needs

    D. Future needs

    E. All of the above

5. What documents should be included in a conceptual design presented to the customer? (There may be more than one answer.)

    A. Narrative of the project scope

    B. Identification of the customer's needs and desires

    C. Conceptual design diagram

    D. Specific cable specifications and costs

6. What is typically the first activity when developing a structured wiring project plan?

    A. Approval of customer wish list

    B. Consolidation of cable requirements

    C. Estimation of labor charges

    D. Site survey

7. Which of the following project phases is not typically addressed in the project plan?

   A. Conceptual design

   B. Rough-in

   C. Pre-wire

   D. Customer training

8. When preparing a project budget, which of the following should be verified?

   A. Blueprints

   B. Local, state, and national building and cable codes and standards

   C. Customer's budget

   D. Availability of quality installers

9. What are the most important characteristics of the project timeline? (There may be more than one answer.)

   A. Reasonable

   B. Aggressive

   C. Vague

   D. Can be accomplished

10. What method should be used to present a project proposal to a customer?

   A. E-mail

   B. Fax

   C. In person

   D. Telephone

Answers

1. **B.** Active listening means that you provide feedback to the speaker and work to gain an understanding of what's being said.

2. **C.** It will be very hard to estimate the materials needed or to anticipate any design challenges without a review of the blueprints or a site survey of a partially completed or existing home.

3. **E.** Hopefully, this was a no-brainer. Actually the list could be much longer; you may need to consult vendors, manufacturers, and other specialists during an installation project.

4. **A, B,** and **D.** Unspoken needs should not be confused with hidden needs, which are needs a customer may not know exist, such as wiring requirements, and so on. Typically, if a customer doesn't mention a system need, you won't include

it. However, you may want to clear up any ideas you have for the system, just to be sure.

5. **A, B,** and **C.** During the conceptual design phase of an HTI project, it is premature to begin estimating the cost of cable.

6. **B.** The lifeline of any HTI project is structured wiring, and a clear identification of all of a project's wiring requirements is the only way to install the wiring efficiently and effectively.

7. **A.** The project plan is developed after the conceptual design plan has been approved.

8. **B.** Blueprints should be verified during the conceptual design phase and, while you may have interest in the customer's budget and the availability of workers, one is none of your business and the other is only your business.

9. **A** and **D.** If a project timeline is too aggressive, it is typically guaranteed to fail. Be reasonable and only promise what can actually be delivered.

10. **C.** Only when meeting face-to-face can you avoid the problems that remote conversations invariably create.

User Interfaces

In this chapter, you will learn about:
- Types of user interfaces
- Handheld, wall-mount, tabletop, and remote control technologies
- User interface issues

Our love of remote controls is evidenced by our viewing and listening activities. In fact, it is not unusual for someone to spend several minutes searching for a misplaced remote control, rather than taking a few seconds to just walk over to the TV, DVD player, VCR, or stereo to change the program, station, disc, or track.

Despite what this may say about us, when you're working with a distributed audio or video system or a whole-house control system, managing the source or control devices can mean walking to a room that may be on the opposite side of a home. One of the primary justifications for installing an integrated home control system is convenience. And handheld remotes, keypads, and other local controls are some of the most important conveniences the system provides.

In this chapter, we take a look at the various types of controls that can be used with automated home systems, including how they work and what are the issues with different types of user interfaces.

Types of User Interfaces

Nearly all consumer electronics these days come with some type of remote control. This includes stereo equipment, televisions, DVD and VCR players, and even video cameras. In addition, home systems, such as lighting, audio, video and even computer systems can also be operated from some form of a remote control. Types of remote control devices range from simple to complex (and expensive) including:

- Handheld remotes and key fobs
- Keypads
- Touch screens
- Voice-activated controls
- Telephone

- Computer
- PDAs and Web pads
- Remote access devices

Handheld Remote Controls and Key Fobs

There are a wide variety of remote controls with many sizes, shapes, and functions. Here we are talking about wireless remote controls only. Essentially, any small remote control that will fit into a normal-sized person's hand can be considered a handheld remote control. However, some of the remote controls that could be included in the handheld category are larger in size and are better categorized into the user interfaces that I describe below.

Handheld remote controls are usually infrared (IR) or radio frequency (RF) devices that are 1.5 to 3 inches wide and from 4 to 10 inches in length. There are models that control a single device and some that have the capability to control multiple devices, although only one at a time.

Figure 38-1 shows a basic single device, in this case a television, handheld remote control.

Remote controls that are small enough to attach to a key ring are categorized as key fob remote controls. These types of remote controls are typically single device remote controls

Figure 38-1

A single device handheld remote control

Photo courtesy of Universal Electronics, Inc.

that are used to open doors, turn on lights, control appliances, and similar type functions in a home.

Most key fob remote control devices transmit RF signals to an RF receiver built into the device or devices they control. However, because this type of control typically has a fairly narrow broadcast range, they are considered to be line-of-sight devices.

Some key fob remotes are programmed to a single device, but replacement models are available that can be programmed to control any compatible device. Some can be set to control two devices, such as the garage door and the lighting system, at the same time.

Power line communications (PLC) key fob controls have the capability to control as few as one to as many as eight receivers and transceivers and directly control a device plugged into the receiver or use a transceiver communicate with a home automation controller using PLC signaling. Figure 38-2 illustrates a PLC key fob remote control.

Keypad Controls

Although keypads have been covered in several places in this book, they have not been discussed in the context of their function as user interfaces. Keypad controls are typically wall-mounted devices that allow for a single control function, such as raising or lowering the volume of the speakers in a room or zone, or the ability to control multiple devices such as lights in a single zone or throughout the house.

Another type of handheld remote control is the IR devices that communicate with base units that are inserted into an AC outlet and send a PLC signal over the electrical lines to turn electrical devices, such as appliances, lamps, and the like, on or off (see Figure 38-3).

Like remote controls, keypads can have hard keys and soft keys, a single light-emitting diode (LED) or an LCD display, and they can be single function or multiple function controllers. Figures 38-3 and 38-4 show examples of the different levels and configurations of keypad controllers.

Some keypad-style remote controls are full-color touch screen displays that are made to mount in or on the wall or sit on a tabletop like Figure 38-5. The unit shown in Figure 38-2 is a PLC device that communicates using RF signals to a base station plugged into a home's AC circuits. Figure 38-4 shows a wall-mounted, hard-wired security system controller that is typically mounted on a wall.

Figure 38-2
A PLC key fob remote

Figure 38-3

A wall-mounted PLC keypad control that can be used to control the power to an electrical device

Photo courtesy of Skylink Technologies Inc.

Touch Screen Controls

When a user touches a touch screen with a finger, the resulting action is similar to pressing a button, or clicking a mouse. A touch screen device is a video display screen, either liquid crystal display (LCD) or cathode ray tube (CRT) that has been engineered to also serve as an input or interface device. There are two touch technologies that can be used, light pen (an external device) or touch overlay (an internal device), both of which output an XY coordinate signal. Of the two touch screen technologies, the touch overlay is by far the most commonly used touch screen system for residential systems.

Figure 38-5 shows a touch screen multiple-device controller that can either be hard-wired into a centralized home system controller or interfaced using RF or IR signals to a nearby receiver.

Figure 38-4

A multiple zone security controller with LED status lights

Photo courtesy of Honeywell International, Inc.

Figure 38-5
A wall-mounted
touch screen
keypad control

*Photo courtesy of
Home Automation, Inc.*

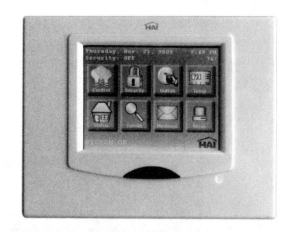

Touch Screen Operation

In most home touch screen devices, the display type is a resistive LCD screen that consists of a flexible outer layer, which is commonly plastic, and a rigid inner layer, which is glass or metal, with a layer of insulating stand-offs on a grid between the outer and inner layers. Both the inner and outer layers are coated on their inside surfaces with a metal oxide coating that conducts a low voltage charge. When a user presses the flexible outer layer, it makes contact with the inner layer, which is detected by the grid controller as a circuit closure. The controller alternates voltage between the upper and lower layers in such a way that it is able to identify the XY location on the grid where the user pressed the outer layer. The XY coordinate is supplied to the touch screen device's controller for processing or transmission onto another device. Other less reliable touch screen technologies are available, but rarely are used on residential devices. They include acoustic wave, capacitive, near field imaging (NFI), and IR.

Touch screen devices are available as wall-mount and tabletop, as well as stand-alone devices that communicate with a base unit using IR or RF signals. The base unit can be self-contained or be connected to a home system controller using PLC or hard-wire connections. Examples of these devices are

- **Wall-mount touch screen devices** An example of a wall-mounted touch screen controller is shown in Figure 38-5. Wall-mounted devices can be small, with only a few touch screen "soft keys" or large with a multifunction, multilayer touch screen program.

- **Tabletop touch screen devices** Figure 38-6 shows an example of a system tabletop touch screen controller. This type of touch screen device is commonly used to control a whole-house system.

- **Stand-alone touch screen devices** Figure 38-7 shows a stand-alone touch screen controller that operates either as a universal IR controller or as a part of a single or multiple zone control system.

Figure 38-6
A multiple-device tabletop home automation controller

Photo courtesy of AMX Corp.

Photo courtesy of Koninklijke Philips Electronics N.V.

Figure 38-7   A stand-alone touch screen controller

Touch Screen Programming

Many wall-mount and stand-alone touch screen devices include a number of preset soft keys. The soft keys themselves cannot be relocated on the screen, but the command or action assigned to each button, and its label, can be changed during a menu-driven programming and setup action.

More elaborate and more fully featured touch screen systems, such as tabletop devices and touch screen systems implemented on a personal digital assistant (PDA) or a tablet PC (see Figure 38-8), typically include a more sophisticated programming routine that allows some custom scripts and programming to be included.

Voice-Activated Remote Controls

If changing the channel on the television or controlling the volume of the stereo without getting up from your chair still involves too much physical effort, new remote control devices are entering the market that allow users to control a variety of devices using only spoken words. While these products seem perfect for the hopelessly lazy, the original intent was to assist disabled or infirmed consumers who are unable to operate a conventional remote control.

Voice-activated remote controls, like the one in Figure 38-9, are voice-recognition devices that digitize and store the sound wave pattern of spoken command words.

Photo courtesy of Hewlett Packard Company.

Figure 38-8   A tablet PC can be used as a remote control for a home automation system.

NOTE Before most voice-activated systems can be used, the user must "train" the device or its controller by recording a list of command sounds or words. On most devices, just about any spoken sound can be recorded to control one of the remote's functions, although most come with a list of as many as 60 suggested voice commands that can be recorded by as many as four family members. After the controller has been trained, whenever it receives sound, it searches through its database of recorded sound prints and when it finds a match, it performs the action associated with that sound, just as if a button had been pressed on a keypad.

Voice-activated remote controls (see Figure 38-9) typically operate either through recognized voice commands or through their keypad. Voice-activated controls continuously receive sounds from their immediate vicinity. Each sound it receives is then converted to a digital pattern and matched to stored digital images of prerecorded sounds. Should the digital image of a received sound match a digital image of a recorded sound, the function or action associated with the recorded sound is activated. For example, if the sound recorded to control turning on a TV set is "Picture," whenever the person who recorded this command speaks the word "picture," the voice-activated remote transmits an IR signal to the TV to turn it on. The words used to designate the remotely controlled actions should be chosen carefully so that normal conversation doesn't create a series of random electronic device events.

Figure 38-9

A voice-activated remote control

Photo courtesy of the Brookstone Company, Inc.

Telephone Controls

If you are away from home and you want to arm your security system, you can turn on a few lights, or interact with any of the other automated functions in your home, if the home automation control system is configured for it. These functions can all be done by the homeowner simply placing a telephone call to the home and pressing a few phone number pad keys.

Many home automation controllers have either built-in or optional phone control modules that allow a homeowner to access the controller and enter commands using a telephone number pad on a phone either inside or outside the home after entering a security code.

Another approach to using a telephone as a remote control is a group of newer devices that combine a cordless telephone with a universal remote control (see Figure 38-10). The handset of these devices doubles as both a cordless telephone handset and a multiple-device IR remote control.

Figure 38-10

A cordless telephone with a universal remote control built into the handset

Photo courtesy of Innovative Telecom Industries.

Computer Controls

Home systems can be controlled through a personal computer through the installation of specialized software and a few peripheral devices added to the computer, such as IR or RF transmitters, Electronic Industries Alliance/ Telecommunications Industry Association (EIA/TIA) 232 or parallel ports, PLC interfaces, Universal Serial Bus (USB) or Institute of Electrical and Electronic Engineers (IEEE) 1394 ports, and the like. A PC can be used to control a home system through a variety of interfaces:

- **Automation** Home automation control software can convert a PC into a home automation controller that can be connected into the home automation network in very much the same way as a stand-alone home system controller. By definition, a PC can be connected into the UTP and coaxial wiring of a home's structured wiring and used to control the home system by transmitting control commands over the cabling. However, a PC can also be interconnected into a PLC network to transmit control commands across the AC wiring of the home to PLC controllers and modules throughout the home. The type of network system installed will dictate the type of software system used on the PC.

- **External control and communication** A PC connected to the Internet provides the option for a homeowner to access the home automation system running on the PC from outside the home using the Internet. This allows the homeowners to check the system status and to make changes to the security, lighting, or other systems or be alerted to certain events while they are away from home. Some of the home automation control software systems include features to send e-mail or to dial a pager or cell phone in the event of an alert.

- **PC control** The computer user can use specialized software to directly control the lighting, appliances, and other PLC devices throughout the home by indicating the desired result to the software that then generates the appropriate commands to carry out the user's wishes.

- **Remote control** With the appropriate transmitters (IR or RF) attached, a PC can also be used as a remote control device to control the on/off switch and other functions of devices within its line of sight (IR) or broadcasting range (RF). Specialized software is required to facilitate this control along with an IR or RF transmitter.

In general, the software used for home automation or device control is designed to run on one or more specific operating systems. However, in nearly every case, the software uses a graphical user interface (GUI, pronounced "gooey") that allows functions to be selected using a mouse. Figure 38-11 illustrates a Lindows (Linux Windows) GUI screen.

PDAs and Web Pads

Personal digital assistants (PDAs), those handheld appointment books, notepads, phone directories, and personal information manager devices, can also be used as a remote

Image courtesy of Lindows.com, Inc.

Figure 38-11   The Lindows GUI

control for several consumer electronic devices, such as a TV, VCR, CD, DVD, and even home control systems. By adding special software (and perhaps a hardware chip) such as the Nevo software from Universal Electronics and proprietary offerings from Sony and Palm, a PDA can be used as a full-featured, customizable universal remote control. PDA remote control systems display (see Figure 38-12) stylus-selectable soft-keys on the PDA display that can be programmed to virtually any device. Communication from the PDA can be via IR or wireless RF that transmits using the IEEE 802.11b wireless communications standard, also called Wireless Fidelity (Wi-Fi). The benefit of using 802.11b communications in place of IR or other short-range RF technologies is the device then has a range of about 330 feet (100 meters). To complete the wireless remote control system, the central home automation controller needs to be connected to an 802.11b network access point (NAP) that supports Ethernet networking.

A Web pad is a generic term used for Tablet PCs and other wireless self-contained, handheld computers. Web pads (see Figure 38-8 earlier in the chapter) are generally full-featured PCs that allow users to surf the Internet, receive and send e-mail, and perform

Figure 38-12

A PDA configured as a home automation system remote control with the NEVO add-on software

Photo courtesy of Universal Electronics, Inc.

most PC-based functions, including data entry. By loading software on the Web pad, the computer can become a control device and touch screen.

Web pads are wireless RF devices that transmit using the IEEE 802.11b wireless communications standard, Wi-Fi. Just like the PDA with wireless control, Web pad devices, or the central home automation controller it is controlling, need to be connected to an 802.11b NAP that supports Ethernet networking.

Remote Access Control

It is also possible to control an automated home system remotely, in this case from outside the home, using the Internet or a connection from one PC to another. However, this does require some special software, in most cases.

If the home automation system is controlled by software running on the home computer network, then all that is required is PC remote control software, such as pcAnywhere from Symantic or GoToMyPC from Expertcity. This allows you to either dial up using a modem-to-modem connection or a broadband connection. You then access the home network either directly or over the Internet, as illustrated in Figure 38-13.

Once the remote PC is connected to the home network, the home automation controller can be managed and the settings changed on any of the subsystems linked to the controller.

Special telephone modem interfaces are also manufactured for specific home automation subsystems. For example, Honeywell offers a product called the Telephone Access Module (see Figure 38-14) that allows remote computer access to control the Heating, Ventilating, and Air-Conditioning (HVAC) subsystem of a home.

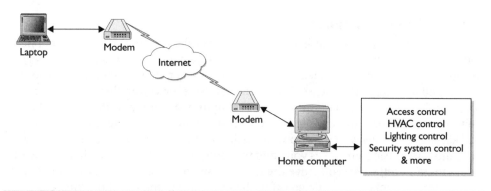

Figure 38-13   A home automation system can be managed and controlled remotely using a modem to access the home controller or on a home network.

Figure 38-14

The Honeywell Telephone Access Module is used to provide remote telephone modem access to a HVAC system.

Photo courtesy of Honeywell, Inc.

Hands-Free Controls

When you hear the phrase hands-free, you must wonder how the control can happen if you don't use your hands in some way, like touching a handheld remote button, keypad, or touch screen. Hands-free means the control is triggered by motion sensors located throughout the house. They sense the presence of someone within their scan pattern and act according to a preset plan initiated by the input of a command through traditional user interfaces earlier. An example would be turning on the music in the kitchen on the wall keypad, then when you walk down the hall from the kitchen and into the living room, the lights and music come on as you enter the room and go off in the kitchen because no one is there. Later, when you leave the living room and head back to the kitchen, the reverse occurs: lights and music go off in the living room and on in the kitchen.

Control Characteristics

There are some characteristics that are common to all types of remote controls, regardless of their size, their shape, or the device or devices they control. The most common of these characteristics are

- **Hard key**   A key or button on the remote control activates a fixed function and is linked to a single command code. The term hard key is derived from "hardwired." Hard keys are permanently labeled on the face of the remote or on the key itself for the function it performs. As shown in Figure 38-15, the hard keys are the buttons that have been printed or silk-screened with their associated function.

- **Soft key**   On some remote controls, especially multiple device controls (see Figure 38-5), the buttons on the side of the display screen are not typically preassigned as hard keys. These buttons are "soft keys," and their functions are assigned logically, depending on the device selected for control. The soft key's function is displayed adjacent to the button on the screen. When a soft key is pressed, it performs different functions for the device currently selected depending on the settings displayed on the remote's user interface.

- **User feedback**   On many remote controls, the user feedback is only an LED that lights when a button is pressed and a command code is activated. On other remote controls, an LCD is used to give visual feedback and can display status messages, command functions, show the device menu, and, on some remote devices, assign the functions of soft keys. Some models have auditory feedback, such as a click or sound when the button is engaged. On some models, the user interface is both hard keys and a touch screen offering a full array of soft keys.

The operating characteristics that all forms of remote control devices use to determine if a particular type of remote control is appropriate in a given situation are

- **Display**   Depending on the type and size of a remote control device, its user feedback display could be as simple as a single LED or an LCD display, or as advanced as a full-color touch screen display.

- **Ease-of-use**   A remote control should be easy to use, intuitive, and its keypad should be logically laid out, including its hard keys and soft keys. Related keys should be grouped together and clearly labeled. Consistent placement of the same keys on every keypad or screen (LCD or touch screen) is critical for ease of use. The graphics should be easy to read and pleasing to the eye along with being easily read by those who might be "small font-size challenged."

- **Two-way versus one-way communications**   Many higher-end remote controls (wall-mounted keypads and tabletop controls) are two-way devices that are able to display system feedback and status information. Most handheld remote control devices are capable of only one-way communications. The benefit of two-way communication is obvious; you know if the command you sent was received and gave the desired result. With one-way communication, you will often hear the saying "Send and pray" because you have no idea if the command sent was received and executed.

Figure 38-15
Hard keys and
soft keys on a
remote control
device

*Original photo courtesy
of Universal Remote
Controls, Inc.*

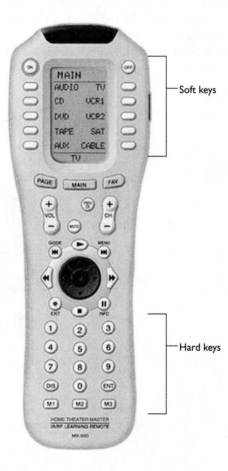

Remote Control Technologies

Handheld remotes come in a wide variety of shapes and sizes, but only two types of signal transmission technologies are used:

- Infrared (IR)
- Radio frequency (RF)

The basic difference between an IR remote control and an RF remote control is line-of-sight and operating range. An IR remote control uses a light beam to communicate with the device being controlled and must have a direct line-of-sight to operate within a fairly limited area. On the other hand, an RF remote control broadcasts radio waves and doesn't require a line-of-sight. In fact, many RF remotes don't even need to be in the same room as the devices they control, because they have a much larger operating range.

IR Controls

The core technology of an IR device is, of course, IR signaling. Infrared light is invisible light that is just below the red band of the visible light spectrum. On virtually all IR devices, a red glass or plastic lens or filter is placed over an LED to produce the red color most people associate with IR devices. Figure 38-16 shows an IR remote control and its base unit receiver.

Figure 38-16
An IR remote
control and
a base unit

*Photo courtesy of
Streamzap, Inc.*

IR Command Codes

Each button on an IR remote control's keypad (see Figure 38-17) is associated with a command code. When a button is pressed, the circuitry inside the remote modulates the frequency of the light beam to send the number associated with its command function for that button in a binary-encoded format. For example, if the number one is pressed on the keypad, the remote modulates the light beam to send the command value of two as a binary number.

Command Code Sets   Unfortunately, no standard command code set exists and many manufacturers use a proprietary code set to control their devices. The Infrared Data Association (IrDA) has developed a standard coding scheme for computers and peripheral devices, but in the home entertainment market, several different command code sets are in use. Table 38-1 lists a sample of IR command codes used by the Sony Corp for its television systems.

Figure 38-17

Each button on an IR remote control has a command code associated with it.

Photo courtesy of Intrigue Technologies, Inc.

Table 38-1	Command Code	TV	DVD
Sony IR Command Codes	0	1	1
	3	4	4
	11	Enter	Enter
	14	Channel guide	Return
	16	Channel up	Search reverse
	19	Volume down	Channel up
	21	Power	Power
	30	Brightness up	Program
	43	Clock, time	Play mode
	59	Jump, last	Step forward
	66	Video 3 select	Disc 3
	78	Cable select	Mega control
	96	Menu, guide	Slow reverse
	107	Auto program	AV center

Notice in Table 38-1 that the codes for a television and the codes for a DVD have only a few basic commands in common, demonstrating that even within the products of a single manufacturer, the IR command codes can vary for different devices.

Command Code Modulation   The most common method used for modulating an IR signal combines amplitude key shifting and turning the carrier on and off. When a button on the keypad is pressed, the command value associated with it is generated by the circuitry inside the remote and a modulated signal where the frequency is raised and lowered to represent the binary digits (see Figure 38-18) is sent to the light producing circuitry. The light-emitting part of the remote then transmits the command code values by turning the carrier frequency on and off in a pattern that represents a one, zero, or the short spaces between the digits and the long spaces separating the commands.

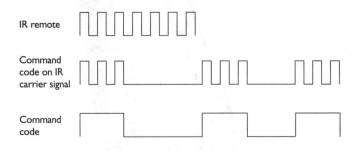

Figure 38-18   The command code is represented in a modulated signal.

Binary Number System

The binary number system represents values using ones (1) and zeroes (0) to indicate whether a position, which has a value of two to a certain exponential power, is included in the number being represented or not.

For example, the binary number 101 indicates that 2 to the power of 0 and 2 to the power of 2 are included in the value it represents, which in this case is the decimal number 4. The positional values of a binary number are listed in Table 38-2.

In an 8-bit binary number, the positional values of each bit are as follows:

2^7	2^6	2^5	2^4	2^3	2^2	2^1	2^0
128	64	32	16	8	4	2	1

When a one is present in a position, it indicates that the positional value of the position is included in the number represented. For example, in the number 00010010, the values included are

2^7	2^6	2^5	2^4	2^3	2^2	2^1	2^0	– Powers of two
128	64	32	16	8	4	2	1	– Positional values
0	0	0	1	0	0	1	0	– Binary digits
0	0	0	16	0	0	2	0	– Included values

So, in this example, 00010010 represents 16 plus 2, or 18.

Table 38-2 Binary Positional Values	Position in Binary Number (Right to Left)	Power of Two	Decimal Value
	8	2^7	128
	7	2^6	64
	6	2^5	32
	5	2^4	16
	4	2^3	8
	3	2^2	4
	2	2^1	2
	1	2^0	1

Using the information in Table 38-1, the IR command code of 18, which is volume up on a Sony system, would be modulated and transmitted as the binary value of 10010.

RF Controls

Radio frequency devices, including remote controls, emit an alternating current electromagnetic field (radio wave) using a wide range of frequencies and wavelengths. RF devices, such as cordless and cellular telephones, televisions, radios, baby monitors, and most garage door openers, are found in most homes.

A garage door opener is a commonly used example of an RF remote control. When the button on the handheld device is pressed, the unit transmits a radio wave signal in a fixed frequency. The receiving device is searching for signals in just that frequency and when it detects the right radio waves, it closes the contact, which opens or closes the door. Of course, this type of system isn't foolproof because the garage door opener's receiver has no way to sense the identity of the source of the signal, only that it was in the proper frequency.

RF remote control devices include a transmitter with an encoder circuit and the controlled device includes a receiver and a decoder circuit. The operation of an RF remote control is very similar to an IR remote control (discussed earlier in the chapter). Pressing a button on the remote activates the encoding circuit and the transmitter sends out radio waves. The receiving device decodes the transmitted signal and applies the command transmitted.

Most handheld RF remote control systems, especially the all-in-one and universal models, replicate the IR command signals associated with each device controlled after receiving the RF command. Because so many consumer electronic devices are equipped with IR receivers for use with IR remote controls, to use an RF remote control with any IR device, the RF signal must be converted into an IR signal, as illustrated in Figure 38-19.

An RF remote control is typically a universal or an all-in-one device with the capability to control up to ten different source devices from anywhere in a home. The remote control unit communicates using RF signals to the base unit (see Figure 38-20) placed in a line-of-sight to the source devices to be controlled. The RF base then issues IR control signals to the source device selected on the remote control.

RF remote controls can also be integrated with PLC systems to control centrally located devices such as those that change the media (music or video) being delivered to a room or zone. These systems work much the same way as the universal remote control described in the preceding paragraph. RF receivers are either base stations like the one shown in Figure 38-20 or they are built into wall-mounted keypads, switches, or just receivers that convert the RF signals into IR signals that are PLC based. These signals transmit over the AC lines in a home to another PLC device that converts the PLC-based signal into an IR signal that is "flashed" to the equipment to be controlled.

Chapter Review

Nearly all consumer electronics and most home control systems include some form of a remote control. Types of remote controls include handheld remotes and key fobs, keypads, touch screens, voice-activated, telephone, computers, and PDAs and Web pads.

A small remote control that fits a normal-sized person's hand is considered a handheld remote control. Handheld remote controls are usually IR or RF devices that range from 1.5 to 3 inches in width and from 4 to 10 inches in length. Some models control a single device and some control multiple devices one at a time.

Figure 38-19
The operations of
an RF to IR base
unit and remote
control

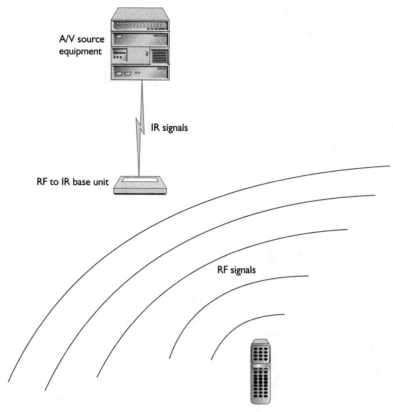

A/V source
equipment

IR signals

RF to IR base unit

RF signals

Keypad controls are wall-mounted devices that allow for a single control function or the ability to control multiple devices. Keypadds have hard keys, soft keys, or both as well as one or more LED indicators, and some have LCD isplays.

Figure 38-20
An RF-to-IR
base unit

*Photo courtesy of
Onkyo USA Corp.*

A touch screen device is a video display screen engineered to also serve as an input or interface device. Most home touch screen devices use resistive LCD screens. Other touch screen technologies are acoustic wave, capacitive, NFI, and IR.

Voice-activated remote controls are voice-recognition devices that digitize and store the sound wave pattern of spoken command words. After a voice-activated control is "trained," it searches through its database of recorded sound images for any sound it receives. If it finds a match, the action associated with that sound is activated.

Many home automation controllers have either built-in or optional phone control modules that can be used to access the home system controller and enter commands over a telephone.

Home systems can also be controlled through a PC with specialized software and the appropriate peripheral devices used to execute the desired commands. PCs can be used to control in four ways: automation, external control, PC control, and remote control.

PDAs and Web pads can be configured for use as remote control devices. A Web pad is a generic term used for tablet PCs and other wireless self-contained, handheld computers. It is also possible to control an automated home system remotely from outside the home, using the Internet or a connection from one PC to another. However, this does require some special software, in most cases. Special telephone modem interfaces designed to work with home automation systems are also available.

Several characteristics are common to all remote controls: hard keys, soft keys, and user interfaces. Remote controls use two types of signal transmission technologies: IR and RF. The difference between an IR remote control and an RF remote control is the line-of-sight and operating range. The core technology of an IR device is infrared light. Each button on an IR remote control's keypad is associated with a command code. RF devices emit an alternating current electromagnetic field (radio wave) using a wide range of frequencies and wavelengths. RF remote control devices include a transmitter with an encoder circuit and the controlled device includes a receiver and a decoder circuit. Pressing a button on the remote activates the encoding circuit and the transmitter sends out radio waves. The receiving device decodes the transmitted signal and applies the command transmitted.

Questions

1. What are the two communications technologies generally used by handheld remote controls?

   A. IR

   B. PLC

   C. RF

   D. Bluetooth

2. Which of the following communications technologies can be used together in a remote control system?

   A. IR

   B. PLC

    C. RF

    D. HomePNA

3. What type of remote control key has a fixed function and is linked to a single command code?

    A. Hard key

    B. Soft key

    C. Touch screen key

    D. Virtual key

4. What action must be taken before a voice-activated remote control is fully operational?

    A. IR range test

    B. RF range test

    C. It must be trained.

    D. None of the above; voice-activated controls are ready for use out of the box.

5. Which of the following can be considered to be remote control devices?

    A. PDAs

    B. Touch screens

    C. Key fobs

    D. All of the above

6. What is the common term used for a tablet PC used to control a home automation system?

    A. PDA

    B. Notebook PC

    C. Laptop PC

    D. Web pad

7. What are the two ways that a PC outside the home can access a home automation controller?

    A. By modem

    B. Hard-wired

    C. Over the home network

    D. Via the Internet

8. What is the operating range of a wireless 802.11b system?

    A. 3 meters

    B. 30 meters

    C. 50 meters

    D. 100 meters

9. Which of the following is not a commonly used display type on keyboard controls?

   A. LCD

   B. CRT

   C. LED

   D. Plasma

10. A PC can be used as a system controller with which of the following system types?

   A. PLC

   B. EIA/TIA 232

   C. RF

   D. IR

   E. All of the above

Answers

1. **A and C.** PLC communicates over household AC wiring, but is not directly used in remote controls, and Bluetooth is a type of RF technology used to create a PAN.

2. **A, B**, and **C.** IR and PLC can be used together to access centralized devices from anywhere in a home. RF has the operating range to provide remote access throughout a home. HomePNA is not used for remote control.

3. A hard key is in effect hard-wired to a specific function. Soft keys and touch screen keys are virtually the same, can be programmed by the user to a desired function, and are typically aligned with a display that indicates their function.

4. **C.** Training a voice-activated device involves recording the user's spoken voice for a series of command words.

5. **D.** Any device that has some control over another device's operations, configuration, or function can be considered a remote control.

6. **E.** Actually, all of the devices listed could be used as remote controls with a home automation system.

7. **A and D.** Once a connection is made to the system controller or to a home's data network, the effect is the same as if the remote unit were directly connected to the controller or network from within the home.

8. **D.** This is the technology used with PDAs and Web pads.

9. **D.** Plasma screens are being used in television monitors, but they have not yet made their way into user interfaces on keypad controls.

10. **E.** All of the choices can be interfaced to a PC equipped with system control software and the appropriate interface ports.

Home Automation Controllers

In this chapter, you will learn about:
- The features of home automation controllers
- The communications technologies used by controllers
- Configuring a controller

At the heart of an integrated home automation system is the controller. It is like a conductor of an orchestra, directing when each instrumental section plays, how loud or soft they play, and so on. In a similar manner, the controller of a home automation system directs when each subsystem is activated and provides its settings, such as the volume, operating patterns, and the like. The home controller creates the total experience for the occupants of the home, just as the orchestra creates the total experience.

A home automation controller is the integrator of the independent systems in the home. It pulls the home's subsystems into a single integrated system and through its control settings and programming manages a home's total environment.

This chapter focuses on the different types of home automation controllers and their components, functions, and configuration. Essentially, all home automation controllers perform the same basic tasks. However, it is how they go about performing these tasks that this chapter is about.

Controller Features and Characteristics

The primary feature of any home automation system controller is control. More specifically, this means the controllers capability to interface, interact, and communicate with the different subsystems in an automated home.

The true benefit of installing a controller in a home system is that it consolidates the functions of the separate subsystem controllers into a single interface for the homeowner. In home subsystems such as lighting control systems, Heating, Ventilating, Air Conditioning (HVAC) systems, security systems, distributed audio/video systems, and any other systems a home may have installed, each usually has its own separate controller with unique user interfaces. Often, the convenience gained from each subsystem is lost in the complexities, and possible overlapping, of the controls.

Integrating the subsystem controls into a single home control system means there is only one user interface for the homeowner to learn. For example, a single button on a room controller might dim the room lights, turn on the audio, turn up the room heat, and turn on the outside lighting. Or a button labeled "Outta Here" could turn down the heat, lower the house lighting, and arm the security system. With independently controlled subsystems, each of these actions would require the homeowners to take several steps; they would need to remember each step instead of using a single button, leaving nothing forgotten. The capability to set whole house environmental scenes through the push of a single button is perhaps the biggest advantage a controller-based home automation system provides.

Hardware- and Software-Based Controllers

Home system controllers can be either hardware-based or software-based. However, in either case, the system controller involves a computer microprocessor. A home system controller doesn't have to be a separate device installed in a control box or panel in a central location along side of the structured wiring distribution panel. The controller can be a home PC running home system control software.

Hardware-Based Controllers   Hardware-based controllers are specialized devices with a microprocessor for processing inputs and providing control. They are equipped with relays, input and output jacks, a variety of optional communication ports and have embedded processors to provide stand-alone functionality for the home control system.

Hardware system controllers provide a variety of features, including:

- **Communications**   A home control system controller typically has relay or contact closures, infrared (IR) ports, radio frequency (RF) port, serial RS-232 and RS-485, Universal Serial Bus (USB), or RJ-45 connections for Ethernet that are used to communicate with local controls, devices, and subsystems directly.

- **Macros, modes, and scenes**   The better system controllers have the capability to set the operating levels and functions of different combinations of local devices to create a local scene, also called a mode or a macro.

NOTE   A macro is a setting on a controller that can be enacted with the press of a single button to send numerous commands and settings to several different devices as a part of a single control sequence.

- **Multiple-zone control**   System control units have the capability to control devices in more than one room or zone of a home.

- **Reliability**   Many types of hardware-based system control units have the capability to modulate the signal strength to overcome interference on the communications lines.

- **Remote access**   Quality home system control units also provide the capability to access the control system remotely, using the phone line, remote portable computer, modem, or over the Internet via TCP/IP.

- **User interface**   A home control system is typically operated through either local keypad control, touch screens, or through software running on a web-enabled device such as a PDA or PC.

Software-Based Controllers

Several types of home control system software are available that can be installed on a PC and connected to the home network, be it the power line control (PLC) type or Ethernet home network.

Many of the home automation control software products available are designed to work with Ethernet networking, regardless of the transmission media or technology in use. Some are specific to certain media, such as PLC, but the better systems are designed to work over any hard-wired home network operating on Ethernet protocol.

PLC software products interface to the AC powerlines using Electronic Industries Alliance/ Telecommunications Industry Association, or EIA/TIA (RS) 232 or 485 serial interfaces and typically use a DB-9 connector or a USB interface. Using one of these serial connections, the PC is connected to a PLC interface that provides the link to the AC electrical lines and any other PLC devices connected to the AC system. Some software control systems provide an IR interface to allow the PC to control devices with a line-of-sight connection.

Communications

A home system controller, as shown in Figure 39-1, can be connected directly to the devices it controls or connected for communication with the subsystems it is sending control commands to. There are four possible ways to connect the controller to the devices or subsystems that it must communicate with:

- Hard-wired
- IP-connected
- PLC
- Wireless

Controllers communicate with devices and subsystems and their control modules in either a one-way or a two-way direction. A home system controller may communicate with the lighting system using a one-way direction, but it may communicate with the room control requesting a lighting scene change using a two-way direction. When the room control requests the scene change, the controller signals the lighting control module to activate a preset lighting configuration (one-way) and then notifies the room control (two-way) to confirm the change has been made.

One-way communications are used to transmit control signals to devices or sub-system controllers or to receive signals from subsystem controllers. The home system

Photo courtesy of Crestron Electronics.

Figure 39-1   A home system control panel

controller may have only one-way communications with a subsystem controller, which then has two-way communications with the devices under its control.

Two-way communications are used to send or receive command requests to and from subsystem controllers and room control devices and then to transmit command signals and status information to these same devices.

When the controller issues commands to a subsystem controller, it must use the signal format and coding scheme understood by the subsystem. Most robust control systems are able to communicate in a variety of ways including relay/contact closure, IR, RF, RS-232, RS-485 and TCP/IP. So, in some ways, a home system controller also acts as a translator and interpreter between the various components and subsystems connected to it.

Hard-Wired Controllers

Some subsystems, such as telephone, security, and surveillance systems, have their own unique signal formats that require a direct connection to the controller and to a subsystem module. The subsystem module can either be integrated into the controller or act as a stand-alone controller connected to the home system controller. It receives, interprets, and transmits signals in the proper format. The subsystem module can also communicate with the controller's main circuitry, often a microprocessor, to hand off signals with a system-wide impact. For example, if a disarm signal is received by the security system control module, this signal is passed to the home system controller, which then first communicates with the lighting module to turn up the house lighting and then back to the music system to play jazz.

Hard-wired control systems are the most reliable type of communications links that can be used to connect a system controller to subsystems and room controls. However, they usually work on proprietary communications protocol. In addition, they are usually the most expensive of the available options.

Most hard-wired systems communicate over the Cat 5e cabling installed as a part of a structured wiring system or over a proprietary cabling system. The controller can be connected to the network cabling using two primary methods: using a network adapter that is either built into the device or available as an add-on module (see Figure 39-2) to the controller or through a connection made in the distribution panel (see Figure 39-3).

Photo courtesy of Crestron Electronics.

Figure 39-2   A controller network interface add-on module

Another advantage of a hard-wired control system is that it is able to perform multiple tasks at one time. Because of the data speeds supported by unshielded twisted-pair (UTP) cabling, a hard-wired system is able to communicate at a faster data transfer speed and still maintain its reliability. Hard-wired systems are best installed during new home construction, as they are difficult to install with the necessary wiring as part of a retrofit or remodel project.

IP-Connected Controllers

A variation on the hard-wired approach to communications in a home control system is an Internet Protocol (IP) control system. IP control systems interconnect the home system controller and the room controls into the home computer network (see Figure 39-4) to create what amounts to a home intranet that is called a controller-attached network

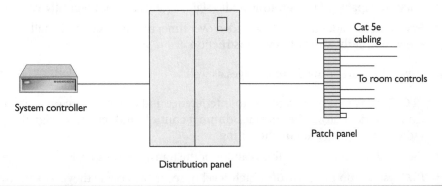

Figure 39-3   An illustration of how a hard-wired home system controller connects into a home's structured wiring

Figure 39-4

An illustration of a home system controller connected to a home computer network.

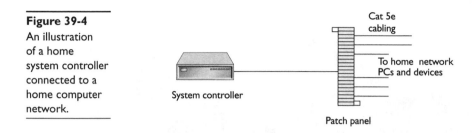

(CAN). An intranet is a network contained within a home, as opposed to an Internet, which extends way beyond a single home.

On an IP control system, the communication protocol is Ethernet-based TCP-IP. Each device connected to the network is assigned an IP address and the network communicates with it using that address.

PLC Controllers

Perhaps the most affordable type of home control system is powerline carrier control (PLC) systems, which are more commonly known as X-10 or CEBus. PLC uses a home's existing AC powerline to communicate.

The heart of a PLC home control system is its network control unit (see Figure 39-5), which serves to integrate and control the various PLC units and modules. A variety of PLC system controllers are available ranging from software for PC to stand-alone controllers. And PLC systems are easy to install, because the network media is already installed in the walls of a home (the electrical wiring). Here's an overview of the advantages of PLC communications advantages, along with the disadvantages.

The advantages of PLC communications are

- They use existing AC powerlines for communications media.
- Access is available to the PLC network through any AC outlet.
- They are compatible with data transmission and control signal transmissions.
- They are capable of transmitting audio signals (although not typically very well).
- System can be added to and expanded over time; not necessary to install everything at the time of new construction.

However, there are some disadvantages as well:

- PLC signals are very susceptible to interference and electric noise on a circuit from electric motors, thermostats, dimmer controls and television signals, and radio signals picked up by the wiring.
- Electrical noise on the AC lines can lower the transmission speeds of PLC signals.
- PLC systems do not provide a high-level of security because they transmit over insecure media.

- Attenuation can be an issue because of line noise and interference.

- PLC-enabled devices can be more expensive than their standard networking counterparts.

- They are only capable of transmitting one signal at a time, which is transmitted sequentially, since the signal requires time to travel over the electrical lines.

- No standard has been established for PLC communications.

- Windows computer operating systems do not include drivers for PLC products.

Photo courtesy of Home Automation, Inc.

Figure 39-5   A PLC network control unit

In spite of its disadvantages, PLC can be used in certain situations fairly effectively, such as controlling light fixtures and electric devices in a single room or smaller-size home (less than 2200 square feet).

Wireless Controllers

Wireless control systems can communicate using IR, RF, or IEEE 802.11b standards. Most often, wireless control systems, room, zone, and whole house remote controls transmit command and control signals to the central home system controller through the air using radio waves.

The IEEE 802.11b standard, also known as Wireless Fidelity (Wi-Fi), is a wireless communications standard that operates in the 2.4 GHz RF band. The 802.11b offers up to 11 Mbps of bandwidth in a range of around 150 feet indoors. At the present time, 802.11b is the most commonly used wireless networking standard. Table 39-1 lists the characteristics of the wireless networking standards on the market.

The advantages of wireless networking include the elimination of cabling between a remote control device and the system controller, and the portability provided by the lack of wiring. Another advantage is that the system is fast enough to provide bandwidth to overcome most interference problems, which are highly probable.

The disadvantage of wireless networking is its operating frequency. All of the 802.11 standards, and the Bluetooth standard, operate at 2.4 GHz, the same frequency used by many cordless phones, some garage door openers, baby monitors, and other wireless products commonly found in a home. In addition, wireless digital subscriber lines (DSL), or wireless Internet access to a home, also operates on this frequency. So, the possibility for interference is real, but as mentioned earlier, the bandwidth and data speeds are high enough that in most cases, interference can be overcome, though it's not always true in all cases.

In its best application, the use of wireless communications should be limited to transmissions between room and zone controls and the system controller only. This is for two reasons. First, there aren't many wireless subsystem interface modules available; and secondly, the traffic stream between the system controller and the subsystem control unit needs to be reliable. In this case, wiring is the best option. In a home that has structured wiring installed, the best approach is to interconnect the home system controller into the hard-wired environment for communications between the system controller and the subsystem controls over the structured wiring (see Figure 39-6).

Table 39-1	Standard	RF Band	Bandwidth	Indoor Range
Home Network Wireless Communications Standards	802.11a	5 GHz	54 Mbps	25 to 75 feet
	802.11b	2.4 GHz	11 Mbps	150 feet
	802.11g	2.4 GHz	54 Mbps	150 feet
	Bluetooth	2.4 GHz	720 Kbps	33 feet

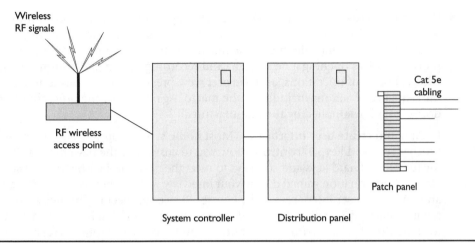

Figure 39-6 A home system controller in an RF wireless network relays signals to subsystem modules and devices over the integrated wiring system.

Controller Setup

When installing a home system controller, there are some basic steps you should followed to ensure the control system meets the needs of the homeowners and the installation goes efficiently. On all systems, you should work on much of the system configuration prior to visiting the site for installation and setup. The programming needs to be done very carefully. It is much more effective to find the problems and resolve them at the workbench then out in the field. Troubleshooting on-site is inevitable, but you want to keep it to a minimum.

The steps you should use to set up and configure a home system controller are

1. **Interview the homeowners** To be sure that the controller will best serve the needs of the homeowners, you should discuss the lifestyles and desires of the homeowners to help define the setup of the system. Also discuss system options and capabilities in detail to gain an understanding of the homeowners' expectations of how the system will perform once it is in place.

2. **Set Up control devices and programs** Here is where you layout the devices to be controlled and the desired programming. Be sure to follow the basic configuration of the controller according to the manufacturer's specifications and guidelines. Documentation is critical at this point because you will probably need to refer to it in the field. Remember, it is much easier to pre-program the controller in advance and off-site and then just install it on-site and upload the programming as necessary.

3. **Program macros and scenes**   During this step of the process, you should program and document any scenes or macros into the controller for testing on-site. Some systems include interactive macro creation software, but for most, the process involves opening a new macro and recording the keypad buttons using a logical order of operations, as if the user were pressing the buttons to request the sequence of actions included in the macro. Again, follow the programming documentation supplied by the manufacturer.

4. **Design and create user interfaces**   Most home system controls and many touch screen and keypad controls allow you to customize the placement and the function of hard keys and soft keys to meet the needs and wishes of the users. Using the information gained during your interview with the homeowners, design and set up the user interfaces on the control devices to meet the homeowners' requirements. Again, remember that documentation is critical. It is often beneficial to share the physical layout of the buttons on keypads and touch screens (an actual drawing of the control device with buttons labeled) with the homeowner prior to programming them, as they may have changes they would like and it is easy to make them initially.

5. **Install controller**   Now is the time to visit the site and physically install the controller unit or the control software on a local PC. Load the setup and programming you've done previously, and you're ready for the next step.

6. **Connect communications links and test local controls**   You should now connect and test the communications links with the control functions for both the local controls and the system controller, at least at a basic operational level. For example, does the request to dim the lights in a room result in the lights actually being dimmed? The settings may not be exactly right at this time, but the objective is to ensure the controller and the local controls are able to communicate and function together. Also check that any status messages that should be returned to a local control with a user interface display are displaying properly. You should test all controls thoroughly and correct any problems you encounter before proceeding to the next step.

7. **Acceptance testing**   When the system is completely set up and configured properly, perform a complete test of the system to ensure none of the homeowners' requirements have been overlooked or aren't working properly. Once you are satisfied that the system is working as specified, assist the homeowners in a complete run-through of all of the system's functions and actions. If the homeowner requests adjustments or changes, make the modifications and perform this step again completely.

8. **System maintenance**   Chances are that the homeowner will want some changes to the system or the user interfaces within the first 30 days of the system's operation. In anticipation of this, you should make some arrangement, with

an appropriate fee schedule, with the homeowner for a warranty, system changes, and ongoing system support.

On many systems, modifications can be made without the need for a house call, or what the communications people call a "truck roll." On systems that provide remote access, most problems or minor changes can be done by accessing the system through a modem or over the Internet and gaining access via a security code (which should be kept top secret at all times). A house call should be necessary only for major reconfigurations of the system or hardware problems, and if the system has been properly installed to the homeowner's wishes, it shouldn't be a common occurrence.

Chapter Review

A home system controller consolidates the functions of the separate subsystem controllers into a single user interface for the homeowner. Home system controllers can be hardware-based or software-based.

Hardware-based controllers are specialized devices with a microprocessor for processing inputs and control. They are equipped with relays, input and output jacks, a variety of optional communication ports, and have embedded processors to provide stand-alone functionality for the home control system. Many home automation control software products work with Ethernet networking, regardless of the media in use, although some are specific to certain media.

Home system controllers can be connected directly or can use communications media to transmit signals to the devices controlled. Four methods used to connect a controller to the devices or subsystems it controls are: hard-wired, IP-connected, PLC, and wireless. Home system controllers use either one-way or two-way communications.

Hard-wired control systems are the most reliable of the communications links that can be used to connect a system controller to subsystems and room controls. However, they usually operate on proprietary communications protocol and are usually the most expensive of the available options. IP control systems interconnect the home system controller and the room controls into the home computer network. On an IP control system, each device connected to the network is assigned an IP address and is communicated to across the network with that address. The most affordable home control system is PLC, which uses a home's existing AC powerline to communicate. Wireless control systems communicate using IR, RF, or IEEE 802.11b standards.

When installing a home system controller, some basic steps should be followed to ensure the control system meets the needs of the homeowners and the installation goes efficiently. The steps that should be used to set up and configure a home system controller are: interview the homeowners, set up control devices and programs, program macros and scenes, design and create user interfaces, install the controller, connect communications links and test local controls, perform acceptance testing, and provide system maintenance.

Questions

1. Which of the following best describes the basic function of a home automation system controller?

    A. Centralized maintenance

    B. Centralized interface

    C. Consolidation of separate subsystem controller functions into a single user interface

    D. Remote access for system maintenance

2. Of the following, which is not a commonly used communications technology or protocol for home automation control systems?

    A. Hard-wired

    B. IP-connected

    C. PLC

    D. HomePNA

3. Of the media configurations common to home control systems, which is considered to be the most reliable?

    A. Hard-wired

    B. IP-connected

    C. PLC

    D. HomePNA

4. On what cable media are hard-wired home control systems typically installed?

    A. AC powerlines

    B. Coaxial cable

    C. UTP cable

    D. 2-conductor 22 AWG wiring

5. What technology does the popular home automation protocol X-10 operate on?

    A. Ethernet

    B. IEEE 802.11b

    C. PLC

    D. Wi-Fi

6. What is the indoor range of an 802.11b network access point?

    A. 25 to 75 feet

    B. 50 to 100 feet

    C. 300 to 500 feet

    D. 330 meters

PART I

7. What is the primary disadvantage of using IEEE 802.11 networking?

   A. Interference with other 2.4 GHz devices

   B. Limited system controller offerings

   C. Line-of-sight

   D. Operating range

8. Which of the following is not typically a feature of a hardware-based home system controller?

   A. Communications with standard protocols

   B. Local access only for security reasons

   C. Macros

   D. Multiple-zone control

9. What should be the first step performed when preparing to install a home systems controller?

   A. Perform acceptance testing

   B. Install controller

   C. Interview homeowners

   D. Connect communications links and test local controls

10. A command sequence of several actions that can be enacted through a single button is called a(n)

    A. Automated local control

    B. Macro

    C. System interface

    D. Program

Answers

1. **C.** The other choices listed are features of a home system controller, but the home automation controller's primary purpose is to consolidate the control of the subsystems.

2. **D.** HomePNA is primarily used for data networking, although some advancements are being made to apply this technology to home control systems.

3. **A.** Hard-wired systems are the least susceptible to interference.

4. **C.** UTP cable is installed as part of a home's structured wiring system.

5. **C.** Powerline control (PLC) protocols include X-10 and CEBus.

6. **A.** The range of this technology depends on the construction of the home and its furnishings.

7. **A.** None of the other choices are factors with 802.11 wireless communications.

8. **A** and **B.** Although local access for security may sound right, most of the better home control systems offer remote access that is gained only after a security code is entered and nearly all systems are compatible to standard communications standards.

9. **C.** It's hard to know exactly what the homeowners' vision or expectations are for the control system without first discussing their lifestyles, the system, and its functions in detail with them.

10. **B.** Also called a mode or a scene, macros group a sequence of commands together so they can be executed as a single command stream.

Programming

In this chapter, you will learn:
- The different approaches used to program a home automation system controller
- The areas of a controller that require programming or configuration
- The processes used to back up and secure the controller's configuration

When you configure and set up a home automation system controller, as discussed in Chapter 39, the detailed steps you take to configure the controller require you to program the system. This doesn't mean programming in the sense of computer programming necessarily, but it does mean you need to specify the hardware connected to the controller, set system parameters, identify scheduled events, and create any desired macros.

This chapter provides an overview of the programming methods used on a cross-section of home system controllers, including those programmed directly on the controller, those that support a user interface for programming, and those that are programmed through interactions with PC-based software.

Programming Methods

Programming or setting up a home automation control system is first and foremost an exercise in organization. First you need to identify what the system is supposed to do and what you need to organize in terms of sequence and hierarchy before actually beginning to program.

Planning Ahead

Before beginning the actual programming on the controller or its programming software, draw a sketch of how the functions should flow logically; this can help to organize the steps. In the sketch shown in Figure 40-1, a "Home" key is planned for a keypad control placed near the front door of a home. The sketch shows a simplified version of what should happen in the controller when it receives a signal from the keypad that the "Home" key has been pressed. As illustrated, a "Home" macro is to be activated, and the controller issues command signals to the lighting, Heating, Ventilating, Air Conditioning (HVAC), and music systems to take certain actions.

With the sketches or perhaps an outline of what actions are included in what functions, you have a road map to follow to complete the programming. Planning out the

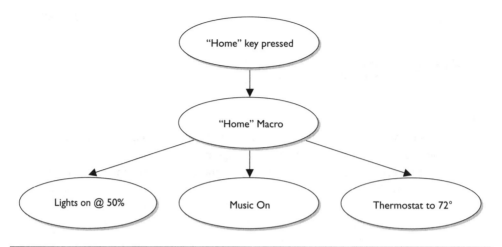

Figure 40-1   A sketch of the logical flow of the actions that should be performed by the system controller when a key is pressed on a keypad control

process in this way helps to prevent overlooking any of the required actions planned for the system. It also helps you to identify repeated actions that can be turned into macros or subroutines and called by different buttons, saving on programming time.

When setting up and programming a home controller, you usually take the following steps. By always following this procedure, you will minimize programming time and ensure that most, if not all, items are completed the first time around.

1. Set up controller parameters and user information
2. Define and set up all devices to be controlled (should already be done in previous documentation)
3. Identify and enter all programmed events
4. Define and enter all macros
5. Test, test, test

Ways to Program

There are essentially four ways to program a control system: standard code programming, proprietary code programming, wizards, and application driven programming.

Standard code programming requires the knowledge of standard programming languages such as C++ or PERL. Few systems exist today that use standard programming languages; almost all have been simplified with either proprietary code programming or wizards, or they have applications already set up.

There are also a variety of independent devices that can be custom configured to create a home control system, but we are not addressing this option in this book. This requires the creation of a programming language script and extensive programming. This type of system is very dependent on the programmer's abilities and can take longer to debug and test, which is why a proven system from a well-known manufacturer that offers a warranty should be installed in a customer's home.

Most of the higher-end home automaton control systems have built-in proprietary software interfaces for programming and configuring of the controller. These utilities are typically menu-driven or structured as a function or device hierarchy, as illustrated in Figure 40-2.

Whenever working with propriety programming software, it is strongly recommended, and often required, to participate in the manufacturer's training courses before selling, installing, and programming a home control system for a customer.

The manufacturers of the most popular systems, also typically the most expensive, have designed their systems with the end user and installer in mind. This effort is reflected in their programming interfaces. The programming interface on these systems is either embedded in the system control unit as firmware or is software that is installed on a PC with a hardwired or wireless interface for uploading and downloading to the control unit.

If the controller's programming software is PC-based, it usually incorporates several features to simplify the process and to aid in the navigation within the programming software. For example, menu bars, drop-down menu options, utilities, and wizards (see Figure 40-3) guide the programmer through the process of setting up devices and

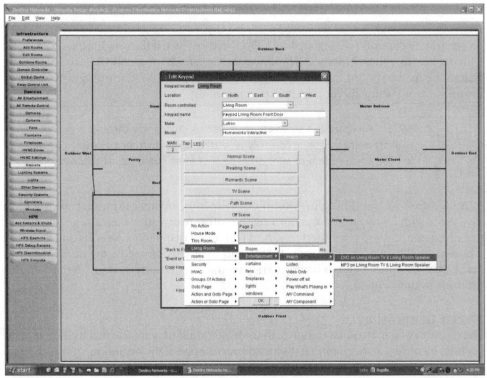

Image courtesy of Destiny Networks, Inc.

Figure 40-2   A sample configuration menu for a home system controller

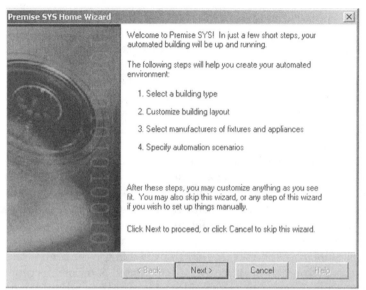

Figure 40-3   An example of a wizard utility in the setup software for a home automation control system

programming controls (see Figure 40-4). On these systems, if the programmer is familiar with the interfaces on a Microsoft Windows, Macintosh OS, or a UNIX/Linux X-Windows system, he or she should have little trouble navigating the programming software that includes wizard setup and application programming.

NOTE   A wizard is a software routine that guides you through a process, such as programming lighting controls or setting up audio zones. A wizard allows you to configure a system or subsystem by answering questions or choosing options.

Application programming uses drop-down menus, making inputting information easy. Also, with application programming the software can automatically generate control programming and user interfaces. And it is much easier to make edits and changes, which is good for the programmer and the end user. This can allow the homeowner to make changes without always having to rely on the installation company to make modifications to their system.

Macro Generation

The creation of a macro first requires an understanding of what the macro is to accomplish, as identified at the planning discussion mentioned at the beginning of this chapter.

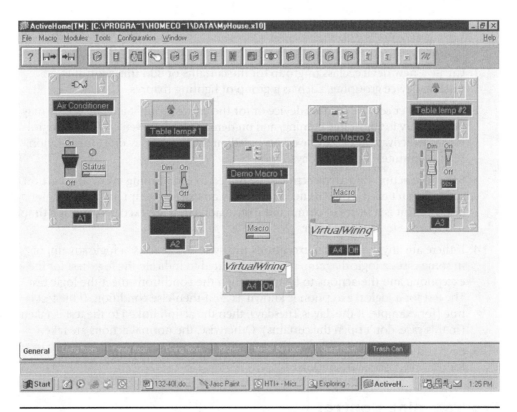

Figure 40-4   The configuration interface of a PLC home system control software package

Once you are sure you know what the macro is to do, the process of creating the macro in the home system controller's programming software is usually a straightforward process.

Many programming systems offer applets (mini-applications or utilities) to assist with creating a macro or scene. In some cases, the applet is a wizard and in others it is a series of questions with check boxes and fill-in-the-blank spaces. At the completion of the input process, the applet generates the macro, control sequence, or scene. It can then be tested and tweaked until it is exactly what you intended.

Some systems include templates that can be used to re-create new or modify standard devices, groups, and scripts, which can be timesavers for installers. On the logical control level, many homes require the same types of device controls, and after a few installations a programmer can build up a library of portable and reusable devices, templates, and macros.

A Programming Example
Here is an example of how to program a device control, including the general steps used in a sample home control software system.

To create a macro to control the powered curtains in a home theater room, you use the following general steps:

1. Create a new device, class or group for the curtains or add this control to an existing device grouping, such as a group of lighting fixtures.

2. Set the timer control for this device or for the entire group. Separate events may be necessary for morning, evening, and on-demand timing events. A timer control is used to activate or deactivate events based on the time of day or a time duration, such as minutes, hours, or days.

3. Select the action or activity script to be linked to each timing event. If an action script doesn't exist, you will need to modify an existing script or create a new one. A script is a series of command instructions that are executed one at a time in sequence by the controller.

4. If there are any conditional exceptions to any of the actions, a logic stream, or in some cases a logic diagram, should be created to indicate the logic test for the exceptions and the actions to be taken when the conditions meet the logic test. The test for a logical exception is known as an if-then-else condition. If the test is true (for example, if the day is Tuesday), then the action linked to the test is taken (in this case, don't open the curtains). Otherwise, the normal actions are taken.

5. Save and name the new macro. Macros can also be exported on some systems for use with other installations.

Programming Control

The purpose of the home controller is to control the devices in the system. These devices can be controlled in any of the following ways:

- Direct Device control
- Scheduled events
- Conditional control

As illustrated in Figures 40-2 and 40-4 earlier in the chapter, the programming interfaces on home system control configuration and programming modules typically include a menu, dialog box, or tree format for selecting specific devices for configuration, timing, and functions.

Provided that little or no scripting has been included in the system, the device interfaces are where most debugging and later modifications are typically made. How intuitive a user interface or menu system is should be a key criteria when selecting a system for a homeowner or yourself.

Direct Device Control

The simple ON/OFF control of a device can happen directly through programming or remote keypads, or touch screens can be set up to always control if a device is ON or OFF. The key word here is *always*; this means that whenever the button is touched, it *always* controls the device it is defined to control. An example would be the top center button on the keypad in the kitchen that controls (turns ON or OFF) the kitchen ceiling lights every time it is pushed.

Scheduled Events

Timer routines are at the heart of any home control system. Once the cable, wire, devices, and interfaces are installed and working properly, much of the remaining programming involves setting timer events (what comes on or goes off at what time of the day) or grouping devices into scenes.

The system timer continuously scans its list of configured timer events, also called scheduled events on some systems, looking for a match. Items it checks for a match include the current time, day, date, sunrise or sunset, and the scheduled event times. This kind of programming is often referred to as "When statements" because when the timer detects a match for a scheduled event, it passes control of the event to the system's processor and the commands, scripts, and actions defined in the event are then performed. For example, if the outside lights of a home are to come on at 6:30 P.M., a scheduled event is predefined to execute this action, "When 6:30 P.M. turn on outside lights." At 6:30 P.M., the timer would detect that the time criteria is met, this event is to be executed, and notifies the system processor, which then executes the event's commands to turn on the outside lights. The same sequence of actions takes place to execute another timed event that turns off the lights the next morning at the designated time.

Conditional Control

Conditional control is just what it sounds like it is: the control of the device depends on one or more conditions being met. The conditions are tested and if all are met, the command is executed. This type of control is often referred to as *If/Then* programming because the statement reads, "If <condition is true> then <perform command>." An example would be, "If security system is AWAY, then turn ON sink light at 6:30 P.M." Conditional statements can be nested and combined with *AND* and *OR* statements. An example would be, "If security is Away AND temperature in living room is greater than 80 degrees, then close drapes." This would protect the house from heating up from direct sun and fading the furniture fabric. Remember that with an AND statement both conditions must be met for the command to be executed. With an OR statement only one of the conditions must be met for the command to be performed.

How Boolean Logic Works

Boolean logic has three operators: AND, OR, and NOT, but the basic premise that only true is true is applied to all three. Here are some simple examples of how the Boolean logic operations work:

- AND logic: True is represented in the computer as a one (1) and false is represented as a zero (0). So, if an expression tests if two values, say value A and value B, are both true, the statement is likely to be "if A and B equal true." This expression is the same as testing "if A and B are both equal to 1." If A and B both happen to be equal to 1, the result is a 1, which means "true." If either A or B are 0 (the only other value they can be), then they aren't both equal to true and the result is 0, which means "false."

- OR logic: The OR operator tests for any one of the values to be true. So, if A is equal to 1 and B is equal to 0, the result will be true. True would also be the result if A is equal to 0 and B is equal to 1. An OR test is true if only one of the values is 1 (true). However, if neither A nor B is equal to 1, the result is false (0).

- NOT logic: Boolean NOT logic tests only a single value for true or false, meaning it tests a value for either a 1 or a 0. If value A is equal to a 1, then NOT A would result in a false. The NOT operator asks the question, "Is the value not true?" If the value is true (equal to a 1), then the answer to the question is, "No, the value is true." However, if the value is equal to a 0, the answer to the question is, "Yes, the value is not true."

Documentation and Preventive Action

The complete documentation of the entire configuration and programming of a home system controller is required. The procedures used to back up and restore the controller after modifications are made or in case of a system failure need also to be documented. These are the final pieces of any programming and setup job.

Documentation

No matter how well executed a manufacturer's documentation is, this documentation is general in nature and cannot possibly cover each specific installation. Every home control system must be treated as if it is a completely unique and custom installation, and the documentation you make should record everything about the system. Documentation should exist in two places: your office and on-site at the home with the installed control system.

The documentation you provide to the homeowner should address any concerns the customer may have after the system is installed and operating. This doesn't mean you can't include documentation supplied by the manufacturer, but the final documentation of the system should include all of the information the homeowner needs.

A full copy of the documentation should be stored on-site for reference by a technician applying upgrades or making modifications to the system. Another full copy of the documentation should be stored in your company's files for future reference. Storing copies of the documentation at both the home and your office ensures that it is available when it's needed, in either location.

The documentation for the programming, configuration, and setup of the system controller should include at least the following:

- A narrative description of the system including details on the devices controlled and any special features supported. In effect, this is a summary of the information gained from the customer during the pre-configuration interview.

- A diagram of the hardware components of the home automation system, including all controlled or monitored devices, including their connections.

- A list of the locations of each of the software modules used to create and maintain the system's programming. By location, I mean the PCs or the controller(s) where any copies of the configuration files are located. If the software is located only on the original programmer's PC, a note should be included to this effect. However, if this is the case, a backup should absolutely be created and its location noted as well. If the configuration software is embedded as firmware in the controller itself, this should be indicated, along with the commands used to access and start the configuration routines. Any passwords required should also be documented.

- An overview logic diagram of the control system and its relationships to controls or events defined for each major subsystem.

- A logic diagram of all timer and conditional events that have been configured or scripted.

- A maintenance and version log that tracks the date and technician for all installation, troubleshooting, upgrade, additions, and modifications made to the system beginning with its initial installation.

- A hard copy of the system configuration, setup, and programming should be created, if at all possible. In many cases, these files can be saved to a text file and printed. A copy of the hard copy should be stored at the office in the customer file and another kept on-site for a maintenance and debug reference.

- A hard media (floppy disk or CD) backup that contains copies of all programming and configuration files specific to the system.

Preventive Action

Throughout the programming process, the system controller's programming should be copied electronically to create a backup of the programming created to a certain milestone or development point. You can't create too many backups, and the relatively small amount of time it takes to create a backup is an investment in your ability to recover the data or programming in the event of a catastrophe that strikes during the programming process.

Backups

Any number of things can happen to wipe out the programming: power failure, somebody tripping over the power cord, the press of the wrong button, or even bad controller hardware or software.

The control systems that run on a PC typically include backup, restore, and reset functions that are used to copy the system configuration to a removable medium (such as tape, disk, or CD), restore the configuration should the PC where the controller is running fail, and remove any configuration changes made to the standard or default configuration, respectively.

The backup function should be used after each major event or device is programmed, at the end of each day of programming activities, and finally when all programming is completed. The final backup of a system should be created even before the system is tested. If any changes are made during testing, additional backups should be created. Creating these electronic backups ensures that should the system fail, the programming is lost, or you simply wish to start over, the fallback point is not too far in the past.

If the homeowner will also have the ability to make changes to the system, the documentation should include instructions on how to create and restore backups. Of course, the best scenario is that you or your company is contracted to make all future programming changes, which ensures that all changes have been tested and the system backup has been created.

Upgrades

Periodically, manufacturers release upgraded or improved versions of their software and hardware products. There are two schools of thought on upgrades: the first believes that "if it ain't broke, don't fix it," and the second believes that all upgrades should be installed regardless of need or the customer's configuration. The best approach to upgrades falls somewhere in the middle of these two philosophies. You should analyze the upgrade's documentation carefully to determine if a new feature or function will improve a customer's system or provide better performance with regard to the homeowner's expectations of the system. If the answer is yes, the upgrade will improve the customer's system, the upgrade should be applied. However, if the upgrade has no effect on the current configuration or performance of a customer's system, it is probably better to not install this particular upgrade at this time. Don't worry about losing track of which customer has which version; if the maintenance log part of the documentation is steadfastly maintained, there should be no mysteries.

Chapter Review

Programming a home automation control system is an exercise in organization. Before beginning the programming on a controller, draw a sketch of the logical flow of the control activities to be set up. The sketch proves a road map to completing the programming. Planning out the process in this way helps to prevent overlooking any of the required actions planned for the system.

Most higher-end home automaton control systems have built-in graphical user interfaces (GUIs) that are typically menu-driven or displayed as a function or device hierarchy. User interfaces on home system control configuration and programming modules typically include a menu, dialog box, or tree format for selecting specific devices for configuration, timing, and functions.

The programming interfaces on controller systems are either embedded as firmware or installed on a PC linked to the controller. Many systems offer applets or wizards to assist with programming a macro. Some include templates that are used to re-create new or modify standard devices, groups, and scripts.

The documentation of the completed programming and the procedures used to back up and restore the controller a system failure are key pieces of a programming and setup job.

A manufacturer's documentation is general and cannot cover each specific installation. It can be included, but the final documentation for a system should include the information needed by the homeowner and the next technician to work on the system.

Any number of things can happen to wipe out the programming: power failure, somebody tripping over the power cord, the press of the wrong button, or even bad controller hardware or software. The backup function should be used after each major event or device is programmed. The final backup of a system should be created before the system is tested. Creating backups ensures that the fallback point to which the system can be restored is not too far in the past.

The best approach to home controller hardware and software upgrades is to analyze the release information to determine if new features or functions may improve a customer's system. If the answer is yes, the upgrade should be applied. If it's no, don't install the upgrade.

Questions

1. What should be completed prior to programming a home system controller?

    A. Backup of system software

    B. User wish list

    C. Sketch or outline of system controller functions to be created

    D. Programming language training

2. Which of the following aids can be found in home system controller programming software?

    A. GUI

    B. Menu-driven options

    C. Device tree

    D. Wizard

    E. All of the above

3. A module that groups together several actions that are activated through a single command or button is called a(n)

A. Event

B. Macro

C. Program

D. Wizard

4. What is the last step in the actions used to create a macro?

A. Create if-then-else logical relationships

B. Create new classes or groups

C. Create scripts

D. Create timer events

E. Export macro

F. Save and name macro

G. None of the above

5. A sequence of logical programming statements that specify a certain action is a(n)

A. Device event

B. Macro

C. Script

D. Timer event

6. What type of home system controller action is executed based on the system clock?

A. Device event

B. Macro

C. Script

D. Timer event

7. What should be created at the end of the programming to communicate a system's history to programmers in the future?

A. Macro listings

B. Maintenance activity log

C. User instructions

D. Printout of all system programming

8. The manufacturer's documentation is generally sufficient for documenting a home system controller and its configuration.

    A. True

    B. False

    C. It depends on the system

9. Which of the following is typically not included in the system documentation?

    A. Description of the system

    B. Diagram of hardware components

    C. Price list of system components and software modules

    D. Logic diagram of the control system and the relationships to controls

10. During the programming process, when should backups be created?

    A. Only after the system is complete, fully tested, and debugged

    B. After completing each major milestone

    C. At the end of each work session

    D. At the end of the programming project

Answers

1. **C.** You don't really need to sketch out the system functions, but some form of a sequenced outline should be created. Any of the other choices could be done before you begin programming, but some form of an outline or sketch should absolutely be created.

2. **E.** Not that any system will necessarily have all of these features, but chances are good that a quality system has most of them.

3. **B.** Macros are comprised of events, which are created during programming, which is accomplished through a wizard in many cases.

4. **F.** The other steps listed are used to create and control the macro's functions.

5. **C.** Not to be confused with a macro, which may involve more than just logic statements.

6. **D.** Timer or scheduled events are executed based on a clock time.

7. **B.** If the next programmer to work on a customer's system is a year or more after the initial programming is completed, chances are nobody will remember what the last action completed was or what version of the software is installed.

8. **B.** And it really doesn't depend on the system.

9. **C.** This information belongs on an invoice or an accounting statement, but not in the documentation.

10. **B, C,** and **D.** In other words, just about anytime you need the peace of mind.

Integrating the Connected Home

In this chapter, you will learn about:
- The integration of a home control system to the home data network
- The interfacing the networks
- The home technology in the future

In this chapter, how the computer network (and its PCs) are integrated into the home automation system and then connected to the outside world is the focus. This discussion looks at the methods, connections, and cabling used to connect a data network into the home automation system controller and the related benefits and hazards.

 CROSS-REFERENCE See Chapters 10, 11, and 39 for more information and discussion on the role of a home computer network in an automated home environment.

There are several PC-based home automation controllers that can be used to integrate home control system technology, especially for powerline control (PLC) and Home Phoneline Networking Alliance (HomePNA) systems. However, using a PC as a stand-alone controller integrated into these systems is not what is meant by integrating a home network into the home automation system.

This chapter covers interconnecting the home data network, its computers, and peripheral devices and the whole-house control system to the outside world via the Internet.

Interfaced Is Not Always Integrated

Just because a device provides an interface to another device or a cable connecting to another device, doesn't mean the devices are integrated. When two devices are connected using common cable or wire, the devices are interfaced. However, to be integrated, the devices must have onboard functions that support a specific communication between the devices using a common coding system or protocol. In a typical home automation system, the home system controller provides integration support, but it can be distributed to local controllers and, in some cases, to specific devices themselves.

A home PC and some specialized software can be used together to control and command a distributed home automation system. On these systems, software running on a PC allows the user to set up zones and areas for controlling audio, video, lighting, and other home systems. The PC communicates to these types of systems typically through a serial, Universal Serial Bus (USB), or IEEE 1394 interface to a signal converter device that provides transceiver services to the distributed controls and modules of the system. For example, a PC running software to control an X-10 lighting control system transmits its signals through either a serial or USB port to an X-10 interface module that transmits and receives signals to and from the electrical wiring of the home.

 CROSS-REFERENCE   See Chapter 39 for more information on home system control software.

The home automation control software typically runs on a single PC, which may or may not be connected into the home data network. Even if the PC is connected to the home network, in a peer-to-peer network arrangement that is common to home networks, the control software is not likely to be accessible from other network computers.

Interconnecting the Networks

The first step involved with connecting the data network to the home automation network is of course connecting the cabling or media of each system. After the physical connection is made, the signal format of the two systems must be converted in either direction to allow the systems to communicate. Typically, the home data network is installed on structured Cat 5 or Cat 5e unshielded twisted-pair (UTP) cabling, on one of the wireless media standards (IEEE 802.11a, 802.11b, or 802.11g), and operates on Ethernet protocol. To connect the home automation controller to the home network, the controller must have a compatible jack or transceiver to operate on an Ethernet network.

Not all home automation controllers are designed for, or equipped with, a connection to an Ethernet data network. Some have optional third-party modules that can be installed to provide an Ethernet connection directly to the data network distribution panel. In any case, the arrangement used to connect a home data network to a home automation controller should look something like the configuration shown in Figure 41-1.

Connecting the Links

However, to achieve true integration of a home controller into the home network, the two systems must speak the same language. Just like two people who don't speak each other's language will have trouble communicating, integrating an Ethernet data network to a proprietary home automation controller can prove troublesome.

Ethernet to Serial Bridges

In some cases, this may mean that a signal converter or bridge must be used between the two systems, such as an Ethernet to serial bridge, an Ethernet to RS-485 converter, or an

Figure 41-1

Connecting
the home data
network to the
home automation
controller

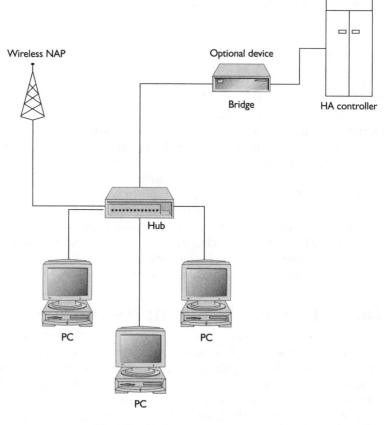

Home Data Network

Ethernet to PLC module. The bridging device shown in Figure 41-1 is only necessary in cases where the Ethernet/TCP/IP data network link must be converted to an Electronic Industries Alliance/Telecommunications Industry Association (EIA/TIA) 232, 422, or 485 serial format for use by the home automation controller. In cases where the home system controller has an RJ-45 jack and is able to connect directly to the Ethernet/TCP/IP link, an external bridge is not needed.

Newer and developmental home automation systems include microprocessors that are able to control home systems over Ethernet and Internet networks. These systems overcome the limitations that have prevented the easy interface for data networks and home automation systems in the past.

NOTE   EIA/TIA (RS) 485 is a serial communications standard that like Ethernet requires dedicated media, but unlike Ethernet which uses eight wires, requires only two wires (one wire pair). This standard, with a bandwidth of about 10 megabits per second (Mbps), is also topology free and so can be easily installed in homeruns.

Controller-Attached Network (CAN)

Another interface technology that can be used to integrate a computer network and home automation controllers is the controller-attached network (CAN) protocols. CAN is a serial bus system designed to interconnect smart devices into smart systems and networks.

Interfacing the Networks

Why integrate a data network to the home automation system? Good question. Even though the homeowners may not wish to control or monitor their home automation systems from any networked PC in the home, the capability exists. Having a link to the home automation controller from any networked PC in a home provides the possibility for monitoring, programming, troubleshooting, and controlling the home automation controller and the distributed devices it controls.

In addition, if the Home Automation Telephone Interface (HATi) protocols are in use, a link to the home automation controller can also allow the telephone system to be controlled from a PC, including placing and receiving telephone calls to any line in the home.

The bottom line is that someday everything will be an Ethernet/TCP/IP enabled device. That is where the future is going, just read on.

The Future of the Connected Home

This book has covered all the parts that lay the foundation for a connected home: structured wiring, home networking and of each of the subsystems that can be installed in the home (audio; video; lighting; telecommunications; Heating, Ventilating, Air Conditioning or HVAC; water management; security; and access control and other automated devices). It has discussed controls for these systems and integrating the systems under a whole-house controller. The benefits behind a connected home exist: the system offers efficiency, convenience, safety, financial savings, and ease of use.

The real advantage of a networked and integrated controlled home is yet to come. When the home is connected to the Internet, the options are endless. This trend has already started with the introduction and rapid adoption of IP-addressable devices.

IP-Addressable Devices

With the Ethernet protocol becoming prevalent in the home, new IP-addressable devices are coming on the market. These include digital cameras, digital media servers for both audio and video content, and digital art and picture frames, to name just a few.

 CROSS-REFERENCE   Chapter 42 discusses new and emerging IP-addressable devices.

IP-addressable devices have built-in Ethernet network adapter capabilities and can be connected to a TCP/IP network as a fully addressable device. However, a device that is IP-addressable typically cannot be configured across the network and may or may not be Web-enabled.

Web-Enabled Products

A Web-enabled product is first and foremost an IP-addressable product that is able to communicate directly over an Internet connection. These devices include extra hardware and software that gives it the capability to transmit and receive Hypertext Transfer Protocol (HTTP) messages. HTTP is the primary data transfer protocol of the World Wide Web (WWW) or, as it is better known, the Web.

The primary benefit of a Web-enabled device is that it can be viewed, controlled, or configured over a Web connection. This capability gives not only the installer but also the homeowner the opportunity to connect over the Internet with a device to control its function, settings, and status.

Wireless Extension of Networks

More and more home networks are becoming wireless. New wireless solutions work over existing wiring in the home such as coaxial cable, telephone, and electrical wiring. As the wireless Ethernet standards, 802.11a, 802.11b, and 802.11g, gain acceptance in the home market, more devices are emerging with wireless communication capabilities. In the future, other mediums may be delivering services to the home, such as the electrical powerline coming into a home also carrying broadband data communications services.

Sample Integrated Home Network

Home networks are becoming more prevalent and more and more devices are becoming IP-addressable. The Internet is a necessity in life at home and inter-connectivity of systems and devices in the home is occurring. Figure 41-2 shows a home system that incorporates nearly all of the subsystems discussed in this book.

Chapter Review

Two devices that are connected by a cable or wire are interfaced. To be integrated, the devices must share a specific communication method and a common coding system or protocol. Integration may require a signal converter or bridge between the two systems. A bridging device is used in cases where the signal format between the devices is different and the signals must be converted for each device to communicate with the other. An interface technology that can be used to integrate a home computer network with a home automation controller is a CAN.

A link to a home automation controller from a networked PC provides an additional access resource for monitoring, programming, troubleshooting, and controlling the home automation controller and the distributed devices it controls.

The full advantage of a networked and integrated controlled home may still be in the future. Connecting the home to the Internet provides virtually endless options. As IP addressable products, Web-enabled products, and wireless networking products continue to emerge, they add additional functionality and capabilities to home networks and home automation systems.

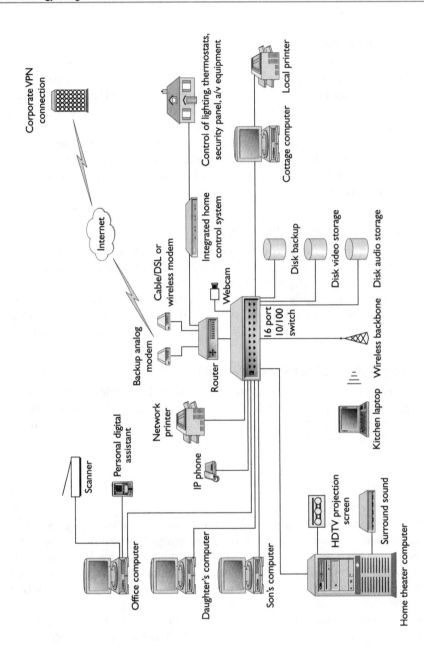

Figure 41-2 A diagram of a comprehensive integrated home network

Image courtesy of CyberManor.

Questions

1. Two devices that are connected by a cable and are able to communicate are

   A. Interfaced

   B. Interlinked

   C. Integrated

   D. Interoperable

2. Two devices that share a common communications coding scheme or protocol so that one device is able to control the functions of the other are

   A. Interfaced

   B. Interlinked

   C. Integrated

   D. Interoperable

3. What type of device is required to interface an Ethernet device to an EIA/TIA 232 device?

   A. Bridge

   B. PLC module

   C. Network adapter

   D. TCP/IP converter

4. What home system protocol can be used to integrate a computer network with home automation controllers?

   A. CAN

   B. HAN

   C. LAN

   D. WAN

5. What telecommunication protocol allows a PC to control the internal telephone system?

   A. HATi

   B. HAVi

   C. NID

   D. PSTN

6. Which of the following is not an advantage of integrating a home data network into the home automation system?

   A. Emergency backup

   B. Monitoring

C. Programming

D. Troubleshooting

7. Home automation devices that have the built-in capability to communicate on a TCP/IP network are called

A. Ethernet-ready

B. IP-addressable

C. IP-compatible

D. TCP-addressable

8. A home automation device that can be viewed, controlled, or configured through an Internet connection is called

A. Internet-ready

B. IP-addressable

C. Network-capable

D. Web-enabled

Answers

1. **A.** All that is required for two devices to be interfaced is the capability to communicate, which is only slightly different than being interlinked.

2. **C.** Integrated devices have the capability to communicate control data and commands that each device is able to interpret and understand. Interoperable devices also have this same capability using a common protocol.

3. **A.** An Ethernet to serial bridge converts the communication signal into the formats required by each of the communication protocols in use.

4. **A.** A controller area network interconnects home system control devices, as opposed to a home area network (HAN), which is a form of a local area network (LAN). A WAN is a wide area network and extends outside the home.

5. **A.** The Home Automation Telephone interface (HATi) allows a home's phone system control to be passed to a PC.

6. **A.** A PC may be configured to automatically provide a backup to a home system controller. However, this is not typically done and is therefore not a likely advantage of the integration.

7. **B.** IP-addressable devices can be connected into a TCP/IP network.

8. **D.** Web-enabled means that a device can be accessed through an Internet connection from inside or outside a home.

CHAPTER 42

Other Home Technology Integration Devices

In this chapter, you will learn about:
- Automated audio visual (AV) cabinetry
- Automated screens and projector lifts
- Automated fans
- Automated skylights and windows
- Automated window treatments
- Other new home technology products

In addition to the various communications, audio, video, lighting, Heating, Ventilating, Air Conditioning (HVAC), and security devices discussed in this book, there are several other home technology devices that can also be integrated into a home system. While some or all of these devices may seem frivolous at first, remember that so did television, computers, and even electric can openers at one time. The devices discussed in this chapter are included to demonstrate the ever-expanding world of home automation.

This chapter is a bit different from other chapters in this book in that it doesn't contain a summary. In many ways, the products, services, and devices described in this chapter provide insight to technologies of the future. While all of the products included in the chapter exist today, they also indicate what is yet to come in the area of home systems and home automation.

Automated Audio/Video Cabinetry

As the depth of television monitors continues to become shallower and shallower, it is now possible to conceal the TV and other AV devices inside furniture quality cabinets. The ability to retract AV equipment into a cabinet, or even the wall or ceiling, can add to a room's décor because this equipment isn't visible when it isn't in use. Specialized automated cabinetry and systems, including speakers, source devices, and more, are also available for a wide-range of AV equipment.

Figure 42-1 shows a closed and an open view of an automated plasma TV cabinet and Figure 42-2 shows a projection screen that can be raised and lowered into a cabinet.

Photos courtesy of Cabinet Tronix.

Figure 42-1 An automated TV cabinet showing the TV unit retracted (left) and elevated (right)

Both of these products can be opened or closed remotely using a relay control connection on a home automation controller, power line control (PLC) signals, or an infrared (IR) remote control.

Photo courtesy of Vutec Corp.

Figure 42-2 A lift raises and lowers a projection screen from a cabinet

Automated Screens and Projector Lifts

A variety of motorized products are available that can be added to a home theater or AV area to enhance its convenience and performance. Motorized screens, lifts, and windows (see "Automated Windows" later in the chapter) can be used to hide away screens and projectors when they're not in use and to darken or lighten a room as needed.

Motorized Screens

Although they have been more common in boardrooms and classrooms in the past, motorized screens can add to the aesthetics of a home theater or video viewing area by hiding away the screen when it is not in use. Various models of motorized screens are available that can be mounted on a wall or the ceiling, or be recessed into the ceiling.

Wall mounted or ceiling mounted motorized screens, like the one shown in Figure 42-3, require only on/off control, either through a hardwire connection to a toggle switch, a PLC control, or an IR or radio frequency (RF) remote control module. The screen retracts into a housing that is either directly mounted to the wall or ceiling or is suspended by chains.

If the homeowner wishes to completely hide the screen and its housing when it is not in use, a recessed ceiling-mounted screen (see Figure 42-4) is what is needed. This type of screen is mounted above the ceiling with a large slit hole provided for the screen to descend from and retract into. Some models are completely self-contained and others require some trim work around the screen slit.

Self-contained units typically include an enclosure cover that opens when the screen is lowered and closes when the screen has been completely retracted. This helps to blend the screen and its housing into the room and may even enhance its aesthetics.

Most manufacturers of motorized recessed screens engineer their product so that the housing and the screen fabric can be installed separately. This ensures that the screen fabric is not damaged during rough-in installation.

Figure 42-3

A motorized wall-mount projection screen is retracted into its housing when it's not in use.

Photo courtesy of BEAMAX.

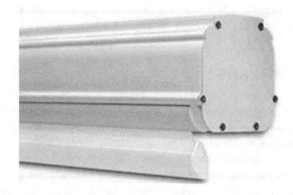

Figure 42-4 A motorized recessed ceiling mounted projection screen is hidden away when it's not in use.

Projector, TV, and Equipment Lifts

The projection screen is not the only piece of AV equipment that can be hidden from view when it's not in use. Motorized lifts are available for virtually any object that the homeowner wishes to hide away when the item is not in use.

A variety of motorized lifts are available: ceiling drop-downs, console or kiosk lifts, and lifts that don't actually lift, but slide side-to-side out of a wall. Figure 42-5 shows two of the more popular lift styles. As I discussed earlier in the chapter, motorized lifts can also be used for other devices as well.

Automated Fans

Although they've been common in commercial buildings for some time, automated fan systems are becoming available for residential use as well. These systems can be found in commercial greenhouses, grain elevators, and other large structures where they are used to provide automatic aeration, airflow, or exhaust application.

In residential applications, any number of sensors can be used to activate automated fans, but the most common are temperature sensors and carbon monoxide (CO) or smoke detectors. Typically placed in attics or below the roof spaces of a home, an automated

Figure 42-5
Two different
motorized lifts:
a projector ceiling
mount lift (top)
and a kiosk
projector lift
(bottom)

*Photo courtesy
of Vutec Corp.*

fan can be activated to supply airflow in or out when the temperature reaches a certain air temperature, either in the same area or outside the home. When it's used with a CO or Radon detector, an automated fan can be used to exhaust gas fumes whenever they are detected.

An automated fan can also be used in parts of a home that may not be included on the home's Heating, Ventilating, Air Conditioning (HVAC) system, such as a garage or storage space.

Automated Skylights and Windows

Many newer homes now include one or more skylights to supply natural sunlight into the home. However, there are occasions when the sun is directly over a skylight and too much light (or heat) can enter the home.

Skylights

Automated skylights can be opened to allow airflow into or out of a home or closed automatically using a handheld remote control or a home automation control system. Typically, most opening skylights open with a long handle, but many new models are available that include a motor that can be controlled using an IR remote control or a home control system.

Another way to control the light and heat passing through a skylight is to apply an automatic window treatment to the inside of the fixture. Several types of motorized shading systems are available, with pleated or cellular shades or blinds being the most common. An automated shading system (see Figure 42-6) controls the amount of sunlight entering through a skylight.

Photo courtesy of the Velux Group.

Figure 42-6   A skylight shading system is used to control the amount of light coming into a home.

A motorized track system is installed on the sides of the skylight or window that includes either an alternating current (AC) or a direct current (DC) motor in the head rail to open or close the shade. The shading system can also be independently linked to a light sensor, temperature sensor, or a home control system to which a sensor is connected. The sensor or the control system can then be used to limit the amount of light (and corresponding heat) that enters through the skylight. The operation of the shading system can be controlled using PLC signals, a handheld IR remote control, or a relay control on a home automation controller.

Automated Windows and Ventilation Systems

An automated window system or an automatic opening ventilation system can be used for room ventilation in everyday use or in the case of an emergency.

Automated Windows

Automated or motorized window systems allow the homeowner to open or close framed windows through the use of a wall switch, an IR or RF remote control, or a relay controlled by a home system controller. The primary purpose of motorized window systems is to provide convenience and ease for opening and closing windows.

Automatic Opening Ventilation Systems

Automatic opening ventilation (AOV) systems can include motorized window systems and automated fans that are used to open, close, and, if necessary, secure windows and provide emergency situation exhaust ventilation for a home based on the situation and the programming configured on the system controller. Most AOV systems require a dedicated control cabinet that can be connected to a home system controller or a security system controller through a relay. AOV systems are designed to interface with glass break panels, smoke detectors, wind and rain sensors, wall switches, and fire sensors and alarm systems, either directly or through a control system.

Odds and Ends

In the category of devices that are either cutting edge or just plain frivolous are a few home innovations that could be integrated into a home, but typically only at the homeowners' request. For the sake of completely representing the "state-of-the-art," I've included such devices in the following sections.

Digital Art and Picture Frames

With the development of flat plasma and liquid crystal display (LCD) high-definition television and video display devices, comes the digital picture frames, also called digital art displays. Basically, these devices are thin, flat screen displays that can be mounted on a wall (see Figure 42-7) much like a painting or photograph (see Figure 42-8). However, unlike a static painting or photo, digital picture frames are electrically powered and connected to a home network or directly to the Internet.

Photo courtesy of Vutec Corp.

Figure 42-7   A digital art frame halfway through a image change

The image displayed on the screen can be virtually any digital graphic image the homeowner wishes, such as fine art, family photos, television, digital home movies, and so on. The image is transmitted to the digital picture frame from a computer on the home

Photo courtesy of Pacific Digital Corp.

Figure 42-8   The front (left) and back (right) views of a digital picture frame. It looks like a standard picture frame but can connect to a network.

network or by an Internet service. Some digital picture frames also offer simple IR remote control and some can be integrated with motion detectors, Wiegand card or badge readers, and voice-control systems to allow the occupants of a room to choose the image displayed, or based on the information on the Wiegand card, customized to the occupant automatically.

Digital Media Servers

A variety of products are available that allow downloaded audio and video content to be shared across a home network or distributed through the audio system. Stand-alone radios and monitors that play streaming AV from the Internet can be integrated into a home network to play music, radio broadcasts, live video broadcasts, and video on demand files downloaded from providers on the Internet.

There are literally thousands of Internet radio stations from around the world available and these devices expand the radio reception boundaries of a home to include stations from around the globe. Several video broadcast sites are available and more are coming online virtually everyday. Digital media and audio server devices designed specifically for the purpose of downloading, storing, and distributing downloaded media provide the best solution and management in a home network.

Internet radios and digital media or audio servers work on the same principle as audio and video broadcasts and streaming media. Digital media services relieve network computers of the processing required to reproduce the transmitted audio or video signals. This provides for better network performance and audio, video, or multimedia reproduction quality.

An advantage of using a centralized digital media server, like the one shown in Figure 42-9, is that the downloaded media can be shared throughout the home and not just where the computer is located. Figure 42-10 shows the connection jacks on the back of a digital media server.

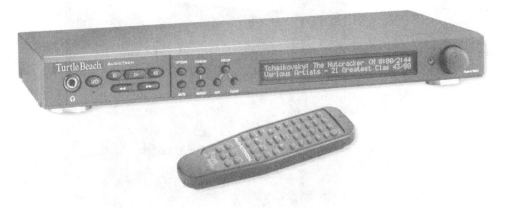

Photo courtesy of Voyetra Turtle Beach, Inc.

Figure 42-9 A digital audio server can be used to download audio content from the Internet for distributed playback over the home network.

Figure 42-10
A digital audio server provides connection jacks for almost any connection requirement.

Photo courtesy of Voyetra Turtle Beach, Inc.

Satellite Radio

Digital broadcast satellite (DBS) television has been around for some time now, but in the past few years, a new digital satellite media has emerged: digital audio radio service (DARS). DARS systems, such as XM Satellite Radio and Sirius Satellite Radio, use geostationary satellites (satellites that remain over a fixed portion of the Earth) to broadcast signals to earth station antennas using microwave S-band frequencies.

Both XM and Sirius will be broadcasting more than 100 commercial-free radio stations coast-to-coast in the United States in the near future. This means that a DARS subscriber traveling in a car can listen to the same radio station coast-to-coast, as well as at home. In addition to car radio adapters that convert a standard car radio into a DARS receiver, converters exist for home use. In fact, some models allow the receiver to move from the car to home and back.

Figure 42-11
A DARS (satellite radio) receiver with a home use adapter

Photo courtesy of Delphi Technologies, Inc.

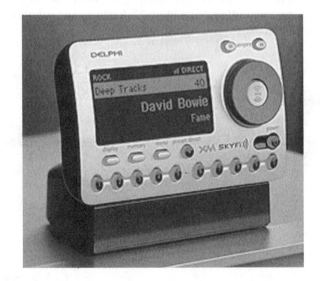

Emerging Devices

New Internet and network-ready products are continually being announced. Recent product announcements, typically at consumer electronics trade shows or at stockholder meetings, include:

- Wireless radio frequency flat-panel television monitors that receive their signals from an RF transmitter centrally located in a home that supports up to three TV monitors, each of which is displaying a different channel.

- Internet-ready toasters that can be controlled across a network or a home automation controller. For the person who wants his toast ready at an exact time, the toaster can be controlled to lower the bread, toast it, keep it warm, and pop it up at just the right moment. Several other Internet-ready home appliances, such as coffee pots, ovens, and the like, are also being readied for the market.

- Microwaves that can be accessed over the Internet to start a dish or meal cooking (see Figure 42-12).

- Refrigerators with television and Internet displays built into their doors that can be controlled across a network or the Internet to display messages and even change their settings (see Figure 42-12).

- Robotic vacuum cleaners that can be accessed via the Internet (and an RF wireless connection) to start or stop the appliance and change its settings (see Figure 42-12).

- In Japan, millions of "smart" toilets are being sold. What makes this toilet "smart" is its capability to analyze solids and fluids for possible health problems of users and to transmit the results across the Internet to the family's medical care provider for analysis.

Photos courtesy of LG Electronics.

Figure 42-12   A microwave oven, refrigerator, and robotic vacuum cleaner—all Internet accessible

PART X

Appendices

Home Technology Project Management

Both the HTI+ and CEDIA exams include questions that deal with the organization and management of a home systems project. The project management information in this appendix reflects a combination of the procedures prescribed in the exam objectives of both the Home Technology Integrator (HTI+) and the CEDIA Installer I certification exams.

Whether a project is technical or nontechnical, the project manager must plan, organize, direct, control, and document several activities. In virtually every aspect of a project, the project manager must decide how best to apply limited resources and work within the constraints of budget and time. The project manager is directly responsible for ensuring that all required activities are performed and that the outcomes of the project meet the expectations of the customer.

Often the project manager of a home systems project plays a dual role as both the technician and a manager. However, these roles aren't necessarily mutually exclusive. As a technician *and* a project manager, you must have the ability to work with the customer and ensure the project activities are performed timely and that the technology is appropriately, effectively, and efficiently installed, tested, documented, and demonstrated. To fulfill these duties, the project manager/technician must also be able to estimate, plan, communicate, lead, and motivate, and be adept at problem solving.

As you proceed through a project, there is no activity more important than creating documentation as you go. Detailed documentation provides not only a reference point for earlier activities and decisions, but a historical record of the events, choices, and activities of the project. The documentation produced and retained should include all of the forms, diagrams, checklists, plans, and other project-related documents.

These project management skills are necessary in most projects:

- Project planning
- Project scheduling
- Supervising the project team
- Documenting the project
- Communicating with the customer, contractors, and team members

Project Planning

The activities included in the planning phase of a home technology integration project are:

- Identifying the customer's current and future needs
- Defining the project's scope of work
- Preparing a work plan that addresses equipment, budget, and time constraints
- Conducting a project survey that determines:
  - Any existing systems in the home
  - Location of any existing equipment or devices
  - The type of construction activity
  - The coordination required with other contractors
- Developing preliminary system designs and a proposed work plan
- Reviewing project planning and preliminary designs with the customer
- Finalizing the required equipment and devices list
- Purchasing all necessary materials and devices
- Preparing wire charts, schematics, and equipment layout diagrams

Project Management

Once the project is underway, there are certain tasks the project manager must perform to ensure that the project plan is followed and that any deviations from the original plan are documented, presented to the customer in advance, and approved by the customer.

The tasks of the project manager during the work phases of a project include:

- Preparing and presenting progress status reports to the customer
- Preparing and verifying all change order requests in writing
- Ensuring all technicians observe applicable job safety rules and guidelines
- Direct, or perform and document, pre-wire and rough-in activities
- Direct, or perform and document, trim-out and testing activities
- Direct, or perform and document, wiring testing
- Direct, or perform and document, finish activities
- Direct, or perform and document, device testing
- Direct, or perform and document, subsystem and system configuration or programming activities
- Direct, or perform and document, system testing

- Direct, or perform and document, backup of system configuration or programming
- Develop initial system maintenance log
- Train customers on equipment and system operations
- Prepare and offer ongoing preventive maintenance support contract to customer
- Schedule post-installation follow-up with customer

Post-Project Management

After a project completes, the documentation created or gathered during the project should be collected and filed both at the project site, meaning the home, and at your office in a project file. Each time any additional work is performed, for whatever reason—routine maintenance, repairs, upgrades, and so on—both sets of documentation should be updated.

You should maintain some contact with the customer after the project completes for a variety of reasons:

- To ensure the system is working properly and the customer is satisfied with the system
- To ensure even minor unreported problems are solved quickly
- To advise the customer of available upgrades, recalls, and error corrections provided by the manufacturers
- To advise the customer of newly available products or services
- To advise the customer of impending warranty expirations

The preceding list is far from complete, but it presents some of the more common reasons for contacting the customer after the system has been completed. Another important reason, especially with a warranty due to expire, is to advise the customer of maintenance or repair programs your company may offer.

It is also important for the customer to understand the issues involved with warranty or maintenance program transfers, should the home be sold while either of these programs is still in force.

Home Technology Integration Glossary

The following are the terminology, phrases, and most of the major standards publishers you will most probably encounter or should know for working as a home technology integrator or a installer.

 Cross-reference For a more complete list of the organizations you should be acquainted with as a home technology professional, see Appendix D.

0–9

10Base2 (Data Networking) The IEEE 802.3 standard for 10Mbps thin coaxial cable Ethernet networks that have a maximum segment length of 185 meters. Also known as Thinnet or Cheapnet.

10Base5 (Data Networking) The IEEE 802.3 standard for 10Mbps thick coaxial cable Ethernet networks that have a maximum segment length of 500 meters. Also known as Thicknet and Yellow Wire.

10BaseT (Data Networking) The IEEE 802.3 standard for 10 Mbps Ethernet baseband networking over unshielded twisted pair cable.

100BaseT (Data Networking) The IEEE 802.3 standard for Fast Ethernet or 100 Mbps Ethernet baseband networking over unshielded twisted pair cable.

100BaseFX (Data Networking) The IEEE 802.3 standard for fiber optic Ethernet networks with 100 Mbps bandwidth.

100BaseT4 (Data Networking) See 100BaseTX.

100BaseTX (Data Networking) The IEEE 802.3 standard for UTP Ethernet networks with 100 Mbps of bandwidth. Also known as 100BaseT4.

1000BaseTX (Data Networking)   The IEEE 802.3 standard for UTP Ethernet networks with 1000 Mbps of bandwidth. Also called Gigabit Ethernet.

110 block (Data Networking/Structured Wiring)   An IDC system used to terminate telephone and data cables. Also referred to as a 110 connector or 110 punchdown.

110 punchdown tool (Data Networking/Structured Wiring)   A special tool that is used to press wires into the IDC terminals on a 110 block.

568A (Data Networking/Structured Wiring)   The EIA/TIA standard defining RJ-45 jack pin-to-wire attachment for telecommunications wiring in commercial buildings.

568B (Data Networking/Structured Wiring)   The EIA/TIA standard defining RJ-45 jack pin-to-wire attachment for data communications wiring in commercial buildings.

570 (Data Networking/Structured Wiring)   The EIA/TIA standard defining standard telecommunications wiring in residential buildings.

802.3 (Data Networking)   The IEEE reference standard that defines media access, cabling standards, and connectivity for Ethernet networks.

802.11a (Data Networking)   An IEEE standard for wireless networking.

802.11b (Data Networking)   An IEEE standard for wireless networking.

802.11g (Data Networking)   An IEEE standard for wireless networking.

A

A-line lamp (Lighting)   A standard incandescent lamp used in indoor residential lighting.

AC (alternating current) (Electricity)   An electric current in which the flow of the current is alternatively reversed. The frequency of AC electricity in the U.S. is 60 hertz (Hz), and in many parts of the world, it is 50 Hz.

Accent lighting (Lighting)   Lighting used to highlight a particular object or room feature.

Accumulator air coil (HVAC)   A coil on some heat pump types that can be used as either an evaporator or condenser.

ADSL (Asymmetric Digital Subscriber Line) (Data Networking)
A broadband DSL-telephone line technology that transmits voice, video, and data over existing copper telephone wires at very high speeds. ADSL provides faster data transfer speeds for download and slower data transfer rates for upload.

Air change (HVAC)   The amount of air needed to completely replace the air in a room, zone, or building.

Air diffuser (HVAC)   An outlet through which airflow is directed into a desired direction.

Air handler (HVAC)   The fan, blower, filter, and housing of an HVAC system.

Air infiltration (HVAC)   Air that leaks into a room or building through cracks, windows, doors, and other openings.

Air terminal (HVAC)   An air distribution outlet or diffuser.

Airflow (HVAC)   The distribution or movement of air.

AM (Amplitude Modulation) (Audio, Video, Data Networking)
The transmission method that merges a transmitted signal into a carrier signal by modulating the amplitude of the carrier.

Ambient lighting (Lighting)   The general lighting of an entire area or room made up of natural and artificial light.

Ampere (Electricity)   A standard unit measure of the rate of electron flow or electrical current in a conductor.

Amplifier (Audio, Video)   A device that increases the amplitude of a signal retaining the same waveform pattern of the original signal. Amplifiers are analog devices.

Amplitude (Audio, Video, Data Networking)   The wavelength of a transmitted signal that represents the strength or volume of the signal measured in decibels.

Analog/analogue (Audio)   The electrical representation of a signal that retains the properties of the original data.

ANSI (American National Standards Institute) (Standards)
A standards organization that administrates standards for the United States and represents the United States at the International Standards Organization (ISO).

Appletalk (Data Networking)   The network protocol suite used on proprietary Apple Computer networks.

Artifacts (Audio, Video)   Image or sound distortion that can occur when an audio or a video signal is compressed to a low bit rate. Also referred to as noise.

Armored cable (Electricity)   Electrical cable assembly in which two or more insulated conductors are protected by a flexible metal conduit.

ASCII (American Standard Code for Information Interchange) (Data Networking)   The 8-bit character encoding scheme that is the standard for computer data interchange.

ATSC (Advanced Television Systems Committee) (Video)
An international standards organization that establishes voluntary technical standards for advanced television systems.

Attenuation (Data Networking)   The decibel loss of signal that occurs when a signal is transmitted through a medium.

Attenuator (Audio, Video)   A passive transmission device used to reduce signal strength.

AWG (American Wire Gauge) (Standards)   A standard guideline used to measure wire diameter. Lower AWG values represent larger wire diameters.

B

Backbone (Data Networking)   The primary media of a data network that runs the length of the network and interconnects all network segments.

Backmount (Structured Wiring)   The mounting method used for attaching add-in modules inside a structured wiring distribution panel.

Balance point (HVAC)   The lowest outdoor temperature at which a heat pump is able to meet the heating demands of a home without using a supplementary heat source.

Balanced line (Electricity)   A cable with two conductors with identical properties that provide common symmetry to ground.

Ballast (Lighting)   An electrical device used in fluorescent or HID fixtures to supply sufficient voltage to start and operate a lamp. A ballast also limits the electrical current during lamp operation.

Balun (balanced to unbalanced) (Electricity)   A device that is used to convert an unbalanced electrical line into a balanced line.

Bandwidth (Data networking)   The amount of data that can be transmitted over a medium in a specific period. The standard bandwidth measurement is megabits per second (Mbps).

Bare wire (Lighting)   An electrical conductor wire that has no covering or insulation. Commonly ground wires in prewired lighting fixtures are bare wires.

Baseband (Data Networking, Video)   A transmission mode that transmits digital data using time division multiplexing (TDM). Baseband transmissions use the entire capacity of the transmission media.

Baseband video (Video)   Video signals that are unmodulated, such as NTSC, PAL, SECAM, and others, and carry no audio component.

Battery backup (Electricity)   A rechargeable battery that is maintained in stand-by mode to supply power when an interruption in the normal power supply occurs.

Bend radius (Structured Wiring)   The angle to which a cable can be bent without damaging the cable or affecting its electrical properties.

Bit (binary digit) (Data Networking)   The representation of a binary one or zero using positive and nonpositive electrical values, respectively.

Bit rate (Data Networking)   The transmission speed of a network media expressed in bits. Bit rate is equivalent to bandwidth.

Blocking (Structured Wiring)   A horizontally placed wooden or metal brace set between two wall studs.

Bluetooth (Data Networking)   A wireless RF communications technology used to link mobile devices into ad hoc networks.

BNC (Bayonet Neill Concellman) (Audio, Data Networking)
A standard coaxial cable connector that uses barrel and T connectors to join coaxial cables or connect to a networking or source device.

BPS (bits per second) (Data Networking)   A measurement of the number of bits transmitted over a medium in one second.

Branch circuit (Electricity)   A household electrical circuit that branches from the main electrical panel to an outlet box or a device.

Bridle ring (Structured Wiring)   A cable management device that is used to loosely hold cabling in a loop, or plastic, wire, or other flexible materials.

Breaker (Electricity)   A toggle switch device that is used to connect and disconnect the power to an electrical circuit by nonautomatic means and also to pen a circuit by automatic means when a predetermined level of current passes through it. Circuit breakers can be reset.

Broadband (Data Networking)   The high-speed transmission media that transmits data at speeds of 1.544 Mbps or faster. (Audio, Video)   The transmission mode for data, voice, and video using frequency division multiplexing (FDM) such as is used with cable television systems. Broadband transmissions use a single medium to carry several channels at once.

BTU (British Thermal Unit) (HVAC)   A heating system measurement that measures the amount of heat required to raise the temperature of one pound of water one degree Fahrenheit.

Byte (binary digit?eight) (Data Networking)   A grouping of eight bits that is used to store or represent numeric values or ASCII characters in computer storage.

BX Cable (Structured Wiring)   A legacy cable type that is now illegal for use in homes.

C

Cable (Structured Wiring)   A bundle of separated insulated wires wrapped with a single protective outer jacket.

Cable clamps (Structured Wiring)   Metal clips inside a distribution panel, outlet box, or other electrical box that are clamped down on a cable using screws to hold the cable in place.

Cable tie (Structured Wiring)   See Tie-wrap.

Capacitance (Electricity)   The capability of a material to store an electric charge. Capacitance is measured in farads.

Cat (category) 3 cable (Structured Wiring)   A four-pair TP cable once used for telecommunications and data networking that is now replaced by Cat 5 or Cat 5e cabling in the standards. Cat 3 cable is the minimum cable requirement for 10BaseT Ethernet networking.

Cat 5 cable (Structured Wiring)   A four-pair TP cable that provides a higher standard than Cat 3 cable because of an increased number of twists on the wire pairs and better resistance to interference. Cat 5 cable is the minimum cable requirement for 100BaseT and below Ethernet networking.

Cat 5e (expanded) cable (Structured Wiring)   The currently recommended category TP cable for use in residential cabling systems. Cat 5e cable is compatible with 1000BaseT and below Ethernet standards.

Category cable (Structured Wiring)   TP cabling is rated into several numbered categories, ranging from category 1 (Cat 1) to category 7 (Cat 7), as specified by the EIA/TIA 568 cabling standard. The higher the category number, the higher the information capacity of the circuit.

Cathode (Lighting)   An electrode in a fluorescent lamp that emits or discharges electrons to the cathode at the opposite end of the lamp.

CATV (Cable Access Television) (Video)   An RF distribution system that distributes television broadcast programs, original programs, premium programming, and other services using a network of coaxial cable.

CCD (Video)   Light detecting circuit arrays used in video cameras, scanners, and digital still cameras. Advantages include good sensitivity in low light and the absence of the burn-in and phosphor lag found in CRTs.

CCTV (Video)   A closed circuit television distribution system that limits the reception of an image to those receivers directly connected to the origination point by coaxial cable or microwave link.

Central monitoring station (Security) A facility of a privately owned protection service company that receives remote alarm signals and acts based on customers requests.

Central monitoring station (Surveillance) A central location in a home where surveillance images captured by video cameras are viewed and monitored.

CEDIA (Custom Electronic Design and Installation Association) (General) A global trade association of companies that specialize in planning and installing integrated electronic systems in the home.

CFM (cubic feet per minute) (HVAC) A standard measurement for airflow that measures the amount of air passing a stationary point.

Chandelier (Lighting) A hanging light fixture that is often used as the focal point in a room or area.

Channel (General) A single path for communications. Channels may be one- or two-dimensional.

Channel (Video) A defined band within the 6 MHz RF spectrum that transmits the audio and video carriers of a television signal.

Circuit (Electricity) A continuous loop of electrical current.

Circuit breaker (Electricity) See Breaker.

Cladding (General) A low refractive index material that surrounds the core of an optical fiber causing the transmitted light to travel down the core and protects against surface contaminant scattering.

CO (carbon monoxide) (Security) An odorless and colorless gas that is often called the "silent killer." Faulty furnaces can emit CO gas, which can poison the occupants of a home and can be lethal after extended exposure.

CO (central office) (Communications) A term for the local telephone system's switching center. The nearest CO to a home is also called an end office (EO) or a local exchange (LE). The telephone lines that enter a home at the NID are terminated at the CO.

CO detector (Security) A sensor that can detect the presence of CO gas in a home and alert the occupants of the hazard.

Coaxial cable (Communications/Video) A two-conductor copper cable made up of a solid central conductor, a dielectric layer, and a second conductive layer that is usually a metal braid or mesh, all of which are inside an insulating jacket.

CODEC (Compress/Decompress) (Video) An algorithmic video service that encodes and decodes video files for transmission over network media.

Color temperature (Lighting)   A measure of the appearance of the light produced by a lamp that categorizes the light as either warm or cool.

Compact fluorescent lamp (CFL) (Lighting)   A small, single-end fluorescent lamp that can be installed into an incandescent lamp socket.

Composite video (Video)   The complete video signal including the brightness (Luminance) signal, the blanking and sync pulses, and the color (Chrominance).

Compressor (HVAC)   A pump used to increase the pressure of a refrigerant or gas between low-pressure and high-pressure cycles.

Conductor (General)   A material that offers little resistance to the flow of electrical current.

Conduit (Structured Wiring)   A metal or plastic tube that is used to protect the cabling running through it.

Connecting block (Communications)   A plastic block containing metal wiring terminals used to establish connections from one group of wire to another with insulation displacement connections (IDC). Also called a terminal block, a punchdown block, a quick-connect block, or a cross-connect block. Used in residential wiring for terminating CPIW and provides a means for a telephone set to connect to the CPIW through a modular jack.

Control (General)   A multiposition mechanical device, usually wall mounted, that allows for adjustment (attenuation or amplification) of the signal from the source or distribution device to an end device.

Concealed wiring (Structured Wiring)   Cable installed in a wall, between floors, in attics, or I in crawlspaces to prevent the cable from being tampered with and to improve the aesthetics of the home.

Condenser (HVAC)   A pump that receives vaporized refrigerant from an evaporator and compresses it into a liquid state for return to the refrigerant control unit.

Contacts (Security and General)   Electrically conductive points, or sets of points, that open and/or close circuits that ultimately control electrical loads.

Contrast (Video)   The range of dark and light values in a picture or the ratio between minimum and maximum brightness.

Control panel (Security)   A device that arms, disarms, and supervises an alarm system at the user's premises.

Controller (General)   A device or group of devices that serve to govern, in some predetermined manner, the electric power delivered to the apparatus it is connect to.

Convergence (Video)   The alignment of the red, green, and blue video on a projected display such that the lines produced by the three "guns" appear to form one clearly focused white line and the perceived single image is clearly focused.

Cove lighting (Lighting)   A type of architectural lighting that uses light sources shielded by a ledge or recess to distribute light across a ceiling or wall.

CPIW (Customer Provided Inside Wiring) (Communications)   Any and all telephone wiring inside a home and beyond the NID.

Cross-connect (Structured Wiring)   A physical connection made between patch panels or punchdown blocks that interconnects cable runs from source devices and end devices.

Crossed pair (Structured Wiring)   A wiring termination error on TP cabling in which the two conductors of a wire pair are attached incorrectly exchanged with the conductors of a different wire pair at one end of a cable.

Crosstalk (Structured Wiring)   Interference on a cable caused by electrical energy being absorbed into adjacent conductors of a cable that may cause signal loss.

CRT (Video)   Cathode ray tube.

Current (General)   The flow of electricity in a circuit, measured in amperes.

D

Daisy chain (Structured Wiring)   A wiring technique in which multiple terminations are made on a cable or wiring branch that interconnects one device on the branch to the next.

Damper (HVAC)   A device located inside a duct that is used to adjust the airflow.

Data Rate (Data Networking)   The number of bits of information that can be transmitted per second.

dB (Decibel) (Electricity, Audio)   See Decibel.

DC (direct current) (Electricity)   An electrical current that has no alternations or reversals.

Decibel (dB) (Electricity, Audio)   A measurement for the loudness or strength of a signal. One decibel is considered to be the smallest amount of difference between two sound levels that a human ear can detect. One Bel indicates that an input signal is 10 times quieter or weaker than the output signal. A decibel is one-tenth of a Bel.

Definition (Video)   The fidelity of a video picture reproduction. The clearer the picture, the higher the definition.

Demarc (Demarcation point) (Communications)   The point at which a telephone company's lines terminate and are interconnected into a home's CPIW. Typically, the demarc of a home is the NID.

Device (General)   Any electrical or mechanical equipment attached to a cable or wire.

DHCP (Dynamic Host Configuration Protocol) (Data Networking)
A networking protocol that allows network nodes to self-configure for IP address, subnet masks, default gateways, and more.

Digital Communicator (Security)   A device that can be triggered automatically to electronically dial one or more preprogrammed telephone numbers using digital codes and report alarm or supervisory information to a receiver.

Dimmer control (Lighting)   An electrical device that controls the brightness of one or more lamps by varying the electrical current flowing to the lamps.

DIP (Dual Inline Package) switch (Data Networking)   A set of toggle switches, rockers, or slides that are used to select settings on a modem or electronic circuit board.

Distortion (Video)   An undersized change in a wave form or signal.

Distribution panel (Structured Wiring)   A centrally located panel that organizes and interconnects cable-based technologies, including data, voice, audio, and video signals throughout a home.

Dolby Pro Logic (Audio)   Advanced surround sound system for the home using two front speakers, two rear-channel speakers for ambiance reproduction, and a front center channel speaker for dialog and "logic steering."

Door contact (Security)   A two-part magnetic sensor that detects when a door is opened and generates a trip signal.

Downlight (Lighting)   A light fixture that is typically recessed into a ceiling or an architectural feature that concentrates its light in a downward direction. Also called can or recessed can.

Drop wire (Communications)   A cable used to connect a home to telephone services that may either be underground or above ground and terminates at the home's NID.

Drywall (General)   Also called Sheetrock (a brand name) or wallboard, drywall is a gypsum-based wall covering material that is installed in large sheets as a substitute for plaster on interior walls.

DSL (digital subscriber lines) (Data Networking)   A broadband DSL-telephone line technology that transmits voice, data, and video over existing copper telephone wires at very high speeds. See ADSL.

DSL modem (Data Networking)   A type of modem that connects a computer to a DSL network that connects to the Internet. Once connected, DSL modem users usually have a continuous connection to the Internet.

Duct (HVAC)   A pipe or enclosed conduit used to control and direct the flow of air from an air-handling device.

Ductwork (HVAC)   The system of ducts in a home.

Duplex receptacle (Electricity)   An electrical outlet that includes two AC power plug-in sockets.

DVD (digital versatile disc) (Video)   An optical disc system using MPEG-2 compression technology and the side of a CD-ROM that can store about 133 minutes of digital video.

E

EIA (Electronic Industry Association) (Structured Wiring)   A trade association of electronic equipment manufacturers that develops and publishes standards.

EIA/TIA 568 (Structured Wiring)   See 568A and 568B.

EIA/TIA 570 (Structured Wiring)   See 570.

Electrical box (Structured Wiring)   Also called outlet box, an electrical box is a metal or plastic box that is mounted to wall studs to hold electrical receptacles, light switches, and structured wiring jacks and outlets. Structured wiring runs terminate at electrical boxes.

ELV (Extra low voltage) (Electricity)   Electricity with voltage not exceeding 50 volts AC or 120 volts DC.

Emergency lighting (Lighting)   Lighting, typically powered by battery backup, that is used when the normal electrical supply is interrupted and the lighting system is not available.

EMI (Electromagnetic Interference) (Structured Wiring)   Interference in signal transmission or a reaction on a cable caused by low-frequency waves emitted from electromechanical devices.

Entry delay (Security)   A timer in most security system controllers that provides a homeowner time to disarm the security system before an alarm is sounded.

Ethernet (Data Networking)   A star or bus topology networking technology for computer data communication defined in the IEEE 802.3 standards that operates over twisted-pair, coaxial cable and RF at speeds up to 1000 Mbps. See 10BaseT.

Exit delay (Security)   A timer in most security system controllers that provides a homeowner with time to leave a home after arming the security system and setting off an alarm.

Expansion slots (Data Networking)   Slots or spaces inside a computer or controller that are used to connect additional circuit boards (cards).

F

F-type connector (Structured Wiring)   A threaded barrel connector used to terminate coaxial cable in video applications.

Fiber Optics (Structured Wiring)   Plastic or glass cable that carries a large capacity of information suing light (modulated light waves) and is immune to electrical noise, lightning, and induced voltages.

Firewall (Data Networking)   Dedicated hardware and/or a software system that protects against intrusion on a network from systems external to the network.

FireWire (General)   A reference to IEEE 1394 1995 standard. A data communication scheme that manages digitization, compression, and synchronization processes.

Fish tape (Structured Wiring)   A coil or steel tape that is used to guide a cable through a wall from above or below.

Fixture (Lighting)   A permanently installed and connected light or electrical device that consumes electrical power.

Fluorescent lamp (Lighting)   A low-pressure mercury electric-discharge lamp that has a phosphor coating on the inside of a glass tube to transform UV energy into visible light.

Foot-candle (fc) (Lighting)   A measurement for the amount of light reaching an object in the United States.

FPS (Frames per second) (Video)   The number of video frames captured or displayed in one second.

Frequency (General)   The number of cycles per second in an electrical signal, measured in Hertz.

FDM (Frequency division multiplexing) (Data Networking, Communications)   A communications technology that transmits multiple signals over a single communications link, such as cable television systems and wireless networks. Each signal is assigned a separate frequency.

FT4 (Fire Type 4) (Structured Wiring)   A cable jacket material rating for non-toxic, nonflammable materials used for the insulation and outer jackets of low voltage cable, such as speaker wire.

Furnace (HVAC) The part of a heating system that converts gas, oil, or electricity into heat.

Fuse (Electrical) A removable device that completes a circuit at the fuse box that will break if the circuit should have an overload or a short occurs on the circuit.

Future-proofing (General) The practice of designing and installing wiring and/or a system that provides a home with the flexibility, expandability, and adaptability to support new and emerging technologies without requiring new wiring.

G

GA (gauge) (General) Identifies the physical size of a wire. The lower the AWG (American Wire Gauge) number, the bigger the wire.

Gain (Audio) A measure of amplification on a device expressed in dB for the highest frequency of operation.

Gateway (Structured Wiring) The entry point of services in to a residence.

General lighting (Lighting) Uniform ambient lighting of a room or area without using special lighting, such as task lighting or accent lighting.

GFCI (Ground Fault Circuit Interrupter) (Electricity) Sometimes called GFI (Ground Fault Interrupter), this is a specific circuit protection outlet or breaker that protects homeowners from shocks. GFCI outlets are typically installed in kitchens and bathrooms.

Ghosting (Video) Positive or negative images displaced in time from the actual image caused by signal interference from multiple paths of signal reception.

Gigahertz (GHz) (Data Networking) A network frequency of one billion cycles per second.

Glare (Lighting) Light coming into an eye directly for a light source that can harm vision and cause visual discomfort. Indirect glare is light reflected into an eye from a nonlight source surface.

Glass break sensors (Security) Sensors that detect the sound or vibration of glass breaking and generate a trip signal.

Ground (Electricity) A conductive entity with a zero electrical potential that is neither positively nor negatively charged.

Ground wire (Electricity) One of the three common circuit wires. The ground provides a safety route for returning current. The ground circuit is joined with the neutral conductor at the main service panel.

Ground fault (Electricity)? Current that has been misdirected from a hot or neutral lead to a grounding element such as a wire, box, or conductor.

H

HA (home automation) (General)   The use of a computer or microprocessor-based controller to control the functions and scheduling of home systems.

Halogen lamp (Lighting)   A type of incandescent lamp that contains halogen gases, such as iodine, chlorine, bromine, or fluorine, that impede the degradation of the tungsten filament. Also called a tungsten halogen lamp or a quartz lamp.

HAN (home area network) (Data Networking)   A local area network (LAN) inside a single home.

Handheld remote (General)   A portable handheld control device.

Hand-over section (Security)   If the security system detects an entry or exit through the primary entry/exit point, the entry or exit delay feature is engaged. However, if an entry or exit is made through any other point, the alarm is sounded.

Hardware (Data Networking)   The physical components of a computer or network system, including the Internet gateway, monitor, hard drive, printer, modem, network adapter, keyboard, etc.

HDTV (high-definition television) (Video)   A high-resolution, wide-screen picture format and transmission standard.

HID (High-Intensity Discharge) (Lighting)   Lamps that produce more lumens per watt and have longer lives than most other lamp types. HID lamps include mercury vapor, metal halide, high-pressure sodium, and low-pressure sodium.

High temperature sensor (Security)   A sensor that detects a rise in the ambient temperature of a room or area beyond a certain preset level and generates a trip signal.

Heat loss (HVAC)   The amount of heat lost from a space to be conditioned, measured in BTUs.

Heat pump (HVAC)   A compression cycle system that uses the heat in outdoor air to supply heat to a home or to remove heat from the home to cool it.

Hertz (General)   A unit of signal frequency equal to one cycle per second.

Home network (Data Networking)   A peer-to-peer network that allows users to share data, peripheral devices, and Internet resources on a common network inside a home.

Home run (Structured Wiring)   A wiring method where every cable is terminated at a central distribution facility and pulled directly to a single device, hub, or group of devices wired in series.

Hot wire (Electricity)   One of the three common circuit wires with neutral and ground. The current flow travels on the hot wire.

House Code (Lighting)   An alpha character (A-P) setting on an X-10 PLC device that is used to indicate an item or area/zone within the home. This code setting is combined with a Unit Code (1-16) to uniquely identify the X-10 device.

HTI (home technology integration) (General)   The integration of a home's control and entertainment and other systems based on a structured wiring system and through the use of automated controllers.

HTI+ (General)   The certification examinations produced by the Computer Technology Industry Association (CompTIA) that certify the abilities of an HTI technician to install, troubleshoot, and maintain home automated systems.

Hub (Data Networking)   A network clustering device that connects several network-ready devices to the network media using a shared bandwidth.

HV (High voltage) (Electricity)   Electrical lines that carry voltage in excess of 1,000 V AC or 1,500 V DC.

HVAC (Heating, Ventilation, and Air Conditioning) (HVAC)   The integrated system that heats, cools, and ventilates a home.

I

IEEE (Institute of Electrical and Electronics Engineers) (Data Networking)   IEEE is a trade organization of engineers, scientists, and students that develops standards for the computer and electronics industry.

Internet gateway (Data Networking)   Also called a residential gateway or a home gateway, an Internet gateway provides a link between a home network and the Internet.

IP (Internet Protocol) address (Data Networking)   A 32-bit binary logical address that identifies a computer on a TCP/IP (Transmission Control Protocol/Internet Protocol) network.

IDC (Insulation Displacement Connector) (Data Networking, Structured Wiring)   A type of wiring terminating connection where the insulating jacket is removed from the connector when the wire is inserted/pushed/forced into the split connector with tines. This eliminates the need to strip wires first.

Impedance (General)   The resistance and reactance of a conductor or component measured in ohms. The lower the ohm value, the better the quality of the conductor.

Incandescent lamp (Lighting)   A filament heated to the point of incandescence by an electric current inside of a glass bulb produces Light.

Induction (General)   Creating an electric current on a circuit from the magnetic influence of an adjacent circuit.

Instant start (Lighting)   A type of fluorescent lamp that starts without the need for preheating the cathodes or a starter.

IP Telephony (Data Networking)   Using Internet protocols to exchange voice, fax, and other forms of information traditionally carried over dedicated circuit-switched connections of the public switched telephone network.

IR (infrared) (General)   A transmission technology that uses infrared light to transmit command signals and data. IR signals are also used in motion detectors and IR beam trip sensors.

Internet (Data Networking)   An internetwork of networks around the world that provides access to information, electronic mail, graphics, and other media on content servers connected to the network.

I/O (Input/Output) (Data Networking)   The operations of a computer that accept data inputs and transmit data outputs to and from peripheral devices.

ISDN (Integrated Services Digital Network) (Data Networking)
A telephone system of digital voice and data transmission services carried over the PSTN.

ISO (International Standards Organization) (Standards)   An international membership organization that develops computer and telecommunications standards, among others. ANSI represents the United States at the ISO.

ISP (Internet service provider) (Data Networking)   A company or organization that provides Internet connection services to subscribers.

Isolation (Video)   The amount of separation or loss between two channels or signals.

J

Jack (Structured Wiring)   The female component of a jack and plug connector that is attached to a cable as a terminator at an outlet or interconnect.

Jacket (Structured Wiring)   The outer protection covering of wire or cable that may also provide additional insulation.

K

Knockout (Structured Wiring)   A plug or piece of an electrical box or panel that can be removed to provide a pass-through for cable to enter or exit the box.

Kilohertz (KHz) (Data Network)   The equivalent of a frequency of 1,000 cycles per second.

Keypad (General)   User interface and input devices that are used to control the functions of one or more integrated systems. In a security system, a keypad is used to arm or disarm the system. In an audio/video system, keypads are used to select source devices and control volume.

Kilowatt (kW) (Lighting)   The equivalent of 1,000 watts.

Kilowatt hour (kWh) (Lighting)   The amount of kilowatts used by a device in one hour of operation.

Kilobyte (KB) (Data Networking)   The equivalent of 1,000 bytes of data.

L

Lamp (Lighting)   A light source, such as an incandescent, a halogen, a HID, or a fluorescent lamp. Also called a light bulb.

LCD (liquid crystal display) (Video)   Utilizes two transparent sheets of polarizing material with a liquid containing rod-shaped crystals between them that respond to electrical currents and align to create dark images. LCD panels do not emit light but are often backlit or sidelit for better viewing.

LCD Projector (Video)   Utilizes LCD technique, separating red, green, and blue information to three different LCD panels where the appropriate colored light is then passed through and combined before exiting through the projector lens.

Lead (Structured Wiring)   A short length of conductor wire loose in a box or service panel.

LED (light-emitting diode) (General)   A small electronic device that produces light when electricity is passed through it. LEDs are commonly used as indicator lights on keypads and other control devices.

Light fixture (Lighting)   A complete lighting device that consists of a lamp, housing, and power connection.

Line Conditioner (General)   Contains multiple protection devices in one package to provide electrical noise isolation and voltage regulation.

Line Doubler (Video)   Doubles the number of scan lines in a video picture. Fills in the space between the original lines, making them less noticeable and increases the brightness of the picture.

Line voltage (Electricity)   The normal or nominal voltage level of a line. In the United States, the line voltage of a home is typically 120 volts AC.

Local area network (LAN) (Data Networking)   A computer network in which two or more computers are connected with a communications medium for the purpose of sharing resources. Local area networks are typically created in a small geographical area, such as a home.

Load (Lighting)   Applies to all current-carrying devices on a given electrical circuit or feeder.

Logic circuit control (Security)   The system used with PIR devices to analyze changes in signal frequency to generate a trip signal, such as in a motion sensor, to determine movement before sounding an alarm. Also determines whether the object detected is a person or a pet to prevent a false alarm.

Loss (General)   The energy dissipated by a transmission line.

Louver (Lighting)   A diffuser made of opaque or translucent material in a geometric design to prevent a lamp from being viewed directly and to minimize glare.

Low temperature sensor (Security)   A sensor that detects decreases in the ambient temperature of a room or area to a preset limit and generates a trip signal.

Lumen (Lighting)   The amount of light produced by a lamp is measure in lumens.

Luminaire (Lighting)   An architectural lighting effect or fixture.

LV (low voltage) (Electricity)   An electrical circuit that carries voltage not exceeding 1,000 volts AC or 1,500 volts DC.

M

MATV (Multiple Access Television) (Video)   The method used for broadcasting television signals through the air.

Mbps (Megabits per second) (Data Networking)   The equivalent of one million bits of data transmitted in one second.

MHz (MegaHertz) (General)   The equivalent of a frequency with one million cycles per second.

Mixer (Audio)   A device that will "mix" two or more input signals to form a combined outlet signal.

MMOF (multi-mode optical fiber) (Structured Wiring)   Transmission medium that uses glass or plastic strands to carry light impulses.

Modem (modulator/demodulator) (Data Networking)   A telephone communications device that modulates digital data into analog data for transmission over a telephone line and demodulates the analog data into digital data at the receiving end for use by a computer.

Modulation (Audio, Video, Data Networking)　Raising a signal to a higher frequency by changing amplitude, frequency, or phase.

Motion detector (Security, Lighting)　A sensor that can detect movement or the presence of a person in a room or area to sound an alarm or merely turn on or off the lights.

Mounting bracket (Structured Wiring)　A bracket attached to a wall stud during rough-in that allows the mounting of a faceplate during trim out. Also called a low-voltage mounting bracket.

Mud ring (Structured Wiring)　A bracket attached to a wall stud during rough-in that ends up mounted flush with the drywall for the attachment of a faceplate during trim-out.

Multizone (General)　A home automation or home technology integration system set up that allows separate areas of a home to operate independently of other areas of the home.

Modular outlets (Structured Wiring)　Multiuse outlets that allow for a variety of jacks to be mixed into a single outlet faceplate. Modular jacks are snapped into the faceplate in any pattern desired.

N

NEC (National Electric Code) (Standards)　The NEC is a guideline for electricians, electrical contractors, engineers, and electrical inspectors put out by the NFPA that is generally accepted as the building wiring standard in the United States.

NEMA (National Electrical Manufacturer's Association) (Standards)　An association of manufacturers that develops technical standards for electrical products.

Network (General)　Two or more computers or peripheral devices connected by a communications medium.

Network adapter (Data Networking)　The device that provides the interconnection and transceiver services to connect a computer or network-ready device to a network.

Network cable (Data Networking)　The physical wire medium used to connect two or more computers or peripheral devices.

Neutral wire (Electricity)　One of the three common circuit wires. The neutral wire returns current to the power source. The neutral conductor is joined with the ground at the main service panel.

NEXT (near-end crosstalk) (Data Networking)   Interference caused by the induction of a signal from one wire pair into another pair at the transmitting end of a cable.

NIC (network interface card) (Data Networking)   A network adapter that is installed in a computer as an expansion card and manages the flow of information over the network.

NID (network interface device) (Communications)   The interface device where the telephone company's lines interconnect with the residential wiring. Also called the demarc.

NM (nonmetallic) cable (Electricity)   An electric service cable that is sheathed in a plastic material.

NMC (nonmetallic, corrosive) (Electricity)   An electric service cable that is sheathed in a solid plastic jacket for use in wet or corrosive areas, but is not approved for underground use.

Node (Data Networking)   Any network device where a network cable terminates.

Noise (General)   In a cable or circuit, any extraneous signal that tends to interfere with the signal normally present in or passing through the system.

Noise reduction (Audio, Video)   Processes used to reduce the amount of noise in an audio or video signal.

Normally Closed (General)   Circuit or switch where the contacts are closed during normal operation.

Normally Open (General)   Circuit or switch where the contacts are open during normal operation.

NTSC (National Television Standards Committee) (Video)   A color television broadcast signal standard that is used in North America and Japan.

O

Occupancy Sensor (Security and Lighting)   Control device that detects the presence of a person in a given space. Commonly used to detect intrusion in a security system or control lighting systems and HVAC.

Ohm (General)   The unit of measure for the resistance in a conductor.

Off-air (Video   RF signals (typically TV) that can be received by a conventional antenna system, including VHF and UHF broadcast stations.

Ohmmeter (General)   An instrument for directly measuring resistance in ohms.

P

PAN (Data Network)   Personal area network.

Parallel circuit (General)   Circuit interconnection where all components share a common positive and common negative connection.

Patch cords (Structured Wiring)   The cabling used to interconnect terminations at the central distribution panel.

Patch panel (Data Networking)   An interconnecting device that is used to terminate home-run cabling and connect it to distribution devices using patch cords.

PAL (Phase Alternation by Line) (Video)   The television signal format used in Europe and several South American countries.

PCI (peripheral component interconnect) (Data Networking)   An internal communications and expansion bus on computers. Most network interface cards are PCI compatible.

PCMCIA (Personal Computer Memory Card International Association) (Data Networking)   PCMCIA is a standard for hot-swappable cards developed for use with portable PCs.

Peer-to-peer (Data Networking)   A simple kind of network that sets up a conversation between two machines without a middle man.

Pendant light (Lighting)   Lighting fixtures used for either task or general lighting that are suspended from a ceiling.

Peripheral device (Data Networking)   External computer devices that are attached to the computer, such as CD-ROM drives, modems, and printers, through an interface cable.

PIP (Picture-In-Picture) (Video)   Display of a small picture with a larger picture, each from its own video source.

PIR (passive infrared) sensor (Security)   A detector device that senses changes in the radiation in the infrared band.

Pixel (picture element) (Video)   A video image is composed of individual dots called pixels that create the image patterns and colors.

PLC (powerline control) (Data Networking)   The use of electrical AC wiring for networking transmissions of signals.

Plenum (General)   Airflow space between the actual ceiling and a drop ceiling where ductwork for an HVAC system is installed.

Plenum-rated cable (Structured Wiring)   A cable that has a fire retardant coating that complies with local and national building codes and is suitable for installation in air ducts and plenum spaces.

Plug pack (Security)   A transformer that converts 120 or 240 volts AC to 16 volts DC to power a security system controller.

Port (Data Networking)   A receptacle on a computer or patch panel.

POTS (plain old telephone system) (Communications)   Analog telephone service that runs over copper wires based on the original Bell telephone system.

Prewire (Structured Wiring)   The installation of structured wiring in a home before the drywall is installed during new construction.

Protocol (Data Networking)   A set of rules or guidelines that govern the communication between two applications, computers, or networks.

PSTN (Public Switched Telephone Network) (Communications)
The switched telephone network that carries long distance calls and point-to-point network communications.

Punchdown (Structured Wiring)   A method for securing wire to a contact where the insulated wire is paced in a terminal groove and pushed down with a special tool. As the wire is seated, the terminal displaces the wire insulation to make an electrical connection.

Punchdown block (Data Networking)   See 110 block.

Punchdown tool (Data Networking)   A spring-loaded tool that is used to insert conductors into IDC contacts when terminating on a 110 block.

PVC (polyvinyl chloride) (General)   Material most commonly used for the insulation and jacketing of cable.

R

Raceway (Structured Wiring)   A metal or plastic channel used to hold electrical or structured wiring in a floor.

Rapid start (Lighting)   A fluorescent system without starters that requires one to two seconds of warm-up before beginning to emit light.

Rated life (Lighting)   The time in which 50 percent of a large quantity of a certain lamp burns out.

Reactance (General)   Measure of the combined effects of capacitance and inductance on an alternating current.

Recessed downlight (Lighting)   A light fixture that is recessed into a ceiling that concentrates its light downward.

Refrigerant (HVAC)   The substance used in a refrigerating mechanism that absorbs heat in an evaporator by changing its state from liquid to a gas and then releases its heat in a condenser as it is returned to a liquid state.

Register (HVAC)   A device that combines a grille and damper to cover an air opening.

Relay (General)   An electromechanical switching device.

Remodel box (Structured Wiring)   An electrical box designed for use during remodeling projects for installing electrical receptacles such as HYPERLINK "http://www.netday.org/" \l "jack" jacks or light switches in existing walls.

Remote alarm (Security)   An alarm signal that is transmitted to a remote central monitoring station.

Repeater (Data Networking)   A network device that amplifies and regenerates signals so they can travel for longer distance on a cable.

Reset (Security and General)   To restore an electrical component or a alarm to its original (normal) condition after improper performance or an alarm signal.

Residential gateway (Data Networking)   See Internet gateway.

Resistance (General)   The amount of opposition a cable has to the flow of electrical current that is measured in ohms.

Resolution (Video)   The density of lines or dots for a given area that make up an image. Resolution determines the detail and quality in an image.

Retrofit (General)   A modification to an existing building.

Return air (HVAC)   Air drawn into a heating unit after being circulated in a room by the HVAC system supply.

RF (radio frequency) (General)   Transmission of wireless signals over a high-frequency carrier.

RFI (radio frequency interference) (General)   Interference inducted into a conductor from radio frequency signals on a nearby carrier.

RG6 (radio grade 6) coaxial cable (Data Networking)   Type of coaxial cable with a 20-gauge center conductor that is the current standard for data communications over coaxial cable as it allows for higher bandwidth than RG59.

RG59 coaxial cable (Video)   A type of coaxial cable typically used for video signal transmission.

RGB (red, green, and blue) (Video)   The chroma information in a video signal. The basic components of the color television system.

RGB monitor (Video)   A color monitor that accepts separate red, green, and blue input signals to produce a high-quality picture.

Rheostat (General)   A variable resistor.

Ring (Communications)   The side of a two-wire circuit that is connected to the negative side of a power source at the telephone company CO.

RJ-11 (Communications)   A modular jack/plug connector that accepts a single pair of conductors. Used for single line telephones and modems.

RJ-31X (Security)   A modular jack/plug connector that is used to interconnect a security system to a telephone distribution panel and allows for seizure of an in-use phone line.

RJ-45 (Data Networking)   A modular jack/plug connector that is used to terminated twisted-pair cabling per EIA/TIA 568 termination standards.

Romex (Electricity)   A brand of nonmetallic-sheathed cable that is also the generic name used for NM sheathed cable.

Rough-in (Structured Wiring)   The phase of a structured wiring project in which the boxes, cables, and in-wall connections are installed. Rough-in occurs before the dry-wall is installed.

Router (Data Networking)   A device where the basic function is to efficiently route network traffic from one network to another network.

Run (Structured Wiring)   The path of a length of cable from a distribution panel to an outlet or other termination point.

S

Secam (Systeme Electronique Couleur Avec Memoire) (Video)   A color TV standard developed in France.

Sensor (Security)   A device designed to produce a signal or other indication in response to an event or stimulus within its detection.

Serial Interface (Data Networking)   An I/O port that transmits data one bit at a time in contrast to parallel transmission that transmits multiple bits simultaneously. RS-232 is a common serial signaling protocol.

Series wiring (Structured Wiring)   See daisy chain.

Server (Data Networking) An application running on a centralized computer that processes requests from network clients (nodes).

Service drop (General) The overhead conductors between the electrical supply, such as the lat pole, and the building being served.

Service loop (Structured Wiring) A length of cable coiled near the end of a cable run to facilitate future changes in the wiring system.

Service entrance (SE) (Electricity) The point where the incoming electrical line enters a home.

Service lead (Electricity) An incoming electrical line that supplies power to a service panel. Also called supply lead.

Service panel (Electricity) The distribution facility that ties the service lead to the interior electrical circuits of a home. The service panel is typically a main circuit breaker panel or a fuse box.

Set point (HVAC) The temperature setting a thermostat is to maintain in a room or area.

Setback thermostat (HVAC) An electronic programmable thermostat that can be set to provide different temperature settings for different times of the day.

Set-top box (Video) A generic term for a device connected between the television set and the cable service coming in. It performs selection and decryption processes.

Sheetrock (General) A brand name for drywall material. See Drywall.

Shield (Structured Wiring) A metal braid, mesh, or foil placed around a cable to conduct return current and to prevent signal leakage or interference.

Short circuit (General) The condition caused when a current flow is interrupted short of or before reaching the device terminating the cable. A short circuit is caused when a hot conductor comes into contact with neutral or ground conductors.

Shunt (Security) To remove some portion of an alarm system from operation, allowing entry into a protected area without initiating an alarm signal.

Signal (Security and Communications) Any visible or audible indication that can convey information. Also, the information conveyed through a communications system.

Signal strength (General) The intensity of a signal measured in volts (V), millivolts (mV), microvolts (uV), or dbmV.

Silent alarm (Security) A remote alarm without local indication that an alarm has been transmitted.

Single-zone (General)   A whole-house system in which all devices operate from a single controller.

Siren (Security)   A sounding device that emits a harsh and loud sound when a trip signal is received from a directly connected sensor or the security system controller.

Skin effect (General)   The tendency of alternating current to travel only on the surface of a conductor as its frequency increases.

SMOF (single-mode optical fiber) (Structured Wiring)   A type of fiber optic cable that carries a single signal stream over long distances.

Smoke detector (Security)   A device where an electrical circuit runs through a chamber where two electrodes are placed very close together to allow electricity to cross the gap, completing the circuit. Should smoke particles collect on one or both of the electrodes, the circuit is broken and a trip signal or an alarm is generated.

Snow (Video)   Visual noise displayed on a television screen caused by excessive signal noise on a circuit.

Speaker siren (Security)   A siren that receives audio signals from the security system controller for playback.

Spike (General)   A momentary increase in electrical current that can damage electrical equipment.

Splice (General)   The joining of two or more cables together by connecting the conductors pair to pair.

Splitter (Video)   A device that divides (or combines) the RF energy on the coaxial cable to two or more cables. Splitters are also two-way and they combine as well as divide.

Star topology (Structured Wiring)   A wiring pattern where each cable run emanates from a central distribution facility and is terminated at a single device. See Home run.

Starter (Lighting)   The electrical device that works with a ballast to start a fluorescent or HID lamp.

Stereo (Audio)   A process of using separate signals on separate channels for the left and right audio, thereby giving depth, or dimension, to the sound.

STP (shielded twisted-pair) (Structured Wiring)   A type of twisted pair cable that includes a foil shielding around each wire pair.

Streaming media (Video)   This type of network-download video file allows a user to watch the media content of a file without first downloading the entire file. The user is able to watch the content while the download is in progress.

Strobe light (Security)   A high-intensity light that strobes when an alarm is activated.

Structured wiring (Structured Wiring)   A system of installing home wiring in which all cable runs are distributed from a central distribution panel using a star topology and home-run cable pulls.

Subwoofer (Audio)   A loudspeaker that reproduces very low sounds usually in the range of 20 Hz to 1000 Hz.

Super VHS (Video)   A video tape player that combines with compatible S-VHS tape to produce images featuring an increase in HRLS and a sharper picture.

Supply (HVAC)   The ductwork that carries conditioned air to a room.

Surge (General)   A rapid rise in current or voltage usually followed by a fall back to a normal level.

Surround sound (Audio   A system that separates the various components of the sound track, then disperses them to speakers placed around the room. Four to five speakers are incorporated and a surround sound processor is used to create the effect.

SVGA (Super Video Graphics Array) (Video)   Term used to denote resolutions higher than VGA (640 x 480). SVGA computer graphics cards have a resolution of 800 x 600 pixels (480,000 pixels) but may be able to output resolutions of up to 1280 x 1024 and 16 million colors.

S-VHS (Super Video Home Systems) (Video)   A high band video recording process for VHS that increases the picture quality and resolution capabilities.

S-Video (Video)   The composite video signal is separated into the lum (Y, black, and white information) and the chroma (C, color information)

Switch (Data Networking)   A LAN switch is used to efficiently forward messages on a network. In addition to several other features, the advantage of a switch over a hub is that each port has its own dedicated bandwidth.

Switch (General)   A two position wall-mounted device that toggles between the completion or interruption of a circuit between two devices.

System (General)   A group of electrical devices that processes inputs into outputs, allowing for feedback and control. For example, an audio system includes audio source devices, audio distribution and amplification devices, cabling, speakers, and controls.

Systems integration (General)   Having intelligent subsystems that communicate with each other and act upon the information shared.

PART X

T

T1 (Communications)   A standard for digital transmission in North America. T1 lines are used for connecting networks across remote distances.

Tamper sensor (Security)   A sensor or switch used to detect the unauthorized tampering with a sensor or contact.

Tap (Communications)   A device inserted into a communications line that allows the line to be shared.

Task lighting (Lighting)   Lighting specifically placed to illuminate an area used for a particular activity.

TCP/IP (Transmission Control Protocol/Internet Protocol) (Data Networking)   The primary protocol suite for networks that use IP addressing.

TDM (time division multiplexing) (Data Networking)   A communications technology that transmits multiple signals over a single communications link, assigning each signal a certain time slice.

Telecommunications (Communications)   Any transmission, emission, or reception of signs, signals, writing, images, and sounds or information of any nature by cable, radio, visual, optical, or other electromagnetic systems.

Terminator (Structured Wiring)   A resistive device that is attached to the end of a cable run. A terminator must match the impedance of the cable to which it is attached.

Thermostat (HVAC)   A set point device used to control the operation of a HVAC system.

Thinnet (Data Networking)   See 10Base2.

TIA (Telecommunications Industry Association) (Standards)   A trade organization that develops and publishes standards for the telecommunications industry.

TIA/EIA (Standards)   Trade associations that collaborate on communications, electronic, and cabling standards. See EIA and TIA.

THX (Video)   A trade name of Lucasfilm Ltd for a movie sound enhancement technology that sets the standard of performance for Dolby sound; originally THX represented Tomlinson Holman Experiment.

Three-way switch (Lighting)   A switch that allows control of power from two or more locations.

Tie-wrap (Structured Wiring)   Plastic or nylon strapping used for binding or bundling cables together or holding them in place. Several styles of tie-wraps are available cinching, hole-mounted, and adhesive closure.

Tip (Communications)   A conductor in a two-wire telephone circuit that is attached to the circuit leading to a positive power source at the telephone company's CO.

Ton (HVAC)   A cooling system unit of measure that is the equivalent of 12,000 BTUH. Single-family residences typically are equipped with air conditioning units that provide between 2 and 5 tons of cooling.

Topology (General)   The physical or logical pattern of a cabling system. These include star, ring, and bus configurations.

Touch screen (General)   A visual display terminal screen that responds to instructions as the user touches the screen.

Transformer (General)   An electrical device used to reduce or convert the current of an electrical circuit.

Traveller Wires (Lighting)   Wires interconnecting switches when more than one switch can control circuit power independently.

Trip signal (Security)   A signal generated by a sensor or contact and transmitted to an alarm or the security system controller when an out-of-norm condition occurs.

Troffer (Lighting)   A large recessed luminaire that is typically flush-mounted on a ceiling.

Tuner (Audio)   A device used to select signals at a specific radio frequency for amplification and conversion to sound.

Twisted pair (Structured Wiring)   A communications cable made up of one or more wire pairs that have been looped around each other. An increased number of twists in the pair reduce the vulnerability of the wire pair to external interference and signal radiation.

TVSS (Transient Voltage Surge Suppressor) (General)   A device designed to protect connected devices from transient voltages.

Tweeter (Audio   A loudspeaker designed to reproduce high-pitched or treble sounds.

U

UF (underground feeder) cable (Electricity)   A cable designed and rated for underground and outdoor use that is molded into solid plastic.

UHF (ultra high frequency) (Video)   Off-air signal frequencies that carry television channels 14 through 69.

UPS (uninterruptible power supply) (General)   Provides protection against all power disturbances.

Upstream (General)   The transfer of data from an in-house device to elsewhere in the home.

USB (Universal Serial Bus) (Data Networking)   A standard high-speed interface mode for attaching peripheral devices to a PC.

UTP (unshielded twisted-pair) (Structured Wiring)   A type of twisted pair cable that does not include additional shielding to resist EMI or RFI.

UV (ultraviolet) radiation (General)   Invisible light that is composed of electromagnetic radiation with a wavelength of less than 400 nanometers (nm) and greater than 100 nm. UV radiation can be harmful to humans and pets.

USOC (Universal Standards Ordering Code) (Communications)
A standard coding scheme for registered jacks used in telecommunications.

V

Valves (HVAC)   Devices inserted into air ducts that are used to open or restrict the air resistance of a HVAC system.

VHF (very high frequency) (Video)   Off-air signal frequencies that carry television channels 2 through 13.

VHS (video home service) (Video)   The half-inch video cassette format originated and developed by JVC and adopted by different manufacturers.

Volt (General)   Unit of electrical measure that indicates the amount of electrical pressure on a circuit.

Voltage drop (General)   A loss of the power level of a circuit caused by the electrical resistance of the wire.

Voltmeter (General)   An instrument designed to measure a difference in electrical potential in volts.

W

Wall sconce (Lighting)   A decorative wall-mounted light fixture.

Wall washing (Lighting)   A lighting technique used to illuminate a wall.

WAN (wide area network) (Data Networking)   A computer network that interconnects LANs over a large geographic area.

Watt (General)   An electrical unit measure that indicates the amount of electrical power on a circuit.

Wattage (Lighting)   The amount of electricity consumed by a lamp.

Wi-Fi (Wireless Fidelity) (Data Networking)   A certification awarded to IEEE 802.11b wireless networking products that meet the standards developed by WECA (Wireless Ethernet Compatibility Alliance) aimed at ensuring interoperability.

WEP (Wired Equivalent Privacy) (Data networking)   The encryption protocol used to encode data transmitted over an 802.11b wireless network using either 40-bit or 128-bit encryption.

Whole-house controller (General)   A computer-based system dedicated to integrating and managing all home electronics systems.

Whole-house network (General)   A network designed to allow any appliances, electronic products, or systems to communicate directly with any other electronic product or system also on the network, regardless of application.

Wire (Structured Wiring)   A single solid metal conductor or a multiple strand metal conductor used to carry an electrical signal or a current.

Wire clamps (Structured Wiring)   see Cable clamps.

Wire stripper (Structured Wiring)   A tool used to remove portions of insulation from a wire.

Wiremold (Structured Wiring)   A brand name for surface-mounted cable raceway.

Window contact (Security)   A magnetic device used to detect when a window is opened and generate a trip signal to an alarm or the security system controller.

Woofer (Audio)   A loudspeaker that reproduces bass frequency.

X

X-10 (Data Networking, Security)   A popular powerline carrier (PLC) technology that transmits signals over AC power lines to transfer data on a network or to control lights, appliances and other devices.

XLR Connector (General)   A type of audio connector featuring 3 leads; 2 for the signal and one for overall system grounding. A secure connector often found on high quality audio and video equipment, also called a cannon connector.

Z

Zone (General)   A single room, a group of rooms, or an entire house in which automated or centrally located devices are controlled from a single controller. For example, in an audio zone all occupants hear the same audio playback.

Home Technology Industry Associations and Organizations

The associations and organizations listed in this appendix contribute trade practices, regulations, standards, guidelines, and certifications for the various building, design, contracting, and technical aspects of a home technology integration or home automation project. The associations and organizations listed (in what is a long but hardly a complete list—new groups emerge every day) can provide you with education and information concerning new developments, practices, and standards that affect the installation of home systems.

I have listed the associations and organizations alphabetically with a brief overview of their mission or function, along with their Web site address.

1394 Trade Association
www.1394ta.org
Promotes the 1394 standard for data communication, which establishes a scheme that manages the digitization, compression, and synchronization processes of data sent over twisted-pair wire.

Air Conditioning Contractors of America (ACCA)
www.acca.org
The ACCA is the U.S. trade association for heating, ventilating, air conditioning, and refrigeration (HVACR) contractors.

Air Diffusion Council
www.flexibleduct.org
The Air Diffusion Council is an industry association that represents the manufacturers of flexible air ducts in North America.

American Lighting Association

www.americanlightingassoc.com

The American Lighting Association is a trade association made up of lighting manufacturers, retailers, distributors, manufacturer representatives, component manufacturers, and lighting industry companies that provide residential lighting.

American National Standards Institute (ANSI)

www.ansi.org

ANSI is a private, nonprofit organization that administers voluntary standards for the U.S.

American Society of Heating, Refrigerating and Air-Conditioning Engineers (AHRAE)

www.ashrae.org

AHRAE develops and publishes standards for uniform methods of testing and rating equipment and accepted practices for the HVAC industry worldwide.

Association of Home Appliance Manufacturers (AHAM)

www.AHAM.org

AHAM is a trade organization representing the manufacturers of household appliances and the products/services associated with household appliances.

Bluetooth Special Interest Group (SIG)

www.bluetooth.com

The Bluetooth SIG is a trade association consisting of members from the telecommunications, computing, automotive, industrial automation, and network industries working together in the development of the Bluetooth wireless technology.

Builder Officials and Code Administrators International (BOCA)

www.builderonline.com

One of the three national building codes for residential and commercial construction.

Canadian Home Builders' Association

www.chba.ca

Canada's residential construction industry association.

Canadian Standards Association (CSA)

www.csa.ca

CSA is a nonprofit membership-based association that operates in Canada and around the world to develop standards that enhance public safety and health.

CEBus Industry Council (CIC)

www.cebus.org

The CIC provides information to the design and development community on CEBus and CEBus Home Plug & Play.

Computer Technology Industry Association (CompTIA)
www.comptia.org
CompTIA is a global trade association that promotes industry standards, professional expertise, skills education, and relevant business solutions to the information technology industry. CompTIA is the sponsor of the HTI+ certification exams.

Construction Safety Council (CSC)
www.buildsafe.org
The CSC is a nonprofit organization dedicated to the advancement of safety and health interests in the field of construction throughout the world.

Consumer Electronics Association (CEA)
www.ce.org
The CEA is made up of more than 1,000 companies in the consumer technology industry, providing information, market research, and education.

Continental Automated Buildings Association (CABA)
www.caba.org
CABA is a nonprofit industry association that promotes advanced technologies for the automation of homes and buildings in North America. Its mission is to encourage the development, promotion, pursuit, and understanding of integrated systems and automation in homes and buildings.

Council of American Building Officials (CABO)
www.iccsafe.org
A subsidiary of the International Code Council, CABO provides residential-only building codes that are compiled by BOCA, Southern Code, and UPC.

Custom Electronic Design & Installation Association (CEDIA)
www.cedia.net
CEDIA is a worldwide trade association that focuses on the planning and installation of residential electronic systems. CEDIA is the sponsor of the CEDIA Professional Certification program.

Door and Hardware Institute (DHI)
www.dhi.org
DHI serves as a resource for education and information on doors, hardware, security, and specialty products for the architectural openings industry.

DSL Forum
www.dslforum.org
An international consortium of nearly 200 service providers and equipment manufacturers focusing on developing broadband DSL to its full potential.

PART X

Electronic Industries Alliance (EIA)
www.eia.org
The umbrella association that includes the Consumer Electronics Manufacturers Association (CEMA), the Telecommunications Industry Association (TIA), and CEBus (Consumers Electronics Bus) Industry Council, and produces the CES show. EIA activities include standards creation and government lobbying.

Energy Information Administration (EIA)
www.eia.doe.gov
Independent agency within the Department of Energy (DOE) that develops surveys, collects energy data, and does analytical and modeling analysis of energy issues.

Ethernet User Alliance (EUA)
www.science.edu/EUA
The Alliance's purpose is to promote development of Ethernet standards and the interoperability of hardware platforms, operating systems, and applications.

European Commission (EC)
The products and services directorate for the European Union.

European Home Systems Association (EHSA)
www.domotics.com/homesys/Ehsa.htm
EHSA is an open organization that supports and promotes the home systems industries in Europe.

Extend the Internet Alliance (ETI Alliance)
www.emware.com/partner/eti %20alliance
The ETI Alliance provides networking and remote management solutions that allow timely and accurate transfer of information between devices, people, and enterprise business systems.

Federal Communication Commission (FCC)
www.fcc.gov
Regulates the radio frequency spectrum within the United States. The FCC is responsible for allocating empty frequencies to new HDTV broadcasters who in turn will phase out the use of their current VHF/UHF and SHF frequencies.

Federal Energy Regulatory Commission (FERC)
www.ferc.gov
An independent federal regulatory agency in the Department of Energy. Has jurisdiction over interstate electricity sales, wholesale electric rates, and hydroelectric licensing, as well as natural gas pricing, oil pipeline rates, and gas pipeline certification.

Fiber to the Home (FTTH) Council
www.ftthcouncil.org

The FTTH Council is a market development organization working to educate, promote, and accelerate fiber optic cable to homes.

HiperLan2 Global Forum (H2EF)
www.hiperlan2.com
HiperLAN2 is an open forum to promote a global interoperable standard for high-speed wireless LAN products.

Home Audio Video Interoperability Association (HAVi)
www.havi.org
The HAVi Association is a member organization that promotes the use and development of the HAVi standard for home entertainment AV networks on the IEEE-1394 digital interface.

Home Phoneline Networking Alliance (HomePNA)
www.homePNA.org
The HomePNA is a nonprofit association of companies that work together to ensure adoption of the HomePNA phoneline networking standard.

HomePlug Powerline Alliance (HomePNA)
www.homeplug.org
The HomePlug Alliance is a member organization that promotes and develops the use of HomePlug standards and products.

Infrared Data Association (IRDA)
www.irda.org
Trade association of computer and chip manufacturers creating standards for high-speed communications for infrared media.

Institute of Electrical and Electronics Engineers (IEEE)
www.ieee.org
International professional society that issues standards and rules for electrical and electronic devices. It is a member of ANSI and ISO.

International Code Council
www.icc-es.org
The focus of this council is to develop technical reports containing descriptions of building construction materials, products, systems, or subsystems and how they meet the model codes.

International Committee on Information Technology Standards (INCITS)
www.incits.org
INCITS is the primary U.S. organization for standardization in Information and Communications Technologies (ICT). INCITS serves as ANSI's Technical Advisory Group to ISO.

International Communication Industry Association (ICIA)

www.infocomm.org

ICIA is a worldwide organization that provides education, training, and certification for communications technologies.

International Electrical Testing Association (NETA)

www.netaworld.org

The National Electrical Contractors Association, founded in 1901, is the leading representative of a segment of the construction market that includes over 70,000 electrical contracting firms. NETA is an accredited standards developer for ANSI and defines the standards by which electrical equipment is deemed safe and reliable.

International Organization for Standardization (ISO)

www.iso.ch/iso/en/ISOOnline.openerpage

A network of national standards institutes from 148 countries working in partnership with international organizations, governments, industry, business, and consumer representatives.

Konnex Association—Convergence of EHSA, BCI, EIBA

www.konnex-knx.com

Konnex was created from the merger or BCI (Batibus Association), EIBA (EIB Asssociation), and EHSA (European Home Systems Association) to promote KNX, a standard for electrical, HVAC, telecom, and related services.

Mechanical Contractors Association of America

www.mcaa.org

A trade organization with a membership of more than 2,000 contractors that is dedicated to excellence and committed to quality in mechanical contracting.

National Association of Home Builders (NAHB)

www.nahb.org

The NAHB is a federation of more than 850 state and local homebuilder associations in the U.S.

National Association of Plumbing and Heating Contractors

www.naphcc.org

A professional trade association for contractors who work in the plumbing/heating/cooling industry.

National Association of the Remodeling Industry (NARI)

www.nari.org

NARI is a professional association for the residential remodeling industry that provides education and member networking.

National Burglar and Fire Alarm Association (NBFAA)
www.alarm.org
The NBFAA is the trade association offering services and representation to the electronic security systems industry.

National Center for Standards and Certification Information (NIST)
www.nist.gov
NIST is a non-regulatory federal agency within the U.S. Commerce Department's Technology Administration.

National Conference of States on Building Codes and Standards (NCSBCS)
www.ncsbcs.org
NCSBCS provides the public and private sectors with a national forum for coordinating building code and public safety interests and concerns about building construction codes and regulations.

National Electrical Contractors Association (NECA)
www.necanet.org
NECA represents over 70,000 electrical contracting firms and 650,000 electrical workers in countries around the world and provides continuing education and current information.

National Electrical Manufacturers Association (NEMA)
www.nema.org
Establishes standards and ratings to be followed in the construction of electrical components and materials. Primarily determines sizing requirements based on electrical power for such items as receptacles and enclosures. Its goal is to ensure high safety ratings and interchangeable parts.

National Fire Protection Agency (NFPA)
www.nfpa.org
NFPA is a non-profit organization that is the worldwide leader in providing fire and electrical safety standards and guidelines to the public.

National Safety Council
www.nsc.org
A nonprofit membership organization focused on protecting life and promoting health through a wide range of information, training, products, programs, and advocacy.

Open Mobile Alliance (OMA)
www.wapforum.org
The Open Mobile Alliance was established by the consolidation of the WAP Forum and the Open Mobile Architecture Initiative to drive the growth of the mobile wireless industry.

Security Industry Association (SIA)

www.siaonline.org

The SIA is a full-service, international trade association focused on promoting growth, expansion, and professionalism within the security industry by providing education, research, and technical standards.

TechHome Division of CEA

www.ce.org/div_comm/division_main.asp?DivisionID=19

The Home Automation and Networking Association (HANA) merged with CEA to become the TechHome Division of CEA, an association for professional home system integrators and manufacturers of home control and networking products.

Telecommunications Industry Association (TIA)

www.tiaonline.org

A branch of the CEA, the TIA is a communications and information technology association that focuses on standards development, domestic and international advocacy, and market development and promotion programs. TIA works in conjunction with several organizations, including EIA and ANSI, to develop and publish telecommunications and networking standards.

Underwriters Laboratories, Inc. (UL)

www.ul.com

UL is an independent, nonprofit product safety testing and certification organization that tests products for public safety worldwide.

Universal Plug and Play Forum (UPnP)

www.upnp.com

The UPnP Forum is an industry initiative to enable simple and robust connectivity among stand-alone devices and PCs from many different vendors.

Window and Door Manufacturers Association

www.wdma.org

The Window and Door Manufacturers Association promotes the interests of the window, skylight, and door industry.

Wireless Ethernet Compatibility Alliance (WECA)

www.wi-fi.org/OpenSection/index.asp

The Wi-Fi Alliance is a nonprofit international association formed to certify interoperability of wireless LAN products based on IEEE 802.11 specification.

Wireless LAN Association (WLANA)

www.wlana.org

The Wireless LAN Association is a nonprofit educational trade association of the leaders and technology innovators in the wireless LAN technology industry.

CompTIA HTI+ Exam Objectives

CompTIA HTI+ Exam Objectives

Exam One: Residential Systems

DOMAIN 1.0: Computer Networking Fundamentals
1.1 Basic network design considerations and information distribution methods through diverse media

1.2 Equipment location considerations when designing a computer network

1.3 Physical devices (hardware) that comprise networking technology

1.4 Core configuration and settings for the networking technology hardware and software

1.5 Standard methods of device connectivity in networking technology

1.6 Shared in-house services of networking technology

1.7 Sources of externally provided data services found in networking technology

1.8 Current industry standards of networking technology

DOMAIN 2.0: Audio and Video Fundamentals
2.1 Design considerations of a connected audio/video system

2.2 Audio and video equipment location considerations

2.3 Physical audio and video products and components

2.4 Standard configuration and settings of audio/video components

2.5 Methods and components involved in device connectivity

2.6 In-house services

2.7 Sources of externally provided audio and video services and their associated technologies

2.8 Current standards and industry related organizations

2.9 Installation plans and procedures for audio/video system components

2.10 Maintenance plans and procedures for audio/video system components

DOMAIN 3.0: Home Security and Surveillance Systems
3.1 Basic home security and fire alarm design considerations

3.2 Equipment location considerations when designing a security or fire alarm system

3.3 Physical devices that comprise the security and surveillance alarm systems

3.4 Core configuration and settings for the home security and surveillance alarm systems

3.5 Standard methods of device connectivity in the home security and surveillance alarm systems

3.6 In-house services available in the home security and surveillance alarm systems

3.7 External services available in the home security and surveillance alarm systems

3.8 Current industry standards relating to the home security and surveillance alarm systems

3.9 Installation plans and procedures for home security and surveillance alarm systems

3.10 Maintenance plans and procedures for home security and surveillance alarm systems

DOMAIN 4.0: Telecommunications Standards

4.1 Telecommunications design considerations of the home network

4.2 Telecommunication equipment location considerations when designing a home network

4.3 Physical telecommunications products of the home network

4.4 Standard configurations and settings of telecommunications components in a home network

4.5 Standard methods of device connectivity of telecommunications equipment in a home network

4.6 In-house services available in telecommunications technology

4.7 External services available in telecommunications technology

4.8 Current industry standards for telecommunications technology

4.9 Installation plans and procedures for home telecommunications systems

4.10 Troubleshooting and maintenance plans and procedures for home telecommunications systems

DOMAIN 5.0: Home Lighting Control and Management

5.1 Design considerations of the networked home lighting control and management systems

5.2 Equipment location considerations of the networked home lighting control and management system

5.3 Physical products of a networked home lighting control and management system

5.4 Standard configurations and settings of a networked home lighting control and management system

5.5 Standard methods of device connectivity with networked home lighting control system

5.6 Current industry standards related to the home lighting control and management

5.7 Installation plans and procedures for home lighting control and management

5.8 Troubleshooting and maintenance procedures for networked home lighting control system

DOMAIN 6.0: HVAC Management

6.1 Design considerations of for a home HVAC system

6.2 Equipment location considerations when designing a home HVAC system

6.3 Physical products and components of for a home HVAC system

6.4 Standard configurations and settings of the products and components of a home HVAC system

6.5 Standard methods of device connectivity with the equipment and components offor a home HVAC system

6.6 Current industry standards related to the installation and maintenance of home HVAC systems

6.7 Installation plans and procedures for home HVAC systems

6.8 Troubleshooting and maintenance plans and procedures for home HVAC systems

DOMAIN 7.0: Home Water Systems Controls and Management

7.1 Design considerations of networked home water system control and management systems

7.2 Equipment location considerations of a home water system control and management system

7.3 Standard configurations and settings for a home water system control and management system

7.4 Standard configurations and settings for a home water system control and management system

7.5 Standard methods of device connectivity for equipment in a home water system control system

7.6 Current industry standards related to the home water system control and management system

7.7 Installation plans and procedures of the home water system control and management system

7.8 Troubleshooting and maintenance plans and procedures for home water system control system

DOMAIN 8.0: Home Access Controls and Management

8.1 Design considerations of the home access control and management systems

8.2 Equipment and component location considerations when designing a home access control system

8.3 Physical products and components of the home access control and management system

8.4 Configurations and settings of the components in a home access control and management system.

8.5 Methods of device connectivity for equipment in a home access control and management system.

8.6 Current industry standards related to a home access control and management system

8.7 Installation plans and procedures for a home access control and management system

8.8 Troubleshooting and maintenance plans and procedures for a home access control system

DOMAIN 9.0: Miscellaneous Automated Home Features

9.1 Fundamental design considerations of connected home system features

9.2 Telecommunication equipment location considerations for connected home system features

9.3 Physical products and components of identified connected home system features

9.4 Standard configurations and settings of components providing connected home system features

9.5 Methods of device connectivity for equipment and components of connected home system features

9.6 Current industry standards related to the identified connected home system featuresVisit www.comtia.org for most current objectives

Exam Two: Systems Infrastructure and Integration

DOMAIN IA: Structured Wiring, Low Voltage

1A.1 Standard structured wiring design considerations

1A.2 Standard structured wiring location considerations

1A.3 Physical structured wiring connection components

1A.4 Core configuration and settings for low voltage structured wiring design

1A.5 Standard methods of device connectivity for low voltage structured wiring design

1A.6 Current industry standards for structured wiring design

1A.7 Standard installation plans and procedures for structured wiring design

1A.8 Maintenance plans and procedures for structured wiring design

DOMAIN IB: Structured Wiring, High Voltage

1B.1 Design considerations for high voltage structured wiring

1B.2 Audio and video equipment location considerations

1B.3 Physical high voltage structured wiring connection components

1B.4 Core configuration and settings for high voltage structured wiring design

1B.5 Standard methods of device connectivity for high voltage structured wiring design

1B.6 Current high voltage structured wiring standards and industry related organizations

1B.9 Installation plans and procedures for high voltage structured wiring design

1B.10 Maintenance plans and procedures for high voltage structured wiring design

DOMAIN 2.0: Systems Integration

2.1 Standard system integration design considerations

2.2 Equipment location considerations in system integration designs

2.3 Core components found in system integration designs

2.4 Configuration and settings for the components found in system integration designs

2.5 Methods of device connectivity for the components found in system integration designs

2.6 Current industry standards for system integration designs

2.7 Standard installation plans and procedures for structured wiring design

2.8 Maintenance plans and procedures for structured wiring design

CEDIA Installer Level I Classification System

Installer Level I
Classification System
Domain 1 - Wire the Dwelling – 20%

- Wire/cable types and their applications
- National Electric Code (NEC)
- Structural basics (e.g., drilling studs)
- Basic installation techniques (e.g., opening sizes and device/component placements, etc.)
- Basic wire dress (e.g., final trim lengths, labeling, etc.)
- Safety practices and procedures (including ongoing job site maintenance and cleanliness practices and procedures)
- Outside service provider drops (e.g., Telco, CATV, ISP, etc.)
- Diagrams, documentation and instructions

Domain 2 - Wire/Cable Preparation – 10%

- Wire/cable types and their applications
- Wire/cable preparation techniques
- Wire/cable/connector tools and their use

Domain 3 - Connector Identification – 8%

- Connector types and their uses

Domain 4 - Connector Installation – 12%

- Wire/cable/connector tools and their use
- Connector installation techniques
- Connector pinout standards
- Diagrams, documentation and instructions

Domain 5 - Install and Mount Devices (including, but not limited to, interface devices, control devices, transducers, structural/mechanical devices, mounting devices, aesthetic devices, architectural devices, display devices, etc.) – 20%

- Wire/cable types and their applications
- National Electric Code (NEC)
- Structural basics (e.g., drilling studs)
- Basic installation techniques (e.g., opening sizes and device/ componentplacements, etc.)
- Safety practices and procedures (including ongoing job site maintenance and cleanliness practices and procedures)
- Connector installation techniques
- Connector pinout standards
- Diagrams, documentation and instructions

Domain 6 - Install Components/Equipment (including, but not limited to, transducers, displays, lighting fixtures, control components, source components, signal processing, electrical power conditioning and management components, telephony components, data management components, etc.) – 20%

- Wire/cable types and their applications
- National Electric Code (NEC)
- Structural basics (e.g., drilling studs)
- Basic installation techniques (e.g., opening sizes and device/component placements, etc.)
- Basic wire dress (e.g., final trim lengths, labeling, etc.)
- Safety practices and procedures (including ongoing job site maintenance and cleanliness practices and procedures)
- Outside service provider drops (e.g., Telco, CATV, ISP, etc.)
- Wire/cable preparation techniques
- Wire/cable/connector tools and their use
- Connector types and their uses
- Connector installation techniques
- Connector pinout standards
- Thermionic management
- Power management
- Diagrams, documentation and instructions

Domain 7 - Verify Operations (i.e., verify that all subsystems and controls function and list exceptions) – 10%

- Safety practices and procedures (including ongoing job site maintenance and cleanliness practices and procedures)

- Outside service provider drops (e.g., Telco, CATV, ISP, etc.)

- Basic system operations (e.g., start-up procedures, etc.)

- Diagrams, documentation and instructions.

About the CD

The CD-ROM included with this book comes complete with three MasterExam practice exams: one for each of the two HTI+ exams and one for the CEDIA Installer Level I Certification exam. The CD-ROM also includes a CEDIA Planning Icons PDF document (created and provided by CEDIA) that shows a set of design icons useful for mapping out home technology systems.

The MasterExam software is easy to install on any Windows 98/NT/2000/XP computer. You may access the CEDIA Planning Icons directly from the CD-ROM with no installation necessary.

System Requirements

The MasterExam software requires Windows 98 or higher and Internet Explorer 5.0 or above and 20 MB of hard disk space for full installation.

Installing and Running MasterExam

If your computer CD-ROM drive is configured to auto run, the CD-ROM will automatically start up upon inserting the disk. From the opening screen you may install MasterExam by pressing the *MasterExam* button. This will begin the installation process and create a program group named "LearnKey." To run MasterExam use START | PROGRAMS |LEARNKEY. If the auto run feature did not launch your CD, browse to the CD and Click on the "RunInstall" icon.

MasterExam

MasterExam provides you with a simulation of the two HTI+ exams as well as the CEDIA Installer Level I exam. Note that these HTI+ and CEDIA practice exams are designed to help you assess your understanding of the book material. Be aware the question types, exam duration, and number of question on the real exams are subject to change and this software is not intended to precisely mirror the actual exams.

Within MasterExam, you may take an open book exam, which provides the option of receiving hints, references, and answers; a closed book exam; or the timed MasterExam simulation.

When you launch MasterExam, a digital clock display will appear in the upper left-hand corner of your screen. The clock will continue to count down to zero unless you choose to end the exam before the time expires.

Help

A help file is provided through the help button on the main menu page in the lower left hand corner. Individual help features are also available within the MasterExam application.

Removing Installation(s)

MasterExam will install to your hard drive. For best results for removal of programs use the START | PROGRAMS | LEARNKEY| UNINSTALL options to remove MasterExam.

Technical Support

For questions regarding the content of the MasterExam, please visit www.osborne.com or email customer.service@mcgraw-hill.com. For customers outside the 50 United States, email: international_cs@mcgraw-hill.com.

LearnKey Technical Support

For technical problems with the software (installation, operation, removing installations), please visit www.learnkey.com or email techsupport@learnkey.com.

INDEX

Numbers

2+2 bundled cabling, features of, 19–20

2+2+2 bundled cabling, features of, 20

97 aspect ratio, significance of, 360

5.1 surround sound system, features of, 296–297

10-1000Base IEEE standards for Ethernet, descriptions of, 104

329 aspect ratio, significance of, 360

24V AC power, using with video surveillance cameras, 667

25-pair cable, using with telephone systems, 539

66 block IDC contacts, using, 49

66-style punchdown tool, using, 41

110 block IDC contacts, using, 49

110 punch-down blocks, terminating at, 165–166

120V AC power, using with video surveillance cameras, 667

208V, significance of, 5

240V feed, significance of, 5

568 cable standard, overview of, 259–260

568 EIA/TIA pinouts, overview of, 44–48

568 standard, significance of, 100

568 wiring configurations, diagrams of, 43–44

568a and 568b standards, overview of, 102–103

568a cable termination, EIA/TIA standard for, 102

569 standard, overview of, 102–103

802 standards, responsibilities of, 97

1394 connectors, using with PCs, 58–60

1394 standard, description of, 110

1926* sections of SCOR, topics associated with, 106

A

"A" default house code, advisory about, 459

absorbtion, relationship to light and objects, 426

A-BUS technology, using with audio systems, 315–317

AC (alternating current), significance of, 3–4

AC circuits in UPS units, purpose of, 143

AC power
   installing for distribution panels, 179
   and phase shifts, 505

accent lighting, description of, 431, 433

access control
   role in interior security, 604
   role in perimeter protection and detection, 605

access control systems
   biometrics, 690–692
   card readers, 682–686
   driveway entry detection systems, 692–695
   electric door lock systems, 688–690
   electric door strikes, 690
   electronic key systems, 687–688
   installation considerations, 695–696
   keypads, 686–687
   overview of, 681–682
   wiring, 695–696

ACD (automatic call distribution)
   in digital residential telephone systems, 528
   relationship to call routing, 525–526

ACLs (access control lists), relationship to network security, 240–241

acoustic glass break detectors, installing in security systems, 632–633

acoustical design, issues associated with, 326

acoustical rooms, issues associated with, 325

active bipole speaker enclosures, description of, 308

active hubs, explanation of, 228

active speaker crossovers, description of, 305

active ultrasonic sensors, using with wired lighting control systems, 488

actuators, purpose in water management systems, 591

ADC (analog-to-digital converter), description of, 293

addressing. *See* network addresses

alarm monitoring services, features of, 613

alarming switchers, using in video surveillance systems, 671

alarms, types of, 607–608

ambient lighting, description of, 431–432

AM/FM tuners, using in audio systems, 302

amperes chart for wire gauge to circuit, 9

amplification, relationship to video signals, 349–350

What is CEDIA?

The Custom Electronic Design & Installation Association (CEDIA) is a global trade association of companies that specialize in planning and installing electronic systems for the home. These systems include home networking, home automation and communication systems, media rooms, single or multi-room entertainment systems, and integrated whole-house subsystems providing control of lighting, security and HVAC systems. The association was founded in September 1989 and has a total membership of approximately 3,100 member companies.

Who Benefits from CEDIA?

Consumers benefit because they can obtain referrals through CEDIA to find qualified, reputable and insured design and installation contractors to counsel them and work in their homes. They also benefit by having CEDIA promote professionalism and honorable business practices in the field of custom installation.

Custom installers benefit in several ways. Consumers, builders, architects, interior designers, etc., recognize them as a professional resource. Through CEDIA education conferences and training programs, they can obtain continuing education in both technical and business skills to enhance the growth of their employees and their business. They have access to data, publications and other materials that can enhance their business practices and marketing services. They also have an open line of communication to manufacturers, industry officials and colleagues to address challenges and exchange information. Through CEDIA certification, installers now have a benchmark in their industry against which to measure themselves. Being a CEDIA Professional Certified Installer lends even more prestige to membership.

Manufacturers benefit from CEDIA because equipment specified, installed and serviced by CEDIA members will satisfy customers, lead to enthusiastic referrals, and help the industry grow. CEDIA provides manufacturers with feedback that will help them create products that perform more efficiently, are easier to install, and satisfy changing customer demands.

CEDIA Consumer Referral Service

In addition to its many member services, CEDIA provides consumers with an online Finder Service (http://www.cedia.org/homeowners) for free referrals to custom design/installation specialists throughout the United States and other countries throughout the world.

Why Do Companies Join CEDIA?

Custom design and installation is the cutting edge of a rapidly growing field, and only recently is becoming more widely known outside the consumer-electronics industry. Among consumers, there is little awareness or appreciation for the specialized knowledge and skills of the custom designer/installer. Builders and home designers are better informed, but most are not aware of the breadth of custom-installation services, or of all they and their clients stand to gain by using custom installers.

CEDIA's purpose is to build recognition and acceptance for this specialized field, and to speak up for its interests in addressing the industry, government, and the marketplace.

How Does CEDIA Advance the Interest of Custom Designer/Installers?

Through educational programs, trade shows, publicity, advertising, technical meetings and other methods, CEDIA helps its members in many ways:

- By building awareness of custom installation among consumers, and promoting CEDIA members as the most qualified contractors to perform design and installation of home electronic systems.
- By generating leads and referrals.
- By establishing contacts with allied industries, professions and trades including building, architecture and interior design.
- By assisting members in improving their management and technical skills.
- By working for the establishment of industry standards with respect to the design and installation of home-electronic systems.
- By protecting members' interests in matters affected by government regulation.
- By monitoring and guiding the growth of our industry for the benefit of all its members and customers.

Additional information is available by contacting CEDIA, 7150 Winton Dr. Ste. 300, Indianapolis, IN 46268, Phone: 800-669-5329 or 317-328-4336; Fax: 317-280-8527 Email: member@cedia.org; and Web site: http://www.cedia.org

Internet Home Alliance

Internet Home Alliance is a cross-industry network of leading companies advancing the home technology market. A non-profit organization founded in 2000, the Alliance provides member companies with the cross-industry collaboration, research and real-world testing opportunities they need to bring their home technology products and services to market more quickly, successfully and cost effectively.

Principal members of the Alliance are Best Buy Co. Inc., Cisco Systems, Inc., General Motors, Hewlett-Packard Company, IBM, Invensys, Microsoft, Panasonic (Matsushita Electric Corporation of America), SBC Communications, Sears, Roebuck and Co. and Whirlpool Corporation.

A thought leader in the connected home space, Internet Home Alliance is the architect of the Ecosystems Framework, a breakthrough business tool that helps companies in the home technology space mitigate market risks and identify the most promising market opportunities. It also serves as a common blueprint and language for industry players—which is critical to developing nascent markets—encourages greater industry collaboration and benefits consumers.

The Alliance's Ecosystems Framework is comprised of three ecosystems—Family, Career and Entertainment – that correspond to discrete consumer needs. Within each ecosystem, consumer demand, products and services and enabling technologies are aligning to create market opportunities.

To learn more about the three ecosystems, the Alliance conducts a series of pilots, home solutions trials that enable members to come together and test their home technology products and services in real-world settings. This program provides a way for leaders from across industries to collaborate on developing and testing new, innovative home technologies under real-world conditions and represents a unique venue for cross-industry collaboration. Through the pilot process, companies can create and refine new products outside their typical and often confining frames of reference. Both the technical results and consumers' reactions to the piloted prototypes help member companies identify new market opportunities and accelerate product development.

Internet Home Alliance is also committed to developing the home integrator channel and worked with CompTIA in 2002 to launch the Home Technology Integrator (HTI+), a nationwide certification program for technicians who install and network digitally-based security, audio and video, computer, heating and air conditioning, cable and satellite, and telecommunications systems. Developed in response to the growing need for qualified technicians to install and maintain networked home entertainment, environment and security systems, the new certification serves as a trust mark to assure homeowners that professionals have mastered the complexities of networking diverse products.

For more information about Internet Home Alliance, please call 831-648-1001 or visit www.internethomealliance.com.

Electronic Systems Industry Consortium (ESIC)

Electronic systems industries (such as telecommunications, video/audio, fire/security, entertainment and building automation) traditionally have a shortage of qualified electronics field technicians. In 1998, national and international industry trade associations formed the Consortium for Electronic Home & Building Systems Installation Training. The purpose of the consortium was to identify the skill sets and training required for electronic systems technicians (ESTs). Since the organizations inception, the consortium has co-developed a 500+ hour training curriculum, helped create the federal industry occupational code for Electronic Systems Technician, and worked with consortium members to establish an Electronic Systems Technician apprenticeship program with the US Department of Labor.

In 2004 the organization broadened it's scope and changed the name to the Electronic Systems Industry Consortium. In addition to promoting the Electronic Systems Technician curriculum to schools and technical training centers, the consortium also accredits organizations that teach the curriculum, offers knowledge and skills assessments for individuals entering the industry, and monitors legislation that may impact licensing, training, apprenticeship or other workforce issues.

The associations that are members of the consortium represent over 700,000 persons employed in electronic systems industries. In 2003 more than 213,000 electronic systems technicians were employed by electrical and electronic systems contractors, integrators, suppliers and manufacturers. Technicians earned over $6.4 billion in wages in 2002 (average of $27,000 for entry level and $60,000 for those with an average of 5 years installation and design experience). Projected growth rate for technicians is 25% in residential and slightly less in the commercial sectors for 2004.

Electronic Systems Technicians are defined as skilled individuals who design, integrate, install and provide field maintenance on products that:

- Transport voice, video, audio, data signals in commercial and residential premises.
- Capture and display or otherwise annunciate signals or control signals.
- Use signals to control mechanical and electrical apparatus.

Electronic Systems Technicians typically work for:

- Data and telecommunications companies
- Electronic security and alarm companies
- Home theater designers/contractors
- Sound and communications contractors
- Electrical contractors and systems integrators
- Home and building automation companies
- Communications cabling contractors
- Manufacturers, distributors and equipment suppliers

Members of the consortium include:

- Building Industry Consulting Services International (BICSI) www.bicsi.org
- Consumer Electronics Association (CEA) www.ce.org
- Continental Automated Buildings Association (CABA) www.caba.org
- Custom Electronic Design & Installation Association (CEDIA) www.cedia.org
- Entertainment Services & Technology Association (ESTA) www.esta.org
- National Burglar & Fire Alarm Association (NBFAA) www.alarm.org
- National Systems Contractors Association (NSCA) www.nsca.org
- International Communications Industries Association (ICIA) www.infocomm.org
- Security Industry Association (SIA) www.siaonline.org
- Lincoln Technical Institute

For more information about the Electronic Systems Industry Consortium, contact Managing Director Joe Jones at 813-962-7987 in Tampa, Florida, or go to the consortium web site at www.hightechjobs.org.

CompTIA and HTI+ Certification

The Computing Technology Industry Association (CompTIA) is a global trade association representing the business interests of the information technology industry. For more than 22 years, CompTIA has provided research, networking, and partnering opportunities to its more than 19,000 members in 89 countries. The association is involved in developing standards and best practices, and influencing the political, economic, and educational arenas that impact IT worldwide.

In the early 1990s, the major computer suppliers and resellers approached the CompTIA services section, looking for a way of pooling resources to develop a set of standards for hiring and retaining PC technicians. These suppliers and resellers not only defined the problem but worked closely with CompTIA to develop a solution. The result of this industry effort was the CompTIA A+® certification, widely regarded as the most successful "vendor-neutral" certification in the world.

Other vendor-neutral certifications like CompTIA's Network+™, Server+™, Security+™, and HTI+™ (Home Technology Integrator) followed. Vendor-neutral certification ensures that technicians understand the "whys" of technology and promotes technician flexibility. The suite of CompTIA vendor-neutral certifications is recognized today for its overall excellence. More than 600,000 individuals globally hold one or more CompTIA certifications.

To keep pace with technology change, all of CompTIA's certifications undergo thorough and ongoing revision. Furthermore, steering committees of industry's leading suppliers and educations guides the direction of each certification ensuring confidence in CompTIA certificates.

Home Technology Integrator (HTI+) certification

CompTIA HTI+ certification assures architects, builders, and homeowners of the knowledge mastery of the home-integration technician — from first interaction to the installed and supported system. CompTIA HTI+ certified personnel have demonstrated knowledge mastery of best practices equivalent to six months on-the-job experience in home integration by passing two comprehensive exams. The certification emphasizes how these systems interoperate so that personnel can optimize performance and troubleshoot problems. For more information on CompTIA and HTI+ please visit www.comptia.org.

INTERNATIONAL CONTACT INFORMATION

AUSTRALIA
McGraw-Hill Book Company
Australia Pty. Ltd.
TEL +61-2-9900-1800
FAX +61-2-9878-8881
http://www.mcgraw-hill.com.au
books-it_sydney@mcgraw-hill.com

CANADA
McGraw-Hill Ryerson Ltd.
TEL +905-430-5000
FAX +905-430-5020
http://www.mcgraw-hill.ca

**GREECE, MIDDLE EAST, & AFRICA
(Excluding South Africa)**
McGraw-Hill Hellas
TEL +30-210-6560-990
TEL +30-210-6560-993
TEL +30-210-6560-994
FAX +30-210-6545-525

MEXICO (Also serving Latin America)
McGraw-Hill Interamericana Editores
S.A. de C.V.
TEL +525-1500-5108
FAX +525-117-1589
http://www.mcgraw-hill.com.mx
carlos_ruiz@mcgraw-hill.com

SINGAPORE (Serving Asia)
McGraw-Hill Book Company
TEL +65-6863-1580
FAX +65-6862-3354
http://www.mcgraw-hill.com.sg
mghasia@mcgraw-hill.com

SOUTH AFRICA
McGraw-Hill South Africa
TEL +27-11-622-7512
FAX +27-11-622-9045
robyn_swanepoel@mcgraw-hill.com

SPAIN
McGraw-Hill/
Interamericana de España, S.A.U.
TEL +34-91-180-3000
FAX +34-91-372-8513
http://www.mcgraw-hill.es
professional@mcgraw-hill.es

**UNITED KINGDOM, NORTHERN,
EASTERN, & CENTRAL EUROPE**
McGraw-Hill Education Europe
TEL +44-1-628-502500
FAX +44-1-628-770224
http://www.mcgraw-hill.co.uk
emea_queries@mcgraw-hill.com

ALL OTHER INQUIRIES Contact:
McGraw-Hill/Osborne
TEL +1-510-420-7700
FAX +1-510-420-7703
http://www.osborne.com
omg_international@mcgraw-hill.com

Sound Off!

Visit us at **www.osborne.com/bookregistration** and let us know what you thought of this book. While you're online you'll have the opportunity to register for newsletters and special offers from McGraw-Hill/Osborne.

We want to hear from you!

Sneak Peek

Visit us today at **www.betabooks.com** and see what's coming from McGraw-Hill/Osborne tomorrow!

Based on the successful software paradigm, Bet@Books™ allows computing professionals to view partial and sometimes complete text versions of selected titles online. Bet@Books™ viewing is free, invites comments and feedback, and allows you to "test drive" books in progress on the subjects that interest you the most.